To ? & Mrs. Patrick Kenn

very best wishes

Alfred A. Low

The Anschluss Movement, 1931–1938, and the Great Powers

By

Alfred D. Low

EAST EUROPEAN MONOGRAPHS, BOULDER
DISTRIBUTED BY COLUMBIA UNIVERSITY PRESS, NEW YORK

1985

EAST EUROPEAN MONOGRAPHS, NO. CLXXXV

To the memory of my parents
Samuel and Klara Löw and to
Rose, Suzanne and Owen, Ruth,
David, and Matthew

Previous books published by the author:

Lenin on the Question of Nationality, 1958.

The Soviet Hungarian Republic and the Paris Peace Conference, 1963.

The Anschluss Movement, 1918–1919, and the Paris Peace Conference, 1974.

Die Anschlussbewegung in Österreich und Deutschland, 1918–1919, und die Pariser Friedenskonferenz, 1975.

The Sino-Soviet Dispute. An Analysis of the Polemics, 1976.

Jews in the Eyes of the Germans. From the Enlightenment to Imperial Germany, 1979.

The Anschluss Movement, 1918–1938: Background and Aftermath. An Annotated Bibliography in German and Austrian Nationalism, 1984.

Table of Contents

Acknowledgements

Among the archives and libraries I consulted for my first book on the Anschluss (union between Austria and Germany; 1974) as well as the present one were the British Public Record Office and the British Museum, London, the French Foreign Ministry Archives and the Library of the French Foreign Ministry, Quai d'Orsay, and the Bibliothèque Nationale, Paris, the German Foreign Ministry Archives and the Library of the German Foreign Ministry, Bonn, and the German Federal Archives, Koblenz, the *Allgemeines Archiv* and *Geheimes Staatsarchiv*, Munich, and the microfilm copies of the German Foreign Archives, most of which are located in the National Archives, Washington, D.C., and of the League of Nations Library, Geneva, Switzerland. Last but not least, I have made extensive use of the resources of the *Neues Politisches Archiv, Österreichisches Staatsarchiv*, and of the *Nationalbibliothek* in Vienna, as well as of the library of the University of Vienna. I greatly appreciate the assistance of all persons who gave permission for the use of these materials.

I owe a special debt to the staff of Marquette University's Memorial Library, to Rev. J. Philip Talmadge and Mr. Harry J. Onufrok, and particularly Mrs. Patricia Bohach and the invaluable inter-library service, the library staffs of the University of Wisconsin, Madison, and of the University of Wisconsin-Milwaukee, the staff of the Library of Congress and the National Archives, Washington, D.C., of the University of Washington, Seattle, where I enjoyed Visiting Scholar's privileges for three consecutive summers, and the library staff of the Hebrew University of Jerusalem, where I lectured during the autumn session of 1984 and also made last-minute corrections.

Acknowledgement is also due to the editors of the following journals for permitting partial reprint of my articles which had earlier appeared in their pages, the editors of the *Canadian Review of Studies in Nationalism, Slavic Review, Jahrbuch des Instituts für Deutsche Geschichte* (University of Tel-Aviv), and *East Central Europe.* In proper order the articles in question are "Otto Bauer, Austro-Marxism, and the Anschluss Movement 1918–1938" (spring 1979, pp. 33–57), "The Soviet Union, the Austrian Communist Party, and the Anschluss Question 1918–1938 (March 1980, pp. 1–26), "The Anschluss Movement 1933–1938 and the Policy of France" (1982, pp. 295–323) and "Edvard Beneš, the Anschluss, and the Policy of Czechoslovakia 1918–38" (1983, vol. X, pp. 46–92). Finally, my annotated bibliography on the Anschluss Movement (1984) which appeared in the series of Bibliographical Studies on Nationalism under the auspices of the foregoing *CRSN* and was suggested and edited by Professor Thomas Spira, acquainted me with the most recently published literature in the Anschluss field, which proved very helpful in putting finishing touches on the present study.

I am also indebted to Columbia University Press for granting permission for the reproduction of a map from Robert Kann's *The Multinational Empire,* I, pp. 39–40, and to the American Philosophical Society for that of a map of my study *The Anschluss Movement, 1918–19, and the Paris Peace Conference,* 1974; to the Verlag Herder, Vienna, for the reproduction of pictures of I. Seipel and O. Bauer on page 311 of the work *Spectrum Austriae,* 1957, and to the Österreichischer Bundesverlag, Vienna, for the use of the pictures of Engelbert Dollfuss and Kurt von Schuschnigg from the book by H. L. Mikoletzky, *Österreichische Zeitgeschichte.* The *Bildarchiv* of the *Österreichische Nationalbibliothek* also graciously permitted the use of these photographs. Last but not least, the Austrian Institute, New York, N.Y., by making a generous contribution for the publication of this study, deserves my sincere thanks.

As usual, I owe a debt of gratitude to my wife, Dr. Rose S. Low, for numerous kinds of help and for her unfailing patience and support while I was engrossed in research and writing.

Alfred D. Low
Milwaukee, Wis.

Preface

Ever since completing my earlier study THE ANSCHLUSS MOVEMENT, 1918–1919, AND THE PARIS PEACE CONFERENCE* I felt tempted to write a sequel to it. As it turned out, two other works of mine which had preoccupied me since the completion of the Anschluss study "interfered" with this plan, delaying its realization. During the last years, however, I was able to turn again to the Anschluss topic, publishing several articles on the interwar Anschluss movement and *The Anschluss Movement 1918–1938: Background and Aftermath. An Annotated Bibliography in German and Austrian Nationalism.* Garland Press, New York, 1984, while continuing to work on a book-length study of the Anschluss movement in the 1930s.

The "Anschluss," climaxing in March 1938 in Hitler's annexation of Austria, will soon pass the half-century mark. Though virtually every textbook writer on European history and Twentieth Century History has touched on the problem, and others have focused on it, the best known and most widely used study in English on the Anschluss in the 1930s remains a thin volume by Jürgen Gehl, *Austria, Germany, and the Anschluss 1931–38,* which has appeared as long as two decades ago (London, 1963). There exist a fair number of more specialized works on the Anschluss movement in German, dating back to Ulrich Eichstädt's study, *Von Dollfuss zu Hitler. Geschichte des Anschlusses Österreichs 1933–38,* Mainz-Wiesbaden, 1955, and more recent ones, all of which I discussed in my *Annotated Bibliography.* After having examined the entire Anschluss literature, I concluded that a follow-up study, treating the Anschluss and its various aspects in the 1930s, was

---

*American Philosophical Society, vol. 103, *Memoirs,* Philadephia, 1974; an abbreviated German version appeared in Vienna, Braumüller's Universitaetsbuchhandlung, 1975.

desirable on several grounds. Not only were there numerous primary sources which had been published in the meantime or had been made accessible, sources which needed to be explored and fully utilized. There were also substantial gaps in secondary literature and an obvious need for new and comprehensive interpretations. Last but not least, the likely European-wide ramifications and repercussions of the Anschluss movement in regard to the continent's balance of power and security had on the whole been paid not quite adequate attention. The reasons were quite obvious: Austrian postwar historians were mostly preoccupied with the defensive struggle of the Dollfuss and Schuschnigg regimes against the *Third Reich*, while National Socialist spokesmen and propagandists and German postwar historians—most of the latter critical of the *Third Reich*—tended to focus on the right of self-determination rather than on the European balance of power, which attracted their interest to a lesser extent.

The German literature on the Anschluss is unquestionably richer than the one in English, but it is not free of shortcomings. Few of the authors make extensive use of primary sources available outside of Central Europe, and some tend to ignore the secondary literature published abroad, concentrating rather on Austrian and German archives and publications. Furthermore, most of these studies center on Austrian domestic politics (though less on political parties), the German-Austrian diplomatic duel with its special pan-German and National Socialist ideological overtones rather than on the Anschluss as part and parcel of the European diplomatic struggle. The history of the Anschluss, however, is not part of Austrian and German history alone; it belongs to Europe and European history in its entirety.

In this study I am trying to place the struggle over Austria into the larger framework of European diplomatic history and to elucidate the interests and policies of the Great European Powers as they relate to the Anschluss as well as those of the smaller neighbors of Austria and Germany. The history of the Anschluss movement in the 1930s is not just a bilateral affair; in all its ramifications it encompasses not only the aggressive thrusts of the *Third Reich* and the defensive moves of its victim, the hapless Austrian Republic, but involves all of Europe. Therefore the foci of this work are twofold: the growing German-Austrian confrontation and the attitude and policies of the major, primarily

European, powers. The latter focus is a relatively new one for the 1930s and would by itself have justified another work on this topic. Actually, the present study also in respect to this focus—Austria, Germany, *and* the Great Powers—is a continuation of my earlier book on the Anschluss, which centered attention both on the two Central European states immediately affected, Austria and Germany, as well as on the policies of the Great Powers prior to and during the sessions of the Paris Peace Conference.

The history of the Anschluss movement in the 1920s forms part of several chapters of this study. There seemed to be good reasons for not discussing the movement in he 1920s more fully. First, the work would simply have become unwieldy. This appears to have been a major rationale for most historians confining their works on the movement for union to the 1930s. Secondly, European diplomacy in the 1920s, as compared to the following decade, moved at a more sluggish pace, and the Anschluss, while occasionally much talked about, never reached the level of becoming an acute threat to Austria's independence and to the neighbors of Austria and Germany.

The first two chapters of this work cover the period 1918–1931, ending with the abortive German-Austrian Customs Union project of 1931, when the Anschluss concept was strongly revived; chapters three and four deal partially with this time span. The movement for union in the 1920s was, however, by no means in a state of continuous slumber; to the contrary, it had some notable spurts during this period. Still, no knowledgeable contemporary observer expected its fulfillment then or in the foreseeable future.

Chapters three and four focus attention on Austria's political parties covering also their position on the Anschluss in the early 1930s as well as their interaction with the corresponding German parties. In the early 1930s Austria's political parties were still operating and the *grossdeutsch* orientation of virtually all of them, even of the majority of the Christian Socials, was to remain ideologically and politically the outstanding factor of Austrian politics even after the submergence or prohibition of these parties. In chapters five and six attention is centered on the relations of Hitler's *Third Reich* with the Dollfuss regime and that of Schuschnigg until the Berchtesgaden Conference, while chapters seven to nine focus on European interstate relations and international affairs, with Central Europe and Austria in particular being in the spotlight. The main purpose of this section lies in analyzing the interests and policies of the major Powers, of France, Great Britain, and Italy in regard to the Anschluss. The Soviet Union and the United States which for reasons of history, geography, and power politics, were more remote from the tug-of-war of Anschluss politics and have been largely neglected for this reason, have been treated separately in chapters ten and eleven. The following chapter deals with the interests of the smaller European states in an independent Austria and the causes of their often wavering policies toward the union. Chapters thirteen to sixteen focus on the last phase of the hopeless struggle for saving Austria's independence against the mounting pressures of the *Third Reich*. Major interest here is again divided between domestic developments before the climax and foreign apologia, after the tragedy, for remaining aloof. A conclusion marks the end of the study.

Old *grossdeutsch* dreams stretching back to 1848 have influenced the thinking of most Austrians in the interwar period. German nationalism had secured a stranglehold even on conservative and Catholic circles and produced the ambivalent attitude to the Anschluss by Dr. Ignaz Seipel, priest and Christian Social Party leader. Even to the young Engelbert Dollfuss the Anschluss appeared as a national ideal. Similarly Chancellor Kurt von Schuschnigg always underlined the German character of Austria. In his book *Mein Kampf gegen Hitler* (1969) he later lamented that an entire Austrian generation had grown up with a distorted picture of Austrian history and of their fatherland, the "captive" of an unceasing pro-union propaganda: "The opponents of the Anschluss felt more or less overwhelmed." Austrians lived under the shadow of the *grossdeutsch* legacy, brought up-to-date in the Austrian historian's Heinrich Ritter von Srbik's *gesamtdeutsch* ("all-deutsch") interpretation. This made the union of the German remnant of the Habsburg Empire with the German Republic appear as an historical and ethical imperative, and as the very fulfillment of Germany's national unification.

Austrian patriotism was only a weak plant in the First Republic. All three major political camps—the Social Democratic Party, the *Grossdeutsche Volkspartei*, and even the Catholic, conservative and seemingly most patriotic party, the Christian Socials—were ensnared by Pan-Germanism. The belief that Austrians were a separate nationality, distinct from the German one, that they had a national character of their own and that they were entitled to live in their own independent state, was not widely shared in the interwar period.

Hitler himself was keenly aware of the ideological and political weakness of the Austrian government and state. In a German cabinet session held as early as May 1933 he considered the Austrian Government's resolve to propagandize the Austrian concept, instead of the German national idea, as dangerous to the realization of German goals; Austria, equipped with a militant patriotic ideology, might become another Switzerland, largely German in culture and language, but free from the Reich's political control. He correctly assessed the power of ideology and propaganda which might be unleashed by his Austrian opponent. But for reasons stated, such Austrianism never captivated the majority of Austrians in the First Republic.

It is a major thesis of this work that the lack of an Austrian patriotic ideology contributed to the ultimate demise of the First Austrian Republic. An analysis of the foreign policy programme of Austria's major political parties—which forms the first part of the present study—reveals the depth of the commitment of all Austrian parties to the German cause and the Anschluss in particular. Given these political and ideological circumstances, the Austrian resistance to Nazism and Pan-Germanism was undermined from the very beginning. In view of the strong pro-German trends even among Christian Socials and the Austrian Fatherland Front and their leaders such as Engelbert Dollfuss, Kurt von Schuschnigg, and Prince Ernst Rüdiger von Starhemberg, the possibility of a successful defense of Austria against the *Third Reich*—the disparity of natural and manpower resources of the two countries aside—was always sharply circumscribed.

This disparity was never balanced by any support of Austria by the Great Powers. The latters' aid, as this study shows, proved to be inadequate and in the end turned out to be an utter phantasmagory. Austrian and German contemporaries had few illusions about the imbalance of forces confronting each other over the Anschluss issue. But for long Austrian political leaders and others clung to the hope that somehow Europe's overwhelming moral support for Austria would block Hitler's relentless drive toward annexation. Yet no effective international collaboration and alliance was forthcoming. Narrow interests prevailed over

long-range national and all-European considerations. Considering
the magnitude of the Hitler threat—which became soon evident
to most European countries—a realistic perception of their states'
true interests and a statesman-like leadership should have overcome adverse economic and strategic-military considerations and
should have compelled France, Britain and Fascist Italy to try to
bridge their differences, to coordinate more effectively their policies,
and to stem the aggressive thrusts of the *Third Reich*. As far as
Fascist Italy was concerned, short-sighted selfish nationalism made
her overlook the basic threat emanating from Germany once the
latter would reach the Brenner Pass; Rome rather set its hopes
on uncertain gains in the Mediterranean region.

In discussing the role of the Great Powers concerning the
Anschluss issue, I make no claim of presenting a novel thesis—
rather unlikely almost half a centry after the annexation. I believe,
however, to have unearthed a considerable amount of new materials
and perhaps delineated more sharply the interests of France, Italy,
and Great Britain in regard to Austria and their Anschluss policy,
a "policy" largely of retreat and procrastination.

As far as the great Powers were concerned, it is my view,
along with that of many other students of the interwar period,
that the policy of appeasement and surrender was bound to lead
to further debacles and make the outbreak of World War II
inevitable. The ideological and political split between Paris, London, and Rome made a close diplomatic cooperation and alliance
between their peoples unlikely.

Hitler's policies of course were aggressive both in methods
and goals; the Third Reich always aimed at the total incorporation
of Austria and her complete submergence which would destroy
Austria's very identity—all in accordance with the Nazis' totalitarian *Weltanschauung*. The Führer always considered Austria's
annexation as a mere stepping stone toward the subjugation of
the rest of Central Europe, the penetration and domination of
the Balkans, and ultimately as a jumping-off board toward the
hegemony over the entire continent. The Austrian National Socialists approved these goals, though before their country's annexation by the *Third Reich* their energies were absorbed in the
internal Austrian struggle. In the different political climate of the
postwar period, attempting to belittle their actual role and to
reject their historic guilt, most Austro-Nazis stressed their devotion

to the German rather than to the Nazi cause. In reality they had served as a willing instrument of Hitler's radical goals in undermining Austrian independence and sovereignty. If the Third Reich itself pursued at times a seemingly more moderate course than the radical impatient Austrian National Socialists, and attempted to restrain them, it did so primarily for tactical reasons.

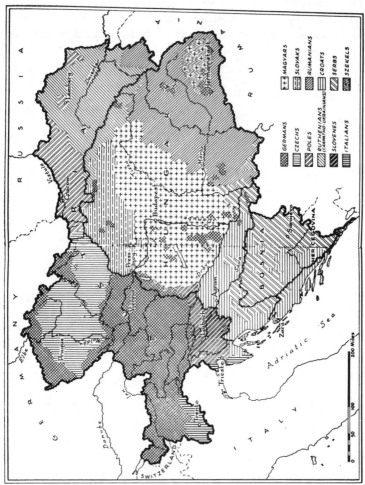

Map 1. Austria-Hungary, National Groups (only national groups representing more than 50 percent of the population in a given area are shown on this map)

Part I
Austrian Politics, the Anschluss and the Third Reich

Chapter 1

Austria, the Great Powers, and the Paris Peace Conference

Alternatives in Central Europe

During World War I British and French postwar planners had contemplated the possibility—and toward the end, the desirability—of the dissolution of the Habsburg Empire and pondered about the Anschluss of German Austria. When the war ended, pro-Anschluss views had still some support in the foreign offices of the Western Powers. Yet the suspicion against Germany ran high and few in the West wanted to strengthen a seemingly unregenerated *Reich*. As Otto Bauer, the Social Democratic Foreign Minister of the First Austrian Republic observed in *Die österreichische Revolution* (1923), in the English Government the Austrians faced an Anschluss opponent hardly less determined than the French government.[1]

The major postwar alternatives before Austria were independence, Anschluss, or the establishment of a Danubian Confederation. France and Great Britain favored Austrian independence over the Anschluss, but held the creation of a Danubian Confederation to be even more preferable. The latter project would embrace the newly established independent national states of Central and East Central Europe. It promised them as well as German Austria the greater economic benefits accruing from a wide region, one more or less identical with that of the former Austro-Hungarian monarchy. In 1918 there seemed to be little danger that the planned confederate structure could be dominated by its German neighbor as the old Dual Empire had been.

In the wake of the war the policy of the Western Powers, of both Great Britain and France, was based upon the prevention of the impending Anschluss threat. It was also concerned with calming the aroused passions in Central Europe, preventing the outbreak of hostilities between the nationalities of the former

Dual Monarchy and urging them to cooperate. Thus the old territorial realm would reemerge, though under new political auspices. This new Danubian Confederation would be based upon a just and realistic balance of power between the nationalities concerned; thus the grave would be dug for the Anschluss movement. The Austrian people in the very exercise of national self-determination—a principle which plagued the Allies because they had curtailed it in several recent pronouncements—would join a Danubian federated bloc. The creation of such a federation as a counterweight against the *Reich* was a major motivation of France.

During the year 1918–1919 English and French policies toward Austria and the Anschluss seemed to converge: both nations moved toward prohibition of the Anschluss. But while the French wished to make it permanent, the British hinted at the possibility of a later revision of the Peace Treaty.

At a meeting on February 21, 1919, British and American delegates agreed that the union between Austria and Germany could not be recognized until the peace treaties had been signed. Soon thereafter a parallel recommendation on the Anschluss was made by a joint group of French and American experts. The prohibition was clearly limited to the immediate future. For the more distant future the hope was held out that union might be permitted under certain conditions, depending mainly on the consent of the Council of the League of Nations which of course included France.

Still, in the early postwar period the situation surrounding the Anschluss issue was fluid. Numerous prominent politicians and diplomats claimed unfamiliarity with the policies of the governments of the victorious countries. This included Czechoslovakia's President Dr. G. T. Masaryk, Austria's Foreign Minister Dr. Otto Bauer, and such knowledgeable British diplomats as Horace Rumbold in Berne and Colonel Thomas Cunninghame, British representative in Vienna.[2] Allied policy in regard to Austria and the Anschluss remained vague, indecisive, and inclined to procrastination.

After the German and Austrian peace treaties had been submitted to the German and Austrian delegations in Paris in early May and June 1919, Sir Francis Oppenheim, at the request of the Chancellor of the Exchequer, wrote two memoranda on Austria, warning against "a policy of drift" and against the Anschluss in particular, since it would give a "great stimulus to German expansion toward the Near East," would lead to the establishment of a German-Italian bloc and would isolate France from her eastern allies; it would also prepare "the isolation and destruction of Czechoslovakia." He pleaded that the Western Powers grant extensive economic assistance to Austria. The memoranda were subsequently endorsed by the Foreign Office and the War Cabinet. British concern at this late stage was a clear indication that in their view the treaty submitted to Austria was not the ultimate solution and that it urgently needed economic and political supplements. Even if Western economic help were provided in adequate measure, there seemed to be some doubt that the chasm separating Austria from the new succession states could be bridged in the reasonably near future. If it was not, Austria's continued economic, national, and political isolation and the attraction of belonging to a Greater Germany were likely to grow stronger.[3]

Before 1914, it had been France's major interest to preserve the Austrian monarchy at least in its historic core. When in 1918 the Austrian Empire disintegrated and Germany went down in defeat, the French government, victorious, but haunted by fear for France's security, was determined to prevent Germany from annexing German Austria. A continental power and immediate neighbor of the *Reich*, France was always more directly involved in continental problems than the island nation Great Britain, which was more concerned with imperial and overseas problems. As a sharp opponent of the Anschluss concept in the last days of the dying Habsburg Empire appeared also the influential *Le Temps*, which was known to express views closely akin to those of the *Quai d'Orsay*. In late December 1919 Foreign Minister Stephen Pichon in the Chamber of Deputies opposed Austria's union with Germany, since it would enable the *Reich* to recover through the Austrian population "what she will irrevocably have lost" through the Allied victory.[4]

Clearly, France's policy, notwithstanding protesting voices on the Left, was based on the rejection of the Anschluss. This course was to remain unchanged in the following months and years. The French government squarely opposed that Germany, through the backdoor of the Anschluss, was to gain "compensations" for losses which she might incur at the Peace conference and that French and European security would once again be endangered.

The activities of Henri Allizé who arrived as France's new Ambassador in Vienna on March 29, 1919—only days after the Bolshevik seizure of power in Hungary—were designed to block the union with Germany or Communist Hungary.[5] French traditional diplomacy of encouraging German particularism and separatism, favoring the creation of a South German-Austrian Catholic state, played also a distinct role in shaping France's stance on the Anschluss. Through an ingenuous solution of the German Austrian problem Germany might be reduced in size and even split in two. This would diminish the danger of a German revanche.

Anxieties over the growth of Germany's population as compared to that of France and related concerns of security lay heavily on the French mind and determined France's policy on the Anschluss. Commenting on a speech in Mainz by the leading Majority Socialist Eduard David who had put forth a claim to Austria, a leading French daily wrote: "Here is revealed the deep and secret thought of all German statesmen without exception. Yet . . . if Germany is much bigger and stronger than before the war, will this war not have been without purpose? Then it will be in vain that France, serving as rampart of civilization, will have lost in its defense 1,400,000 men of her best sons."[6] French concerns over Germany's "numerical imbalance" in relation to her neighbors and to herself as well as British interest in the long-range balance of power on the continent outweighed in the end primarily British considerations for the principle of national self-determination.

Italy had entered the war on the side of the Western Powers after wresting territorial concessions from the allies which had crystallized in the Treaty of London in 1915. At the Paris Peace Conference therefore she demanded German South Tyrol, the Brenner pass as well as Dalmatian territories. The wrangling with the victorious allies was to lead to the precipitate departure of the Italian delegation from Paris and its return to Rome.

Italian opinion on the future of Austria which was to emerge from the catastrophe in Central Europe was divided from the beginning. S. Sonnino and many other Italian political leaders were opposed to the aggrandizement of Germany at Austria's expense. In the words of the French consul in Milan, many Italian law-makers estimated that "in the last analysis Italy would badly accommodate . . . to the annexation of German Austria by

Germany."[7] While France feared an Austrian and German *fait accompli* in the form of an Anschluss, Italy was alarmed at the prospect of the *fait accompli* of a French-sponsored Danubian Confederation. The leading Milanese daily *Corriere della Sera* (Jan. 24 and May 15) was opposed to a *"paix française"* in Central Europe. In 1918–1919 the Italian and French press carried on an extensive polemics on the future of Austria. Ultimately, the Great Powers, Italy included, agreed on the prohibition of the Anschluss.

Italy's ultimate switch of policy toward opposing the Anschluss was motivated by the realization that she would fare much better with weak little Austria as a neighbor than with a strong, potentially threatening power like Germany. A German irredenta in South Tyrol would be a much greater threat to Italy if she had a common boundary with the *Reich* than one with Austria. Germany, having swallowed all of Austria, would come menacingly close to the Adriatic Sea and challenge Italy's domination over it. Italy would then lose any influence in Hungary and even Rumania. Germany would gain entrance to the Balkans and become a rival of Italy in southeastern Europe. On the other hand, by opposing the Anschluss, Italy would join the Western Powers in their opposition to German expansionism into Central Europe and ingratiate herself with the Entente.

In the course of the year 1918, the United States and her allies reached the conclusion that the Austro-Hungarian Monarchy, in Secretary of State Robert Lansing's words, should be "blotted out" as an Empire.[8] All its nationalities were to satisfy their national aspirations, in accordance with their wishes. For a brief moment in September 1918, Lansing—perhaps driven by the inner logic of the situation and the seemingly universal validity of the principle of national self-determination—had toyed with the idea of endorsing the Anschluss; but he quickly backed down. The United States seemed to have no policy on the union issue until early 1919. Then, however, her leaders gave unstinting support to the Anschluss prohibition and never wavered subsequently.

Early in 1919 American experts at the Paris Peace Conference moved rapidly toward the French position on the Anschluss. This becomes clear in a communication of W. C. Bullitt to Secretary Lansing on February 19: "In opposing the union, a welcome opportunity is afforded to the U.S. of supporting a vital point of French policy at a time when American prestige in France is suffering because of divergence of views on other important subjects."[9] And in early March 1919 E. L. Dresel of the U.S. Peace Commission suggested in a memorandum that the Council of Ten of the Conference publicly declare that it considered the Anschluss "under present abnormal conditions . . . premature and precipitate."

While the American position on the Anschluss prohibition was especially pleasing to France and also to Great Britain, the one relating to German South Tyrol was favorable to Italy. Yet Italy was hardly pacified by it and remained resentful of the American stand on Adriatic questions. Though the United States contributed to thwarting Austria both in the matter of the Anschluss and of German South Tyrol, she managed to earn and retain the goodwill of the great majority of Austria's population partly by various forms of economic assistance and partly by speaking softly and tending to shift the burden of unpleasant decisions onto France's shoulders. After the peace treaty of St. Germain had been signed, Chancellor Karl Renner voiced Austria's gratitude to Great Britain and the United States for their impartiality during the peace negotiations, as contrasted with the attitude of France and Italy. Although the treaty had been harsh, he said, it had been mitigated by the Anglo-Saxon Powers to whom the new Austria now looked for friendship and assistance.[10] Austria's Foreign Minister Dr. Otto Bauer expressed himself similarly in appreciation of the American and British attitude immediately after his resignation in July 1919.

Dissolution of the Habsburg Empire and Criticism of the Peace-Makers

The Paris peace-makers have been severely criticized for the breakup of the Austrian Empire. Clearly, had the Empire survived and its nationalities decided to continue their political coexistence, perhaps on a new and egalitarian basis, the German Austrians would have remained within the larger political framework and not gravitated toward the German *Reich*. The Anschluss would not have been placed on Europe's agenda, and the political fragmentation of Central Europe, which ultimately played into Hitler's hands, would have been avoided.

But the history of the breakup of the Habsburg Empire shows that its dissolution occurred in October and November 1918 and thus preceded by three months the opening of the Paris Peace Conference in mid-January 1919. The Empire had long disintegrated by the time the Peace Conference opened its doors. Obviously the demise of the Empire was not the work of the Peace Conference.

Could the victorious powers have attempted to revive the Empire in a new form? Such an attempt would have been a hopeless undertaking. The new succession states which in the meantime had sprung up, had done so in response to centuries-old desires for liberty and independence and the political dreams of their peoples. They would never have considered relinquishing their newly won independence and never voluntarily accepted subordination to a higher central authority of uncertain national and political character. The mistrust of centuries, the historic legacy of domination and oppression by the German element, and later also by the Magyars, could not have been swept away by any pious declarations of the former master nations. Not even the threat of force by the victorious Great Powers would have provided the necessary strength to change the mind of the liberated peoples of Central and Eastern Europe. It was utterly unrealistic to expect the victors to furnish such forces or to expect Western public opinion to tolerate the use of force against friendly and allied nations, all for the sake of creating a new Central European federation to take the place of the defunct Habsburg Empire. At a time when the West lacked the resolve to use force against the menace of Russian Bolshevism and to mount an intervention on a larger scale in the Russian Civil War, the prospect of a Western military intervention to restore in a new form the old Austrian Empire—long a reliable ally of the hostile German *Reich*—was virtually nil.

If the dissolution of the Austrian Empire was not the result of hasty decisions of the Paris Peace Conference, perhaps Allied war-time diplomacy was the real culprit. After all, during the year 1918 Western diplomacy embraced the goal of dissolving the multinational monarchy pledging support to the spokesmen for Czechs, Poles, Rumanians, South Slavic peoples, Italians, and others, all of whom demanded independence. Neither the Great Powers nor the smaller European nationalities can basically be faulted for the dissolution of the Austrian Empire. One might as well blame powerful natural forces such as hurricanes, floods, and earthquakes, for creating havoc and destruction. It was during the desperate struggles of World War I that the Allied Powers had made the fateful decision to strengthen their military and diplomatic association with the subjected peoples of Central, Eastern, and Southeastern Europe. These subject peoples became thus cobelligerents and allies. It was the struggle for freedom and national self-determination which was the primary cause of the disintegration of the Austrian Empire. When World War I came to an end, the Habsburg Empire's disintegration was unavoidable, a political, national, and ethical imperative which no one could disregard.

With the advantage of hindsight it is easy to blame the peacemakers for the Balkanization of Central and Southeastern Europe and lack of foresight in regard to the economic future of the liberated peoples of these regions. Yet the plans of the British and French for a Danubian Federation in Central Europe to take the place of the defunct Empire showed that the Western Powers were aware of the serious economic problems likely to grip the area in the immediate postwar period. But should they bear the blame for Italy's opposition to a Danubian Federation and for the obstructions and errors of the new nations of Central and Southeastern Europe and their leaders who feared a resurrection of the old Empire under new disguise? For the new nations or those greatly enlarged after the war, political goals—independence and sovereignty—far outweighed any contrary economic considerations and criteria. The new economic barriers erected hastily by the new states after the war would turn out to be more than just temporary obstacles to the needed economic unity of Central Europe.

The extreme postwar nationalism in Germany and Hungary, their desire to recapture their former hegemony in Central Europe and beyond it, and the opposition of chauvinist forces in Italy to an economic reconstruction of Central Europe under the auspices of France or even of Czechoslovakia buried all prospects for a replacement of the economic unity which the Habsburg Empire had represented. To all this must be added the shortsightedness of strongly nationalist forces in the new succession states which did not fully appreciate their own long-range national and economic interests all of which pointed toward cooperation. Most importantly, neither the Great Powers at the Peace Conference nor the states of Central Europe immediately affected could have anticipated the rise of fascism. Neither Western statesmen nor political leaders of the succession states could have foreseen the emerging political and national cauldron when revisionist nationalism joined forces with a counterrevolution such as German National Socialism and Italian fascism.

Revisionism, Nationality Problems, and the Anschluss

The peace treaties imposed on recalcitrant Germany and Hungary and accepted under protest even by economically dependent Austria determined the history of Europe's interstate relations in the interwar period. Germany's objection though was caused by her own territorial losses rather than by the Anschluss prohibition. German Austria had not been part of Imperial Germany and was not "lost" by the *Reich*. Therefore, Germany in 1919 was on the whole rather cautious in promoting the Anschluss, leaving the initiative in this matter to the Austrians. Germany tried to hold on to her former territories rather than to push for the Anschluss. Weimar Germany was wary that a more vigorous propagandistic pursuit of union would only raise the fears of the Western Powers that the *Reich* was once again travelling on the highway of *Grosse Politik*, trying to establish hegemony in Europe. This would have had adverse repercussions for the *Reich's* 1914 boundaries which remained to be decided upon.

The peace treaties of Versailles and Trianon resulted finally in severe losses for Germany and for Hungary. Both countries lost not merely non-German and non-Magyar minorities who were liberated from centuries-old alien rule: Germany lost Frenchmen, Danes, and Poles. Hungary had to relinquish Slovaks, Rumanians, and Southern Slavs; Austria at St. Germain was definitely to abandon control over Czechs, South-Slavs, and Italians. These losses aside, Germans and Magyars had to relinquish some of their own kinsfolk to neighbors who invoked not only national criteria, but also historic, economic or strategic-military ones, which the Great Powers in turn recognized. It was also often impossible to draw ethnically just boundary lines in nationally hopelessly mixed regions.

To permit Germany to receive any "compensation" for territorial losses by turning over to her 6½ million Austrians would have strengthened the *Reich* in manpower, resources and geopolitics far beyond the power which she had wielded in 1914: 1) Germany would then dispose of more ethnic Germans than she possessed when war broke out, since Austria was, nationally speaking, relatively homogenous. 2) By securing Austria, Germany would have improved her geopolitical and strategic situation over that of 1914: 3) the *Reich* would have come into striking distance of the Balkans and the Adriatic Sea and would have completely surrounded the new Czechoslovakian state.

The principle of national self-determination was widely observed at the Paris Peace Conference, far more than at past Eurpean peace conferences. But in a number of cases it was deliberately overruled by the Conference in favor of other principles such as economic viability, historic claims, and especially considerations of military exigencies and national security. Few historians would justify all territorial cessions and changes which were stipulated in Paris. German and Magyar revisionism, which became prominent in the interwar period, harped on flagrant "injustices"; actually many Germans and Magyars aimed at the restoration of their pre-war hegemony and at undermining the new independence and national liberation which the War's end had brought to the formerly oppressed non-German and non-Magyar peoples.

Was Austria a revisionist state such as Germany, Hungary and, to a considerable extent, Italy? Austria's situation was unique. With the exception of claims for greater autonomy in German South Tyrol—and of claims to parts of the Burgenland (the province remained an apple of discord between Austria and Hungary)—the country's political course was hardly set on territorial revision. Revisionism seemed to Austria a hopeless cause, considering the power of the Italian neighbor to the south and the militancy of Hungary to the east. Austria's sight was rather set on union with Germany. But the policy of Austria, militarily a negligible factor, to gain concessions in these areas was in the 1920s primarily of a declaratory and programmatic character, and geared toward the distant future. The Anschluss movement in the 1920s and early 1930s was a potential rather than an immediate threat to the stability of Central Europe.

Revisionism and the Anschluss movement seemed to link forces when Germany aimed not merely at regaining lost territories but also at overturning the Anschluss prohibition, as stipulated in the treaties of St. Germain and Versailles. In reverse, the new states which were beneficiaries of the peace treaties opposed any attempt at modifying the treaties and were therein firmly supported by France. Italy, though sympathetic toward Hungarian revisionism, opportunistically opposed revisionism in regard to her own northern boundaries at the Brenner pass and in regard to the Anschluss prohibition, out of concern over acquiring too powerful a German neighbor. British public opinion and policy leaned toward moderate revisionism, but Britain did not come out for cancelling the prohibition of Austria's union with the *Reich*. The states of the Little Entente led by Czechoslovakia were on the whole set against revisionism, especially that of the Magyars. Poland, however, while vigorously opposing German revisionism along her own border, was more favorably disposed toward Hungarian demands and more indifferent about the Anschluss prohibition. Each state, in pursuit of its own national and territorial interests, shaped largely by the outcome of the war, the subsequent peace treaties, and its new multinational character, pursued its particular course of policy and action.

On the whole, the lines were sharply drawn between the former victorious powers, largely interested in preserving the *status quo*, and persistently revisionist Germany, Hungary, and, with regional and timely modifications, Italy. The latter was anxious to magnify its European role as champion of territorially and nationally dissatisfied states.

Chapter 2

The Anschluss Movement 1919–1931

The new Austrian Republic, the peril of secession, and the Anschluss

The disintegration of the Austro-Hungarian Dual Monarchy created a vacuum in the center of Europe. It was filled by the new Succession States—Czechoslovakia, Poland, Hungary, Rumania, Yugoslavia—and by the new Austrian Republic, the latter calling itself first "Deutsch-Österreich." German Austria, in the words of Clémenceau, comprised what was left from the Habsburg Empire. There were strong Anschluss currents in this German-inhabited remnant of the Austrian monarchy. But following the prohibition of the Anschluss of German Austria with the *Reich* by the Entente, which was ultimately crystallized in the peace treaties, the new Austrian Republic faced not only domestic revolution but also the threat of further disintegration of the country.[1] The threat of secession from the new Austria arose especially in outlying provinces such as Vorarlberg, Tyrol, Salzburg, and Styria. At the root of this secessionist movement lay the economic distress of the new Austria, her lack of cohesion, the disappointment over the failure of the Anschluss and of the creation of a new large economic realm comparable to the old Empire, and opposition to and fear of "Red Vienna." But Austria weathered the storm and preserved her integrity.

On May 11, 1919, Vorarlberg held a plebiscite on the question of union with Switzerland. About 80% of the people voted in its favor. Thereupon, the Provincial Assembly of Vorarlberg prepared to negotiate with Vienna, Berne, and the Peace Conference about the implementation of the union. The instructions of Dr. Otto Bauer, Austrian Minister of Foreign Affairs, to the Austrian Peace Delegation in St. Germain contemplated the possibility that special delegations would represent some of the Austrian *Länder*, including Vorarlberg, at the Peace Conference in Paris. The Swiss government actually raised the question of the constitutionality of Vorarlberg's secession from Austria. On December 6, 1919, nevertheless, the Vorarlberg *Landtag* by a vote of 20 to 7, with the Socialist Party in opposition, decided to hold a plebiscite on the issue.

From Vorarlberg the secessionist movement spread to other Austrian provinces, including neighboring Tyrol. The Tyrolese pretended to ignore the virtual prohibition of the Anschluss in the just concluded treaties of St. Germain and Versailles. Pointing to the desperate economic situation of Tyrol in regard to food, coal, and other necessities, the Tyrol *Landtag* passed a resolution in which it drew attention to its dire needs and appealed to the Entente for help. But at the same time it also threatened the Western Powers that it would proceed with the union with Germany and urged the Austrian federal government to obtain the consent of the Supreme Allied Council for the secession of Tyrol and the link-up with the *Reich*.[2]

On December 16 the Salzburg *Landtag*, in a unanimous motion, asked for economic union with Bavaria rather than with Germany in her entirety and also appealed to the Vienna government to act as an intermediary. The Supreme Allied Council, however, in line with Allied policy at the Peace Conference, was determined to prevent a further breakup of German Austria, and vetoed such a move. Clémenceau spoke for the entire Council when he, pointing to the need for the preservation of the Austrian territory, warned that her disappearance would destroy the balance of power in Central Europe. The very argument, previously used in behalf of Austria's separate political existence and against the Anschluss with the *Reich*, was this time repeated against the further breakup of the remains of the Austrian Empire, of German Austria proper. The Supreme Allied Council let Chancellor Renner know that he "must uphold the provisions of the treaty of St. Germain and prevent any development likely to prejudice the political and economic independence of Austria."[3]

The government of Tyrol, however, ignored the Allied decision. Early in March 1920 it insisted on Tyrol establishing political union with Germany. This Tyrolese drive toward union with Bavaria, supported by Governor Schraffl, was partly motivated by a virtual famine in the provinces. On March 16 the Tyrol *Landtag* passed a unanimous resolution to the effect that the provincial government enlist the assistance of the Vienna government so that the Great Powers cancel the prohibition of the union with Germany. Representatives of the three major Tyrolese political parties journeyed to Vienna in support of the resolution. Chancellor Karl Renner, however, informed the Tyrolese delegation that any movement aiming at the revision of the St. Germain treaty had little chance of success. He also appealed to all Austrians to refrain from any precipitate demonstrations which would needlessly aggravate the situation. While the various *Landtage* continued their splitting activities, they called upon the federal government in Vienna to support their steps at Geneva; the separatist propaganda and agitation in the provinces continued unabated. In late April, 1920, the Vienna government was compelled to point out to the Tyrolese authorities that their planned plebiscite on the Anschluss with Germany was unconstitutional, since Austria's fundamental law placed the subject of union squarely into the field of foreign affairs which were outside the jurisdiction of the *Länder*.[4] Faced finally with the threat by the French government to withhold financial assistance to Austria unless Vienna terminated its support of the Anschluss, the Austrian government was forced to demand the cancellation of the Tyrolean plebiscite. Still, the plebiscite was held, as scheduled, on April 24, 1921; 98.9% of all votes cast were for union with the *Reich*.

The Allies were dead-set against any Anschluss of Austria with the *Reich* whether in its totality or in parts. Preservation of Austria's independence was essential to the security of Austria's neighbors as well as their own security. Even a mere partial Anschluss would leave the remainder of German Austria economically less viable than before. It would also establish a dangerous precedent for the political stability of other states and of Europe as a whole. The recently signed peace treaties were not to be hurriedly revised at the dawn of the new day. In the event the prohibition of the Anschluss was disregarded, the Allies were resolved to apply even military sanctions. To discourage the Salzburg *Landtag* from holding an Anschluss plebiscite, the Entente spokesmen threatened Vienna with the occupation of Carinthia by Yugoslavia.[5] Chancellor Mayr warned Austria's Constitutional Committee that, if full or partial Anschluss was contemplated, badly needed foreign credits would be withheld. In vain did the Chancellor convoke the Commission for Foreign

Affairs on May 28 to warn it about the danger of the projected plebiscites in Salzburg and Styria, pointing to the protests submitted to the Austrian cabinet during the last five weeks by France, Italy, Great Britain, Rumania, Czechoslovakia, and Poland.

The vote taken in Salzburg on May 29 revealed an overwhelming approval of the union with Germany; of 102,000 votes cast 95,000 were for the link-up with Germany. Thus the Vienna government was unable to dissuade the *Landtag* of Styria to cancel the plebiscite scheduled for May 31. In dire need of credits, but encountering stiff Allied opposition to the plebiscites and to the union agitation, Mayr saw no other exit but resignation.

Postwar Austrian governments and German political parties

The new government, formed on June 21, was headed by Johann Schober and supported by the Christian Social Party, still the strongest Austrian party, and the *Grossdeutschen*. The latter, however, were compelled to pledge to continue the reconstruction program of Austria through the League of Nations, to oppose further provincial plebiscites, and to approve the cancellation of the Styrian plebiscite. The announced foreign policy of the Schober government included pledges for the faithful observation of the Peace Treaty. Austria was to avoid the perils of the Anschluss policy and establish cordial relations with all states. The economic reconstruction of Austria became the primary objective.[6]

With the accession to power by the Schober cabinet in June 1921, the provincial movement for union which had recently characterized the Anschluss movement, came to an end. Differently from the 1918–19 era, when the Anschluss movement was under socialist auspices, the period 1919–1921 was politically under "bourgeois" and *grossdeutsch* influence and, socially speaking, the petit bourgeoisie, the peasants, and in particular the provincial intelligentsia had become most assertive. The progressive and socialist current which had first driven the Anschluss stream ahead had been replaced by a strong current of petit bourgeois ideology. The Social Democratic support for union with the *Reich* continued, though with less enthusiasm and élan than in the immediate postwar period. Dr. Otto Bauer, the theoretical and political leader of the Social Democratic Party and champion of the Anschluss movement, while serving as Austrian Foreign Minister from November 1918 to mid-summer 1919, himself pointed to the changing political complexion of the Anschluss movement in the early twenties.

Numerous Anschluss demonstrations took place in Austria in the early postwar era, though with less vigor than in 1918–1919 and also with diminishing hope of immediate success. The more gripping the economic problems in Austria became, the more strident the call for the Anschluss. In February 1920, the small National Democratic party and the somewhat larger *grossdeutsch* (Pan-German) party in Austria with Franz Dinghofer as President, emphasized that the only solution for Austria was union with all the Germans of Central Europe.[7] It seemed as if, notwithstanding the fierce Anschluss debate in Central Europe and the arduous labor of the Peace Conference, the champions of union still thought that the case could be reopened, the opponents be persuaded to change their views, and France in particular be isolated.[8] Illusions have sometimes a hard way of dying.

In Germany the political parties overwhelmingly favored the Anschluss. In the twenties, democratic parties such as the Social Democrats, the Democrats, and the Catholic Center, were among those who were most vociferous and persistent in favor of union; it was as if they wished to remind their political opponents at the Right that despite their "international" ties with either Socialists or Catholics in Europe and their ideological sympathies for the Western Powers, they could be fully trusted, since they were also fighters for a preeminent national cause such as the Anschluss. Smarting under the accusation by extreme rightists and conservatives, that in 1918 they had stabbed Germany in the back and that they entertained sympathies for the Western enemy, and for Western liberalism and democracy, the German democratic Parties tended to be critical of the peace treaties and of the prohibition of the Anschluss in particular.

If the Entente had permitted the Anschluss, the *Reich* would have acquired boundaries more favorable than those in 1914; expecting such an outcome was obviously devoid of all realism. Still, many Germans had set their heart on it. Though they realized that German revisionism would arouse bitter hostility and insuperable obstacles among Germany's neighbors, such as France, Belgium, Denmark, Poland, and others, they persuaded themselves that Anschluss with Austria would encounter less resistance. Faced with the apparent endorsement of union by a majority of Austrians, they hoped that the Western Powers, with Great Britain and the even more distant United States taking the lead, would bow to the insistent clamor for national self-determination.

The Anschluss, some German Democrats held, would redound to the advantage of the Weimar regime, bestow prestige and glory upon it at home and abroad, and strengthen German democracy against its internal enemies. These German democrats included German Socialists who were national-minded and Austrian Socialists who favored union also on grounds of party politics. These Germans were fearful of not being considered good patriots and of being not responsive to German needs. The accusation of being indifferent or hostile to German national demands might prove calamitous at the ballot box. The endorsement of the Anschluss concept by German democrats and socialists was to dispel once and for all the unjust charge of lagging German nationalism. At the same time the possibility of an early union, despite the recurring publicity, seemed remote and not likely to produce an immediate international crisis. In the twenties, the Anschluss issue, though continuing to attract attention, generated neither in Austria nor in Germany the feverish emotional intensity among its proponents which had characterized it at the end of the war. On both sides of the Inn river it was understood that union was not the first item on the agenda.

Still, the link between the Anschluss issue and the strength and survival of German democracy puzzled politicians abroad. French political leaders such as Paul-Boncour were perplexed that in the *Reich* it was not the parties of the Right, Pan-Germans and nationalists, who favored annexation, but "the parties of the pacifist Left," Socialists, Democrats, and the Catholic Center.

In espousing the Anschluss, the German democratic parties of the Weimar era were also influenced by the historic past, the link between the national movement of 1848–49, which had aimed at creating a *Grossdeutschland*, and nineteenth century German democracy. German and Austrian liberals pointed repeatedly to the links between the Anschluss program and German democracy. In the immediate postwar period the *Deutsche Demokratische Partei*, including prominent leaders such as Friedrich Naumann and Theodor Heuss, had loyally worked in behalf of the Anschluss and continued to give vigorous support to the union concept.[9] Political considerations, too, played a considerable role in their championship of the Anschluss. In the event of union with Austria, the SPD and the Center Party in the *Reich* would each add about 1½ million voters to their rolls, while the German Nationalist People's Party (DNVP) would have secured only about half a million votes.

In 1920 several propaganda organizations championing the Anschluss idea sprang up in Vienna, among them the *Deutsch-Österreichischer Volksbund*[10] and the *Deutsche Arbeitsgemeinschaft*. For some time to come they confined their activities to Austria, but later extended them to the *Reich*. The *Deutsche Arbeitsgemeinschaft*, founded on June 5, 1920, counted among its first members Professor Karl Hugelmann, the director of the *Deutsches Volksblatt*, General Alfred Krauss and numerous Austrian deputies, among them Walter Riehl. An address by Dr. Karl Seitz, President of the Austrian Republic and prominent Social Democrat, to the teachers of Lower Austria, though pro-Anschluss in its over-all tendency, indicated already a distinct shift in the Social Democratic position. The Austrian Republic should be "preserved" for the moment, until "that great historic day arrives when Austria shall be incorporated into the great intellectual[!] community of the German *Reich*." No immediate Anschluss! And his emphasis was on mere intellectural ties with Germany. A debate in the Austrian National Assembly showed a similar reluctance on the part of deputies of different political persuasions. Dr. Wagner of the Christian Social Party cautioned not to press the Anschluss issue, since the agitation for union had already injured Austria's interests. He protested, perhaps too sharply, when he disputed that Austrian Catholics were afraid of union with the *Reich* because the latter had a Protestant majority. Indeed, the very reluctance of the Christian Socials on the Anschluss issue was the target of criticism by *grossdeutsch* deputies and others.

Austria and the League of Nations

The pressing economic problems of Austria, impoverished heir of the defunct Habsburg Empire, were dealt with by the League of Nations in March 1921. After a conference in London, France, Great Britain, Italy, and Japan informed the League of Nations that they would permit all claims against Austria to lapse for several years, provided that all other concerned states would consent to do the same and provided that Austria would agree to turn her assets over to the League. By February 1922, Great Britain, France, Italy, and Czechoslovakia advanced considerable sums of money to Austria to save her from bankruptcy. The Austrian government made an additional appeal for help to enable it to meet not only the country's current needs but also to carry out thorough financial reforms. On August 15, 1922, Lloyd George held out the prospect of further financial assistance to Austria on condition that a reconstruction program include definite guarantees for far-reaching financial improvements. On September 6, 1922 finally, Chancellor Ignaz Seipel, after several visits to Prague, Berlin, and Verona, presented the Austrian case to the Council of the League of Nations. Pointing to the depreciation of the Austrian currency and to the fears of the Austrians for the country's future, he underlined the financial and economic misery of the moment. As an early postwar Austrian government in which Socialist influence prevailed had cautioned, so Seipel now warned of the grave perils which would arise in all of Central Europe if one refused to come to grips with the Austrian predicament. Shrewdly he reminded the victorious Powers of the high stakes they had in the stabilization and survival of Austria. The disappearance of Austria, one of the oldest centers·of culture and civilization, would be a "serious blow to the peace treaties" and would demonstrate that Austria was simply not viable. All of her neighbors would be "drawn into the catastrophe and would thus upset the balance which, apart from Austria, is even now maintained only with difficulty."[11] Seipel conceded that some control of Austrian finances by the League would be inevitable, but basically Austrian sovereignty would not be affected. An Austrian Committee, created by the Council of the League and consisting of 5 members, represented Great Britain, France, Italy, Czechoslovakia, and Austria; Lord Balfour headed the Committee. On October 4, the representatives of these states appended their signatures to altogether three protocols on the restoration of Austria. Eighty percent of the necessary loan was granted by the foregoing four powers. The guarantors for the proposed economic and financial restoration solemnly promised that they would respect the integrity and sovereignty of Austria and would not seek to obtain any special or exclusive advantage. Austria, in accordance with the terms of Article 88 of the Treaty of St. Germain, pledged not to alienate her independence. In 1919 German Austria, reduced to poverty and impotence, had had no choice but to accept the treaty of St. Germain with its prohibition of the Anschluss. In 1922, driven by financial need, the Austrian government was compelled to accept the Geneva Protocols thus renewing its obligation to preserve Austria's independence for the duration of the loan—until 1943.

From Geneva to Locarno

During the next four years the Anschluss Movement made little headway in either Austria or Germany. Austria had to pull herself out of her financial mire and Germany faced the tribulations of an unprecedented inflation, of the pressing problems of reparations, and of the Ruhr occupation. German National resistance against France was raised to new heights. Though Anschluss was no longer a prime and acute concern of the Austrian and German governments and of the Western Powers, popular demonstrations in behalf of union continued to dominate Central Europe's political life, and Anschluss oratory did not abate. In January and February 1923, when French and Belgian troops occupied the Ruhr, voices from Austria—such as the utterances of the President of the *Nationalrat*, Dr. Weisskirchner, and a proclamation to the Austrian people by members of the Christian Social Party, of the *Grossdeutschen* and the *Landbund*, all of which protested the occupation—boosted the morale of the German people, as the German Minister in Vienna, Dr. Pfeiffer, gratefully acknowledged. On May 18, 1923, on occasion of the 75th anniversary of the German Parliament of 1848, a delegation from the Austrian Parliament, headed by Dr. Dinghofer and Dr. Seitz, one a *Grossdeutscher*, the other a Social Democrat, travelled to Frankfurt a.m.; Seitz held out the hope that one day the longing of the German nation for union would be fulfilled. Leaders of virtually all Austrian political parties thus voiced their hopes for a union with Germany, though many were realistic enough not to expect it in the foreseeable future.

In March 1924 Chancellor Wilhelm Marx and Foreign Minister Gustav Stresemann journeyed to Vienna to discuss mutual economic problems with members of the Austrian government; Stresemann took this opportunity to point out that this was their first visit outside the *Reich*. The visit was returned in January 1925 when Dr. Dinghofer, President of the Austrian *Nationalrat*, and the former Vice-Chancellor Frank, both *Grossdeutsche*, travelled to Germany to meet with President Ebert and Stresemann. There followed other visits by members of the *Deutsche Volkspartei* and the *Deutschnationale Volkspartei* (German National People's Party). Similarly, a delegation from the Austrian Social Democratic *Schutzbund*, headed by Dr. Julius Deutsch and Dr. Pichler, attended the meeting of the *Reichsbanner*, the noted socialist-oriented paramilitary organization in the *Reich*, at Magdeburg on February 22, 1925. On this occasion both the German ex-Chancellor Dr. Wirth and Dr. Deutsch, Social Democratic deputy in the Austrian *Nationalrat* and leader of the *Schutzbund*, voiced their hope for union. On July 29, 1925, an Austro-German convention decided on the reciprocal abolition of visas.

In the mid-twenties the Anschluss problem was frequently discussed, usually in the context of several alternative solutions for Austria and Central Europe, especially the project of a Danubian Federation under French auspices, the restoration of the Habsburg Monarchy, even the projection of Italian influence into Austria and Hungary. The Czechoslovak Foreign Minister Edvard Beneš, in a speech in the Czechoslovakian Senate on April 1, 1925, rejected both the Anschluss proposition and the Confederation concept, but did not exclude a closer economic relationship with Austria and other neighbors, provided the Central European states concerned would preserve their full economic and political sovereignty.[12] But many Austrians suspected that what Czechoslovakia aimed at was a Danubian Confederation in which she herself, and indirectly France, would play a dominant role.

On April 2, 1924, German ex-Chancellor Wilhelm Marx, a declared candidate for the presidency, came out in favor of the Anschluss;[13] no similar declaration was issued by other candidates. Under these circumstances, the election of Hindenburg as President of the German Republic was looked upon by many Austrians at least as a temporary defeat for the union movement.

During the year 1925 several Anschluss organizations displayed an increasing activity. In June of that year the *Schutzbund*, a Social Democratic paramilitary organization, met in St. Pölten, demonstrating in favor of the Anschluss. On the same day the *Alldeutscher Verband* at a Congress in Villach, came strongly out in favor of union with the *Reich*. Hardly less intensive was the propagandistic activity in behalf of the union movement on the German side of the border. During the month of July the German conservative deputy and noted historian Otto Hoetzsch, and the Social Democratic deputy Rudolf Breitscheid, leader of his party in the *Reichstag*, championed the Anschluss. Both men, however, exhibited a certain caution, favoring for the moment only an economic and cultural rapprochement between Germany and Austria. The same reluctance to push forward toward a political union was also displayed by ex-Minister Koch, leader of the Democratic Party in the *Reich*.

Both German Democrats and Socialists and their Austrian counterparts participated in one of the largest, allegedly spontaneous, pro-Anschluss demonstrations in Vienna; it coincided with the arrival of about 30 members of the *Reichstag*, led by its President, the prominent Social Democrat Paul Löbe. Löbe, representing the progressive, democratic and pacifist wing of the Anschluss movement, assured his audiences and the world at large that the Anschluss was "not a question of victory of one power over the other but a peaceful movement which would ensure the pacific collaboration not only of Austria and Germany but of all [!] the nations of the earth."[14] Other speakers at this meeting held in the *Rathaus* on August 30, 1925, were the Austrian right-wing Social Democratic deputy Karl Leuthner, Dr. Theodor Heuss, *Reichstag* deputy of the German Democratic Party, destined to become President of the German Federal Republic after World War II, and Dr. Gustav Stolper, noted Austrian economist, writer and Anschluss champion since the early postwar era. In 1926 members of the socialist opposition in the Austrian *Nationalrat*, Dr. Karl Leuthner and R. Austerlitz, attacked the Austrian Foreign Minister Heinrich Mataja for his alleged weakness and unfriendly attitude toward the *Reich* and the Anschluss.

Anschluss Organizations

The most important of all German Anschluss organizations was the *Österreichisch-deutscher Volksbund* (People's League); still it has been estimated that as late as 1924 it had no more than

21,600 members. It displayed a lively propagandistic activity especially among the intelligentsia and professional elements of the *Reich*. The organization reflected the political complexion of the Weimer coalition, comprising the SDP, the Center and the DDP. Among its leaders, representing especially the democratic Left, were Paul Löbe, SPD Chairman, dubbed the "General Field Marshal" of the Anschluss movement, and Wilhelm Heile, Vice Chairman,[15] of the DDP.

The *Volksbund*, sponsoring the publication *Österreich-Deutschland: Heim ins Reich*, emphasized its ideological distance from the Pan-German League and vehemently denied that it was annexationist. Its first President had been the historian and Social Democrat Ludo Hartmann, the first Austrian Ambassador to the Weimar Republic and dedicated champion of the union movement in the immediate postwar period. Apparently this Socialist and Austrian background of its first President, made a lasting impression upon the *Volksbund*. A continuing complaint addressed to the organization was that it was allegedly socialist-dominated. Another accusation levelled against it was that most of its members were Austrians who resided in the *Reich*. In the mid-twenties, an Austrian diplomat admitted that 80% of the membership of the Berlin chapter of the *Volksbund* consisted of Austrian and other foreign residents in the *Reich*. Only after 1926, in post-Locarno Europe, when the chances of union were on the increase, did the German membership of the *Volksbund* increase rapidly.

Another organization working toward the Anschluss was the *Deutsch-Österreichische Arbeitsgemeinschaft*, created in 1925. It denied that it competed in any manner with the *Volksbund*. Its purpose, it insisted, was not to focus on propaganda or lobbying activities: it was rather engaged in the preparation of specialized studies on the problems of the eventual union between Austria and Germany. As late as 1928 it counted in all of Germany fewer than 400 members. Its first President, Freiherr von Branca, wished to shift major activities of the new organization away from Berlin to Munich, apparently in the hope of attracting supporters for union with Austria in the Catholic South. Both the *Volksbund* and the *Arbeitsgemeinschaft* received some financial support from Berlin.[16] The appeal of the Anschluss movement in both Austria and Germany was, as seen, not limited to distinct political groups, but extended to ideologically diverse elements covering a broad ideological spectrum. Though this circumstance lent the movement strength, it was in some respects also a source of weakness.

The Anschluss movement in both countries, though occasionally bridging the internal political differences, was most often dominated by domestic disputes and mutual distrust. In practice, the Austrian Christian Socials, led by Monsignor Ignaz Seipel, opposed the Anschluss. Theoretically, however, the Party trod a narrow path avoiding to run counter to the widespread pro-union sentiments in the new Republic, existing even within its own party. Since 1922, the Christian Socials were joined in a domestic alliance with the *Grossdeutschen* in which the latter made greater compromises on the union issue. Anti-Socialist policy held the coalition together and prevailed over continuing differences between the two bourgeois parties on the Anschluss question, the issue of church schools, and other religious and cultural questions.

Seipel and the Christian Socials

The most influential leader of the Christian Social Party and Chancellor of the First Republic, Ignaz Seipel, had actively opposed the Anschluss in 1918–1919 and had renounced it again in the Geneva Protocols of 1922. He wrote privately that while he was "unsympathetic" to the German-Austrian *Arbeitsgemeinschaft*, he "completely rejected" the *Volksbund*. Though the latter was basically conservative in tone and had a middle-class following, it was in Seipel's eyes tainted by its partly socialist membership, partly by its Anschluss fervor. As far as the pro-union Christian Socials and the *Grossdeutschen* were concerned, they intensely disliked the participation of the paramilitary socialist *Schutzbund* in Anschluss demonstrations. The position of Seipel on the union was always ambiguous, at times hostile toward union, and the program of the Christian Social Party itself was frequently straddling the issue. Many Christian Socials favored linking up with the Succession states and shied away from the Protestant, unitary, if not increasingly centralistic *Reich*.

Seipel himself, while stressing the German *Kultur* of the Austrians and the existence of a single German nation, was bent on defending Austria's independent existence. In April 1925, Seipel rejected the political form of the Anschluss concept: "I am not against a union, but I do not see a solution of Austria's problem in such a union."[17] And he observed: "As long as treaties exist, there can be no discussion of a union." His ideal was a "United States of the whole of Europe."

In August 1925, Seipel, after his return from a Catholic Congress in Stuttgart opposed the union concept, though he paid lip-service to the cultural community linking Austria and Germany. Austrian Catholics, he asserted, were "conscious of the unity of culture of the German Nation."[18] Recalling the views expressed in an earlier wartime study, Nation und Staat (1916), he restated that Germans should "not attach too great an importance to political frontiers, because they know by experience that the nation and the state do not by necessity coincide." Again on a visit to Berlin on February 5, 1926, Seipel came out in criticism of a policy of mere demonstration for union, which seemed to have become popular in Austria. He himself would favor establishing closer ties, especially economic ones, with the Reich, but oppose political union with Germany, since he considered it impossible of attaining it.[19] With Seipel's hands at the steering wheel of the Austrian ship of state, there was little chance that, whatever pronunciamentoes were made in behalf of union, Austria would sail into Anschluss waters. As far as the German side was concerned, notwithstanding Foreign Minister Stresemann's stronger ideological commitment to the Anschluss concept, union under his stewardship was not high on the agenda of the Weimar Republic. Germany's conciliation with France and Great Britain, which led to the Locarno treaty and Germany's entry into the League of Nations, had a definite priority and it compelled the Reich to postpone playing the Austrian card.

Seipel was the more concerned that Austrian and German Anschluss propaganda was to be kept in bounds and that union with the Reich be not considered an immediate and urgent problem, as the prospects for Austria's regaining full control over her finances looked bright in 1925. This was then the very gist of the reports of the foreign experts W. T. Layton and Charles Rist made after an investigation of Austria's economic and financial condition. Their report to the League of Nations, The Economic Situation of Austria pointed out that Austria had shown "slow but definite improvement."[20] Though the Austrian Republic was in some respects still compared to "a convalescent," the often-posed question whether Austria was a viable state was answered affirmatively. This report enabled the League to restore to Austria financial self-control in 1926.

Polemics on Austria's economic Viability

Next to national, ideological, political, and cultural motivation, economics figured large in the development of the Anschluss movement, though this is not always reflected in the documents and the archives. The economic dislocations in Central Europe which occurred as consequences of the demise of the Habsburg Empire and in postwar Austria in particular, have been frequently analyzed in contemporary writings and in scholarly works. Though the descriptions of the sad state of affairs exceeding that of most European countries do not greatly differ from each other, the analysis of the major problems and especially recommendations for their cure diverged widely.

It was no surprise that the foregoing favorable report on Austria's economy by Layton and Rist was sharply criticized by Austrian pro-Anschluss propagandists for whom the political goal of union took precedence before all others. Friedrich Kleinwaechter, a tireless champion for the Anschluss and author of several pro-union books and pamphlets on the union issue, claimed that the German Austrian lands were the "directing brains"[21] of the entire economic region of the former Habsburg Monarchy and compared Austria's postwar situation of being cut off from the new succession states which had become the heirs of the defunct Empire to New York state which would be suddenly separated from the rest of the USA. The union propagandists pointed especially to German Austria's need for the import of foodstuffs and raw materials and the country's inability to pay for these imports, the continued growth of a trade deficit, and the depletion of Austria's credit. Their exaggerations and often one-sided analysis caused consternation and fear among the business community, small as well as heavy industrialists, and both retailers and wholesalers. K. W. Rotschild in his study *Austria's Economic Development between Two Wars* (London, 1947) was convinced that Austrian businessmen, gripped by discouragement and anxiety, actually underestimated Austria's potentialities and that their pessimism was a primary issue for the slowness of the recovery in the 1920s. Another writer, Ferdinand Tremel, similarly concluded that "Austria's capability to live was at that time not an economic but a psychological problem," a view also endorsed by Stanley Suval in his book *The Anschluss Question in the Weimar Era*.[22]

Conceding that Austria faced serious economic problems, it is, nevertheless, noteworthy that different economists responded differently to the question as to their solution. Those leaning toward union with Germany became enthusiastic proponents of the Anschluss, foremost among them, Friedrich F. Kleinwaechter, *Selbstbestimmungsrecht für Österreich* (Stuttgart, 1929), Gustav Stolper, *Deutsch-Österreich als Sozial-und Wirtschaftsproblem*, Munich 1921, Herbert Kniesche, *Die grossdeutsche Wirtschaftseinheit*, Leipzig, 1929, Siegmund Schilder, *Der Streit über die Lebensfähigkeit* Österreichs (Stuttgart, 1926) Adolf Günther, *Die wirtschaftliche und soziale Seite der deutsch-österreichischen Anschlussfrage* (Munich, 1926),[23] and others. On the other side, Friedrich Hertz, a noted writer and civil servant, who after 1938 became a leading sociologist and political scientist in England, siding with the League of Nations' economists Layton and Rist, argued that the Austrian deficit was only a bookkeeping problem and that the unfavorable trade balance could be reduced—a view quickly challenged by Gustav Stolper.[24] Hertz insisted that Austria could emulate the example of Switzerland as a model for concentrating her efforts on tourism and light industry.

A good number of those who were convinced of Austria's economic viability came from believers in free international trade, from champions of Pan-Europe or at least of a Danubian Confederation, while their opponents, Anschluss propagandists, considered such goals too distant and virtual illusions; they held with Kleinwaechter that Austria could "not wait until the ideal of Pan-Europe is achieved."[25] Many of the proponents of union with Germany were not only German nationalists but simply convinced that the large state held out numerous advantages over the small Austro-German remnant of the Habsburg Empire and looked upon solutions other than union with Germany as utopian. Their decision in behalf of the latter was unquestionably politically motivated.

Next to Pan-Europe was the more modest plan of a Danubian economic federation of which Johannes Barodin became a champion. Barodin too became the target of sharp criticism by Anschluss propagandists, especially Stolper who questioned whether the

states of Central Europe which had just been created were prepared
to relinquish their newly-won national and political independence.
In hyperbolic fashion, Stolper called upon Austrians to build "a
paradise in the garden of Europe,"[26] just before changing his own
residence from Austria to the *Reich*'s. Chancellor Seipel himself,
though favorably inclined toward the Danubian federation project,
entertained serious doubts about its practicality on account of
the new states' likely opposition.

Hertz and Barodin insisted that the Anschluss would have a
deleterious impact upon Austria by depriving her of the last few
trump cards vis-à-vis the *Reich*, and warned that Austrian wages
would have to be raised to the German level with the result that
Austria would lose its competitiveness in the European market.
The German political scientist Moritz Bonn, on the other hand,
pointed to alleged Austrian slovenliness[27]—a frequent observation
by some Germans—which could not compete with North German
thoroughness. Most Anschluss proponents, however, argued that
the union would benefit Austria in the long run. Even they,
however, had to concede that Vienna would never reach the
preeminent status of an imperial capital, that at best it would
become the "Hamburg of the East."[28]

There were times during the 1920s when the state of German
recovery made the Anschluss unattractive and dampened the spirit
of the Austrian union enthusiasts. This was the case at the time
of the 1919 revolutionary turmoil and especially of the 1923
German inflation crisis. The Anschluss fervor in Austria reached
then rock bottom. The strength of the Anschluss movement, other
potent forces aside which gave birth to it in the first place, was
also a function of the economics of both Austria and Germany
and the relative advantages which Anschluss promised to the
other country. Germany's economic recovery after the acceptance
of the Dawes plan and after Locarno brought substantial changes
in the Austrians' drive toward union. By 1928, Austrian manufacturers' associations for most branches of light industries and
of foreign and internal commerce became more articulate, and
the increasing links of Austria's heavy industry with German
industry through direct investment of the latter in Austria produced
a further change of climate in Austria. Anton Apold, director of
the *Alpine Montangesellschaft* which had been acquired by the

United Steelworks Trust of Germany, considered the Anschluss "an economic necessity."[29]

Slow Progress: Cultural, legal, and economic rapprochement 1926–1929

Demonstrations and speeches continued to keep the Anschluss issue before the eyes of the Austrian and German people and the rest of Europe. There followed occasional journeys of Austria's business and political leaders to the *Reich* and return visits of German officials and spokesmen to Austria. Representatives of various other Austrian and German organizations crossed frequently the boundary, and student journeys and travels of guest professors also strengthened the numerous sentimental and cultural ties between Austria and Germany. On November 12, 1925, the Socialist leader of the German *Reichsbanner*, participating on the seventh anniversary of the proclamation of the Austrian Republic, praised such paramilitary social democratic organizations as the *Reichsbanner* and the *Schutzbund*. These "protective" organizations should be preserved until the German nation became a united state and all boundary posts still separating Austria and Germany had been removed. These organizations, actually created to meet the threat from the Right in both countries, were thus endowed with a national task to make them more acceptable to public opinion.

The year 1926 became a turning point in regard to the status both of Austria and Germany. In the summer of 1926, after the stabilization of the Austrian currency and the balance of the state budget had been achieved, the League of Nations terminated its control of Austrian finances. Similarly, the entry of Germany into the League of Nations and the signing of the Locarno treaties radically altered the position of the *Reich* in Europe. But these changes, notwithstanding their far-reaching effects, did influence the Anschluss movement only little. In the views of the two leading politicians in Austria and the *Reich*, Monsignor Seipel and Foreign Minister Stresemann, both pragmatists, the over-all situation in Central Europe and in Europe in its entirety did not encourage any Anschluss movement. Actually, as long as Stresemann lived, no policy change bearing on the movement for union of Austria with Germany did take place.

Despite the unceasing propaganda, continuous demonstrations and frequent mutual visits in the nineteen twenties, little progress was made toward political union of Austria and Germany. While a political move toward fulfillment of the union seemed even to the most ardent partisans of the Anschluss out of question, legal *Angleichung* (assimilation) and closer economic and cultural ties appeared feasible and the most promising road for both Austria and Germany. With the Austro-German treaty of June 1, 1923, each of the two countries gave special recognition to the decisions of the civil courts of the other.[30-31] The German code of Civil Procedure, especially the law of February 13, 1924, was greatly influenced by the Austrian code. In 1928 an agreement was reached between Germany and Austria regarding railroad regulation; the Austrian lower House saw in it "an accelerated assimilation of the legal and economic relations of German Austria to those of the German Reich."[32]

Similarly, in January 1929, the *Nationalrat* appealed to the government that it introduce a bill to cover the "*Angleichung* of the Austrian marriage law to German law."[33] The most important example of legal rapprochement was probably the reform of the criminal code. In 1919 there had been worked out in the German criminal law field the so-called *Entwurf von 1919* (Draft of 1919); at the same time Austrians published the *Österreichischer Gegenentwurf zu dem Deutschen Strafgesetzentwurf von 1919*. Since then both the Austrian and German Departments of Justice worked closely on a reform, with a definite view of making the draft rather identical.

While the steps in the late twenties toward juridical *Angleichung* and diplomatic rapprochement were rather cautious, continuous pro-Anschluss demonstrations during the years 1926–29 exerted unrelenting pressure. On October 2, 1927, 75,000 *Grossdeutsche* organized an Anschluss demonstration in front of the old Imperial Palace in Vienna, in honor of von Hindenburg's 80th birthday.[34] Count Lerchenfeld, German Ambassador to Austria, assured the audience that Germany would always welcome Austria into a German confederation. In April 1928 a Committee for the Economic Union of Austria and Germany was created in Vienna. Between July 19–22, 1928, the *Deutscher Sängerbund* arrived in Vienna to celebrate the Schubert festival, which turned out to be one of the most grandiose Anschluss demonstrations in the Austrian capital. The political overtones of this meeting were apparent from the very beginning. Therefore, the reception in the former Imperial Palace at Schönnbrunn was demonstratively boycotted by the Ministers of the Entente countries. An oration by Minister Siegert culminated in the ominous threat, "Germanic countries will not know real peace until the cry resounds 'One fatherland, from the Rhine to the Danube'"![35] The Nazi slogan "*Ein Volk, ein Führer*," was a mere development of this very concept. On July 22, 200,000 people paraded over the Ringstrasse in Vienna, and Reichstag President Löbe, a Social Democrat, at a reception in the Socialist-controlled *Rathaus* warned that the rejection of the Anschluss by the Great Powers signified "the annihilation of the principles of the right of self-determination." The Parisian *Le Temps* cautioned that what surfaced in the Vienna demonstrations was not a mere matter of community of language and culture. What was at stake, was the "new European political order created through the Allied victory"; what was threatened was "peace in Central Europe, based upon existing treaties."[36]

Politicians and Historians

Yet the Austrian and German barrage of speeches and pronunciamentoes in behalf of union continued. At various times personalities of different political persuasion, Dr. Renner, ex-Chancellor of Austria, the Austrian Minister of Commerce Dr. Schürff, the President of the Austrian Republic Dr. Michael Hainisch, another former Austrian Minister Dr. Heinrich Mataja and Count Ottokar Czernin, Imperial Minister, came out for the union, voicing especially the need for an economic link-up between Austria and Germany.[37] From the German side Dr. Held, President of the Bavarian Council, Count Lerchenfeld, German Minister to Vienna, and the German Chancellor, the Social Democrat Hermann Müller, spoke in behalf of union, though the latter sharply restricted his goal; he merely wished to bring Austrian and Germans closer together. Somewhat farther went his Party colleague the German Minister of Interior Carl Severing, though he too drew back from full political union. At about the same time many other prominent Germans expressed themselves in favor of the Anschluss, perhaps not of an immediate union, but of one in the distant future.[38] Among them were the *Reichstag* deputies Dr. Ludwig Haas, Dr.

Otto Hoetzsch, and R. W. Kahl, Wilhelm Marx, deputy and former
Chancellor, and Erich Koch-Weser, Minister of Justice; Marx held
that a satisfactory solution of the Anschluss problem would remove
the tension from which Europe suffered, and that a "real peace
would emerge."[39]

Otto Hoetzsch and R. Wilhelm Kahl were not only German
deputies but also professors at German Universities. In Austria
University professors and especially professors of history were
in the vanguard of the Anschluss movement, articulating and
crystallizing Austrian thought on the union. Long before the rise
of National Socialism with its renewed and fanatic emphasis on
the Anschluss, based not only on historic, national, and cultural-
linguistic grounds, but also on considerations of race, power, and
expansionism, German and Austrian historical writing was thoroughly in favor of the union concept. The intellectual and middle-
class constituencies to which historiography in both countries
especially catered, had been brought up in veneration of the
nation state, and the Anschluss appeared to them both as an
inevitable as well as a desirable fulfillment of their dearest
aspirations. Just as the concept of the inevitability of the proletarian
socialist Revolution powerfully strengthened the drive toward
socialism, the earlier notion of the inevitable victory and realization
of the nation state had given political nationalism an unprecedented
impetus.

Friedrich Meinecke's support of "union with our Austrian
brothers" was echoed by numerous German historians already
in the nineteen hundred twenties such as Hans Delbrück.[40] Though
Meinecke hoped to attract Austria to the *Reich*, he wished nevertheless to preserve the unitary character of the new German
Republic.[41] German historians such as Hermann Oncken, Willy
Andreas, Martin Spahn, Erich Brandenburg, Wilhelm Schüssler,
and others were enthusiastic supporters of the union movement.
Many of these historians had to overcome the *kleindeutsch*, Prussian
myth which prevailed in Germany after Bismarck's unification
movement, reached its climax in 1871, and insisted on Austria's
separate political existence. Though the Austrian Empire had been
dissolved, many *kleindeutsch* historians continued to harbor prejudices not only against the Habsburg dynasty, but also against
the Austrian people and state, adding a touch of the widespread
popular bias relating to the supposedly inferior Austrian character

and manners (*Schlaffheit*) and the alleged inadequacy of the recent wartime ally. Some German historians were patently jealous of Austria's eminent cultural role and in particular of Vienna's intellectual and artistic splendor.

Austrian historians in the First Republic, on the other hand, were, in spite of Germany's defeat, too enamored of imperial Germany's military preeminence and political and cultural achievements to be resentful or critical of anything German. To the contrary, most of them saw the solution of all of German Austria's problems in the Anschluss. The Anschluss concept strongly attracted many Austrian academicians. German national convictions aside, the very poverty of Austria, her material insecurity, and the relatively better financial situation of German Universities contributed to the high esteem in which Germany was held by the Austrian intelligentsia and their promoting close cultural and political ties with the *Reich*. But economic advantage was not the only, surely not the primary cause, why "all Austrian University professors of history professed the Anschluss," as Herbert Dachs in his study *Österreichische Geschichtswissenschaft und Anschluss, 1918–1930* concluded.[42] Many among the Austrian historians, Alfons Dopsch, Ludo M. Hartmann, and Heinrich Kretschmayr rejected the theoretical alternative of a Danubian Confederation. They were convinced that the Anschluss of Austria would serve national interests and should be supported by all Austrians, irrespective of party and religious affiliation. Among the leading members of the *Österreichisch-Deutscher Volksbund*, founded in Vienna on June 4, 1925, were Professors of History Wilhelm Bauer, R. F. Kaindl, L. M. Hartmann, and Hans Voltellini. The program of the club was also subscribed to by other historians such as Heinrich Srbik, Oswald Redlich, Ludwig Bittner, Herman Wopfner, Hans Uebersberger, and others.[43]

The majority of the Austrian intelligentsia, conservative and German-minded, followed the lead of the *grossdeutsch*-oriented University Professors of all fields, historians often in the vanguard. Though not overly enthusiastic about union with a revolutionary postwar Germany in 1918–19, they became, in the course of the 1920s, increasingly committed to the Anschluss concept.[44] Oswald Redlich spoke of the "closest cultural community" between the two German states as likely to lead to political unity.[45] Intensive German national and cultural education among both Germans and Austrians was necessary to overcome the differences of character and outlook and focus upon the common traits and interests. The Anschluss should be prepared through cultural, economic, and *völkisch* rapprochement and through *Angleichung* (assimilation) in law and administration.

Both in Austria and Germany University professors, and historians in particular, continued to enjoy great intellectual prestige. They were the real molders of the political philosophy of prospective teachers in history and other fields in Austrian and German secondary schools. As Dachs aptly remarked, the students listened raptly to the teachings of the German nationalist professors. Their views on the Anschluss were to shape the political opinions of the future leaders of the German and Austrian intelligentsia, of civil servants, of lawyers, and of the entire educated bourgeoisie. At the same time these educators proclaimed the German national point of view not as a mere wishful political image but as strictly scientific and as corresponding to the demands of highest objectivity.

Austrian historians in the 1920s looked upon the First Republic as a transitory phenomenon. They saw in Greater Germany a kind of political utopia from which they fervently expected the solution to all Austrian problems.[46] Thus hardly one of them came to grips with the concrete difficulties of interwar Austria, her political problems and her economic survival. Srbik considered the Anschluss concept as a "rescue anchor" of Austria and the Austrians caught in deepest misery. While historians tried to illuminate Germany's and Austria's past and pointed to political union as inevitable, as well as desirable, German and Austrian contemporaries placed patiently stone after stone upon the structure of the future unitary *Reich*, often deluding themselves as to the actual progress made. At the same time Germany's foreign minister Gustav Stresemann attempted to improve Germany's relations with the West in preparation of further German progress in other respects and along the *Reich*'s other boundaries.

The Locarno Accords of 1925 had raised new hopes for the Anschluss. Both the *Volksbund* and the *Arbeitsgemeinschaft* welcomed the Locarno agreements and Germany's entrance into the League of Nations; they saw in them stepping stones toward the revision of the peace treaties, a revision likely to remove also the obstacles to the Anschluss. They overlooked that only a unanimous decision of the Council of the League could reverse the specific prohibitions of the union in article 80 of the Versailles Treaty and article 88 of the Treaty of St. Germain.

On the other hand, a noted French journalist, Pertinax, thought it unlikely that Germany would be held back by a mere legal provision in the Covenant of the League and had little doubt that the *Reich* would be prepared to challenge the League of Nations. Partisans of the Left in France were often as opposed to the Anschluss as French Conservatives. They were aroused that Paul Löbe, a German socialist, was a champion of the Anschluss movement. On occasion of an international Conference in Paris, Edouard Herriot, President of the French Chamber of Deputies, refused to share the same platform with Löbe, Stresemann and others of the German Foreign Office who were all articulate on the union issue.

After Locarno: From Mussolini and Stresemann to McDonald, Briand, and Coudenhove-Kalergi

In the negotiations leading to Locarno Mussolini had attempted to impress his views on the English government. He held it to be shortsighted to judge only the Rhine border as a potential source of European instability, while ignoring that the dispute over the Anschluss might spark a war. But Britain's Foreign Minister Austin Chamberlain seemed satisfied with German assurances that the *Reich* did not contemplate the Anschluss. In the end France sided with Britain, and Mussolini's Italy suffered a diplomatic setback. In the mid-nineteen hundred thirties Austria, by then the object of German aggressive thrusts, would have been in a much stronger position if she had been the beneficiary of such early collective assurances. A diplomatic opportunity for guaranteeing Austria and South Tyrol was thus missed in the mid-twenties when Germany was not yet able to offer effective opposition. Again, at Locarno Mussolini brought up the matter of a guarantee for the Brenner pass, but Chamberlain dismissed it in a rather cavalier manner.

Mussolini's increasing concern for Austria and adjacent South Tyrol and Germany's, especially Bavaria's, growing interest in the South-Tyrolese minority that Fascism tried to italianize, produced at times intolerable tension between Rome and Berlin. Stresemann even held the possibility of an Italian *Putsch* against Tyrol proper not unlikely, a coup which would have established a joint Italo-German frontier. He solemnly warned Il Duce to deter him from such an adventurous course. Besides, in an address to the *Reichstag* on February 9, 1926, Stresemann warned Italy that, though the *Reich* would not directly interfere in South Tyrol, Germany had "cultural concern for a *Land* and people who had been German for centuries."[47] This time it was the *Reich*, not Austria, which protested against Italian "cultural" encroachments and established a joint German-Austrian front against Italy in respect to German South Tyrol. On the other hand, behind the scenes Streseman tried to terminate the boycott movement against Italian goods which was organized by the *Andreas Hofer Bund* in Munich, and to calm the aroused public anger to avoid a further escalation of the quarrel. While Stresemann was pitted against Mussolini, National Socialism adopted early a pro-Italian and pro-Fascist stance. This was in accordance with the Führer's willingness to write off South Tyrol and in conformity with the thesis developed in *Mein Kampf*, aiming at the creation of an Italo-German alliance.

After Locarno, Germany was most anxious that France withdraw her troops from the Rhineland. But, despite some suggestions, the *Reich* was in no mood to renounce the Anschluss in exchange for a French withdrawal. France felt little assured that Germany, following the evacuation of the Rhineland, would not turn eastward and feared that thereafter the *Drang nach dem Osten* would only gain momentum. Austria seemed a stepping stone in Germany's thrust against Czechoslovakia as well as into the Balkans.

While under Stresemann's stewardship German interests along the Western borders were by necessity paramount, he never ignored or wrote off the *Reich*'s long-range ambitions in regard to the East, especially those concerning Poland and Austria. Historians are not agreed as to his priorities between the two latter countries, but do not question that Stresemann attributed greater importance to both of them than his predecessors.

The Anschluss issue figured prominently in a discussion held between Stresemann and Poincaré on occasion of the former's visit to Paris in August, 1928. While emphasizing, as was customary for most German statesmen in the 1920s, that the *Reich* did not contemplate an immediate Anschluss, Stresemann, not very diplomatically, indulged in philosophical excursions on the German and Austrian soul. "We [Germans] seek our lost souls in these people [Austrians] who are of the same blood and have the same feelings as we."[48] Poincaré countered that Germany and Austria could have a common cultural identity as long as they remained politically separate states. Toward the end of the year, on December 4, 1928, Foreign Minister Briand stated even more bluntly that France would never consent to Austria's political suicide.

Realizing Germany's limitations, Stresemann apparently did not contemplate more than a customs union with Austria. He also appears to have placed greater importance on the revision of the Polish-German frontier than on pushing the Anschluss issue; the former move concerned of course territory which had been German before 1914. His utterance in the 1920s on Austria and the Anschluss created contradictory impressions but left no doubt that the problem was potentially acute. Still, Stresemann's prevailing tone and the essence of his policy toward Austria and the Anschluss were marked by restraint; this was unavoidable in view of the opposition to the union concept by the Great Powers.

In the late 1920s the leading West European statesmen were not disposed to encourage the Anschluss movement. In a cabinet session in Rome on August 1, 1927, Mussolini opposed both the creation of a Danubian Confederation and a move toward the Anschluss, since neither of these propositions was in line with the existing peace treaties. Particularly the union of Austria and Germany would "profoundly alter the political map of Europe," as laid down in the Peace of Paris in 1919.[49] In an interview in Berlin on October 1928, Ramsey MacDonald, later head of the British Labor government, claimed that the Labor Party held no definite views on the subject. But two months later, on December 14 and 15, 1928, when Briand, Stresemann, and Austin Chamberlain engaged in conversations in Lugano, even Briand, known for his policy of striving toward "conciliation" with Weimar Germany, made clear France's resolute opposition to the Anschluss. An appeal to the Council of the League would not result in unanimity, he warned, since France would vote against union in Central Europe: "Now if there occurred a *coup de force* on the part of Germany to annex Austria, which I do not believe, Germany should not ignore the fact that this doubtless would mean war."[50]

Such a warning emanating from a French moderate was indicative both of what Frenchmen considered a strong push of Austria and Germany toward economic rapprochement and union and of the threat which they perceived in the Anschluss movement to the peace of Europe and the security of France. But after a severe admonishment addressed to Germany and Austria, Briand held out to them the possible participation on an apparently equal basis in his project for a United States of Europe, a Pan-Europe.

The Pan-European concept was actually propagated by an Austrian, Count Coudenhove-Kalergi, who in the interwar period was the very inspiration and main driving force of this movement. The plan aimed at the creation of a federation of all European states, with the exception of England and Russia. In the Eighteenth Assembly of the League of Nations Aristide Briand elaborated upon his own Pan-European plan which showed Coudenhove-Kalergi's influence. His project was further elaborated upon in a memorandum of the French Foreign Office, dated May 1, 1930. Ironically, both the Austrian and German governments responded to Briand's project most favorably. The Austrian government recalled that the unsatisfactory political and economic position of present-day Europe was nowhere more clearly and painfully felt than in Central Europe. Pointing to the Great Depression, it hoped to make a strong impact. The German government seemed hardly less enthusiastic about the Briand project. No country, it asserted, could feel the defects in the structure of Europe more strongly than Germany, situated as she was in the center of the continent; she was therefore "very ready to cooperate" in the solution of the problems affecting Central Europe. It was clear from the beginning of Briand's campaign that the various European states envisaged Pan-Europe differently; none entertained serious doubts about the compatibility of the Pan-European idea with its own particular national interests.

The Austro-German Customs Union Project and Europe's Reaction

The Austrian Foreign Minister Johann Schober was reputed to be more pro-German and pro-union than Monsignor Ignaz Seipel, had ever been. Similarly, the German Foreign Minister Julius

Curtius turned out to be more daring in the conduct of foreign affairs than Gustav Stresemann. After the latter's death in the fall of 1929, the chances of German revisionism seemed better than ever. Negotiations concerning the Young plan were brought to a successful conclusion. Foreign financial control on German soil was to be terminated, and the last occupation troops were withdrawn from the Rhineland in 1930, three years ahead of schedule. In the German Foreign Office Bernhard von Bülow, Deputy Director of Department II, anticipated already during the summer of 1929 that the issue of the Corridor, of Upper Silesia, and of the Anschluss, would, in this order, be dealt with by international diplomacy.[51] He suggested not to work for an Anschluss "in the fullest sense of the word, but rather to undertake resolute steps in regard to preferential tariffs and similar things."

Soon after assuming his post, Curtius had taken the initiative in broaching the Anschluss question with Schober when the latter visited the German capital between February 22–24, 1930. The German foreign minister was fully aware of the strong opposition of the Great Powers to the union issue. Still, the opportunities for German progress vis-à-vis Austria were alluring. Only three days after the withdrawal of the last French troops from the Rhineland, on July 3, 1930, the German Foreign Office suggested to Vienna that an Austro-German technical discussion concerning the formation of a customs union begin in earnest. Notwithstanding the warnings from German representatives in Paris, Prague, and Rome, Curtius decided to press ahead. As often before, German leaders underestimated France's vital interests in Austria's continued independence and her ability to impress Great Britain and Italy with her arguments and resolve.

On March 1, 1931, it was Foreign Minister Curtius' turn to visit Vienna; Chancellor Brüning too had intended to undertake the journey, but was detained in the last minute. The Christian Social journal *Weltblatt* agreed with other Austrian dailies that Austria was not in the position to consider a serious political link-up with any other state in Central Europe. In its opinion, the best precept for future relations with Germany was that of Dr. Schober, "one nation in two states." Actually, this had been Seipel's program and it was reformulated by Curtius in his farewell address.[52] There seems little doubt that mutual economic problems were the major concern of the Vienna discussions in which far-reaching decisions were reached. Sixteen days after Curtius' departure, Vienna and Berlin published a protocol climaxing in the assertion that they had agreed to create a customs union.

This was startling news for Europe and especially affected France, England, Italy, and Czechoslovakia. The communiqué, signed on March 19, but not published on that date, asserted that the Central European customs union between Germany and Austria was actually a move toward the establishment of a European-wide customs union.[53] A second communiqué, issued from Vienna on March 22, further insisted that the customs union project was in accordance with the recommendations of the Geneva economic conferences. Both Austria and Germany were ready to enter into analogous agreements with all other European states!

On March 22, before the publication of the communiqué, the ministers of France, Italy, and Czechoslovakia had already expressed concern about the customs union. Making their presentations at the *Ballhausplatz*, they warned Dr. Johannes Schober that the treaty was in violation of the Geneva Protocols of October 1922. Dr. Schober, however, replied that Austria, in conformity with Briand's Pan-European project, had merely reached a "regional understanding."[54] A few days later, Sir Eric Phipps, British Minister to Vienna, visited Dr. Schober, who in turn assured him that Austria had no intention of creating a *fait accompli*. Still, several days later, the British government too, in a formal request to the Secretary-General of the League of Nations raised the question of the legality of the Austro-German customs union. This issue was dealt with in detail by the 63rd session of the Council of the League in Geneva, on May 18, 1931. The French position, expounded in a Memorandum critique, focused on the restrictions imposed upon Germany and Austria by the peace treaties and the Geneva Protocol and disputed the legality of the customs union project. Speaking for the British Government, Arthur Henderson suggested that the Permanent Court of International Justice be asked for an advisory opinion.

In his rejoinder, Schober denied that Austria and Germany were in violation of established treaty provisions and reminded the Powers that the Geneva Protocol not only obligated Austria to preserve her independence but also bound the powers to respect it. In the end he assured the Great Powers that Austria did not object to having the issue referred to the World Court. Briand agreed with Henderson that the problem was primarily a legal one, but he also warned that under some circumstances European peace could be most seriously imperiled. It was impossible to distinguish between political and economic independence.[55] Briand quoted Metternich to the effect that no state could preserve its independence if it had close relations with stronger powers. The Italian representative Dino Grandi, while agreeing with Henderson's draft resolution, nevertheless asserted that the Council should reserve the right to decide the issue at hand on its political merits, underlining once more the World Court's purely advisory function. Still, he did not want Germany to be arraigned before any public body as a "disturber of the peace." The then President of the Council of the League, German Foreign Minister Dr. Curtius, stated that it was primarily the Austrian Government's international obligations which had been challenged, though the German government too was much interested in the issue of a custom's union. While he consented to the referral of the disputed question to the World Court, he refused to recognize the right of the Council to deal with the political aspects of the problem. The Council reached no decision on the question of its right to judge the political side of the case.

The French reaction to the announcement of the Austro-German customs union had been swift and devastating. On March 22, *Le Temps*, expressing the views of the government, wrote thus: "The *Drang nach dem Osten* could easily be resumed under cover of close regional economic interests." Two days later the daily voiced its conviction that the economic Anschluss would turn out to be the "preface to political Anschluss," a plan of the Berlin government aiming at the conquest of Central Europe.[56] Aristide Briand, criticized by some French Senators as pursuing too moderate a course, defended his policy in the Senate.[57] The Czech reaction to the customs union was one of sharp opposition.[58] Italy's stance, however, was ambiguous. It was not until June 1931, when Grandi addressed the Senate that Rome's position became somewhat clearer. Though he spoke with warm words about both Austria and Germany, he too voiced the fear that economic union would lead to a political union.[59] In Great Britain, Foreign Minister Arthur Henderson, recalling many conversations with Aristide Briand relating to a customs' union in Central

Europe, defended his policy of originally turning the issue over to the Council of the League of Nations.[60]

In a session of the *Reichstag* on March 31, 1931, Foreign Minister Curtius, referring to the customs union project—the brainchild actually of the Brüning government—asserted that, whatever the circumstances of the moment, the project was strongly supported by the German people.[61] Curtius, pointing to the economic hardships of Austria and Germany and its 5 million unemployed workers, concluded that Germany was imperiled by many economic and social dangers. Austria and Germany had acted in accordance with the principles of European cooperation and attempted to build it up from the bottom. Their plan did not exclude other nations, and the purely economic character of their agreement was not in conflict with the international obligations of either country. He sharply disputed the point of view that the plan was a danger to European peace, and seemed particularly concerned about the accusation that the Central Powers had created a *fait accompli.*

The German press approved heartily of the position taken by the Berlin government. Only a few protests were raised on economic and technical grounds rather than on grounds of international politics. Dr. Schober, Austrian Vice-Chancellor and Minister of Foreign Affairs, facing objections to the customs union project from abroad, attempted in an interview in the *Neue Freie Presse* to shift the discussion to the dissolution of the old Austrian Empire back in 1918, pinning the blame for it on the Czechoslovaks![62] Thus he absolved Austria and Germany from any responsibility for the customs union project of 1931. The latter was only designed to fill the newly arisen postwar economic needs. In a formal declaration to the press on March 30, Dr. Schober assured his audience that Austria and Germany in agreeing to a customs union had not wished to disturb the peace of Europe by any means.[63] Dr. Renner, then President of the Austrian *Nationalrat*, defended the project as a "first step" toward the "reorganization of all of Europe" and the then Austrian Minister of Agriculture, Dr. Dollfuss,—soon the bitter foe of the Socialists—felt similarly that the German-Austrian customs union was "only the beginning" of an evolution toward the formation of large economic blocs in Europe.[64] Facing an aroused public opinion in

Europe, Austrian politicians of all colors attempted to give the customs union project the most innocuous character.

Many Austrian journals, however, took a critical attitude toward the customs union.[65] They raised questions about the economic desirability of the project and expressed concern over its legality and timeliness. The Austrian Communists as well as the Monarchists opposed the plan outright, the former suspecting the hand of German capitalism in the union project,[66] the latter fearing that the Anschluss concept lurked behind it and that it would quickly bury all restoration plans of the Habsburg dynasty.

Two months after the customs union had been proclaimed the Austrian *Kreditanstalt*, the largest bank of the country, faced bankruptcy. In dire straits, the Vienna government turned to the League of Nations for emergency help. It soon became obvious that France would play a key role in the financial salvation of Austria and that the customs union would turn out to be the sacrificial lamb. German financial circles too faced utter disorganization and gloomy prospects. Following the publication of President Hoover's plan for a moratorium on war debts and reparations for one year, there was organized the London Conference of July 20–24, 1931, which representatives from Belgium, France, Germany, Great Britain, Italy, Japan, and the United States attended. The Conference averred that maintaining German financial stability, threatened as it was by the withdrawals of capital, was a prerequisite to a healthy global economy. The report of a Committee of Experts, appointed by the London Conference, pointed to the need for long-term credits for Central Europe. Both Austria and Germany understood the signs of the times and the necessity of winning France's favor; continuing to pursue the customs union project was, however, bound to alienate France.

These were the circumstances when on September 3, on occasion of the meeting of the Commission of Enquiry for European union, Dr. Schober declared that it had been clear "from the beginning" that the Austro-German customs union would be successful only if other states were ready to join it. Since in the meantime the opposition of other states to the project had become apparent, the Austrian government had decided no longer to pursue this objective. To overcome the economic depression not only in Austria but also in a large number of other European states, the Vienna government thus renounced the customs union project.[67] After

Dr. Schober's address, Dr. Curtius associated himself with the observations of his Austrian colleague. The German government informed the League of Nations that Germany too had decided to discontinue working toward the creation of a customs union with Austria.

Though the Austrian and German governments had yielded, public opinion in both countries was outraged and in a bitter mood. The socialist *Arbeiter-Zeitung* in Vienna, though cool to the timing and other aspects of the customs union, struck an anti-French note and criticized Foreign Ministers Schober and Curtius for having yielded to French pressure. The *Neues Wiener Journal* reproached the government for having compromised the idea of a customs union for years to come.[68] The German socialist *Vorwärts* was no less nationalistic than its Austrian counterpart, denouncing "French imperialism" and its "domination" of Europe. The *Frankfurter Zeitung* criticized the German government for not having in advance properly weighed the chances of success of the project.

There is little doubt that the decisive blow against the customs union plan was administered by France and that the financial distress of Austria and Germany made the defeat of the project inevitable. Yet in view of the known determined opposition of the Great Powers to the project, as it was expressed in the debates of the League of Nations, the prospects for the customs union had always been dim indeed. The decision of the Permanent Court of International Justice at The Hague, which had been called upon by the League to give its advisory opinion on the Union, sealed its fate also juridically. The opinion of the Court was made public on September 5, only two days after Germany and Austria had renounced the Customs Union! By a most narrow 8:7 decision, the Court declared that the customs union project violated the economic independence of Austria and therefore was incompatible with the Geneva Protocol No. I of October 1922.[69] On the other hand, the Court held that Austria's political independence would not be encroached upon within the meaning of Article 88 of the Treaty of St. Germain. Since Protocol No. I was not to expire before 1943, on repayment of the 1922 loan, Austria was obligated to observe until that time the restrictions placed upon her economic freedom. In view of new loans and of the agreements signed by Austria on July 15, 1932, Vienna obligated itself once more to the preservation of Austria's economic independence for a period of at least 10 years and promised not to grant exclusive advantages within this time span to any state.

The abortive customs union project represented the vain attempt of Austria and Germany, both still democratic states, to circumvent economically the postwar prohibition of the Anschluss. It constituted the climax of the movement toward union which had gripped both states ever since 1918 and had won numerous adherents in Austria and the *Reich*. The next major attempt to bring about their union, by whatever means, was made after Hitler came to power in Germany. But it found neither the support of Austria's government nor that of the great majority of its people. Buoyed by his startling success in the *Reich*, the Führer quickly turned his attention toward Austria in the hope of overwhelming the resistance of the Dollfuss regime. The latter opted to fight simultaneously Austrian National Socialism as well as the Social Democratic Party.

Chapter 3

Austro-Marxism, Otto Bauer, and the
Anschluss Movement 1918–1938

An Overview: Austrian Socialism and
the Anschluss Movement in the 1920s

Before World War I, the Austrian Socialist leadership, especially Otto Bauer and Karl Renner, had pondered the theoretical and practical implications of the nationality problem in the multinational Austrian Empire. Both men had become persuaded that the polyglot Monarchy merited to be preserved. But after the demise of the Empire in 1918, the Social Democratic Party steered the Austrian working class into Anschluss waters. Its leaders were mightily influenced by the historic vision, inherited from Karl Marx and Friedrich Engels, that the unification of most German-speaking groups in Central Europe was a necessary way station on the road to socialism. In 1871, only Bismarck's limited *kleindeutsch* solution had prevailed. Germans in the Habsburg Empire had remained citizens of the Dual Monarchy. Within Austrian Social Democracy, Bauer emerged as a prime mover of the Austrian orientation, until the break-up of the Monarchy prompted him to embrace the *grossdeutsch*, or Austro-German, solution of the German question.

Shortly after war's end, Bauer became Austria's foreign minister and, after Viktor Adler's death, he also emerged as Social Democratic Party leader. In these twin capacities, Bauer espoused the Anschluss concept. With the disintegration of the Empire, the Socialists' Austrian patriotism thus yielded to German political nationalism, by way of their traditional *gross-deutsch* imperatives. For over a decade, they viewed the Austrian working class as a branch of the German proletariat, and envisioned the foundation of a Socialist Greater Germany that would also encompass Austria. But with the decline of the Party's power and influence, and with the growing preponderance of "bourgeois" parties both in Austria and the *Reich,* Socialist enthusiasm for Austro-German unification diminished. Most Austro-Marxist leaders became far more interested in partisan political, economic, and ideological problems; they wished, in particular, to accelerate the creation of a socialist order in the heart of Europe. Hitler's assumption of power finally led to the adoption of different tactics by 1933. Socialist leaders thenceforth strove to prevent the destruction of Austria's sovereignty and freedom, in order to avoid enslavement by the *Third Reich,* and to forestall the loss of hard-won working class rights in the First Austrian Republic.

In the interwar era Austrian nationalism and patriotism had been a tender plant. None of Austria's political parties cultivated it, none held it close to its heart. A small minority of Austrian patriots loved the imperial past, but not the new Republic. Only after Hitler's tyranny in Germany had triumphed, did a gradual though inconclusive Austrian patriotism reassert itself. Socialists also became persuaded that the defense of Austria, imperfect as its system still appeared to them on political, social, economic, and national grounds, was a tactical imperative. If nothing else, preserving Austria's territorial and national integrity meant stopping Hitler, saving Austria's remaining freedoms, and maintaining European peace. Yet, to its own champions, Austria's survival appeared moot. When the country succumbed in 1938, few Austrians were foolhardy enough to believe that Austrian nationalism and patriotism would be resurrected only a few years hence.

A national movement tracing its roots to the German and Austrian 1848–1849 Revolution, the Anschluss drive held a powerful grip on the people of the First Austrian Republic and that of Germany as well. The movement encountered only weak ideological resistance in the First Republic, which doubted its own economic viability and separate existence. Notwithstanding the flurry of Austrian official propaganda since the mid-1930s, Austria failed to develop a convincing patriotism of her own, rooted in the belief that a distinct Austrian nationality existed and that Austria's political future should not include any sort of political affiliation with the *Reich.* To the contrary, the conviction that a *gesamtdeutsch* (all-German) community of interest existed, compelling Austria to march shoulder to shoulder with the *Reich,* hampered Austria's intellectual defenses against Weimar Germany and later encouraged the *Third Reich*. During the First Austrian and the Weimar Republic union was not the exclusive programme of any particular Austrian or German political party, but often that of virtually all parties on both sides of the Inn river. Depending on the political winds blowing in either country, the movement had different political sponsors and varied political objectives depending on time and circumstances. The close link forged between German nationalist and Austrian Socialist ideology in 1918–1919 was somewhat loosened—though never completely severed—and in the early 1920s it was replaced by a connection linking German conservative nationalists and Austrian provincial and reactionary elements. This was especially true of Tyrol and Salzburg, both of which sought an association with anti-communist Bavaria. In the later 1920s Austrian industrial and banking interests felt increasingly attracted by the economic upsurge and compatible conservative political trends in the *Reich*. After 1932 National Socialism took the Anschluss movement under its wings, distorting what its adherents considered to be its progressive past and character, and finally, in March 1938, established its tyranny over Austria with the annexation of the country.

In the immediate postwar period, the Austrian Social Democratic Party became the leading force in the Anschluss movement. Compared with it even the *Grossdeutschen*, representing the national-minded middle class and the Austrian intelligentsia but fearful of the revolutionary trend in Germany, appeared rather reluctant about union with the *Reich*. The Christian Social Party, partly prompted by similar hesitations and partly influenced by the fear of a renewed anti-Catholic *Kulturkampf*, paid largely lip-service to the union concept; its leader, the priest-politician Ignaz Seipel, actually operated behind the scenes against it.[1]

In early November 1918, Otto Bauer became the helmsman of the Austrian ship of state. In March 1919, while the Peace Conference deliberated in Paris, he visited Berlin and negotiated a largely secret union agreement with Germany's foreign minister Ulrich von Brockdorff-Rantzau.[2] But he ran afoul of the Entente Powers. Not only France and England but Italy too came ultimately to oppose the Anschluss, because it would strengthen Germany, unbalance the precarious European equilibrium, and threaten the succession states which had emerged on the ruins of the Habsburg Empire.

The national posture on the Anschluss question of Austrian and also of German Socialism during the entire interwar period was not a matter of mere political opportunism and tactics; it harked back to the revolutionary national legacy of 1848–1849. Before 1914, national feelings and thoughts had gripped not only the Austro-German intelligentsia and the bourgeoisie but also Social Democratic circles. They had found support in the *grossdeutsch* views of German Socialist leaders, such as Karl Marx, Friedrich Engels, and Ferdinand Lassalle. The latter had pointed to the overthrow of the dynasties in both Vienna and Berlin as a prerequisite of the desired Central European German unification. Similarly, Engels had insisted that the *grossdeutsch* solution might become a reality in the event the Austro-Hungarian Monarchy should break up: "The complete dissolution of Austria is the first prerequisite for the unity of Germany!" The *grossdeutsch* tradition continued to be strong in German Socialism under the leadership of Wilhelm Liebknecht and August Bebel. Liebknecht, who remained an "irreconcilable *Grossdeutscher*," hated Bismarck not only because he had failed to create a German republic; he also could not forgive his *kleindeutsch*, Prussian solution of the German question when he threw a portion of Germany to the Habsburgs.[3]

After Otto Bauer's resignation in July 1919, when Chancellor Karl Renner, a right-wing Social Democrat, also assumed the post of foreign minister, Austrian foreign policy lost its abrasive edges; while continuing to proclaim his Party's and Austria's interest in the union with Germany, Renner nevertheless toned down the Anschluss concept to soothe the Western Powers. Throughout 1919 Paris and London considered him much more pliant, less doctrinaire and less insistent on the Anschluss, and also no radical Socialist like Otto Bauer. Still, the Social Democratic Party continued to cling to the Anschluss idea in the early 1920's, though once the peace treaty of St. Germain was signed, it understood that the chances for an early union were virtually nil. In 1920 Bauer continued to favor the Anschluss with a bourgeois, even with a "reactionary Germany," since the union would ultimately bring about the "necessary connection" with the German proletarian Revolution. "The economic and social preconditions in the great German *Reich* are incomparably more favorable than in German Austria."[4] However distant the prospects of Revolution in Germany and Austria, they apparently justified the Anschluss even under less attractive circumstances. What clearly was not and could not be anticipated yet was the rise of a National Socialist Germany.

In 1920 Bauer still considered the Anschluss as unlikely as in the preceding two years. Its prospects remained dim as long as the German and French bourgeois social order was not overthrown. The German Social Revolution would complete the German National Revolution of 1848–1849, and, by inspiring the French workers with the example of Social Revolution, it would push aside French "imperialist obstacles." Among the points in favor of union which Bauer stressed were Austria's precarious economic existence as a *Kleinstaat*, the heavy yoke of French imperialism in Central Europe and elsewhere, as well as the alleged preparedness of the German and French working class to embrace a proletarian, Socialist Revolution. Bauer's conviction that the German and French Social Revolutions were near constituted a cardinal part of his socialist "faith" and activism, rather than being borne out by a detached assessment of the revolutionary capacities of their working classes. But it was part of the Marxist legacy to believe in the striking force of the German proletariat, the strongest section of international socialism, and it deluded virtually all German and Austrian socialist leaders.[5]

Marx's and Engels' views that a close connection existed between political and social Revolution and the fulfillment of the German National Revolution continued to grip Austrian Socialism. Austrian Social Democrats remained convinced that the Anschluss would speed the cause of Social Revolution in *Grossdeutschland* as well as be contingent on its progress. Yet the rapid change in Austria's and Germany's early postwar political situation influenced the character of the Anschluss drive. Conservative Austrians resented socialist Vienna and the influence of Socialism in Austria in general. This, combined with the victory of the Bavarian counterrevolution, altered the outlook of many Austro-Germans toward the concept of union with the *Reich*. In 1921 the Tyrolese *Landtag* decided to conduct an Anschluss plebiscite. This movement, which fought under a conservative banner, displaying quite different colors from those of the early postwar period, nonetheless threatened Austrian integrity.

According to Bauer, the Tyrolese *Landtag* had initiated a new type of German unification movement: "The Anschluss movement of 1921 was of a reactionary origin. . . . In 1921 the movement was led by the government of the alpine *Länder,* was aimed against the Vienna government, and their goal was the separation of *Länder* from the federation."[6] In 1919 the Tyrolese government had fought the Anschluss, whereas in 1922 it placed itself at the head of the unification movement. Following Tyrol's example, similar movements were also organized in the other Austrian *Länder.* But Great Power opposition had not abated, and the government headed by the Christian Social Tyrolese Professor Dr. Michael Mayr was toppled. In the words of Bauer, the provincial bourgeoisie now learned first-hand that, in view of the prevailing European power balance, the Anschluss could not be realized.[7] The Socialists had encountered similar obstacles in 1918–1919; Otto Bauer had been forced out of office in July 1919.

Although the 1921–1922 Anschluss movement in the Austrian *Länder* had failed, the unification drive did not slacken. On both sides of the Inn river it was supported by most, if not all, parties, ranging from the extreme Right to the Left. In Germany, as seen, Paul Löbe, the presiding officer of the *Reichstag* and a leading Social Democrat, played a major role in the union movement. The Austrian organization was led by Dr. Hermann Neubacher, who was to become the first Nazi mayor of Vienna after the 1938 annexation of Austria. In the 1920s, the Anschluss movement aimed not at immediate realization but at keeping the "idea" alive.

In view of Bauer's preeminent position in Austria's Social Democratic Party, his view on the Anschluss in the later 1920s and thereafter represented not only his personal point of view but also the Party's. His original motivation aside—socialist and national imperatives pointing toward union—Bauer then and later was also influenced by tactical considerations. He feared that an outright Socialist rejection of the Anschluss would be construed as a "betrayal"[8] by Austria's nationalist elements.

Throughout the 1920s, the Austrian Social Democrats continued to cling to their pro-Anschluss position, both theoretically and practically. At the noted Linz Party Conference between October 30 and November 3, 1926, Otto Bauer submitted proposals which became the basis of the new programme of Austro-Marxists, as the leftist-oriented Austrian Socialists were called. They considered the Anschluss of *Deutschösterreich*—the Allies previously had prohibited the official use of this suggestive name—"as necessary conclusion of the national Revolution of 1918," but stressed that the Party strove for the Anschluss "by pacific means."[9] It was not until October 1933, after Hitler had come to power in the *Reich*, that the Austrian Social Democratic Party relinquished its pro-Anschluss policy.

The Austrian Socialists and Political Democracy

Despite its radical language and its general leftist orientation the Austrian Social Democratic Party was dedicated to the preservation of the First Republic and of its democratic constitution. When in 1919 some of its members had been tempted to embark on the Bolshevik course, the Party had made a clear choice for political democracy and against neighboring Hungarian and Bavarian Bolshevik adventurism. It resisted the early radical postwar urge of many workers to join Hungarian and South German Bolshevism and establish a Communist political bloc in the heart of Europe. Even the Party's opponents acknowledged its positive role during the revolutionary turmoil of 1918–1919. Demagogues of the extreme Right, however, and Chancellors Schuschnigg and Dollfuss, pictured the Socialists and their leaders as Austro-Bolsheviks, ignoring their positive attitude toward establishing Austrian political democracy and the basic differences between them and the Russian Bolsheviks. In a study published in 1921, *Bolschewismus oder Sozialdemokratie*,[10] Otto Bauer, political and theoretical leader of the Austrian Socialists, had actually well laid out the fundamental differences for both friend and foe to see. Still, within European democratic socialism Austrian Social Democrats unquestionably belonged to its left wing.

Austrian democratic Socialism became known throughout Europe and the world for its many positive achievements in governing the municipality of Vienna, and for having prevented a split in its organization which, following the November Revolution in Russia and the end of the War, had occurred in virtually all other European social democratic Parties. Despite their leftist orientation, the Austrian Social Democrats were dedicated democrats and also widely respected for their weighty theoretical contributions to democratic socialism. An influential member of the coalition government since the birth of the Republic, they became an opposition party in 1920, but remained a power in the country, especially in Vienna.

In 1926 the Socialists adopted the so-called Linzer Program. Ever since, the opponents of Austro-Marxism claimed to discern in it the endorsement of the Marxist concept of "proletarian dictatorship" and the Party's repudiation of political democracy. Though no foes of dictatorhsip themselves, ultraconservatives used the Linzer Program as vindication of their own anti-democratic and semi-fascist political concepts. Actually, in the section of the Linzer program entitled "The Struggle for Power in the State" the Social Democratic Party program stressed the task of the working class to use the democratic republic in order to attain its ultimate objective.[11] It should gain the support of the majority of the people to "overthrow" the class domination of the bourgeoisie. The goal was not to abolish democracy but to put it to the use of the proletariat.

The Socialists were convinced that the bourgeoisie would not freely relinquish its power position but would rather be tempted to undermine the democratic republic to establish a monarchist or fascist dictatorship whenever the working class, through use of the universal suffrage, was about to seize power in the state. It was therefore necessary to keep the workers in continuous physical and spiritual preparedness to defend the Republic, to foster loyalty to it, and to enable the proletariat to break the bourgeois rule at the polls. After attaining power, the Social Democratic Party would respect "the forms of democracy." If, however—and this was the critical point—the bourgeoisie by "conspiracy with alien counterrevolutionary powers" should resist the social transformation desired by the majority of the electorate, the working class would be "compelled to break the resistance of the bourgeoisie by means of a dictatorship." The latter, it claimed, would be a "dictatorship" of the majority, the resistance of the bourgeoisie, however, one by a minority, illegally obstructing the majority's will. There is little doubt that the radical language—based on Marx's terminology—did strike fear into the hearts of bourgeois and peasant groups, tough others recognized the hyperbole for what it was—primarily radical rhetorics.

From 1927 to the Customs Union Project, 1931

Rhetorics affected also the Anschluss movement in the 1920s. It could be argued that in this entire decade, notwithstanding the at times mounting oratory, all Austrian adherents of the Anschluss, whether Socialists or not, understood well that an early realization of the union with Germany was years away.

In 1927 some decline of the postwar socialist Anschluss fervor was already noticeable. In July of that year, Bauer observed that during the last months Austrian industrial and agricultural entrepreneurs had effusively demonstrated on behalf of the Anschluss. Dr. Anton Apold, Director of the *Alpine Montangesellschaft*, had recently concluded a startling pro-union speech with the words: "The Anschluss is for us an economic necessity, and we must achieve it." Spokesmen of industrialists in the *Nationalrat* had repeatedly proclaimed that Anschluss was Austria's "only salvation." Similarly, the Christian Social Farmers, in their first announcement after the recent national election, had revealed that customs union with the *Reich* was the goal of Austrian agriculturists. With these striking demonstrations on behalf of the Anschluss by the upper bourgeoisie a "very important change" had taken place within the Austrian Republic. The Austrian bourgeoisie now looked "with envy" upon the *Reich*, where the domination of the bourgeoisie had been strengthened and made more secure.[12]

Still, Bauer saw no decisive change as yet in the attitude of the Great Powers toward Central European union. The main hindrance to the realization of this concept lay in the international power configuration. Since Germany's disarmament, Europe west of the USSR had only two mighty forces—the great military power of France and of her allies, Poland, Czechoslovakia, and Yugoslavia, and the armed power of Italy. The overthrow of the French bourgeoisie and of Italian fascism was the prerequisite of German Austria's Anschluss with the *Reich!* Union with the *Reich* was thinkable only in the greater context of revolutionary changes on the entire continent. This assessment of the European situation was no doubt correct in the 1920s. However, it was no longer accurate after the mid-1930s, when France's power sharply declined, her alliances in Eastern Europe crumbled, and when Germany heavily rearmed and Italy became exclusively preoccupied with the Ethiopian war and thereafter the Spanish adventure. As far as Bauer's assessment of West European socialism and its likely attitude to the Anschluss movement was concerned, it harbored many elements of wishful thinking. Could one really assume that social revolution in France and Italy would persuade the citizens of those countries to lose all fear of the German colossus and approve its further aggrandizement, all because the issue at stake was allegedly the German Social and National Revolution?

In 1919, the Entente, controlled by the bourgeoisie, had blocked the National and Social Revolution of the German people. In 1927 Bauer still believed that through the Anschluss the German and Austro-German National and Socialist Revolutions would merge. With the French bourgeoisie and Italian fascism overthrown, the Social Revolution of the Central European proletariat would also secure the union and freedom of the German people.

Barring such revolutionary changes in France and Italy, the Anschluss, according to Bauer, would materialize only in the event of a European war. France and Italy, their forces pinned down at a distant front, would be unable to prevent the Anschluss. In any event, war would usher in the Proletarian Revolution in much of Europe, which in turn would pave the way for Austria's union with the *Reich*. Since in 1927 neither Social Revolution nor war was in sight, Bauer actually removed the Anschluss issue from the immediate political and national agenda of the Austrian Social Democratic Party!

But theoretically, Bauer and the Austrian Socialists continued to adhere to the Anschluss concept. True, the leadership of the Anschluss movement had passed to the Austrian bourgeoisie, which was making many workers suspicious. Bauer paraphrased them: "Can this be the goal of the proletariat if Apold waxes enthusiastic about it? Will the bourgeoisie not strive toward the *Reich* because it holds its dominance within Germany more secure? Would we [Austrian Workers] not be weaker in the *Reich*? Would not the Anschluss deprive us of many of our achievements?" Nonetheless, Bauer was convinced that it would be "dangerous" for the Austrian proletariat to entertain doubt about the Anschluss concept as such.

In his biography of Otto Bauer, his disciple Otto Leichter mentioned Bauer's "cautious attempt"[13] in this article to question the advisability of continuing to embrace the Anschluss concept. But Bauer had to abandon his doubts, because he was criticized by the friends of Anschluss of whom there were many in the Party, including its leadership ("Parteivorstand"). These unification enthusiasts misinterpreted Bauer's caution as hesitation: they had not understood that what in one historic situation might be revolutionary and progressive, at another historic moment might be just the opposite.

According to Bauer in 1927, Anschluss in the near future, with the *Reich* of Hindenburg, with bourgeois Germany and the *Bürgerblock* (coalition of bourgeois parties), would not succeed. But Austrian Social Democrats should not turn away from the Anschluss idea only because the Austrian national bourgeoisie— which, incidentally had battled the Social Democratic Anschluss movement back in 1918–1919 in a "traitorous manner"—now appeared to fight shoulder to shoulder for the same goal. "There is no joint national front linking them and us. . . . Not the German Austrian bourgeoisie, but the French proletariat and the Italian democracy are our allies. . . . Only in closest company with them, only in courageous battle and loyal service to the great international fighting army of the proletariat do we serve effectively our national task."[14] For domestic political reasons Bauer minimized the similarity, if not identity, of the views of Austria's political parties on the Anschluss issue and exaggerated, if he did not outright misjudge, the common interests of the German and Austrian working classes and democratic parties on this question.

Bauer and the Austrian Socialist Party did not favor the latter stage of the Anschluss movement nearly as much as its initial stage in 1918–1919, when Social Democracy had played the leading role and when it had considered union to be the *sine quo non* of socialist growth. But the Social Democratic Party certainly did not reject the Anschluss movement in 1927. To the contrary, Bauer still supported it and appealed to the workers not to desert it but to hold the Anschluss concept high, though its chances of realization were at the moment admittedly nil. But very differently from 1918–1919, for Bauer and the Austrian Social Democrats the Anschluss was no longer an item on the immediate political agenda; it remained a distant, long-range objective, just like the proletarian revolution. Socialists continued to pay lip-service to it as they did to other slogans, but union with the *Reich* had ceased to be a burning issue as it had been in the immediate postwar period.

Yet the Anschluss issue was revived in 1931 in the guise of the customs union project sponsored jointly by the *Reich* and Austria. It was an ill-timed move, as even friends of the Anschluss conceded. In Austria the past fervor had vanished. The Austrian Socialist Party was neither the initiator of this customs union project nor was its heart in it; but for tactical reasons it cooperated, expecting that the project would fail, owing to the continuing opposition of the Western Powers and the neighbors of Austria and Germany.

In Bauer's view, the attempted customs union was launched "in a most awkward manner." The right-wing social democratic leader Karl Renner, Chancellor in the First Austrian Republic and President of the Second, though favoring the Anschluss, expressed the same view; "The best thing in the world can be initiated at the wrong time, the wrong road be chosen, and success can be endangered." But for Renner all these errors remained topics for subsequent discussion. He recalled that both the German and Austrian Social Democratic Parties, though criticizing some aspects of the customs union project, approved its essence. Renner himself had no doubt that union was progressive. He also condemned the "unbearable hypocrisy" and "injustice" of the 1919 settlement, which had denied to the Germans national self-determination, one granted to virtually all other nationalities.[15] Renner preferred to overlook, if not to ignore, that "self-determination," as interpreted by many Germans and Austrians, would have given the Germans dominance in Central Europe. It would have made them victors despite their having suffered a military debacle, and would have left their neighbors, especially the Central and East European nations, at their mercy. According to Renner, Austria was the victim of the European customs anarchy and it was thus natural that she agitated the loudest for European economic reorientation. Austria just could not wait any longer. It was a difficult road which Austria and Germany had recently trod upon, but the two states had to persist: "The European developments will mature toward our plan."[16]

German Socialists and the Anschluss

The policy of Austrian Socialists on the Anschluss was to some extent influenced by that of German Social Democrats with whom they often engaged in a dialogue about it. On the whole German Socialism was always more lukewarm on the union issue than the Austrian Social Democratic Party. True, until Hitler came to power, both parties favored the Anschluss in theory, though they had to postpone it in practice. The number of union supporters in the SDPD (Social Democratic Party of Germany) was always smaller than in Austria and they were also less ardent. The union issue obviously was a cardinal issue for all Austrians, but, in view of the multiplicity of domestic and foreign policy problems facing the *Reich*, only a secondary one for most Germans.

Still, German Socialists created a mass movement for union in the *Reich*, their chief instrument being the Austro-German *Volksbund*: it was close to the paramilitary social-democratic oriented *Reichsbanner*. In the 1920s the German Social Democrats, as the *Volksbund*'s journal *Österreich-Deutschland* shows, encouraged the movement for union in a national, multi-partisan, class-cooperative manner. But after the terms of the Versailles Treaty were published, its propaganda was toned down. Still, some of the most prominent leaders of German Socialism belonged to the Executive Committee of the *Volksbund*, among them Eduard David, Konrad Hänisch, Rudolf Hilferding, Marie Juhacz, August Knoll, Paul Löbe, Heinrich Müller, Carl Severing, Friedrich Stampfer,[17] and others; some of these men were new arrivals from Austria. The very vocabulary used especially by right-wing Socialist leaders, who represented the bulk of Socialism in the *Reich*, was frequently based upon nationalist terms and slogans such as "völkisch," Blutgemeinschaft," "Stammesbrüder," "deutsche Zunge," "Schicksalsgenossen," etc., a language which in turn was to inflame chauvinism.

The leftist Independent Socialists (USPD), who played a key role in the early postwar period, largely opposed the Anschluss,[18] as did, from the other end of the political spectrum of Socialism, the ideologically revisionist journal *Sozialistische Monatshefte* and its editor Eduard Bernstein himself. As so many other groups the USPD was actually divided on the union issue: though theoretically it stood for *Grossdeutschland* and for self-determination, and even linked the Anschluss issue to world revolution,[19] claiming that it would further it, it clearly wanted to leave this problem to the Peace conference, and abide by its decision; it avoided the nationalist and *völkisch* terminology of the *Vorwärts* of the early postwar period.

When at the time of the *Sängerbundesfest* in Vienna in 1928 the Anschluss fever reached a dangerous level, the Allied press criticized the participation of Paul Löbe, presiding officer of the *Reichstag*, and the support given to this demonstration by the Hermann Müller government and Carl Severing.[20] Rudolf Breitscheid, on the other hand, the Party's specialist on foreign affairs, former leader of the USPD, and member of the German Delegation at the League of Nations in Geneva, tried to assure the Western Powers that the political unification of Germany and German Austria was "far away" and that, in any case, while it primarily involved two peoples, it was obviously also "a problem of European interest";[21] but he protected his Socialist colleague Löbe against the accusation that he was an imperialist.

The Social Democratic Party supported Gustav Stresemann's policy of fulfillment and wished to remain on good terms with the West; it tried therefore to calm Paris and London on the issue of the Anschluss. The left Socialist Paul Levi in his journal *Sozialistische Politik und Wirtschaft* took issue with an article of the Austrian socialist leader and theoretician Otto Bauer in the journal *Der Kampf* (Vienna);[22] though starting out with the same Marxist view, he reached conclusions contrary to those of Bauer. While Bauer for the first time had raised herein some doubts about the Anschluss, including about some of the chauvinist fellow-travelers of the Anschluss concept, Levi concluded that, while the present boundary between Germany and Austria did not disturb the peace, its elimination would definitely lead to war! Thus the Anschluss would be a disaster for Germany. The German bourgeoisie would use Austria as a springboard for its imperialistic drive into the Balkans. Others on the left of the SDPD, however, for instance George Ledebour—former leader of the USPD—considered union a justified and desirable goal,[23] but did not think its implementation likely as long as capitalism held sway over Europe.

In 1930 Breitscheid made it clear that he himself supported union only under some favorable conditions, namely when Austria and Germany formed a "bloc of peace." As he told Austrians: "Because just as you seek no Anschluss with Hitler-Germany, we desire no Anschluss with Starhemberg-Austria."[24] But Breitscheid's voice was a lonely one against the opinions held by Severing, H. Múller, Löbe and the leading socialist daily, the *Vorwärts*.

During the 1920s and especially while Hermann Müller headed the government (June 26, 1928 to March 30, 1930), the SDPD frequently reaffirmed its commitment to the union with Austria. Apparently a good deal of planning toward the customs union, as ultimately presented by Minister J. Curtius, originated with the Social Democrats. But when the customs union was announced, it raised great confusion and perturbation among German Social Democrats.[25] The *Volksbund* Director Robert Mischler explained the difference between the Anschluss and a mere customs union project, pointing out that the latter theoretically was "an international project."[26] Most leftists in the Party criticized the union as something similar to the *Mitteleuropa* concept, popularized at the beginning of World War I, as a scheme providing for German hegemony. Paul Löbe and others on the other hand supported it wholeheartedly,[27] with most socialists standing half-way between these extreme positions.

At the time of the 1931 Customs Union project German Socialists were divided about it as they had previously been. Three days after Curtius and Schober announced the agreement, Breitscheid in the name of the SDPD denounced the German Foreign Office for its methods of secret diplomacy and also for having flouted the authority of the *Reichstag* Committee on Foreign Affairs. But the broadside was mostly directed against the methods used by the German and Austrian governments rather than against the union itself.[28] In a subsequent article in the *Arbeiter-Zeitung* Breitscheid claimed that the customs union was only a step toward the "economic and political pacification of Europe"—which did not tally with the European-wide interpretation of the move. He also asserted that the German-Austrian customs union must be "Europeanized"—which had hardly been the original intention.[29] At the Party Convention of the SDPD in June 1931, Heinrich Ströbel, one of the leaders of the Party's left wing, however, criticized the Party for its failure to take a negative stance on the customs union. Similarly, even the right-wing Socialist Wilhelm

Sollman held that the *Reich* should not risk Anschluss at the price of alienation and isolation from the rest of Europe.[30] Otto Bauer in the *Arbeiter-Zeitung* announced that at the moment the Socialist International demanded of both Austria and Germany that they subordinate their interests to those of Europe.[31-32]

Even the abortive customs union project did not erode the traditional commitment of the German Social Democrats to the *grossdeutsch* ideal to any great extent, but, faced with a critical decision in 1931, most Social Democrats chose Europe over *Grossdeutschland*.[33]

A Turn-about of Austrian Socialism?

Actually, it was in the midst of the customs union project crisis that the Austrian Socialists performed what some contemporaries considered to be a *volte-face*. In March 1931 the Austrian Social Democratic Party had made a pro-Anschluss gesture when, in a secret session in the main Committee of the *Nationalrat*, its representatives approved the customs union plan sponsored by Dr. Johannes Schober.[34] But later that year Social Democratic enthusiasm measurably cooled in view of the political developments in the *Reich*. In a closed session the Party Executive Committee commissioned Bauer, its permanent reporter on foreign policy, to formulate anti-union guidelines.[35] According to P. Erdöly, the Vienna correspondent of *Lidové Noviny*, which was close to the Hradčany in Prague, the Austrian Socialists no longer steadfastly adhered to the Anschluss concept![36]

Erdöly saw proof of the change in a 1931 article, "Danubian Confederation," written by Paul Szende, which appeared in the influential Viennese socialist theoretical monthly *Der Kampf*.[37] With this publication the Austrian Social Democratic Party had shifted its position on the Anschluss question and had entered the political arena against union and for the Danubian Confederation. The *Prager Presse* similarly interpreted it as a turn-about and reprinted the article in full, as did *České Slovo*, Edward Beneš's official newspaper.[38]

Szende's article advanced persuasive arguments on behalf on the Danubian Federation plan. In the past the project had been favored by some Christian Socials and, abroad, by France and Italy. France supported a broader Danubian Federation and Italy a smaller one, confined to Hungary and Austria. Szende rejected economic and statistical arguments which had been marshalled against the Danubian Confederation, convinced that it offered tangible advantages for Austria and Austrian Socialism. Since France was dead-set against the Anschluss, its prohibition by the Western Powers would remain a fact of international life in the foreseeable future. Consequently, Austria had to pursue the policy of the lesser evil, that is it had to work toward a larger Danubian Federation rather than preserve the *status quo*. Though a federation was theoretically not the best of all solutions, at least it need not be dominated by any great power. A Danubian Confederation should be able to assert itself even against the Western Powers by establishing a special economic relationship with Germany. Austria's presence would ensure that the Federation could not be turned into a political instrument against Germany. A Federation would serve not only economic purposes, but also would guarantee the pacific coexistence of nationalities and thus would contribute to the solution of the extremely complex nationality question in Central Europe. Within the structure, Austria would confront two major tasks: to foster German-Austrian *Kultur* and German language and to aid the development of Social Democratic parties and of Socialism in Hungary, Yugoslavia, and Rumania.

The publication of Szende's article in *Der Kampf* was perhaps another trial balloon to test whether Austrian Social Democrats were prepared to shelve the Anschluss concept and to embrace a rather contrary plan of Danubian Confederation, next to, but outside of, the *Reich*.

The "Two-Front" War of Dollfuss and Austrian Independence

In 1933, the Austrian government, headed by Engelbert Dollfuss, became strongly influenced by events in the neighboring *Reich* and by the anti-democratic waves sweeping over Europe, and wished to emulate the extreme rightist, anti-democratic and anti-parliamentary movement by striking a deadly blow against Austrian democracy. In his book *Im Kampf gegen Hitler* Kurt Schuschnigg claimed that Austria's defense against Nazism also necessitated the struggle against the Social Democrats. He admitted though that Dollfuss had fought for a "new order." Even a leader of the Christian Social democratic wing such as Dr. Otto Ender thought that it was time to seek new approaches if Austria was to survive.[39] But the "new ways" in fact made Austria's survival even less likely.

In 1933–34 the Austrian Social Democratic Party was fighting a rear-guard action defending the democratic Republic against Chancellor Dollfuss's Christian Social Party, which had increasingly fallen under the domination of its authoritarian right-wing and closely cooperated with the armed fascist *Heimwehr*. During 1933 the Austrian Nazi Party, buoyed by Hitler's power seizure, displayed vigorous activity in the various German nationalist and anti-Semitic organizations and became the political heir to the *Grossdeutsche Volkspartei*. The triangular Austrian politics emerged more threateningly than ever. Dollfuss believed, however, that he could save Austria's independence against the opposition of a majority of the Austrian population by fighting a political two-front war: an unavoidable struggle against the Nazis on the Right, and another one which needlessly complicated the war for independence, against the Social Democrats on the Left.

Austrian Socialism too was fighting a two-front war: against indigenous Austrian fascism and against National Socialism within Austria and across the border. It battled Dollfuss and the *Heimwehr* and tried to preserve Austrian democracy. At the same time it was fully aware that the threat from the National Socialist *Reich* was growing by leaps and bounds. In October 1933, when the Nazi regime was already firmly entrenched in the *Reich*, the Austrian Social Democrats held a Party Convention which revised the 1926 resolution of the *Linzer Parteitag*: "In view of the situation of the German people altered [by the seizure of power] by Fascism in the Reich, the Party Convention resolves: Point four of the sixth section of the Party program which demands the Anschluss of German Austria with Germany is annulled."[40] The abandonment of the Party's Anschluss programme in 1933 was the logical outgrowth of changed conditions in the *Reich* and in Europe in general. The Nazi dictatorship signified the end of political and economic freedom for the German working class and the establishment of tyranny over the entire German people; it also threatened the freedom of all other peoples and continental peace itself. Under these circumstances the Social Democratic Party turned its back on the union concept and began to stress Austrian patriotism instead of German nationalism.

The newly awakened interest in Austrian patriotism came admittedly as an afterthought. An independent Austria in 1918, impoverished remainder of the once powerful Empire, had been the object of first love of only a minority of Austrians. Many Austrians, including Socialists, doubted then the country's viability. They questioned also its tradition which, in their view, was too closely associated with the Habsburg dynasty, militarism, and the Empire with its national quarrels, national and political oppression, and opposition to the demands of the working class. Only after the demise of German democracy did Austria's Social Democrats acknowledge that their country had lasting value. But at that very moment Austrian freedom was already threatened by an indigenous fascism! Under these circumstances it was rather difficult to cultivate the socialist workers' Austrian patriotism. In league with the Dollfuss regime Austrian native fascism was bent on destroying the democratic foundations of the state and eliminating democratic socialism. The Dolfuss government ultimately accomplished these goals when it suppressed the 1934 February revolt. Austrian patriotism thus remained stunted. It took Nazi domination and World War II with its total oppression to develop an appreciation among Social Democrats and others for a separate Austrian political status, for Austrian *Kultur*, freedom, and independence.

The Social Democrats maintained that the working masses would defend only a democratic Austria but not one that was about brutally to repress the Party and to exclude it from any political and economic influence in Austrian life. Indeed, Social Democrats would not stand idly by while the Dollfuss government eliminated Austria's democratic order. Only a return to parliamentarianism and the multipartite state could have brought a conciliation with the Left. A political imperative, it unquestionably posed difficult problems for Schuschnigg and would have required statesmanlike vision and courage. With the Christian Socials controlled by antiparliamentary and antidemocratic forces, Schuschnigg probably would have risked a schism with powerful forces in his own party and the Fatherland Front, especially with the paramilitary semifascist organizations. A return to democracy would undoubtedly have aroused suspicion and hostility also in

Berlin and Rome. By his own account, Schuschnigg tried to conciliate the Social Democrats. But he was primarily interested in having the Social Democrats rally to the Fatherland Front on his and the Front's narrow terms which excluded the reestablishment of a democratic order.

In retrospect, Schuschnigg still accused the Socialists of political extremism ("*aufs Ganze zu gehen*"), of wishing to overthrow the new political order[48]—the constitutionality of which was in fact highly questionable. According to Schuschnigg, the Revolutionary Socialists and Social Democrats before them, whatever their immediate goals might have been, ultimately desired the dictatorship of the proletariat. This, in his eyes, justified the continuance of his own regime; its very establishment had been only a defensive measure. This echoed Mussolini's and Hitler's earlier claims of having saved Italy and Germany respectively from Bolshevism. It is true, of course, that the elimination of Austria as a political democracy in 1933–1934 had substantially contributed to ideological radicalization and to the sharpening of tone and language, for which Austro-Marxism was already known.

The Dollfuss and Schuschnigg regimes had made the fateful decision of waging war not only against the Nazis but also against the Social Democrats. Meanwhile, National Socialist Germany, watching events closely from beyond the border, was ready to intervene at the first sign of the Austrian government's faltering. Encouraged by the opportunities of the political struggles in Austria, the Nazi regime began vigorously to increase its Anschluss propaganda, which traditionally had a wide appeal among Austrians of different political persuasions. The Socialist response in 1933 in particular was, as seen, to annul the Anschluss clause in its 1926 Linz programme. Before, during, and after the 1934 February Revolt the Austrian Social Democrats, in self-defense and trying to shield the democratic Austrian constitution, battled the dictatorial Dollfuss government. The major shafts of its criticism were aimed against the Austrian regime, Schuschnigg's "clericofascism," and the *Heimwehr*.

The February 1934 Socialist Uprising

In January 1934, Vienna expected the arrival of Fulvio Suvich, Italy's Under-Secretary of State for Foreign Affairs. Perhaps to gain support from the Austrian Left, Dollfuss, in a speech on January 18, 1934, appealed to the Austrian working class and "honest Labor leaders"[42] to participate in the construction of a new Austria and in the defense of Austrian independence. The oration apparently was to remind Mussolini that a rapprochement with the Austrian Social Democratic Party and indirectly with the Western Powers and Czechoslovakia was a tangible alternative for Austria. The Social Democratic *Parteirat* (Party Council), not unaware that Dollfuss's speech had been a trial balloon, declared on January 28, its readiness to participate in the defense of Austrian independence. It repeated earlier declarations that it was prepared to make concessions regarding a new constitution, but insisted on universal and equal suffrage as well as on the right of workers to form trade unions.[43] The February 1934 uprising destroyed the remnants of Austrian democracy and shoved aside workers' rights. It led to the destruction of the Social Democratic Party as well as of the democratic foundations of the First Republic.

The new Austrian dictatorship which emerged in 1933–1934 had battled both against Austrian National Socialism and Social Democracy. It severely curtailed the free press and limited the right of assembly to government parties. It enlarged the juridical powers of the police and diminished the powers of juries. It annulled workers' collective agreements, lowered wages, and reduced unemployment compensation. It deprived the city of Vienna of more than a third of its income. This counterrevolution set the stage for the popular explosion of February 1934, which aimed at reversing the process of consolidating the authoritarian regime of Dollfuss.

The Social Democratic Party had bitterly denounced the trenc toward Austrian dictatorship and its support by Il Duce. But at the same time the Socialist leadership realized that the likely ultimate beneficiary of the errors of Austria's political leadership would be National Socialism, an incomparably stronger, more brutal, and more dangerous foe than the home-grown fascism, marked by interminable domestic rivalry, internal confusion, and inherent instability. Austria needed mass support for her independence against the combined threats of Nazi Germany from without and the Austrian Nazi Fifth Column from within. The Austrian government which lacked this support was admonished to create it by moving toward conciliation with Socialists and democrats by restoring political democracy.

In the last free elections in the early 1930s the Social Democratic Party still obtained about two fifths of the popular vote. Nevertheless, after the February 1934 uprising the Party was dissolved. With the exception of Otto Bauer and Julius Deutsch who were able to reach Czechoslovakian soil, many prominent leaders of the Social Democratic Party were arrested and the Party press prohibited. Eleven Social Democratic members of the *Nationalrat* and *Bundesrat* and deputies to the *Landtage* and towns' and cities' councils were deprived of their mandates. The Vienna City Hall, the *Rathaus*, proud citadel of Austrian socialism, was occupied; the elected socialist mayor Karl Seitz was deprived of his post and Richard Schmitz appointed mayor in his stead. The Free Trade Unions were dissolved as were also all auxiliary workers' organizations; not even the Religious Socialists escaped the oppressive measures of the government headed by Engelbert Dollfuss.

Anschluss and the *Third Reich* in Austro-Marxist Thought

After the February 1934 civil war the political thought of broad currents of Austrian Socialism in general and of its still most prominent leader and theoretician Dr. Otto Bauer in particular about the *Third Reich*, Central Europe, and the Anschluss can best be ascertained by an analysis of the illegal press, the *Arbeiter-Zeitung*, which was published in Czechoslovakia and smuggled into Austria. In view of the destruction of the Social Democratic Party and Austria's democracy, the paper looked upon Austrian patriotism and propaganda of the Dollfuss government and later of the Schuschnigg regime with utter disbelief and upon the replacement of the democratic First Republic by an authoritarian semi-fascist state with bitter disappointment.

According to the *Arbeiter-Zeitung*, the Austrian government had not erected a strong bulwark against the *Third Reich*, to the contrary. It charged that Germany need not break down Austria's gates: the Austrian government "itself opens to her the door." The rule of clerical fascism in Austria, it claimed, had resulted in every Austrian despising the regime and desiring its overthrow. A growing part of Austria's population was ready to endorse any other regime, if it was only freed from the insufferable arbitrariness of the present rulers. This mood penetrated all circles of the population, extended to the state organs themselves, to the administration of justice, to the police and army; even the clerico-fascist organizations themselves were "Nazi-diseased" (Nazi-verseucht). "This was the problem of Austria: a state in which nobody believes, a regime for which none feels any other sentiment then indifference, hatred, and contempt."[44] The Austro-Nazis, despite the failure of their coup in July 1934, were still very strong. "Herr von Papen, the German Ambassador, can travel in Austria, address audiences, and conduct secretive negotiations with the *Landeshauptleute* (governors of the Länder)." A regime such as the Austrian nurtured even in the circles of the rulers, cautious, calculating politicians and secret helpers of Hitler, contempt. The present Austrian regime thus was no shield against the Nazis.

The *Arbeiter-Zeitung* maintained that Schuschnigg and Starhemberg, far from being able to hold off Hitler, paved the way for him. "The hope to fight one fascism through the other was a fateful error." There was only one means of preserving Austria as an independent state: to restore that majority of the Austrian population as a political factor which rejected every oppression and opposed every fascism; namely the majority of Austrian workers under the leadership of socialism. Only one force in Austria can prevent the conquest by the Nazis and ward off the catastrophe of *Gleichschaltung* to Hitler: the socialist proletariat. "To throw this force onto the scales, to bring the power of the working class to bear on the struggle for the fate of the country—this is the cause for which we fight."[45] The defense of Austria, as argued here, grew out especially from the need for preserving a base of freedom against Nazi tyranny. But it was difficult, if not virtually impossible, for the Socialists to evolve quickly a love for Austria, particiularly in view of the repression of freedom and democracy in the country.

In spite of its sharp opposition to Austrian fascism, the Austrian Social Democracy knew quite well that "Austrian fascism was weaker than the Italian one." The threat to Austria by foreign conquest was considered in January 1935, not very serious, the real threat lay in that an "undeniably large part of the Austrian people wishes the *Gleichschaltung* with Hitler-Germany." Only proletarian socialist masses were an effective and reliable defense against Nazism within and beyond the Austrian borders; neither the weak clerico-fascist forces in Austria nor even Italian fascism abroad would do. The latter forces were utterly unreliable as allies and defenders of Austrian sovereignty and independence. Austrian clericalism and fascism could not defend Austria's integrity.

The Austrian government, in justificatin of its repressive measures at home, continuously pointed to the Nazi threat. This threat, according to the *Arbeiter-Zeitung*, was an exaggeration, a "subterfuge." But it admitted that "the danger of a new attack of brown barbarism against Austria, was undoubtedly very great, "very serious." But in the event of Nazi aggression, Socialists will support none "who will not open the doors of our prisons" to release political opponents of democratic and socialist persuasions.[46]

Between 1934–1938, the *Arbeiter-Zeitung*, published in Brno, Czechoslovakia, and later in Paris, never lost sight of German fascism. The latter, after all, had dealt the death blow to German democracy, had crushed all political parties in the *Reich*, including Socialists and Communists, and made preparations for the annexation of Austria. Similarly, while the Austrian Social Democrats criticized the Western Powers and Fascist Italy—the latter because of its "dominance" over the Vienna regime—it increasingly came to realize that Germany represented a formidable imperialist threat far surpassing any other danger.

According to the *Arbeiter-Zeitung* in early 1935, Austrian fascism was the foe, but German Nazism was the most dangerous enemy of the Austrian working class and of Austria. Nevertheless, Austrian Socialists could not support the Austrian government unless it promised to open its jails and was ready "to restore lost freedoms."[47] The Socialist newspaper was highly skeptical about the Austro-German July 1936 Agreement, in which Schuschnigg promised that Austrian foreign policy would follow the German course.[48] When prior to the Agreement, Prince Rüdiger von Starhemberg, leader of the *Heimwehr* and Austria's fascist champion, was dropped from the government, the *Arbeiter-Zeitung*, recalling that he had been a "mortal foe," rejoiced but briefly. It warned of the great "perils of today"[49] and the risk of Austria's absorption by Germany. There was serious danger that Austrians might become "mere cannon fodder" and be dispatched to the battlefield for the prestige of tyrannical despots against Western democracy and Eastern Socialism; that they would spill their blood to serve alien fascist tyrants.[50] This was a prophetic prognosis of what was to happen to Austria during World War II!

The *Arbeiter-Zeitung* feared that a Berlin-Rome Axis was likely to be forged at the expense of Austria, with Rome sacrificing Austria's independence. The paper had few illusions about Austria's ultimate prospects, though for apparent tactical reasons it could not bare its deep-seated pessimism. Yet it did raise the question: "What shall we do when war erupts?" and replied:

> We do not fight at the side of Hitler and Mussolini, not for Hitler and Mussolini. One will tell us: "You are Austrians after all. As Austrians you must fulfill your duty. . . . By no means. If the coalition of fascist powers wins the war, then Hitler will be master of Europe! Then Austrian independence is lost! Then Austria will become a province of the *Third Reich!* They will tell us: "You are Germans, after all. You must fulfill your duty if the German nation is fighting for its existence." By no means. Yes, we are Germans. But just on this ground we hate German fascism, which has debased the German workers to being slaves without rights. For this very reason we hate the German rulers who lead the German people into the bloody catastrophe of a new war.[51]

In the mid-thirties the Socialists did not claim that their struggle was in defense of the Austrian fatherland and a confrontation between Austrian and German nationalism—they denied the existence of a distinct Austrian nationality! Still, they clearly rejected the loss of Austrian "independence" to German fascism, an incomparably greater danger, the sacrifice of Austrian lives in a war of conquest unleashed by German fascism and aiming at Germany's domination of all of Europe, including the permanent subjugation of the Austrian people.

From Berchtesgaden to Austria's Annexation: First Socialist Reaction

In the last days of the Austrian Republic, especially after the Berchtesgaden crisis, Schuschnigg initiated discussions with the Socialist opposition. He also extended the promised amnesty not only to Austrian National Socialists but also to the Left. This strategy, intended to deepen support for the Austrian government, was followed by negotiations with the Revolutionary Socialists, all aiming at strengthening the ramparts of beleaguered Austria. Cabinet changes in the wake of the Berchtesgaden Conference made the former Social Democratic officer of the Free Trade Unions, Adolf Watzek, Secretary of Welfare and Protection of Workers. On March 3, 1938, in a four-hour-long discussion in the Chancellery with the action committee of the illegal socialist workers' organization, the agenda contained four points: 1. Political equality of Social Democrats with the National Socialists. 2. Free elections in the trade union organizations. 3. Permission to publish a socialist daily, and 4. Guarantees in regard to improved social legislation. In Schuschnigg's judgment these negotiations were very fruitful.[52] The Revolutionary Socialists, though less satisfied especially with the pace of Schuschnigg's concessions, were apparently optimistic. In a later proclamation they warned that the 13th of March, the day Schuschnigg had designated for the plebiscite to thwart the rising Nazi threat, was not the appropriate day to present the bill to the Austro-fascists; the issue rather was "to testify to the hatred of Hitler." They therefore urged their followers to vote for Schuschnigg's plebiscite with a resounding 'yes'; "such a vote would not be a vote of confidence for Schuschnigg and the authoritarian Austrian regime, but one against Hitler and *Gleichschaltung*."[53]

In the days prior to and after the announcement of Schuschnigg's desperate plebiscite call, the Austrian Left was in a buoyant mood; it hoped that the republican constitution and the democratic liberties of the pre-1933 era would be restored. But the state of euphoria ended quickly on March 11 when Schuschnigg, presented with a German ultimatum, was compelled to resign. On March 13 Austria was annexed.

The Social Democratic position toward the *fait accompli* of Austria's annexation and the end of Austrian independence was clearly stated by Bauer. German political union, however accomplished, should not be reversed by the Revolutionary Socialists, because the German and Austrian Revolutions would benefit from it in the future. This Socialist stance, to prevail at least for the next five years, sharply separated Austrian Socialists from fellow Socialists in non-German states which had also been destroyed by the Nazi colossus: these Socialists wanted to restore their national independence. In 1938, Austrian Socialism proclaimed no such goal for Austria.

Bauer realized that in the event Hitler unleashed a war, Germany might be defeated and the *Reich's* debacle result in Austia's liberation. But the term he used twice, "losreissen" (tear oneself away), seemed to anticipate considerable domestic reluctance, if not outright opposition to the restoration of Austrian independence at that moment; this in spite of the resolute opposition of Austria's Socialists to the 1938 annexationist coup. Clearly, Austrians of all political persuasions were no more enthusiastic about Austrian independence in 1938 then they had been in 1918. This hesitance undoubtedly determined the attitude of Bauer and other Socialists even after the First Republic had reached the end of its road. Bauer assumed that a *gesamtdeutsch* (all-German, embracing also German Austria) revolution would be feasible only in the event of Germany's defeat. In that event there would no longer be any need for the Austrian working class to unfold the separate banners of Austrian Socialism and of the restoration of Austrian independence. Austria's union with the *Reich* might have been brought about by Hitler and by fascist reactionaries in violation of genuine national self-determination and of democracy, but, in the event of Germany's defeat and the ensuing German Revolution, Socialism would surely emerge as the ultimate victor. The example of World War I, which had enthroned Socialism as the domestic winner in the vanquished countries, doubtlessly influenced Bauer's thinking. As it turned out, in view of Germany's total defeat, the seizure of all her territory in 1945, the occupying foreign armies rather than the German revolution were the victors.

The "Counterrevolutionary" Annexation: Otto Bauer's Political Testament

Though Bauer did not proclaim the restoration of Austrian independence as the postwar goal of Austrian Socialism, he did nothing to assist Hitler in the plebiscite, unlike the right-wing socialist leader Karl Renner. Following Austria's annexation, Hitler had ordered a plebiscite to be held on April 10 both in Austria and the old *Reich* to ratify the Anschluss. It was to give the appearance of popular approval and democratic blessing to an act of brute force. On the eve of the plebiscite, the *Neues Wiener Tagblatt* published an interview with Renner in which the Socialist leader welcomed the Anschluss: "As Social Democrat and therefore as champion of the right of national self-determination, as first Chancellor of the Republic and former presiding officer of its peace delegation to St. Germain, I shall vote 'yes'." Shortly thereafter Bauer, referring to Hitler's "plebiscite comedy," accused Renner of having distorted the situation to an extent "which even the terror under which now all Austrians live and suffer can hardly excuse."[54] Renner's statement at that particular moment was indeed a hardly concealed recommendation to Social Democrats to vote in favor of the annexation! Genuine self-determination and Hitler's plebiscite were of course mutually exclusive. Renner's interview was rendered barely a few weeks after Austria's Revolutionary Socialists had been ready to defend Austrian independence with everything they had! To many Austrians Renner's interview appeared as a cowardly surrender, dictated either by pressure, intimidation, or by political opportunism.

On April 1 1938, some important Austrian Socialists in the underground movement convened at Brussels, then the seat of the World Socialist organization. Most participants unconditionally supported Bauer's political exposition. Friedrich Adler, Secretary of the Second International, even more decisively than Bauer, championed the *gesamtdeutsch* revolutionary ideas of 1848. Only Otto Leichter, according to his own account, and to a lesser extent K. H. Sailer, saw a danger in a one-sided orientation, in viewing the Anschluss as an "irrevocable fact." Oscar Pollak, former editor of the *Arbeiter-Zeitung,* also endorsed the Anschluss, though not without inner reluctance.[55] The decisive sentence in the Brussels resolution was almost identical with Bauer's statement in *Der Kampf:* "In view of the *fait accompli* we proclaim: 'The Austrian workers cannot struggle for their liberation, the Austrian people cannot be freed from the despotism of the *Third Reich,* by any other means than through the *gesamtdeutsche* Revolution.'"[56]

Still, after March 1938 the Austrian workers' organization did not merge with the illegal German Social Democratic emigrant organization. Nothing was further from its mind. As again Leichter observed: "In accordance with Bauer, the Declaration of Brussels preserved the organizational independence of Austrian Socialism." The Austrian Socialists, the Declaration asserted, will be able to "accomplish the union with the German socialist movement only when the political and organizational preconditions for it will have been created. Until that time the Austrian Socialists will remain an independent organization within the framework of the Socialist Workers' International."[57]

Bauer previously had pointed to the disunity among German social democratic organizations, which obviously made Austro-German Socialist union more difficult. In the 1918–1919 Revolution, the Austrian S.D.P. had been able to retain its hold upon Austrian labor; Austrian Communism was and remained rather insignificant. While German Socialism had succumbed to Hitler's fascism without a struggle, the Austrian Social Democrats in February 1934 had battled the Austrian fascist enemy heroically. The recent traumatic historical experiences had radicalized both German and Austrian Social Democrats, without bridging, however, their previous political and tactical differences. This consideration aside, the underground effectiveness of Austrian Socialists might be diminished rather than enhanced by any organizational merger— which was an additional reason to opt for organizational independence. The Austrian workers, who were increasingly chafing under German impositions, could be expected to trust an Austrian rather than a *gesamtdeutsch* Social Democratic leadership. The decision to retain a separate Austrian party organization did indicate an unconscious Socialist desire to support a separate Austria, or at least to keep this option open. In his last articles written in Paris, Bauer continued to maintain that it was necessary to preserve a separate Austrian Workers' Party.

In 1918–1919 Otto Bauer had considered the Anschluss as the fulfillment of the German National Revolution and as the harbinger of Austria's Social Revolution. But in April 1938, he observed bitterly that it was the "tragedy of German history" that the counterrevolution utilized ideas which originated with and were fostered by revolutionary people's movements, that it distorted them and "completely transforms thus originally revolutionary ideas into means of stabilizing and solidifying the counterrevolution."[58] The Anschluss now served Revolution no longer, but its very opposite, Counter-Revolution. Bauer entertained no doubt that the immediate consequence of Austria's annexation was reactionary—even though in the indeterminate future the German Revolution would turn it to its advantage. He juxtaposed the idea of the *gesamtdeutsch* (embracing all Germans) revolutionary democracy of 1848, of Bismarck's still progressive unification of Germany in 1870–1871, and of the Anschluss attempt of 1918, with the perversion of the Anschluss idea through the annexation of 1938.

In view of his conviction that the 1938 Anschluss was counterrevolutionary, and that the new German imperialism constituted a mounting danger to the peace and stability of Europe,[59] it is surprising that neither Bauer nor the Socialist Party proclaimed the restoration of Austrian independence as their political goal. True, most Austrians, whatever their political leanings, acquiesced in the permanency of Austria's absorption by the *Reich* at that historic moment; they were too stunned and paralyzed for bold and independent thought. Socialists, in addition, were burdened with Marx's and Engels' positive nineteenth-century thought about German unification and convinced that it was bound to lead ultimately to German Socialism.

The Austrian Communist Party, a mere splinter, was actually less burdened by this Marxist legacy. Taking its cue from Moscow, which was less concerned with genuine Marxist orthodoxy and more worried about the growth of National Socialist strength in the heart of Europe, it perceived the absorption of Austria as a threat to Czechoslovakia's independence and as a step toward war; it proclaimed, in accordance with Moscow's instructions, the restoration of Austrian independence as its goal! In the Second Republic, long after all Austrian political parties had approved the restoration of an independent Austrian state, the Communists boasted that theirs had been the only Austrian party in 1938 to have announced its intention to nullify the Anschluss and to restore Austrian independence.[60] In contrast, Austrian Socialists had adopted a vacillating, even contradictory position in 1938. Though they had been willing to battle the Nazis at home and abroad in defense of their country, taking the side of the Schuschnigg government and its following, the *fait accompli* of the fusion with the *Reich* and of Austria's absorption was, according to the Socialists, not to be undone.

It was Bauer's view, expressed in his April article in *Der Kampf*, that Austrian Socialism could not and should not attempt to reverse the irreversible link-up: "We cannot turn back the wheel of history [!]. Only a defeat of Germany in the war could tear

Austria away from the *Reich;* but such a defeat would unleash
the German Revolution and from this Revolution Socialism could
not tear itself away. . . . The future of the Austrian working class
is the future of the German Revolution." As it turned out, a
German Revolution never erupted in 1945; no German plan had
a chance of improving upon the pattern of 1918 and linking up
with Austria. In 1945 neither the Austrian nor the German
proletariat was a decisive political force to contend with; nor did
the Austrian working class wish to continue the German union.
None of this could be foreseen in 1938. Though Bauer expected
an Allied victory, he still thought that in its aftermath the chance
for a "proletarian" Revolution would improve. Did he believe
that the victorious Western Powers would be unable to reassert
their Anschluss veto, first enunciated in 1919? He left the question
open—or had no time to answer it.

In early April 1938 Bauer had returned from Brussels to Brno.
But with Czechoslovakia becoming ostensibly Hitler's next target,
his removal to Paris toward the end of the month became
imperative. In May the Austrian Socialists established an Austrian
Socialist Bureau (*Auslandsvertretung*) in the French capital, where
Otto Bauer began to publish *Der Sozialistische Kampf* (*La lutte
socialiste*), the first issue of which appeared on June 2. The slogan
in one of his articles, "critical, but not reactionary," were Friedrich
Engels' words in a letter to Marx, dated December 9, 1867,
regarding the Austro-German problem after Königgrätz and concerning what the correct Socialist policy against Bismarck ought
to be. Engels had criticized Wilhelm Liebknecht, who had negative
thoughts regarding the *kleindeutsch* solution of the German question, because it excluded Austria from the North Germanic Confederation. Bauer too raised the question as to the correct Socialist
policy concerning the completed annexation of Austria and the
country's future. After a new war, would Austrian Socialism wish
to cut loose from the German Social Revolution? Again, he replied
in the negative.

It had seemed pragmatic at the moment of Austria's annexation—the "fulfillment" of Germany's national drive which Socialists had always deemed as progressive—neither to wish to
undo the *fait accompli* nor to attempt to restore the irretrievable.
Bauer also wished to concentrate all socialist energies on the
impending *gesamtdeutsch* Revolution, as unrealistic and distant a

goal as the latter then seemed to be. He still envisioned an eventual all-German Revolution, though the German working class had not exhibited great skill and ardor in staging revolutions in 1848, 1918–1919, or later in defending the Weimar Republic. Was a pooling of the more militant and leftist Austrian proletariat with the German working class likely to enhance the fighting capabilities of the latter, or to increase the revolutionary opportunities of the former?

In his June article Bauer had cited the growing hostility between German fascists and the Western "capitalist-imperialist powers." He omitted to state that the latter also represented political democracy. In his last article, however, he sharply distinguished between German fascism and the Western democracies; he championed Friedrich Engels' 1848 distinction between "revolutionary" and "counterrevolutionary" nations, and this time placed the Germans at the head of the latter category.[61] Bauer's last article, published a few days before his death, was written after the late May 1938 crisis which arose over the alleged threat of Germany's invasion of Czechoslovakia. Faced with the possibility of another world war, in which the issue of the right of the Sudeten Germans to self-determination would figure prominently, Bauer returned to a problem with which he was thoroughly familiar, and with which he had theoretically and practically grappled in the old Austrian Monarchy when at the age of 25 he had established his reputation with the book *Die Nationalitätenfrage und die Sozialdemokratie* (1907). During his entire life, as with most German and Austrian Socialists, a partiality for the German point of view had marked Bauer's outlook, perhaps only subconsciously, notwithstanding the strong internationalist bent of his thought. That— in his belief—the German nation was now, under Hitler's stewardship, a "counterrevolutionary" nation, indicates the length of the road which he had traveled.

Writing after the annexation of Austria, while the Führer proclaimed once again the right of the Sudeten Germans to self-determination, Bauer recognized that this concept was being abused and distorted by National Socialists, whose real objective was the destruction of Czechoslovakia. Since the fascist victory in Germany, coupled with the rearmament and the revival of German imperialism, the international situation had radically changed. "The struggle for the right of self-determination of the Sudeten

Germans twenty years earlier and the struggle of the German Revolution against imperialism has now turned into a tool of the most dangerous and most formidable imperialism." Proclaiming the right of the Sudeten Germans to self-determination was "only a propagandistic means that is to serve as vindication of a war of conquest." Turning to the Western Powers and their great labor parties, still shackled by pacifist thought, Bauer castigated the policy of appeasement: "Therefore today one can not warn urgently enough against that pacifist sentimentality which falls into the trap prepared by Hitler . . . one must warn against the fateful error of persuading the Czechoslovak government to yield important political power in the German-inhabited territories of Czechoslovakia to the Sudeten German Nazis."[62]

On the eve of the Munich Conference—he was to die prior to it—Bauer thus warned the democracies not to succumb to the empty Nazi slogan of national self-determination, which Germany exploited only to undermine the independence of Czechoslovakia. He cautioned against the dangerous Western policy of appeasement long before this word acquired its sinister meaning. Having drawn a new distinction between the "most formidable" Nazi imperialism and the old-fashioned imperialism of the Western democracies, a new Otto Bauer had emereged. What he recommended to the West's Social Democratic Parties and to the governments of the Western "capitalist and imperialist" states was to risk war rather than to continue on the slippery road to surrender. This message was a far cry from Bauer's 1933 position when he had criticized Socialists favoring a Western "preventive war" against Hitler's Germany. At that time he had warned bluntly that a war against fascist Germany, one perhaps unleashed by the West, would come "against the will, the resistance, and the impassioned protest" of Austrian Socialism.[63]

But the conquest of Austria and the mounting threat against Czechoslovakia had radically altered the European and world situation. Bauer no longer feared a war by the West, he dreaded one unleashed by Hitler, aimed at the domination of Europe. His new slogan was "revolutionary nations versus counterrevolutionary nations." The latter included the Germans at this particular historic moment, the former the Czechoslovaks and apparently also the Poles, the French, and the English. The "capitalist-imperialist" Western nations had been transformed at least into "progressive" nations, because they blocked the Führer's march toward hegemony over Europe. The adequacy and the full applicability of terms such as "revolutionary" and "counterrevolutionary" nations were perhaps debatable, but about the change in Otto Bauer's political thinking, especially concerning the German working class, there could be little doubt. Ever since Marx and Engels, the Germans had been considered to belong to the progressive nations, moving forward toward the Proletarian Revolution. The Austrian working class in particular was now informed that German imperialism, which had swallowed Austria and destroyed any chances for the revival of Austrian democracy and of Austrian Socialism, was not only their enemy, but also that its defeat in a new world war, likely to erupt in the near future, was imperative if international reaction was to be vanquished.

The Nazi annexation threat to Austria in the late 1930s and the *fait accompli* of the Anschluss in March 1938 radically altered Bauer's and his Party comrades' thinking about the European and international situation. This, admittedly, did not lead to an early and bold pronunciamento proclaiming the will of Austrian Socialism to restore the independence of Austria. It took years of Nazi occupation and supreme wartime sacrifices by Austrians of all classes to exorcise the *grossdeutsch* incubus which had lain oppressively on the Austrian mind for so long. It was not before 1943, largely following the Allied Moscow decision to restore Austrian independence, that Austrian Socialists also adopted this course. But the road to this decision had been prepared long before. Though Bauer in 1938 had held that the Anschluss was irreversible and that the *gesamtdeutsch* Revolution was the goal of the Austrian revolutionary working class, he had nonetheless held fast to the organizational independence of Austrian Socialism. Also, by denouncing Hitler's imperialism before the Munich Conference, he had, theoretically at least, prepared for the later dismantling of Hitler's Empire. Its foundation stone had been laid, as Otto Bauer had come clearly to perceive, with the annexation of Austria in 1938.

Ignaz Seipel, 1876–1932, chancellor, priest, and prominent leader of the Christian Social Party.

Otto Bauer, 1881–1938, Social Democratic champion
of the postwar Anschluss movement and principal
ideologue of Austro-Marxism.

Chapter 4

Austria's "Bourgeois" and National Parties and the Movement Toward Union

A. The Christian Socials, the *Grossdeutsche Volkspartei,* the *Landbund,* and the *Heimwehr*

The Christian Social Party, 1918-1919: Seipel opposes the Anschluss

In the course of March and April 1919, while the Peace Conference continued its work in Paris, fear and uncertainty gripped many minds in Central Europe. The specter of social revolutions in Hungary and southern Germany, where Soviet republics were emerging, cast its shadow also over Austria. A good number of highly-placed Austrian politicians, leading industrialists, and professors, suggested privately that one method of blocking the movements toward revolution or Anschluss would be for the Entente to dispatch troops to the unsettled areas and to send food and raw materials. They felt that the Entente should dissuade the Austrian people from seeking closer ties with Germany. One of these calls for British troops and supplies and for a differentiation in the treatment of Germany and Austria came from the eminent leader of the Christian Social Party, Dr. Ignaz Seipel. His plea was directed to Professor Heinrich Lammasch, a former Prime Minister of Austria, who shared Seipel's view of these matters. The letter, of course, was not made public.

An appeal similar to that of Dr. Seipel was made by Professor Joseph Schumpeter, Minister of Finance and a well-known theoretical economist, in a conversation with Professor A. C. Coolidge, head of the American mission in Vienna. Schumpeter asked the Entente to bring pressure to bear on the Austrian government— of which he himself was then a member—and in particular to disband the socialist-controlled *Volkswehr.* The conversation took place about ten days after the Bolshevik coup in Budapest.

Schumpeter was apparently convinced that Vienna would shortly follow in the footsteps of Budapest, claiming that some of the Austrian Social Democrats were already negotiating with the Communists.[1] Schumpeter feared that "if things were allowed to drift, as at present, the result must inevitably be Bolshevism." Yet Schumpeter was equally concerned about the Anschluss with Germany. In his talk with Professor Coolidge he pointed out that "the radical elements, if they came to power, would press for the union with Germany more urgently than ever, and all hope for a Danubian confederation would definitely have to be abandoned."[2]

To many of Schumpeter's conservative contemporaries in Austria and abroad, it appeared that the Anschluss movement and the radical socialist current were converging into the same stream and that its waters were becoming dangerously swollen.

The only party opposed both to Bolshevism and the Anschluss was the Christian Social party. As far as the Anschluss was concerned, it opposed it on grounds of Austrian patriotism and hostility toward socialism, then seemingly dominant in Germany. Yet at times the wind of the Anschluss movement blew so strongly that the party did not dare to unfurl its true flag of opposition. The party program of December 15, 1918, was conditional and ambiguous regarding the Anschluss. It read: "An essential prerequisite [of the return, *Wiederanschluss*], is that Germany succeed in transforming herself into a truly free commonwealth which does justice to the special character and the economic necessities of German Austria."[3] The attached conditions offered the party an easy way out to avoid its *grossdeutsch* and national commitments. In the midst of the revolutionary turmoil and on the eve of the Spartacist attempts to seize power in the *Reich*, Germany seemed a long way from developing into a "truly free commonwealth."

The Christian Social party's position on the Anschluss question had been rather equivocal from the very beginning; even the pro-union forces felt little passion for their cause. As the London *Times* remarked, the Christian Socials were "never eager for union at heart."[4] Trends favoring the Anschluss were stronger in the *Bundesländer*, while opponents of the union were prominent in Vienna. Yet the division of Christian Socials in regard to the Anschluss movement by no means followed strictly these geographic lines. In 1918 a Christian Social Circle, opposed to the anticipated union, had already formed around the composer Ludwig Bittner; the author Hermann Bahr was also closely involved with this group. The writers Anton Wildgans, Robert Müller, and Oscar A. H. Schmitz spoke out against the union.[5] But the most important opponent of the Anschluss among the Christian Socials, although less known as such, was Dr. Ignaz Seipel.

Seipel was the most outstanding leader to emerge from the Christian Social party between the wars. Priest and professor of theology in Salzburg and later at the University of Vienna, he became a champion of political Catholicism. He did not conceal that at heart he was still a monarchist. In 1918 and 1919 Seipel was definitely opposed to the Anschluss which would bury any chance for the restoration of the Habsburg empire. Like numerous other German Austrians, he had earlier hoped that the polyglot empire could be saved. He had not considered the growth of the nation state the only possible form of modern development. Seipel had been, and still was, an Austrian patriot with a strong sense of German nationality and belief in the values of German civilization. But these views were tempered by his Christian universalism and his appreciation of Austria's cosmopolitan historical tradition. Elected in February, 1919, into the Constituent Assembly as well as into the Presidium of the Christian Social Association, Seipel soon became the undisputed leader of the party to a degree which perhaps even the Vienna mayor Karl Lueger had never reached. In spite of the ideological gulf separating Ignaz Seipel from the socialist leader Otto Bauer, they had much in common. Both were looked upon as doctrinaires by some elements in their respective parties. Seipel was a statesman of "European caliber" (to use Bauer's words), but by force of circumstances he had to confine his talents to the narrow political framework of a small country; this could also be said of Otto Bauer.

In 1916 Seipel had published his major theoretical work *Nation und Staat*. He concluded that since the beginning of the modern period ethnic boundaries and political frontiers had largely coincided in Western countries such as England and France. But Seipel dared to question the historical necessity, absolute value, and inherent superiority of the national state, which seemed to him by no means the highest principle of political organization.[6] He criticized "the exaggerated belief that nationality, the fact of belonging to a particular nation, is man's highest good."[7] Seipel continued to cling to this idea even after the breakdown of the Habsburg monarchy. To him the multinational empire had not only an important function; it had also a mission. It was the prototype of a state carrying a vital message for all of Europe and the world: the need for cooperation among different peoples and the establishment of peace. Also in accordance with his concepts in this war-time book that nation and state were not identical, he developed later the thesis of two separate German states.[8]

Seipel, later Chancellor of five governments of the First Republic (1922-29) and Foreign Minister in 1931 was largely responsible for the increasingly authoritarian course after 1927. In the midst of the First World War, however, Seipel, astute and politically flexible, in several articles published between March and December 1917, prepared for the change-over toward republicanism and subsequently criticized the Habsburg Monarchy for its "sins," militarism, bureaucracy, the remainder of feudalism and absolutism, and the "sins" of capitalism.[9] Though on November 12, 1918, the Christian Social Party along with all other parties voted for the Republic *and* the Anschluss with Germany, Seipel at the same time seemed proud of being the best-hated man in Vienna, because he was considered the leader of the monarchists *and* of the opponents of the Anschluss. His position on these and other questions was often ambiguous.

Seipel's devotion to the Old Austrian Empire did not exclude love for the German nation or the conviction of the preeminence of German culture and its educational value for non-German peoples. The German nation itself had reaped great advantages by being able to spread German *Kultur,* through the medium of the Austrian realm, to the East and South and into the Balkans. "If . . . the German Austrians," he wrote in 1916, "were to join the German empire, it would only gain a couple of milion [sic] more inhabitants . . . Austria would have disappeared,"[10] and with it, by implication, the carrier of German *Kultur* and civilization.

On November 18, 1918, Seipel disclosed his views in the *Reichspost:* "The German Austrians have been members of a great state for so long that they cannot suddenly confine their spirit to the narrow interests of a small state." Seipel saw the only solution for Austria's problems in a link-up with a "great state," "but of course only as a fully privileged member of some confederation, not as a mere part."[11] He thus clearly criticized the Anschluss resolution passed by the Provisional National Assembly on November 12—just six days earlier.

Seipel raised the point that Austrians "did not know yet" where they could best serve the German people. He reminded his countrymen of the historic German Austrian mission in Central Europe: to be Austrian was not merely to be German. Ignoring the recent Anschluss resolution, Seipel pointed to the alternative, a link-up with other peoples of Central and Southeastern Europe in a new confederation, a new political structure which could become the heir of the Habsburg Empire.

Yet the outcome of the war spelled doom for the multinational state structure, while giving a fresh boost to the nation state. Though beset by doubts, Seipel himself held out against union with Germany and was sympathetic to the Allies who likewise combatted both the Anschluss and the threat of Bolshevism in Austria. While Seipel, along with many others, had misgivings about the viability of German Austria, he was consistently critical of what he called a merely declaratory policy on union with Germany, which was not and could not be followed up by a meaningful deed. He therefore opposed the plebiscites on the Anschluss which were organized in some of the Austrian Länder. In 1926 in a talk to the Vienna *Politische Gesellschaft* he remarked:

> To us [Austrians] the nation, irrespective of citizenship, is the great cultural community; to us Germans, it is dearer than the state. . . . If we see the life of our nation consumed in the creation of a unitary state, then somehow we can also find consolation in living in a German state which does not belong to the German *Reich*.[12]

This had also been very much his view in 1918-1919.

On January 14, 1919, Ludo Hartmann, Austrian Ambassador in Berlin, had forwarded to Secretary Dr. Otto Bauer a confidential letter which Seipel had written to a German friend. Though Bauer asked Hartmann on February 6 to obtain permission to quote the letter, the request was denied and Bauer abstained from making political use of it. The letter, if published, would no doubt have been highly embarrassing to Seipel at a moment when proclaiming one's interest in the Anschluss was virtually a political imperative.

In the letter Seipel pointed to the absence of a German "echo" to Austria's offer for union and to the contrast between the interest displayed by Austrian journals in the Anschluss and the indifference shown by the great German newspapers toward union and Austria in general. It was still uncertain, Seipel developed, "where the good Lord wanted to have us German Austrians."[13] "Old Austria was by no means dead and the Danubian federation will certainly materialize and will invigorate Austria." It appeared that economic considerations as well as the interests of the entire German people would compel Austria to opt for the federation.

A union prior to the conclusion of peace would be "disastrous," resulting in the loss of German South Tyrol. The Anschluss movement in Austria had already led to the loss of German Bohemia to Czechoslovakia. Finally, Seipel expressed unwillingness to link up with "Germany of today in which there is the terror of soldiers' councils and a socialist dictatorship." Thus "we have every reason to use the brake." The Anschluss would only play into the hands of those who always had prophesied that Germany even in the event of an unhappy outcome of the war, would profit through the annexation of Austrian territories. "Only if Austria has definitely succumbed, shall we be morally free to find new associations."

Another letter of Seipel, if known, would have become an even greater political liability. It was a letter written in March, 1919, to Professor Heinrich Lammasch, who had earlier gone to Berne at the invitation of Entente leaders, to inform him of the turbulent course of events and growing radicalization in Austria.[14] Both men had been ministers in the short-lived imperial cabinet in late October and early November of 1918. Describing in dark colors the situation in Vienna with its requisitioning, *Volkswehr* excesses, general insecurity, and government weakness, Seipel told Lammasch that he anticipated an imminent upheaval in Austria more along the lines of the Russian Revolution than the German Revolution.

> A serious danger threatens the very moment when the government's policy of union collapses in the sight of all. . . . Under Otto Bauer's leadership the government . . . placed its entire stake on this one

card [Anschluss.] When it becomes known that South Tyrol and German Bohemia have become separate states, without [Austria] having achieved union with Germany, then a most terrible despair will grip this people whose ideals have all been shattered and which is now a prey to hunger; not only will the government be overthrown, but doors will be flung open to Bolshevism which up to the present has not been able to obtain a firm foothold. . . .

In his letter to Lammasch, Seipel also pleaded for aid:

Under these circumstances help can only come to us from the Entente. In my opinion this is what should be done; 1) a clear and decisive position must be taken on the union question, and at the same time a strong differentiation made in regard to the treatment of Germany. It would be a very good thing if this government which has compromised itself by its one-sided pursuit of the policy of union were advised to make place for another government which enjoys the confidence of the Entente. . . . 2) The safeguarding of public peace and order by means of a small contingent of British or American troops which could be transferred to Vienna. Some 3,000 men would suffice and would render the numerous guards harmless; the mere presence of the troops would suffice, and it is very improbable that there would be fighting of any kind. . . . All these measures of precaution must be taken before the Entente's decision on the Anschluss is made public.

Seipel's third request was for an adequate supply of provisions and his fourth for coal to be used for industrial purposes. "It is only by work that social revolution can be averted."

These demands represented Dr. Seipel's minimum program to combat effectively the Anschluss movement. He was well aware that the dispatch of troops was advisable before the Entente made its negative decision on the Anschluss—a decision which was likely to swell dissatisfaction to a dangerous level.

Dr. Seipel emerged here as a determined opponent of the Anschluss movement in 1919 on the grounds that it was bound to fail and that failure in turn was likely to usher in Bolshevism. One wonders whether under different conditions in Germany, with no threat of social revolution on the horizon, Seipel might have looked favorably upon the union with Germany. How attractive could a predominantly Protestant, republican and moderately social democratic Germany be to the spokesman of Austria's political Catholicism, who still favored monarchist concepts?

Conservatives in Austria on the whole were basically cool toward union with Germany. They were pinned between Hungarian and South German Bolshevism and fearful of Austria's own radical socialists who were pushing toward Anschluss with a *Reich* in which the Social Democrats were well entrenched. Though critical of the anticipated harsh treatment of Austria by the Western Powers, Austrian conservatives were dependent on the West for political, economic, and possible military support against the dangers from both East and West, Bolshevism and the Anschluss movement.

Heinrich Lammasch

The man to whom Dr. Seipel had written, Professor Heinrich Lammasch, was a well-known and widely respected authority on international law and organization. In the summer of 1918 he had been considered for the post of Austria's imperial chancellor and was finally chosen for it in the dark October days of 1918.[15]

Lammasch considered pacifism a "Christian heritage." During the war, when waves of national antagonism lashed Austria continuously, he mercilessly castigated "national hatred." Author of a work entitled *Para Pacem*, he spoke out several times in 1917 and 1918, in the Austrian *Herrenhaus*, pleading for a peace without annexation and for the equality of all nations.[16]

His conservatism, his interest in continued links with the peoples with whom the Austrian Germans had so long been associated, his opposition to German nationalism, and his Western orientation, all combined to make Lammasch oppose the Anschluss. In addition, one of his major aims was the salvation of German South Tyrol in behalf of which he had worked in Berne since March, 1919. He was convinced that Italy would be prepared to relinquish South Tyrol only as the result of "pressure" by the Entente and attempted to win over to his cause the American, English, and French envoys to Switzerland. Under these circumstances he considered Vienna's strident demand for the Anschluss as "untimely and menacing to the fate of South Tyrol." Later, as member of the Austrian delegation in St. Germain, Lammasch became fully aware of the contrast between his views and those of the leaders of his delegation who endorsed the union with Germany.[17]

Foreign Secretary Dr. Otto Bauer considered Lammasch to be loyal, though a monarchist, and mistakenly thought him sympathetic to the Austrian government's pro-German orientation. He suggested that Lammasch, aside from treating questions of the law of nations, use his influence in behalf of German Bohemia, the Sudetenland, German South Tyrol, and the threatened border regions in Carinthia and Lower Styria. Lammasch should also speak in behalf of the Anschluss and a plebiscite in Austria and against the Danubian federation.[18]

On the eighteenth of March a disappointed Baron de Vaux, Austrian Ambassador in Berne, replied to Dr. Bauer informing him that Lammasch's sympathies belonged to the Danubian confederation. He was also favorably disposed to the project of the neutralization of the Alpine republic and resigned to the loss of German Bohemia. If neither the Danubian confederation or Austria's neutralization was feasible, he would favor the Anschluss with a South German republic—a concept which Dr. Bauer earlier had sharply rejected.[19]

It was evident that the scholar, great individualist and conservative Lammasch, who had been suggested by Entente politicians as a middleman, was not cut out to be Dr. Bauer's diplomatic agent or a spokesman for German national demands. Convinced of the necessity of building some multinational structure at a time when nationalism was rampant, he was unsuited to represent the foreign policy of the new socialist, republican, and above all Anschluss-minded Austrian government.

To sum up, in the immediate postwar period Seipel and the Christian Social Party, despite the professed sympathies of some Christian Socials toward the union concept, were set against the Anschluss. Numerous other distinguished Conservatives, among them Lammasch and the economist Schumpeter, displayed the same aversion toward the union.

German Political Parties in the 1920s. Austrian Connections

Immediately after the War, German political parties came out in support of the Anschluss, but with much less ardor than the

Austrian parties. The German government and nation were then burdened by numerous social, economic, and political problems. Many Germans feared that an Anschluss with Austria through a *fait accompli* prior to the Peace Conference would result in retaliàtion by the victors, taking the form of harsher economic terms and greater territorial losses. After the War's end, Germany was more concerned about the expected losses in East and West, the Polish Corridor, Upper Silesia, and Alsace-Lorraine and the Saar—all of which were German before 1914—than she was about Austria, which had not been part and parcel of the *Reich*'s patrimony when war broke out.

Still, on February 6, 1919, Majority Socialist Friedrich Ebert, soon President of the Weimar Republic, and Eduard David, first President of the Constituent Assembly, heartily welcomed the November 1918 proclamation of the Austrian Provisional National Assembly which proclaimed the Austrian Republic part of the German *Reich;*[20] at that moment the Anschluss enthusiasm clearly gripped the Assembly. Only later did cooler temperaments and contrary political considerations gain the upperhand. The Heidelberg program (1925) of the Social Democratic Party of Germany came out for self-determination of peoples, though it refrained from specifically mentioning the Anschluss. The Party's separate *Erläuterungen* (Explanations), however, demanded that the Austrian *Stämme* (tribes) be granted free self-determination.[21] The German Communist Party abstained from coming to grips with the Anschluss problem, though on some occasions Communist speakers demanded the right of self-determination for Austria, echoing the Soviet Union's opposition to the "capitalist-imperialist" dictate of the peace treaties of Versailles and St. Germain.

On January 19, 1922, at its second Party Convention, the German Catholic Center Party endorsed guidelines which demanded freedom of decision for German Austria in the Anschluss question and self-determination for all German *Stämme,*[22] the latter apparently relating to the former German border regions which had been seized by Poland, France, Belgium, and Denmark. Similarly to the *Zentrum* (Center Party), the Bavarian People's Party, which also stressed Christianity, claimed self-determination for Austria. It specifically demanded assimilation of legal and economic institutions between Austria and Germany, considering it a "stepping stone" toward the Anschluss.

The German Democratic Party, which showed strength in the early postwar period, though it gradually declined later, in its last electoral appeal in 1928 came out in support of the "great goals of German foreign policy," especially the creation of a *grossdeutsch*-national state, comprising "all Germans of close German settlement," but obviously diluted this call by warning "that this could not be achieved by saber-rattling and high-sounding phrases." According to its *Principles* of 1922, the German People's Party strove for conciliation of nations but considered this goal unattainable as long as a "union of all Germans torn from our side or of those who wished to be part of the Reich, including German Austrians, was prevented."

In its electoral appeal of 1928, the important German National People's Party, close associate of the Nazis since 1930, stridently demanded union with the Germans of Austria.[23] During the Bismarckian and imperial era these conservative circles had espoused the *kleindeutsch* program, but since 1918 they had changed over to the *grossdeutsch* point of view, insisting on the implementation of the right to self-determination for the entire German nation, primarily the Anschluss of German Austria; due to old traditions, the Party emphasized freedom and federalism, though the meaning of these words had been eroded. In its program of 1928 the German NSDAP finally bluntly announced: "We do not renounce any German in the Sudeten German area, in South Tyrol,"[24] in Poland and in Austria; the last-named was declared to be a "colony of the League of Nations."

Austrian political parties entertained close relations with their sister parties in the German Weimar Republic. This held true, as noticed, for the leftist parties, Social Democrats and Communists, but applied also to democratic and liberal parties, to the Nationalists and National Socialists, and also to the Catholic parties, as shall be seen in the following.

Division Among Christian Socials. Austria's "Mission." Seipel's Contradictions

As late as July 1920, as well as thereafter, the Christian Socials in Austria remained divided on the union issue. On July 11, 1920, Leopold Kunschak, leader of the Christian Social workers and Trade Unionists, wrote thus in the *Reichspost:* "I know that there are people in the Christian Social Party who simply rave [schwär-men] about the Anschluss. I also know that there are others who have the Danubian Federation in their programme;"[25] and there was a third group, rejecting both options, desiring rather "a great Catholic South German state."

However contradictory Seipel's speeches and other utterances on the union issue turned out to be in the 1920s and remained so until his death in 1932, he was strongly pro-German culturally, but never a German nationalist. He always remained a Christian theologian, dedicated to universalism rather than to excessive nationalism, and never ceased to question the general validity of nationalism as the main organizing political principle. While a devoted German, he stressed the values of German civilization, not those of the German race. One of the early interpreters of his ambivalent attitude toward the Anschluss concept, Miss Barbara Ward, held that if Seipel had lived long enough to witness the annexation of Austria, he would, despite occasionally approving earlier remarks about Austria's union with Germany, have turned out "as determined an opponent" of National Socialism as Cardinal Faulhaber.[26]

In 1922, prior to the signing of the Geneva Protocols, Seipel saw his primary task in keeping Austria's economy on an even keel and saving the country and its people. The issue then turned not on independence or Anschluss, but on something more basic, survival of the Austrians. In the event of a domestic breakdown, alien occupation of the country seemed unavoidable. To obtain help from the West, he considered it essential that Austria live up to her treaties, including the prohibition of the Anschluss. Whatever his thoughts about St. Germain, the wishes, interests, and fears of other European Powers had, according to Seipel, to be taken into account. At the same time he never wearied to repeat his old distinction between nation and state, stressing the community of "culture and language," of "blood [!] and destiny" which ought to be "preserved at all costs, even though we do not form a single state."[27] This primacy of culture over state and politics left the door open, of course, to the development of a "single state," but did not make it a command, nor a political or moral imperative! The idea of Austria's historic and cultural mission in Central Europe, either in connection with the former co-citizens of the Austrian Empire, or in a new combination with the German nation, continued to crop up frequently. Occasionally Seipel seems to have come rather close to the concept not only of an Austrian but also of a German mission, though his view of the latter was never that of the National Socialists. "Austrian Germans . . . together with the whole German nation must be champions of our people's mission, guardians of the truth that it is the Germans' duty [!] to rebuild Europe."[28]

References to "blood" and a German mission with overtones of German preeminence may, admittedly, sound irreconcilable with a truly democratic Europe and genuine national equality; but they recall the traditional 19th century superior attitude of the Germans of the Habsburg Empire in Central, Eastern and Southeastern Europe toward other nationalities rather than anticipate the blatant national and racial arrogance of the Nazis and their wide-ranging claims to German hegemony and domination.

After forming his first cabinet Seipel came out against a "policy of mere declarations" against the Anschluss. He welcomed the coalition with the *Grossdeutschen* who in forging this alliance had demonstrated "some confidence in my national [German national] conviction." He appreciated that they did not relinquish their national point of view but that they also acknowledged that for the duration of the coalition with the Christian Socials they considered it their duty to work with full strength against the breakdown of the existing *status quo;* whatever one's belief in the future ideal, the Austrian people must continue to survive.[29] According to Schuschnigg, Seipel, due to the coalition with the *Grossdeutschen* in mid-1922, was in regard to the Anschluss question in a "difficult situation." "He himself was from the start certainly not a politician in favor of the Anschluss." The *bon mot* "always talk about it, never think of it," (actually an inversion of Gambetta's remark in regard ot the reconquest of Alsace and Lorraine: "Always think of it, but never talk about it") was occasionally ascribed to Seipel, though incorrectly. The saying, according to Schuschnigg, was actually that of Karl Renner who in his debate about the Geneva Protocols thus tried to ridicule the views and practices of the Austrian Foreign Ministry at the *Ballhausplatz.*[30]

On December 31, 1926, the Christian Social Party, adopting its first authentic programme since the birth of the First Republic—

it was referred to as the "Sylvester-Program"—was still very cautious about union with Germany. Point 8 of its programme had this to say about the union: "As national-oriented Party, the Christian Social Party demands the cultivation of the German character and fights against the superiority [Übermacht] of the destructive Jewish influence in the intellectual and economic realm. It demands in particular equality of rights for the German *Volk* in the European family of nations and the development of the relationship with the German *Reich* on the basis of the right to self-determination."[31] Clearly, both German nationalism and anti-Semitism were here deliberately emphasized, but the word "Anschluss" was definitely avoided, though the right to national self-determination for Austria left the door open to a later union with the *Reich*. The Christian Social Party, apparently to avoid internal dispute, aimed at satisfying both opponents and partisans of the Anschluss. Professor Karl Hugelmann, a prominent Christian Social himself but also a champion of the Anschluss movement, was attempting to claim Seipel for the latter group, but felt compelled to quote a speech of the Chancellor in which the latter revealed his view that Austrians should refrain from deciding quickly on a solution, whether it was an all-European, *mitteleuropäisch*, or German solution, "the moment the door opens to us in this or that greater economic realm."[32]

Seipel called the period between 1922 and 1928 a "time of waiting." But in an article, "Das wahre Antlitz Österreichs," he warned that under some circumstances, continued lack of economic unity and the persistence of old hatreds and hostilities, Austria might not be content with the mere development of "cultural unity" and with the old *Reich* idea, the Austrian state concept; she might be forced to turn to the Anschluss, to the "one nation, one state" idea, long established in the West, the "union of the one nation in one state."[33]

As Ward described Seipel's attitude in 1928: "Painfully and sadly—for it meant the desertion of a principle and a hope— Seipel came to recognize the necessity of an Anschluss"; she also spoke of Seipel's "tardy but undoubted conversion to the inevitability" of the Anschluss.[34] In a letter to Bishop Frind, written on August 16, 1928, Seipel, it is true, admitted that in the question of the Anschluss doubts had seized him. Once more he raised the notion of a "special mission" which German Austria had cultivated for Central and Eastern Europe.

> [He] admitted that he did not know whether it had been gambled away or not. If we have, then we shall be simply sent home to the *Reich* to become a province among provinces under the leadership of Prussia, for God has no further use for us. . . . With every ounce of strength in me I hope and pray that they will find it [the special mission] again. But if this is not the case, we must take the punishment upon ourselves and be happy that we can serve in our father's house.[35]

This certainly was no enthusiastic endorsement of union with the *Reich*, a union taking the form of "punishment" rather than liberation, and coming only as a result of Austrian failure, in consequence of the German Austrians' loss of their true mission. The appeal to the Austrians to be "happy" in case of union, to "serve in our father's house," sounded rather like a religious command, since the thought of Austria being a mere "province among provinces under the leadership of Prussia" held no attraction for Seipel. Yet if God "has no further use for us" in Austria, it was clearly obligatory upon Austrians to "serve" where the Lord had assigned them to serve. What it all probably boiled down to was the advice to make the best of a bad situation. Two years later, in 1930, in reply to a question on the attitude of the Anschluss, he answered, "I accept the Anschluss, but not because I regard . . . the national state as an ideal to be attained, but because the Anschluss seems to me to be the only possible way out for Austria."[36] Seipel thought for a time that the Austrian National Socialists might be harnessed to the vehicle of the state as the Socialists had been in 1918-1919, and as he tried to "domesticate" the *Heimwehr* movement after 1927. But in 1931 he expressed serious doubts as to the possibility of cooperation with the Nazis and later attacked the "blasphemous language" of Nazism "against the whole of Christianity."[37]

A most interesting and illuminating private letter by Seipel on the Anschluss to one Dr. W. Bauer, dated July 30, 1928, has been published by Paul R. Sweet in the *Journal of Modern History*, 1947, the original of which is in the Austrian State Archives. Seipel therein disputed that the Anschluss would be a threat to peace, since an alliance with Germany could place the inhabitants of Austria at the side of Germany "in time of war as effectively as though we were united in one state." Furthermore, the Peace treaties "anticipated" the Anschluss, stipulating the consent of the League to a possible union. Seipel dismissed arguments against the Anschluss, such as "the understandable aversion to the congenital characteristics of the Prussian nature or the effect the Anschluss would have on particular business enterprises, or the fear of political difficulties or economic advantages," as not decisive criteria. "So far as our future position in the world is concerned, only the task which we recognize as assigned to us can show us the way." The mission which Austrians designed for themselves was the primary yardstick which ought to be applied![38]

The only argument against the Anschluss which, according to Seipel, had any validity, was "that it might perhaps alienate us from a higher calling!" Though this argument was rather drowned by others adduced by him, it cannot be entirely dismissed. By its very nature it is antithetical to the nationalist point of view, which of course does not recognize a "higher calling," none higher than nationality and nationalism! Or as Seipel put it in the same letter: "The question of whether or not the Anschluss ought to come at any time is bound up with the other question of whether or not the Austrian Germans have trifled away their historical task for all time. This mission might be placed before them once more, either as an Austrian, an Eastern European, a central European, or a pan-European task." In other words, any of these alternate self-imposed tasks or missions would do! Seipel continued: "Whether or not the old task has been trifled away, I do not know—here I speak in the actual sense of myself as a person. So long as I do not know, my *Hic Rhodus, hic salta* implies the obligation to hold both possibilities (Anschluss or independence) open for the Austrians and to educate them so that they will be prepared to follow either possibility." The Austrians must thus ascertain their alternatives and choose their true mission—which Seipel himself as late as 1928 did not yet seem to know!

Yet at the same time Seipel, as he made clear, was "against an agitation for the Anschluss," since, as he revealed, he mistrusted the character of the Austrian people: They "are not very energetic and do not like self-discipline, they get considerable satisfaction from bewailing the 'wretched times' and in waiting for the wheel of fortune to be turned from the outside, by a *deus ex machina*." Issues surrounding the union ought to be weighed "seriously . . . when a question so great as that of the Anschluss is involved." Ten years after the establishment of Austria's independence Seipel still feared to rush into union and opposed "a superficial and premature [!] agitation to determine the decision." No wonder that both proponents of Austria's independence as well as the champions of the Anschluss were able to find ammunition in some of Seipel's ambiguous remarks on the topic!

Catholic Nationals, Clergymen, and the *Schönere Zukunft*

The national elements received support from the Catholic Nationals. Since the summer of 1932 when the Lausanne loan and the attached demands were widely discussed, many of the Catholic Nationals became critical of the foreign policy course of the Christian Social Party, which seemed to postpone *ad infinitum* the implementation of the Anschluss. Leaders of this group were the Vienna University professors Karl Gottfried Hugelmann, who like his colleagues Hans Eibl and the well know sociologist Othmar Spann placed nation above state.[39] Activists of this orientation were members of the Catholic youth movement, the student league "Academia," and other student organizations. This group published in 1932 the volume *Bekenntnis zu Österreich*. The following year the newly founded *völkisch Arbeitskreis* of Austrian Catholics published the work *Katholischer Glaube und das Volkstum in Österreich*. In the same category belonged the book *Österreich's Erbe und Sendung im deutschen Raum*, edited by the Vienna University Professors Josef Nadler and Heinrich von Srbik.

Srbik, champion of the *gesamtdeutsch* conception of history, which aimed at overcoming in the intellectual realm the traditional divisive Austrian-Prussian, *grossdeutsch-kleindeutsch* concepts of history, was a lifelong devotee of the Anschluss. According to his book *Deutsche Einheit*, the army of the Habsburg Empire, German to its core, "was the great carrier of German *Kultur* for the nationalities of a lower culture (absinkendes Kulturgefälle)."[40] After 1866 began the struggle for the self-preservation of the Austrian branch of the German nation. The Germans of Austria, the builders and preservers of the state, feared lest the Danubian Monarchy would become a Magyar-Slav state. From German Austria came the great idea of placing the nation above the state, the *"volksdeutsch* idea," a concept which came close to Nazi thought. National Socialism in turn welcomed the concept of *Gesamtdeutschtum* and Srbik's support of the Anschluss.

What were the intellectual origins of the Catholic National group? According to the Austrian historian Adam Wandruszka, their political philosophy was rooted in the "German Movement" at the turn of the eighteenth century and thereafter, in Romanticism, Classicism and German idealism. A few professors at the University of Vienna such as the Germanist Husing and the art historian Strzygowski had endorsed Houston Stewart Chamberlain's north-Germanic racial thought. Many others expressed the *grossdeutsch* view which considered the *"Reich* concept" as the noblest expression of German political-metaphysical thought. Many of the Vienna professors dedicated their life's work to exploring and elaborating the *Reich* idea, such as the geographers Machatschek and Hugo Hassinger. To this group belonged also the mediaevalist Hans Hirsch who looked with admiration upon the *Sacrum Imperium,* the Holy Roman Empire, and the protective leadership of the small nations in medieval Europe by the Germans as a valid ideal for the contemporary era; the historian Heinrich von Srbik, the biographer of Metternich, whose opinion of Metternich's *Mitteleuropa* conception and sponsorship of the *gesamtdeutsch* historic view recreated in a spiritual sense the *Reich* idea; the German literary historian Josel Nadler whose organic concept and division of the German people into *Stämme* and *Landschaften* (tribes and provinces) became the critical principle in his *Literaturgeschichte der deutschen Stämme und Landschaften,* and the historians of law and philosophers Karl G. Hugelmann, Hans Eibl, and Othmar Spann, mentioned before, displayed similar tendencies. What linked these men were the ideas of the Holy Roman Empire, of Catholic universalism and the concept of Romantic organism, all long and deeply rooted in Austria and especially Vienna, the seat both of the Emperor and of the highest authorities of the *Reich.*

To most students of the University of Vienna and the Austrian intelligentsia in general some of these concepts and ideas, despite their indigenous roots, seemed to come close enough to the extreme views of German nationalism and National Socialism in particular, to Hitler's and Rosenberg's racial thought; the emphasis placed by the Catholic Nationals on German preeminence and cultural, economic, and political superiority and the right of the Germans to be the dominant people in the broadly conceived "*Mitteleuropa*," their rejection of parliamentarianism and political democracy (*Formaldemokratie* and *Parteidemokratie*) and of Socialism, especially in its Austro-Marxist variety, spoke volumes. Joined to it was a traditional anti-Semitism, in turn linked with German nationalism, Christianity, and anti-Marxism. This composite ideology found expression in the party program both of the Christian Socials and the *Grossdeutschen* (Nationals), whatever their differences.

Claiming Seipel for themselves, the Catholic National author Franz Ried in his book *Kanzler Seipel, ein Vorkämpfer volksdeutschen Denkens*, considered him a "precursor" of this extreme nationalist and racial orientation. The political philosophy of the Catholic National Professors was propagated by Catholic National groups. Still, their influence upon Austria's national youth in the early thirties was as limited and circumscribed as that of the *Grossdeutschen* (Nationals).

Catholic Nationals spoke less of an "Anschluss" than of a "Zusammenschluss" of the two German states—actually an illusion in view of the plain economic and political imbalance between Austria and the *Reich* and the ten-fold numerical preponderance of *Reich* Germans over Austrians. What Catholic nationals desperately hoped for was a union with the *Reich* which would leave Austria as a partner—an equal partner—obviously mere wishful thinking in view of the inherent centralism of Nazi totalitarian philosophy. The activities of the Catholic Nationals extended to the *Deutsch-Österreichischer Volksbund*, founded by Ing. Hermann Neubacher. Seyss-Inquart who came from the Iglau linguistic island and Glaise-Horstenau, both prominent in Austrian politics in the Schuschnigg era, were close to this group. So was Dr. Wilhelm Wolff, for a brief moment Foreign Minister in the cabinet headed by Seyss-Inquart.[42]

But for all practical purposes these "betont Nationalen" were "camouflaged" National Socialists. A penetrating report about the dubious political game of Seyss-Inquart which reached the British Foreign Office in 1937 had this to say about him: Politically,

Seyss-Inquart described himself as a " 'legal' National Socialist, i.e., he is opposed to anything savoring of terrorism, and aims, through the medium of negotiations, at finding a *modus vivendi* between the Government and the nationalist elements in Austria. He holds that the realization of an Austro-German union cannot be brought about from inside Austria and that a union is entirely dependent upon the degree of success attained by Germany in her foreign political programme. Dr. Seyss is one of the best camouflaged persons amongst the Nazi leaders. Formerly a member of the Christian Socialist [sic] Party he has been careful to keep up the appearance of still being in this camp, and denies that he was even a member of the NSDAP. But he has always been active behind the scenes of the Nazi movement here."[43]

The views of the Catholic Nationals were well expressed by the leading Catholic weekly in Austria *Schönere Zukunft* which was also widely read in Germany. Peter Eppel in his recent study *Zwischen Kreuz und Hakenkreuz. Die Haltung der Zeitschrift Schönere Zukunft zum Nationalsozialismus in Deutschland 1934-38*, (Vienna, Hermann Böhlaus Nachf., 1980), has examined the policies of the journal to illuminate the relationship between Austrian Catholicism and the *Third Reich* and to focus on the affinities as well as the differences between the Catholics and the Nazi programme. In the 1920s, he concluded, the journal rejected the Anschluss and propagated a Danubian Federation. With Hitler's seizure of power, Austrian Catholics, excepting the Catholic-Nationals, drew a sharp line against the Anschluss. But in the mid-thirties the journal began to flirt with the union concept, feeling attracted by the ideas of common blood and language with the *Reich*, the denunciation of the Peace Treaties and emphasis on *gesamtdeutsch* and anti-Semitic thought, while still claiming to support Austrian independence. According to Eppel, the journal's propagated nationalism was a religiously tainted national chauvinism, not dissimilar to Nazi nationalism, and spiritually prepared the Anschluss.[44] Papen considered the journal *Schönere Zukunft* as serving Nazi power policy.

To the Catholic Nationals in the broader sense of the word belonged also a few representatives of the Austrian Catholic clergy, among them the controversial Austrian bishop Dr. Alois Hudal: in the 1930s he worked in Rome and in Austria for a conciliation between Christianity and National Socialism. His book *Grundlagen des Nationalsozialismus. Eine ideengeschichtliche Untersuchung*, "written from my heart," was dedicated to the "internal peace of our German people" and designed "to pave the way toward an understanding of National Socialism from the Christian point of view." The teaching of race contained "valuable thoughts" and National Socialism was by no means identical with Bolshevism. No one in the Catholic camp "denied the positive, the great, the lasting element which is in this [National Socialist] movement." "We believe in the unconditional necessity of a close association [!] between Christianity and Germandom, support unconditionally [!] the declaration of the Führer of the German Revolution. Our next task lies in battling in the West for Germandom and Christianity."[45]

An even more significant role than Bishop Hudal played Cardinal Theodor Innitzer, who was also sharply criticized because of his attitude on the Anschluss and the Third Reich. He has been reproached for not uniting the church membership, and, in fact, for causing confusion within its ranks. When Innitzer who came from the Sudetenland, a border region which inflamed nationalist passions, was made Cardinal, he gave the unusual assurance that next to being a loyal son of the church, he was also a loyal son of the German nation.[46] When in 1933 he spoke of German soil and blood as sources of strength of nation and fatherland, he was promptly applauded by the press in the *Third Reich*. The assassination of Dollfuss transformed his dissident attitude into a definite rejection of Nazism. But prior to and during the first months after the 1938 annexation, the Cardinal's attitude toward the Anschluss was most ambiguous and brought him criticism from the Vatican.* Victor Reimann commented about the Innitzer phenomenon that in almost every Austrian there lived two souls, one belonging to Germany, the other to Austria.[47] This of course weakened the forces of resistance to the *Third Reich*.

---

*In the early weeks after Austria's annexation this author personally observed the Cardinal flanked by two SS officers cross the pavement and step into a car; he gave the impression of being a virtual prisoner. But this episode hardly explains his earlier support for the Anschluss.

Dollfuss, Schuschnigg, and "grossdeutsch" thought

In the split which after Seipel's death rent the Christian Social Party, Dr. Engelbert Dollfuss, member of a younger generation, the *Frontgeneration* which fought in the war, became leader of the Party. Of diminutive stature,—the "Millimetternich" as he was later referred to—was, as many of his fellow students, greatly influenced by the teachings of the Vienna University Professor Othmar Spann on the *Ständestaat* and his anti-democratic orientation. Dollfuss also played a major role in the *Deutsche Studentenschaft* and displayed pan-German views. Thereafter he was impressed by the contemporary dictatorship, authoritarian and outright fascist regimes, which had risen to power in other European countries such as Italy, Yugoslavia, Hungary, Rumania, Portugal, and of course Germany herself. Using later the fascist *Heimwehr* for his own political purposes, he also organized the Fatherland Front to inject new strength into and broaden the basis of the Christian Social Party, and to stem thus the rapidly growing Austrian NSDAP.

In his speeches, *Dollfuss an Österreich. Eines Mannes Wort und Ziel*, Engelbert Dollfuss stressed Austrian patriotism as well as Austrian dedication to Europe and to world peace. The unfriendly relationship with Germany, he assured everybody, was not Austria's fault.[48] The citizens of Austria were both Austrians and Germans: "As much as we are Austrians, as much are we all Germans." Regional differences among Austrians were fully acknowledged, as were those between Germans. The Tyrolese was different from the Vorarlberger, the Carinthian from the inhabitant of Salzburg, still they were all Austrians. For centuries Austrians had the mission to be the cultural bearer for other peoples, but "we Germans in Austria" had "not lost our national characteristic in this polyglot community." Being German in Austria also meant being Christian.

While struggling for the preservation of Austrian sovereignty and independence against the Nazi juggernaut, Austria's intellectual armor under Dollfuss was highly vulnerable. The absence of the concept of an Austrian nationality; the contrary view that Austrians were Germans, though entitled to a separate state; the assertion of the existence of an indissoluble tie between Austrian patriotism and the German and Christian character of the state, with the inevitable exclusion of Jews and their relegation to a second-class status*—all this, instead of constituting a roadblock to the advance of National Socialism, prepared the way for Austria's intellectual conquest by the Nazis.

Kurt von Schuschnigg, son of a professional army officer, served in World War I and toward the end became Italian prisoner of war. Thereafter, the youngest member of the *Nationalrat*, he was considered Seipel's "crown prince." An intellectual, slightly doctrinaire, he was temperamentally restrained, but politically not without considerable skills. Heir to Dollfuss in 1934, he concluded the July 1936 Agreement with Nazi Germany, convinced that he had no alternative; after all, geopolitical necessity aside, Mussolini's Italy, due to her preoccupations in Africa and the Mediterranean, was retreating from Central Europe, and the Western Powers practiced a policy of appeasement toward the *Third Reich*. Also, ideological considerations, the traditions of the old *Reich* idea, of the "grossdeutsch" legacy from the era prior to 1866, the influence of Professor Srbik's *gesamtdeutsch* historical view—all these factors shaped his decision and pushed him onto the "German road."[49] He was anxious to stem the Nazi tide in Austria, but bent on avoiding a civil war, on preventing any repetition of the fratricide struggle of 1866 or of the civil war of July 1934.

Though Schuschnigg rejected the *"völkisch"* and racist ideology of National Socialism, he was firmly convinced of the closeness of the cultural and intellectual ties linking the entire German community, though many of its members lived widely dispersed beyond Germany's boundaries. He was anxious to terminate, if possible, the intolerable pressures of the *Third Reich* upon Austria and to establish an acceptable relationship with Hitlerite Germany. In his drive to enlist the support of the *betont-Nationalen* for Austria's sovereignty and independence, he was probably unduly influenced by the long political collaboration of the Christian Socials under Seipel with the *Grossdeutschen* (Nationals); he ignored their radicalization since and the growing contrast between

---

*Anti-Semitism under Dollfuss and Schuschnigg was not comparable to that of the *Third Reich*. Austria's relatively limited anti-Semitism was in the tradition of the Jew-hatred of mayor Karl Lueger.

them and their new radical *völkisch* ideas and his own conservative pro-Austrian conception of Austrian independence. His naiveté and illusions in regard to Seyss-Inquart and Glaise-Horstenau and other *Betont-Nationale* were striking. Though he understood the need for broadening his increasingly narrow political base, he failed to understand the significance of modern mass movements and the importance of fighting them effectively.

In his struggle against the Third Reich, Schuschnigg was hampered by his pan-German credo. His Pan-Germanism was not of the Prussian variety, but was rather the historic Pan-Germanism patterned after the Holy Roman Empire and centering in Vienna. Historical or mystical in character rather than practical, it belonged to the irretrievable past. Schuschnigg's predecessor Dollfuss had not been immune to German *völkisch* sentiments either, but after 1933 he effectively gave vivid expression to Austrian patriotism and helped to revive it. In this regard Schuschnigg, more rigid and also a less warm personality, was never able to similarly touch the heartstrings of the Austrian people, and to juxtapose Austrian patriotism persuasively with German nationalism. This lack of confident patriotic assertiveness was a general Austrian weakness, widely shared among the Austrian intelligentsia.

The pro-German feelings of the Austrian government under Dollfuss and especially under Schuschnigg, which hindered the struggle against National Socialism from within and without, were aptly described by the American Ambassador in Austria, George Messersmith, in 1935: "In order to appreciate the realities of the Austrian situation, one must constantly keep in mind that the men who are today directing the government of Austria were brought up with the idea that the closest cooperation between Austria and Germany was essential and to whom the doctrine of political unity with Germany was taught as a desirable goal."[50] Only recently had they come out fighting for a separate Austrian existence, for its sovereignty, but they were still "timorous in their attitude" and were cautious to avoid "irritating the Germans."

While pitted against the Nazis, resolute opponents who attacked Austria and the concept of her independence and sovereignty, Schuschnigg feared being blamed by them and other *grossdeutsch* circles for having unleashed a civil war among Germans, or repeating the fratricide struggle which too often had pitted blood brothers against each other. The only patriotism he sympathized with was the one extolling past glories of the Empire and the Habsburg dynasty. But legitimism had limited popular appeal, despite the revival of interest in the Habsburg dynasty in the mid-thirties. The rebirth of the old Austrian Empire, feared by the new succession states which had arisen on its ruins, and on different grounds opposed by the *Third Reich*, was out of the question.

Since Schuschnigg did not broaden his domestic base by striking a bargain with the Social Democrats, he had little choice but to attempt to appease the Nazis in the *Reich* and within Austria. This policy was partly dictated by the mounting pressure brought against Austria from across the border, the country's increasing diplomatic isolation in Europe, and Italy's abandonment of the guard at the Brenner. But this struggle against the Nazis was weakened by the lack of a militant Austrian ideology and patriotism. This lack in turn was only the reverse side of the wide appeal of German nationalism: after 1918 the latter captured broad segments of the Austrian population, not only rightist nationalists, but also liberal, democratic circles, which were traditionally devoted to the concept of German national unity, and also Social Democrats, who had formed the spearhead of the Anschluss movement in the immediate postwar period. Schuschnigg himself may have lacked the charisma of the great leader and failed to arouse Austrian patriotism. But the truth of the matter was that the bulk of the Austrian middle class and intelligentsia felt attracted to the cause of German nationalism and failed to respond to the appeal of Austrian patriotism in the crucial thirties. It was only the *fait accompli* of the Anschluss and the painful aftermath of life under the *Third Reich* which revived the flagging Austrian patriotism.

Starhemberg, the *Heimwehr*, and Austrian Independence

Like Dollfuss and Schuschnigg, Prince Rüdiger von Starhemberg, the most prominent leader of the fascist *Heimwehr*, had in his youth close ties with the Hitler movement. In the immediate postwar period he volunteered for the German nationalist cause to fight in Upper Silesia against the Poles. Despite repeated attempts to bridge the gulf between the *Heimwehr* organization and the Austrian Nazis as well as the German NSDAP, Starhemberg failed to reach a settlement. Aside from the Styrian *Heimwehr*, which was strongly pan-German and in 1933 went over to the Nazis, there were also strong nationalist and pan-German currents in the *Heimwehr* in the other Austrian *Länder*. This circumstance as well as the common fascist outlook partly explain the repeated attempts in 1933-34, made by Starhemberg, Fey, and other *Heimwehr* leaders, not to mention Dollfuss himself, to engage in frequent negotiations with the Nazis in Austria and those in the *Reich*.[51] But they all failed. According to Starhemberg's own account, he was cast by Hitler for the role of Quisling. Especially since 1934 he feared and opposed any deal with the Nazis, objecting in particular to the July 1936 Agreement.

In the era of its flowering the Austrian *Heimwehr* comprised many diverse political groupings, Christian Socials, Nationals, and members of the *Landbund;* among them were friends and opponents of the Anschluss.[52] Linked by a destructive negativism, the rejection of Marxism, increasingly also of political democracy, they often split along Christian Social or national lines, as well as between friends of the Anschluss and adherents of the Habsburg Restoration. In 1930 Richard Steidle and other *Heimwehr* leaders adopted the teachings of the "true state" which Professor Othmar Spann preached, the doctrine of the *Ständestaat*, though Steidle admitted that it was a "nebulous" concept. At the same time the *Heimwehr* rejected parliamentarianism and "Formaldemokratie" and proclaimed the need for seizing power in the state. The movement was frequently paralyzed by internal feuds and personal squabbles, by the rejection of its attempt of a military coup by Johann Schober, and by the inability and the lack of maturity of its leaders. After fruitless negotiations with Austro-Nazis and the German NSDAP, the Starhemberg-led *Heimwehr* emerged finally as a special political party in the electoral campaign of November 1930, gaining 8 seats in the *Nationalrat*. In September 1931 the Styrian *Heimwehr* under the leadership of Walter Pfrimer attempted an abortive *Putsch*. In 1933 the Styrians linked up with the Austrian NSDAP, supporting thereafter fully the Anschluss idea. Many other *Heimwehr* men, due to the interminable internal fights and impressed by the apparent successes of Hitler's regime across the border, flocked to the Austrian Nazi camp, unfurling the swastika.

Starhemberg himself had by no means always been a consistent opponent of Hitler and the Austro-Nazis; at times he was not averse to building bridges toward them. Already in 1935, while still in the Austrian Government, Starhemberg had thought of reaching an agreement with Germany, though without damage to Austria. On occasion of a secret meeting with Seyss-Inquart in September 1936 in Raab, Hungary, the latter had made a proposal of cooperation between the *Heimatschutz* and the Nationals in order to compel National Socialism in Austria to become more independent from Berlin. In his *Memoirs* Starhemberg disclosed that Seyss's views that an Anschluss of Austria was out of question and that Berlin's influence upon Austrian domestic policy must be prevented had greatly appealed to him."[53]

Toward the end of November 1937 Starhemberg met with Chancellor Schuschnigg but reached no agreement with him. According to the Prince, this was his last meeting and talk with Schuschnigg. A few weeks later he left with his wife and child Austria to spend the winter in Switzerland. Starhemberg expected in the near future a strengthening of the National Socialist position in the Austrian government and the gradual Nazi conquest of the country, but not as suddenly as it was to occur. He anticipated returning to Austria on March 10, 1938.

Before the Austrian crisis reached its climax, Austrian *Heimwehr*-men and other friends approached Starhemberg voicing the wish that he become again actively engaged in Austrian politics. Among the former, Wenninger, close friend and confidant of Starhemberg, expressed on January 17, 1938[54] the belief that Austria's rapidly worsening situation had opened the road for a political reactivation of the *Heimatschutz*. In another letter to Starhemberg dated February 26, 1938, Wenninger informed him that "even those who were absolutely our foes, now in the hour of need were calling for help."

One day after the fateful meeting between Hitler and Schuschnigg at Berchtesgaden, the German race truck driver Hans von Stuck, who served the *Deutsche Nachrichtendienst* (German News Service), reported a conversation with Starhemberg, dated from Davo Dorf, Silvetta Kulm. In the near future the Prince would not accept any political post in Austria without previous consultation with Berlin; he would not want to take any responsible post, since Schuschnigg was Jesuitic and unreliable. Starhemberg asserted that Austria must always remain an independent state. He held that "a very close collaboration" between Germany and Austria "taking the form of an alliance" would be advisable; both countries could even pool their armed forces under a joint command, creating a relationship similar to the one which had existed in the old Austro-Hungarian Monarchy. (This of course disregarded the circumstance that Cisleithanian Austria was an equal of the Hungarian half of the Habsburg Empire, while the First Austrian Republic was a mere dwarf compared to Germany). The Austrian historian L. Jedlicka interpreted Starhemberg's foregoing utterances as being in support of Austria's political independence.[55] Actually, Starhemberg seems to have gone even further when he asserted that Austria could become "great" only through a "bloodless but decisive change of government." "If people would need him to revive the Austrian spirit, he would be ready to serve. He would like to elaborate about this matter. But he would not undertake anything without Berlin." Surely, this was a rather late offer of his services to Hitler; it was also giving his blessing to a Nazi coup against the tottering Austrian government, provided a limited independence of Austria would be preserved.

In the letter of February 26, 1938, Wenninger had again urged Starhemberg to return to Austria and place himself at the head of a movement to reactivate the *Heimatschutz.* Wenninger went on to tell Starhemberg that the *Heimwehr* circles "absolutely insisted upon Austria's independence and freedom." Starhemberg, however, replied that after Berchtesgaden he had to decline any activities or any function which did not give him the opportunity to "take decisive influence" upon Austrian developments. He did not want that in the political play against the Nationals and National Socialists he personally and the *Heimwehr* movement be exploited. He did not wish to avoid responsibilities [Mir liegt fern mich drucken zu wollen] and to neglect his "patriotic obligations."[56] He considered any other course harmful to himself, his family, his future, and directed against the expectations and interests of his friends. He did "not know from Wenninger's communications whether the *Heimatschutz* actually still existed [!]" and, if not, whether it could resume its former role. In any case, any activities of the *Heimatschutz* were "possible only on condition of a certain understanding also with the National Socialists." Actually Starhemberg then despaired of the chances to redress the Austrian situation; thus he entered into correspondence with the former Austrian Minister Franz Hueber, brother-in-law of Herman Göring, to seek protection for his men.

After the march into Austria, the Berlin government appears to have made the attempt to maintain some contact with Starhemberg and vice versa. Through a Berlin lawyer, Graf von Medem, Starhemberg informed the Reich Commissar Josef Bürckel of an appeal he was to make to former members of the *Heimatschutz*, urging participation in the impending plebiscite.[57] In his *Memoirs* Starhemberg recalls correctly that many personalities previously active in Austrian politics had then advised their former followers to vote affirmatively for the union. He told those who asked for his advice, to vote "yes," since a "no" meant self-sacrifice. "Now the task was to seek cover and to survive until the day when rising against National Socialism is possible."

On March 27, 1938, with the S.S. and the German Army firmly entrenched in Austria, Starhemberg wrote a personal letter to Hitler in which he pleaded for leniency toward his followers, recalling that they had merely loyally followed his, Starhemberg's, orders, the command of their "Führer," taking personal responsibility for their action. He traced the origins of the *Heimwehr* movement which had fought not only Bolshevism but also the bourgeois parties, dedicated to the "system," and striven for "political ideas very close to those of the NSDAP." The Austrian *Heimatschutz* had "always served consciously the *grossdeutsch* idea and had aimed at the realization of the *grossdeutsch* goal." Though, in accordance with the then prevailing conception, this did not mean "a complete renunciation of Austria's separate political existence," still a goal of the movement was to link Austria with the German *Reich* in some political union.

Starhemberg urged Hitler not to punish the *Heimwehr*men who had proven to represent "fighting Germandom" and also to accept them into the ranks of his own following. He blamed the previous Austro-Nazi leadership for having shown complete lack of understanding for the *Heimwehr* movement; he also tried to minimize his own political past which of course had pitted him frequently against the NSDAP. He was basically a soldier and leader of a movement, who had been pushed into politics! In 1923, as a young student, he himself had belonged to Hitler's most ardent followers and, from the moment he became active in the *Hei-*

matschutz, he had hoped one day to lead his adherents into the Hitler-led movement for Germany's rebirth; even at the time of sharp differences he had never abandoned the hope for a reconciliation between the NSDAP and the *Heimatschutz* and the creation of a common front between them. In 1936 he had also planned a meeting with Field Marshal Hermann Göring which however never materialized, since he left the Austrian cabinet. Recently Hitler, at the moment of the complete breakdown of Austria, had saved the country from a civil war. Therefore the Führer could be assured of the sincere and unlimited gratitude of the *Heimatschutz* men.[58] Hitler never answered this letter directly. But on April 30 the Führer directed Himmler to give Starhemberg "the advice not to return to Austria but to stay where he is."

Austria's National Parties of the 1920's

One of the short-lived political parties of the early post-war period was the National People's League (*Volksverein*) which in January 1919 tried to enter the political arena as the *Bürgerlich-Democratic* Party (Citizens Democratic Party). On occasion of a pro-Anschluss demonstration held on February 2, 1919, the League published a pamphlet "Sollen wir den Anschluss an Deutschland fordern?"[59] (Should we demand an Anschluss with Germany?) It posed the alternative: Anschluss with Germany or subjection to "alien Slavic domination." Though aided by democrats in Austria and the *Reich*, the *Party* in its 1919 electoral campaign stressed the idea of *Volksgemeinschaft*, a concept later developed and bent to suit its own purposes by the *Grossdeutsche Volkspartei*.

The League, or Citizens Democratic Party, was supported by *Reich* authorities interested in strengthening the Austrian Anschluss movement. In January 1919 the German Foreign Office had a direct hand in the attempt to create in Austria a middle-class democratic party; ideologically, it was to correspond to the Democratic Party in Germany, and its guiding spirits were to be in favor of the Anschluss. In the view of the German Foreign Office, the new party was to attract bourgeois elements of liberal inclinations to the Anschluss concept, in the expectation that they would not find a suitable political home either in the Social Democratic or Christian Social Party. The party was to be led by the eminent Austrian jurist Dr. Franz Klein. He and Dr. Gustav

Stolper, editor of the *Österreichischer Volkswirt*, received considerable financial support from Germany for this purpose.[60]

In January 1919 the German *Aussenamt* notified Ambassador Botho von Wedel in Vienna of the impending journey to Austria of Baron von Riepenhausen. His plan was to purchase two Viennese papers to carry on a more effective Anschluss propaganda. Dr. Walter Schotte, editor of the German magazine *Mitteleuropa*, and the German Major Fleck were also instrumental in creating a German agency which was to play an important role in boosting the pro-union movement, the *Deutsch-Österreichische Mittelstelle*, which was to function partly under the direction of the Vienna Embassy and partly under that of the German Foreign Office; the latter held the purse strings.[61]

In addition to this aid, individual Germans tried vainly to boost the electoral prospects of the new Citizens Democratic Party. Among them were the historian Theodor Heuss (destined to become President of the German Federal Republic after World War II), Hjalmar Schacht, later noted for his financial wizardry and rightist sentiments, though at the time a Democrat, and the distinguished sociologist Max Weber.[62]

Closely associated on the Austrian side with Dr. Franz Klein, Gustav Stolper, and his friends in the political campaign in early 1919 was also Dr. von Wettstein, Professor of Botany at the University of Vienna, and the Austrian civil servant *Sektionschef* Richard Riedl. In his *Erinnerungen, 1905-1933* (1963) Theodor Heuss[63] recounted how he once came to the help of the scheduled speaker Dr. Franz Klein by climbing through a window into the crowded assembly hall, stepping on the table and beginning his oration by paying respect to the late Dr. Viktor Adler and talking about the Anschluss of which he was an enthusiastic proponent.

A revealing glance of the *grossdeutsch* and still democratic Austro-German point of view in the immediate postwar era is offered by Fritz Fellner and Heidrun Maschel, *St. Germain im Sommer 1919* (Salzburg, 1977), a study focusing on Dr. Franz Klein,[64] who in 1918 was considered by the socialist Foreign Secretary Dr. Otto Bauer to head the Austrian peace delegation to St. Germain; though he lost out to Dr. Karl Renner, he went along to Paris nevertheless. In 80 letters dispatched from Paris to Vienna he revealed his political thought, including his Anschluss fervor. The letters show special hostility to the emerging peace treaty and in particular to the prohibition of the Anschluss. Dr. Klein's philosophy is rightly held to be representative of the *grossdeutsch*-oriented bureaucracy of the Habsburg Empire, which was bitterly resentful of the loss of the traditional hegemony of the German Austrians, refused to accept radical postwar changes, and never ceased to contrast the insignificant Austrian *Kleinstaat* with the imperial splendor of the Habsburg Monarchy. The evil of the German-Austrian situation, according to the editors, lay primarily in the inability or unwillingness of the intellectual and political elite of German Austria to overcome its own deficiencies, while lamenting its harsh and "unjust" fate. The defeat and dissolution of the Austrian Monarchy was rooted in the false pride of the German Austrians, in their belief of German superiortiy and the apparent contempt toward the other nationalities of the Dual Monarchy; this attitude and outlook spilled over into the First Republic and became a source of nourishment for the Anschluss movement.

The *Grossdeutsche Volkspartei* (*Grossdeutsche* People's Party. thereafter the *Grossdeutschen,* or Nationals) was founded in the last days of the disintegration of the Austrian Empire, on November 2, 1918. Support for the endorsement of the Anschluss is listed most prominently in the *Guidelines* (*Richtlinien,* 1919) of the *Grossdeutschen*. They emphasize that the Party is "a national-anti-Semitic, social, and libertarian [!] Party."[65] During the following years other guidelines of the Party had this to say about the union: "The unchanging guiding star of our foreign policy is the Anschluss of Austria with the German *Reich* . . . the union of all *Volksgenossen*" (members of the *Volk*). The Anschluss is to "prepare and and facilitate" the assimilation of the two countries legally, economically, and administratively.[66] All problems—apparently both domestic and international ones—have either a beneficial or harmful impact upon the union. Thus the Anschluss is the main, virtually the unique goal of the policy of the *Grossdeutschen*, and everything else is subordinated to it. Once union would be attained, the party and its programme become utterly superfluous. Thus the *Grossdeutsche Volkspartei* was, one student observed, "a time-limited Party" (Partei auf Zeit) and, historically judged, it only paved the way for National Socialism.[67]

The general program of the Party stressed that it considered itself democratic, but at the same time was distinctly anti-Semitic.

The same stance, incidentally, was taken by another national Party, the *Landbund*. According to the *Grossdeutschen*, theater and press must be "liberated from Jewish influence." Despite their obsession with the Anschluss, they did compromise in this respect by entering in 1922, as mentioned, into a coalition with the Christian Socials, driven by the urgent need to save the Austrian state and economy from ruin. For about a decade they closely cooperated with the Christian Socials, though they found the acceptance of Austria's financial control by the Entente "humiliating."

A small group under the leadership of K. H. Wolf, the "Union [Verein] of the German Nationals," challenged the close working cooperation with the Christian Socials, fearful that the daily association with Seipel, the declared foe of the Anschluss, "and with his associates" could harm the Party in the pursuit of the Anschluss and its realization at the "decisive moment";[68] they might also forget the program of racial anti-Semitism.

In view of the political alignment between Christian Socials and *Grossdeutschen*, the latter's actual Anschluss policy in the 1920s did not greatly differ from that of the Christian Socials. On occasion, however, for instance the journey of two leaders of the Party, Dr. Dinghofer and Dr. Frank, to Germany and their meeting with President Hindenburg and Foreign Minister Stresemann in 1925, the Austrian repercussions were serious, though the alliance with the Christian Socials survived this test as well as others. Though Schober's customs union project of 1931 proved abortive, the *Grossdeutschen* called the plan "the only constructive and fruitful idea" of the last years.[69]

Toward the end of the democratic phase of the First Austrian Republic, the *Grossdeutsche Volkspartei* exhibited the same contradictory attitude toward parliamentary democracy as previously. In its name Dr. Hermann Foppa denounced the dictatorial endeavors of Dollfuss, but was also critical of the past practices of Austrian parliamentarianism.[70] In the matter of union with Germany, in March 1933, several weeks after Hitler had come to power in the neighboring *Reich*, the *Grossdeutschen* approached the *Third Reich* authorities for financial support for the still expected national elections in the fall of 1933. The German leaders, however, deciding in the end in the negative, wanted to know more about the Party's relations with the Austrian Nazis; they had raised the question of the political future of the Nationals in Austria.[71] Theo

Habicht, Hitler's Austrian deputy, wanted to use them for negotiations with Dollfuss. For all practical purposes, in the course of 1933-34, the Nationals, who always had more leaders than followers, simply melted away, its members flocking to the Austrian NSDAP. When Dollfuss claimed that the Austrian Parliament in March 1933 had "eliminated itself," Foppa, prominent leader of the Nationals, protested against the lawlessness of his regime.[72] Under protest the Party's leaders walked out from the rump parliament, which accepted the new constitution and thus virtually dissolved itself. There was some irony in the circumstance that the Austrian *Grossdeutschen*, increasingly admiring the *Third Reich* and its totalitarian principles, opposed the latter on Austrian soil when implemented by Dollfuss. In the period 1936-38 the former *grossdeutsch* deputies Prodinger and Mittermann wrote against the Nazis, taking a stance at sharp variance from that of the great majority of their former Party members. After the Anschluss they were arrested, placed into concentration camps, and died there during the war.[73]

Another national party in the First Austrian Republic was the *Landbund*. In a program laid down in 1921 it came out in support of the corporate state, stressed the Christian *Weltanschauung*—though simultaneously criticizing political clericalism—and the national idea as foundation stones of "the German state." Appealing primarily to small and middle peasants and the middle class in general, it denounced, like the *Grossdeutschen*, Marxism and displayed an openly anti-Semitic attitude by blaming—like the Nazis later, though perhaps with less fanaticism—Social Democrats who accepted the teachings of a "Jew," Karl Marx, but discovered "Judaism" also in international finance capital. The *Landbund* considered itself "a national [völkisch] party," and asked for the "*Zusammenschluss*" (link-up) of all German tribes in the closely circumscribed German linguistic realm into a unified German *Reich*, the latter "an unchangeable foreign policy goal."[74] The *Ostmark* (Austria; Austria's original designation, meaning the eastern borderlands of the Germanies) must become "the border region of the Great German Reich." At the same time, notwithstanding the apparent inconsistency, the *Landbund* promised to guard and protect the existing Austrian state constitution. There were other contradictions in its political and economic philosophy, the primary being that the *Landbund* considered itself not only national-minded, but also "liberal" and democratic.

In the elections of 1923 the *Landbund* gained 5 seats, 2 in Carinthia, 2 in Upper Austria, and one in the Burgenland, and its deputies took their seats in the Austrian Parliament. Throughout the 1920s there were repeated efforts at creating a national unity front among Austria's national parties, including the *Landbund*, but in the end, on November 28, 1926, the *Landbund* declined to join the front, fearful of losing peasant votes to the other parties of the new national alignment.[75] After Dollfuss established the *Ständestaat* and a new constitution, leaders of the *Landbund* expressed their doubts and warned the Austrian President Wilhelm Miklas in regard to the new political course. In this context they deeply regretted "the brothers' dispute" between Austria and the Reich[76] which, they claimed, alarmed broad Austrian circles and was also harmful to Austria's economy; they thus criticized both the Nazis and the *Third Reich* as well as the Austrian government, distributing blame equally among them for the deterioration of their relations! In May 1934, two months before the July *Putsch* of the Austrian Nazis, the leadership of the *Landbund* decided to dissolve itself, prompted by the flight of its members to the NSDAP.

B. Austrian National Socialism and German Union

The Origins of Austrian National Socialism

During the last decades of the nineteenth century German national sentiments grew by leaps and bounds in the Austrian half of the Habsburg Empire. This was partly the result of the strong cultural and national community of feelings between the Germans of the Habsburg Monarchy and the *Reich* Germans, the consequence of the pride with which the former looked upon their kinsfolk in neighboring unified Imperial Germany, and partly the outgrowth of their own precarious, seemingly threatened position in the Habsburg Monarchy. The ruling national minority in the Cisleithanian part of the Dual Empire, the German element, a plurality of approximately 35% of the population, felt increasingly challenged by the rapid cultural and economic growth and development of the Slavic and Latin ethnic groups within the Monarchy.

No movement expressed the fears, desires, and vague ambitions of the Pan-Germans in Austria better than the movement headed by Georg von Schönerer; while boosting the German race, it castigated Jews and Slavs as well as Liberals and Socialists and depicted them as enemies of the German nation; Adolf Hitler later greatly admired Schönerer. After the disintegration of this racist movement by the turn of the century, its ideology, especially its hatred of the Slavs and its virulent anti-Semitism, survived in the German national movement which then took new forms. It assumed a specially venomous character in the mixed German-Czech northern Bohemian region. It was there that Austrian National Socialism was born and from that area that it ultimately spread to Germany.

In 1903 there originated in Trautenau in northern Bohemia the *Deutsche Arbeiterpartei* in Austria.[77] It developed among workers, partly in response to the fierce competition by cheap immigrant Czech labor. Contrary to the hopes of the Austrian Marxists that the international ideology of labor would overcome national grievances and antagonisms, the inroads made by German and Czech nationalism into labor ranks seemed to fly into the face of the Socialist dogma. But the struggle between nationalism and internationalism did not reach a decisive stage. The *Deutsche Arbeiterpartei*, favoring a *völkisch Weltanschauung* and voicing its desire for a link-up with Germany obtained only three seats in the 1911 election to the Austrian *Reichsrat*. Its program showed hostility not only to capitalism, liberalism, and clericalism, but also to the Social Democratic Party and Marxism in particular. It claimed to espouse not only nationalism but also socialism, though it limited itself to the socialization of large concerns. Extremism and chauvinistic pride in German achievements were its trademark. At a congress in May 1918 it modified its name to *Deutsche Nationalsozialistische Arbeiterpartei* (DNSAP, German National Socialist Workers' Party).

Following the dissolution of the Habsburg Monarchy, the DNSAP split into two branches.[78] The Czechoslovak branch of the Sudeten Germans was established in November 1919. The leader of the Austrian branch was Dr. Walter Riehl. There were also early contacts between the German NSDAP, founded in 1919, and the

Austrian branch through a speakers' bureau, the Interstate National Socialist Bureau of German-speaking Areas, which was also headed by Riehl. The Austrian Party, however, supported political participation in the parliamentary system and also endorsed intraparty democracy rather than the leadership principle. But the growth of the German party generated demands for the subordination of the Austrian branch. In August 1923 an open rift evolved between the pro-Hitler factions in the Austrian party and the independent-minded Riehl group. Thereupon Riehl resigned from the party and founded a rival organization, while the Austrian partisans of Hitler finally linked up with the German party. But it was not before May 1926 that the Austrian Hitler followers in Vienna subscribed to the 25-point program of Gottfried Feder, author of the official program of the *Reich* NSDAP. At the following Weimar Party Congress of the same year the Austrian Nazi movement finally merged with the NSDAP. The binding agreement was signed by Adolf Hitler and Hermann Reschny, the latter in his function both as leader of the Austrian Party and of the S.A. units. The agreement specifically emphasized that *Reich* Germans were not to obtain positions in the Austrian Party, economy, and state administration.

All in all, after 1918 the Austrian Republic inherited a National Socialist Party that was mostly Sudeten German in origin and character and was shaped by the *völkisch* and fanatic outlook of the borderland. Its growth was rather slow; it remained a splinter group during the 1920s, compared to the powerful *Grossdeutsche Volkspartei* and a *grossdeutsch* Party such as the *Landbund*. According to Alfred E. Frauenfeld, prominent Austrian Nazi leader, until about 1929 the NSDAP in Vienna had only between 500-600 active members.[79] It was only after the spectacular Nazi gains in German electoral campaigns in 1930 that the Austrian Party began to reap benefits from the successes of the *Reich* NSDAP. This trend continued as a result of German political developments until the election of March 1933.

Austro-Nazis since 1933

Though the impact of Hitler's seizure of power in the *Reich* upon neighboring Austria was far-reaching, it also contained an unmistakable immediate warning to the Dollfuss regime; the latter, at that very moment, became the main foreign-policy target of Hitler and the NSDAP. To save Austrian tradition, independence, and Catholicism, Engelbert Dollfuss, taking advantage of what he conveniently called the "self-elimination" of the Austrian Parliament in early March 1933, proved an adept disciple of totalitarian theory and practice from across the border, though bending it to suit his own political interests. The defeat of Austrian democracy became part and parcel of a European-wide trend away from traditional parliamentarianism. Dollfuss accomplished this in a gradual but still radical fashion, and in violation of Austrian constitutional law. A parliamentary democracy was transformed into an alleged Christian *Ständestaat*, depriving in the process all parties, the numerically powerful Social Democratic Party as well as the rapidly growing Austrian NSDAP, of all influence.

The Austrian Nazis drew recruits from the *Grossdeutsche Volkspartei* and other *grossdeutsch* and pro-Anschluss oriented political groups. Morally encouraged and materially supported from Berlin and neighboring Munich, the Austro-Nazis mounted a relentless attack upon Dollfuss, resorting to propaganda, terror, and general lawlessness. The Austrian Chancellor responded vigorously by finally prohibiting the Austrian Nazi Party. Thus Dollfuss, though not aided by a mass Party such as the *Reich* NSDAP, relying on the hierarchy of the Catholic church, the peasants, and the bourgeoisie, founded an authoritarian, semi-fascist regime. Simultaneously he fought against the Nazis and the Social Democrats, and was also often in dispute with the fascist *Heimwehr* organization as well as democratic-oriented circles of the Christian Social Party. Thus democratic parliamentarianism was defeated not only in the *Reich* but also in Austria; in the latter country, however, the Nazis, ironically, were one of the immediate targets. The attempt to suppress Austrian National Socialism was a justifiable, basically defensive move against the Austrian Nazi minority which was ready to overthrow the government by force and ultimately to bring about *Gleichschaltung*, annexation, and the country's extinction.

Austrian and German National Socialism, though later not always in agreement on tactical problems, were in 1933 and until the Nazi coup of July 1934, basically in harmony as to the desirability and urgency of a "final solution" of the Austrian problem. Among the foreign policy goals of Nazi Germany the Anschluss of Austria played a preeminent role. No other country was as frequently mentioned in the *Völkischer Beobachter*, the main Nazi organ in the *Third Reich*, as early as 1933.[80] The political leaders of no other country were as often and as violently denounced as Chancellor Engelbert Dollfuss, and no other Nazis beyond the borders of the *Reich* were given as strong ideological and propagandistic support as those of neighboring Austria. Austria was considered a highly vulnerable target, and this notwithstanding the lack of German rearmament in 1933 and Germany's general unpreparedness to engage in a major foreign-policy adventure. With relatively little cost, an early success in Austria would give the Nazis unprecedented prestige and power and strengthen the newly constructed foundations of the Third *Reich*. It was not before the Austrian Nazi *Putsch* on July 25, 1934, when Dollfuss was assassinated and Schuschnigg assumed his post, that Hitler and the German foreign office, temporarily, beat retreat, disavowing responsibility for the abortive coup and the ensuing short-lived Austrian civil war. Thereafter the Führer pursued a more cautious policy toward Austria, at least until mid-1936, opting for an "evolutionary" course vis-à-vis the country of his birth.

But after the *Machtergreifung* on January 30, 1933, buoyed by the long-sought, yet sudden victory, National Socialism was cocky and in an exuberant mood; it was disposed to ignore all obstacles on the road ahead. Since the early spring, prospects for Austria seemed most promising; the Austrian Nazis were especially encouraged by the flounderings of the Austrian government and the growing hostility between the latter and the Social Democrats. The ranks of Austrian National Socialism were swelled by former members of the *Grossdeutsche Volkspartei* and strengthened by the support from other *grossdeutsch* oriented elements of the Austrian population. A report from Linz, dated February 2, 1933, three days only after Hitler's assumption of power, informed the readers of the *Völkischer Beobachter* that German Austria paid due honor to the "Chancellor of Grossdeutschland."[81] Five weeks later, on March 10, a few days after the electoral victory of the NSDAP and its German allies in the *Reich*, the Austrian Nazis reported, somewhat prematurely, that they were on the eve of their own "seizure of power." Hitler's success had been "experienced here

[Austria] with a passion, as if there were no longer any dividing borders and as if Austria were a part of the German *Reich.*"[82] According to the Nazi daily, Austria's liberation was close.

The addresses of the *Landesinspekteur* of the Austrian NSDAP, Theodor Habicht, a personal appointee of the Führer, over the Munich sender were given closest attention and were virtually endorsed. The agreement between the Austrian NSDAP and the paramilitary Styrian *Heimatschutz* which surrendered to the former was hailed by the *Völkischer Beobachter* as an indication that Austria was "awakening."[83] The daily castigated the "unbelievable terror acts" against National Socialists in Graz. In May 1933 the paper raised the question whether Austria was still a "Kulturstaat." The Austrian police was being reduced to being the servant of the Christian Social Party.[84] Everything pointed to the circumstance that the final battle in Austria had begun.

From the thirties on "moderate" and "radical" Austrian Nazis had sharply opposed each other.[84b] Until the summer of 1934 the struggle between them had focused on the criticism of the Munich *Landesleitung* of Theodor Habicht and of the external German leadership of the Party in general. The moderates, at one time led by Walter Riehl, one of the founders of the Austrian NSDAP, still aimed at the exclusion of German influence and German domination. Anton Reinthaller, a "moderate" National Socialist peasant leader in Upper Austria, became one of the main bourgeois Nationals who favored the pacification endeavors under Schuschnigg, and was in turn favorably looked upon by the Chancellor. Radical National Socialists, on the other hand, considered Reinthaller's endeavors as being merely of transitory significance. Soon after the failure of the July *Putsch*, they had started to rebuild the illegal Party. Under the leadership of the Gauleiter of Lower Austria, Captain Josef Leopold, recently released from prison, the radicals opposed the political activities of the "moderates" which aimed at a rapprochement with the Austrian government.

The differences between "radical" and "moderate" Nazis and the latters' increasing contact with the bourgeois representatives of the National Opposition split the nationalist camp into several parts. The shift of the moderate Nazis toward the National Opposition, led as it was by Seyss-Inquart and Glaise-Horstenau, gave the latter group additional weight. Hitler's new tactics of gradualism, adopted after July 1934, were endorsed by the National

Opposition and Austria's "moderate" Nazis; it was, if not actually opposed, only grudgingly acknowledged by the radical Nazis.

The assassination of Dollfuss on July 25, 1934, left the governmental dualism in Austria, consisting of the ruling Christian Socials and the paramilitary forces of the *Heimwehr*, unchanged. In accordance with it, Kurt von Schuschnigg became Chancellor and Prince Ernst Rüdiger von Starhemberg Vice-Chancellor.[85] The headship of the Fatherland Front, which was originally designed to absorb the remaining parties in Austria, was also bestowed upon Starhemberg. While for some time to come Starhemberg remained the political favorite of Mussolini, Schuschnigg, a South Tyrolese by birth and an Italian prisoner during World War I, retained a skeptical attitude toward Italy which was characteristic of many an Austrian from the border region. On the other hand, he too entertained no doubt that Austria needed Italy's support against encroachments by the *Third Reich*.

The flight of many radical Nazis, participants in the Austrian civil war of July 1934, to Germany and the mass arrest of others brought the more moderate Nazi element and the former *Grossdeutschen* to the foreground. Among them was the agricultural engineer Reinthaller, originally a member of the *Landbund*, who in 1930 had defected to the Nazis. Differing in tactics from the Hitler-appointed *Landesinspekteur* Theo Habicht, he had in 1933 approached Schuschnigg, then Minister of Education, to discuss a possible conciliation with the Austrian government, but without avail. The following year he resumed these activities, pretending to support Austrian independence, and continued such activities thereafter.[86]

A major force blocking the rapprochement between Schuschnigg and the Austrian Nazis was the *Heimwehr* leader Prince von Starhemberg. He had attempted to stop the occasional mutual advances of both Dollfuss and the Nazis toward each other, though he had not always staunchly opposed those between the *Heimwehr* and the Austro-Nazis. Austrian patriotism and Party interest as well as concern for the future of the *Heimwehr* and for his own power base moved Starhemberg. Informed of an impending conference between Dollfuss, *Nationalbetonte* and Austrian Nazi leaders, such as Reinthaller, Glaise-Horstenau, Seyss-Inquart, Bardolf, and Neubacher in the Chancellery, Starhemberg, on October 27, 1934, made an unexpected appearance, startling the audience with his blunt talk.[87] The planned rapprochement came to naught. Through Preziosi, Italy's Minister in Vienna, Mussolini gave support to Starhemberg.

Negotiations between Reinthaller of the NSDAP, Foppa of the Pan-German Party, and Hueber of the national-minded Styrian *Heimatschutz*, continued, however. In March 1935, these three groups adopted in Linz a joint program for the National Front, that acknowledged the independence of Austria—unquestionably a mere tactical move.

Toward the Abortive July 1934 *Putsch*
The New Tactics

Austrian National Socialists appear to have first conceived the plan for an overthrow of the government in the summer of 1933, soon after the Party was prohibited. For many months pressures and intimidation were built up from beyond the border and terror unleashed in Austria. The Austrian Nazi plots were helped along by Anton Rintelen, Austrian Ambassador to Rome, whom Dollfuss, suspecting his machinations and schemes, had "elevated" to the post abroad. Rintelen, closely cooperating with the Austrian Nazis, counted heavily on differences within the Austrian government, and on rivalries between Dollfuss and the *Heimwehr* and among *Heimwehr* leaders themselves.

On March 29, 1934, the German Ambassador to Austria Rieth sent to the Berlin Foreign Office a memoir of an Austrian Nazi, Hans Kohler, which asked for Hitler's approval to stage a coup against the Austrian government. Rieth urgently recommended that the Foreign Office "stop this action."[88] During these months the Austrian NSDAP felt frequently let down, if not outright betrayed by Habicht and the *Landesleitung* of the Party in Munich, by German diplomacy in Berlin, and even dared questioning Hitler's policy itself.

In early April Hüffer of the German Foreign Office prepared a memoir dealing with the Austrian situation and possible alternative policies which might be pursued in the event of the impending meeting between Hitler and Mussolini.[89] The questions raised therein were also broached in a *Denkschrift* authored by Bülow. Bülow considered closest relations between the NSDAP in the *Reich* and the Austrian Party as crucial if Germany was to make any progress in Austria. Problems could be solved only by Hitler himself.[90] Bülow thought it imperative to make clear "what our ultimate goal ought to be."[91] At present, in view of the international situation, the Austrian question could not be solved "in the German sense." This applied both to the Anschluss as well as to mere *Gleichschaltung*. He himself would consider an explicit renunciation of the union an "extremely unfavorable" development. Actually no Nazi gave any real thought to this alternative; the NSDAP considered *Gleichschaltung* at best a mere transitory phenomenon, a stepping stone to complete union.

Austrian policy was still on the agenda when, on April 10, 1934, Hitler met with von Neurath, Blomberg, Bülow, and Hassel.[92] The absence of Habicht and Party politicians from this meeting was the more striking, since so far they had set the tone and given direction in the formulation of Austrian policy. Hitler asserted that he was completely disinterested in Austria politically and economically—words which his entourage had not previously heard from him. It would be necessary, the Führer elaborated, to invest great sums for rearmament. This then was his main worry, and in view of the apparent difficulties in Austria, Hitler gave the Austrian problem a low priority. The Führer was "quite prepared to write off Austria for years." Hassell alone wanted Hitler to give Mussolini, in the interest of better Italo-German relations, assurances along these lines. However, the Führer refrained from proclaiming the new policy ("neuer Kurs") for public opinion abroad. He was unwilling to retreat from his ultimate goals either in theory or long-range policy.

The radical Austrian Nazis, however, were insistent on early action and plotted to bring matters to a climax in the hope that, if faced with an unexpected opportunity, Hitler would be compelled to go along and take prompt advantage of it. To the champions of a more radical course belonged, strangely, the former *Landbund* politician Winkler and the chairman of the *Grossdeutschen* Hermann Foppa. In mid-April they met Habicht in Zürich and came out in favor of Germany's adoption of more stringent economic measures against Austria. A comrade-in-arms of theirs was Anton Rintelen who privately criticized Germany's "restraint" as a violation of National Socialist principles. His eyes set upon the succession to Dollfuss, Rintelen was closely supported by the Italian military Attaché in Vienna, Colonel Fabbri. In spite of the "new course" Hitler had decided upon, he had not yet severed his ties with Habicht who in a meeting with him, on April 18, attempted to win him over to a more radical policy. Though the Führer made some minor concessions to Habicht, he indicated that it might take an entire decade before he obtained his goal in Austria.[93]

On May 24 General Wolfgang Muff, Military Attaché in the German Embassy in Vienna, reported about the Austrian situation to the German Chief of the Army, Colonel-General Werner von Fritsch.[94] Though he questioned that resort to force in Austria would produce favorable results in the National Socialist sense, he thought that Austrian Nazis were prepared for action. They were only confused about the *Third Reich's* decision-making in Austrian affairs; they did not know whether the NSDAP or the German Foreign Office made policy. Muff also pointed to the peril of serious clashes along the Bavarian-Austrian border between the "Austrian Legion," assisted by the Bavarian Political Police, and the Austrian army and police. Similarly, Germany's Minister Wilhelm Frick remarked on June 14 that the situation along the Austro-Bavarian border had become "intolerable."[95] The Party and the S.A. attempted to shift responsibility for any collision arising out of this dangerous situation upon each other. Habicht once again planned to talk with Hitler about the question of the "central direction" of the forces of Austrian National Socialism, making sure that orders of the political leadership—his own— were obeyed by the Austrian S.A. He considered the situation among Austro-Nazis disorganized and chaotic; most Austrian Nazis were bent on pursuing a "policy of opposing each other."

On May 29, 1934 a leading National Socialist, Wächter, reported to Renthe-Fink of the German Foreign Office that it was becoming increasingly difficult for the Austrian Nazi leadership to remain in control of its followers and to prevent all attempts at insurgence.[96] He suggested that an "organized uprising," one directed by the Party, was preferable to uncontrolled individual actions. Recently, radical elements were more actively stirring than ever before. They claimed that Hitler's "neuer Kurs" had been announced only for tactical reasons, but that the Führer was really agreeable to any courageous deed of the opposition. The S.A., Wächter continued, did what it wanted, "often against the will of the political leadership."[97] "A unified leadership" could only be restored if Hitler said "the redeeming word."

The resort to lawlessness and outright violence in the *Third Reich* which had reached a climax in Hitler's killing of Röhm and of virtually the entire S.A. leadership in June 1934 found a quick replica in the Austrian Nazi *Putsch* of July 25, 1934. According to the official Austrian version in the *Braunbuch* (1934), Austrian Nazis in disguise had penetrated the Chancellery and had occupied it. Otto Planetta's two shots felled Chancellor Dollfuss who died about 15:45 P.M. In accordance with a cabinet decision, General Wilhelm Zehner presented an ultimatum to the rebels at the *Ballhausplatz*. When this ultimatum was drawn up, no one outside the Chancellery knew that in the meantime Dollfuss had died.[98] It demanded the surrender of the hostages, promising the rebels in return the crossing of the border into the *Reich*, provided that no life had been lost.

Dollfuss had become the victim of his determination to save Austria's independence by awakening Austrian patriotism and juxtaposing it to extreme German nationalism and full-blown totalitarianism of the *Third Reich*. President Wilhelm Miklas had telephoned Schuschnigg appointing him successor to the martyred Chancellor Dollfuss.

After the catastrophe of the Austrian Nazi *Putsch* of July 25, 1934, the Führer was compelled to pull back and disavow any responsibility for the abortive coup. Hitler drew the same lesson from this failure in the foreign policy field which he had earlier drawn from the failure of the November 1923 *Bürgerbräuhausputsch* in the domestic field, namely to radically change his tactics. In July 1934 the Nazi attempt at accomplishing *Gleichschaltung* from within Austria had clearly suffered a fiasco and had to be abandoned. The *Gleichschaltung* could only be accomplished by waiting for a more favorable international development, for German rearmament and for applying power at the suitable political and psychological moment.[99]

Following the new tactical decisions reached in the *Reich*, the Austrian Party bureau was promptly dissolved. The former Austrian Nazi leaders were strictly forbidden to participate in illegal associations or activities of any sort. The Austrian Nazi organization in Germany, the *Kampfring*, was to refrain from any interference in internal Austrian affairs. Neither Party nor government leaders were to discuss in the press or on the radio questions relating to Austrian policy unless prior consent had been obtained from both Goebbels and von Papen, the new German Ambassador to Austria.[100] But Hitler's new order to disband the Austrian Legion was not enforced, probably because of the Führer's known ambiguous attitude on this point. Even so, Hitler's new policy was bound to alienate some of his radical Austrian followers who were disillusioned and felt betrayed: the Führer had violently criticized the Austrian insurgents. Rudolf Hess, deputy leader, disclosed that the Führer had found it "very difficult to adopt this harsh attitude" toward Austrian comrades, but Germany's vital interests and therefore indirectly also the "interests of the German-speaking peoples, and not the least of the Austrian NSDAP itself, are at stake."[101]

Berlin's new tactics were actually decided on while the civil war was still raging in the Austrian provinces. On July 26, Papen was appointed as the new Minister Extraordinary to Austria. In a letter to Papen which was immediately made public, Hitler "most sharply condemned and regretted" the attack on the Austrian Chancellor, admitting that it had "aggravated," though allegedly "through no fault of ours,"[102] the already labile political situation in Europe.

The debacle of the July *Putsch* of 1934 had shattered the Austrian Nazi organization. But at a meeting of Austrian Nazi chiefs as early as September 1934 in neighboring Bavaria preparations were made to resume activities in Austria. The combat readiness of the Austrian Legion in Bavaria, then the main instrument of the Nazi spearhead against Austria, was steadily enhanced. At the same time, however, negotiations with the Austrian government, the political weakness of which was well perceived, were by no means spurned.

After the Nazi victory in 1938, Rainer, then *Gauleiter* in Salzburg, in a report written to Seyss-Inquart, dated August 22, 1939, has told the history of the drawn-out struggle in Austria.[103] Following the 1934 debacle the Führer had liquidated the first stage of the battle over Austria and charged von Papen to work in Vienna toward normalizing relations between the two German states. The *Landesleitung* of the Austrian Nazi Party in Munich was dissolved and the Austrian Party for some time to come left to its own devices. At no time, however, were the political goals of

National Socialism in regard to Austria altered; what was changed for the next years of anticipated lack of German military preparedness were only the means and methods of the struggle.

In the wake of the July 1934 *Putsch* there was no generally acknowledged leader of the NSDAP for all of Austria. New leaders emerged only in the individual nine *Gaue,* with virtually no liaison existing between them. Rivalry became the hallmark in the underground life of the Austro-Nazis. The first acknowledged speaker for virtually all *Gaue* in the autumn of 1934 was Ingenieur Reinthaller. He created an illegal organization at the head of which he placed Ingenieur Neubacher. While officially there were no contacts between the Führer and the Austrian Nazis, actually, secret contact was maintained with the Austrian Party as well as with Nazi fellow travellers, in accordance with Hitler's wishes. The Austrian Nazis remained for all practical purposes an illegal organization, ready to spring into action in the event of an "emergency."

Chapter 5

From Hitler's Seizure of Power to the Assassination of Dollfuss

Political Changes in Austria, 1933

On January 30, 1933, Hitler assumed power in the *Reich*. After the German election in March, the coalition government, consisting of Nazis and German Nationalists, though having attained only a small majority, was, nevertheless, firmly entrenched in power. During the following months Hitler transformed Germany's parliamentary democracy into a full-fledged one-party totalitarian state, destroying the multi-party system, the Weimar constitution, and the concept of the *Rechtsstaat*.

The political developments in Austria since March 1933, when Austrian parliamentarianism too was given a deadly blow by the Dollfuss regime, were hardly less turbulent. One day before the elections in the *Reich*, on March 4, 1933, a series of bizarre incidents—the resignation of all three presiding officers of the *Nationalrat*—gave the Dollfuss government the welcome opportunity of claiming that the Austrian Parliament had eliminated itself. Following a cabinet session on March 7 which lasted seven hours, the Austrian Government decided to establish itself as a Presidential government and through emergency decrees promulgated new laws.[1] The Austrian government, disturbed by the outcome of the German election, the apparent political stability in the *Reich*, and the implied threat to Austria, had taken a leaf from the German experience, ready to create its own version of authoritarian government. In Austria this blatant violation of constitutional law encountered not only the most pronounced opposition of the Social Democrats but also, for different reasons, that of the National Socialists. The latter, while hostile to political democracy, had for the moment only to gain from the preservation of Austria's democratic structure. When the Austrian NSDAP failed in its endeavors, it began a campaign of terror against the Dollfuss government and Austria.

What was the Austrian Government's attitude to the new developments in Germany? It feared of course the likely impact of January 30, 1933, upon Austrian domestic politics, though it did not expect any immediate threat to its independence and sovereignty. While Vienna could not close its eyes to the new menace, at the moment no National Socialist deputies had a seat in the Austrian Parliament, though they dominated some provinces and frequently demonstrated in the streets of some Austrian towns and even of Vienna.

As far as the international situation was concerned, there was of course a community of ideological and political interests between Italy, Hungary, and Germany, based upon the sweep of fascism and totalitarianism throughout Europe. Austria's situation and interests, however, were clearly different from those of Germany, Hungary, and Italy. With the exception of South Tyrol, an un-attainable target, territorial revisionism was virtually non-existent in Austria, or insignificant. While after Hitler's seizure of power Austria was clearly gripped by anxiety, government circles in Italy and Hungary were hopeful of a favorable change of the inter-national scene in their favor. The thought that a new political combination was emerging, was apparently in the mind not only of Hungary's Minister President Gömbös, but also in that of Mussolini. In a message of February 6, 1933, Gömbös emphasized his expectation for a closer cooperation with the new German Government. On the same day Il Duce voiced his conviction that Berlin and Rome would be able to agree on a "closely attuned policy."[2]

The German Foreign Minister Konstantin von Neurath, however, in a letter to Ulrich von Hassel, German Ambassador in Rome, pointed rather early to the divergent interests of Germany and Italy. Von Hassel, sketching his political ideas in a detailed report, suggested a German-Italian cooperation in the Danubian area to close the gap of their differences. H. held that German and Italian interests would always coexist in this region and that Germany therefore should accommodate herself to this geographic fact of life.[3] This would help forging a closer diplomatic link between Berlin and Rome, so essential to both powers. The German Foreign Office, however, though not yet activist in regard to Austria, seemed skeptical in regard to the possibility of an agreement between Berlin and Rome.

German-Austrian Relations February–March 1933

Soon after Hitler's seizure of power in the *Reich*, the German Foreign Ministry thought of treading cautiously, continuing along the road of Stresemann's and Curtius' general Austrian policy. The latter was based upon encouraging union between the two German-speaking populations at an indefinite future. On February 18, 1933, the German Minister in Vienna, Kurt Rieth, requested in a letter to State Secretary Bernhard von Bülow financial support for Professor Hermann Foppa, leader of Austria's *Grossdeutsche*, who had recently returned from Berlin, where he had engaged in talks with Alfred Hugenberg, the leaders of the *Stahlhelm* and other personalities of the political Right—the very coalition partners of the Nazis in the *Reich*. While in Berlin, Foppa had also pleaded at the German Foreign Ministry for financial help "of the kind," Rieth wrote, "repeatedly received in the past either upon the instigation of Herr Stresemann, Herr Curtius, or directly through the Foreign Ministry." The *Grossdeutsche Volks-Partei*, in Rieth's view, represented primarily the civil servants, a circumstance which was "precisely what makes the party valuable to us, because it will advance our point of view regardless of the current issues of domestic policy at any given moment. It also occupied in the Austrian Parliament a very important position."[4] In May 1933, Foppa, Presiding Officer of the *Grossdeutsche Volkspartei*, speaking for his party, acknowledged Hitler as leader of the entire German nation, linking the *Grossdeutschen* thus with Austrian National Socialists.[5]

Official German foreign policy thought in regard to the Anschluss is clearly revealed in a letter, dated March 22, 1933, from Gerhard Köpke of the German Foreign Office to Ambassador Rieth in Vienna.[6] Referring to a visit by some Austrian gentlemen, especially Richard Riedl, Austrian Ambassador in Berlin between 1922 and 1925 and adherent of the Anschluss concept, Köpke repeated his warnings lest the *Reich* "under the pressure of events might perhaps act too impulsively" in the Austrian question: it might, he feared, prematurely place the Anschluss on the agenda and thus, just as in 1918, risk a dangerous setback; or the *Reich*, because of the urgency of reaching a political alignment with Italy, might be induced to renounce the pan-German goal altogether. Köpke assured his correspondent that such anxieties were unwarranted.

The former Austrian Ambassador Riedl was received not only in the Wilhelmstrasse, but also by Hitler himself. Köpke, in a communication to two ambassadors abroad, referred to Hitler's conversation with the Austrian Ambassador: this conversation was one of the earliest recorded on the subject of Austria after the Führer had assumed the post of Chancellor. Hitler expected a stabilization of Austria's precarious situation only if the Austrian National Socialist movement was "given the place to which, commensurate with its strength, it is entitled"; he asserted that holding new elections was the proper method to determine the extent of the participation of the Austro-Nazis in the Austrian government.[7] When the Italian Ambassador Vittorio Cerruti conveyed to Hitler Mussolini's warning that he would never permit the Anschluss, the Führer disclaimed any intention of wishing to take over Austria. Among other matters, the likely strengthening of the Center Party, which would be a consequence of the Anschluss, seemed dangerous to him. He did not even aim, he claimed, at *Gleichschaltung* with the *Reich* through the formation of a 100% National Socialist Austrian government.[8]

The demand of Hitler and the Austrian National Socialists for new elections had actually been raised before, particularly in a letter of the *Landesleiter* of the Austro-Nazis, Alfred Proksch, to the President of the Austrian *Nationalrat*, Karl Renner. Proksch had pointed out that the composition of the *Nationalrat* no longer corresponded to the political shifts in the Austrian electorate. Hitler's insistence on new Austrian elections in 1933 constituted of course an interference in Austria's domestic affairs. In March 1933, Hitler, heading a coalition government in the *Reich*, favored the creation of a similar coalition in Austria. He expected no doubt such a government to be only a short-term solution to be followed by an exclusively National Socialist government, similar to the one he already contemplated for the *Reich*.

In his foregoing letter of March 22, 1933, to Rieth, Köpke of the *German Aussenamt*, stressed that German policy must absolutely avoid broaching the Anschluss question prematurely, especially "at a time when we ourselves are politically still powerless."[9] This would only give the Great Powers who were hostile to the Anschluss idea a pretext for joint intervention and would facilitate the establishment of a united front against Germany. More importantly, Germany must try to avoid an open conflict with Italy over Austria. But Köpke apparently considered the distinct possibility that the political development in Austria might be "favorable to us" and that under National Socialist leadership a *Gleichschaltung* with the *Reich* would become feasible. This view reflected the prevailing long-range optimism in German official circles as well as the belief that the *Reich* pattern, coalition government under Nazi leadership, would also be the most likely and most successful model for Austria.

Austro-German and Italo-German Confrontations

On April 11, 1933, Dollfuss arrived in Rome. According to von Hassel, German Ambassador in Rome, extreme reserve was maintained regarding the substance of the talks between the Chancellor, Mussolini, and Fulvio Suvich, Italian Under-Secretary for Foreign Affairs.[10] The Austrian Minister of Justice Kurt von Schuschnigg had arrived a few days earlier. Austria evidently was seeking to obtain Italy's support against the growing National Socialist movement and the rising Anschluss threat across the Inn river.

Mussolini not only assured Chancellor Dollfuss help but also urged him to block indigenous National Socialism by all means. However, as a most "efficient means to this end," Mussolini, according to von Hassel, "insisted on launching an energetic campaign against Marxism," since it constituted "at the moment the greatest [!] threat to Austria, not the least because of the pro-Czech inclinations recently exhibited by the Austrian Social Democrats."[11] Thus Austrian Nazism was to be battled and the Anschluss threat met head-on by drawing the sword against Austro-Marxism! This convoluted reasoning grew out directly from Mussolini's innate ideological prejudices against democracy, especially Social Democracy, and from his deep-rooted bias in behalf of German fascism, which he considered at least as a temporary ally.

In his report from Rome Hassel cautioned that Italy "still maintains her opposition to the Anschluss."[12] The German Ambassador recommended therefore that German political action be directed at bringing about the widest possible meshing of German and Italian interests in the Danubian basin so as to preclude the forging of an Italo-Austro-Hungarian bloc excluding Germany. He confidently expected that the "similarity of their political orientation" would "progressively facilitate a German-Italian understanding even in the question of Austria."

Dollfuss, according to von Hassell, was quite optimistic regarding the future: "The Austrians, to be sure, had the *Reich*-German experience before their eyes, but this did not mean that developments would follow an identical course; on the contrary, what had been witnessed [in Germany] served more as a warning."

Italian concern for Austria was much alive in the months after Hitler had come to power. When, on March 18, 1933, the Bavarian Minister of Justice Hans Frank in a speech over the Munich radio warned the Austrian government not to force German National Socialists to come to the support of the threatened "liberty" of their Austrian comrades, Dollfuss promptly demanded of the German Minister Rieth an authentic text of Frank's speech. The Italian Ambassador Vittorio Cerruti, at the instruction of Rome, also brought the matter up in Berlin.[13] A few weeks later he point-blank asked the German Foreign Minister Neurath about German policy toward Austria. Neurath replied that Germany would "let things take their course." "Support for the present Dollfuss government was not to be expected of us; a visit by Dollfuss in Berlin, which he had mentioned to Herr von Papen, was out of the question at the present time. But as far as the Anschluss was concerned, I could tell him reliably on the basis of a discussion with *Reich* Chancellor Hitler only the previous day, that this was not an acute question for us, and I asked him to tell this also to Mussolini. We had other and bigger matters to be concerned about than the question of the Anschluss."[14]

Whatever the real significance of the Anschluss for German policy in the spring of 1933, and of Neurath's disclaimer, Austro-German relations were far from placid. Following the complaint of the Austrian Minister about the appearance of a cartoon in the *Völkischer Beobachter*, critical of Dollfuss, and about other German press attacks on the Austrian Chancellor, Hitler, on May 10, received the Austrian envoy Tauschitz in the presence of Foreign Minister von Neurath. With sharp words the Führer drew his attention to an article in the Vienna *Reichspost* which had called the presence of members of the German Government in Austria undesirable. When the conversation grew "more and more irritable," Neurath interceded stressing the need for mutual restraint and moderation in the press. But he also asked the Austrian Ambassador to address future complaints to the German Foreign Ministry. According to an official Austrian publication, Hitler, on this occasion, informed Tauschitz that Berlin contemplated a one-year prohibition of visits by German tourists to Austria.[15]

This very threat was repeated by Hans Frank II, *Reich* Commissar for Justice and Bavarian Minister for Justice, at a gathering in Graz on May 14; on this occasion he alluded to Dollfuss, a man of diminutive physical stature, as the "little Metternich." (Earlier, on March 18, Frank II, as noticed, had made a similarly critical remark in Vienna.) Privately, Köpke of the German Foreign Ministry considered Frank's remarks "insulting"; as a member of the *Reich* cabinet he, while on Austrian soil, should have exercised greater restraint. In general Köpke expressed "great concern"[16] about the assignment of Party members to the German Legation in Vienna.

The obvious "deterioration" of the German-Austrian relationship produced further warnings from the German Foreign Office addressed to German policy-makers. Victor von Heeren, author of a memorandum suggested by Department II, took for granted that the two following objectives were paramount with the makers of German policy toward Austria: 1. the strengthening of the Austrian National Socialist movement; 2. The avoidance of anything which could give France and Italy a pretext for intervention and for accusing Germany of interfering in Austria's internal affairs and of openly violating the terms of the peace dictate. Reprisals against the Dollfuss regime would merely play into the latter's hands and "mobilize in its favor the self-respect of large sections of the Austrian population which at this moment are still undecided in their attitude toward National Socialism." Bringing the Austrian problem to a head "at this time by means of official policy entails very considerable risk for us." There was "no adequate justification for accepting such risks at a time when we are so dependent . . . on an atmosphere as favorable as possible for the solution of other problems of vital importance to the German people which have greater priority."[17] The National

Socialist movement, due to its inherent momentum, will undoubtedly reach its goal in Austria sooner or later. Heeren, the author of the foregoing report, observed that appointing the activist Theodor Habicht, German *Landesinspekteur* and highest official of the National Socialists in Austria, and one Cohrs as attachés to the Legation in Vienna, in order to give them diplomatic protection against expulsion, furnished actually no assurances of this kind. As Heeren had predicted, the Austrian government continued to denounce Habicht's transgressions and finally had him and Cohrs arrested. In retaliation, Hitler ordered the head of the press section of the Austrian legation in Berlin, Dr. Wasserbäck, to be expelled from the *Reich*.

The Italo-Hungarian attempt in February and March 1933 to lay the foundations for a new political axis, linking Rome, Budapest, Vienna, and Berlin, had failed. In spite of the ideological kinship of the above four countries, which Mussolini and Gömbös underlined, Hitler was unwilling to command that the Austrian Nazis make a turn-about and support Dollfuss.

Though Hitler realized Germany's limitations in 1933, he was in no mood to repudiate the union concept for all times to come. In *Mein Kampf* he had unconditionally come out for the Anschluss; now he was unwilling to opt for a political freeze in Austria. But he remained confident that ultimately he would be able to create a political bloc linking Berlin, Budapest, Rome, and Vienna, an axis on his own terms, one which would be based upon the prior incorporation of Austria into the *Reich*.

Mussolini renewed the pledge to Dollfuss to support his struggle for Austrian independence on occasion of the latter's week-long visit to Rome in April 1933. As Hassell reported, he had learned from a "reliable source" that Mussolini and Dollfuss were agreed to suppress Austrian National Socialism "under all circumstances" in order to prevent it from seizing power.[18] Still, the Austrian Chancellor, while in Rome, voiced the wish to personally journey to Berlin. But Hitler was little interested in meeting Dollfuss. He virtually rejected the conclusion of an impending Austro-German commercial treaty, asserting that he could not sign a preferential treaty with the Austrian government.[19] He asked that Neurath explain to Vienna the discontinuance of negotiations by offering "non-political reasons."

Habicht, Hitler, and German Tourist Traffic

Theo Habicht, deputy of the NSDAP in the *Reichstag*, became in 1931 *Landesinspekteur* of the *Reichsleitung* of the Nazi Party in Austria. He represented thus the German rather than the Austrian NSDAP. It was primarily through Habicht that Hitler kept abreast of developments affecting the Austrian NSDAP. Habicht's assignment to Vienna conformed also to the preference Hitler generally gave to party over state organs. According to Neurath, Habicht had become Hitler's "absolute confidence man." He had scored a major triumph when he succeeded in forging an alliance of the Austrian Nazis with the Styrian *Heimatschutz* under the leadership of Walter Pfrimer, an opponent of Starhemberg. The joint "combat association" acknowledged Hitler as Führer of the German nation."[20] In the following weeks Habicht further managed to bring together several organizations under the roof of the "National Opposition," among them the *Grossdeutsche Volkspartei* which had eight deputies in the *Nationalrat*. This gave the Austrian NSDAP a strong impetus and also persuaded Dollfuss to establish indirect contact with Habicht—which Mussolini had earlier suggested. Negotiators for the Austrian Government were then Minister of the Army Carl Vaugoin, Finance Minister Karl Buresch, and Minister of Justice Kurt Schuschnigg, the latter serving in the capacity of "special confidant" of Dollfuss. A major initiative in these negotiations was taken by Anton Rintelen, Minister of Education under Dollfuss and Landeshauptmann of Styria, an ambitious politician who hoped to strike a bargain with the Austro-Nazis and to replace Dollfuss as Chancellor. The negotiations in May 1933, aiming at the inclusion of the Christian Socials, the *Heimwehr*, and Austrian Nazis in a new cabinet, failed however.

When Hitler became Chancellor, in addition to being Führer of the NSDAP in the *Reich* and in Austria, Austro-German relations were bound to grow more complex and tense. The Austrian Government believed to be able to strike a deal with the German Chancellor, ignoring or minimizing his role as leader of the Party for both the *Reich* and Austria. Though Hitler pledged non-interference in Austrian affairs, his racist *Weltanschauung*, extreme nationalism, as well as the totalitarian structure of the NSDAP made intervention in Austria an ideological and organizational imperative. Later on German diplomacy often claimed that a victorious National Revolution could not possibly stop at the artificial borders which separated Germany from neighboring kinsfolk. Everything else aside, the mere intermingling of State and Party interests on the German side made the ultimate expansionism of Hitlerism in Austria and the final clash between the *Third Reich* and Austria a foregone conclusion. The Nazi terror in Austria, petty diplomatic complaints and grievances, and Nazi economic warfare could only embitter Austro-German relations.

The German cabinet session of May 26, 1933, produced the final decision about the prohibiton of Germans to travel to Austria;[21] Hitler reiterated views voiced five years earlier in his second book. The real overlords in Austria were allegedly "Vienna's half-Judaism and the Legitimists," both of whom were hostile toward the *Reich*. Their policy was to extirpate the German national idea and replace it with the Austrian concept. Austria thus risked to become another Switzerland, another German country lost to the *Reich*. Therefore, yielding to the present Austrian government, showing even a mere readiness to negotiate with it, was out of the question, since it would only weaken Austria's National Opposition. To the contrary, the time had come to give battle. Hitler realized that even after an Austrian election, National Socialism would "not be the largest Party." The strangling of German tourist traffic, however, the introduction of a one-thousand Mark fee for traveling to Austria, would most likely lead to the downfall of the Dollfuss government. "This would in turn bring about the inner *Gleichschaltung* of Austria, without making a formal Anschluss necessary." Hitler even thought that the confrontation could be brought to a head "this summer."[22]

In view of the speed with which events, in Hitler's erroneous estimate, were likely to unfold and his own "restraint" in not insisting upon a formal union, the Führer thought that international complications over the Austrian course could be avoided. To minimize adverse reactions by the Western Powers, he was also prepared not to arouse needlessly Italy's suspicions and to avoid, as far as possible, any "*grossdeutsch* arguments." The Führer was convinced that the Dollfuss regime was internally weak and expected that decisive and rapid moves against Austria at some critical moment would lessen or even eliminate the possibility of international complications. These suppositions of Hitler were hardly challenged in the cabinet or outside of it. Briefly, and rather tamely, Foreign Minister Konstantin von Neurath and Minister of Economics Alfred Hugenberg raised merely questions about some of these assumptions, especially the effectiveness of economic sanctions, and cautioned that German politics would elicit "general bitterness," but Hitler found it not necessary even to reply to them. Most importantly, Neurath uttered not a word of criticism about the Nazis' patent ultimate goals in regard to Austria's "internal *Gleichschaltung*" and thereafter the outright abolition of Austria's independence.[23] Papen raised a question about Germany's interference in Austrian affairs, which was only aimed against Habicht, but the role of the *Landesinspekteur* was otherwise not directly questioned.

In this cabinet session of May 26, 1933, Hitler clearly wanted the *Reich* to support traditional Party objectives in Austria. His victory in assuming power only a few months previously, its consolidation, and the outcome of the German elections had buoyed his spirits, and he expected Austria to fall like a ripe fruit into Germany's lap. As it turned out, he underestimated Austria's internal resistance, fascist Italy's concern for and interest in Austria's independence and in retaining South Tyrol, and the West's sharp opposition at that moment. He also overestimated the strength of Austrian National Socialism and the applicability of radical and "revolutionary" methods in the solution of the Austrian question. In 1933–34 both Hitler's judgment as to correct tactics and as to the actual interests and strength of all states, political parties, and statesmen with a special interest in Austrian affairs was faulty. The German Foreign Minister Neurath and his staff were rather doubtful and even pessimistic regarding Germany's Austrian policy but could not muster the necessary courage to strongly assert their partly divergent views. They confined themselves to hints of mild criticism of the tactics that Hitler seemed to prefer but did not dare question the ultimate goals— *Gleichschaltung* and Anschluss; they undoubtedly approved of them.

Beyond the border, Austrian National Socialism under Habicht's stewardship veered erratically between assurances respecting Austria's sovereignty and open preparation for union. Following a search of Habicht's quarters in Linz on May 31, 1933, Berlin, fearful that he might be expelled, wanted to prevent this by assigning Habicht to the Vienna German Embassy, thus conferring upon him, as previously stated, diplomatic immunity. But the Austrian Government refused to extend recognition to Habicht and Cohrs—a refusal to which it was fully entitled in accordance with common rules and procedures of international law—and ordered Habicht's arrest, following the spread of Nazi terrorism. During the second week in June 1933 even moderate Austrian Nazis such as Alfred Frauenfeld and Walter Riehl appeared at the *Ballhausplatz* to express their regret over recent terror acts.[24] After bloody clashes at Krems on June 19, 1933, the Austrian Government prohibited all activities of the NSDAP and of its auxiliary organizations throughout the country.

The upsurge of Nazi terrorism in Austria produced a *démarche* in Berlin by the apostolic Nuntius who as doyen of the diplomatic corps voiced to Bülow its "great concern."[25] Neurath, writing from London where he attended the World Economic Conference, warned in stronger than usual terms of the international "sensitivity"[26] concerning Austria, which was greater than Berlin had anticipated. Similarly, the German Ambassador in London cautioned that the sharp methods of the *Reich* versus Austria had produced an "anti-German mood." From the start of the Austro-German dispute Nazi propaganda had stressed that it was only an "internal," a family affair and of no legitimate concern to the rest of Europe and the world.[27] German aggressiveness against Austria, however, had turned the issue into one of general European scope.

Austria Between Two Dictators

The meeting of Dollfuss and Mussolini in Rome on June 2, 1933, stood under the sign of the growing Nazi terror in Austria.[28] Due to Hitler's and the Austro-Nazis' opposition and radical demands, Dollfuss's scheme to include some Austrian National Socialists into a coalition cabinet had come to naught. Mussolini's project of creating a bloc linking Rome, Budapest, Vienna, and Berlin, as seen, had likewise failed. Dollfuss had yielded to Mussolini's pressure tactics to follow a new, anti-Marxist domestic line. Austria and Hungary were closely to cooperate and be "under the protection and active help of Italy," against the peril of an open or camouflaged incorporation by either Germany—

or the Little Entente! Now Il Duce, differently from his earlier scheme, pursued an Austrian policy of his own, and persuaded Dollfuss to adopt it. The Austro-Nazis were to be effectively combatted by striking against "Austro-Marxism," the Social Democrats. This allegedly would deprive the National Socialists of the "anti-Marxist weapons."*[29] Both Mussolini and Dollfuss preferred to minimize, if not to ignore, that Austrian National Socialism with its totalitarian philosophy and the Führer-cult was as bitter an enemy of even an authoritarian Austrian government, of Catholicism, of the *Ständestaat* (corporate state) and of Austrian independence, as it was of Austro-Marxism. With Austria's southern flank protected by Italy, Dollfuss was prepared to resume talks with the *Reich*. The Austrian Chancellor undertook such an attempt on July 1, 1933, in a longer conversation with the German Ambassador Rieth. But it was the Ambassador who poured cold water on Dollfuss's hopes when he left no doubt that the *Reich* government would not leave the Austro-Nazis to their own devices by relinquishing any further moral and financial aid to them; this, he made clear, was a mere "illusion" of Dollfuss.[30]

Habicht's Munich Campaign.
Concerns of the German Foreign Ministry

In an order dated June 22, 1933, the *Reichsleitung* of the NSDAP made it clear that the Austrian Nazi Party was part and parcel of the German NSDAP. Habicht started his new propagandistic activities over the Munich sender with an address on July 5. There are no indications that prior to it the Berlin Foreign Office was consulted or that it favored this course. But Neurath, while in London the month before, had apparently been disturbed by the impact there of Jewish persecutions in the *Reich* and of Austrian developments upon public opinion, and promptly made presentations to the *Reichsstatthalter* of Bavaria.[31] After having received promises that a more restrained propaganda campaign would be waged, the Foreign Office retreated; but Habicht resumed his vitriolic campaign. There followed the wide dissemination of Nazi propagandistic materials by German planes over Austrian

---

*See also p. 213

territory, including of flyers signed by Habicht and Reschny, the leader of the Austrian S.A. Thereupon, on July 17 the Austrian Ambassador Tauschitz presented a protest at the Wilhelmstrasse. Ten days later followed his second démarche. When Bülow and Köpke of the German Foreign Office attempted to counter the complaint by distinguishing between State and Party activities, the Austrian Ambassador plainly rejected this subterfuge.[32]

Privately Bülow was sufficiently concerned about the deteriorating relations to write to Neurath who happened to be on vacation. He considered the situation quite serious, raised questions as to the effectiveness of Nazi propaganda in Austria, and informed Neurath that he had ordered Habicht to discuss with him the "limits" of propagandistic activity.[33] He recalled that the struggle with Austria, "which has already lasted so much longer than we had expected, is extremely costly to us." Germany was losing the sympathies of all the smaller countries which must be telling themselves that we might some day proceed against them with similar methods. We are antagonizing the larger Powers." He especially drew Neurath's attention to the apparent desire of Mussolini, conveyed by Ambassador Cerruti, to obtain a written renunciation of the Anschluss from Berlin. Referring to Austrian complaints regarding acts of terror and the dissemination of Nazi propaganda over the wireless, Bülow claimed that Germany was entirely guiltless; in any case, Habicht had promised that such acts would not be repeated. Radio propaganda could be limited in scope and acrimony. The flights over Austrian territory, he admitted, could not be justified under international law. Regarding Austrian fear of a Nazi coup, there were, according to the Austrians, 5,000–6,000, according to Habicht about 1,000 Austrian Nazi refugees concentrated in a camp where they were performing " 'labor service.' " As Habicht recounted, in the event of an uprising of Austrian National Socialists, the party comrades now in Bavaria would "move back across the border only in small groups and in such a way that they could not be detected." All the Austrian complaints, Bülow asserted, were of rather minor importance compared to the "question whether we will succeed in overpowering [!] Austria." "Overpowering" Austria—this was the goal of the "moderate," partly non-Nazi diplomats of the German Foreign Office, which was supposed to restrain the Nazis!

In reply to Bülow, Neurath, on August 4, reported to him that he had just talked to Hitler on the Obersalzberg. "Result: He will summon Habicht and order him to observe 'still greater moderation' (weitere Mässigung) in radio propaganda and forbid the use of airplanes for propagandistic purposes. A *coup de main* by the refugees was out of the question. The economic struggle, however, was to be continued "with all severity."[34] Acts of terror from across the German border had already been strictly prohibited. Neurath ordered Bülow to summon the Italian Ambassador and to inform him that Germany rejected any intervention. For the present, no compromise could be reached with Dollfuss. Only the other day Hitler had declined giving any written commitment on the Anschluss. On August 5, 1933, Bülow told Cerruti that any interference by third states in the German-Austrian discussions was to be rejected.[35]

Clearly, Hitler flouted accepted international law. While making the most of the national and cultural ties between Germany and Austria, he minimized any dispute between their governments as being a sort of domestic quarrel which was of no legitimate concern to any third parties. Here was a sharp difference between the German and Austrian points of view, which remained unreconciled until the very absorption of Austria in March 1938; also, Italo-German differences over Austria were not solved.

Once Habicht had departed from Berlin, all the doubts about the former *Landesinspekteur* and his and the Austro-Nazis' radical policies were once more expressed by experts of the Foreign Office. Bülow and Neurath questioned Germany's Austrian policy, her aggressive methods, and ambitious goals, perhaps to a greater extent than they had dared before.[36] But this was largely limited to intra-office communications. In his letter to Neurath, Bülow enclosed notes by von Heeren wherein the Foreign Minister was urged to impress upon Hitler the "extraordinary perils" of Germany's Austrian policy; it had reached dimensions apparently never anticipated. On the same day, August 1, a letter from Neurath arrived in the Foreign Office in which the already deeply concerned leading German diplomats and "policy-makers" were informed of the setback suffered in the attempt to enlist Hitler in ordering a change of policy to the Austro-Nazis. The Führer had "categorically rejected" Mussolini's intervention in Austrian affairs.[37]

Démarches of the Western Powers and Il Duce's Policy

But faced with a new Italian démarche, Hitler promised Neurath on August 4 that he would impress upon Habicht "further moderation."[38] The Foreign Office had thus achieved a modest success, though Hitler was not prepared to consent to its suggested "compromise" with Dollfuss. Hitler's slight concessions might have temporarily soothed Italian sensibilities, but did not prevent further démarches by the French and English on August 7, 1933. On August 9 the Italian News Agency Stefani let the world know that the *Reich* government had promised the Italian Ambassador that radio and airplane propaganda against Austria would be "prohibited."[39] But Hitler's promises were dubious. Habicht still attacked the Austrian Government on account of its mere appeal for help to the Great Powers and their diplomatic intervention.[40] The address aggravated the already tense relations between Mussolini and Hitler. Once again the aggressive Austrian course brought embarrassment to the German government and focused international attention upon Austria—which Hitler had strenuously tried to avoid.

The démarches of August 7, 1933 by the French Ambassador and the English chargé d'affaires in Berlin were based on recent Austrian complaints regarding the *Third Reich*'s support of Austro-Nazi propaganda and terrorist activities.[41] On August 12 Foreign Minister Neurath in conversation with Hitler brought up Habicht's latest Munich broadcast and the Italian protest over it. The Chancellor, according to the German Foreign Minister, "was very indignant over the manner of Mussolini's intervention and declared that he would not stand for that sort of tutelage." Habicht's speech, Hitler asserted, was not in contradiction to the promises that had been made; it consisted merely of a recital of facts and historical retrospects. He, Hitler, had given Mussolini no promise to the effect that the propaganda to strengthen the National Socialist Party in Austria would be abandoned, but only that it would be kept in check.[42]

Next to Nazi propaganda, it was the actual threat of an invasion by Austrian Nazis from across the border, trained and stationed on German soil, and under German command, which increasingly concerned the Austrian government. The first alarm regarding the rearmament of the Austrian Nazis on German soil near the Austrian border was rung by the German Ambassador Rieth on July 26. On August 17, 1933, Rieth repeated his warnings to State Secretary Bülow, referring to the rumor that an SA formation made up of Austrians was being readied in Bavaria for use in Austria when the occasion should arise; September 5 was frequently mentioned as the target date.[43] In an earlier letter, dated July 27, he himself had expressed the view that these rumors seemed to some extent based on facts. The crossing over the border into Bavaria by Austrian National Socialists seeking to join the "Austrian Legion" had, he reported, virtually become a permanent item in some of the Viennese newspapers. The *Reichspost* in a special edition had revealed documents of the NSDAP *Landesleitung* which showed the involvement of Party circles in Munich and Berlin in these activities.[44] Though Habicht had denied any aggressive plans, he had admitted that "persecuted" Austrians were gathered in German labor camps so as to keep them from roaming throughout Germany.

Rieth himself cautioned Berlin that the prospects of a forcible intervention of these people in Austrian affairs could not be regarded as very promising. The German military attaché General Muff, offering a military assessment of the chances of such a coup to the *Reichswehr* Ministry, doubted that such a venture would be successful. The political repercussions of intervention by an SA force which consisted of Austrians, but was equipped in Germany, could be "disastrous." Rieth himself concluded with the unmistakable warning: "The Austrian question could then be raised on the broadest front against Germany, not to speak of the possibility of military moves by other powers."[45]

While, according to Habicht, in the summer of 1933 only 2,000 Austrians were quartered in Camp Lechfield near Augsburg and nobody planned an invasion of Austria, Bülow himself entertained little doubt about their real role: "Should there be a *Putsch* in Austria from any quarter, it would of course be impossible to prevent these Austrians from individually disappearing over the border again, the way they came. So much for Herr Habicht." According to Bülow, "subordinate Party officials" pursued their own goals with the Legion. "I am concerned," he wrote, "that some day in Austria the internal political situation may lead to attempts at a *Putsch*, perhaps entirely unaided by us and that then, before it can be prevented, heedless elements among us

may let themselves be carried away into action" that might greatly
embarrass the *Reich* and, at the same time, have a "disastrous
influence" on the Austrian situation. "But even if such an explosion
should not occur, what is happening in Bavaria today is nevertheless
a serious liability for us with respect to foreign policy." The
quartering and employment of Austrian refugees should be handled in such a manner that it "no longer feeds the suspicion that
we are preparing for an armed invasion of Austria." He recommended that they should be quartered in the north of Germany,
at a greater distance from the Austrian border and that all military
training of the Austrian refugees should cease. "We have already
tried to influence Herr Habicht to that effect. I believe, however,
that no essential change can be effected without a strong word
from the Chancellor."[46] But that word was not coming until July
25, 1934, the day of the abortive Nazi *Putsch*.

It was in a letter dated July 1, 1933, addressed to Dollfuss,
that Mussolini had developed his ideas about Austrian domestic
policies—ideas virtually identical with those he had outlined to
Starhemberg in February 1933. Il Duce urged Dollfuss to react
to the "criminal excesses" of Austrian National Socialism "in the
most energetic fashion." To battle "the peril of Nazism," Dollfuss,
according to Mussolini's convoluted logic, had to fight Austrian
Social Democrats first! If Dollfuss would battle Austro-Marxism,
many of those now active in the ranks of the Nazis would switch
to the side of the government. In any case, only through "an
intimate association with Italy" would Austria escape an "im-
moderate pressure" from the German side.[47] Mussolini's relentless
urgings were not lost on Dollfuss.

In his reply Dollfuss reminded Mussolini that Austro-Marxism
was already pushed back to an extent which only half a year
earlier had appeared unimaginable and that he considered the
continuation of the struggle against the Nazis unavoidable. A
cooperation with such a movement, using anarchist methods was
out of the question. Dollfuss rejected thus an earlier suggestion
of Mussolini, which he had previously endorsed, namely forging
a political alliance with the Austrian Nazis as junior partners,
with himself retaining effective political control. An amicable
relationship with Germany was only possible if Berlin would
uphold Austria's sovereignty. The *Reich* and the NSDAP would

have to consider Austrian National Socialism as an Austrian movement and completely refrain from any intervention in Austria's internal affairs.[48] While there was a large area of agreement between Mussolini and Dollfuss, each of them placed emphasis on different matters. Dollfuss endorsed Mussolini's formula, "Independence of Austria, externally, and renewal of Austria, internally speaking." But he saw in National Socialism the greater danger. While Dollfuss sharply opposed Austro-Marxism and wished to take full advantage of the widespread anti-democratic trend in Europe, he still moved against the Social Democrats under the pressure of Mussolini; this was the price Il Duce asked in exchange for support against the National Socialist *Reich* and its Austrian Fifth Column.

To some extent, Mussolini, as he virtually admitted, had become a prisoner of his own ideology. In a letter to Dollfuss he disclosed that National Socialism had always blamed him because Italian Fascism supported in Austria a government which "had not overcome Marxism." Thus Italian pressure upon the Dollfuss government actually originated in German pressure upon Rome! Dollfuss, for the sake of Italy's, as it turned out, rather short-lived support of Austrian independence sacrificed the broad support of the Austrian population and hopelessly alienated the followers of Austrian Social Democracy; the Austrian Socialists had frequently polled more than 40% of the Austrian electorate and bitterly opposed the Anschluss with the *Third Reich*.

Hitler, like Mussolini, was a captive of his own thought processes. His rejection during the first months of his Chancellorship of the Great Powers' suggestions concerning Austria grew out of an overconfidence, nourished by his spectacular success in coming to power in January 1933, and by his *völkisch* ideology, nurturing his belief that the Austro-German dispute was a "family affair," of no concern to anyone else in Europe and the world. Similarly, during the initial phase of the *Third Reich* neither the Party nor the Foreign Office had any clear concept of German strategy and tactics relating to Austria. The cautious advice which the Wilhelmstrasse from time to time conveyed to the Chancellery was ignored by Hitler. His seizure of power merely fed Nazi optimism and totalitarianism and gave radical tactics and goals unquestionable priority over more cautionary procedures.

The *Third Reich*'s Austrian Policy

During the first half year of Nazi rule, the *Reich*'s diplomatic initiative came from the NSDAP rather than from the German diplomats who were inherited from the Weimar period. Actually, the Foreign Office and the NSDAP were frequently at loggerheads, though the Wilhelmstrasse refrained from giving open battle. The Nazis complained about the "idiots" (Trottel) in the Foreign Office who thought that "Austria would fall into their lap,"[49] while the *Auswärtiges Amt* criticized the Party men who were incapable of anticipating the foreign policy consequences of their acts. In spite of such altercations, the NSDAP and *Aussenamt* shared some basic conceptions in regard to Austria. Both were convinced that a German-Austrian union was desirable and in many ways beneficial to both states—views that were also held by most German politicians and parties of the Weimar era. As far as Hitler and the Austrian Nazi leadership were concerned, there was again a far-reaching consensus, though for tactical reasons Hitler wanted the Anschluss "for the moment completely shelved,"[50] while Habicht, expressing Austro-Nazi yearnings, was less patient and restrained. Hitler and the Party's leadership had first counted on a quick overthrow of the Dollfuss government and had also underestimated the Western Powers' resistance. But Dollfuss displayed greater staying power and the Entente states demonstrated far greater interest in the preservation of the *status quo* of the Danubian realm than the Nazi leadership had expected. Especially the Italian government took a major interest in Austria and Central Europe—which greatly irritated Hitler.

By September 1933, the attempt to reach an agreement between Dollfuss and Habicht had ended in failure. Mussolini, however, continued to urge the Austrian Chancellor to pursue this course. Actually, neither Il Duce nor the Austrian Chancellor was interested in helping Austrian National Socialism to secure a position of real power but rather "to bring the National Socialist movement in Austria under control."[51] New attempts of Dollfuss to establish contact with Habicht and finally through Langoth of the *Grossdeutsche Volkspartei*, proved also abortive. This party, as previously mentioned, had entered into a closer association with the Austrian National Socialists, creating a "National Front," in contradistinction to the Fatherland Front established by Dollfuss. Langoth and his friends expected that Dollfuss would take members of the National Front into the government. Even people in Dollfuss's entourage anticipated that the entry of National Socialists into the government would serve as a counterweight against the *Heimwehr*. Schuschnigg, then Austrian Minister of Justice, made an effort to meet Foreign Minister von Neurath in Geneva, but each was fearful of the likely impact of this encounter, the one on the *Heimwehr*, the other upon the Austrian National Socialists, and in the end the meeting failed to materialize. In early October negotiations commenced also in Ödenburg (Sopron), Hungary, between the *Heimwehr* leader Graf Alberti, a confidant of Fey, rival of Starhemberg, and the Austro-Nazi leaders Frauenfeld and Schattenfroh,[52] the latter a plenipotentiary of Habicht. About a week later Habicht flew to Berlin to secure Hitler's approval for continuation of the negotiations. The Führer gave his consent, but the negotiations failed to make any progress. During October Habicht seemed to lose his role as authorized German spokesman and negotiator for Austrian National Socialism.[53] Dollfuss himself wished to block Habicht who in past months had become even more closely identified with anti-Austrian activities. Toward the end of October Dollfuss tried to establish direct contact with Berlin by exploring the possibilities of holding conversations with von Alvensleben, presiding officer of the Berlin *Herrenklub* and through Ernst Hanfstaengl, NSDAP Chief for the foreign press. The latter suggested that the *Reich* NSDAP cut its ties with the Austrian brother Party. Dollfuss seemed elated, but Hitler, in response to an inquiry by von Neurath called the proposals of Hanfstaengl "an idiocy."[54] On October 30 Schuschnigg journeyed to Munich, where he met Rudolf Hess who seemed to have been surprised at his visit. The meeting resulted in a mere restatement of the mutual positions and in Schuschnigg's being more than ever convinced that Habicht could not be circumvented.

Continuing negotiations in Vienna between the Government and Langoth and Foppa appeared only slightly to narrow the differences, but not to remove basic disagreements. In November Dollfuss still rejected the possibility of carrying on negotiations with Habicht.[55] The rejection of Habicht's conditions and of the man himself, even in view of Austria's subsequent development, can hardly be considered a political mistake. A good case can rather be made that each of the various political alternatives of Dollfuss contained serious political risks.

Dollfuss himself wished to establish contact with Hitler to reach "a direct agreement with Berlin" on the assumption that no meaningful understanding could be attained with mere underlings. But Hitler declined dealing with Dollfuss, referring him again to Habicht. At the same time Hitler in a talk with Suvich once again denied that the Anschluss was an acute problem for Germany or even desirable. A union would be a heavy financial burden to Germany. Hitler claimed that he had always held that Germany and Italy should jointly assist Austria. Germany and Italy were to prevent that Austria form a bridge between Poland, Czechoslovakia, and Yugoslavia. The Führer claimed one could not negotiate with Dollfuss since he had virtually no support in Austria. In vain did Suvich remind the Führer of the ideological kinship between Austria and Germany. Hitler demanded that the prohibition of the Austrian NSDAP be lifted and that the "persecution" of the Austro-Nazis cease. He again asked not only for new elections in Austria but also for the restoration even of the Austrian constitution! At the same time he held out the olive branch to Italy: Austria was too insignificant an object to be permitted to influence adversely the relations between the *Reich* and Italy.[56]

German-Italian relations were the focus of a bitter exchange between Hassell, German Ambassador in Rome, and Habicht. The latter was angry over Mussolini's Austrian course, his support of Dollfuss and opposition to himself, and attributed all this to the inadequacies of German diplomacy and to von Hassell in particular. Hassell in turn flatly rejected Habicht's accusation and blamed him for his extremism.[57] Though Italy considered the union in the long run unavoidable, she was resolved "to unconditionally prevent it for the moment." Rome was convinced that a total or partial seizure of power by the Austrian National Socialists would not promptly lead to a complete union. For Habicht, however, his Austrian policy and personal prestige were closely tied up with each other and his failure in being accepted as a suitable coalition partner was bound to doom his political chances.

Despite Germany's military weakness in 1933, Hitler and his men pursued an aggressive course.[58] Austria's policy, on the other hand, while unyielding in the immediate future, was far from being resolute for the longer stretch. In a talk with the German Ambassador in Vienna, Dollfuss spoke of his hope that an agreement could be reached "step by step," taking the form of a "successive evolution."[59] It would have to start with a reduction of tension and would usher in a political system in Austria that would be "comparable" to that of Germany and Italy.

These remarks of Dollfuss about an "evolutionary solution" of the Austrian questions, were virtually indistinguishable from those developed about these very concepts in the *Reich*. Thus both Hitler and Dollfuss claimed to have adopted the evolutionary course, Hitler to reach his goal of *Gleichschaltung* and ultimately Anschluss without having to resort to force and incurring international complications and Dollfuss to procrastinate matters in the hope perhaps of permanently frustrating the linkup. But in doing so, Dollfuss committed the fatal error of theoretical retreat; he conceded that Austrian independence was not a permanent objective and that, ultimately, Anschluss was probably unavoidable. Such a theoretical stance doomed any chances for the fostering and growth of a genuine and strong Austrian patriotism and was bound to plant only doubts in the Austrian mind.

Hitler's socalled "evolutionary" policy in regard to Austria had been preceded by a radical revolutionary course. Initially, the Führer had tried taking Austria from within by storm. But the abortive July 1934 Putsch, the assassination of Dollfuss, and the adverse international reaction produced a switch of policy and the adoption of new tactics. Yet before the ink with which the Austro-German July 1936 Agreement was signed, had become dry, the *Third Reich* again pursued a more aggressive line, while claiming that it was all rooted in an evolutionary course. Official Nazi propaganda was not likely to publicly admit its intransigent character. Theodor Habicht, Hitler's appointed deputy for Austria, had best expressed Hitler's ruthless and radical bent when in April 1934, after an hours-long conference with the Führer, he told a high-placed official in Department II of the German Foreign Office that Hitler "would not consider yielding in the Austrian question, even if the conflict were to last ten more years."[60] Others have testified that in two questions, those relating to Austria and to the Jews, Hitler was always unbending and unwilling to yield an inch. This stance found again clear expression in the Führer's blunt threat to Schuschnigg at Berchtesgaden that he was going to take Austria "so oder so," one way or another.[61] Four years lie between the two foregoing accounts of Hitler's attitude toward Austria. Its common denominator was the Führer's unrestrained radicalism—which official German policy merely tried to disguise.

The Dollfuss-Habicht relationship reached an anti-climax in January 1934. When on January 7, on the eve of Habicht's scheduled arrival, Dollfuss informed some members of his government of the impending talks with Habicht, Starhemberg, supported by two other *Heimwehr* leaders, including Fey, threatened that their ways would part.[62] At the very last moment Dollfuss, calling first Munich and then the Wilhelmstrasse, canceled the meeting. It appears that Habicht himself had been prepared to undertake the journey against the wishes of the Foreign Office and without the approval of Hitler. In the end, Hitler had no choice but to recall Habicht who was already in a plane over Austrian territory, when he changed course and returned to Munich.[63] But the Führer approved an attempt of Habicht to send a representative, Prince Waldeck, to Vienna to explore matters further. However, due to arrests in the Austrian capital, no meeting took place and Prince Waldeck returned to Berlin on January 12. Once again the *Heimwehr* had vetoed any negotiations with Habicht's men.

Dollfuss's motivation in reaching an agreement with National Socialism was complex. First, he chafed under the increasing pressure of the *Heimwehr* and felt the need for a political counterweight against it. Secondly, Germany, though weak at the moment, was bound to grow stronger, and an early settlement of outstanding issues would enhance the prospects for peace. On the other hand, Dollfuss obviously mistrusted Habicht and most other Austrian National Socialists.

Germany's Over-all Foreign Policy

In the framework of the foreign policy of the *Third Reich*, Austria played an important role. The first months of 1933 had revealed National Socialist Germany's Austrian policy as reckless; it was especially in marked contrast to the relative caution displayed by the *Third Reich* toward other neighbors. To the Austrian and German NSDAP, Austria apparently had seemed an easy prey.

But facing international disapproval on account of its domestic policies and isolation, when on October 14, 1933, Germany left the League of Nations, she was bound to pay close attention to the improvement of her relations at least with Fascist Italy. This in turn imposed some restraints upon Berlin's drive against Austria.

Neurath and Bülow had drawn the Führer's attention to the circumstance that other foreign policy issues deserved a higher priority than Austria and promised greater and quicker returns. Though the *Third Reich* was fast developing into a centralized totalitarian state and was thus likely to conduct foreign policy in a steady manner, its intransigent policy versus Austria revealed great confusion; too many German hands were involved in its making and in its execution. Austrian Nazis themselves frequently worked at cross purposes, not to mention their tactical and other differences with the Foreign Office and with Hitler himself. But beginning late summer and September 1933, Germany's foreign policy seemed to pursue more moderate goals.[64] As an early objective, Anschluss was virtually shelved; so was the more modest goal of a mere *Gleichschaltung*. What was now talked about was only a participation of the Austro-Nazis in a coalition government headed by Dollfuss. After September 1933 German foreign policy toward Austria appeared to have lost some of its adventurism and was seeking slightly more realistic goals.

The visit of Fulvio Suvich to Vienna on January 14, 1934, became a turning point in Austrian affairs.[65] Suvich first reiterated Mussolini's demand that Dollfuss strike a major blow against the Austrian Social Democrats; secondly, he demanded a stronger cooperation of Austria with Italy and Hungary. Contrary to earlier ideas floated in Rome, Italy then was not bent on establishing an ideological and political bloc linking the foregoing states with the *Third Reich*, but rather on creating a dominant position in Austria for herself. Dollfuss himself seemed to have second thoughts about Suvich's demands; behind Italy's back he attempted once more to establish contact with Habicht. But after his recent disappointments with Vienna Habicht judged the prospect very pessimistically. In an article of January 27 in the *Österreichische Presse-Dienst*, a Munich-based publication which he himself edited, he called for the "final battle over Austria."[66] The article was actually much more critical of Starhemberg and Fey than of Dollfuss. Tactical consideration moved also Hitler when he, on occasion of the first anniversary of his assuming the Chancellor post, assured the world that the Austro-Nazis had never entertained the idea of using force and were prepared to respect Austria's integrity, a stance almost opposite to that of Habicht.[67] At that very moment it was wildly rumored that the Austrian S.A. prepared a coup for March 15. Though Lieutenant-General Muff, Military Attaché in Vienna, held that such reports were based upon "idle talk,"[68] Hitler himself ordered measures to be taken in the event they proved to have some solid foundation.

Early in February 1934, Hitler received for the first time Rieth, his Ambassador in Vienna. In a manner quite uncharacteristic of him, he listened to Rieth rather than indulging in his usual lengthy monologues. The Ambassador warned of Italy's resolve to carry on the struggle against Austrian National Socialism "with un-diminished harshness." To overcome Italy's resistance and that of the Austrian ruling circles, Rieth recommended that Germany give special assurances to Dollfuss for "a certain length of time."[69] Without them Vienna would not be ready to form a coalition with the Austro-Nazis nor would Rome support such a course. Rieth did not go so far as to suggest relinquishing the Anschluss concept; he merely wanted to win Hitler over to an evolutionary tactic, to voicing his opposition to staging a violent *Putsch* in Austria.

The February 1934 Socialist Uprising and the Austro-Nazis' "Waiting Attitude"

In the critical February days of 1934, just before the Austrian government was to crush the Social Democratic workers, it ap-peared that both Rieth in Vienna and the Austrian Ambassador Tauschitz in Berlin had set once again their hopes upon a direct settlement of the outstanding Austro-German issues by the Chan-cellors of the two German states. The Führer ordered the German Military Attaché, Lieutenant-General Muff, to explore the pos-sibility of a compromise with Austria. This was the second time since he had come to power that Hitler assigned to a German diplomat rather than to a Party loyalist such a major task. But again Hitler developed second thoughts. Muff journeyed to Vienna only to be notified by telephone that his most recent assignment had just been withdrawn.[70] After some hesitation, the Führer once again had given the assignment to a Party man, a contact man of the SA in Vienna, Gilbert In der Maur.

The February days of 1934 were critical for the fate of Austrian democracy as well as of the Social Democratic Party. Ever since the summer of 1933, the Austrian Government, pressured by Mussolini and the *Heimwehr*, had methodically moved against the strongholds of the Social Democratic Party. Dollfuss was resolved to eliminate what was still left of Austrian democracy. On February 12, the day the workers' uprising commenced, an important gathering of leading Austro-Nazis took place in the private quarters of In der Maur in Vienna to discuss the outbreak of the Civil War, which was fraught with far-reaching consequences for the NSDAP. Participants at the meeting were the Chief of Staff of the Austrian S.A., Kirchbach, the representative of the S.A. in Austria, Türk, the National Socialist Prince Schönburg, and In der Maur himself. Though the possibility of an "independent action" during the conflict was discussed, the group decided to adopt a "waiting attitude."[71] It voiced the hope that the embitterment of Social Democrats over the repression by Dollfuss would swell the ranks of Austrian National Socialism. On the other hand, the Austro-Nazi group wanted to exploit the still raging civil war; it held out the olive branch for the Austrian government, offering it a sort of truce. An attempt to reach Dollfuss via Glaise-Horstenau, failed, however. On the very day the resistance of the Social Democrats crumbled, February 16, Glaise informed the Nazis of Dollfuss's rejection.[72] At the moment of victory over one enemy, the government saw no longer an urgent need of making substantial concessions to the other foe, the Austrian Nazis.

The Reaction of the Great Powers.
Germany's "new course"

The Austrian crisis of February 1934 produced different reactions among the Western Powers. On the one hand, it caused resentment, since Paris and London were opposed to the destruction of what was left of Austria's democratic and parliamentary institutions. On the other hand, the fighting in Austria brought home to France and Great Britain how precarious the Austrian situation was; they feared that the political chances of Austrian Nazism were likely to increase by leaps and bounds in the near future. Despite their criticism of Dollfuss's policies and action they continued to support his anti-Nazi government.

Fascist Italy rather welcomed the suppression of the Austrian workers' uprising and the destruction of the remnants of Austrian democracy. Mussolini had pushed Dollfuss toward this very course, claiming that it would rally all anti-Marxist forces in Austria around the government. But Italy's diplomatic action in the very midst of the uprising seemed to belie Mussolini's concepts. In the midst of a crisis for which he was largely responsible, Il Duce discovered the German threat to Austria and its implications.

On February 15, Suvich informed Germany's Ambassador Hassell of the impending separate declarations of France, Great Britain, and Italy, recognizing Austria's independence and her right to defend herself against attacks from without.[73] The following day Cerruti impressed upon Neurath that Mussolini had "very seriously" talked about the Austrian question and had again stressed that he would not tolerate the Anschluss.[74] He added that he considered the *Gleichschaltung* of Austria as being equivalent to a formal Anschluss. On February 17, Rome, Paris, and London issued separate though identical declarations rejecting the "German interference in the internal affairs of Austria."[75] and underlined the joint attitude of the Powers in support of preserving Austrian independence and integrity in accordance with the treaties.

But Habicht was little deterred by the policy declarations of the Great Powers. In an address of February 19 over the Munich sender he claimed that the "terrible catastrophe"[76] would not have occurred if the Austrian government had in time reached an agreement with Austrian National Socialism. He offered a so-called armistice for the next eight days during which the Austro-Nazis would abstain from any criticism of the Government in word or print "or by other means." Yet the address, whatever its form, had all the earmarks of an ultimatum, since it climaxed in the threat that in the event of an unsatisfactory reply or of none at all, the battle against the Dollfuss regime would be resumed. Coming on the heels of the policy proclamation of the Western Powers on Austria, it infuriated them. Considering Habicht an agent of the *Third Reich*, they interpreted his speech as a sign of German intransigence. Mussolini suggested to Hassell that

Habicht be placed into a lunatic asylum and warned Berlin that in the light of the Habicht ultimatum, Italian troops might be given the order to march. When Hassell claimed that it was "difficult" for Hitler to take a position against Habicht, Mussolini rejected this excuse out of hand as "politically untenable."[77] On February 26 Cerruti warned Neurath that German-Italian relations were worse than they had been for a long time and that Italian policy toward the *Reich* would be adversely affected if German policy toward Austria would undergo no change.[78] Dollfuss himself ordered then the strengthening of Austrian troops along the German border.

On February 27, 1934, Cerruti, in an exchange with Neurath, warned the German Foreign Minister that in view of Germany's attitude toward Austria, Italy would consider a rapprochement with France. Neurath rejected "advice coupled with threats," and countered with one of his own, namely contemplating a possible rapprochement with Yugoslavia, then Italy's potential enemy.[79] Rome seemed to consider any agreement between Rome, Budapest, and Vienna merely as a stepping stone toward broader talks culminating in "cooperation" between the Little Entente, Austria, and Hungary. Italy then held out to France the possibility of a joint leadership in the Danubian realm. Berlin understood that the cause which united Italy and France was concern over Austria's independence and integrity and her defense against Germany. Germany thus faced growing isolation.

This is the background of the "new" policy pursued by Habicht and the German NSDAP following the suppression of the February uprising of the Austrian workers. In a letter to Hassell, Neurath spoke of the allegedly "new course" upon which Austrian National Socialism had embarked, pointing out that Habicht had extended the armistice for an indefinite period and had forbidden all press attacks upon the Austrian government and the use of force against the state. The German Foreign Minister interpreted these changes as a turn-about from "direct activity" to a development "in the long run." While Habicht still preserved his credibility in Hitler's eyes and his leadership of Austrian National Socialism, Hitler this time backed his Foreign Minister Neurath, declared the old methods of fighing the Austrian government outdated, and rather advised that the German example and German accomplishments be extolled to the Austrian people by Nazi propaganda. He told

Neurath "specifically . . . that we neither wished the Anschluss of Austria nor intended to bring about the *Gleichschaltung.*"[80] As often before, during the political struggle, Hitler knew how to beat temporary tactical retreat.

Germany's "new course," was a mere sham. The *Third Reich* again adopted "new" tactics following the abortive July 1934 *Putsch*. Even then the change-over to an "evolutionary" policy was merely designed to create a false sense of security in Austria; it turned out to be a mere subterfuge until the moment when the *Third Reich* was ready to strike.

From the February Revolt to the Austrian Nazi *Putsch* (July 1934)

Immediately after the suppression of the revolt of the Socialist workers in February 1934, Dollfuss's position was strengthened by the three-power declaration on Austrian independence of February 17 by Italy, France, and Great Britain. Italy especially moved vigorously to shore up Austria's defense and strengthen the ties between Rome, Vienna, and Budapest. On March 17, 1934, Austria, Hungary, and Italy, presented by Dollfuss, Gömbös, and Mussolini, signed the "Rome Protocols"; there were three of these protocols, one on political, the other two on economic questions.[81] Both Hungary and Austria, prior to their signing, were concerned about the reliability and loyalty of each other. The question of Hungarian revisionism bothered Austria, the issue of Habsburg restoration caused concern in Hungary. But section three of the Roman Protocols relating to the Habsburgs stated that, in the view of the Austrian Chancellor, the question of restoration was not a current problem and that Italy and Hungary were definitely opposed to it.

1934 turned out to be a most troublesome year for Austria. On the heels of the fighting between the regular Army and *Heimwehr* units against the Socialist workers in February 1934 followed in July 1934 a second civil war, prompted by the Nazi coup of July 25, 1934, which climaxed in the assassination of Dollfuss. Mussolini dispatched troops to the Brenner Pass, thus sending a clear warning signal to Hitler that a German intervention in behalf of the Austrian Nazis might lead to a military confrontation with Italy and even war. The German government was compelled to disavow the coup and the Austrian government was able to suppress the Nazi revolt.

It was Otto Planetta who had fired the fatal shots against Chancellor Dollfuss. The death of the Chancellor who was refused even the administration of the last sacraments, occurred on July 25, apparently at 15:45 P.M. Kurt von Schuschnigg, Minister of Education in the Dollfuss cabinet, was appointed Chancellor by President Wilhelm Miklas over the telephone. The new Chancellor promised the rebels the freedom to cross the border into Germany provided that no human life had been lost. While making the pledge, Miklas was unaware that in the meantime Dollfuss had been assassinated. According to the report of the Germany Military Attaché Muff to the German Ministry of Defense on July 26, he himself had known for long that a disguised S.A. unit planned to break into the Chancellery at the *Ballhausplatz* to take members of the Austrian government prisoners.[82]

In the critical July days the new Austrian government maintained firm control over the armed forces; Secretary for Defense, General Zehner, had escaped imprisonment by the conspirators. The fight with the rebels erupted also in Carinthia, Styria, Upper Austria, and Salzburg; the military encounters in the provinces dragged on until July 28. The assassination of Dollfuss gave Austria a martyr, created a wave of sympathy for the cause of Austrian liberty at home and abroad, and strengthened the struggle for the country's independence.

The Aftermath of the July Revolt in Germany and Austria

On August 8, 1934, about two weeks after the abortive July *Putsch*, Hitler in a letter to Ministers Hess and Goebbels, von Papen, and the Office of the Secret State Police, ordered that neither Party authorities nor anyone else discuss, either on the wireless or in the press, questions on German-Austrian policy, unless previous agreement had been reached between the *Reich* Propaganda Minister and von Papen. This was to ensure a "uniform policy."[83] Apparently, the absence of such policy had contributed to the recent Nazi debacle in Austria.

On the same day, Hassel, Ambassador to Italy, in a report to the German Foreign Ministry referred to the purge of Röhm on

June 30, 1934, as well as to the Putsch in Vienna on July 25, which had doubled the impact on Austria. "Like a fungus wedged between Germany and Italy, it had caused a wide rift between their policies."[84] The "reverse" which our relations with Italy have suffered has by no means been retrieved. Even those in the Italian Foreign Ministry who have hitherto been outspoken in their friendship for Germany, were now profoundly pessimistic. Germany had wanted to solve the problem of Austria "regardless of Italian interests," in the interest of Greater Germany. Italy had long observed restraint. Only very recently, when the German pressure on Austria had threatened to prevail, had Italy made clear that she would defend Austrian independence: Rome would oppose all German attempts to lay hands on Austria. If by appointing Papen to the Vienna Legation Germany intended to pursue the designs which violent intervention in Austrian internal affairs had failed to accomplish, Italy would be found at her post. "Germany must seriously consider the consequences of a brusque action in Austria." Many Italians in all walks of life felt that French hegemony in Europe would be "preferable to German dominance which involved special dangers for Italy." This description of the prevailing mood came, according to Hassel, from one in an official position. He had also learned from a very well-informed private source, that Mussolini had been greatly affected by the murder of Dollfuss and, under the pressure of the pro-French clique in the Palazzo Chigi, was weakening.

Germany still had the chance of regaining Italy's friendship. The Italian Government envisaged itself as Austria's protecting guardian and hoped to obtain from Germany a non-interference pledge, "if only a short-term one, that is to say something approximating a non-intervention promise in Austria's internal affairs."

Though Hitler did not renounce ultimate Nazi goals in Austria, he made some minor concessions. Under the impact of the failure of the Austrian Nazi coup on July 25 and its consequences, the Führer issued the order that the *Kampfring* of Austrians in the *Reich* be converted into a Relief Society and cease to carry on political activities in the future. The Foreign Ministry copy of this order was provided with a note by Lammers that bore the following marginal note: "For purposes of foreign policy it would have been more effective to disband the *Kampfring* completely."[85]

On August 19, 1934, Papen, while in Berlin, wrote the "Guiding Principles for German Policy vis-à-vis Austria in the immediate future,"[86] stressing that these principles had been given approval by Hitler only a few days before, on August 13, 1934. The prerequisites for guiding German-Austrian relations once more to a "normal and friendly course" were for the *Reich* to avoid "even any appearance [!] of meddling in Austria's internal affairs" and for Austria "to stop the fight from Austrian soil against the National Socialist regime in Germany" as well as to restore peace with those sections of the Austrian people whose sympathies were with Greater Germany. To deal with the Austrian question was the exclusive concern of those persons whose function it was to conduct foreign policy. Party offices in the *Reich* were thus excluded from dealing with the Austrian issue. Similarly, no "Austrian fighting organization of any kind will be tolerated" if it attempts to intervene in Austrian developments; specifically listed in this context were the Munich *Landesleitung*, the Austrian Legion, and the *Kampfring*. A complete separation as regards the organization of the Party in the *Reich* and the Austrian Party was imperative. All persons, "compromised by having been leaders of the past struggle, were to be excluded from the leadership of the Austrian Party. They also should not be "rewarded" for their services by being appointed to important posts in the *Reich*, for they have committed "serious political crimes and murders!" The best thing would be if Austria would be given as much silent treatment as possible; this would block the work of counter-propagandists.

In the following conversation in August, 1934, with Schuschnigg and Foreign Minister Berger-Waldenegg, Papen, notwithstanding his initial difficulties in Vienna, adopted an aggressive line, complained about Colonel Walter Adam, Austrian Commissar for Propaganda, who had warned his compatriots that he, Papen, though now "in tails," could be expected to continue the "brown-shirt" policy, hitherto pursued by the *Reich*. While Papen reasserted the Führer's determination, "for the sake of détente in Europe, to respect Austria's formal independence," he also made clear that "now that National Socialism had taken possession of Germany, this ideological revolution must naturally [!] also have repercussions beyond the frontiers of Germany, especially in a country with the same culture, customs, language, and traditions.

One could not hope to dam the flow and ebb of spiritual struggles by barricading the frontiers."[87] He expressed concern, that if the present Austrian policy and the "severe persecutions" continued, "fresh revolts might perhaps result, responsibility for which the German government must decline in advance." He, Papen, mentioned in this connection also the persecution of those national elements who for 15 years had loyally and honestly advocated the idea of the Anschluss, but who had never been formally members of the NSDAP.

In his reply, Schuschnigg, according to Papen's account, strongly reasserted his will to preserve Austria's independence. He emphasized that, as a Tyrolese by birth, he always felt a special sympathy for Austria's German role and for his country's *volksdeutsch* tasks. Nevertheless, he was firmly resolved not to allow Austria to become "a colony and province of the German *Reich*. It remained to be seen whether the *Reich* government's promises to safeguard Austria's integrity at home and abroad" would be kept. Schuschnigg indicated that it was impossible to abandon the investigation and punishment of the actual instigators of the July *Putsch*, but also that he was determined to let the "small fry," "the stooges," and the "fellow-travellers of the action of the 25th" off easily.[88] Papen's over-all impression was that there existed in Austria an "abysmal distrust" of Germany and of any promises made by the *Reich* government. As far as political recommendations were concerned, Papen doubted that a fresh declaration by Hitler regarding Austria's independence would give any real assurance, since it would be suspected by all sides.

In consequence of Hitler's decision to shelve, if not completely remove, the former Austrian Nazi leadership, the latter was in a state of agitation and turmoil. This mood found expression in the correspondence between Alfred Frauenfeld and the Führer's deputy Rudolf Hess. In a blunt missive Hess reminded the former that the Führer and the German Party must have nothing at all to do with the National Socialists in Austria, "and warned of dire consequences," "severe punishment," and "even imprisonment," if Hitler's specific orders were disregarded.[89]

Hess assured Frauenfeld that the Führer and his entourage found it very hard "to adopt this harsh attitude, but Germany's vital interests are at stake. As you know, after November 19, 1923, the Führer took the decisions which led to an entirely new and absolutely lawful policy being pursued by the NSDAP in Germany, decisions to which he adhered and which were later to prove justified and to achieve success. Let me assure you that, despite everything, the decision now taken by the Führer in respect to National Socialism in Austria will make possible that one day all your wishes and ours regarding Austria will be fulfilled, and in a perfectly legal manner."

Among those pleading for a new "evolutionary" German policy toward Austria, avoiding revolutionary methods and resolved to shelve wrong tactics of the past, was General-Lieutenant Muff, German Military Attaché in Vienna.[90] In a major analysis of the policy and tactics of the NSDAP he concluded that the Party's struggle for Austria, while provoking ever sharper counter-measures on the part of the government, had led from constitutional to unconstitutional methods, from propaganda to terrorism, and had unavoidably ended in an attempt at a *Putsch* in the incitement to open revolt. The *Landesleitung* in Munich bore sole and full responsibility for the Austrian debacle and had furnished proof of its political ineptitude. But Muff left no doubt as to his own ultimate goals: "Should Austria in the long run remain separated [!] from the *Reich*, then the latter would be encircled, Italy would press on her southern frontier, Hungary would be completely driven into the Italian camp, and the Balkan states would lose their political importance for the *Reich*, and the *Reich* for them. An Austria lost to the German cause would, however, become a direct threat to the *Reich*'s internal policy, for she would constitute a breeding-ground for all the destructive forces desiring to undermine from thence the structure of the National Socialist state. The struggle for a 'German' Austria must therefore continue. What mattered now was first of all regaining a foothold in Austrian affairs, in order to stem foreign influences and by slow and hard work to recover lost ground." Once having discovered a clear line of action, this policy "must be pursued, not deflected by emotional factors." This very idea corresponded closely to Hitler's foreign policy thought on Austria after the July *Putsch*.

Just as Papen earlier had done, so Muff now pointed to the "tremendous amount of mistrust" on the Austrian side, which must be overcome. There were rumors current in Austria that the *Landesleitung* in Munich and the Austrian Legion continued to exist, though "in disguise." There were also fresh and alarming reports concerning the formation of an Austrian Legion under German leadership in Yugoslavia. In conclusion Muff recommended that the *Reich* abandon its passivity in these matters and "cautiously go over to an active policy" in the broadly indicated sense.

The publication of the Austrian Brown Book, *Beiträge zur Vorgeschichte und Geschichte der Julirevolte*, on October 3, 1934, saw the *Third Reich* partly at least on the defensive still. Neurath recorded that the Führer had advised that the publication be "ignored as far as possible."[91] The Austrian evidence appeared strong and unassailable, and, in any case, the Austrian coup was still too recent and the assassination of Dollfuss too vivid a memory to make any German attempt at claiming aloofness and innocence believable. Papen had similarly recommended that the publication of the Brown Book be allowed to be forgotten. But neither Hitler, Neurath or Papen was in a contrite mood, to the contrary, in a hardly concealed manner, they were in an aggressive state of mind. Neurath wanted the Austrian Ambassador in Berlin, Tauschitz, to be told bluntly that because of "misuse of his reports in the Brown Book, conversations could no longer be held with him." Hitler and Papen pursued another bizarre line, namely to shift responsibility for the abortive July Putsch to the S.A. and the followers of Röhm, who only recently, on June 30—well before the Austrian coup—had been purged. Hitler himself had given the cue to Papen when he informed him that the July *Putsch* "must be viewed in close conjunction with the Röhm affair."[92] Papen had willingly endorsed the Führer's thesis which tended to acquit the *Reich* government from complicity in the Austrian Nazi *Putsch*; he was quick to see the propagandistic advantages of blaming the murdered Röhm and his associates, among other matters, also for the uprising of July 25. As he wrote: "There is no doubt that there were very strong links between the Supreme Command of the SA and certain quarters here," though, as he conceded, "it would be difficult to establish the facts of the matter now." "It might at any rate be worth considering," he suggested to Hitler in his letter of October 4, 1934, "whether, in view of the publication of the Brown Book of various happenings which were contrary to international law, it would not be advisable [!] for us to make a statement to the effect that the *Reich* government had no knowledge of these happenings, nor did they approve them, and that they had long since been atoned [!] in full measure by the liquidation of Röhm and his conspirators."[93] Papen surpassed even Hitler by suggesting that the execution of Röhm, other alleged guilt aside, was also an "atonement" for the S.A. leader's, rather than for the Austrian and German Nazis', "sins" against Austria.

International Repercussions. The Question of the Habsburg Restoration

In the wake of the abortive Nazi *Putsch*, in late July 1934, on occasion of a meeting of Mussolini with Schuschnigg, Dollfuss's successor, in Florence, Il Duce asked the Chancellor point-blank what he would do if the Germans would repeat the *Putsch*. Schuschnigg replied that he did not believe that an open break between the two German states was likely, but did not entirely exclude such a possibility. But even if the Austrian Legion should be used against Austria, the Austrian government would be able to defend itself. The thought that Germany might intervene by dispatching her own troops, did apparently not yet occur to Schuschnigg. However, he suggested to Mussolini that in an emergency Italy's assistance, taking the form of an armed demonstration along the borders, would be of inestimable value. Yet he warned that for reasons of domestic politics a full-fledged intervention by Italian troops would be unbearable for the Austrian government.[94] Besides, Czech and Yugoslav troops would quickly follow suit. According to Mussolini, Schuschnigg could not count on Germany leaving Austria alone, but could under all circumstances depend on Italy's help; Italy was a great power, Mussolini proclaimed. The restoration of the monarchy posed no problems for Italy. The final communiqué of August 22, 1934, expressed "complete agreement" between Italy and Austria regarding the means for the preservation of Austrian independence and integrity; such preservation was in the interest of the Danubian region and of all of Europe.[95] On September 27, 1934, Italy, France, and Great Britain reconfirmed the Three-Power Declaration of February 17, 1934,[96] voicing their interest in maintaining Austrian independence in accordance with existing treaties. Austrian diplomacy would have preferred to secure a more binding policy statement, but had to accept what it could get.

In April 1935, the Stresa Conference attempted to coordinate more closely the interests of France, Great Britain, and Italy.[97] Italy stressed her opposition to the unilateral abandonment of all treaties, including the treaties of Versailles and St. Germain which virtually prohibited the Anschluss. The Austrian Government was pleased about the formation of the Stresa Front. But soon thereafter, on June 18, 1935, Britain and Germany signed a naval treaty which demonstrated Britain's political and diplomatic wavering and was a major victory for the policy of appeasement. It raised doubts about Britain's resolve to put a stop to Germany's contemplated expansion in Central Europe. Vienna's resistance to German demands was from now on primarily contingent upon Italy's assistance. Austrians and Italians closely synchronized their military plans to thwart any German military adventure aimed against Austria.

Italian help seemed the more needed since Yugoslavia in her general policy and her policy toward Austria veered increasingly to the German side. According to the Yugoslav Ambassador in Vienna, Nastasijević, King Alexander, before his departure from Belgrade in October 1934, had instructed him to inform Papen that despite Yugoslav ties with France, Belgrade would never participate in a coalition for the settlement of Central European problems which aimed at Germany's exclusion.[98] Yugoslavia was especially opposed to a Habsburg restoration in Austria—a first step, Belgrade feared, toward reclaiming former Austrian territory. In 1935 the Ambassador had suggested to Papen a secret military agreement designed to thwart a legitimist coup in Austria.[99] On October 26, 1936, Göring bluntly revealed to the Austrian envoy in Berlin, Ingenieur Tauschitz, which German army corps in such an event would invade Austria and informed him that the invasion would take place simultaneously with that of Yugoslav troops from the South.[100] For a time the French Government tried to overcome the objections of her European allies against Restoration, but in the end warned Schuschnigg against pressing this issue. On occasion of his visit to London, Starhemberg, who had come to endorse the legitimist cause, backed down after two meetings with Eden.[101] London apparently held that if Austria would only drop the Restoration issue, the Little Entente would be prepared to enter into agreements with Austria. When Sir Austen Chamberlain visited Vienna in April 1936, he recommended to the

Austrian government a rapprochement with the Little Entente,[102] by softpedalling the Restoration question.

The Restoration question was not the only issue separating Austria from the Little Entente. Hungarian revisionism was the other. The combination of the two blocked the rapprochement between Austria, Hungary, and Italy on one hand and the Little Entente on the other. To Hitler and National Socialism both issues were a godsend. They made it difficult, if not impossible, for these two blocs of states to achieve a rapprochement. On the other hand, Berlin succeeded in diverting Hungary's attention from Yugoslavia and in focusing her revisionist demands on Czechoslovakia and Rumania. The Magyar-Czechoslovak tension, nurtured from the *Reich*, always frustrated plans for a Danubian Confederation. Both the Austrian Foreign Minister Guido Schmidt as well as the Director of the Austrian Foreign Office, Theodor Hornbostel, blamed the Hungarian Government for sabotaging the Danubian Pact[103]—which in their view might have given stability to central Europe and fortified it against Germany. But other Austrians criticized equally the opposition of the Little Entente to the return of the Habsburgs to Vienna for the failure to create a Danubian Confederation.

At heart and by conviction Schuschnigg too was a monarchist. In 1935 the Austrian Chancellor established close contact with Otto von Habsburg who resided then in Steen-Eckerzeel in Belgium. At times Vice-Chancellor Starhemberg, leader of the fascist *Heimwehr*, also gave legitimism strong support, dispatching for instance in December 1935 three delegates to the Habsburg pretender in Belgium.[104] As Schuschnigg later disclosed, he considered the Austrian monarchists "100% reliable Austrian patriots,"[105] convinced opponents of the Nazis and of the Anschluss, who could effectively be used against National Socialism. As a pragmatist, however, Schuschnigg soon came to realize that pressing the Restoration issue was bound to produce only adverse repercussions. It was likely to generate hostility in Czechoslovakia and to bring about outright military intervention by Germany and Yugoslavia. He repeatedly warned against provoking the *Reich*. Even some French and British circles, which might have favored the return of the Habsburgs as a means of strengthening Austrian resistance and preventing the Anschluss, drew back when faced with the determined opposition of the Little Entente.

Thus Schuschnigg increasingly underlined his purely theoretical interest in the monarchic question. Toward German representatives and spokesmen he minimized the issue, though he insisted that legtitimism was basically a domestic problem, affecting Austrian sovereignty, and therefore to be decided only by Austrians. Czechs and Yugoslavs feared, nevertheless, the expansionist and revisionist forces which were linked with and supported by legitimism. They had much more reason to fear the threat of ruthless Nazi expansionism than the more distant and partly imaginary peril of Habsburg expansionism.

Germany, on the other hand, expected that the Restoration might strengthen Austria's independence and impede the Nazi thrust toward Anschluss and incorporation. Berlin was dead-set against it. At the same time the *Reich* had a stake in inflating the Restoration issue to divert attention from its own aggressive schemes against Austria.[106] It liked to present itself as an innocent party and the Schuschnigg regime of little Austria as deliberately provoking the *Reich*.

For years Nazi propaganda exaggerated the importance of the Restoration issue and inflated the peril of legitimism, while the Nazi goals in Austria were presented as being in accord with self-determination and democracy. The stress on the danger of Habsburg Restoration was also certain to arouse sympathy among the Little Entente states, appeal perhaps also to anti-Habsburg Austrian Social Democrats and to some circles in the West. In 1934, the French Foreign Minister Louis Barthou in Geneva gave to the Austrian representatives the admonition: "Ne restaurez pas les Habsbourgs!"[107]

Allusions to the Habsburg restoration recur continuously in the diplomatic reports and in Nazi propaganda. Schuschnigg was quite correct when he wrote: "The question of the alleged intentions aiming at the restoration in Vienna is like a red thread in the German anti-Austrian propaganda."[108] Berlin pretended to be concerned about it, though it is doubtful that it would ever have considered a monarchist *fait accompli* a serious obstacle to Austria's annexation. But the alleged danger of a return of the Habsburg dynasty served as a camouflage for making all necessary preparations for Germany's military intervention. It was a means of placing an intimidated Austria on the defensive and divert accusations of aggressiveness from Germany herself. Under the code

name "Operation Otto" the *Reich* readied itself to use military
force to prevent the Habsburg Restoration and seize the golden
opportunity of occupying Austria, all for the sake of allegedly
defending the Austrian Republic and republicanism, in addition
of course to defending German *Volkstum* in Austria. While aiming
at the complete reversal of Austria's domestic and international
status quo, the *Third Reich*, until the very end of the Austrian
Republic, had the impudence to arrogate to itself the role of the
self-proclaimed defender of Austria's "constitution"—to ward off
various threats, including that from the legitimist side. In the
order of the *Oberkommando* of the *Wehrmacht*, Hitler, on March
11, 1938, 2 P.M., declared: "Re 'Operation Otto': extremely secret.
If other means prove unsuccessful, I intend to invade Austria
with armed forces in order to restore [!] the constitutional order."[109]

Dr. Engelbert Dollfuss, Assassinated Austrian Chancellor, 1932-1934

Chapter 6

Austria under Schuschnigg. From the Austro-German Agreement (July 1936) to Berchtesgaden

Franz von Papen becomes Ambassador

Following the assassination of Dollfuss, Schuschnigg assumed the post of Chancellor to continue his country's struggle for independence. One day thereafter, on July 26, 1934, Hitler notified Franz von Papen that in view of the events in Vienna he had been compelled to propose to President Hindenburg the recall of the German Ambassador Dr. Rieth from the Austrian capital: without consulting Berlin he had consented to an arrangement between the Austrian cabinet and the insurgents regarding the latters' safe-conduct to the *Reich*. Thus, "without any reason," he had implicated the *Reich* in an internal Austrian affair. The Führer sharply condemned the "attack" against Chancellor Dollfuss rather than his assassination—which had aggravated the instability in Central Europe. Since he, Hitler, wished to bring Germany's relations to Austria once more back to "normal and friendly paths," he requested that Papen undertake the important task of serving "for a limited time" as German Ambassador in Vienna. As a member of the German cabinet, he had contributed to the creation of "the government of national resurgence" and had gained Hitler's "full and unlimited confidence."[1]

If the *Reich* seemed embarrassed by the Austrian developments and general suspicion of its own involvement in the tragic affair, such feelings had no lasting effect. When only a few days later, in early August, Germany's President Paul von Hindenburg died, the Austrian government sent only a chargé d'affaires, instead of its Foreign Minister, to express condolences. On that occasion State Secretary Bülow thought it fitting to take the Austrian government to task for having not yet issued the agrément for Herr von Papen, denouncing the refusal or delay as an act of "unfriendliness." The "generous [German] gesture of reconciliation

[!]," Bülow put it, had "obviously not been correctly understood in Vienna." If Vienna would consider Papen *persona non grata,* Germany would have to regard this as "a declaration of diplomatic war"![2] Browbeaten and threatened, the Austrians assured Bülow that the agrément would be granted. They expressed their appreciation for the attendance of von Papen and several officials of the German Foreign Ministry at the requiem mass for Dollfuss, held on August 2. This bizarre sequence of events—the assassination of the Austrian Chancellor followed by German accusations and Austrian expressions of gratitude for hypocritical German proprieties—were clear indications of the insolence of the *Third Reich,* of the extent of Austria's intimidation, and precursors of a bewildering array of puzzling German and Austrian moves in the years to come.

In many respects the appointment of von Papen as Germany's Ambassador to Austria seemed a shrewd choice. A former leader of the Catholic Center Party, he had on occasion of the massacre of the SA leaders in June, 1934, himself barely escaped with his life. He could not be fully identified with Nazi aspirations some of which he had dared criticize. On the other hand, he had played a key role in bringing Hitler to power. In the wake of Dollfuss's assassination and under pressure from Italy, the Austrian government procrastinated his confirmation as Ambassador. However, when the German *Aussenamt* disclosed its anger, Vienna finally yielded.[3] It may have committed a crucial mistake: With Germany being on the defensive, the Austrian government should have capitalized on the embarrassment and diplomatic isolation of the Nazi regime following the assassination of Dollfuss.

When Papen first arrived in Vienna, he was a lonely figure. According to his own account, his official reception in the Austrian capital was the coldest he had ever received. Nor was he more warmly welcomed by the diplomatic corps which consisted among others of the French Ambassador Gabriel Puaux, the Chief of the Italian Mission, Gabriele Preziosi, the representative of the USA, George Messersmith. The Papal Nuncio Sibilia greeted him with greatest hostility. Even Cardinal Theodor Innitzer of Vienna and Prince Bishop of Salzburg Waitz were "extremely unfriendly" to him. Catholics saw in him only "the wolf in Catholic garb."[4]

A year later, however, the atmosphere had considerably changed. The German Embassy in Vienna had become a social center, the most influential political salon in the capital. With great ingenuity Papen had created the impression as if he himself had virtually sought refuge in the ambassadorial post in Vienna. In the course of 1934–35 Papen succeeded in establishing friendly contacts and persuading some of his hosts at least of his entertaining best wishes for Austria's welfare. Having adopted novel tactics, he made the Anschluss problem appear as a distant, largely academic question.

Many still considered Papen illoyal, frivolous, and cunning. He himself was apparently insensitive to denunciations of his shady activities and aspersions on his character. He offered the cordial "Du" to Schuschnigg—which the latter, being the offer from an older man, as he later apologetically explained, accepted— in view of his eminent post and political role a patently unwise gesture. Perceiving the hostility of the *Heimwehr* and of Starhemberg in particular,[5] Papen sought to weaken the position of the latter by capitalizing on the widespread Austrian opposition to Starhemberg's pro-Italian stance. In 1935 Papen established also a covert link with Johann Staud, President of the Trade Unions, a former Social Democratic Trade Union leader, and with the Liberty League, a paramilitary organization. Papen frequently reminded Austrian Catholics, including Cardinal Innitzer, that he was a practicing Catholic and determined to save Catholicism in the *Reich*. He diligently wooed Austrian financial leaders and even some members of the *Heimatschutz*, and tried to persuade them that he deserved their confidence. In reality he was bent on undermining Austrian resistance and on preparing the day for an "evolutionary solution" of the Austrian question: this policy was equivalent to a piecemeal surrender of Austria to Nazi Germany. The *Third Reich* would thus obtain its objective without resort to war and without having to disturb the equilibrium in Central Europe by a sudden violent move.

Papen used to appear several times a week at the *Ballhausplatz* either to convey German complaints or because he was summoned to hear Austrian grievances; the latter usually centered on press attacks in German dailies, or were complaints about the support of illegal Austro-Nazi activities through the NDSAP, or even German public agencies, or related to accusations of Germany's aiding the Austrian Legion. While claiming that Austria was on a losing course, Papen tried to win over Austrian officials. Germany would know how to reward her friends and fellow-travelers. He bored from within and without to destroy Austria's integrity and independence. In early 1935, he bluntly told the Austrian Foreign Minister Egon von Berger-Waldenegg that with the help of English and French friends Austria would enjoy independence only a little while longer.[6]

Ambassador von Papen frequently returned for visits to the *Reich* and was often received by Hitler. The Führer gave him specific instructions, all based on the assumption that during the next years nothing should be undertaken which might embarrass Germany externally. The *Reich* would not move against Austria until success was assured. Germany, by all means, was to avoid anything which would give even the mere appearance that she wished to interfere in Austria's internal affairs.[7]

But interfere she did. Papen was told that the *Reich* would make every effort to bring help to the repressed and persecuted Austrian Nazis. The German Minister of Commerce Hjalmar Schacht was authorized to set aside 200,000 marks per month for this very purpose.[8] Soon Papen complained to the Austrian Foreign Minister Baron Egon von Berger-Waldenegg directly that he and the Austrian government in its entirety had adopted a completely negative attitude vis-à-vis National Socialist Germany. Berger-Waldenegg countered that the Austrian government would change its course the moment Germany would acknowledge that Austria was a visible and sovereign German state entitled to an independent existence.[9] Papen himself attributed Austria's willingness to resume talks with Germany to the recent German success in the Saar region. He had made an utterance, to the effect that after the Saar plebiscite the Austrian question should be dealt with from within Austria[10]—a statement with obvious connotations, though Papen promptly disavowed the remark.

A most revealing document from the pen of the German Ambassador was his report to Hitler in the summer of 1935, "Review and Outlook, one year after the death of Chancellor Dollfuss."[11] After reviewing the success that the Austrian Government had scored in proclaiming Dollfuss a martyr and in developing Austrian patriotism, Papen seemed, nevertheless, confident that ultimately National Socialist doctrine and faith would overpower the new Austrian ideology. But he pleaded for making concessions to Austria's "different political make-up" and to "the peculiar Austrian tradition." "Spiritual progress in regard to Austria cannot be achieved" by adopting a method of extreme centralism. Papen also maintained covert contact with Austrian National Socialist groups; he was continually thinking of ways and means of spreading the gospel of National Socialism for "national-gesinnte" (national-minded) Germans beyond the *Reich*'s borders. He thought it more propitious to make use of the ideology of National Socialism than of the centralized Party organization, though he by no means spurned the latter.

At times Papen admitted playing a dubious and deceptive role. This clearly emerged in his reports to Hitler and other communications. He saw his task in softening Austria's resistance to make her vulnerable to the underhanded tactics of the *Third Reich:* in undermining the sovereignty of the very country to which he had been assigned. The American envoy George Messersmith testified that, when once visiting the German Legation in Vienna, Papen blurted out: "Now you are in my Legation and I can control the conversation." "In the most cynical manner," without blushing in the least, he went on to reveal that Southeast Europe down to the borders of Turkey was Germany's "natural hinterland," and his particular task lay in extending Germany's economic and political control over this entire region. He disclosed that the incorporation of Austria was merely the "first step" toward this goal.[12] When Messersmith took him to task for playing such a dishonorable game, while being the accredited representative to a supposedly friendly state, Papen merely grinned. According to Messersmith, his attitude was characteristic of the "absolute candor and directness with which high Nazi officials spoke of their objectives." His treatment of Messersmith also showed the contempt of Nazi diplomacy for American diplomats and for American policy in general which they judged, not incorrectly, as being disinterested in the ultimate destiny of Central Europe and especially as incapable of blocking the *Third Reich*'s ambitions in that part of the world.

Austrian Nazis in 1936. *"Nationalbetonte"* and Trojan Horse Tactics

The Rainer report to Reich Commissar Josef Bürckel in July 1939 gave the following picture of the Austrian Nazi organization as it existed in 1936: "The organization is the instrument of the illegal struggle and the trustee of the idea of creating a secret élite organization . . . and, without making any compromises, it must be available in any emergency."[13] Besides, the German NSDAP was to take advantage of all political opportunities and use all legal means, without, however, revealing any ties with the illegal Austrian organization. All connections with the Party in Germany were to be kept secret, in conformity with the orders of the Führer. Auxiliary centers for propaganda and press, for refugees and welfare, etc. were to be established in the foreign countries bordering Austria.

The Rainer report disclosed the well-known dual tactics of the Austro-Nazis, the operations on two levels, the "legal" and illegal ones, above ground and subterraneously. During this entire time span, especially 1936-38, the Austrian Nazi Party was using men such as Edmund Glaise-Horstenau and Arthur Seyss-Inquart as "front" personalities. Dr. Seyss-Inquart came from the ranks of the Styrian *Heimwehr* and became a member of the Nazi Party when this branch of the *Heimwehr* became incorporated into the NSDAP. Glaise-Horstenau in turn was recommended by Papen to the Führer as a "trusted person."[14] Both Seyss-Inquart and Glaise-Horstenau were considered, and for apparent reasons looked upon themselves as "Nationals," pursuing the goal of functioning as conciliators between different *völkisch* groups, especially between former members of the *Grossdeutsche Volkspartei* and the Nazis. The former represented bourgeois circles and shied away from engaging in violent acts. The latter represented petit bourgeois and proletarian elements and the radical academic youth, and were prepared to continue to challenge the Schuschnigg government.

The rift between the two factions of Austrian National Socialism developed over the struggle for power and personal rivalry as well as over tactical differences. In this rift the Nazi leadership in the *Reich* and Papen in Vienna sided with the "moderate" Nazis in Austria, which included Seyss-Inquart and Glaise-Horstenau. The internal struggle of forces in the National Camp is clearly reflected in a letter dated as late as July 14, 1939, addressed to Marshal Hermann Göring; it was unsigned, but found in Seyss-Inquart's files and was unquestionably written by him; he voiced therein faith in *Grossdeutschland* "[Greater Germany] and the

Führer." Until 1934, Seyss-Inquart disclosed, he had conducted himself as a "regular member of the Party." He had paid his first membership dues, according to a receipt, as early as December 1931—though he apparently left open the question whether he continued to do so. In any case, he could hardly have done any more for the Anschluss than he did. As he wrote himself, "I told myself in July 1934 that we must fight this clerical [Austrian] regime on its own ground in order to give the Führer a chance to use whatever [!] method he desires. I told myself that this Austria was worth a mass." Deception thus was in Seyss-Inquart's eyes warranted for the sake of attaining Austria's union with the *Reich* under the leadership of the Führer! Seyss-Inquart realized that he was following a path which could "not be comprehensible [!] to the masses and also not to my Party comrades,"[15] since he apparently would have to camouflage his extreme nationalist and Nazi convictions. The important thing for him was the opinion which the Führer and the men close to him entertained of him! Seyss-Inquart was resolved to disguise himself as a "Nationalist" (*Nationalbetonter*), hoping thus to render more useful services to the Führer than by being an open follower of the NSDAP. Among those who were deceived in the process, were not only the "masses" and the "Party comrades," but also the Austrian Chancellor Schuschnigg himself.

Schuschnigg, Starhemberg, and Mussolini

Power struggle and personality clashes aside, Schuschnigg and Starhemberg differed substantially in their assessment of the magnitude and immediacy of the Nazi threat. In 1936, this difference was bared in their varied reaction to the politics of the *Nationalbetonten* (Pronounced Nationals), the National Opposition, plans for the strengthening of the Austrian army, and the militant propaganda of the *Heimwehr*.

Starhemberg was sharply critical of the so-called National Opposition and of Schuschnigg's frequently naive view of them. According to his later account, he mistrusted them, doubted their dedication to Austrian independence and sovereignty, and accused them of paving the way toward National Socialism. Their purpose, as he accused them face-to-face, was "nothing but tactics to lull the vigilance of the government and to gain time to prepare the next coup against the independence of Austria."[16] The leading representatives of the *Nationalbetonten*, General Major Bardolff, Glaise-Horstenau, Dr. Riehl, Dr. Langoth, and others attempted to induce Chancellor Schuschnigg to move toward conciliation and "pacification."[17] These men, largely former *Grossdeutsche* (Nationals), now either disguised Nazis or fellow-travelers, were ready to endorse the Nazi creed despite the risks this orientation entailed for Austria's autonomous existence. If some among them had reservations and second thoughts about one or the other aspect of Nazi "philosophy," or the methods applied in practice, the concept of the Anschluss which gripped them powerfully soon silenced all doubts.

Conceding Starhemberg's fascist convictions, fierce partisanship, impetuosity, and early dickering with German and Austrian Nazis, his judgment in 1936 on the new appointments from the National Opposition, was sound. As he wrote: "The word 'inner pacification' became the *Leitmotiv* of Austrian politics. In order to accommodate oneself, one invented expressions such as 'national opposition' or 'betont-Nationale' in order to deceive oneself that one had made a deal with the admittedly bad Nazis."[18] Since the Chancellor knew that Starhemberg clung to his view that every attempt to reach a compromise with the Nazis was equivalent to committing political suicide, he had to rid himself of his Vice-Chancellor before he could move on to the July Agreement with the *Third Reich*.

In the past Starhemberg had been Mussolini's personal protégé and a representative of Fascism and pro-Italian orientation in a country which had strong anti-Italian sentiments dating back to pre-war times and Italy's entry into the war in 1915 against the Central Powers. Italy's Ambassador in Vienna, Dr. Gabriele Preziosi, had been in close contact with the *Heimwehr* and Starhemberg personally; in his *Memoirs* Starhemberg himself freely admitted that he regularly consulted with him, at least twice weekly, to discuss matters which could not be treated in official diplomatic correspondence.[19] Another leading Italian official, Dr. Eugenio Morreale, was "in a way accredited" to Starhemberg personally.[20] After the July 1936 Agreement was signed, Papen requested that Hitler insist on the recall to Rome of "the most unfriendly" Dr. Morreale.[21]

The Italian Ambassador Preziosi once laughingly observed that Starhemberg seemed to follow the course of the Ethiopian War with almost greater interest than an Italian.[22] Starhemberg replied that he feared that Austria's fate could be decided in Ethiopia. He was fearful of the consequences of the African war for Europe and for Austria in particular and that Rome's preoccupation with Africa might ultimately push Italy into Germany's arms. After returning from the coronation of George VI in London, Starhemberg, according to his own account, informed Mussolini personally of his pessimistic report on Austria's future which he had written for Schuschnigg. Mussolini seemed to concur: "With Germany one cannot conclude a treaty. Germany will not keep any treaty, Germany does not want peace . . . Germany wants to conquer, since she wants to pry open the door to the Balkan and the Adriatic coast."[23] Il Duce, however, did take no action in accordance with these insights. The actual trend of Italian policy was toward further rapprochement with Berlin. As Starhemberg noted with some uneasiness, the Italian Propaganda Minister, Dino Alfieri, one of many fascist leaders, pursued in early 1936 the idea of improving relations with Germany at the expense of Austria. Still, when in 1936 Starhemberg took leave from Mussolini, the latter assured him that he could always count on his personal friendship and his goodwill for Austria.[24]

The *Third Reich* labored untiringly to undermine Austria's political structure. German diplomats as well as Austrian Nazis negotiated at times separately with Schuschnigg and with Starhemberg. Papen himself tried to drive a wedge between both men.[25] He enlisted the support of former Nationals who accepted National Socialism as the only feasible contemporary expression of the *grossdeutsch* concept and claimed that Hitler was moved by the desire for conciliation and peace. After prolonged internal quarrels and disturbances such thoughts gripped even many close followers of Schuschnigg and members of the *Heimatschutz*, as Starhemberg himself conceded. The longing among patriotic and activist Austrians to conclude at least an armistice, if not a peace treaty, with the *Reich* Germans was widespread. He who remained skeptically on the sidelines was considered a potential disturber of peace. As Starhemberg put it "The political principle which I represented became increasingly unpopular. The point of view of the uncompromising and unconditional struggle against National Socialism and especially against the *volksdeutsch* idea, so abused by National Socialism, was now increasingly rejected even by my most loyal followers."[26]

Like Papen before him, Seyss-Inquart was bent on enlisting Starhemberg's help on behalf of the formation of a "national group of thoroughly Austrian character and Austrian outlook."[27] Seyss promised to perform an "historic deed by making nationalism in Austria Austrian and independent from Berlin." In his early career Starhemberg himself had actively participated in the German national movement, having fought in Upper Silesia against the Poles. But his fascist convictions notwithstanding, he had in his own manner become an Austrian patriot. He reminded Seyss-Inquart that the difference between Austrian and German national conceptions was indisputable and that they actually stood far apart. "*Grossdeutsche* must strive toward some sort of link-up with Germany . . . , while I as a convinced Austrian reject not only every Anschluss concept, but also any inclusion of Austria into a *grossdeutschh* orientation. . . . For me the independence of Austria is the ultimate purpose, for you only a transitory state."[28] (On this occasion Seyss-Inquart still denied that he wished the Anschluss under all circumstances and assured Starhemberg that he would not tolerate that Austria be ruled by the German government or the *Reich* NSDAP.)

Another issue which separated Starhemberg from Schuschnigg was the question of Austria's rearmament. Schuschnigg favored a far-reaching rearmament, which would not only have a favorable impact upon the Austrian economy by absorbing many of the unemployed, but would also be the best guarantee for internal security and peace.[29] Starhemberg, however, feared that an army based on universal service could be easily penetrated both from the extreme Nazi Right as well as the Left and open the door to many unreliable, if not outright disloyal, elements. *Heimwehr* leaders such as Starhemberg, Stockinger, and others were doubtful that universal service would create a trustworthy army that could be relied upon to suppress an internal Nazi uprising or to loyally serve against the German *Reichswehr*. The socialist *Arbeiter-Zeitung*, smuggled into Austria from Czechoslovakia, entertained similar doubts, being concerned that the Austrian officers' corps would be infiltrated by Nazis.[30]

According to Starhemberg, Schuschnigg once even thought that it was *Heimwehr* tactics rather than Nazi policies which were responsible for the sharpening of tension in Austria, and accused the agitators in the *Heimwehr*, including Starhemberg, of militancy. "The fratricide war would long have come to an end, if one did not incite the Nazis again and again. Pressure produces counterpressure. On the day on which the [Austrian] National Socialists will be liberated from this pressure, they will renounce their terrorist threats."[31] This view was not a permanent element in Schuschnigg's thought about the Nazis, though the remark is indicative of his at least temporary inability to distinguish between provocation and a truly defensive posture and of his inclination toward appeasement.

The immediate cause of Starhemberg's abrupt dismissal from the government on May 14, 1936, was a telegram which the Austrian *Heimwehr* leader sent to Mussolini on occasion of the conquest of the Ethiopian capital Addis Ababa by Italian troops. Starhemberg, in characteristic hyperbolic fashion, congratulated therein Il Duce on the glorious victory of Italian weapons over barbarism, on "the victory of the fascist spirit over democratic dishonesty and hypocrisy and demagogic lies."[32] Schuschnigg had been unaware of this telegram. English public opinion was outraged; the protest of Downing Street, which made a rectification of the diplomatic *faux pas* strongly advisable, played into Schuschnigg's hands. The day after the dispatch of the telegram its sender was dismissed from his cabinet post.

Despite his past alliance with Starhemberg, Mussolini himself, according to the report of the Austrian military attaché Colonel Emil Liebitzky, was by mid-May ready to drop Starhemberg and shift his support to the more flexible Schuschnigg and to work toward a settlement with Berlin which Il Duce considered inevitable.[33] After Starhemberg's dismissal the *Heimwehr* still retained three leading personalities in the Austrian cabinet. Starhemberg, however, shorn of his power, was left with a mere honorary post, the control over Austrian sport organizations. Indignation and bitterness swept through the *Heimwehr* factions which were still loyal to him.

The above differences aside, the raw power struggle between Schuschnigg on one side and Starhemberg and the *Heimwehr* on the other was a major factor which had caused the dispute and had triggered the dismissal. In April 1936 and thereafter the *Heimatschutz* had put forward extremist demands, increasingly extolling the Italian fascist example. The *Heimwehr* apparently aimed at the political penetration of and the ultimate control of the Fatherland Front. It thus brought the rift between Schuschnigg and Starhemberg to a climax, burying the political dualism which had characterized recent Austrian politics.

Schuschnigg himself and others in the Austrian government entertained long only slightly fewer doubts about a possible détente with the *Reich*.[34] While they liked the notion of an "armistice" with Berlin, they were uncertain whether they could achieve permanent peace on the basis of mutual equality, sovereignty, and independence.

As late as March 1936, on occasion of a conference of the three Roman Protocol states, Austria, Hungary, and Italy, in Rome (March 21–23), Schuschnigg's skepticism shone forth in a distinct fashion. Through her delegates, Minister-President Gyula Gömbös and Foreign Minister Koloman Kánya, Hungary came out in favor of broadening the Three Powers Pact by having Germany and Poland join in it. Germany had previously rejected such a step, since it was not likely to further the *Gleichschaltung* of Austria or the incorporation into the *Third Reich*. Speaking for the Austrian government, Schuschnigg insisted at the Conference that a bilateral agreement between Vienna and Berlin, preceding the foregoing five-power link-up was not possible, since Austria, unsupported, could never achieve a satisfactory settlement with the *Reich*.[35] On the other hand, the Austrian government had repeatedly assured spokesmen of the *Reich*, including von Papen, that it would never conduct a policy hostile to Germany and would not participate in possible sanctions against the *Reich*; he, Schuschnigg,, however, rejected under all circumstances any German intervention in the domestic politics of Austria. In spite of differences between Vienna and Belgrade, Schuschnigg declared that Austria was prepared to seek a rapprochement with Yugoslavia; as long as the Austro-German question was unsolved and Austro-German differences continued, Austria was compelled to do so. The same was valid with regard to Czechoslovakia. Indeed, Vienna for some time had attempted to bring about better relations between the Roman Protocol States and the Little Entente. But all these endeavors had failed because of the resistance of revisionist Hungary to enter unconditionally into agreements with the Little Entente, the target of Budapest's territorial ambitions.

Toward the July 1936 Agreement

Though Schuschnigg made clear to his partners of the Roman Protocols Austria's difficult international situation, Mussolini, compelled by the exigencies of the Ethiopian adventure, urged Vienna to seek conciliation with Berlin. He claimed that the Roman Protocols would thus be effectively supplemented and Austrian independence be best guaranteed. Thus Austria was propelled toward the July Agreement of 1936 with Germany. Instead of a multilateral agreement which was to strengthen Austria's independence, the Austrian government signed, against its better judgment, as Schuschnigg subsequently conceded, a bilateral agreement with Germany.

Such an accord had actually been first suggested in a memorandum of the Secretary of State in the German Foreign Ministry, Bernhard von Bülow, on April 9, 1934.[36] This document already contained all the basic points of the later Agreement. It was rooted in the conviction that a radical and militant course aiming at the solution of the Austrian question "in the German sense" was not possible.

On occasion of Schuschnigg's visit in Rocca delle Caminate in June 1936, the Duce stressed the unchanged attitude of Italy toward Austrian independence, but added the important qualification that it would be easier for Italy to help Austria, if both countries entertained friendly relations with Germany.[37] In view of Italy's obligations in other parts of the world, it was necessary that Austria stood on her own feet!

In the postwar treason trial of the former Austrian Foreign Minister Guido Schmidt, in which he was acquitted, witness Kurt Schuschnigg disclosed his and the Austrian government's primary considerations in signing the bilateral July 1936 Agreement with the *Reich*.[38] Schuschnigg emphasized that Austrian National Socialism as such had not been the real danger to Austrian independence; it was dangerous only as the marionette pulled by the *Reich*. The real threat was never represented by the likes of Frauenfeld, Leopold, or other Austrian Nazi leaders, but by Hitler. "For he alone decides. Therefore a way must be found to pin down Hitler." One would have to strive toward the separation of Austrian National Socialism from direct control from Berlin and toward the elimination of German interventionism. As Schuschnigg continued, "I held the view that Austria could not safely survive another civil war or even only latent disturbances."[39]

Hitler himself had to be drawn into the negotiations. Though reliance on Hitler pledges was likely misplaced, Schuschnigg hoped that a treaty might be observed for at least up to two years, "by which time a different world situation might have emerged." In this political struggle Schuschnigg aimed at gaining at least a "breathing space."[40] Austria also hoped that the German market would open up and that radical excesses by Austrian Nazis would be curbed by the *Reich* authorities.

While the Austrian government moved toward signing the Agreement, it did so not without extensive soul-searching. Well aware of the risks it incurred, Vienna felt, however, that it had no real choice. Italy, it realized, had relinquished her guard at the Brenner pass. The terror campaign in Austria had grown more violent and become unbearable. Though Austrians mistrusted the leadership of the *Third Reich*, a treaty with Germany would constitute recognition of Austrian sovereignty and give Austria a firm legal basis in international affairs. Nazi Germany's notorious disregard for the observation of international treaties lay in the future rather than in the past. The non-aggression pact which the *Third Reich* had signed with Poland two years earlier was then still in force.

Other leading Austrian politicians and civil servants, however, opposed the Agreement and warned against its risks and pitfalls. As mentioned, one of its sharpest critics in 1936 was Prince Starhemberg. Looking back in his *Memoiren,* he blamed Schuschnigg and his advisors for political shortsightedness and shameful capitulation. The Agreement, he had warned, was bound to have disastrous psychological and political consequences, since it would deprive "true patriots of the enthusiasm and willingness to undergo sacrifices."[41] To the Italian Ambassador Preziosi, who at the suggestion of Mussolini asked Starhemberg about his reaction to the July Agreement, he gave two words to be conveyed to the Duce: *"finis Austriae."*[42] Preziosi left soon for Rome, being succeeded in Vienna by Ambassador Salata, who was considered by many Austrians a less intransigent opponent of Berlin than Preziosi had been.

Starhemberg aside, Ambassador Theodor Hornbostel, Director of the Austrian Foreign Policy Section, warned the Austrian government on July 12, 1936, the day after the treaty had been signed: "The value of the *modus vivendi* concluded at German initiative cannot be judged yet." It would depend on how the Germans would look upon the years 1933–36, whether they would consider this period as an end of the battle or as the beginning of the final assault. The motives of the Berlin rulers were obviously "to eliminate the tension between Berlin and Rome, to strengthen the position of Germany vis-à-vis the Western Powers and the League of Nations and to effectively demonstrate 'love of peace'." At the same time the loose character of the provisions of the Agreement did not prohibit the ultimate absorption of Austria. Schuschnigg himself did not consider the Agreement a permanent solution, though he, of course, hoped that Hitler would feel bound by it. As he put it succinctly: "He [Hitler] needed calm in foreign affairs, we needed primarily economic progress."[43] After the July Agreement the Austrian volume of trade with Germany increased indeed in a striking manner; after the 1000 mark limit had been lifted, German tourists resumed their travels to Austria, boosting the badly lagging Austrian economy. The cessation of terroristic activities had also a beneficial impact upon Austria.

The most important provisions of the July 1936 Agreement were the following: Schuschnigg would appoint a number of individuals who enjoyed his confidence but were also considered friendly to Berlin to cabinet positions. The Austrian government would also give the "National Opposition" a role in the political life of Austria, within the framework of the Patriotic Front. Austria agreed to permit some Nazi activities on Austrian soil to German citizens who were residents of Austria; these people were allowed to display the swastika and sing the Horst Wessel song.[44] The Berlin government and the Austrian Nazis looked upon the July Agreement merely as an entering wedge to be followed by other concessions and ultimately resulting in Austria's absorption by the *Reich*.

Most knowledgeable Austrian politicians, according to Schuschnigg, considered the Agreement a "necessary evil"; they entertained little doubt that Hitler would continue scheming to annex

Austria. But the Austrian government pointed to what it considered the positive aspects of the treaty: Hitler's assurance of harboring no intention of annexing Austria; the pledge by both signatories to refrain from interfering in the internal affairs of the other; and the acknowledgement that Austrian National Socialism in particular was exclusively under Austrian jurisdiction.[45] The foreign policy of Austria, Vienna promised, would be conducted by taking account of the peaceful endeavors of Germany. This opened at least a theoretical loophole for asserting Austrian independence in the event that Germany pursued a reckless and aggressive foreign policy.

Furthermore, the settlement between both states had apparently been reached on the basis of complete equality and mutual respect for the institutions of the other. The position of the Fatherland Front as "the only organ of political will in Austria" was not affected by the Agreement. Spreading illegal propaganda would continue to be prosecuted and punished. The radical National Socialist press such as the *Völkischer Beobachter* and Julius Streicher's unsavory paper *Der Stürmer* remained prohibited in Austria. Five German newspapers, including the National Socialist Party organ, *Die Essener Nationalzeitung*, were admitted into Austria, while five Austrian dailies were allowed to be sold in the *Reich*. During the next two years the document was frequently quoted by both sides, with each party accusing the other of violating the basic treaty.

Ambassador Papen who considered the Agreement his personal achievement exuded great pride. A year later in a confidential report, summing up why the *Reich* had concluded the Agreement in the first place, he stressed that Germany had aimed at removing Austria as a topic from the international agenda. She had wanted to stop the endeavors to restore the Habsburgs and in turn to prepare the propagandistic penetration of Austria by National Socialism. Along all these lines, Germany, by signing the treaty, had, in his view, scored notable successes.[46]

Officially, not only Vienna and Berlin, but Rome as well, and to some extent the press of other European countries, claimed to be satisfied with the July Agreement. Mussolini, who through his representatives in Vienna was closely informed about the state and issues of the negotiations, disclosed to von Hassel, German Ambassador in Rome, that the pact terminated a state of affairs which left Austria the football of foreign interests. The last obstacle to further betterment of the relations between Rome and Berlin had now been eliminated.[47] He, Mussolini, had recently reminded Schuschnigg that Austria was a German state, which should pursue a course parallel to that of the *Reich* and he had urgently admonished him to let the issue of the Habsburg Restoration rest quietly. There could, however, be no question that Mussolini, in spite of these diplomatic phrases, assessed the new power relationship in Central Europe realistically. Rome's influence had suffered irreparable damage, and Berlin's prestige was on the rise—which none could gloss over. The more surprising, however, was Hitler's personal response.

In his *Memoirs* Papen recounts that after having appended his signature to the Agreement in the Austrian Chancellery, he had rushed to the Embassy in the Metternichgasse and telephoned Hitler. The Führer's reaction was "most puzzling. Instead of expressing to me his satisfaction at the certainly not easy work of two years, he burst into ugly swearing [wüstes Geschimpfe]: I had ill advised him making excessive concessions, while the Austrian government yielded only in a platonic manner. The entire thing appeared to him a deception. . . . Apparently several highly placed Party leaders had criticized the document . . . as containing too many compromises."[48] After the initial disappointment of many Nazis on both sides of the border, many subsequently gave the Agreement a much more favorable interpretation, attempting to put the squeeze on the Austrian government.

Austrian and German political leaders continued to look upon the July 1936 treaty with different eyes. Austrians complained that the Germans did not live up to their specific obligations concerning the Austrian Nazi Party and all its activities as falling within Austrian jurisdiction, and excluding any interference by the *Reich*. Tauschitz, Austria's Ambassador in Berlin, considered the Agreement "the high limit of the concessions granted by us."[49] German and Austrian Nazis, on the other hand, looked upon it as a stepping stone on the road to further concessions which in turn would lead to *Gleichschaltung* or complete annexation, to the extinction of Austria's independence and the demise of her distinct political and cultural traditions.

In August 1936 already it became known to the Austrian foreign office that the notorious Theodor Habicht served once again as a close consultant to the German Foreign Office. The German Secretary of the Interior Wilhelm Stuckart had asked him to present a list of demands which *Reich* authorities in turn submitted as their own to the Austrian government.[50] Still, Austrian national circles were not satisfied with the progress made since the July Agreement. Glaise-Horstenau, "nationalbetonter" member of the Austrian cabinet since the July accord, was already in October 1936, so disappointed by what he considered the absence of meaningful implementation of the July Agreement by the Austrian government that he seriously considered resigning from his post if, as he wrote to Berlin, "he were authorized to do so."[51] This Austrian Minister evidently considered himself responsible to Germany! A clearer case of the sort of dualism which had emerged in Austria after the July Agreement and which was to plague Austrian politics until the very end was hardly imaginable. Since the German Party leaders, however, urged Glaise-Horstenau to continue to play his double role in the Austrian cabinet, he acquiesced and remained at his post. Papen and the Counselor at the German Embassy, von Stein, a dyed-in-the-wool National Socialist, continued also after the July Agreement their scheming against Austrian independence and attempting to bring about personnel changes in Vienna which they considered favorable to the *Reich*.[52] Papen even plotted to enlist Hungarian support in the event of a partitioning of Austria.

In the July Agreement Hitler had pledged non-interference in Austrian affairs. But on July 16, 1936, only five days after the Agreement had been signed, he broke his solemn pledge. According to the later report of Gauleiter Rainer to Reich Commissar Joseph Bürckel, some Austrian Nazi leaders such as Rainer and Globocnik, visited then the Führer at the Obersalzberg where they received a fuller indoctrination and became acquainted with his Austrian plans. The following day Rainer at a meeting in Anif near Salzburg informed all Austrian Gauleiters regarding the Führer's political instructions,[53] and Globocnik gave them organizational guidelines. The Führer had given Lt. General Keppler prime authority over the Austrian Party. Though Keppler was unsuccessful in his cooperation with Captain Leopold, he worked together with Rainer, Globocnik, Kaltenbrunner, Dr. Jury, as well as with the "nationalbetonten" Glaise-Horstenau and Seyss-Inquart.[54]

Continuing Disputes

Soon after the July Agreement, Papen, in a letter to Hitler, dated September 1, 1936, outlined his strategy for destroying Austrian independence: He pointed especially to the important office of the Austrian Minister of Security and his staff; changes in the personnel of this department were of utmost importance. "As a guiding principle I recommend on the tactical side continued psychological treatment, with slowly intensified pressure directed at changing the regime."[55] He, Papen, would attempt to obtain corporate representation of the Nazi movement in the Fatherland Front. For the time being he thought it better not to place National Socialists into top positions, but rather using "nationalist" personalities who had the support and confidence of the movement. "I have a willing collaborator in this respect in Minister Glaise-Horstenau." Close cooperation between von Papen and the representatives of the *Nationalbetonten* in Austria would help pave the way toward the undermining of Austria's independence.

But the radical Nazis were not satisfied with such a gradual course and likely slow progress. In January 1937, Captain Leopold submitted a memorandum to the Austrian cabinet which contained demands of the radical Austrian Nazis.[56] Though the cabinet did not formally acknowledge these demands, it nevertheless considered them. They contained an amnesty for all punishments or privations suffered for National Socialist or National activity or sympathy; equal treatment for National Socialists, including freedom of political and cultural activity; and abolition of all laws and sanctions used by the Austrian Government against Nazi activity. Furthermore, the memorandum advocated a broadening of the Patriotic Front to allow for Nazi penetration, an alliance with the *Reich*, the application of anti-Semitic measures, and an early plebiscite on the Anschluss.

The Nazis continued to bring intensive pressure to bear upon Austria. This was done on July 29, 1936, when the Olympic Torch was carried through Vienna. Similarly, the illegal Nazis massively demonstrated in February 1937, on occasion of the visit of the German Foreign Minister von Neurath to Vienna.[57] In November 1937 the Austrian police discovered the so-called Tavs plan[58] which contained instructions to create unrest at a prearranged time.

Among the concessions made by Schuschnigg in the July Agreement were the appointment of a "Committee of Seven," to discuss with Seyss-Inquart the wishes of the National Opposition and his own appointment as Councillor of State in July 1937. These concessions were dictated to Schuschnigg, as he later revealed, by the critical situation of Austria and made in the hope of at least delaying the Nazi thrust into Austria.

German National Socialism made not only political and military but extensive diplomatic preparations for the conquest of Austria. Berlin launched a vigorous diplomatic campaign designed to weaken Austria externally and internally. External support for Austria was to be undermined and the Austrian state was to be destroyed from within. Divisions were to be created among the states of the Little Entente, Czechoslovakia,, Rumania, and Yugoslavia. Originally all of them were opposed to the Anschluss. The ties between Prague and Bukharest—the latter no immediate neighbor of Germany—and those between Prague and Belgrade—the latter frequently more fearful of the Italian neighbor than of the Germans—were to be weakened. Only Czechoslovakia remained to the very end of the First Austrian Republic a decided foe of the Anschluss; but even the Czechoslovakians were misled when they equated the danger of a restoration of the Habsburg dynasty and of the Habsburg Empire with that of the further envelopment of Czechoslovakia by the German *Reich*.

The German government, as the American Ambassador to Vienna George Messersmith testifies, never hesitated to make generous promises,[59] often quite inconsistent ones from the national point of view, provided it suited its immediate purposes. At times it offered parts of Austrian Carinthia to Yugoslavia to enlist Belgrade's support for the Anschluss. To Italy it pledged that it would consider the Brenner Pass an eternal boundary between Italy and the *Reich*, thus writing off South Tyrol—an act of national betrayal. But most contemporaries, including Messersmith, judged Nazi pledges, including those relating to Austria's sovereignty and independence, to be quite meaningless, relying upon Nazi testimony itself: "High-ranking Nazis with whom I had to maintain official contact, particularly men such as Göring, Goebbels, Ley, Frick, Darré, and others, repeatedly scoffed at my position as to the binding character of treaties and openly stated to me that Germany would observe her international undertakings only so long as it suited Germany's interests to do so. Although these statements were openly made to me as they were, I am sure, made to others, these Nazi leaders were not really disclosing any secret, for on many occasions they expressed the same ideas publicly."[60]

Though Schuschnigg was a firm believer and relentless fighter for Austrian independence, his ideological stance toward the *Nationalbetonten* and in regard to the Anschluss was ambiguous rather than clear-cut. Glancing back, Schuschnigg admitted that for many years he had esteemed many "national-minded" individuals, but politically, he claimed, he had not trusted anyone.[61] Actually, he seems to have been much more gullible than he conceded.[62] His soft attitude toward the *Nationalgesinnten* was admittedly shared by many Austrians of Schuschnigg's generation and general political persuasion. The reason for this attitude was simply the weakness of the Austrian bourgeoisie and of its ideology. They lacked Austrian self-assurance, a combative Austrian ideology, and militant patriotism, and displayed a streak of disbelief and doubts about Austria's independent existence. On the Nazi side, to the contrary, there was an intransigent attitude, a blind faith in the Führer and the NSDAP, in Nazi philosophy and German destiny.

Austrian officials always stressed that Austrianism was Germanism, thus trying to ward off Nazi attacks from the *Third Reich*. Rintelen, though a Nazi candidate in 1933 for the post of Austria's Chancellor, considered Dollfuss, his political opponent, as a "thoroughly German" (durchaus deutsch-fühlend) man. Puaux, French Ambassador in Vienna, looked similarly upon Dollfuss as Austrian "attached" to the "Germanic fraternity."[63] And Secretary General Adam, head of Austria's publicity and propaganda bureau, in an address on April 15, 1935[64] said: "Austria is a German country, and our Germanism is as natural for us as the air we breathe." About the same time, Schuschnigg listed among Austria's tasks "its German mission."[65] On February 6, 1935, the Vienna *Reichspost* asserted that "Austrianism was Germanism of a special character."[66] Thus the German character of Austria was uninterruptedly proclaimed by the Austrian government long before July 1936 when, under the *Third Reich*'s pressure, it pledged to carry out the foreign policy of a German state. This was the policy of Schuschnigg as well as of Austria's Foreign Minister Dr. Guido

Schmidt who, despite his favoring close relations with Germany, retained Schuschnigg's confidence—as did so many other of the Chancellor's associates and confidants.

At the reception of the Austrian Secretary of State Dr. Guido Schmidt by the Führer on November 19, 1936—attended by Foreign Minister von Neurath, the Austrian Minister Tauschitz, von Papen, and State Secretary Dr. Meissner—[67] Hitler, as usual virtually monopolized the conversation; he focused on Bolshevism which in his view aimed at the domination of the world. Most menacing at the moment, he expostulated, was the situation in France and the Lowlands. Germany was perhaps not sufficiently consolidated to withstand the catastrophe of the spread of Bolshevism. Since the *Reich* could not detach itself from "our European community," he, Hitler, could not face with indifference the threat of Communist disaster in neighboring states. Once again he disavowed that Germany had any aggressive designs toward the countries of Central Europe: she wanted "only to ward off Bolshevism." Here was the perennial Nazi scheme of making gains under the camouflage of fighting against the Bolshevik devil, a scenario which cast Germany into a defensive role.

In this context two problems arose: Czechoslovakia and Hungary. He, Hitler, could not possibly allow Germany to become exposed to a threat such as arose from alleged Russian air bases in the German-Czechoslovak frontier region. He did not want war, but neither did he want Germany to be in a position like the one in which she found herself in 1914. While Hitler apparently contemplated a sort of European federation the members of which would be primarily Germany, Italy, Austria, and Hungary, he pointed to the risks of Hungary's "unlimited revisionism" which would alienate Rumania and Yugoslavia. These countries, however, were important "as outposts against Bolshevism." Hitler virtually prodded the Austrian cabinet to dissuade the Hungarian government from making extreme revisionist demands. As if Schuschnigg could achieve what he, Hitler, was unable to do! The Führer also impressed upon Schmidt that Austria consider withdrawal from the League of Nations; all authoritarian states should pull out from the League. Guido Schmidt, however, countered that the situation of smaller nations in regard to the League was different from that of Germany; Austria was still interested in preserving financial ties with Geneva.[68] It was also important, he remarked slyly, that some authoritarian countries remain in the League to defend their point of view against Bolshevism in that forum.

In the talks preceding the signing of the Protocol Neurath had expressed the wish that a National Socialist Party journal be admitted into Austria, possibly the *Völkischer Beobachter*. Though Schmidt insisted that the admission of this leading party paper was not feasible, he held out the possibility of reaching an agreement in regard to selected German papers, including Nazi dailies. Neurath also brought up the matter of "including the National forces in the Austrian bureaucracy" "to a larger extent and at a greater speed than hitherto" and demanded the cessation of "repressive measures" against members of the National Socialist movement. Subsequently he reported that in his conversation with Guido Schmidt he was struck by the latter's apparent "fear of the dynamism" of the National Socialist movement and of the huge resources at the disposal of Germany as contrasted with the meager ones of Austria—reports likely to flatter Hitler's ego. In the final commiuniqué, signed in Berlin on November 12, 1936, the two governments acknowledged that Communism was endangering the peace and security of Europe and pledged to combat communist propaganda in their countries. They further promised to collaborate in the Danubian region; both would refrain from entering into novel agreements in the area.[69] But the economic provisions of the Rome Protocols and their supplements were specifically exempted from this pledge.

After the return of Dr. Schmidt from his Berlin visit, Papen reported to Hitler on November 24 that the Austrian Minister had been especially "touched by the human and amiable manner" in which the Führer had discussed with him the Austrian question.[70] He allegedly was also impressed by his assurance that Germany wanted "nothing but security." In a parting interview Guido Schmidt had quoted from Schiller's *Wallenstein's Lager* Florian Geyer's "beautiful phrase"—'A death-blow to German disunity!'— as the hoped-for goal of his journey.

In a memorandum bearing the same date, November 28, 1936, the German Foreign Minister informed German diplomatic missions abroad of the visit of the Austrian State Secretary Guido Schmidt and of major topics which had been discussed on this occasion: among them he listed the Habsburg restoration and the relations of both German states with Italy, Czechoslovakia, and

Yugoslavia.[71] Neurath had reiterated that Germany was "absolutely opposed" to the Habsburg restoration. Schmidt had not denied the "anti-*Reich* attitude of the Austrian Legitimists," but had assured him that the question of a return of the Habsburgs was by no means acute. The Austrian government, Schmidt had revealed, "intended to rely heavily on Italy for support, as heretofore." Countering the German foreign secretary's observations that a pro-Italian policy would meet with little sympathy from the Austrian people, Schmidt observed that the dislike of Italians in Austria had definitely abated. Though he claimed that the Austrian government had through its good relations with Rome obtained the release of the South Tyrolese who had been imprisoned because of their pro-German views, he freely admitted that Vienna had not succeeded in putting a stop to the Italianization efforts in South Tyrol.

The Czechs, as Guido Schmidt further disclosed, had asked him to sound out Berlin whether it was interested in improving German-Czech relations. Neurath replied that this was only possible if the Czechs would relinquish their close ties with Soviet Russia and if they would accord better treatment to the Sudeten Germans. He again claimed that Germany had proof of the existence of newly Russian-constructed airports in Czechoslovakia. The *Reich* Foreign Minister also observed that the ties between Vienna and Prague seemed to him already close and that he expected Vienna to enter into even more intimate political and economic relations with Czechoslovakia. Guido Schmidt, on the other hand, was concerned about the existence of a military alliance between Germany and Yugoslavia, which made Austria's military situation even more precarious. Although Neurath denied the existence of such an alliance, he admitted that relations with Belgrade were good and that it was hoped that they would continue to improve. He had little interest in assuaging Austria's fears.

A few days later Schuschnigg delivered a somewhat startling speech in Klagenfurt to officials of the Fatherland Front, in which he pointed to three opponents of the front, Communism—which, he held now, represented no acute danger, Nazism, and, last, defeatism within one's own ranks. According to Schuschnigg's analysis, Austrian National Socialism confronted the Austrian government and the Fatherland Front as the main enemy;[72] Hitler clearly could not subscribe to such views. The following day von Neurath, the allegedly moderate German Foreign Minister, whose "prudence" Schmidt had praised only the other day, expressed his astonishment at Schuschnigg's remarks and asked Papen whether the Austrian Chancellor believed he could continue to take ruthless measures against National Socialism in Austria and at the same time follow "a joint course" with the *Reich* "in matters of *Volkstum*"?

Schuschnigg's Klagenfurt speech was, admittedly, an anticlimax to the Austrian Foreign Secretary Guido Schmidt's visit to Germany. At the reception of the Austrian President in Schönbrunn, given in honor of the Hungarian Regent Admiral Horthy, Counselor Stein of the German Legation made this very point to Schuschnigg himself. Stein reminded the Chancellor of his pledge to take members of the National Opposition—which actually consisted "mostly of National Socialists"—into the Austrian administration. Yet in Klagenfurt he had branded National Socialism as the enemy. Schuschnigg attempted to minimize the importance of the Klagenfurt address;[73] the speech allegedly was intended only for a small circle of officials of the Fatherland Front who feared that they would have to relinquish their posts to members of the National Opposition now called upon to participate in the government.

The virtual identification of communism and National Socialism in Schuschnigg's address was bound to arouse National Socialist Germany. But to top matters, Schuschnigg's Klagenfurt speech occurred at the very moment when Germany vigorously pushed the anti-Communist line by signing the German-Japanese anti-Comintern pact. The *Reich* was the more aroused, since the earlier Austro-German agreements, especially the Protocol of November 21, 1936, had underlined the threat of communism to all of Europe.[74] Neurath was so angry that he canceled for the time being a planned return visit to Vienna. He also asked the Austrian envoy Ingenieur Tauschitz, whether Schuschnigg's address showed perhaps gratitude for the recent friendly reception of the Austrian Foreign Minister by *Reich* officials. As late as February 2, 1937, Göring still voiced his disappointment over this speech of the Chancellor.

In his rejoinder to Stein of the German Legation, Schuschnigg insisted that the National Opposition had considerably improved its situation since the July Agreement.[75] However, it was difficult to deal with it, since it consisted of so many diverse groups which were frequently quarreling with each other. Stein, taking a line at variance from his superior Papen and from the *Reich* leadership of the NSDAP, countered that there was really only one large National Opposition in the country, namely the National Socialists who supported Captain Leopold. There followed an exchange focusing on the competency of Leopold, according to Schuschnigg, "a typical former non-commissioned Austrian officer," incapable of holding a ministerial post. But beyond it, the Austrian Chancellor charged that National Socialists demanded "complete control" of the government, and "this was simply not possible in Catholic Austria." Shifting then the discussion to Communism, von Stein in characteristic Nazi fashion returned to the favorite theme of the alleged danger of Communism in Austria, especially the Bolshevik threat in Vienna. That "threat," even in the form only of a return of Social Democracy to its former political position, was a mere chimera. Even Schuschnigg flatly objected to Communism being constantly portrayed as the great peril; one should not talk so much about the devil! The Austrian Chancellor reiterated that the Habsburg Restoration was no current problem. Regarding the Catholic church, he was successfully resisting its excessive demands, but he had to take account of the fact that a large part of the Austrian population was of the Catholic faith. In other context, in reference to the new *"Kulturkampf"* in the *Reich*, he objected that Austria be drawn into the ideological controversies that were a daily occurrence in Germany.

Stein's informal protest to the Austrian government was followed by a formal démarche of von Papen, which had only been delayed by the Hungarian state visit. He too lodged a complaint about Schuschnigg's Klagenfurt address in which he had denounced Nazism.[76] Still, Papen, as he reported to Berlin, had the impression that Schuschnigg regretted having expressed himself in such a way as being "misunderstood." But Papen also criticized the Fatherland Front which, formed during the years of bitter struggle against the *Reich*, was showing no inclination to accommodate itself to the new situation. On the contrary, "in alliance with black clericalism" it apparently was waging war against the integration of national elements into Austria's political life. The regrouping of Europe at a time of most serious tensions "quite

imperatively" demanded the collaboration of all German racial
elements; it would be a "sin against German destiny" if the
leading Austrian statesman considered the July Agreement "only
as a façade" behind which he would continue "a particularistic
Austrian policy." Papen emerged here, as also in numerous other
letters addressed to the Führer and to the German Foreign Ministry
as a single-minded diplomat-politician obsessed with the Anschluss concept, relentlessly aggressive and resorting to intimidation and embarrassment of his Austrian counterparts to achieve
his immediate as well as more distant objectives, the undermining
of Austria's independence and sovereignty. At the same time he
spouted pious utterances on collaboration, peace, and conciliation.
He leveled the usual Nazi invectives against Schuschnigg, gradually
escalating his propaganda campaign and accusing him of procrastination.

The Carrot and the Stick: Austria's "special mission"

Encountering this massive attack which left no doubt that the
Reich would not accept any standstill on the Austrian issue, but
was rapidly moving toward a dramatic climax, the Austrian
Chancellor felt compelled to beat retreat. He was well aware, he
asserted, that the historic position of Vienna had come to its end
and that the focal point of the German mission lay now in Berlin;
he fully recognized that Austria's special historic mission lay
within the framework of the new German Reich.[77] He was determined to place the political and moral forces of Austria at the
disposal of the German nation to help the Reich once again to
conduct Weltpolitik. This went rather far, though Schuschnigg
made this pledge contingent on two conditions. Since the Führer
himself had declared that the historic differences with France had
been settled, the future of the Reich could lie only in Southeastern
Europe. Austria was predestined for this mission by history and
natural capacity. She should therefore be permitted to retain the
character she had forged in the course of a millenium and "not
be yoked to any sort of centralized system, directed from Berlin."
Schuschnigg thus revived a pet idea of Papen himself, a lure
which the latter had repeatedly held out, the resumption of
Austria's traditional expansion into the Balkan. But he combined
it with a greater degree of Austrian independence from the Reich

than the NSDAP and Hitler were ever prepared to grant to Vienna. Schuschnigg made it appear that he was not unreceptive to the advantages likely to accrue to Austria from Germany's *Drang nach dem Osten*. He was willing to acquiesce to some sort of over-all German direction, but not to Austria's complete submergence and ultimate extinction.

In early 1937, glancing back, Papen held that both Austria and Germany had profited from the July Agreement.[78] In its struggle to free itself from the bonds of the Versailles treaty, the *Reich* had acquired new freedom of action. The "German question" had been "reserved for subsequent solution by us"! True, the Agreement was psychologically "not easy on our [Nazi] Party friends and the entire pro-German National Opposition." Yet the overwhelming majority of all pro-German elements realized the necessity of finally putting an end to the course which, on July 25, 1934, had turned to the disadvantage of the *Reich*. They understood that the German question in Austria could not be solved by the Austrian NSDAP. The question of influencing Austrian domestic affairs "would be solved only within the framework of the New Order in Europe as sought by the Führer." If the meaning of these excursions was perhaps not crystal-clear, it was, considering the deliberately nebulous diplomatic verbiage, characteristic of inter-office communications in the Nazi era, reasonably clear.

Still, Papen suggested a further "clarification" of the broad objectives of German foreign policy. The aim of the *Reich*'s policy could "only be the vindication of its historic rights in the Danube basin."[79] He was fearful of any reverses in German-Austrian developments. The leaders of the illegal Nazi Party must recognize that bringing about a new political relationship between Austria and the *Reich* was not their responsibility. They should "rather concern themselves with winning over to a pro-German policy as large sections of the Austrian people as possible to form the nucleus for the domestic National movement"; they will thus create, Papen anticipated, the forces within Austria "to be marshalled by the *Reich* when its dynamic power has been sufficiently developed to solve the problem."

In his report Papen looked both back to the July Agreement and ahead, to assess the distance traveled as well as the one still to be conquered. Once again he recommended to impress upon the Austrian Nazis the *Reich*'s priority in regard to Austrian policy and the necessity of their subordination. The report was also designed to strengthen in Hitler's mind the policy of "gradualism." But there could be no doubt that in the end Papen expected the completion of the Anschluss and even a sudden, explosive burst as climax to the policy of the "evolutionary solution," all admonishment to caution notwithstanding.

Papen assigned to Austria the special mission of serving as the *Reich*'s glacis from which to strike out toward Southeastern Europe.[80] A year earlier already he had made the suggestion of establishing in Vienna a Central European Institute which "under the Reich's intellectual leadership" would concentrate all economic and political resources on this goal. The most extensive preparations should be made for a new and close political relationship between Austria and Germany. Papen also recommended some decentralization which was to take account of Austria's historic individuality, and would allegedly be in accordance with the Führer's wishes. While Papen privately held that the struggle against political Catholicism in Austria was at least as necessary as in Germany, he warned here that ideological controversies in the *Reich* must be terminated. Then the solution of the "German question" and with it the penetration of southeastern Europe will become possible. What he recommended was by no means to shelve the anti-Catholic propaganda, but merely to "reduce" it to the level extant in the *Reich*. This was a stance which would establish in Hitler's eyes the political reliability, if he ever doubted it, of this former prominent leader of the Catholic Center Party. Papen's "moderation" in this and other matters always related to ways and means, never to the goal of the ultimate absorption of Austria by Germany. His political strategy was rooted in preference for "moderate" tactics, which had brought Hitler to power in 1933. The Führer was partial to this tested policy, especially after the Austrian setback in July 1934, when radical tactics had produced utter failure. Thus Papen's policy of "moderation" involved no risk of a clash with the Führer.

The question of the feasibility of the Anschluss in the 1930s was always contingent on several factors; not only on the political and ideological development of Austria and the growing determination and military strength of the *Third Reich*, but also on the international, primarily European, situation, the changing balance of power involving Italy, France, Great Britain, and even the other European states. Italy's quickly changing foreign policy priorities, the switch of Fascism's primary interests from Central Europe to Ethiopia and the Western Mediterranean and Spain affected decisively the chances of the effective defense of Austrian integrity and independence.

Göring Visits Rome

On January 16, 1937, in a conversation with the German Ambassador in Rome, von Hassel, Göring asserted that he would take up the Austrian question with Mussolini in the afternoon of that very day and insisted on need for "complete clarity regarding this problem."[81] Clarity could only mean that Italy should keep hands off Austria and recognize her as a German sphere of interest "so that even an Anschluss could be carried out if we so desired." Von Hassel countered that Mussolini already as early as January 1936 had in principle recognized the German character of Austria and the necessity of her becoming a satellite of her big brother. Mussolini's earlier policy regarding Austria had been pursued "in anger, under the influence of the events of 1934. Perhaps he had actually toyed [!] with the idea of making Austria an 'Italian sphere of influence'." Von Hassel, to soothe Göring, minimized of course the well-known past interests of Italy as protectress of Austria and her opposition to Germany's penetration of the area. According to von Hassel, this represented an earlier, by-passed stage of Italy's foreign policy; still, Mussolini was opposed to the Anschluss even today,[82] first because of Italy's concern for the Brenner boundary and, secondly, because of Italy's fear of further German expansionism, reviving the old Berlin-Baghdad idea and featuring also a German advance toward Trieste and the Adriatic Sea. All this haunted the Italians.

Göring replied that he was prepared to give Italy every possible guarantee in regard to the Brenner boundary: "If Italo-German friendship was firmly established, he would even go so far as to sacrifice [!] the Germans in South Tyrol: they could in any case not be permanently supported"—views which Hitler himself had expressed already in the 1920s. No change in the policy of Italianization was possible, Göring continued pessimistically, and the only remaining solution in the event that German South

Tyrolese wished to retain their national individuality would be re-settlement in the *Reich*.[83] In regard to South Tyrol, Göring and Hitler compared to von Hassel were prepared to pursue a soft line, a policy of acquiescence and appeasement vis-à-vis Rome. Traditional German diplomatic and national views, as voiced by von Hassel, showed greater consideration for this German minority than the allegedly radical national, actually Macchiavellian policy of the Nazis. Both Göring and von Hassel understood of course the tie-up between the Anschluss problem and Italian concern for South Tyrol. Göring also observed that a German advance toward Trieste would be "folly," since, with one stroke, it would create a unified Anglo-Italian front against Germany. Later in his conversation with Mussolini on the Anschluss, Göring, however, having grown overconfident and overly assertive, met with a rebuff. Hassel had advised Göring to promise Mussolini that Germany would never initiate any change in the political status of Austria without prior consultation with Rome. But when Mussolini asked him to put his views on Austria on paper, Göring refused to assume a "unilateral and . . . advance obligation."[84]

According to von Hassel's report—which itself was based upon Göring's account of his meeting with Mussolini—the Duce, "rather hesitantly and reluctantly," had begun by stating that he could not anticipate a change in Italy's Austrian policy, because he was bound by the Rome Protocols. On the other hand, he had been interested in learning the German conditions for really close cooperation between Italy and Germany and had promised that he would persuade the Austrian government to faithfully carry out the Agreement of July 11. According to von Hassel, Göring, while not entirely dissatisfied about his meeting with Mussolini, apparently had expected more.[85] In any case, he seemed convinced that in her Mediterranean policy Italy would remain opposed to the Western Powers and therefore German friendship would be indispensable to her. Göring discounted the risk of a possible leak of his information to Vienna; he had plainly told State Secretary Schmidt that the Anschluss, in any case, was inevitable and had added that if the Austrians did not like the word annexation, they could call it "partnership." Göring always took the lead in undiplomatic bluntness.

With the advance approval of the July 1936 Agreement Mussolini had made major concessions to Germany in Austria, but he did not yet wish to go beyond them, so as to make possible further German thrusts into Austria in the near future. Germany should abide by the key provisions of the Agreement, the recognition of Austrian independence. This Agreement was the basis for such understanding as had been forged between Rome and Berlin. Ciano, on the other hand, saw clearly where, given Nazi ambitions, the Agreement would lead to. He admitted that the German-Italian friendship like all such relationships rested on a row of pillars and would not simply collapse if just one of these pillars, the Agreement on Austria, collapsed. "Permanent value could not be claimed even for the Agreement of July 11."[86]

Clearly, in January 1937 Italian leaders had already written off Austria in principle, but they were not yet ready to abandon it that very moment. They conceded that both the Austro-German Agreement and even the Rome Protocols with their Italian guarantee to Austria were not written for the ages: They virtually gave carte blanche to Berlin, assuring themselves merely the right of being consulted in order not to be totally surprised at the moment of any major German thrust into Central Europe. They virtually assured Berlin that, if only certain technical formalities would be observed and no radical step be taken in the immediate future, Italo-German friendship would "weather even violent storms unleashed by Germany in and around Austria."

Papen Escalates the Pressure: Spring and Summer 1937

In view of the great likelihood, if not certainty, that Germany would no longer encounter Italian troops north of the Brenner pass on Austrian soil, it was hardly surprising that in the following months, February to May 1937, Germany began to mount a new campaign of pressure and harassment against the Schuschnigg government. On February 13, 1937, Papen reported to the Führer about the "growing approval of the concept of [Habsburg] Restoration" and recommended a German action program, but advised against a frontal attack upon legitimism and against disparaging criticism of the Habsburg tradition.[87] Germany should rather make use of the criticism of the Habsburg Restoration by French Socialist and Radical Socialist circles and by the Succession states, and underline the likelihood that restoration of the Habsburgs would revive Hungarian revisionism; the *Reich* should align itself with the powerful non-German opposition to a return of the Habsburgs to Austria. It was also important to point out that the Austrian restoration was being supported diplomatically only by a small clique of Austrian landed proprietors, old government officials, and the clergy.

On February 22 and 23, 1937, the German Foreign Minister Baron von Neurath visited Vienna. Neurath expressed the desire that the wearing of Nazi Party insignia and the giving of the German salute be permitted to citizens of the *Reich*, but Secretary Guido Schmidt refused to make a binding promise.[88] Similarly, Schmidt raised considerable objections to the display of the *Reich*'s flag other than on May day, in view of the internal political tension which still prevailed in Austria. In regard to Hitler's *Mein Kampf*, Guido Schmidt indicated that the sale of the book might be allowed, without, however, permitting window displays or other advertising measures. Von Neurath complained that not even 100 of the 500 refugees whose repatriation had at one time been promised had been allowed to return to Austria.

Among other divisive issues surfacing during the discussion was once again the Habsburg question. Neurath threatened a German military intervention in the event of a Habsburg restoration! Yet Schuschnigg did not give much ground, strongly asserting that the question of the form of government was exclusively a matter for Austria to decide. While conceding this point, Neurath recalled that the Habsburgs did not limit their political aspirations to present-day Austria and, in any case, bluntly told the Chancellor that a Habsburg restoration would be "the best way for Austria to commit suicide."[89] The Austrian government was thus given clear warning that under some circumstances Germany would use brute force against Austria and would terminate her independence. Faced with such a threat, how safe could Austria feel even if she completely suppressed the legitimist movement? On the other hand, trying to blunt Schuschnigg's criticism of some German utterances on the Anschluss, von Neurath assured him that use of force against Austria was out of the question; one should not attach great weight to such belligerent remarks, "for Göring and company are not taken seriously by anyone."

To Neurath's query how the Austrian Chancellor envisaged the future development of German-Austrian developments,

Schuschnigg replied that, while maintaining the complete independence of Austria, he desired close ties with the German *Reich* in the military field as well as in the areas of foreign and commercial policy, and in the judicial sphere. Schuschnigg no doubt talked with tongue in cheek. He must have understood that such close ties on all these levels were bound to lead to the early extinction of the Austrian state. When Neurath called Schuschnigg's attention to the alleged continued persecution of Austrian National Socialism, the Chancellor recalled his recent meeting with Captain Leopold, the representative of the Austrian National Socialist Party, and his endeavors to include National Socialists in the government; he pointed, however, to the difficulties of erasing the memory of the severe conflicts after the assassination of Chancellor Dollfuss.[90]

But the "moderate" Neurath left no doubt about the *Reich*'s ultimate goals concerning Austria. Germany would never sanction a historical development for Austria which would result in the permanent separation of Austria comparable to that of the Netherlands and of Switzerland from the German body politic, since it would weaken the position of the German nation in Europe!

The departure of Neurath was accompanied by an organized mass demonstration by the Fatherland Front—designed to counterbalance the Nazi demonstration a few days earlier when the German foreign minister had arrived in Vienna. In his report to Hitler, Papen later tried to minimize the scope of the anti-Nazi demonstration and once more laid down his program, stressing the need for the stabilization of the Rome-Berlin axis and for inducing the Austrian government to make concessions. He also emphasized "the consistent progress" of the National Opposition and the continuing penetration of Austria by National Socialist ideology. All this was the prerequisite for the "historic progress of the German question."[91] Like the Communists, the Nazis frequently resorted to "Aesopian" language to camouflage their ultimate goals.

Papen gave a full assessment of the situation in Austria, of her prospects and of German policy toward Austria in the following reports covering the months of March to May 1937. In his letter to the German Foreign Ministry dated March 13, 1937, he referred to alleged attempts of Richard Schmitz, the mayor of Vienna, to abandon the pro-German policy and rally all Austrians, including the Socialists, under the banner of a Popular Front Government. As against this scheme Germany had "only the course of supporting the Schuschnigg government—even though we do not like it." Still, Schuschnigg was prepared to continue the policy of pacification toward the National forces. Yet, as Papen pointed out, Schuschnigg stood "between the devil and the deep blue sea," and criticism of Austrian conditions by the German press only weakened the position of the Austrian Chancellor. Since in Papen's eyes Schuschnigg represented the lesser evil, he went so far as to demand that the policy of pinpricks against Schuschnigg be stopped. Most importantly, the "illegal Party must repeatedly be convinced that the ultimate decision with regard to Austria lies outside of Austria," namely with Hitler; the Austrian Party must be persuaded that it played "only a passive role" and that "its first duty is not to disturb the European policy of the Führer." There were too many offices in the *Reich* which concerned themselves with Austrian policy.

In April 1937 Papen reported of two sets of instructions of the Vienna government to the Austrian Minister in London which he had gotten hold of through devious means. According to these instructions, dated April 4, and 15, 1937, Vienna was endeavoring to obtain from London and Paris broader guarantees in regard to her sovereignty.[92-93] While the Italian government underlined that the Vienna cabinet had to avoid anything which might impair the political effectiveness of the Berlin-Rome axis, the Austrian government opposed these arguments: adherence to the course of the July Agreement of 1936, it insisted, was virtually impossible, since the NSDAP constantly and systematically interfered in the internal affairs of Austria and since the Party, a devotee of totalitarian philosophy, struggled against the Catholic church.

Austria's Defensive Policy and Germany's Dissatisfaction and Threats.

The Austrian position had indeed crystallized in the two foregoing documents cited by Papen. According to the first communication (April 4), the Austrian Ambassador in London was to inform the British Foreign Secretary in greatest confidence that Vienna would greatly value London's efforts to secure a lasting peace in the Danubian region.[94] An effective British guarantee for Europe in its entirety would meet with the full understanding and energetic support on the part of Vienna. The British Foreign Secretary was to be reminded of Austria's dependence upon Italy in regard to the preservation and guarantee of her political independence and territorial integrity. But if Britain and France would give effective guarantees on behalf of Austrian independence, Austria would modify her foreign policy, taking account of the West's position. Here was a reminder to London and Paris that Austria's refusal to endorse sanctions against Italy on account of her attack against Ethiopia had very pragmatic rather than ideological roots.

Austria turned to the West when it began to doubt the firmness of Italy's commitment to her independence. In the instruction to the Austrian Ambassador in Rome, Vienna wanted the Italian government to know of the growing rift between Austria and the *Reich* in general and in the interpretation of the July Agreement in particular; Rome was warned that Berlin might denounce the Agreement.[95] In striking departure from its usual compliant manner of treating the Italian government, Vienna noted "with astonishment" the attitude of Rome toward the problem of Czechoslovakia and of the Danubian area, since it extensively deviated from the principles of the Rome Protocols of 1934 and 1936. Realizing that it had little to lose, Vienna concluded bluntly: "The Federal Government must absolutely insist that the Royal and Imperial Italian Government disassociate itself unequivocally from the political objectives of German National Socialism with regard to the Danubian area and adopt a clear and well defined attitude toward the individual states." Vienna had increasingly questioned the Western Powers' attitude toward Austria; now it questioned also Rome's steadfastness as an ally. Indeed, at the very time Mussolini urged Austria to yield to German demands, he warned her against a monarchist restoration[96] or—an almost opposite ideological course—orienting Austrian policy toward Prague or Paris, and establishing a Popular Front government at home; this, he unmistakably threatened, would lead to his taking a stand against Austria. Yet Austria feared little Mussolini's opposition. What she urgently needed was Mussolini's active support; his mere lack of aid would place her in a quandary. Paralleling Mussolini's new stance, Ciano, in speeches in the Italian Chamber, repudiated the idea that the Austrian question could ever disturb the Italo-German friendship.

On May 26, 1937, Papen reported to Hitler a conversation with Guido Schmidt after his return from England, where he had represented Austria in the coronation ceremonies, and from France.[97] It had not been Schmidt's intention, the Austrian Secretary had assured him, to obtain either in London or Paris political guarantees regarding Austria's independence; he had merely wanted to ascertain the extent of the West's interest in the problem of Central Europe. Schmidt revealed to Papen, rather unwisely, that Eden had been particularly pleased that Austria did not ask for commitments of any kind from third countries, but had left no doubt that the Austrian question was arousing England's "keenest interest." In Paris Schmidt had maintained that German-Austrian relations would become normalized, that in any case these relations were "a family matter," which the French, therefore, should refrain from criticizing. Schmidt was apparently on the defensive, having learned that the Führer himself had expressed disapproval of his policies; he also assured von Papen that an English informant's adverse report about him, which had reached Berlin, was a forgery, that the alleged instructions of his to the Austrian Minister in London had never been issued.

It was clear that the highest German authorities took a critical view of Guido Schmidt's attempts to enlist England and France on behalf of Austria, though nothing less should have been expected of Austria's foreign minister. The German officials were well aware that Schmidt's attempts had failed and also that Austria was gradually abandoned by her Italian friend. Thus Papen did not hesitate to browbeat the Austrian Secretary. Papen presented to him "very seriously the Führer's interpretation of the sabotage of the policy of pacification": "I [Papen] said that this constant poisoning of the atmosphere must be stopped at once; otherwise, through some unforeseen incident an explosion would occur, the effect of which on Austria no one could predict." Schmidt and Schuschnigg should not "depend on the possibility that at such a moment the British government would actively intervene on Austria's behalf." Although Schmidt's London impressions in this connection may have been encouraging, the *Reich* government, according to Papen, considered the evolutionary solution of the

Central European problem "a question in which it would not tolerate any interference from England."[98]

The lines were sharply drawn, and the intended victim, Austria, was no longer kept in doubt as to its chances for survival. The date of its demise was not yet set, but Papen made no secret that he wished to move it closer. Germany, he vaguely promised, would not suddenly eliminate Austria; but Vienna should not expect to continue traveling *ad infinitum* on its separate road, since this went counter to the principles of the July Agreement.

The foregoing document, as numerous others, disclosed the cruel frankness of Nazi "diplomacy." The very phraseology used in the *Third Reich*, its hardly concealed arrogance, if not outright brutality, revealed clearly its aggressive intentions and it disposition to ignore traditional international law; but the scarcely disguised undiplomatic language still deceived some foreign politicians, usually those of an appeasing bent, who were reluctant to come to grips with ugly reality and preferred to be hoodwinked. These politicians looked upon Hitler as a German leader in traditional German garb, as another Bismarck. They claimed to understand Hitler and the Nazi philosophy and language better than the Führer himself did. They ignored that when Hitler spoke of a "solution" of the Austrian question, he meant a "final solution" comparable to that of the so-called Jewish problem.

In his dealings with the Austrian Chancellor, Papen continued on the road of intimidation and pressure tactics and of rudely offensive talk. On May 26 he reported to the Führer that, "in accordance with instructions," he had warned Schuschnigg that he, Hitler, had "given serious thought to the question whether in view of the many incidents that had taken place in Austria . . . the retention of a German Ambassador on special mission in Vienna was still warranted."[99] The Austrian political machinery created in 1934 for the purpose of suppressing National Socialism had remained intact. If the policy of insults and rude rebuffs to the interests and symbols of the *Reich* would continue, it "would require only another incident to touch off an explosion." While Hitler was very "anxious to preserve peace as well as to promote the development of German-Austrian relations by evolutionary means," there was a limit to these endeavors, for the Führer "could not tolerate the activities of an anti-German minority in

Austria, which poured ridicule on everything that was sacred to Germandom."[100]

Schuschnigg, according to von Papen, replied that he was fully aware of the "gravity" of the situation. Upon conclusion of the July Agreement it had been his earnest intention to restore in as short a time as possible the former close and friendly relations with Germany. If he had failed therein, then the growing radicalism of the Austrian National Socialists and the reaction it provoked in the Fatherland Front were to blame as well as the church controversy in the *Reich*. Notwithstanding the circumstance that Germany through the July Agreement had acknowledged that Austrian National Socialism was an internal Austrian affair, German authorities had never ceased to exert a continuing influence on it. He had been informed that the Austrian Nazi leader Captain Leopold had only recently been ordered to report to Minister President Göring to receive instructions for a more aggressive course of action. While Papen rejected this interpretation, Schuschnigg insisted that, whatever the attitude and policy of the Führer toward Austria were, the Austrian government knew from numerous documents and communications that had fallen into its hands that the view was widely held in Party circles, that German troops would "soon march into Austria and that such a solution is being urged."[101]

Faced with Papen's, respectively Hitler's, threats against Austria, Schuschnigg stood his ground. But he had to strike a conciliatory note. Thus he expressed his serious intention to improve relations with the *Reich* and to enable the National Opposition to collaborate with the Austrian government. Papen concluded by expressing the opinion that at present the Austrian government would probably not publish the embarrassing material which it had seized in the offices of the Nazi Party in Vienna. These finds included records of conversations of Himmler with the Austrian Nazi leaders Leopold and Kaltenbrunner and threatened to explode the myth that Austrian National Socialism had no foreign master.

There was no end to further "incidents." About mid-June a group of Austrian industrialists were invited to Berlin and met Hitler and Göring. The latter stressed that it was impossible for the German people to continue to live in a politically dispersed manner. A *"Zusammenschluss"* (link-up) of the German people of Central Europe inhabiting different regions was necessary; one must create *faits accomplis*. Informed of these developments through Ambassador Tauschitz, Schuschnigg decided that the journey of the industrialists be abruptly discontinued.[102] When on May 26, 1937, the Italian Ambassador in Vienna, Salata, had inquired of Papen whether he would remain at his post, the latter replied evasively but pointed out that, unless the Austrian atmosphere would be cleared up and the poisonous air hovering over it dispelled, the future of the Berlin-Rome axis would be adversely affected. Such pressures were designed to make the Italian government choose between Berlin and Vienna.[103] Similarly pessimistic were the accounts of Hitler's moods rendered by Papen to the French Ambassador in Berlin, François-Poncet and to the Austrian Ambassador in Berlin Ingenieur Tauschitz. As the latter reported, Papen had revealed that Hitler was "under the possibly worst influence" of Party leaders who advocated an armed intervention in Austria; still, through forcible intercession a final solution could be reached within as few as three days.

Schuschnigg's attempts to bring about a detente during the summer of 1937 resulted from mounting German pressure. He well understood the need for delaying tactics, for avoiding giving Hitler an occasion for venting his pent-up fury and starting a chain of events bound to lead to confrontation and surrender. On the other hand, he had relinquished his earlier belief that German and Austrian National Socialism could be virtually kept apart and that it was possible to come to terms with the German Nazis.

After returning from Berlin in July 1937, Papen encouraged Seyss-Inquart to take an active part in Austria's political life. It was Papen's support of Seyss-Inquart which precipitated the break in relations between the radical Austrian Nazis and the German Embassy. The radicals accused Papen of being an intrigant, of believing that Austrian affairs could be straightened out with the help of the "National Opposition" instead of by Schuschnigg's overthrow, and he was advised to "vanish" from the scene.[104] Schuschnigg was well aware of these internal Nazi feuds on which he hoped to capitalize when he had appointed Seyss in June 1937 as State Councilor. The appointment had made a favorable impression in the *Reich*. In July 1937, during Seyss's visit to Berlin, where he met Göring and Hess, he asked that demands for the legalization of Austrian National Socialism as a

Party be postponed; as individuals, however, Austrian National Socialists should become politically active without delay. Seyss-Inquart wanted that German Party authorities guarantee the "independence" of the Austrian Nazis who were to occupy important posts in the Austrian administration.[105] It was rather obvious that all those who relied or pretended to rely on German pledges had an extraordinary talent for delusion and self-deception.

From October to December 1937. The Inadequacy of Austrian "Passivity"

In a report of October 7, 1937, to the German Foreign Ministry, the German chargé d'affaires in Austria, von Stein, referred to the meeting of Chancellor Schuschnigg with the Czechoslovak Prime Minister Hodža. According to this report, Schuschnigg spoke not only of the necessity of close economic cooperation of the countries of the Little Entente with Austria and Hungary, but also lent a willing ear to Hodža's plea that at the impending meeting in Budapest the Chancellor champion the improvement of relations with the Little Entente. Guido Schmidt, on the other hand, differently from Schuschnigg, always held that close ties with Czechoslovakia, which was politically vulnerable, were dangerous for Austria; the Austrian Foreign Minister rather favored that Austria endorse the Swiss pattern of international politics, non-alignment and neutrality, in close relationship with that country and also with Hungary. Guido Schmidt's orientation, Stein held, was fundamentally West European, but was not pro-Czech.[106]

To Stein it was clear that the Schuschnigg government continued "to travel along several tracks. Fine words and many a phrase feigning sympathy for Germanism cannot conceal that fact." The strengthening of German-Italian relations, instead of inducing Herr Schuschnigg to adopt a line of the Berlin-Rome Axis, has "rather added to his apprehensions concerning what is most important to him, Austrian independence." "Being of Slovene ancestry and from the pro-Habsburg military caste, and educated by the clergy, he [Schuschnigg] does not find it too difficult to pursue rather openly a policy of security directed against the *Reich*, since he is connected with all the forces here working against the *Reich*. Besides the Vatican and France, Czechoslovakia too is one of these forces."

According to von Stein, the Austrian National Socialists had the will to hold out despite all hardships. But in the age of machine guns and light armored cars, the Austrian NSDAP must reject the idea of an armed uprising. While Schuschnigg struggled against National Socialism, he had tolerated Legitimism, which had undoubtedly gained ground. The theme had always been the same: the restoration of the monarchy will bring Austria not only rescue from National Socialism but will also generate economic recovery. Schuschnigg probably hoped to see the legitimist movement in Austria and possibly also in neighboring Hungary so strengthened that outside influences could no longer block it.

On October 22, 1937, Stein recorded a conversation with Minister von Glaise-Horstenau. This representative of the *Nationalbetonten* in the Austrian Cabinet, had apparently no compunction to disclose his conversation with the Austrian Chancellor—a measure of the dubious role he and like-minded leaders of the National Opposition played. As Stein recounted, "Minister von Glaise-Horstenau called on me today and said confidentially that in the last few days he had obtained a shocking insight into the Federal Chancellor's political mentality."[107] Schuschnigg had stated "that, from the point of view of foreign as well as domestic policy, National Socialism was the enemy of peaceful developemnt in Austria. The July Agreement had not fulfilled his expectations: the establishment of a relatively close cooperation with the *Reich* in foreign affairs, and the maintenance of absolute freedom to pursue an entirely independent Austrian—meaning clerical and legitimist—policy in domestic affairs. The Federal Chancellor then stated with relative frankness that he had set his hopes on a new confederation in Central Europe." When Glaise-Horstenau expressed grave misgivings about Schuschnigg's plans, he was assured that such a policy would by no means be directed against the *Reich*; perhaps after the formation of a confederation with several states in Central Europe, first excluding Germany, it would even be easier to arrive at a compromise with the *Reich* along the lines of the pre-war situation. Glaise-Horstenau told Stein that, as Berlin was well aware, he was not clinging to his post and would rather resign from it today than tomorrow. "I asked him to carry on for the sake of the cause; only in that way might he still exert some influence on the course of events and at least keep us informed of possible developments."

What a spectacle! The Austrian Minister ran to the German Embassy to complain about his Chief, only to be persuaded to hold on to his post and continue spying on the Austrian cabinet! What really did "shock" Glaise-Horstenau about Schuschnigg? It was the plan of a Central European Confederation partly reminiscent of the old Habsburg Empire, though the Chancellor stressed that Austrian policy would not be directed against the *Reich*. Apparently, it was Schuschnigg's goal of a fully independent Austrian existence which aggrieved Glaise-Horstenau; in defense of this goal the Austrian Chancellor was willing to establish closer ties with the Succession States. In any case, it was the Reich's policy to strengthen the position of the *Nationalgesinnten* in the Austrian government, not to encourage their resignation.

Glaise-Horstenau was not the only *nationalgesinnte* Austrian Minister closely consulting with the German Embassy in Vienna. On October 23, 1937, von Stein reported to the German Foreign Minister that Dr. Seyss-Inquart had informed him that on the previous day he, accompanied by Glaise-Horstenau, had called upon the Austrian Chancellor and had complained that his task of making proposals for the internal pacification in Austria had been practically undercut; Schuschnigg, however, disputed his drawing such conclusions.[108] According to Seyss-Inquart and von Stein, Schuschnigg had always believed that with the passage of time the views of the current *Reich* leaders would moderate and that this would facilitate the establishment of normal relations between Germany and Austria, such as had existed before 1933. Schuschnigg held that only in the event of a Communist revolution in Germany (!) would Restoration in Austria become a reality; in that case the legitimist concept would even spread beyond Austria into the German *Lebensraum*. Seyss-Inquart felt that there was a seed of expansionism embedded in Schuschnigg's political philosophy. It was not Hitler but Schuschnigg who had expansionist ambitions! Stein concluded that, domestically speaking, Schuschnigg was bent upon preserving the political *status quo* in Austria, and "any improvement for the benefit of the National Opposition" would have to be wrested from him only with greatest force. The views expressed in these reports from Vienna revealed a growing impatience with the Austrian situation and an escalating crisis which boded ill for the future. But for the moment, for the next months as it turned out, Hitler's "evolutionary" cause was to prevail.

On December 21, 1937, Papen reported to Hitler on the subject "Further development of Austria's domestic political situation."[109] Schuschnigg had invited him; in the presence of State Secretary Guido Schmidt, he, Papen, had told him of his apprehensions: "By exerting the best and strongest energies of the *Reich* and by utilizing the present international situation, the Führer was trying to restore the world position of the *Reich*. In this process Germany had to demand more than mere passive assistance from Austria; she had to demand that Austria, with heart and soul, support, wherever possible under existing circumstances, Germany's struggle for her existence. Though the Federal Chancellor had told me repeatedly that his foreign policy nowhere interfered with the policy of the *Reich*, I had to tell him that this was not enough [!]. This passive attitude was itself in effect a negation, particularly so, when every act of foreign policy ended with a new appeal to the world for preserving Austria's independence. The *Reich* did not intend to attack this independence, but it demanded that Austria observe the second part of the treaty with equal conscientiousness and that she lend active support to Germany in the struggle for the existence of the whole race. Both in the Spanish affair and in the fight against Bolshevism through the anti-Comintern Pact as well as in her attitude toward the problem of the League of Nations, Austria had gone her own way. Instead of creating a close and cordial relationship by means of evolutionary development in the sphere of culture, defense, and economics, she would not go a fraction of an inch for fear of displeasing the Western Powers. Quite the contrary, actions such as the setting up of roadblocks, etc., even at the border of the German *Reich*, were bound to prove to the world how little friendship there really was in Austro-German relations."

"The sole aim of my policy," Papen continued, "pursuant to the instructions of the Führer, was to promote a solution of the German problem by way of evolution, in order to forestall any solution by force." Referring to the fratricide war of 1866, he explained that the tragedy of German history lay in the frequent resort to force. But he made it clear that anything short of outright war, namely pressure, intimidation, penetration, and mere threat of force from within or without were quite legitimate methods of the political struggle.

Papen concluded by observing to Schuschnigg that he had come to understand the Chancellor's position after reading his book *Dreimal Österreich,* which, in his view, was based upon a completely false historical conception. The Chancellor's views would be disregarded by history. In his rejoinder Schuschnigg, apparently alarmed at this turn of the discussion, warned that any attempt to solve the Austrian problem by force would meet with considerably stronger resistance than in 1934 and would reduce Austria to a heap of ruins. He suggested that Papen present him with a written memorandum listing the requests which the *Reich* wished to make of Austria with respect to an extension of the July Agreement. Papen concluded his report to Berlin by saying that most national-minded people believed that further progress could be made only by subjecting the Austrian Chancellor "to the strongest possible pressure." Thus Papen not only brought himself pressure to bear upon Schuschnigg, but also, in a hardly veiled manner called Hitler to action!

Austro-German relations shifted rapidly to a climactic point. What Papen in unmistakable terms demanded was a cessation of Austria's calls for help addressed to the Western Powers and to the League of Nations. He also insisted on an end to Austrian neutralism, on the abandonment of Austria's "passivity," on a closer and more enthusiastic coordination with and the endorsement of National Socialist philosophy and foreign policy principles, for a voluntary *Gleichschaltung.* He plainly warned that the evolutionary course of the Führer could always be replaced by resorting to force. In sending this report to Hitler, Papen of course did not act as a special pleader. The ideas which he voiced to Schuschnigg originated with the Führer, as both correspondents fully knew, and were identical with his goals and desires.

Toward the end of 1937 it became clear that the Nazis, with the knowledge of *Reich* authorities, planned new activities in Austria, as the discovery of the Tavs Plan showed beyond doubt. The Austrian government, however, did not exploit this matter propagandistically, because, as Schuschnigg revealed, the material was "precious to us in order to convince Hitler of the lagging good faith of the *Reich.*"[110] Vienna also feared that the public disclosure of the Tavs Documents might merely push Berlin toward a formal renunciation of the July Agreement. It was then that the Austrian government decided to invite Göring to a hunting trip in Tyrol; Schuschnigg entertained the widespread illusion that one could talk with Göring more easily than with other Nazi leaders; yet Göring declined.

In the course of 1937 the illegal Austrian Nazi movement, scenting victory, assumed a more unbending attitude. Schuschnigg, subject to increasing pressures, seemed anxious to win over the more moderate and flexible *Nationalbetonten* in the hope of blunting the growing threat of the radical Nazis. Seyss-Inquart had repeatedly stated that he and his group, especially Jury, Globocnik, Rainer, etc., were prepared to follow a course of reconciliation. Seyss-Inquart was opposed to the radical Nazis headed by Leopold and the so-called "Committee of Seven." In spite of the unquestionably treasonable activities which the seizure of documents in the Teinfaltstrasse in late 1937 revealed, the Austrian Government refrained from moving against the Austrian Nazis, fearful that the German government would accuse it of persecuting them. The Austrian police also feared to drive the Nazis underground, which would merely aggravate the problem of keeping them under close scrutiny.

Since the summer of 1937 the relationship between Schuschnigg and Papen had become rather tense. The Austrian Chancellor did no longer attend any social functions in the German Embassy. Schuschnigg had also lost confidence in Glaise-Horstenau; it was reduced to "zero." He did not think that Glaise-Horstenau was possessed of an evil will, but considered him "politically weak, fearsome, and totally submissive to the influence of the circle of Haushofer in Munich." Schuschnigg also resented his close relations with the German military attaché W. Muff, "our sworn enemy.'" His trust in Seyss-Inquart had also become "very limited." Of all Nazis, Schuschnigg considered Dr. Jury to be the "most honest," yet the Chancellor admitted that even his "faith" in Jury was based upon mere "personal impressions."[111]

Austrian and German Nazism and the
Last Months of Austria's Independence

The outlook and psychology of the Austrian Nazis can only be understood by taking account of two basic facts, first of the failure of their July 1934 Putsch and, secondly, of their subsequent inability to come to power on their own. The Austro-Nazis seemed to be unable to attain victory by their own strength. After July 1934, Hitler and the German NSDAP left no doubt that the Austrian Nazis were at best auxiliary troops for Germany and that strategy, tactics, and timing in regard to Austria were to remain a German prerogative. Papen too expressed the virtually identical view "that the ultimate decision with regard to Austria lies outside of Austria" and that the Austrian NSDAP "therefore played only a passive role."[112] But Captain Leopold, leader of the radicals, hit back. In the Austrian *Völkischer Beobachter*, the official organ of Austria's NSDAP, he revealed that the Austrian Party had temporarily broken off social relations with the Metternichgasse, the seat of Germany's Embassy in Vienna. The mission of the Ambassador, Leopold boldly claimed, had been terminated on July 11, 1936, the day the German-Austrian Agreement had been signed; but this was only his own and the Austrian Party's interpretation. Papen, unable to obtain a retraction from Leopold, retaliated by ordering the members of the Legation to discontinue all official relations with Leopold and his middlemen.[113] Hitler himself, however, preferred not to make a clearcut decision about the respective jurisdictions of his quarreling paladins in the expectation that his own and the Party's interests would best be served by continuing, until further, his ambiguous policies and refraining from alienating any of his supporters.

Counselor von Stein of the German Legation in Vienna was sympathetic toward the radicals and advised Schuschnigg to deal directly with Leopold; the same advice was given to the Chancellor by a member of the Austrian cabinet, Odo Neustädter-Stürmer.[114] Both Leopold and Neustädter-Stürmer contemplated the formation of a new association, called the *Deutsch-Sozialer Volksbund*, which was to gather under one roof all national forces in Austria. Instead, the "Austrian Committee of Seven" was formed, which included three National Socialists, all associates of Leopold; the chairmanship of the Committee passed to the latter. When on February 12, 1937, Schuschnigg met with Leopold for the first time, the latter consented to a formula proposed by the Chancellor that acknowledged the independence of Austria and recognized the Austrian constitution of 1934. The project of forming the *Deutsch-Sozialer Volksbund* was subsequently abandoned.

Though blocked by members of his own party, Schuschnigg continued seeking an agreement with the Austrian Nazis. But the break between Papen and Leopold complicated the implementation of Schuschnigg's plan for a settlement with the radical Nazis. Papen of course wanted German-Austrian relations based on the July Agreement and on trust in the "evolutionary" process; rapprochement was always to be controlled from the German side. German representatives were the *bona fide* authorized spokesmen of the *Reich* and the NSDAP, not Austrian Nazi leaders.

Because of his continuous challenges to the Führer and his incorrigible streak of independence, the Austrian Nazi chief Captain Leopold was not in the good graces of Berlin; nor was he trusted by the more moderate Nationals in Austria. Thus Guido Zernatto, the General Secretary of the Fatherland Front, proposed to Schuschnigg the appointment of Arthur Seyss-Inquart as one who would be able to represent German national interests in Austria and ultimately rally the Nationals behind the Vienna Government. A known lawyer in Vienna, long active in national circles and especially the Anschluss movement, he had continuously avoided the limelight. In April 1937, Seyss-Inquart met Schuschnigg for the first time, and in the Chancellor's apartment.[115] He had the opportunity of expounding his ideas in general and those about the unification of all Germans in a *Volksreich* in particular. Austria would not be submerged, but rather play an important part in the enlarged Germany. Seyss-Inquart held that the *Reich* would probably have a federal, perhaps even a monarchic structure. There is little doubt that Seyss-Inquart was well acquainted with Schuschnigg's pet political ideas and deliberately played up to him. The Austrian Chancellor then decided on terminating his relations with the Committee of Seven and rather use Seyss-Inquart as the new instrument to reach national circles in Austria. In a letter of June 16, 1937, he offered him appointment to the Federal State Council, provided he would join the Fatherland Front; Seyss-Inquart promptly accepted the offer.

Ensconced in his new post, Seyss-Inquart, as Schuschnigg had tried before, attempted to reach agreement with Leopold. Seyss-Inquart's main goal was to build bridges between the Austrian government and the Austro-Nazis, both of which he served[116]— refusing to acknowledge that their interests were irreconcilable. Leopold's inflated conception of his own role, however, required the subordination of Seyss-Inquart. The latter, claiming that he owed his official position to Schuschnigg, was not prepared to accept a lesser role. To counter Leopold, Seyss-Inquart established contact with those Austrian Nazis whom Leopold had previously dismissed, namely Hubert Klausner, Friedrich Rainer, and Odilo Globocznigg. A trip of Seyss-Inquart to Berlin, where he met both Hess and Göring, appears to have given him some encouragement to continue serving in his post and pursuing his policies.

In July 1937 Schuschnigg called a meeting of the commission, provided for in the July 1936 Agreement, which was to implement its program for the further rapprochement between the two German states. The German delegation headed by the SS *Gruppenführer* Wilhelm Keppler, Chief of the Central Party Office for economic questions, met with Schuschnigg and other members of the Austrian cabinet, including Glaise-Horstenau and Seyss-Inquart, but with disappointing results. A week later, on July 12, 1937, Papen and Keppler reported to Hitler personally about the conference. In response to Papen's complaint that too many German officials had a hand in Austrian policy, Hitler gave Keppler sole jurisdiction to conduct relations of the NSDAP with Austria.[117] In addition, he entrusted him with supervising help for Austrian refugees (*Flüchtlingshilfswerk*) and the Austrian legion. Keppler's appointment in Austria showed the growing interference of the *Reich* NSDAP in Austrian Party affairs, all earlier pledges including that in the July Agreement 1936 to the contrary.

A member of the Party since 1927, Keppler had later become Hitler's personal economic adviser and was also responsible for the Four-Year Plan; thus he was in close contact with Göring. Besides he was also engaged in a survey of Austrian industries for proper exploitation after the planned annexation. When Keppler met Leopold on August 7, 1937, he informed him of Hitler's decision, but Captain Leopold rejected Keppler's intrusion in Austrian Party affairs. Only a few days later Leopold forbade Party members to associate either with Keppler or Seyss-Inquart and other top Austrian Nazi leaders.[118] Since Keppler, Seyss-Inquart, and their close associates happened to be members of the S.S., the Austrian intra-Party fight took on the character of a quarrel between the Leopold-led S.A. and the S.S.

Leopold was not one to give up easily. In two letters of late August and early September 1937 he again appealed to Hitler, raising questions of policy and tactics and criticizing his rivals. Toward the end of September 1937 he traveled personally to Berlin to plead his case. But the moment was ill chosen. In these very days Mussolini was expected to arrive in the German capital and the delicate Austrian question, which might prove divisive, was not supposed to be touched upon in the conversations between the two leaders. Thus, at that moment, Leopold was not received and his relations with the Nazi leadership in the *Reich*, Hitler in particular, deteriorated rapidly during the following critical months.

The closer the hour of decision came, the more intransigent grew also the attitudes of the main opposing players in Germany and Austria, Hitler and Schuschnigg. Pressure upon the Austrian Chancellor grew already from several sides toward the end of 1937. But Schuschnigg continued to procrastinate and yielded little. Seyss-Inquart and Glaise-Horstenau became increasingly impatient with him; so did also Foreign Minister von Neurath, when Schuschnigg refused to respond to his suggestions concerning a custom's union. Papen then concluded that Schuschnigg was simply unwilling to carry out the July Agreement and that, if the Chancellor persisted in his policy and tactics, "we shall be very soon in an untenable position." Seyss-Inquart's own conclusions were hardly different. The Austrian proposals for customs and currency union were, he judged, "politically impracticable." He was ready to resign; only Göring's forceful intervention changed his mind. Göring's own attempts to reach a new agreement with Schuschnigg through the Austrian Foreign Minister Guido Schmidt, who visited Berlin, failed similarly. The Vienna government turned a deaf ear to his proposals for a military alliance and customs union. Thus the lack of what the *Third Reich* and mediators such as Papen, Seyss-Inquart, and Glaise-Horstenau, considered as progress in Austro-German relations narrowed the differences between the radical and "moderate" Nazis in Austria and laid the groundwork for the climax in March 1938.

II
Austria and the Great Powers
1933–1938

Map 2. The first Austrian republic—the heart of Europe.

Chapter 7

The *Third Reich* and the Stresa Policy
of the Western Powers

France, the *status quo*, and the Anschluss threat

The Paris Peace Conference of 1919 prohibited the union between Austria and Germany. After a bitter war and major contest for the hegemony of Europe, the Western Powers were determined to weaken rather than to strengthen the German colossus. France, the traditional enemy of the German *Reich*, was fearful for her own security and for that of the smaller or middle-sized European states, which had recently been created or been greatly enlarged, Poland, Czechoslovakia, Rumania, Yugoslavia, Italy, and other neighbors of the *Reich* in Western and Northern Europe. In the postwar era France had become the leader in the defense of the territorial *status quo*. Other major powers, England, Italy, and the United States, had attached their signatures to the peace treaties and were bound by them.

If the Western Powers would have been ready to cancel the Anschluss prohibition, they would have opened the Pandora box of revisionism and would have completely undermined the postwar peace settlement. In the opinion of Henry Bérenger, Chairman of the French Chamber's Foreign Affairs Committee (December 20, 1932), "la raison d'Europe" required the permanent prohibition of the Anschluss. On November 14, 1933, Paul-Boncour, France's Foreign Minister, considered a sovereign Austria an "essential element of the stability and of the equilibrium of Central Europe."[1]

However, there was no complete agreement between France and Great Britain as to how essential Austrian sovereignty and the stability of Central Europe in general was for the security of France and all of Europe. Despite continuous disputes between France and Great Britain during the interwar period, British strategic opinion was based upon the view that the defense of France was in the British strategic and national interest.[2] The

French, however, were by no means satisfied with this British stance, though they agreed of course with the concept that the defense of the Rhine in general was also essential to British security. They stressed the importance of the *status quo*, the demilitarization of the Rhineland, in addition to the stability of Central and Eastern Europe. For France it was not only the Rhine but also the Vistula and the Danube which had to be protected against Germany's overreaching ambitions.[3] Therefore, the Rhine policy had both defensive and tactically offensive purposes, being part of the over-all policy of security for France and for Europe in its entirety. France's Rhenish policy aimed not only at the defense of French soil, but was also designed to hold over Germany the threat of French retaliatory action in the event of a German threat against Poland, Czechoslovakia and/or Austria. As Raymond Poincaré put it: The Rhine offered the Allies an "excellent jumping-off board"[4] for a decisive military demonstration. A French government memorandum, as early as February 25, 1919, stated succinctly that a demilitarization of the Rhineland was "an indispensable protection for the new states to the east and south of Germany."[5] Germany could bring her military superiority over the smaller powers in the East to bear only if France was frozen behind her defense line.

On the whole, British political and military circles endorsed the concept that the defense of the Rhine frontier was in the British national interest. So did for instance Stanley Baldwin.[6] But the English were less concerned about the inviolability of the frontiers of Germany's eastern neighbors. For France, however, her own security was tied up with the sovereignty and integrity of Germany's eastern neighbors, her friends and allies. French politicians and the French press often quoted Woodrow Wilson's having called the Rhine the frontier of freedom.[7] The French, however—excepting some politicians in the late thirties who propagated retrenchment behind the Maginot line—emphasized consistently not only the inviolability of the Rhenish frontier but also their obligations and interests in defending the *status quo* everywhere in Europe, not only in the West but also in East and Central Europe, within the framework of the League and apart from it if necessary.

The British, on the other hand, looked upon the eastern boundaries of Germany not quite the same way in which they judged her western boundaries. Britain, in the words of a close student of French and British policy, welcomed the Locarno Pact "precisely because it differentiated between East and West and because it limited Britain's commitments to a guarantee of the frontier on the Rhine."[8] French opponents of the Locarno Pact vice versa were always concerned that it would not prevent Germany from seeking a change of her eastern boundaries by pacific means. France consistently held to the opinion that threats and moves to weaken her eastern allies, such as Poland and Czechoslovakia, would only strengthen the *Reich*, would destroy the European equilibrium, and threaten French security. As Ybarnégaray expressed it in the Chamber of Deputies in February 1938, the very moment when Hitler would have realized his goals along Germany's eastern borders in *Mitteleuropa*, the fate of France would be "inevitably sealed."[9] French political and military leaders were convinced that France's security depended not merely on the Rhine, but on the integrity and the effective defense of German's eastern neighbors. Most Frenchmen agreed that permitting Germany to expand eastward, standing aside while the *Third Reich* pursued the policy of the *"Drang nach dem Osten,"* would be a suicidal policy for France.

France was not only bent on preventing Austria from joining the *Reich*, but even wanted Austria to become one of the pillars of a Danubian Federation, which was to block Germany's expansion into Central and Southeastern Europe. But her espousal of this project ran into unavoidable obstacles, one of these being Italy's disapproval and resistance. Italy, an immediate neighbor of Austria and geographically so much closer to Hungary, Yugoslavia, and the rest of the Balkan than France, was her natural opponent in Central Europe; Italy ignored the circumstance that France's interests were largely defensive, primarily designed to prevent Germany's thrust into Austria. In view of the common danger of a German expansion into Austria, France and Italy seemed at times prepared to settle their differences and coordinate their policies. But the Stresa Front which they established with Britain in 1935 turned out to be a transitory phenomenon.

France's own allies, the states of the Little Entente, were another roadblock to the creation of a Danubian Federation. These states were so obsessed with the specter of a restoration of the Habsburg dynasty and the rebirth of the old Austrian Empire—perils of the past—that they neglected over it the incomparably greater contemporary danger of German domination of Central and Southeastern Europe.

France often grew impatient with her own allies, Czechoslovakia and the other states of the Little Entente, since they responded only slowly, if at all, to the French-sponsored project of a Danubian Confederation and gave only inadequate economic assistance to Austria. Yugoslavia, Rumania, and Poland had an insufficient comprehension of the geopolitical significance of Austria for Europe's equilibrium and their very own security.

Nor did all the great European Powers fully and consistently appreciate Austria's strategic importance for Europe in its entirety. None of them gave ever any formal and binding military guarantee to Austria. Britain, as mentioned, was never willing to consider making any specific commitment regarding Austria's independence and integrity. Italy showed her deep interest in preserving Austria's sovereignty, but—a consequence of her increasing preoccupation with adventures in Ethiopia and Spain—her military capacity to assist Austria gradually diminished. Similarly, though obviously for different reasons, France's abilities to play a vigorous role in Central Europe decreased strikingly, especially after the 1936 occupation and remilitarization of the Rhineland and Germany's apparent preparation for war. Since the remilitarization of the Rhineland France actually lost her access to Central Europe and to Austria in particular. In the 1930s the Soviet Union had radically altered many of her earlier foreign policy views on Central Europe and the world. She was too absorbed in her own domestic crises to be of real help to Austria; she was also geographically too remote.

After Hitler's *Machtergreifung*

After Hitler's seizure of power in Germany the French government became increasingly concerned about the threat which the *Third Reich* posed to France and her allies, especially Czechoslovakia. This threat was effectively brought home by the vigorous and virulent Nazi Anschluss propaganda which followed Hitler's accession to power. A few weeks only after Hitler had come to power, France's Foreign Minister Paul-Boncour expressed the fear that Italy might relinquish her policy of opposition to the Anschluss and reach an understanding with Germany in regard to union with Austria.[10-11] As it turned out, for the next years his was not a correct prophecy, but in the long run Paul-Boncour's misgivings were well grounded. Both the narrow interests of Italian Fascism and the ideological and political turn of the Austrian government to an extreme rightist position were matters of concern to French political leaders and bad omens for the continued independence of Austria.

The French Ambassador in Vienna, Clauzel, was also worried about the fascist trend in Austria following the so-called "self-elimination" of the Austrian Parliament in March 1933 and the apparent weakening of Austria's internal front against the Nazi threat from within and without. The fear of an Austrian link-up with Italy had seized not only Austrian Socialists but had gripped also officials of the German Foreign Service. On March 21, 1933, Ambassador François-Poncet sent a message from Berlin to Paris to the effect that von Bülow of the German Foreign Office questioned Italy's endorsement of the Anschluss with Germany and he even claimed to know Italy wanted an "Anschluss" of Austria with herself.[12] Clearly, both German policy on one side, Italian and French responses on the other, had not yet been fully crystallized and each of the major Powers tried to carefully assess the likely direction and vigor of the policy of the other states before deciding on its own. While France opposed the German thrust into Austria, she was hardly enthusiastic about the German peril being merely replaced by Italy's dominant position in Austria. But the Austrians urged Franco-Italian collaboration in the defense of their country. When von Pflügl, formerly Austrian delegate in Geneva, arrived in Paris in early April 1933, he promptly called upon the Quai d'Orsay and pointed out that, in Vienna's view, French and Italian interests coincided on the Austrian issue and suggested that Paris commence a conversation with Rome on this matter: "If one permits surprises by events, what is one going to do?"[13]

Paris had a most capable and astute Ambassador in Berlin, André François-Poncet, who followed closely Germany's moves versus Austria. He served as French Ambassador during the critical period from September 1931 to October 1938.* He was the only Western diplomat in Berlin able to talk to Hitler and the prominent Nazi leaders in fluent German without the help of an interpreter. While he was aware of the widespread abhorrence of war in both France and allied Great Britain and shared these sentiments, his was still the voice of eloquent warning against the threats and dangers which the *Third Reich* posed to the West and the civilized world.[14]

François-Poncet and Paul-Boncour

Glancing back at Hitler's early policy after his assumption of power, François-Poncet underlined that while Hitler then pressed energetically forward at home, he acted in general with caution and circumspection in foreign affairs.[15] An exception, however, to this attitude was his Austrian policy. In his early interviews with Hitler, François-Poncet, who had no illusion about the anti-French thrust of National Socialism, concluded that "German nationalism was by definition anti-French, how much more so was Nazism"![16] In an interview of April 8, 1933, Hitler, however, protested his sympathy for France and his esteem for the French character, but despite the French Ambassador's suggestion to soften the most violently anti-French passages of *Mein Kampf*, the Führer never saw fit to do so.[17] The later assassination of Dollfuss, Austria's Chancellor in July 1934, betrayed, according to François-Poncet, the same unforgettable Hitlerian trademark as the *Reichstag* fire and the massacre of Röhm and his associates. François-Poncet believed that, starting out in 1933 and continuing in 1934, Hitler "did not intend to absorb Austria forthwith into the *Third Reich*; he was not going to effect an Anschluss whereby complications might arise abroad at a time when he did not judge himself capable of standing his ground."[18]

The resistance put up by the Vienna government "scandalized and exasperated Hitler and the Berlin Nazis; in their fanatical

---

*Hitler and the Nazis thought they had won François-Poncet over to their cause. In his words, "they could not conceive of a man, speaking German and being familiar with Germany, who was not captivated by them." Actually, he had always found National Socialism "revolting" (*Memoirs*, p. 10).

and sectarian mentality they could not conceive how a country of German race and language could be reluctant to leap into their arms." That Dollfuss, "this little dissenter and pygmy should dare to stand up to them seemed to them at once ridiculous and odious; they were filled with rage and scorn." Hitler, according to François-Poncet, was "no normal being, he was rather a morbid personality, a quasi-madman, a character out of the pages of Fyodor Dostoevsky, a man 'possessed'." Britain, he thought, was "reluctant to dabble in this Austrian business" and held the Anschluss sooner or later for inevitable. France, for her part, "hesitated to take measures without being assured of British collaboration." This basically was to remain the root of English and French attitudes toward the Anschluss until March 1938.

While France's stance toward Austria and Central Europe between 1933–39 was indeed to become increasingly dependent on the position taken by Great Britain, in January 1934 already some French political leaders, such as Joseph Paul-Boncour, were clearly dissatisfied with British policy, especially the "passive attitude" which Britain had adopted in the Austrian question and which aroused "the gravest fears" and "immediate reservations" by France.[19] The intervention of France, Great Britain, and Italy the previous year had remained "without results." Paul-Boncour objected that England apparently wanted to dissuade Chancellor Dollfuss from bringing the Austro-German dispute before the Geneva forum. Paul-Boncour himself had encouraged the Austrian government to do so and even expressed the opinion that it should not have delayed matters. The French Ambassador in London, Corbin, was told to make the French views known to Sir John Simon who was known to follow very closely Austrian affairs.[20] Corbin promptly talked both with Sir Simon as well as with Sir Robert Vansittart, Permanent Under-Secretary of State. The latter denied that he had discouraged the Vienna government to use the Geneva tribune to publicly air its complaints, but revealed that he had "serious fears" in regard to Mussolini and doubted whether he was really contemplating collective action. "Isolated" action by him, however was perilous. Corbin himself compared the situation of Austria with that of a state being "between two fires, the German threat and the fascist pressure."[21] On the eve of the Austrian February 1934 revolt, partly triggered by Mussolini's pressure on Dollfuss, Corbin pointed to the danger of civil war with the Austrian Socialists and its likely harmful repercussions for Austria's struggle for independence.

But while dissatisfied both with English and Italian policy toward Austria, Paul-Boncour and other French political leaders saw eye to eye with many abroad in regard to an over-all agreement among the Western Powers in behalf of the defense of Austria. Through Ambassador Puaux in Vienna the Quai d'Orsay was frequently reminded by Chancellor Dollfuss himself that Austria badly needed both French and English support.[22]

Paris gave direct encouragement to Dollfuss. When on a return trip from London, the Austrian Chancellor visited Paris on June 16, 1933, the Foreign Minister "congratulated" Dollfuss on "the struggle which he pursued for the independence of his country, a struggle which one followed in France with a very lively interest."[23] When Dollfuss then raised the question of a loan for Austria, the French Foreign Minister recalled that if his government demanded certain guarantees regarding internal Austrian politics, the reason was not that he wished to become involved in Austrian domestic affairs. Still, the French attempted to make the loan to Austria contingent on the pledge of Dollfuss and his cabinet to return to constitutionalism and the parliamentary road. In taking leave, Dollfuss emphasized that in the current struggle he defended not only the cause of Austrian independence, but also that of peace in Central Europe.[24] Neither side was ready to make concessions, but there were ominous indications that French support for Austrian independence would continue, irrespective of the internal trend of Austrian politics.

Franco-Italian Collaboration and Dissonances

In 1933, Italy's stance toward Germany was rather ambiguous. According to Charles-Roux, French Ambassador at the Holy See, Cardinal Pacelli* revealed to him that Italy was by no means reticent in regard to its opposition against the Anschluss.[25] Count de Vecchi of the Italian Foreign Office, remarked: "We are with Germany on the Rhine, but not on the Danube." In either case Fascist Italy pursued national objectives, though she favored in

---

*Cardinal Pacelli became later Pope Pius XII.

the first German revisionism—when it was aimed against the West, relating to the Saar and the Rhineland—while opposing it on the Danube when it appeared to threaten Italy's position in Central Europe and at the Brenner pass. Besides, Italian resentment against France's role in European affairs, dating back to the Peace Conference, was still a major factor in Fascist Italy's attitude. Charles-Roux reported to Paris that the Italian ambassador to the Holy See had criticized the excessive French ambitions, which were allegedly reminiscent of the era of Richelieu and of Louis XIV.

During the summer of 1933 Mussolini's attitude toward Austria and Germany was marked by excessive caution. As the political director of the Austrian Foreign Service, Hornbostel, confided to Puaux, Mussolini recommended to Dollfuss to "moderate the tone of the Austrian press vis-à-vis Germany in order to give the latter no pretext for continuing her attacks."[26] When Dollfuss pointed out that all good words had not prevented Habicht from making his attacks, Mussolini, somewhat embarrassed, doubted that the latter's radio propaganda originating in Munich constituted a political danger for Austria. Il Duce did not believe that a German *Putsch* was imminent. At Dollfuss's question what he would do in that event, however, Mussolini, again somewhat evasive, answered that there were enough of the Great Powers interested in Austria's independence and in using military force to restore the *status quo*. In the course of his conversations Mussolini expressed himself often critically and sometimes with scorn about Hitler-Germany, a "bad copy of fascism," "deformed and warped by Slavic [!] influences."[27] Il Duce appeared to Hornbostel a questionable expert on German psychology. He promised, however, the Austrian Chancellor to give Berlin counsels of moderation and pledged that in the event the situation worsened "I shall be quite prepared to join a French-English action." Still, according to Puaux, Dollfuss did not hide the fact that the attitude of the Italian government had long caused him a certain disquiet.[28]

According to Jevtić, Yugoslavia's Minister of Foreign Affairs, Italy's opposition to the Anschluss was beyond doubt. But even he was critical of the uncertainties and "childishness" of the foreign policy of Rome which followed contradictory goals, namely "to prevent the Anschluss and at the same time to dream of an

Italian *Mitteleuropa* without breaking with Germany, encouraging Hungarian claims without encouraging German ones."[29]

In 1933 Mussolini wholeheartedly approved the principle of Franco-Italian collaboration in the Danubian basin. Yet, in his view, the moment had not yet come to present under the aegis of France and Italy a plan which the likely opposition of Germany and Hungary would doom. "Austria herself feels too Germanic for its government . . . to accept without peril a plan which would appear to be aimed against Germany."[30] According to Mussolini, the powers would have to act with "utmost prudence." Once Austria would be tranquil, he, Mussolini, would serve Austin Chamberlain as a guide to convince both Austria and Hungary of the necessity to conclude economic agreements with the countries of the Little Entente. These two camps would not be "rival blocs."[31] But as a result of the foreign adventures in which Il Duce involved himself, his hopes of a Franco-Italian cooperation in the Danubian basin aimed against the *Third Reich* evaporated.

France wished for Italy's support of Austria's independence against Germany, but opposed the destruction of Austria's political democracy and her replacement by a mere political copy of Fascist Italy. The French feared that the Italian government was pushing Dollfuss into a needless and dangerous confrontation with the Austrian Social Democrats, though the latter were resolved opponents of National Socialism within Austria and beyond her borders. Late in January 1934 Puaux reported about his talk with the Italian diplomat Suvich, who was visiting the Austrian capital: "Rather than to proceed against the Socialists," he had suggested, "it was better to let time work" and "rally the working class gradually to the formula of the corporative state."[32] Yet while "Suvich listened with attention, he did not indicate that he approved;" he knew that the suggested "gradualism" would not fit with Mussolini's plans. Two days later, after Suvich had returned to Rome, Puaux had an interview with Dollfuss during which the latter observed that the Socialist leaders had "no political sense and no Austrian patriotism"![33] His course for the next days was apparently set and nothing was to prevent two weeks later the destruction of the "unpatriotic" Austrian Social Democratic Party and with it of the remaining democratic foundations of Austria.

Early February 1934, French authorities apparently got wind of the approaching crisis in Austria. Puaux informed the French Foreign Minister Daladier, that he had discussed with Dollfuss Daladier's concerns.[34] He claimed that the eviction of the Socialists from the Vienna *Rathaus*, the seat of Vienna's municipal government, would actually be a strike "against the National Socialists." In reality, the Chancellor endorsed thus a thesis of Mussolini! Dollfuss assured Puaux that he personally was not the man of the capitalists, but was "horrified by the antipatriotic internationalism and the conception of the class struggle"[35]—alleged attitudes of the labor leaders—rather than by any conspiratorial activities!

Two days later, as if to defend Dollfuss vis-à-vis Daladier, Puaux pointed to the lack of effective diplomatic and military support of Austria by the Western Powers:[36] It was a year now that the Nazis battled against the Dollfuss cabinet "with all means, given by the enormous disproportion in their favor of arms and resources; they have the drive, cohesion, money, enthusiasm, the split among their adversaries; the front against them is organized only slowly, laboriously . . ." Mussolini's solemn pledges to Chambrun in Rome, "We [Italy and France] shall defend Austria together, if necessary in the trenches of Vienna,"[37] remained indeed empty oratory being not translated into binding treaties.

While the French government was opposed to Italy's increasingly evident desire to eliminate Austrian democracy and the Austrian Social Democratic Party in particular, Paris also opposed what it considered British "hesitations in regard to Austria."[38] The British Secretary of State defended British policy pointing to Eden's remarks in the House of Commons where he had supported the right of Austria to oppose the intervention by any government in its internal affairs. But this statement in reality lacked any special thrust against the chief culprit, Nazi Germany.

The very day of the outbreak of the civil war in Austria on February 12, 1934, Barthou in a message to Puaux criticized the decision taken by Dollfuss against the municipality in Vienna as irreconcilable with the Chancellor's earlier assurances that he would take only defensive measures against the Socialists.[39] Barthou wanted the French Ambassador to caution Dollfuss if he planned to ask for "France's assistance." Barthou was plainly aroused by Dollfuss's actions and he may also have entertained doubts whether France's Ambassador conveyed accurately the thoughts and sentiments of the French government to the Austrian authorities. However, the Austrian government ignored this admonishment from Paris as it had ignored earlier ones.

After Austria in February 1934 had moved into the fascist camp, Puaux, never a friend of the Austrian Social Democrats and hardly ever a serious critic of Dollfuss, conceded: "The great danger remains, as it was before the February days, the Hitler peril. It always was the principal danger, though many refused to recognize it as such."[40] Puaux, similarly, questioned the official Austrian optimism as proclaimed by Dollfuss: "There does not exist an Austrian problem." The Chancellor was quickly to learn differently.

France and Her East European Allies

Though France herself was interested in shoring up Austria's defenses against the aggressive tendencies of the *Third Reich*, which operated in combination with the Austrian Nazis' "Fifth Column," she had less than adequate support from her eastern allies, from Czechoslovakia, most vitally affected by the fate of Austria, and from Poland, Yugoslavia, and Rumania.

Neither the Czechoslovak government nor Foreign Minister Beneš in particular had always been consistent in regard to the need for the preservation of Austrian independence and the dangers of the Anschluss. In a talk with the French Ambassador Beneš made remarks which clearly reveal his opposition to the Anschluss but also his complete helplessness vis-à-vis Austria. "I shall do everything to prevent this catastrophe [the Anschluss], but what can one do? . . . . In 1930 I was alone among the members of the Czechoslovak government who thought that everything was not lost yet." The Anschluss would be "the starting point of grave developments."[41]

At times Beneš toyed with the concept of Austrian neutrality, which, if generally accepted, might help avoid the Anschluss. (Neutralization of Austria was to become reality about two decades later, after World War II, in the Austrian State Treaty of 1955, under admittedly different conditions.) Beneš also entertained the idea of a customs union between the states of the Little Entente, a union which might later include Austria and Hungary. But to a union between Austria and Hungary alone he was sharply opposed, hardly less so than to the Anschluss. Such a union appeared to some to be inseparable from the idea of a restoration of the Habsburg dynasty. France shared this position. When Paul-Boncour telegraphed to Laroche, French Ambassador in Warsaw, he asserted that "there can be no question of a union between Austria and Hungary, no more than a monarchic restoration."[42]

Fierlinger, Czechoslovak Minister in Vienna, a "militant socialist," seemed to Puaux "haunted by the fear of a Restoration of the Habsburgs." He told him with vehemence: "Rather Anschluss than the Monarchy."[43] Such a view, which was directly contrary to that of Paul-Boncour and of most French leaders had a grossly distorted vision. The fear of yesterday's enemy, the Habsburg Monarchy, blinded them and paralyzed their action against the incomparably greater immediate threat by Nazi Germany. No wonder that Paul-Boncour showed impatience with Czechoslovakia. In an urgent letter to Noël, French Ambassador in Prague, the French Foreign Minister impressed upon him the importance of Czechoslovakia and the rest of the Little Entente helping Austria and her economy. Paul-Boncour stressed that a "joint and energetic affirmation by France, Italy, Great Britain, and the Little Entente" to the effect that they would never permit the Anschluss was imperative; such a reaffirmation, as he recalled, had been frequently made by Briand, Daladier, and by himself. As he wrote, "Italy on that point at least, is in agreement with us. It is the Little Entente which, for some time, has seemed to demonstrate some disinterest in this so important question." It appears, Paul-Boncour complained, "that now the Little Entente is more preoccupied with the Austro-Hungarian union than with the Anschluss. We want neither the one nor the other."[44]

Referring to a recent private, only partly published, conversation with Beneš and King Alexander of Yugoslavia, Puaux raised the question whether independent Austria was "condemned to die." In this regard the Little Entente appeared to be unanimous, "since I know personally the sentiments of King Carol and M. Titulescu of Rumania. They don't believe, neither one nor the other, in Austria and are ready to accommodate themselves in her disappearance."[45] In defending Austria, France was fighting for the preservation of a system destined to assure her own security as well as that of the Little Entente.

In June 1937 Beneš revealed that he contemplated an economic federation in Central Europe which would make Germany's penetration of the area and of Austria in particular more difficult. He emphasized to a representative of.the *Prager Tagblatt* that the economic interests of the Danubian states were not incompatible with each other. "The old monarchy represented, from the economic point of view, a very sound and solid organism, and I am convinced that sooner or later we shall return, as far as economics are concerned, to the old ties."[46] An economic union between Czechoslovakia, Yugoslavia, Rumania, including perhaps Hungary and Austria, represented a true solution to the problem of Central Europe.

While Czechoslovakia was on the whole opposed to the Anschluss, but at critical moments resigned to "accommodate" herself to the inevitable course of history, the foreign policy and attitude of Yugoslavia, her partner in the Little Entente, toward Austria and the Anschluss was from the start marked by contrary tendencies. On one hand, Yugoslavia feared Germany's proximity in the event of the annexation of Austria, especially in view of her own German minority which was located in the northwestern part of the country. She feared equally the German resumption of the *Drang nach dem Osten* which would make her the springboard for further German expansion. On the other hand, some Germans had held out the tempting lure that in the event of Austria's absorption by the *Third Reich*, Yugoslavia's territorial claims against portions of Styria and Carinthia would be given due consideration in Berlin; a few gullible Yugoslav politicians fell into this trap.

Yugoslavia had also serious territorial differences with Italy, which dated back to the peace treaties and the early postwar period, was fearful of Mussolini's expansionist ambitions, and entertained the illusion that Belgrade would be able to play off the Führer against Il Duce. Yet, in spite of her flirtations with Germany, Yugoslavia still remained France's ally and was also linked with Rumania and Czechoslovakia in the Little Entente. Like its other members, Belgrade was opposed to Hungarian revisionism and, like many Czechoslovaks, had a paranoic fear of the restoration of the Habsburg Empire. Many Yugoslavs were also more hostile to the idea of a return of the Habsburgs than to Austria's Anschluss with Hitler Germany. This fear of a Habsburg restoration, the rapprochement with Nazi Germany, and the subsequent weakening of Yugoslavia's ties with France and the Little Entente, became more pronounced between 1933 and 1938.

According to François-Poncet, Hitler had expressed himself to the Yugoslav Minister in Berlin with bitterness and anger about the Italian attitude toward Austria and Italy's pretensions of wishing to dominate that country; he must have speculated that this line would appeal to Belgrade. As Hitler previously had given assurances to Poland, similarly, when the Yugoslav Minister alluded to the *Drang nach dem Osten* the Führer replied that this was an ambition of the old Austrian Empire, not of Germany! He repeated that he offered to Yugoslavia, as to the other states of the Little Entente, the same pact into which he had entered with Poland.[47] The Yugoslav Minister, however, was struck by Hitler's worried appearance and by "his streak of violence"; he found him "a man both disturbing and disturbed."

Poland was one of France's allies, but was ready to "accommodate herself to Austria's disappearance. Late in 1933 Berlin and Warsaw established contact with each other which in January 1934 was to climax in a ten-year non-aggression pact. Though Poland retained military and other ties with France, there could be little doubt that Hitler had scored heavily and that the system of collective defense laboriously built up by France in the post-war period had received a blow from which it was never fully to recover. Poland, concerned about territorial integrity and survival, made the fateful assumption that Hitler's word could be trusted. Its government was all too willing to watch silently the propaganda campaign of the *Third Reich* against Austria, hoping that her annexation would still Germany's appetite and make her forget the tense and disputed German-Polish border, rather than whet her appetite for an eastward expansion.

There were rumors in Warsaw and elsewhere, confirmed by a report of François-Poncet from Berlin, that at a meeting of Hitler with Lipski, Polish Ambassador in Berlin, the Anschluss had been discussed. The French Ambassador to Warsaw, Laroche, raised the question whether the Polish government had concluded an agreement with its German counterpart that it would refrain from taking sides on the union issue.[48] Though in his opinion this was not "absolutely certain," he found the attitude of the Polish government toward Austria quite ambiguous: "One Bressy during the summer had written an article in *Gazeta Polska* which considered the Anschluss as being in conformity with a natural order of things and indicated that the struggle between Austria and Germany was in reality an internal dispute within the Germanic bloc." Colonel Beck had subsequently expressed the view that Poland, "not directly interested in the Anschluss," had taken no initiative on this issue and that, in any case, it would be difficult to prevent the Anschluss unless France and Italy mobilized. Now, similarly, Warsaw refused to become involved in an affair which it judged as lost in advance. One Pole—referring to the successful Polish rescue effort of Vienna back in 1683 when the Turks had laid siege to it—stated: "We are not going to repeat Sobieski.* As Laroche explained it, Warsaw did not want "to compromise Polish-German relations."[49]

The Polish government's myopia concerning the significance of the Anschluss which was bound to strengthen Hitler's Germany was quite apparent. The Russian Ambassador to Warsaw, Antonov-Owssejenko reported to have heard from Colonel Beck himself, that Hitler had told the Polish Ambassador in Berlin, Lipski, "I am not a Prussian."[50] These words were designed to convey the impression that the Führer would interest himself to a lesser extent than the Prussians proper in problems of the East. Beck and the government of the Colonels banked heavily on such fatuous promises! Hitler, of course, was bent on deceiving the Poles and making them believe that he was more interested in the Anschluss—a "specifically German problem"—than in broaching the question of the eastern frontier of the *Reich*. He also went so far as to blame Bismarck's policy against the Poles![51] Laroche cautioned Colonel Beck that Poland's indifference regarding the Anschluss was not only a "major error" of the Warsaw government, but would also have grave consequences for the policy of France the efforts of which to save Austria were well known to him.[52]

Dollfuss saw through Hitler's game. He understood that the Führer wanted to detach Austria's friends, France, Great Britain, Poland, and others.[53] Referring to Hitler's 1933 address at the Nürnberg Party Congress, he remarked: "Hitler attempts to calm and tranquillize Europe before turning with greater ease to his goals in Austria. He has already succeeded in calming Poland,

---

*The Polish king who led the Polish army for the relief of besieged Vienna.

now he addresses himself to France. Tomorrow it will be the turn of Great Britain. Must Austria resign herself to be victim of these tactics?"[54] Shall Germany be given a "free hand" in Austria? When Puaux assured the Chancellor that the French government would never consent to taking a disinterested attitude regarding the fate of Austria, whatever other benefits might be offered to it, Dollfuss seemed pleased about the congruity of the interests of the two countries, but cautioned: "The day on which Hitler would be master of Vienna, all the other goals of Germany's foreign policy would be simultaneously attained. It is not for us alone that France will work to lend us support." And he complained that, economically speaking, Czechoslovakia, France's ally, had "not done anything for Austria so far."

While the Little Entente and Poland were slow to respond to France's suggestion to help Austria materially and diplomatically, Austria herself under Dollfuss's and Schuschnigg's auspices was by no means free of fault. After the Austro-German July Agreement of 1936 Schuschnigg assured once Puaux that he understood the need for friendly relations with Czechoslovakia which were based upon mutual confidence and that he personally trusted Hodža and had sympathy for him. Yet the "russophile policy of Prague makes impossible an entente between the two countries." And he pictured for Puaux "Czechoslovakia as an immense depot of arms of the Soviet air force from which will develop the inevitable Russo-German conflict."[55] When Puaux replied that the famous camps of the Soviet air force existed only in the tendentious information of Hitler's propaganda, Schuschnigg made the rejoinder that this was also the personal conviction of Mussolini. The Austrian Chancellor, wearing ideological blinders, apparently believed in mere rumors and obvious falsehoods concerning the neighboring Czechoslovak Republic. All this was bound to adversely affect his resolve and resistance to Nazi Germany and to strengthen anti-Austrian sentiments in the countries of the Little Entente.

Il Duce's Early Opposition to the Anschluss

The advance of National Socialism and the formation of a new Austrian government by Dollfuss on May 20, 1932, had produced mixed reactions in Rome. The Italian Foreign Minister Dino Grandi remarked in Geneva that Italy in the event of a breakdown of the Austrian government or an attempt at an Anschluss was resolved to protect her interests "through occupation of the western Alpine lands."[56] Other Italian officials were prepared to go even further and protect all of Austria. Dollfuss assured the Hungarian Premier Gömbös that he was ready to work toward an Italo-Austro-Hungarian economic union and was confident that Italian fascism would revise its policy in Southern Tyrol.[57] Austrian defenses against Germany would thus be strengthened.

After Hitler's seizure of power in January 1933, German National Socialism attempted to crush the Dollfuss regime by a combination of pressures from within and without. When Dollfuss, compelled to turn to Fascist Italy for support, visited Rome on April 13, 1933, Mussolini pledged to him not only economic but also military assistance. On August 20, 1933, at a meeting between Mussolini and Dollfuss in Riccione, the two political leaders took seriously the threat to Austria posed by the Austrian Legion which comprised several thousand Austrian refugees stationed near the border and was militarily in excellent condition and capably led. In September 1933 Mussolini reiterated to the Austrian emissary *Sektionschef* Dr. Schüller the promise made earlier to Dollfuss to resort to military action, if necessary.[58]

One of the earliest voices which had been raised in Fascist Italy against any German orientation of the Palazzo Chigi was that by F. G. Giovannucci, author of two books on Italy and Central Europe, *La Germania di Hitler e l'Italia* (Rome, 1933) and *Il Problema austriaco e l'Italia* (Rome, 1934). In the latter he cautioned that Nazi Germany constituted a threat not only to Austrian independence but also to Italy's' control of South Tyrol and to the very role of Italy as a great power.[59] These views were the official Fascist views for the next years until, starting in early 1936, they were relegated into the background and ultimately sacrificed at the altar of the axis—which in Mussolini's view held out other, though only vague, promises to Fascist Italy.

During the year 1933, while Dollfuss tried desperately to negotiate directly with Hitler, Italian diplomats, such as Cerruti in Berlin and Suvich, visiting the German capital on December 15, 1933, learned first-hand that leading Nazis spoke openly of a possible "forcible solution" of the Anschluss question by the

Austrian Nazis; they had hatched such plans since October 1933 and set a tentative data for a coup for February or March 1934.[59] Such news may have spurred Mussolini to action, urging Dollfuss to lay the foundation for fascism in Austria. The visit of Suvich in Vienna on January 18, 1934, provided the last push for the Austrian government to slide down the road of anti-parliamentarianism toward dictatorship;[60] it provoked the Social Democrats and unleashed, on February 12, 1934, a bloody civil war. Among Rome's demands posed to Vienna in January was one to "step up the struggle against Marxism and to bring about the elimination of parties." The Italian Minister of War issued clandestine instructions to commanders of Italian military units which are listed in the Italian documents under the titles "Plan K" or "Plan 1934." An Italian high-placed official openly admitted that the possible occupation of several select points in Austria by Italian troops would have the purpose of "relieving Austrian troops" to make possible their deployment against Nazi rebels. Other Italian sources, including the Italian Military attaché in Vienna, Colonel Fabbri, however, planned already to reconcile contrary German and Italian interests in Austria and suggested the ambitious national-minded Dr. Anton Rintelen as Austrian Chancellor as the ideal man to harmonize German and Italian aspirations.[61]

While the Austrian Civil War was raging in February 1934, Italian dailies vigorously supported Dollfuss and were sharply critical of both Austrian "Bolshevism" and of the Austrian Nazis. As the American Ambassador in Rome reported to Washington, D.C., during the past week the language of Italian journals toward Germany was an indication that "a change for the worse has come over the relations of the two dictatorial regimes."[62] *Il Messagero* called Habicht's radio ultimatum to Dollfuss in the midst of the fighting against the socialist workers "crazy and a criminal provocation." The influential Italian journalist Virgino Gayda warned in *Giornale d'Italia* that the joint declaration of the three Great Powers, France, Great Britain and Italy of February 17, 1934, served notice on Germany that henceforth the Austrian situation was one of international concern, although the *Berliner Tageblatt* "insolently affirms that it does not know for whom this declaration is intended." Austrian National Socialism, according to Gayda, persisted in preparing the way for the absorption of

Austria by Germany. "This preparation . . . constitutes an infringement of existing treaties. Italy does not oppose treaty revision . . . but does oppose the German method which it considers intemperate, arbitrary and unilateral. Italy does not see how the absorption of Austria can be defended either on grounds of justice or necessity."[63]

The polemics between the Italian and German press was not confined to the above two organs. The *Vossische Zeitung*, to divert attention from the *Reich's* aggressive methods, charged Italy with expansionist plans. An editorial in *Giornale d'Italia* replied "that in her support of Austria, Italy was only discharging her duties and responsibilities as a Great Power."[64] The tone of the Italian press left no doubt concerning the earnestness of Italy's intention to support the cause of Austrian independence. For apparent tactical reasons Mussolini always disclaimed that the expansion of Germany to the Italian border was a source of concern for Italy; he rather stressed that it was essential to prevent the German push eastward toward Belgrade and Constantinople, and possibly beyond it. Belgrade, however, doubted that it could rely on Rome against Berlin. For different reasons Schuschnigg did not want to rely on the military support by Rome against Berlin either. Schuschnigg considered an Italian intervention in Austria for the purpose of protecting her soil, as distinct from a military demonstration on the Italian side of the border in July 1934, not feasible. The Austrians would not tolerate that Italian troops—enemies in the Great War—would "protect" Austria against the German blood brother.[65] Similarly, the following year the Austrian government felt compelled to decline a French offer, made through the French military attaché, to assist Austria by furnishing tanks and planes in return for a pledge to remain neutral in the event of a European war and a promise to defend her soil against a German attack.[66] Austria's military chief, Alfred Jansa, replied in the spirit of Schuschnigg's previous declaration, undoubtedly after consultation with the Chancellor, that Austria could well inform the French about the deployment of weapons, but could not accept a French military mission in Austria or placing her army under the command of the French General Staff. Neither the Austrian army nor the Austrian people would permit either.

The July *Putsch* and Its Consequences Abroad

On July 25, 1934, the Nazis struck in Austria and Dollfuss was assassinated. But the *Putsch* failed and no Austrian Nazi, but Schuschnigg, already Minister of Justice and later of Education in Dollfuss's cabinet, became his successor. Mussolini ordered Italian troop movements along the border, while Yugoslavia, taking Germany's side against Austria and Italy, threatened military movements of her own. For a short moment Carinthia threatened to become the battleground between Italy and Yugoslavia, since both had their eyes on this Austrian *Land*. Yugoslavia's benevolent attitude toward Nazi Germany was also demonstrated by the friendly treatment of Austrian S.A. units which crossed into Yugoslavia and were housed in the noted camp of Varasin. For a brief moment it seemed feasible that a second Austrian Legion, in addition to the one in Bavaria, might come into existence, the latter to be stationed on the southern border of Austria. The Hungarian Chief of Staff proposed then to his government that in the event of the occupation of Austrian territory by Italian troops, Hungarian units too march into former West Hungary, the *Burgenland,* and occupy it.[67]

Il Duce was outraged as well as personally affected by Dollfuss's assassination. He sent Starhemberg, Vice-Chancellor, a telegram saying: "The independence of Austria is a principle for which Italy has fought and will continue fighting with even greater determination" in the difficult days ahead. When Starhemberg expressed to Mussolini the appreciation of the Austrian Government for recent Italian help, Il Duce revealed his innermost thoughts: "What I did, I did for Europe. For it would be the end of European civilization if this nation of murderers and pederasts would spread to all of Europe."[68] He left no doubt of his firm belief that German National Socialism had unleashed this rebellion in Austria and that Hitler was responsible for the assassination of Dollfuss and voiced his deep contempt for the Führer, "a dangerous fool"; he proclaimed National Socialism a "revolution of the Germanic primeval forest against the Roman-Latin civilization."

While admitting that there existed "extensive similarities" between National Socialism and Fascism, Mussolini "passionately" denied that both movements belonged to the same category. National Socialism was "wild barbarism." He hoped that it would be possible to create "a grand coalition against Germany." "I cannot always,' he continued, 'be the only one to march to the Brenner. The others too have to demonstrate that they have an interest in Austria and the Danubian region.'" But the new Chancellor Schuschnigg never developed the closer personal relationship with Mussolini which had bound his predecessor Dollfuss and Il Duce. When Schuschnigg met Mussolini in Florence on August 21, 1934, he voiced his gratitude for Italy's assistance, but made clear that a crossing of the Brenner border into Tyrol by Italian troops would be politically unbearable for the Austrian government.[69] When later, in October 1934, King Alexander I was assassinated by Croatian terrorists, Belgrade was convinced that the conspirators of the Ustascha, the Croatian terrorist organization, were supported by Fascist Italy and by Hungary and that they had made use of Austrian territory. Yugoslavia thus had additional reasons to lean toward Berlin.

It was the abortive Nazi coup in July 1934 and the murder of Dollfuss which shocked Mussolini into realization of the impending Nazi threat to Austria and the northern Italian frontier and led Fascist Italy to establish closer relations with the West aiming at the defense of Austria. But the ideological split between the Western states, their power conflict, and Mussolini's desire for fame and adventure doomed their rapprochement and with it Austria's salvation. Both the Western Powers and Italy were reluctant to make significant concessions to the other side and to move toward a genuine coordination of their policies regarding Austria and Central Europe. Also, the permanent rift between revisionist Hungary and the Little Entente prevented the formation of a Central European bloc of states to stem the German drive and block the Nazi policy of *divide et impera*.

Hardly a week after the July 1934 *Putsch*, on July 31st, Alexis Léger, Secretary General of the French Foreign Ministry, suggested the creation of a standing committee which was to consist of the French and British Ambassadors in Rome and an Italian representative as presiding officer. Such a committee, he claimed, would discourage Germany from launching an attack on Austria, and at the same time prevent Italy from acting on her own. The proposal, coming right after Italian military demonstrations at the Brenner Pass, reflected Italy's preeminence in Central Europe, but British Foreign Secretary Sir John Simon opposed the idea.[70] During the month of September 1934 discussions on Central Europe between representatives of the Western Powers were carried on at Geneva—though not within the framework of the League. Baron Pompeio Aloisi, the Italian representative on the League Council, proposed a trilateral guarantee pact between Great Britain, France and Italy. When he was turned down by the British, he suggested that Italy be given a mandate to act also in behalf of the other two major Western Powers. Barthou favored this Italian proposition,[71] but in the end the French government felt that the opposition of the Little Entente had to be taken into account—which blocked a possible agreement. The net result of these futile endeavors was the mere reaffirmation of the declaration of the Big Three of February 17, 1934. In view of the absence of real sanctions in this declaration, it had merely theoretical significance. On the other side, the attempts of the German Ambassador von Hassell in Rome to persuade the *Aussenamt* to accede to the declaration of the three powers met only with a cold reception in Berlin.[72]

Barthou had intended to visit Rome, but he was assassinated on October 9, 1934. An Italo-French agreement was, nevertheless, concluded on January 7, 1935. The two powers invited Austria's neighbors, Czechoslovakia, Hungary, and Yugoslavia, to sign a non-intervention pact, leaving it open to France, Poland, and Rumania to adhere to it later. All of the signatories were to refrain from interfering in Austrian affairs and not to permit any hostile agitation and propaganda aimed against the territorial integrity of any of the states involved. Besides, France and Italy agreed to consult with each other for the purpose of preserving Austrian integrity. In the event of a threat to Austrian independence, Britain, too, consented to consultation with the two other Great Powers. Here was an attempt to enlist not only the Western Powers but also rival blocs of smaller states in Central, Southeastern, and East Central Europe in behalf of Austria's independence against the pressures by the *Third Reich*. However, the obligations of all three major Western Powers were sharply circumscribed. In a declaration Prime Minister MacDonald underlined this in the House of Commons when stating that the proposals accepted by London with regard to the integrity of Austria involved no military

commitments![73] When Sir John Simon and Eden visited Hitler in
Berlin on March 25 and 26, 1935, the former went even further,
making the gratuitous remark that British interest in Austria was
not comparable to their interests in Belgium!

From the Stresa Conference (April 1935)
to the Ethiopian Conflict

There followed the Stresa Conference, April 11–14, 1935, between France, Italy and Great Britain. As far as Austria was
concerned, the Great Powers reconfirmed the declarations of
February 17 and September 27, 1934, about the urgent need for
preserving Austria's sovereignty and independence. But no new
commitments were entered into to support Austria in the event
of a German threat. While the Stresa Conference condemned
unilateral German rearmament, it did not take issue with the
Italo-Ethiopian war and ignored Ethiopia's recent appeal to the
League for aid against aggression. Still, the new alignment was
most significant, pointing as it did, to the possibility of the two
major democratic powers in combination with Italian fascism
stemming Germany's expansion into Central Europe. Stresa focused on their common interests in preserving the *status quo* in
Austria and Central Europe, and on the possibility of an alliance
cutting across ideological lines and isolating the aggressive *Third
Reich*. But six weeks later it became evident that Britain's commitment to the Stresa Front was quite limited. When London
signed the Anglo-German naval treaty, and without any previous
consultation with Italy and France, it virtually scrapped even
such limited obligations as it had recently assumed,[74] not to
mention those which it had shouldered as signatory of the Peace
Treaties of Versailles and St. Germain.

Britain and France had not objected to Italy playing a major
role in the defense of Austria and in wielding special influence
and power in Central Europe. But when Mussolini reached out
for Ethiopia in October 1935, the Western Powers seemed to spurn
any concessions to Italy either in Ethiopia or in the heart of
Europe. Italy, in turn, was not willing to carry alone military
responsibilities for the defense of Austria's independence, responsibilities which might interfere with the pursuit of her ambitious plans in Africa. Repeatedly Mussolini reminded the West

that the defense of Austria was a joint European task: "The independence of Austria was a European question and not one for Italy alone and he [Mussolini] had no intention of opposing Germany in Austria, unless he was to receive full support from France and England."[75] Great Britain and France, and even the Soviet Union, through Eden, Laval, and Litvinov respectively, cautioned Mussolini that involvement of Italy in Ethiopia would prevent her giving effective aid to Austria against foreign threats. Mussolini came to suspect that the Western Powers wanted Italy's participation in the defense of Austria and Central Europe only to prevent her expansive thrust into Africa.

Il Duce claimed not to be unwilling to continue to play a major role in Austria's defense, but insisted on "full support" by the Western Powers. He left it open whether he expected that "support" in return for a strong Italian stand in behalf of Austrian independence in Central Europe or, more likely, also Western favors or acquiescence to Italy's demands in regard to Ethiopia. Mussolini refused to draw from the geographic accident of Italy's proximity to Austria the conclusion of Italy's exclusive responsibility for the survival of that country. Furthermore, he tried to make the Western Powers understand that "Italy does not mean to limit her historic mission to a single political problem, or to a single military sector such as the defense of a frontier, even such an important one as the Brenner." This was an often repeated warning which should not have been taken lightly. Il Duce's bristling anger at the leaders of the Western Powers was apparent; there were those, he hinted, who wanted Italy to be frozen at the Brenner so as to "prevent us [Italians] from moving in any other part of the world."[76]

Thus, Hitler perceived the possibility of widening the wedge between Italy and the Western Powers. First, the Nazi press had resented Mussolini's recent policy which blocked National Socialism in Austria. In retaliation, the *Third Reich* was hostile to the fascist adventure in Ethiopia; some Germans even entertained the thought of fighting Italians in Africa. But Hitler decided that emotions had no place in German foreign policy. In mid-January 1935, he gave the order that the German press avoid unfriendly comments on Italy's Ethiopian conflict.[77] The new policy was quickly and appreciatively noticed by Mussolini. He was even more pleased about the prohibition of German arms deliveries to Ethiopia.

It became rather obvious that, whatever the Western Powers' thought and sentiments about Italy's Ethiopian adventure, concessions in Africa were imperative if Italy in turn were to make any contribution to the defense of Austria and to the stability of European peace and security. The West should have realized that without Italy's assistance the possibility of an effective defense of Austria was virtually nil. Yet the Western Powers considered Italy's asking price too high, the principles at stake of overriding importance and, last but not least, public opinion in their countries so adamant that they had virtuallly no choice but to reject Italy's bid for major concessions in Africa.

Some Western statemen, however, were ready to strike a deal with Rome. Pierre Laval had secretly conceded most of Ethiopia to Mussolini. Robert Vansittart of the British Foreign Office and Foreign Secretary Sir Samuel Hoare who was greatly influenced by him were for the sake of establishing a common front against Germany in Europe similarly prepared to retreat in Africa. During the summer of 1935, when the peace ballot focused attention on the support of the principles of the League of Nations by the British people, English public opinion strongly asserted itself for peace and stability and against fascist aggression. Sir Hoare came to believe that the government would lose heavily if it dared defying public opinion.[78] Though anxious to strengthen the League, he still hoped to reach an agreement with Mussolini.

England and France pursued different policies vis-à-vis Italy. Paris had welcomed it when, after the abortive July 1934 *Putsch* during which Dollfuss was assassinated, Rome turned toward it. As Laval told Sir Hoare, the Western Powers had "to prevent Mussolini being driven into the German camp."[79] To Laval, punitive action against Mussolini on account of the Ethiopian aggression involved the risk of losing Italy's support for Austria. On September 8, 1935, the French politician asked British authorities point-blank whether they would be prepared to guarantee Austria's independence; Hoare had to decline. Neither of the two major Western Powers was prepared to take the necessary steps in the event of German aggression. Therefore, their policy toward Italy was marked by extreme caution. When on October 3, 1935, Italy launched the invasion of Ethiopia, England under Sir Hoare embarked on a hesitant and ambiguous policy. The publication of the Hoare-Laval plan, which aimed at the surrender of much of Ethiopia to Mussolini, forced Sir Hoare to resign and made Eden his successor. The attempt of some British and French political leaders to buy off Mussolini by yielding in Ethiopia had failed; thus only a short time after the outbreak of the Ethiopian War, Italy gradually turned toward the *Reich*.

The war produced an irreparable split in the Stresa Front which was bound to affect Austria deeply: her possible protectors were involved in a diplomatic and economic struggle that threatened to escalate into a military conflict. Germany of course was interested in exploiting the split. In Geneva when sanctions against Italy were placed on the agenda in October, 1934, the Austrian delegate Pflügl voted with the Hungarian delegate against the application of sanctions. Censure of this vote by the Western Powers aside, this Austrian policy faced also substantial criticism at home, even among members of the Austrian government.

Beleaguered Austria and British Policy

Dollfuss's and Schuschnigg's attempts to instill Austrian patriotism among their fellow-citizens and to ward off Hitler's attacks against Austrian independence from within and without aroused great sympathy everywhere in Europe. In England Eden, then Parliamentary Under-Secretary of State for Foreign Affairs had voiced the support of the British government for the Dollfuss regime to strengthen Austrian finances and "maintain the authority and independence of the state."[80] But the British government had favored that the Vienna authorities come to a peaceful agreement with the Social Democratic Party,[81] the strongest Austrian political group. Despite her concern for Austrian democracy, Great Britain supported Austrian independence and stability in Central Europe and opposed aggressive Nazi behavior. But in June 1933. Britain's Foreign Secretary, Sir John Simon scorned the idea of joint action by England, France and Italy "to persuade the Nazis to abandon their aggressive policy,"[82] naively setting his hopes upon the persuasive force of British public opinion upon the *Third Reich*. About two weeks later, however, Dollfuss, feeling threatened, sent Rost, the League financial advisor of the Austrian government, to London with the suggestion that the three major West European

Powers agree in advance on action to be taken in behalf of Austria, should the country be suddenly attacked. This time Sir Simon favored the suggestion, but Rome refused cooperation, resenting the circumstance that Austria was obviously attempting to free herself from the one-sided dependence on Italy.[83] The need for defense of Austria against the *Third Reich* and the existence of disunity among the other major European Powers, despite their common interest in preserving Austrian independence and integrity, were as obvious already in 1933 as in early 1938, at the time of the German annexation of the country.

The apparently strongest pro-Austrian English move in the late summer of 1933 originated with Sir Robert Vansittart, Permanent Under-Secretary of State for Foreign Affairs who was in charge of the Foreign Office during the six weeks when John Simon was on holiday. In a memorandum "Present and Future Position in Europe" he held that Austria constituted for Britain "a European crisis of the first magnitude." With exceptional clarity he pointed out that Austria had only been "chosen for the first break-through of the renewed Nazi will to power because it is the easiest and weakest point. . . . The future of Europe turns largely on the fashion of our facing the German challenge over Austria, in which we are at present likely to lose." The German challenge over Austria should not be seen "as an isolated case in which the country has no direct interest, but as the first of a series of challenges each of which will carry with it a nearer threat to this country."[84]

On July 24 and 25, 1933, Dollfuss once again appealed to Rome, London, and Paris to support Austrian independence and make representations in her behalf in Berlin. But Mussolini did not react to the British request of July 29 for concerted action in the German capital. To the contrary, he informed Berlin of the contents of the British note and rather suggested to stop any actions that caused major concerns to the Western governments. As a concession of his own to Germany, he went so far as to suggest the creation of an Austrian coalition government consisting of Christian Socials and National Socialists.[85] Even while ready to support Austrian independence, some of Mussolini's suggestions were not infrequently to confuse and disturb his Austrian friends as well as the Western Powers.

In September 1933 when the Nazis accelerated their propaganda and terror campaign to undermine Austria's independence and integrity, a warning was voiced in a cabinet session of the National government under Prime Minister Ramsay MacDonald that supporting Austrian independence was identical with "backing a losing horse." Though the preservation of Austrian independence was considered to be in Britain's interest, questions were raised as to the practicality of an effective British action in the heart of Europe as well as to its overall strategic importance for the United Kingdom. Some Englishmen doubted that Austria was worth fighting for. On the whole, British response in 1933 to Austria's dilemma facing Nazism within the country in combination with the threat from the *Reich* itself, was less promising than France's reaction or even that of Fascist Italy.

On the eve of the February 1934 civil war between the Dollfuss regime and the radical socialists, the Austro-German relationship had reached a critical point. Dollfuss warned the German Government that "unless illegal activities ceased," Austria would have to haul Germany before the court of the League of Nations.[86] While France under Foreign Minister Louis Barthou, differently from a similar previous situation, welcomed the Austrian move, the British Government was hesitant. Prime Minister MacDonald wanted cooperation with Germany; he had even suggested a visit by Hitler to London for November 1933!

In February 1934, Eden, then Parliamentary Under-Secretary of State for Foreign Affairs, was anxious for a return of Germany to the League of Nations. London therefore tried to avoid a struggle over Austria in the League. The British Government had learned through Suvich that Italian fascism intended vigorously to pursue its anti-democratic course in Austria, and had urged Dollfuss to crush the Austrian Socialists; Suvich and apparently also Mussolini looked forward to a possible "invasion by German Nazis of Austrian territory," since this would produce an "energetic reaction" by Italy, Czechoslovakia, and Yugoslavia.[87] While the British Government supported Austrian independence, it opposed Italian domination of the country. Sir Simon warned that in the event Austria's democracy would be shelved, there would be a "very marked cooling in the unanimity of support hitherto given to Austria by the British press and public opinion" and further attempts to help Dollfuss "might be rendered increasingly difficult."[88] Vansittart similarly cautioned that suppression of Austrian socialism was no solution which England or France could approve.

After the February 1934 civil war between the Austrian government and the socialist workers only France was still supporting Austria's attempt to bring her dispute with Germany before the League. The Italian government rather proposed that separate but identical policy statements recognizing Austrian independence be issued. The upshot of these developments, as mentioned before, was a joint declaration made public on February 13, 1934, to the effect that the governments of London, Paris, and Rome took "a common view of the necessity of maintaining Austrian independence and integrity," in accordance with the relevant treaties. But the real significance of this statement was quite limited. Simon, when questioned in the House of Commons on February 21 whether the British government had made clear to the other two parties that England would "not raise a finger to protect" Austria's independence replied that the statement in question was merely proclaiming "general principles" and the final reference ("in accordance with relevant treaties") qualified it substantially.[89]

Soon after the outbreak of the civil war in February 1934, during which the Austrian Nazis stood aloof and waited for the outcome, Anthony Eden and Sir John Simon were on their way to Germany. On February 20 they met Hitler, Neurath, Hess, Goebbels, and the aged President Hindenburg. Hitler, erroneously, held Simon to be a Jew, apparently on account of his biblical name. As Simon recorded, the Führer was "in an excitable and distinctly manic phase."[90] According to Hitler, Germany desired a good understanding with Britain, but "she expects in time to get all Germans within her borders," including Austria (The fighting in Austria may have encouraged Hitler to make this prophecy or reveal his long-range policy). Germany did not fear isolation, opposed collective security, and in general wanted the restoration of the former German colonies before returning to the League. "All this," Simon concluded in his report, "is pretty hopeless." If Germany will not cooperate to preserve the solidarity of Europe, "the rest of Europe ought to cooperate to preserve it in spite of Germany." This might not prevent an ultimate explosion, but it would delay it.

At the very moment of a showdown in Austria British observers saw the situation in a realistic fashion: The German threat to

Austria was indisputable. Their recommendation of international cooperation against the Nazi threat seemed sound, but the chances for its effective implementation appeared slight, even though German rearmament was in its incipient stage.

The British reaction to the suppression of the last shreds of Austrian democracy was as sharp as the reaction in France and throughout continental Europe. The British Parliament and Foreign Office were inundated with questions and policy statements regarding the Austrian situation. For the Labor Party in Parliament spoke Maxton, Wedgewood, Grenfell, Mandes, and Cocks; all denounced the Dollfuss regime and made clear that in their view the Austrian champion of the oppressed had turned oppressor.[91] Sir John Simon, Foreign Minister, however, refused to interfere in what he pointed out were the internal affairs of Austria; but he reminded the Opposition that the English Government had asked Chancellor Dollfuss for clemency and that he had promised leniency to those capitulated.[92] (Similarly, half a year later, on occasion of the July 1934 abortive Nazi *Putsch* the British Foreign Minister, overly cautious, limited his comments on the assassination of Dollfuss by the Austrian Nazis to lamenting the "tragic events.") British policy which played no active role in the preservation of Austrian democracy in 1933–34, played none in the attempt to restore any aspect of it. Spurred by press criticisms and especially Laborite speeches in the British Parliament, Dollfuss and later Schuschnigg tried to counter the accusations aimed against their oppressive policies. When Sir John Simon, Foreign Secretary, assured the Austrian government of continued support for its independence, it was obvious that the British government cared more for Austria's independence than for her liberty and democracy.

The Defense of Austria and Great Power Cooperation

A few weeks only after the suppression of the Austrian workers' February uprising, on March 17, 1934, were concluded the Roman Protocols between Italy, Hungary, and Austria. This consultative pact came as a surprise to France and the Little Entente. But according to Mussolini, the Western Powers should have understood that it was "essential to keep both Austria and Hungary under my influence." He could not offer any other method "to prevent the Hungarians from passing into the German camp."

The relations of Fascist Italy and National Socialist Germany were frequently ambiguous. While ideology played always an important role in their relationship, geopolitics and national power shaped it too. And the latter involved Austria, German South Tyrol, and the access to the Balkans, all constituting differences of interest which were difficult to reconcile. The meeting between Hitler and Mussolini in Venice on June 15 and 16, 1934, focussed on Austria. While Hitler asserted that the Anschluss question was "of no interest, since it was in no way acute and . . . internationally not feasible,"[93] his insistence that a person of "independent outlook," one not bound by any political party, should head the Austrian Government appeared to qualify his disclaimer; it constituted an indisputable intervention in Austrian domestic affairs.

The Führer's reasssurances to Il Duce concerning the Anschluss proved in the light of the quickly following July developments outright deceitful. Hitler's offer to reaffirm Italy's control over German South Tyrol did not satisfy Mussolini; he also wanted Germany's renunciation both of the Anschluss and of a mere *Gleichschaltung*. The final agreement of the two dictators that the Austrian question "must not and would not be an obstacle to the development of their relations" was ominous and revealed weakness on the Italian side. The Nazi coup of July 25, 1934, resulted in the assassination of Dollfuss, but the Austrian government under the new leadership of Kurt von Schuschnigg maintained control of the country. Following this abortive *Putsch*, there was a series of bilateral and trilateral discussions between Britain, France, and Italy for the purpose of strengthening Austria's position toward Germany. But the proposal of Baron Aloisi, the Italian representative at the League Council, to give Italy an Austrian "mandate" authorizing her to act in behalf of all three powers, encountered the opposition of the Little Entente, and forced France to back down. The net result of these developments was the September 27 declaration which was basically a repetition of the February 17 proclamation.[94]

Following the assassination of Louis Barthou on October 9, 1934, Franco-Italian negotiations were resumed and led to the Franco-Italian agreement of January 1935. A consultation pact which had the purpose of maintaining Austrian independence and integrity, it was supposed to bury their past rivalry. The two powers invited Austria's neighbors to join them in a non-intervention pact. First, Czechoslovakia, Hungary, Yugoslavia, and Germany were to conclude such a treaty; at a later stage Rumania and Poland might adhere to it. All signatories were to refrain from interfering in domestic affairs and not to permit any propaganda or agitation aimed at changing the territorial integrity of any of the other signatory states.

In view of the predominance of Fascist Italy in Austria since the February 1934 clashes, if not earlier, the pact constituted also a recognition by Paris of Rome's preeminence and a willingness to subordinate ideology to the needs of Austrian defense against Germany; it rather acknowledged the semi-fascist political course in Austria which Italy had imposed upon the Austrian government. Great Britain was no party to the bilateral agreement. But in early February 1935, in the wake of Franco-British talks an understanding was reached with London to the effect that Britain, in case of any threat to Austria's independence, would consult France and Italy.

There followed in April 1935 the Stresa Conference between France, Italy, and Great Britain. Concerning Austria, the declarations of February 17 and September 27, 1934, emphasizing Austrian independence, were reconfirmed, but not strengthened. But the British virtually torpedoed the understanding reached with the two other Western Powers when they signed the Anglo-German naval treaty. Although Great Britain justified the treaty on the basis of national self-interest, this act constituted an outright attempt at appeasement; by attaching her signature to it, Great Britain ran afoul of the 1919 peace treaties, of the spirit of the Covenant of the League and its underlying principle of collective security, as well as of other agreements relating to Austria.

The Ethiopian War, Britain, and Central Europe

Mussolini's war against Ethiopia which began on October 3, 1935, augured a radical change of Italy's policy not only toward Austria and Central Europe, but also toward the Western Powers and the *Third Reich*. It held out great prospects for new German successes and led to the occupation of the Rhineland in March 1936 and to the crucial Austro-German Agreement of July 1936. The wounds inflicted on the relationship between Italy and the

Western Powers had no time to heal since soon after the termination of the Ethiopian War—which Mussolini proclaimed ended on May 5, 1936—a civil war erupted in Spain in July 1936, pitting Italy and Germany against the West.

The implications of the Ethiopian war became quickly apparent. Not only for its duration but as an aftermath to it, with Italy's resources more widely disseminated, her influence and power in Central Europe were bound to decline while those of the *Reich* were to be strengthened. Beyond the impact upon Austria directly, people everywhere quickly perceived the close connection between this conflict and the future of the League of Nations, of peace, and of collective security. If Ethiopia could be effectively helped by the League, the supposed protector of small and weak states, the value of the Covenant and of international cooperation would be promptly apparent.[95] But economic sanctions which the League belatedly and half-heartedly applied against Italy proved ineffective. Austria and Hungary voted against the sanctions, a vote which caused appreciation in Italy, but bitterness in the United Kingdom. In July 1934 Mussolini had saved the Austrian regime and the country's independence by sending troops to the Brenner pass to keep Hitler at bay and to prevent Germany from supporting the Austrian Nazis. Now Austria demonstrated her gratitude for Italy's help at that crucial moment. While some Englishmen seemed to understand Austria's dire international predicament, others cautioned Austria that strengthening the League was an international obligation and also served her self-interest. Many in Austria and throughout Europe foresaw that Austria's policy was shortsighted and that she might come to regret it.

During the Ethiopian crisis, Eden, while at Geneva, had pointed out to Pierre Laval how British public opinion, the Labor and Liberal parties, the peace and League societies, and the Churches, supported sanctions against Italy. When Laval inquired what Britain would do in case Austrian independence was threatened,[96] Eden was evasive, merely claiming that the building up of collective action would be a precedent for Britain's future action. But when pressed to be more specific, he admitted that he could give no official answer.

While there were forces in the West and in the League which wished to penalize Italy, there were others which tried to bring about a conciliation between them. The Hoare-Laval plan, however, under the terms of which Italy would have received part of Ethiopia with an outlet to the sea, became public knowledge and resulted in the resignation of British Foreign Secretary Sir Samuel Hoare. But not long thereafter, in the late spring of 1936, he was made First Lord of the Admiralty, a sure sign that he was once again in good graces.

When the Ethiopian War neared its end, Eden strongly hinted at the possibility of terminating sanctions and at a turn in British policy toward reconciliation with Italy. But Western hopes to rebuild the Stresa Front were shattered when the Spanish Civil War broke out on July 17, 1936. This date virtually coincided with the July 1936 Agreement between Austria and Germany. The latter, as seen, was not only a treaty between the two German states but one that Rome had fostered for months. In this respect the July Agreement was also a new understanding between Italy and Germany. Involved in his African adventure and anticipating the outbreak of civil war in Spain, Mussolini realized that he could not hold out indefinitely in Austria and Central Europe without making concessions to Germany.

In July 1936, the sanctions voted by the League of Nations against Italy were finally lifted. The Ethiopian War ended thus in defeat of the Western Powers, of the League of Nations, and the principle of collective security, and of all the small and weak states in the world, which were potential targets of the aggressors. The outcome of the conflict held a clear lesson also for Austria. As Colonel Wedgewood put it in the British Parliament: "If one dictator cannot be stopped from attacking Abyssinia, nothing can stop the other from attacking Lithuania, Memel, and Austria."[97]

Chapter 8

The Diplomatic Revolution:
Italy, the Ethiopian War, and Austria

Italy's Turn-About

In an extended discussion with the German Ambassador von Hassel on January 6, 1936, Mussolini suggested that Berlin and Vienna settle their differences by recognizing Austria's sovereignty and independence and signing a treaty of friendship and non-aggression. This suggestion, differing radically from Il Duce's previous Austrian policy which had climaxed in the threat of military intervention in July 1934 augured a veritable diplomatic revolution. He was fully aware that this new course would make Austria "practically a satellite of Germany." He would not object to such a relationship, but would even consider it an "advantage for both Germany and Italy that Germany gets a reliable satellite."[1] Plans for a French-inspired Danubian Pact would thus be shelved. Il Duce's change of heart and mind, coming about half a year after the beginning of the Spanish Civil War, was obviously the consequence of this conflict as well as of the preceding Ethiopian War.

Mussolini's interview left no doubt that a complete reversal in Italian foreign policy was about to take place. Hitler fully understood the significance of this turn-about. Summoning promptly Ambassador von Hassel from Rome, he held, on January 20, 1936, a special conference with him and Foreign Minister von Neurath.[2] Once again he stressed that German policy was not to be shaped by emotions and that Italy's anti-German policy of 1934 had to be disregarded. Resentments engendered in the past should not be permitted to have any bearing on future policy. He even expressed the fear that fascist Italy might be crushed in the dispute arising out of the Ethiopian conflict. Just as in 1933–34, Mussolini, his coolness for National Socialism notwithstanding, had shown concern for Nazi Germany's perceived weakness, Hitler in January

1936 voiced similar anxieties in regard to Italy; he did so on ideological and geopolitical grounds and being fearful of the likely repercussion of a military setback for Italy's fascist power structure. In the event of the collapse of Italian fascism, Germany too would face "more isolation." It was obvious that Hitler was more concerned about a catastrophe befalling Italian fascism than overjoyed at the prospect that Austria was to lose its main champion. A debacle of fascism, he reasoned, would have adverse impact upon National Socialism itself.

In early 1936 it was the Rhineland rather than Austria which was the first item on Hitler's agenda. Italy's attitude on both these issues was important to the *Reich*, though the Austrian issue was not one of immediate urgency. As signatory and guarantor of the Locarno Pact, Italy had a vital stake and interest in helping to preserve the *status quo* in regard to the western boundaries of Germany. Hitler could not well expect that Mussolini, despite his preoccupation with Ethiopia and the Mediterranean, would fully accommodate him on two issues simultaneously. Hitler's occupation of the Rhineland and later refortification and general German rearmament would strikingly alter the military balance on the continent in Germany's favor, and Italy's propagandistic support of this move promised long-range returns also in regard to German policy toward Italy and Austria.

Actually, Il Duce made substantial immediate concessions also on the Austrian issue. Beginning January 1936 he urged Schuschnigg, as noticed, to shake the hand which Hitler stretched out to him. During the next months followed Austro-German negotiations which led to the July Accord between the two countries; these, in turn, opened Austria's doors to further Nazi penetration from the *Reich*. Mussolini had long opposed Germany's thrust into Austria and her ultimate absorption by the latter. Strangely, he was also haunted by the fear of a rapprochement between Austria and the Little Entente, Czechoslovakia in particular, by the specter of a revived Austrian Empire, and the allegedly corrupting ideological consequences of democracy upon Austria. Such strengthening of Austro-Czechoslovak relations was on the agenda when Schuschnigg visited Prague on January 16 and 17, 1936. The extent to which closer relations between these two states concerned Mussolini seemed quite puzzling at times, were it not for reasons of ideological concern which so often outweighed more earthy geopolitical considerations.[3]

The weakening of the Italo-Austrian tie was not lost on Vienna, and the latter was anxious to find, if not a surrogate for Rome in Prague alone, perhaps in a combination of Prague and her allies of the Little Entente. Czechoslovakia's Premier Milan Hodža made then a far-reaching proposition to Schuschnigg, namely, to revive plans for a Danubian pact.[4] Such a pact would have given Austria the security which she had lost after Italy's plunge into Ethiopia. In pursuit of the goal to create a Danubian Pact, Hodža, in February and March 1936, visited Belgrade and Vienna, respectively. He aimed at concluding a treaty which would encompass Austria, Hungary, and the Little Entente, and was to give the area greater defensive capabilities against Germany's threats. The vacuum of Central and Southeastern Europe was to be filled by the states of the region themselves.

It was, as stated, the outbreak of the Ethiopian War in October 1935 that had triggered Italy's diplomatic revolution. Italy, sharply opposed by the Western Powers and the League of Nations and hurt by the latter's economic sanctions, became increasingly isolated and dependent on German economic supplies and diplomatic and other support. Some Austrian political leaders fearfully anticipated the day when the Italo-Austrian friendship would be sacrificed on the altar of Italo-German rapprochement. In early January 1936, the Italian Ambassador in Vienna, Gabriele Preziosi, disclosed to Foreign Minister Berger-Waldenegg that the Stresa Front belonged to the irretrievable past.[5] Papen quickly conveyed the contents of this conversation to Berlin. In March 1936, Mussolini told visiting Chancellor Schuschnigg that, considering Italy's extensive overall commitments, Austria would have to stand on her own two feet.[6] Schuschnigg could no longer entertain any doubts about the limitations of Italy's support for Austria's independence. Nor could he place reliance on the Western Powers. There had been no effective response by the Western Powers to Italy's invasion of Ethiopia or to Germany's occupation of the Rhineland: the security system of the League of Nations virtually broke down. These were the circumstances when Austria's political leadership embarked on the risky course of trying to reach an agreement with the *Reich*.

Mussolini Nudges Austria Toward the July Agreement

The Austrian initiative toward the resumption of talks with German authorities aiming at an Austro-German understanding was taken by Foreign Minister Guido Schmidt. Since the spring of 1936, Schuschnigg had given him several major assignments and a few months later even appointed him Foreign Secretary. While serving in this post, Guido Schmidt in general followed the instructions of Schuschnigg, though his over-all role in negotiations with Germany is disputable and the special privileges accorded to him after the annexation have raised numerous doubts.* Germany, on the other hand, was, after the annexation of the Rhineland, intent on calming the troubled waters, and on creating a better international atmosphere. This was the background for the direct exchange of views between Papen and Schuschnigg concerning a possible Austro-German agreement.[7]

Such an accord was bound to increase German influence in Austria, if not to lay the groundwork for her later absorption by the *Reich*. But in view of the changes in the European balance of power since 1934, and especially Rome's changing priorities in foreign policy, Mussolini was not only in favor of an Austro-German agreement, but even urged Austria to embark on this new course. Still, the new Italian Ambassador Francesco Salata, spokesman of a new more pro-German policy, had been instructed, as he revealed to Theodor Hornbostel of the Austrian Foreign Office, to be at the disposition of Austrian authorities in formulating a conciliatory agreement with Germany.[8] Thus, while negotiating with the *Reich*, Schuschnigg still looked toward Mussolini as his mentor. Italy was not yet ready to completely withdraw from Central Europe. It was also through the services of the Austrian military attaché in Rome, Colonel Emil Liebitzky, a confidant of Schuschnigg, that the Chancellor kept in touch with Italian policy; the Colonel's judgment that Italy would in no case alter her policy toward Austria and would not conclude new friendships at the expense of the old Austrian friend turned out to be fallacious.[9]

As mentioned, Mussolini received contradictory advice on Austria from his two representatives in Vienna, Gabriele Preziosi,

---

*In a postwar trial, however, he was acquitted of charges of treason.

his Ambassador who was close to Starhemberg and the latter's paramilitary organization, the *Heimwehr*, and Francesco Salata, fascist Senator, then head of the Italian Cultural Institute in the Austrian capital, who had access to Schuschnigg and was to become the new Ambassador. Salata, who, like Secretary of State Fulvio Suvich before him, came from Trieste, favored an end to the political dualism Schuschnigg-Starhemberg and the establishment of a regime headed by Schuschnigg alone, while Suvich had been in favor of that dualism.[10] The struggle between the two political rivals, Preziosi and Salata, had also definite foreign policy implications. Starhemberg, notwithstanding his early German nationalist leanings, had become a resolute defender of Austria's independence and an Austrian patriot and sharply opposed any concessions to the Nazis and even to the *Nationalbetonten*, both of whom he deeply mistrusted.[11] Both Schuschnigg and Mussolini held that Starhemberg was thus a stumbling block which had to be removed if a bilateral Austro-German accord was to be concluded.

It was Salata's pro-German view which ultimately won the favor of Mussolini. And it was Mussolini's decision which largely determined the outcome of the Austrian domestic struggle between Schuschnigg and Starhemberg. Il Duce came to support Schuschnigg, since he seemed more inclined to reach an agreement with Hitler than Starhemberg, the latter's loyalty to Mussolini notwithstanding. This new course corresponded closely to Mussolini's changing interests, the growing primacy in fascist thought of Ethiopia and of the Mediterranean area over Central Europe and Il Duce's inclination to gradually yield the latter region to Nazi Germany.

Actually, Starhemberg, in accordance with his early views on National Socialism and contrary to the impression which he later wished to give in his *Memoirs*, had not always been averse to negotiating with the Nazis. As late as February 12, 1936, Papen reported to Berlin that in a recent conversation Starhemberg had hinted at the possibility of erecting a common front between Germany, Austria and Italy. He repeated the idea in a speech before a *Heimwehr* assembly,[12] stressing the danger of Bolshevism and the need of "bringing the Fascist states into one front." Through Franz Hueber, the former Austrian Minister and *Heimwehr* leader, also brother-in-law of Hermann Göring, he attempted to

arrange a meeting with the *Reichsmarschall*.[13] Still, in the end
Starhemberg opposed the conclusion of the Agreement with the
Reich.

When Italian troops captured the Ethiopian capital Addis Ababa,
Starhemberg sent a telegram to Mussolini expressing his heart-
felt congratulations—[14] a last desperate attempt to regain Mussolini's favor. But the telegram alienated public opinion in Austria
and abroad, especially in Great Britain, and placed a weapon
against him in Schuschnigg's hands. The day after the publication
of the telegram, May 14, Starhemberg lost his cabinet post as
Vice-Chancellor and simultaneously that of the leader of the
Fatherland Front; another prominent *Heimwehr* leader, Berger-
Waldenegg, was also dismissed from the top foreign office post,
a post which Schuschnigg added to his other administrative
functions. On May 15 Starhemberg rushed to Rome in the hope
to save his fortunes, though without avail.[15]

When on May 29, 1936, Starhemberg returned to Vienna, the
Heimwehr's political fate was sealed.[16] With Starhemberg toppled,
the Austrian Chancellor turned to Mussolini to secure his help
in negotiating the basic agreement with Hitler. Through Salata,
rather than through the Italian Minister Preziosi,[17] Mussolini was
kept informed of the major provisions of the prospective Agreement. Finally, on June 5–6, 1936, Schuschnigg explained to Il
Duce at the latter's country home in Rocco della Caminate the
basic principles and concrete stipulations of the Austro-German
Agreement. Yet it was Mussolini who had originally suggested
what kind of concessions were to be made to the *Reich*.[18] When
first asked by Schuschnigg about the Austrian government's intentions to reestablish normal relations between Vienna and Berlin,
Mussolini had gone out of his way to support him: "I cannot
too emphatically advise you to come to terms with Germany."
An Austro-German treaty would signify "the final crack-up of
the Western democracies. Austria's place is at the side of the
dynamic Powers. This is how you can best insure your independence."[19] While the latter judgment was more than questionable,
Il Duce's reaction shows clearly that the Austro-German Agreement, in his opinion, paved the way to the establishment of the
Rome-Berlin axis. This alliance was uppermost in his mind, with
Austria being aligned with it. Il Duce had also persistently
reminded Schuschnigg that Austria was too weak a country to

pursue what he called an anti-German policy. He, Mussolini, could more effectively help Austria if not only Italy, but also Austria herself entertained good relations with the *Reich*.

Corresponding to the new pro-German trend in Italian policy, Mussolini made also several changes in the Italian cabinet. Direction of foreign affairs, which up to this moment had been largely the responsibility of Fulvio Suvich, Secretary of State in the Foreign Ministry, changed hands: Count Galeazzo Ciano, his son-in-law, became Foreign Minister at the age of thirty-three and deliberately set out to reverse Suvich's policy.[20]

Having been urged by Mussolini to take the initiative toward Berlin, Schuschnigg approached von Papen who a year ago had made pertinent suggestions relating to a bilateral German-Austrian accord. Schuschnigg's own proposal of June 19, 1936, was actually based upon several ideas previously advanced by Papen. The Austrian Chancellor also engaged in negotiations with Edmund Glaise-Horstenau, a representative of the *Nationalbetonten* in Austria, many of the latter barely disguised Nazis. These activities, proceeding along two different channels were to climax in the Agreement of July 11, 1936.[21]

The Reaction of the Great Powers

The Western Powers and the Soviet Union were by no means unaware of the dangerous trend in Central Europe. In early June the French and Soviet Ambassadors had urged the Italian government to rebuild the system of collective security, suggesting especially a Four-Power Pact between France, Great Britain, the USSR, and Italy. Italy would pledge to defend Austrian independence, while the sanctions against Italy resulting from the Ethiopian War would be terminated. But Italy demanded that the sanctions be unconditionally scrapped.[22] Thus, the combined East-West attempts to jolt Italy and make her align with other major powers in behalf of Austria failed again.

In late June 1936, Anthony Eden and the French Foreign Minister Yvon Delbos made another attempt to block the move toward an Austro-German agreement. They invited Schuschnigg to meet with them in Geneva at the General Assembly of the League. But when Mussolini advised against it,[23] Schuschnigg declined the invitation with the words that "the internal and external position of Austria was of a clarity that left nothing to be desired."[24] The rejection pleased Rome and Berlin. Mussolini, though ready to abandon Austria, was unwilling for her to seek alternate support against Nazi Germany. Schuschnigg actually was well aware of the strong opposition to the impending agreement both within and without Austria. On July 9, two days only before the Austro-German Agreement was to be signed, he ordered the start of a propaganda campaign to counter the expected adverse criticism.[25]

Italy herself was on the defensive. Referring to the 1936 Agreement, *Gazetta del Popolo* claimed that Austria's relations with Italy, as expressed in the Rome Protocols, remained even after the July Accord the fulcrum of Austrian policy.[26] *Tribunal* accused British and other foreign circles of deliberately exaggerating their pessimistic assessment of the situation in Central Europe and in Austria in particular.[27] Only a few months later, in an article in the *Neues Wiener Tagblatt*, on August 25, 1936, V. Gayda, confidant and frequent mouthpiece of Il Duce, directed attention to the Franco-Italian accord of January 7, 1935, as an agreement "for the protection of Austria."[28] Mussolini wanted also to secure the cooperation of Poland, Austria, Hungary, and this time also of the Little Entente. Though Mussolini had urged Austria to sign the July Agreement with Germany, he apparently did not yet consider Austria's cause as completely lost or Italy's role in the defense of Austrian independence once and for all terminated. And he wanted to let Berlin know about it!

The assessment of the new situation in Central Europe by the Soviet Union was more realistic. As the American Ambassador reported the Soviet point of view from Moscow, recent events, primarily the occupation of the Rhineland and the July Agreement of 1936 "have altered the balance of power in the Danubian basin in a way that is far from favorable for Italy. From Italy's point of view, [there was] only one aim to follow, to try to create a dam against German influence."[29]

Italy's Declining Influence in Central Europe

The Agreement clearly showed that Italy had yielded to Germany in Central Europe and in Austria in particular. Still, Göring was not satisfied either in regard to Austria or Hungary. In a

conversation with Hungary's Foreign Minister Kánya, he alluded
to Italy's "exaggerated influence" in Hungary.[30] Von Hassel,
German Ambassador in Rome, also thought that Italo-German
differences were not definitely settled and would still cause many
altercations between the two nations. As far as Austria was
concerned, Italy knew that she had retreated, but was not always
candid. As Ciano reported after his visit to Berlin, the Austrian
problem no longer existed![31] This was wishful thinking and also
indicated that Italy was resigned to play a subordinate role in
the region.

Though since early 1936 Italian fascism had moved toward
accommodation with Germany and toward persuading Austria to
enter into an accord with the *Reich*, Berlin still mistrusted Mussolini's new course; it did not consider the new policy as "de-
finitive."[32] With Italy's foreign policy being in a state of transition,
neither Germans nor Austrians nor others were sure in which
direction Italy's ship of state was steered. While on September
26, the Italian Ambassador in Budapest tried to assure Kánya
that the German-Italian rapprochement had not changed Italy's
policy versus Austria,[33] others were less certain. While Czechoslovakia, favoring support for Austrian independence, was anxious
to enlist Italy's continued help, Italy, through Suvich, advised
Austria to seek closer ties with Yugoslavia rather than with
Czechoslovakia! In view of Belgrade's pro-German and pro-Anschluss orientation, such a course was hardly in Austria's interest.
Nor was it in the interest of Rome. But Rome's hostility to Prague
was largely determined by the anti-Czech orientation of German
foreign policy, not to mention Prague's continued allegiance to
democratic practices.

Austria's Ambassador Pflügl sharply castigated the pro-German
foreign policy of Italy which he considered equivalent to the
complete abandonment of Austria.[34] In general, Prague was as
pessimistic as Vienna in regard to Rome. A report, however, from
the Austrian Embassy in Prague, pointed to new Czechoslovak
hopes in regard to the Danubian realm; these hopes rested on
the irreconcilability of German and Italian interests in Central
Europe,[35] interests that had been only temporarily shelved by the
German-Austrian July Agreement. Much of Europe found it difficult to believe that Rome had permanently renounced its interests
in Central Europe, all for the sake of friendship with Berlin.

In view of Italy's rapprochement with Germany, the former was bound to abandon any thought of supporting Austrian legitimism and the Habsburg Restoration. Even in the earliest postwar era, Rome had been dead-set against the Restoration of the Habsburg dynasty and with it of the Austrian Empire to the north, which had been Italy's historic enemy. As the Italian Ambassador Vinci in Budapest told Kánya, the Restoration was not desirable in view of the Italo-German collaboration.[36] The influential Italian journalist Vittorio Gayda had recently published an article displaying keen hostility to the Habsburg Restoration.[37]

In the judgment of the Soviet Ambassador in Rome, Italy had lost her independence in foreign policy vis-à-vis Germany.[38] Mussolini had completely surrendered Austria to the influence of the *Reich*. The Vice-Commissar of Foreign Affairs of the USSR was convinced that Italy would be compelled to relinquish her entire position in Central Europe.[39]

In the spring of 1937 Rome, as far as Austria was concerned, was no longer in an optimistic mood. Ciano revealed to the Hungarian Minister President Dáranyi and Foreign Minister Kánya that the Anschluss would probably occur sooner or later. In the future, Italy could no longer support the independence of Austria with force of arms. But in the course of his conversation Ciano averred that it was the goal of Italy's foreign policy to postpone the implementation of the union for as long as possible.[40] Neither the absorption of Austria nor the fate of Czechoslovakia would affect Italy's political course, which was tied to Germany.

The declining faith of Austria's leadership in Italian pledges in behalf of Austria made her government turn to the Western Powers. But returning from London and Paris, Guido Schmidt claimed that he had merely wanted to inform the West about Austria's situation and that he had not requested their guarantee for Austria's independence.[41] Papen did not seem convinced that this journey had been devoid of any political purpose. According to his information, the Austrian government had been seeking in London and Paris assurances in regard to the independence of its country.[42]

The meeting in Venice between Mussolini and Schuschnigg on April 22, and 23, 1937, held significance for the quadrangular relationship between Italy, Germany, Austria, and Czechoslovakia. The final communiqué remained silent about the independence of Austria. To top matters, Il Duce committed a studied insult by not accompanying Schuschnigg to the railroad station, while visiting a German cruise ship! His message to Vienna and Berlin could hardly be clearer. Prague was bitter about the results of Venice, since Il Duce had definitely blocked the road to an Austro-Czechoslovak understanding. The Austrian foreign minister Guido Schmidt held that only the end of the Spanish Civil War would terminate the Italo-German collaboration,[43] implying that thereafter Italo-Austrian relations might improve.

Germans, including von Neurath, believed that the problems of the Danubian realm would be solved only through bilateral accords. The *Third Reich* did not wish to join the Roman Pacts, but rather wanted that Austria, Hungary, Yugoslavia, Bulgaria, and if possible, also Rumania and Poland, adhere to the Berlin-Rome axis. In April 1937 Neurath revealed that the fulcrum of the axis lay now in Berlin. He considered the German-Italian collaboration as quite satisfactory,[44] but complained that the Austrian government allegedly did not observe the stipulations of the German-Austrian July 1936 Agreement. This complaint was in the nature of a threat. But the Hungarian Foreign Minister Kánya thought that Germany for the sake of Italo-German collaboration would not employ force against Austria.[45]

The policy not only of Italy but also of Yugoslavia had become ambivalent toward the Anschluss and toward Germany. According to Ciano, the Yugoslav and the Hungarian governments sought security against Germany in the development of a new political axis Rome-Belgrade-Budapest![46] Il Duce displayed a keener resolve to resist Germany's and especially Göring's pressure than Ciano and spoke of the need of pooling Italy's and Yugoslavia's resources, not, he claimed, "against Germany; but we should between us organize collaboration with her." A short time thereafter, Yugoslavia's Premier Stojadinović expressed his actual fear of the Anschluss in stronger terms. In his view, there should be an Italo-Yugoslav rapprochement after the implementation of the Anschluss: "All those countries who must oppose the German descent towards the Adriatic or along the Danube valley will polarize around the Rome-Belgrade axis." Still, in 1937 neither Rome nor Belgrade were willing or felt strong enough to block Germany in Austria; they were already resigned to the loss of Austria and were merely thinking of defensive measures against

Germany—*after* the *fait accompli* of Germany's annexation of the country!

Izvestiia, the Soviet government daily, saw another axis emerging, namely one between Vienna, Budapest, and Prague.[47] Moscow itself was tied to Prague by a defensive pact. About the same time, the Czechoslovak press commented similarly that Germany's threat to both Austria and Hungary compelled both states to take defensive preparations. But many Czechoslovak journals doubted that Hungary, obsessed with territorial revisionism, was likely to create sufficient distance between herself and Germany. Hodža was more optimistic about the possibility of improving Czechoslovak-Hungarian relations, indicating simultaneously his intention not to make Czechoslovakia's treaty with the Soviet Union the cornerstone of her policy.[48]

In Italo-German relations, focused on Austria as they were, the role of Göring with his ruthlessly aggressive manner was comparable to the bulldozer crushing all opposition before it. Arriving in Rome on January 15, 1937, he told Il Duce that it was necessary to clarify the Austrian problem, especially if Italy wished to count on German support at critical moments, such as might arise from her Mediterranean policy. Mussolini asked Göring to put his views on paper. Despite the lack of a positive response by Il Duce, some sort of understanding emerged from their conversations: there would be no revival of Italy's Stresa partnership with the Western Powers and no second "watch on the Brenner." Germany, on the other hand, would strictly adhere to the July Agreement and no change in the German-Austrian relationship would take place without prior notification of Rome.

Chapter 9

Austria Isolated: The Western Powers' Policy of Appeasement. From the Rhineland Occupation to the Eve of Austria's Annexation

The British Foreign Office, the Rhineland and the Continent

Mussolini's success in the Ethiopian War was a boost for Fascism. But by spreading Italian resources thin, he was bound to weaken Italy's position in Central Europe. The winner in this region was bound to be Germany. British foreign policy thought, as expressed in numerous memoranda of the British Foreign Office during 1936 and early 1937 made this quite clear. The chief of the Southern Department of the Foreign Office, Owen St. Clair O'Malley, analyzing on December 1, 1935, the Central European situation in a memorandum entitled "Collective Security," predicted with great accuracy that Germany would first occupy the demilitarized Rhineland and create for herself freedom of movement. He considered it very unlikely that Britain or other nations would block such a move and expected that Germany, buoyed by this success, would then turn against Austria, if the latter had not already dropped "like the proverbial plum into her mouth."[1] Shrewdly assessing France's and Italy's lack of preparedness to risk war for the sake of Austria's independence, he did not even pose the question of resort to arms by the United Kingdom in this context. After stating that Britain had relatively minor interests in the Danubian basin, he even claimed that she should economically "benefit rather than lose" by the economic unification of the Danubian basin under German leadership. The historian and collaborator of the Southern Department of the Foreign Office Edward Hallett Carr, a noted Soviet and International Relations expert, agreed with this strategy proposed by O'Malley and pointed to the advantages of a British-German Agreement on Central and

Southeastern Europe. Germany, he held, "must expand some-where," and her expansion into Central and Southeastern Europe might take place "with a minimum of danger and inconvenience to British interests." He proposed that the British Government let the German authorities know that it disapproved of a forcible link-up of Austria with Germany, "that, however, in the event of an Austrian plea for union, addressed to the League of Nations, she should be ready to act favorably upon it."[2] This view was also largely supported by William Strang, Counselor in the Foreign Office. He recommended that Britain refrain from participating in new joint declarations on Austria's independence and integrity, and added: "Our general obligation under the Covenant to oppose aggression remains. It is to be hoped that the absorption of Austria by Germany, which is probably inevitable in the long run," can be accomplished "peacefully." This was the line of thought and policy course which British governments pursued until Hitler's annexation of Austria.[3]

The British seemed convinced that neither the League of Nations nor France's army would be able to defend Austrian independence. In the cabinet session of January 29, 1936, Eden disclosed that in his view France would never fight for the sake of the principle of collective security, but only to ward off an attack aimed at her own frontiers.[4] The historian Carr concluded that "military action in defense of Austria with—and a fortiori, without—the cooperation of foreign states, is no practical politics, whatever the state of our armaments." Any sanction which might be imposed on Germany would "not suffice to release Austria from the German grip." He drew the further conclusion—"a highly important one for our Central European policy"—"that Austrian independence continues to exist only at the good pleasure of Germany. The same may be said of the independence of Czechoslovakia."[5] Opinions such as these, widely shared among the experts of the Foreign Office and members of the Cabinet, were likely to undermine every will to resist German pressures.

On February 11, 1936, Orme Sargent, Assistant Under-Secretary of State in the Foreign Office, outlined alternatives for British policy aiming at the prevention of the Anschluss, but he definitely excluded British or French military intervention. According to Sargent, Great Britain could rely first upon the system of collective security and the League; she could also attempt to enlist Italy

into a new Stresa Front. England might also try to create a
political and economic bloc consisting of the states of the Little
Entente, Austria, and Hungary. There was furthermore the possibility of restoring the Habsburg dynasty. Finally, the help of
the USSR could be secured to protect Czechoslovakia's and
Austria's independence. Admittedly, "none of these alternative
courses looks very effective or promising."[6]

The British Foreign Office favored negotiations between Czechoslovakia and Austria. Restoration of the Habsburgs, however,
appeared to the Foreign Office dangerous on account of the
pronounced German hostility to this scheme. Czechoslovakia and
her allies of the Little Entente, were also opposed to it. Austen
Chamberlain warned that a Habsburg Restoration would be a
crime against the entire world.[7] The British Foreign Office did
not deny, however, that in the long run the right of self-determination included the right to establish a monarchy. For the time
being, however, the Habsburg question could be regarded only
as "back-page news."

The British Government realized the difficulty of enlisting the
possible support of the Soviet Union for Austria and Czechoslovakia. Already early in 1936, the Foreign Office, not immune to
hostility to the USSR, which originated in the early revolutionary
Soviet phase, and not unmindful of the tortuous Anglo-Soviet
relations of the 1920s, thought it "in the long run uncomfortable
and dangerous" "to be beholden to Russia for undertaking to
maintain the *status quo* in Europe."[8] In occasional talks between
British and Soviet statesmen on Central Europe there was apparent
agreement that an increase of German strength in the area was
in the interest of neither power. But Britain would have considered
a diplomatic or military tie-up with the USSR only "in the event
of an extreme threat," as one official put it,[9] of a deliberate
onslaught by the fascist powers on the Western democracies. While
there were some doubts in British Government circles that the
Soviet Union would become a reliable partner in the defense of
Czechoslovakia, the likelihood that she might render effective
help to Austria seemed even smaller. The anti-Communism of
the generally conservative Foreign Office personnel affected perhaps this judgment on the Soviet Union. Others in the Foreign
Office drew attention to France's weakness, her alleged lack of
resolve, and chronic political instability. In any case, all attempts

to establish a strong anti-Nazi front in Europe against further German expansion in the direction of Austria and Czechoslovakia came to naught. All this made even Lord Vansittart, known for his opposition to German imperialism and Nazism, come out in favor of the return of former German colonies, provided the *Third Reich* would be ready to make concessions of her own and not raise any new demands. He specifically demanded Germany's return to the League, the start of disarmament, and her renunciation of all territorial claims in Europe, including Austria.[10]

Going even beyond this stance, O'Malley, Chief of the Southern Department of the Foreign Office, writing on February 24, 1936, a memorandum for the Cabinet, found it advisable to silently drop the British declarations in support of Austrian independence and sovereignty and to agree to a continuing expansion of German trade in the Danubian states; Germany in return would pledge not to violate the principles of the League or to injure British trade interests in Central Europe. According to O'Malley, only Italy had so far prevented the Anschluss. France, Great Britain, and Italy held the position of Austria "by a system which may not unfairly be described as a mixture of bluff and bluster."[11] The Foreign Office seemed to be increasingly inclined to embrace a policy of compromises vis-à-vis Germany and some were even ready to yield on the issue of the defense of Austrian independence.

This policy met with the approval also of Foreign Secretary Anthony Eden.[12] As some experts in the Foreign Service had predicted, the loss of the demilitarized Rhineland zone made it virtually impossible for France to take military action against Germany and to come to the assistance of her East European allies. Joseph Avenol, Secretary General of the League of Nations, disclosed to Lord Cranborne that the remilitarization of the Rhineland signified that "French obligations in Eastern Europe must be liquidated."[13] About half a year later, on November 25, 1936, he apodictically stated that "French intervention in Central Europe was no longer possible";[14] this opinion was based upon the expert judgment of the French Chief of Staff.

The occupation of the Rhineland was to impress all of Europe with the bold challenge of the *Third Reich*, the weakness and hesitancy of France, Great Britain's unwillingness to give strong support to the French ally, and Italy's growing inclination to lean toward Germany. As far as Austria was concerned, it could hardly strengthen her confidence in effective support by Paris and London or Rome. Yet the Austrian Foreign Minister Berger-Waldenegg in an interview published in the *London Observer* (April 4, 1936) sounded confident, nevertheless: "There was nobody in the Rhineland to oppose the march of German troops into the zone. It is different in the case of our country." "We are convinced that our friends Italy and Hungary, and even others, would assist us."[15] The Austrian Foreign Minister and *Heimwehr*-man exaggerated until the very end Italy's influence, steadiness, and continuing interests in Austria; he trusted less the Western democracies. His skepticism in this respect was shared by a British parliamentarian who visited Vienna in April 1936. Sir Austen Chamberlain, while in the Austrian capital, contrasted British public opinion towards Italy and Germany: while British opinion was "thoroughly incensed against Italy," it was only "placid towards the recent German Rhineland move."[16] This contradiction, rooted in what was perceived to be the primacy of British colonial and African interests over most European interests, was to continue until 1938.

After March 1936, the Foreign Office was fully aware of the deterioration of the Austrian situation. On April 10, 1936, Orme Sargent raised the question of additional guarantees reaffirming Austrian independence, but held that the British public "did not think that its direct interests were involved in Austria." Besides, "by giving these guarantees we would be definitely pledging ourselves to the policy of the *status quo* (e.g., as regards Memel, Danzig, and the Corridor) and at the same time making ourselves responsible for the government or misgovernment of Austria and Czechoslovakia."[17] While Britain was not ready to enter into a new agreement assuring Austrian independence and integrity, she was not prepared to renounce such contractual and other obligations toward Austria which she had voluntarily assumed since the end of World War I. These treaties included the Peace treaties of 1919, the Covenant of the League of Nations, as well as a number of financial arrangements in the postwar period none of which could be easily shirked. But some experts in the Foreign Office were ready to weaken past joint Anglo-French-Italian declarations in behalf of Austrian independence. This stance found expression in a memorandum by O'Malley dated May 7, 1936; Britain should continue to support the independence of Austria, but the British government needed "more room for maneuver"; it should support a modification of article 80 of the Versailles Treaty.[18] The latter suggestion, however, was opposed by his colleagues Orme Sargent and Ralph Wigram,[19] though both shared O'Malley's view that Great Britain's going to war over Austria was "entirely inconsistent with British public opinion."[20] This view was also given expression by Eden in the cabinet session of April 29, 1936, when he declared it improbable that British public opinion, bolstered up by Mussolini, could be against another party which was bolstered up by Hitler.[21]

The British were by no means enamored of Schuschnigg as a political leader. The Labor Party, dedicated to political democracy and to her Austrian sister Social Democratic party, had serious reservations about Schuschnigg's semi-fascist political course, though it supported his struggle for Austrian independence. Most British people appreciated that Schuschnigg was dedicated to the latter course, but did not consider him an inspiring leader. They were also critical of Austria's attitude toward the League of Nations, her support of Italy in the Ethiopian War, and especially her vote against sanctions against Italy. In combination with other weighty geopolitical motives, these considerations were responsible for a strategy of delay. As Eden disclosed, a policy of procrastination on Austria was the consensus of the Cabinet.[22] Any crisis which might arise over her destiny, should be approached with utmost caution: it should not be brought to a head but rather postponed. Tactics of delay might not solve the problem, but might avoid a catastrophe and perhaps in the end lead to a peaceful settlement. Avoiding war over the Austrian issue seemed the best course possible.

Toward the Austro-German July Agreement: Britain's Policy of Procrastination

The tactics of procrastination were fully endorsed by Oliver Harvey, Eden's Private Secretary, Lord Cranborne, Parliamentary Under-Secretary, and J. P. Thomas, parliamentary Private Secretary.[23] Whatever differences existed in the Foreign Office, all seemed to agree on the need for reaching a settlement with Germany, if at all feasible, since the system of collective security enshrined in the Covenant was "no more than a myth." Some, as Sir Alexander Cadogan, believed that Germany could not be held to the "vindictive" clauses of the Peace Treaty.[24] German propaganda, often by endless repetition—the ground being prepared by a guilty English conscience over the Peace settlement—had unquestionably made inroads into English public opinion and had even made an impact upon some experts in the Foreign Office.

The War Office followed the Foreign Office with a memorandum on the likely consequences of the Anschluss, but went far beyond expressing strictly military judgments. It held that German control over Austria might prove economically advantageous "through its resulting increase in the prosperity of Central and Southeastern Europe" and by disposing of the Austrian "bone of contention."[25] The War Office added (July 10, 1936) that German control over Austria might "take place by mutual consent" and, "with adequate guarantees for the rest of Europe," without elaborating on such important points.[26] Leading officials of the Foreign Office, the Chiefs of the Southern and Central Department, joined the War Office in reaching similarly optimistic conclusions: that the prosperity in the wake of German dominance of Southeastern Europe would lead to a stronger demand for British goods. The trade of Great Britain with Czechoslovakia, Austria, and Southeastern Europe amounted only to 2% of the entire British volume of trade.[27] German expansion into this part of Europe would help British traders!

On June 26, Eden proclaimed that Great Britain could not give any guarantees for Central Europe, even if the French Government had concluded treaties with countries in that region.[28] Under these circumstances, an Italian guarantee, at least the existence of a friendly Italy, was "necessary if Great Britain and France are to continue to exercise any effective influence in Central Europe."[29] But neither Eden nor Vansittart had a clear conception of how an Italian guarantee could be secured.

The July 1936 Austro-German Agreement came as a great surprise to the Foreign Office. O'Malley later disclosed that the Office had no information about the preceding Austro-German negotiations.[30] The first reaction of the Foreign Office was favorable: Sir Vansittart even talked about a "diplomatic victory" of Schuschnigg. The British press welcomed the Agreement. In a memorandum entitled "The Austro-German Agreement," written on

July 14, O'Malley went overboard listing a number of alleged advantages which in his opinion warranted that the Austrian government attached its signature to the document. Since Austria had come to realize that no French government was "capable of mobilizing the French army for any purpose other than the defense of French soil," and that Italy was in no shape for a European war, it was "high time for Austria to take out an insurance policy in Berlin."[31] He did not deny, that the agreement represented "a tendency towards *Gleichschaltung*, though it in terms foreswears the Anschluss," but still considered it "quite positive" from the point of view of British interests. In any case, "German action in this matter deserves a public expression of our satisfaction and respect."[32] Positive, though not as exuberant as O'Malley's, was also the assessment of the Agreement by the British Ambassador in Vienna, Sir Walford Selby.[33] And Lord Cranborne in the House of Lords, in the only official declaration of the Foreign Office on the July Agreement, welcomed the alleged strengthening of Austrian stability and the removal of frictions in Central Europe.[34] Sargent, Under Assistant Secretary of State, in an inter-office assessment, found fault only with the bilateralism of the Agreement and Eden similarly recognized the dangerous implications of the Austro-German document. But in a major foreign-policy address on July 27, 1936, he placed Austria definitely beyond the zone of British interests.

But thereafter criticism of the Agreement mounted rapidly, though skepticism was restrained and not always publicly expressed. Some held that the July Agreement represented "a sort of half-Anschluss." Only toward the end of 1936 did the Southern Department reach the conclusion that in the long run the Agreement would benefit only Hitler. He had put the Austrian question "on ice until Germany was ready for . . . *Gleichschaltung* or Anschluss."[35] Similarly pessimistic, in a memorandum dated August 24, 1936, were now the judgments of Ralph Wigram, Chief of the Central Department, of Orme Sargent,[36] also of the Foreign Office, and of Sir Thomas Inskip, Minister for Coordination of British Defense. According to the latter, Great Britain would at no time fight for Austrian independence. Looking forward to 1940 when British plans for rearmament would be substantially carried out, "an automatic liability to engage in war in which our vital interests were not concerned, probably in Southeast Europe, would

cause me," he wrote, "a great deal of apprehension."[37] Despite
the strong position which Sir Vansittart took in regard to the
defense of Western Europe, for Central and Southeastern Europe
he too favored only a policy of procrastination and caution. He
presented his views in a letter to the British Minister for Air,
asserting that he had "never contemplated further commitment
in Central Europe," but it was a "very different thing to appear
overtly and in advance to leave it to fall."[38] In a private talk
with Litvinov, Eden similarly confined British commitments specifically to Western Europe. The British Government's position
was finally made quite clear by Eden on December 2, 1936, in
the House of Commons when he limited the development of
British arms to the defense of Britain, France, and Belgium. The
next days the Foreign Minister also approved of the Foreign Office
memorandum of August 24, 1936, that, if Austria was to survive,
she would "undoubtedly have to rely very largely, perhaps entirely,
on herself."[39] By 1936, British public and expert opinion had
come to oppose military assistance to Austria and Central Europe
as not being possible; it was not likely to be effective, and, in
any case, not needed for the defense of what were judged to be
only vital British national interests.

The Foreign Office's leading West and Central European experts
were increasingly opposed to advise the British government to
risk war for the sake of Austrian independence. In December
1936, Admiral Alfred E. M. Chatfield in a letter to Lord Vansittart
confirmed the need for "British military assistance to Western
Europe . . . France, Belgium, and Holland," but continued: "If
Germany tried to expand to the Southeast, we must accept it."[40]
France should be told confidentially that Great Britain can't support
her in a general European conflict. There seemed to be a growing
consensus of opinion that England and France, even if acting
jointly, would not be able to stop German expansionism in Central
and Southeastern Europe. By the end of 1936, Eden believed that
Central and Southeastern Europe could be held only through
close cooperation with Italy. On December 16, 1936, he voiced
the hope to be able to reach "a real Anglo-Italian Entente. There
is nothing I should like better. . . ."[41] Sir Vansittart similarly
considered Italy's help in the defense of Austrian independence
crucial in view of mounting German pressure and the Nazis'
Trojan Horse tactics. As he wrote: "Let us never disparage

Mussolini, but pray on the contrary that he may endure; for he is our best hope . . . in this world whose imperfections may thus be measured."[42]

Early in 1937 the British Foreign Office had to a large extent accepted the thesis that German expansion should not be halted forcibly in Central and Southeastern Europe. It insisted, however, that the *Third Reich* observe certain diplomatic proprieties, namely refraining from armed aggression and resort to force. The memorandum "British Foreign Policy toward Germany" of May 1937 stressed[43] that as long as the national integrity and independence of Germany's neighbors remained secure, the British government possessed no right to object to the *Third Reich's* hegemony in regions which, in any case, Germany, through resident German population, German industry, and her army, could easily dominate. In the case of Austria, however, Great Britain need not insist even on national independence and territorial integrity. The British government in the end may face in Austria a *fait accompli*. Surely, the author of this memorandum of the Foreign Office, nine months before the resignation of Eden in February 1938, had reached a dismal conclusion in regard to Austria and virtually recommended surrender. Even Eastern Europe was here assigned to become Germany's sphere of influence. It was after all no vital British sphere of interest, "and the German is certainly more civilized than the Slav and in the end, if properly handled, also less potentially dangerous to British interests."[44] Needless to point out that such judgments fell far short of needed objectivity, revealed a spineless attitude and constituted an unprecedented retreat compared to earlier British positions. Germany had simply become "too powerful" for Britain to prevent "a certain German predominance eastward," a trend which after all was inevitable.

An examination of the documents originating in the British Foreign Office as well as official pronouncements of the Government in the course of 1935–36 shows thus clearly the weakening of the British position on Austria in particular and Central and Southeastern Europe in general. The British Government, it is true, maintained its interest in Austrian integrity and independence, but began to make numerous qualifications. Britain grew reluctant to commit herself firmly and without reserve. Many of its officials, privately at least, frequently raised questions about the justice of the Peace Treaties, the wisdom of the Anschluss prohibition, the fairness of denying self-determination to Austria, and some even acknowledged Germany's right of expansion into Central and Southeastern Europe and East Central Europe. They were resolved to protect only "vital interests" of the British people, limiting these to Western Europe. They assumed that National Socialism, if treated gently and not "provoked," would turn out to be "moderate" and would abandon its far-reaching goals and aggressive methods.

Long before the March crisis of 1938 not only Austrian politicians but also several British political leaders were unquestionably intimidated by aggressive National Socialist foreign policy and behaved in an overly cautious manner.[45] The Austrian Foreign Minister Guido Schmidt was no paragon of straightforwardness. Fearful of the repercussion of a strong British policy statement on behalf of Austrian independence, he advised that Great Britain proclaim her interests in the stability and the *status quo* of Central Europe in general rather than those in Austria in particular; the latter might needlessly irritate Hitler. Eden did not need such a warning. While he claimed that British policy could not "disinterest" itself from Austria, he never indicated the extent of British interest and what he considered the limits of tolerable German behavior in regard to Austria. He tried avoiding being "imprudent." What actually was needed to deter Hitler was more than a mere policy declaration by Britain in behalf of Austria or a wider Central European area, namely an iron-clad guarantee by Britain, France, and Italy, supported by a credible and steadfast foreign policy, and adequate rearmament. Also needed of course were courage, determination, and opposition to appeasement.

The Policy of Appeasement; the Cliveden Set, Nevile Henderson, and the *Times*

Appeasement started long before Austria was annexed and it did not die until the outbreak of World War II. But an understanding of British policy toward Austria and Central Europe must take full account of the ideology and methods of the policy of appeasement which deeply affected the policy of British cabinets even before Neville Chamberlain became Prime Minister in May 1937. It prevailed at the time of the annexation of Austria, climaxed in the Munich Conference, and flourished even thereafter.

Foremost among the group of British appeasers was the so-called "Cliveden set." Without formal organization, inclined to criticize French rather than German policy, sharply critical of the Peace Treaties and the *status quo* and willing to ignore or gloss over the Nazi domestic record, they were long bitterly opposed to the policies of the Foreign Office and especially to Sir Robert Vansittart, its permanent head, as one likely to alienate Hitler by his "rudeness." The Astors, Margot Asquith and others objected especially to Vansittart's "hatred" of Nazism rather than to Hitler's and the Nazis' well known dislike of and contempt for most European nations. The Cliveden set included both Tories and Liberals of distinction and men of eminent social status. They rejected going to war for the sake of small distant and relatively little known European peoples. The ideology and politics of the Cliveden set were widely shared in the United Kingdom; they were by no means limited to country houses, but also well represented at Westminster. Other Germanophile Englishmen gathered around magazines such as the *Anglo-German Review*. While some Britishers judged Hitler wild and unpredictable, the appeasers were confident that British patience and kindness would duly impress him and bring him to reason.[46]

The appeasers made a point arranging journeys for influential Englishmen to visit Germany and to be received by Hitler. Lloyd George, himself not a member of the Cliveden set, but often leaning toward appeasement, after a visit to the Führer found him "the greatest living German" and, a year later, expressed his admiration for him.[47] While British Ambassadors such as Sir Horace Rumbold, Sir Eric Phipps, and Ivone Kirkpatrick, First Secretary of the Embassy in Berlin, and numerous experts were increasingly anxious about the trend of German developments and foreign policy, an unending stream of British appeasers, according to Vansittart, deceived themselves on the basis of the flimsiest evidence and the shortest conversations with the Führer, of the possibility of Anglo-German rapprochement and of the settlement of deeply divisive issues between both nations; they rejected any thought of Britain's defense of the *status quo* in Central and Eastern Europe. J. L. Garvin, editor of *The Observer*, which Astor owned, wrote that one of the conditions of a "constructive peace" was that a "large part of Eastern Europe proper should be reconstructed under German leadership. Germany's drive to Eastern Europe would bring new unity and order to that chaotic region.[48]

A prominent champion of appeasement was Lord Lothian who had met Hitler in 1935. While the Führer lectured him on the evils of Communism, he informed Hitler that he personally did not rule out a "change in the political status of Austria."[49] In response to Hitler's suggestions for a plan for Anglo-German cooperation, Lothian promised to talk with leading British statesmen about a possible "plan designed to stabilize Europe for ten years." Though enthused, even he seemed doubtful that the *Third Reich* could be appeased for a longer period. After his return to London, Lord Lothian in a letter to *The Times* voiced his conviction that Germany did not want war. When he met the Führer a second time in May 1937, he told him that "Britain had no primary interest in Eastern Europe."[50] Again Lothian assured Hitler that he considered the "obstacle" to a solution of the Austrian question not England, but rather Mussolini and the Pope!

Joachim von Ribbentrop, German Ambassador to the Court of St. James since October 30, 1936, was introduced to the Cliveden set by Thomas Jones, an influential member of the group. At Lady Nancy Astor's house at Sandwich—"a south-coast Cliveden"—Ribbentrop lectured to a group consisting of Lothian, Inskip, and the Astors about the importance of Anglo-German collaboration and talked with Lord Lothian about Austria. Lothian expressed the hope that if Austria fell to Germany,[51] it would not come to a "breach of faith" between Britain and Germany— to which Ribbentrop promptly agreed. As Thomas Jones had told Stanley Baldwin a week earlier: "We do not mean to fight for Austria any more than for Abyssinia. We are not going to impose sanctions against Germany under any formula of collective security."[52] Another close friend of Ribbentrop was Lord Londonderry who became especially receptive to the Ambassador's scheme of an Anglo-German alliance against Communism.

The appeasers worked cautiously and carefully, and behind closed doors. The English people in the opinion of M. Gilbert and R. Gott, close students of British appeasement (*The Appeasers*, 1963), "knew little of their surreptitious work before 1937, and in the three following years were not to discover anything at all."[53]

A key post in British-German relations was held by an outspoken appeaser, Nevile Henderson. He was appointed to his post of Ambassador in Berlin by Stanley Baldwin, not without misgivings by many British officials,[54] and arrived in Berlin toward the end of April 1937. In an address at a dinner given in his honor by the *Deutsch-Englische Gesellschaft*, which Heinrich Himmler and Alfred Rosenberg personally attended, he emphasized that far too many people had an erroneous conception of what the National Socialist regime really stood for. "If Germany could guarantee peace, she would find that she has no more sincere and, I believe, more useful friend in the world than Great Britain." "Peace" seemed to him more important than other traditional English values, including the age-old British concept of balance of power, so vital for British security and that of the Commonwealth. According to the American Ambassador, historian William Dodd, Henderson "informed the German government that England would make no objections if Hitler seized Austria and Czechoslovakia." He also told Dodd, "Germany must dominate the Danube-Balkan zone which means that she is to dominate the seas jointly with the United States." England and Germany must enter into close relations, economic and political ones, and control the world. Though Henderson disavowed this conversation, he made similar comments to many of his friends.[55]

Of all British dailies, none was more influential in matters of foreign affairs than the *London Times*. Its editor Geoffrey Dawson was a proponent of appeasement long before Chamberlain assumed the post of Prime Minister. Dawson knew Chamberlain well and was also a close neighbor of Halifax in Yorkshire. Responsible for foreign affairs in *The Times*, he actually relied on Lord Lothian whose expertise on Germany apparently dated back to his visit to Hitler.

Though the policy of appeasement and that of Neville Chamberlain have become identified in the minds of most people, appeasement actually preceded the assumption of power by Chamberlain on May 28, 1937. In the preceding month Nevile Henderson had become British Ambassador in Berlin, replacing Eric Phipps who was known for his anti-Nazi orientation. Now the Prime Minister and his Ambassador were both enthusiastic champions of the policy of appeasement. They also had something else in common: both were permeated by the belief that Providence

itself had chosen them. They were thus able to discount the keen
opposition which their policy encountered in Great Britain. Their
desire for peace at any price placed human and civil rights, the
parliamentary and democratic system of government, British national interests in Central, Southeastern and East Central Europe,
at correspondingly lower levels. They extolled international tran-
quility, even if it had only a transitory rather than permanent
character.

Neville Chamberlain at the Helm

It was ironic that Neville Chamberlain who throughout his life
had disliked and mistrusted Germany became the champion of
the policy of the appeasement of the *Reich*. While on a holiday
in the Black Forest in 1930 he had revealed that "on the whole,
I loathe the Germans." He was quite critical already of the first
performances of the Hitler regime and convinced that Germany
was up to her old tricks again. His private comments on the
Nazi leaders were sharp: Hitler was "a lunatic" and "half-mad,"
Goebbels a "vulgar common little mind," and Ribbentrop "stupid,"
"shallow," and "self-satisfied;" he was "horrified" by the German
behavior toward the Jews. In March 1938 in the House of Commons
he disclosed that "for the preservation of democracy I myself
would fight."[56]

When Neville Chamberlain came to power in May 1937,
England, in his view, was not ready to fight; even in the summer
of 1938 experts held that it might take one to two years before
England would be prepared to wage war on more or less equal
terms. The lack of military preparedness was undoubtedly a major
factor in shaping his policy versus Germany, but there were
others.[57] After Eden's resignation on February 22, 1938, Chamberlain voiced his disbelief in the League's collective security.
With other Englishmen he had developed doubts about the justice
and the wisdom of the stipulations of the peace treaties of Versailles
and St. Germain. Neville Chamberlain had been Prime Minister
Baldwin's chief advisor for several months before he succeeded
him to the top post, a post for which his own father Joseph
Chamberlain had considered him completely unsuitable. While
Stanley Baldwin's foreign policy was marked by lack of initiative
and drive, Neville Chamberlain gave it great impetus and energy,

but the over-all direction of the political course was hardly altered. As his policy of appeasement took on more definite shape, he was to earn a French sobriquet "Monsieur j'aime Berlin." He expressed frequently his lack of confidence in France which, he charged, changed governments every nine months,[58] and he lamented the "absence of any powerful ally." His mistrust of Russia formed part of the background of his desire for friendship with Germany. Dircksen, who succeeded Ribbentrop as German Ambassador to Britain, pointed out that the Neville Chamberlain cabinet was the first postwar cabinet which had included agreement with Germany as one of the major points of its programme. Chamberlain's cabinet included numerous docile men who shared the Premier's wishful thinking about the *Third Reich* and echoed his general political philosophy. Men of more independent character and judgment, Eden, Duff Cooper, and Hoare-Belisha, were all destined to leave the Cabinet. A dominant figure in Chamberlain's circle and one to gain influence also in foreign affairs, was Horace Wilson, though he was hardly knowledgeable of the German and general European scene. All in all, the philosophy of appeasement had deeply penetrated British government circles.

Driven by a sense of personal mission to reach a friendly agreement with both Fascist Italy and Nazi Germany, Chamberlain wanted to demonstrate to both Rome and Berliln that Britain could be generous and was willing to trust them; in return he apparently anticipated a sort of *noblesse oblige* behavior, without insisting on definite pledges and guarantees. Chamberlain was willing to recognize Italy's conquest of Ethiopia and to offer African colonies to the *Third Reich*. Eden, not trusting the behavior of the Fascist aggressors who had already demonstrated their territorial greediness, held Chamberlain's course unwise, demoralizing to British and European public opinion, and perilous at a moment British rearmament was conspicuously lacking.

In November 1937 Chamberlain wrote to his sisters: "I don't see why we should not say to Germany 'Give us satisfactory assurances that you won't use force to prevent the changes you want, if you can get them by peaceful means.' "[59] After Halifax's visit to Germany and his conversation with Hitler in November 1937 he concluded, as his diary showed, that he was prepared to hand over to Germany Tanganyika (German East Africa before 1914), with some territorial adjustments. Chamberlain's benign assumptions about the moderate character of Hitler's and the Nazis' ambitions were completely erroneous, as every realistic and unbiased observer of the *Third Reich* in the 1930s could testify to. But Chamberlain light-heartedly dismissed the knowledge of eminently qualified British contemporaries, stubbornly relying on his intuition. He was supported by leading British dailies which endorsed the policy of appeasement, especially *The Times*, the *Daily Express* of Lord Beaverbrook, the *Daily Mail* of Lord Rothermere, and many others. As Mowat wrote in *Britain between the Wars*: "In retrospect everyone was against appeasement; at the time not so many."[60] But a determined political leader with perspicacity, foresight, and courage could probably have produced a timely change in the attitude of the British people and with it of the British press.

Greatly encouraged by Neville Chamberlain's accession to power, the appeasers continued their struggle against their opponents. Franckenstein, Austrian Ambassador at the Court of St. James, held that while recent speeches in the House of Lords had shown that many recognized the necessity of making certain colonial concessions to Germany, it appeared that the "great majority of members of both houses of Parliament continued to be unyielding." They were convinced that Germany would not be pacified and would make increasing demands.

In November 1937 Lord Halifax who was considered "moderately friendly to Germany" and maintained good relations to the Germanophile circles in Britain was journeying to Berlin.[61] Eden had warned against Halifax's trip and withdrew the threat of resignation only after the task of drawing up instructions for Lord Halifax was entrusted to the Foreign Office.

When Halifax met Hitler in November 1937, he made clear Britain's interest in peaceful evolution in Central Europe rather than in the application of force or the threat of force; he mentioned in this context Danzig, Austria, and Czechoslovakia.[62] This policy actually amounted to a surrender, provided Hitler only chose the proper method of action; it permitted Germany to ignore the Peace Treaties and to create a new European order. Halifax, however, seemed satisfied that Hitler claimed to adhere to the Austro-German July 1936 Agreement in which he had pledged to respect Austrian sovereignty and integrity. Without touching upon the long dispute between the two parties in interpreting the Agreement, Halifax in his report stressed the importance of continued Austro-German conversations; this bilateralism was of course close to Hitler's heart. Not only to Hitler but also to the German Foreign Minister von Neurath, Halifax revealed too many of his cards: he assured Neurath for instance that the English people would never approve going to war over the mere issue of union between the two German states; Chamberlain, however, considered Halifax's visit a great success.

Abroad, Chautemps sharply criticized Halifax for having made in his conversation with Hitler a "blunder" of the first order. Halifax, according to Chautemps, had begun by saying that he had not come to discuss matters in Central Europe and had accepted without protest Hitler's reply that "Great Britain was indeed very little interested in what might happen in Central Europe."[63] In England herself there were also critical voices raised. Lord Londonderry, an appeaser who, however, had developed second thoughts about this policy, castigated the British Government's "shilly-shallying policy."[64]

In late November 1937, Chautemps was scheduled to visit London. The diary note of Chamberlain for November 26, 1937, shows what was in the Prime Minister's mind at that moment. Chamberlain promised not to use force in dealing with the "Austrians and Czechoslovaks if Germany can get the changes she wants by peaceful means." Again he did not object to changes in substance, merely to some methods Germany might employ. Chamberlain agreed with Chautemps on opposing "any forcible change in Austria."[65] But Eden in his *Memoirs*, contested that anything was said on this occasion about Austria; Czechoslovakia, was the main topic of discussion.

That the issue of Austrian independence was largely ignored on occasion of the Chautemps visit is confirmed by the meeting of Eden and Ribbentrop in the Foreign Office on December 2. Eden reported that he had told Chautemps that the Austrian question was "of much greater interest to Italy than to England." (This of course was passing the buck!) Again, this was a discouragingly weak statement, making it highly unlikely that Britain would ever resort to effective military action to check a possible German attack against Austria. This policy was hardly different from the dubious reflections of Lord Halifax about Austria at Berchtesgaden in November 1937. In both cases the pledge of

British passivity was given to the highest officials of the *Third Reich!*

Whatever differences in policy and approach existed then between Lord Halifax and Eden, they hardly extended to the Austrian problem. In regard to Austria, they both travelled along the highway of appeasement. Three days earlier Delbos had warned Chamberlain that the "absorption of Austria" and of part of Czechoslovakia by Germany would have adverse consequences for the peace of Europe. It was necessary that treaties be respected, for this was the basis of the law of nations. Whatever France's weakness, here at least was a clear conception of the major issues posed by the challenge to Austrian independence and sovereignty. Compared to this insight, which was admittedly not supported by adequate force and resolute will, the conceptions and actions of English statesmen, whether Halifax or Eden, appear pale and weakly. The overall English position versus Germany on Central Europe lacked strength and firmness.[66]

French Policy, 1937, Austria and Czechoslovakia

France's self-doubts and doubts about her allies increased during the year 1937. While the French government itself continued to assure friends and allies of her loyalty toward Czechoslovakia and dedication for the preservation of the territorial *status quo* based on the peace treaties, it made repeatedly a distinction between France's treaty obligations to Prague and the absence of comparable obligations to Austria. The declining faith of leading Frenchmen in the policies and capabilities of France became evident to Bullitt in his talks with both Delbos and Léger of the French Foreign Office. In their view, the likely purpose of von Papen's impending visit to Paris had been to ascertain whether France would react more violently to an aggression against Czechoslovakia or to one against Austria.[67] Delbos disclosed that after Berchtesgaden Papen had been informed with complete honesty that France would fulfill to the limit her treaty obligations to Czechoslovakia and that she would view with disfavor any change in the status of Austria. As Delbos put it to Bullitt: "France has no obligations to protect Austria." There would, however, be a different reaction if French territory or that of an ally of France would be invaded.[68] At the beginning of the new year the French

Foreign Minister had thus few hopes for Central Europe; he did not expect that either the United States or Italy would side with France in this region. Delbos believed that if Hitler should decide to make any move in Central Europe at the present time, it would be directed against Austria and not Czechoslovakia. He thus had already written off Austria. The French government was also fully aware that Poland, Czechoslovakia, and other states in Central and Eastern Europe were beginning to lose confidence in the effectiveness of French support.[69] Still, these very states, Delbos and Léger asserted, had no confidence in German pledges of non-aggression and would continue trying to obtain support from the Western Powers.

Both Delbos and Léger considered it "highly improbable" that Germany would risk war during the next twelve months, since she will need this time to make changes in weaponry the defects of which had become apparent during the fighting in Spain. They were both apprehensive, however, that Hitler might possibly decide sometime during the next twelve months to provoke a Nazi revolt in Austria and support it by so-called "volunteers" from Germany.

About Austria's dire political and military situation neither Delbos nor Phipps, the new British Ambassador in Paris, had much doubt. They were of the opinion that Hitler could now take Austria any time he might choose without creating serious international complications.[70] In the course of a long conversation on May 5, Bullitt reported that Delbos had expressed to him his "despair" of being unable to invent a working foreign policy which might preserve peace in Europe. He said that "day and night he was worried how he could keep Central Europe from falling into the hands of Germany," that he was "unable to invent any scheme which seemed to him likely to achieve success. Every time that he suggested to Czechoslovakia, Rumania, Yugoslavia, or Austria that they should together with France more strongly oppose Germany, the reply was: "We should be very glad to do so if England would join France in guaranteeing us against Germany. France is not strong enough to protect us alone, especially in view of the new status of Belgium. We cannot therefore carry out an anti-German policy." Phipps, however, British Ambassador to Paris, had made it clear to Delbos that "Great Britain would not guarantee either Czechoslovakia or Austria, to say nothing of Rumania."[71]

The more immediate German target in Delbos' view was, as mentioned, Austria rather than Czechoslovakia. In his interview with Bullitt Delbos went on to say that Schmidt, the Austrian Foreign Minister, would reach Paris on May 19th and he, Delbos, would not know what to say to him. France alone could not possibly march to the support of Austria. Mussolini had made it clear to Schuschnigg that he would do nothing to keep Austria from falling into Germany's hands. Mussolini, furthermore, had told Schuschnigg that he was entirely opposed to the project of a rapprochement between Austria, Czechoslovakia, and Hungary. It was he, Delbos, who had initiated this rapprochement and he hoped that Schuschnigg and Beneš would go ahead with it in spite of Mussolini's disapproval. He still had some faint hopes that such a rapprochement might become the nucleus around which other states of the Danubian basin could group themselves, but he was by no means optimistic. He had failed to draw Poland into better relations with Czechoslovakia despite a recent French loan to Warsaw.[72]

Delbos went on to say that Schuschnigg had shown great courage in his conversation with Mussolini at Venice. He had said to Mussolini that he could not and would not detach Austria from Czechoslovakia, that they were both equally menaced by Germany, that if one should be swallowed, the other would shortly after, that "they might be weak but they should stand or fall together." Delbos also thought that "Schuschnigg would hold out to the end against absorption by Germany because he was sure of the Pope's complete support against the Nazis." Though Delbos was quite frank and realistic regarding the extent of aid, if any, which Vienna could expect from Paris, he expressed only slightly more optimism, "faint hopes," regarding a rapprochement between the Danubian states; actually, he exaggerated the possibility of an Austro-Czechoslovak rapprochement. For a fleeting moment only Schuschnigg may have held it possible for Vienna and Prague to stand together, but, when the moment of decision approached in March 1938, Prague was bound to follow its separate course!

While the French Foreign Minister emphatically stated that in the event of a German attack against Czechoslovakia, France would immediately declare war on Germany, on the other hand he admitted to Bullitt that the Rhine was strongly fortified by the Germans and that the only line of attack against the *Reich* was a line of 150 km between Karlsruhe and Luxembourg. "This front was so short that a small portion of the German army could hold up the French army, leaving the major portion of the German army to operate against the Czechs and Austrians."[73] In his discussion of this question, Delbos appeared to Bullitt very gloomy. As the American Ambassador wrote: "For the first time I caught a note of irresolution and I suspect that after Delbos' unsuccessful visit to Belgium and his apparent inability to obtain the approval of its government for a march through Belgium against Germany, the decision of the French Government to go to war on behalf of Czechoslovakia might "weaken"—which turned out to be a correct prognosis. In conclusion, Delbos admitted that "France was no longer strong enough to maintain the *status quo* in Central Europe against an opposition composed of Germany and Italy. France could take a strong position only if she should have the absolute support of England. But until England would be "fully rearmed," he feared that she "would not take any strong position with regard to Central Europe. He was at his wits end. . . ."[74] The implications of this analysis for Czechoslovakia, not to mention Austria, were quite clear, France was caught in a vicious circle.

Delbos apparently was in better spirits after the joint visit of Premier Chautemps and his own to London in late November 1937. After his return he was to leave for a journey to Poland and the states of the Little Entente: Neville Chamberlain had "authorized" him to represent also Great Britain in the capitals of these states! In reply to a question, however, whether Britain had promised to "support France completely in Central Europe" he was evasive, saying that neither France nor England would announce in advance that they would go to war and that "only the event could prove what would happen. The case of Czechoslovakia was different. . . . The British had declared that they were not disinterested," but "had made no promises."[75] Actually, no basic change in Franco-British relations had taken place in London, the divergence of their plans regarding military help to Czechoslovakia in the event of an emergency was as deep as ever. Possible help to Austria had, as a matter of fact, been rejected by Chamberlain. As the American Ambassador to Poland, Francis Biddle, wrote to Secretary Hull on December 8, 1937, according to Delbos—as he had revealed to the Soviet chargé while in Warsaw—France was "seriously concerned over . . . Britain's indication to Germany that she would consider standing aside under certain conditions in the event Austria elected to turn to Germany culturally and otherwise. France did not like this."[76] Still the French Premier Chautemps had not abandoned all illusions. He claimed to look "with considerable equanimity on the possibility that Germany might annex Austria, because he believed that this would produce an immediate reaction of Italy against Germany."[77] This frail optimism was based upon the hope that Italy's Stresa policy, a policy long abandoned after the Ethiopian War and Italy's involvement in the Spanish Civil War, could be revived. Chautemps had no false hopes in regard to possible help in the approaching Austrian crisis from the U.S. or other states. The United States, he remarked, "sits happily on the outside, and every other nation in the world sighs with hands folded."[78]

In spite of this criticism French Premier Chautemps expressed his pleasure at the remarks on foreign affairs by President Roosevelt in his message to Congress, though basically he remained skeptical.[79] He then reiterated to Bullitt, as the Ambassador reported, that the only effective intervention of the United States in world affairs would be if the President should be able to state that the United States would take up arms against an aggressor or at least cut off exports to an aggressor and send supplies to any nation or nations attacked. He added at once that it was impossible for the President to make any such statement or take any such position. "He felt that this was unfortunate, as he was convinced that such a declaration by the President of the U.S. would be sufficient to stop the aggressor states and therefore would end the risk of the U.S. being involved in war. He was convinced that the U.S. would be drawn into war, if war should start in Europe, and suffer tremendous losses which could be avoided by taking a strong position which would prevent war." In reply to Bullitt's question whether he, Chautemps, had done anything in the way of developing a rapprochement with Italy, he said, "that with Mussolini in his present state of mind it was virtually impossible to do anything with Italy," in fact diplomatic relations had "practically been severed by France and Italy."[80] Chautemps' realistic assessment of Mussolini's stance toward the mounting Austrian crisis bode ill for the possible blocking of German ambitions in Central Europe.

Britain Gives Confusing Signals

While Germany's foreign policy in regard to Austria, especially since the summer of 1937, moved at greatly accelerated tempo and showed growing signs of impatience and radicalism, France, playing more and more the role of a "brilliant second," looked anxiously toward Britain. British policy toward Central Europe and Austria seemed quite contradictory. The remarks of a conservative Member of Parliament, Enrys Evans, in the Commons on June 25, 1937, and the utterances of Anthony Eden made, according to a report from the Austrian Embassy in London, considerable impression in Britain. Evans recalled that Great Britain throughout her history had never permitted any power to militarily dominate the continent and Eden cautioned that Great Britain could as little disinterest herself from Central Europe as from developments in other parts of the world. The preservation of peace in that region must be paid unceasing attention. Eden rejected the accusation that the general guidelines of British policy on Central Europe were unclear,[81] the very charge revealing of widely held beliefs. But the French Embassy in London was convinced that an attack by Germany on Czechoslovakia or Austria must necessarily lead to France's intervention and that Great Britain in turn would be compelled to side with her ally. This, according to the Austrian Ambassador in London Franckenstein, himself leaning to an optimistic interpretation of English affairs, was the view of many other contemporary observers. The Permanent Under-Secretary of State in the Foreign Office and later Ambassador to Paris, Lord Tyrrell, confirmed that it was important to make Britain understand the significance of preserving Austria's independence for the sake not only of the latter but of European peace in its entirety. Czechoslovakia's survival and France's system of alliances were also at stake.

At the so-called Hossbach Conference on November 5, 1937, Hitler revealed to a select group of high-placed Nazi officials and military leaders his scheme for aggression in Europe in the near future. A few days thereafter, Lord Halifax, ready for his journey to Berlin, but unaware of these plans of aggression, expressed to

Ribbentrop his "pleasure at having the opportunity of becoming acquainted with the Führer . . . whose work he admires."[82]—an inexcusable and dangerous flattery. On November 13, the *Evening Standard's* diplomatic correspondent reported that, according to the information of the British Government, Hitler was ready to offer Great Britain a ten-year "truce" during which period Germany would not raise colonial issues. "In return for this agreement Hitler would expect the British Government to leave him a free hand in Central Europe." Both the French and the British public were alarmed; there followed hasty disavowals from the Foreign Office. Still Chamberlain, as seen, was already prepared to surrender Central Europe to Hitler, provided he would only use peaceful means; he confirmed as much on November 26, 1937, in a private letter to his sisters.[83] But once Austria and Czechoslovakia were within the German orbit, however peaceful the procedure, what was to prevent Hitler from using new threats and force to make new gains? Britain would have no sanctions to prevent further German expansion.

British public opinion was not fully aware of every slight shift of governmental policy. But the mutual impact of public opinion on Austria and public policy toward her was undeniable. On November 22 began to appear in *The Observer* a series of articles by Garvin which were widely commented upon also in the Foreign Office. Garvin claimed that the incorporation of Austria aimed at by Germany was no less natural and inevitable than the union of the German states under Bismarck's leadership had been. It was simply "crazy to interfere." He furthermore called Czechoslovakia an "unnatural and unhistoric state," in behalf of which Great Britain should "under no circumstances raise arms."[84] The Austrian Ambassador in London Franckenstein commented: "No doubt that Garvin's thesis would find approval of the by far great majority of the population—if it would be consulted."[85] Former veterans, according to prominent British generals, had a fanatic abhorrence against any war, feelings which were widely shared among the populace. The League of Nations had great support in the British Isles. While German policy in the religious field was widely disapproved, the criticism was counterbalanced by Britain's ardent desire for conciliation and peace with the *Reich.*

High-placed British military officials did not share Garvin's view that Britain was as weak as pictured in his articles.[86] British politicians also informed the Austrian Ambassador that while the Government must take account of public opinion, it had also means of influencing the population and of persuading it to go along. In the British Foreign Office Franckenstein was told that Great Britain "as a Great Power could not disinterest herself on the Continent."[87] George Lansbury, the known Labor deputy, explained to him that, though political gatherings in which pacifists spoke, attracted large audiences, it would be erroneous to conclude that the working class and the people in general were not affected by the situation on the Continent. "Sacrificing Austria in the interest of an agreement between Great Britain and Germany contradicted their views."[88] Whatever the contrary strands in British public opinion, Chamberlain and the strategically placed fellow-travellers of his foreign-policy course gained increasingly the upper hand.

Chapter 10

The Soviet Union, the Austrian Communist Party, and the Anschluss

Revolutionary Expansionism and the Peace Treaties

Soon after the Bolsheviks seized power in Russia in October 1917, they came to grips with the problems of the foreign policy of the new state. In March 1918 they signed a separate peace with the Central Powers. After the conclusion of armistice between the Entente and the Central Powers in November 1918 they came face to face with political and social revolution in many parts of Europe and the spread of Bolshevism to Budapest and Munich. Under these circumstances the Anschluss question in the immediate postwar period was not a central, but rather a minor and distant problem for Soviet Russia.[1]

In the 1920s the movement for German union in Central Europe, never reaching a real climax, was again one of many, though never one of the primary diplomatic concerns of the Soviet Union. It was part and parcel of the German question, to be placed into the larger framework of her Rapallo policy; it was also tied up with Soviet opposition to the peace treaties. The USSR opposed the victorious imperialist Western Powers and criticized their peace treaties as dictates; not invited to join the League of Nations, the Soviet Union denounced it as a league of capitalist and imperialist oppressors. In accordance with this stance, the Communists attacked the prohibition of the Anschluss. In the 1930s, however, after Hitler's seizure of power in Germany, it became increasingly clear to the USSR that Austria held the key to German domination over Central Europe and to German penetration of the Southeast of Europe and that the Anschluss would create an imbalance on the European continent. The Soviets especially feared that Austria would become a jumping-off board for the resumption of the *Drang nach dem Osten* (drive toward the East). Revamping their foreign policy under the threat of fascism, they finally reversed it and came to oppose Hitler's thrust against Austria.

Hitler's accession to power substantially altered the political situation in Central Europe and in Europe in its entirety. In view of the open hostility of National Socialism toward Communism and the USSR, a revamping of Soviet foreign policy was only a matter of time. In accordance with such changes, Soviet policy on the Anschluss also veered from one extreme to the other.

In 1931 and 1932, at a time of the rising threat of Hitler fascism in Germany, Soviet policy still favored the Anschluss and pointed once again to the Danubian Federation, an alleged tool of French imperialism, as a possible threat to both Russia and Germany. France wanted to broaden the federation to include all of East Central Europe and establish its hegemony. The editorial of *Izvestiia* of February 29, 1932, entitled "Danubian Federation," pointed to a regrouping everywhere of the Great Powers and their small allies and vassals, including a regrouping in Central Europe.[2] France wished to broaden the Little Entente through the inclusion of Austria and Hungary and to have Poland join it. But the USSR saw in this projected bloc merely a broadening of the military alliance between France, Poland, and Rumania, which was aimed against the Soviet Union. According to *Izvestiia*, the Danubian bloc was also a permanent threat directed at Germany. A month later, on March 27, 1932, *Izvestiia* continued its comment on "the Danubian Federation Plans." France, by sponsoring such a project allegedly wanted to shore up fascist dictatorships which, under the blows of the economic crisis, began to crumble in Central Europe and the Balkans. Furthermore, France wished to create a powerful bloc extending from the Danube to the Baltic area comprising a population of 120 million and thus to perpetuate her own hegemony and the Versailles settlement.[3] According to the Austrian envoy in Moscow, the Soviets held that the French plan aimed at linking Austria and Hungary to the chariot of the Little Entente.[4]

The Soviet leadership, obsessed then with the struggle against left and right "deviation" at home, had apparently less time for foreign affairs: it underestimated the appeal and strength of National Socialism in both Germany and Austria, and the staying power of the authoritarian Austrian government. In 1932 the Soviets gave the Dollfuss regime only a few months of life.

Austrian National Socialism would take over the reins in Austria; but the Soviets apparently also held that a Nazi regime would be only of brief duration and represent a mere transition to communist seizure of power. According to the Austrian envoy in Moscow, Stern, Director of the Second Western Division in the *Narkomindel* (Commisariat for Foreign Relations), held that National Socialism in Austria was not in a retrogressive stage, but rather in a growing one and that the present Austrian regime could not last long. "A national socialist government in Austria would perhaps not be so bad, one must give this Party the chance to demonstrate its capacities." The Austrian envoy could hardly believe his ears, but noticed the unquestioned serious intent of Stern.[5] He entertained no doubt that Stern expressed not merely a personal point of view but rather one held widely throughout the Communist Party of the Soviet Union, though this could not be publicly revealed.

Gradual Changes of Soviet Policy

At the time of the abortive Nazi coup in July 1934 and the assassination of Dollfuss, the Soviet press, according to the Austrian envoy, took no clear-cut position on the Austrian events—in sharp contrast to most of the European press. The Soviet press rather pictured the Austro-German tension and the defense against National Socialism in Austria as "a scuffle between different varieties of fascism." Most Soviet papers seemed to gloat that the "capitalist world" encountered serious perils on account of the Austrian problem. Paralleling the recent francophile turn of their policy, however, the Soviets, according to the Austrian envoy, expressed greater sensitivity to the growing threat of Hitler Germany to world peace.[6] The Soviet press, he criticized, held no eulogy for Dollfuss nor voiced a word of indignation over the abominable murder. *Izvestiia* was indeed quite restrained about the role of German officialdom in the assassination; it held that the recent unrest in Austria was the work of domestic Nazis rather than the result of manipulation and unceasing agitation and propaganda from across the border. It looked, however, with special satisfaction upon the deterioration of German-Italian relations following the assassination of Dollfuss.

The Soviet Union's ambivalence toward Nazi Germany, marked by increasing awareness of the threat the *Reich* constituted to her own security and perhaps by fear of arousing Nazi ire, characterized her attitude also toward the question of the restoration of the Habsburgs versus Anschluss. Officially, the Soviet Union was then opposed to both propositions, but unofficially its opposition to the Habsburg restoration was apparently slackening, especially if the Anschluss danger would thereby be reduced or eliminated.

In close connection with the crisis in Austria, many foreign, especially French, dailies had raised the question of the restoration of the Habsburgs in Austria. The Soviets apparently did not share the viewpoint of those in Austria or abroad who thought that Restoration would definitely remove the danger of German fascism to Austria. While according to *Izvestiia*, Czechoslovakia and Yugoslavia preferred the Anschluss as the "lesser evil" to a Habsburg restoration, the Soviets considered the Anschluss a peril to peace. For this reason perhaps some officials in the USSR were not dead-set against the Habsburg Restoration.

According to the Austrian envoy in Moscow, a high functionary in the Foreign Commissariat had expressed himself to the Austrian envoy in a manner quite different from the official *Izvestiia*. "The restoration of the Habsburgs as a means to do away once and for all with all Anschluss endeavors, was not to be lightly dismissed," he held. The Austrian envoy concluded that in his view such utterances again did not express mere personal views, but reflected a widely held opinion in official Soviet circles,[7] though it was not the one which prevailed at the moment.

Held in the same vein is another report almost a year later in which the Austrian envoy, in a communication to the Austrian Foreign Minister Berger-Waldenegg, referred to articles by the Moscow correspondent of the Viennese *Neue Freie Presse*, Basseches, about Soviet policy toward Austria.[8] Officials of the *Narkomindel*, Stern and his deputy Linde, had allegedly expressed "very great understanding for Austria's Catholic policies" in the struggle against National Socialism and had indicated Soviet readiness to assist Austria's economic needs.

The Czechoslovak-Russian rapprochement, climaxing in a military alliance in 1935, fortified Soviet policy in support of Austrian independence, in spite of the ideological polarity existing between the two countries. Moscow recognized, just as Prague and Vienna did, that the defense interests of Czechoslovakia and Austria were intertwined. In talks with Soviet politicans in June 1935, Beneš repeatedly stressed the need for the preservation of Austrian independence. According to the correspondent Basseches, the tie with Czechoslovakia forced the Soviets to a more activist policy both in the Danubian area as well as in the Balkans. After the November 1918 Revolution in Germany, Soviet policy first had extolled rapprochement with Germany and had favored the application of Bolshevik theories of the nationality problem to Central Europe, including the Anschluss. But in the course of the last months there had occurred pronounced changes. Some Soviet circles were still of the opinion that the fate of Austria did not affect the interests of the USSR. Yet it was characteristic that "on occasion of Beneš's visit here your correspondent had frequent occasions to discuss this question with Soviet diplomats. A highly responsible Soviet diplomat explained . . . that the Soviet government placed a great value on good relations with Vienna."[9] On October 31, 1935, the Austrian envoy assured the Foreign Minister in Vienna that the démarche of the Foreign Commissar Litvinov in Geneva against those states which refused to apply sanctions against fascist Italy on account of the Ethiopian war, meaning Austria and Hungary, was "by no means an intended criticism of Austria."[10] Litvinov himself on occasion of a social gathering had also assured the envoy that he had not meant to hurt Austria.

On January 16, 1936, the Austrian envoy seemed puzzled that for a longer period no unfriendly articles on Austria had appeared in the Soviet press. Previously, hostile articles from the pen of former *Schutzbündler*, now living in the USSR—the organ was named after the socialist para-military organization of freedom fighters of February 1934—had been published in the Moscow *Deutsche Zentral-Zeitung*. An article on Austria in *Izvestiia*, January 27, 1936, omitted any reference to "Austro-fascism." The author emphasized that the Austrian Chancellor Buresch's visit to Prague was the first Austrian state visit since 1922, when Chancellor Seipel, "the known proponent of a close collaboration between the succession states of the former Austro-Hungarian Monarchy," had visited the capital of Czechoslovakia.[11] The journey of Buresch to Prague was, according to *Pravda*, the more significant, since

Austria, as was known, was the first of several states "which, according to the plan of German fascism, are to be swallowed by the *Third Reich* one way or the other."[12]

In his report of April 21, 1936, the Austrian envoy pointed to the inherent contradictions in the Soviet attitude toward Ausrian affairs. The Soviets continued their criticism of Austria's domestic policies on political and ideological grounds, while at the same time expressing concern about the "security of our [Austrian] state," considered an essential goal of Soviet policy.[13] Despite this apparent dichotomy, in July 1936 the Austrian envoy believed that the policy of the USSR was basically and relatively simple. "They apply only one measuring rod to every political event, to every political question: Does it harm or does it benefit Germany?" German-Soviet relations had reached a point where it was superfluous to add that if, in Soviet opinion, it harmed Germany, it benefitted Russia, and vice versa. On July 14, 1936, in an article entitled "The Iron Fist in the Diplomatic Glove," and referring to the just concluded July 11, 1936 Agreement between Austria and Germany, *Pravda* held that Austria would have to pay for the recognition of her sovereignty by Germany with "real concessions."[14]

The Austrian envoy considered the restraint in the Soviets' assessment of Italian policy and of the Ethiopian conflict "puzzling," though he himself found the clue to it. The Italian ambassador in Moscow had assured him that "Litvinov did not relent any time in offering his services in behalf of Italy," in order to lift the League sanctions against her. He had done everything to prevent a definite non-recognition of Italy's seizure of Ethiopia to pave the way for Italy's return to the Stresa front. Thus it was evident that Soviet policy had not relinquished the hope "to include Italy in the ring of hostile encirclement of Germany."[15]

But at other times *Izvestiia* seemed to have lost all hopes in regard to Italy. Commenting on the Communiqué issued by the Roman Protocol states Italy, Austria, and Hungary, whose representatives had met on November 11 and 12, 1936, *Izvestiia* pointed to the declining role of Italy in Central Europe and conversely to the growing might of Germany in this area.[16] The Conference hardly justified the hopes of Italian politicians. Besides, Italy, in *Izvestiia*'s view, "becomes more and more a vassal of

Germany." In March 1937, *Izvestiia*, commenting on Schuschnigg's journey to Budapest, held that he apparently was concerned about Italy's diminishing strength in Central Europe and tried to compensate for it by establishing ties with Prague via Budapest and also be seeking a rapprochement with Paris and London. He attempted to "Europeanize" Austrian policy, but it was still too early to talk of a "turn-about" in Austrian foreign policy.[17]

What was deemed essential in Moscow was not only a "turn-about" in Austria's foreign policy, but also one in her domestic affairs. Commenting on an editorial in *Izvestiia* which appeared on August 22, "Policy of the Axis, of Circles and Triangles," the Austrian envoy Schwimmer pointed to the hypocritical concern with which the Soviet press followed the struggle of the Austrian government against the Nazis;[18] it regularly considered the penalties meted out to Nazi disturbers of law and order much too mild. It strongly recommended the overthrow of Austro-fascism and the proclamation of a Soviet dictatorship.

Soviet Foreign Policy and Austrian Nationality

Like other Communist Parties in Europe and the world, many of the leading members of the Austrian Communist Party had found refuge in the USSR. Austrian Communists were ideologically, organizationally, and materially clearly dependent on Moscow and received instructions and directives either directly from the Kremlin or through the Comintern; they served as Moscow's political agents in Austria. It was since early 1937 that the small illegal Austrian Communist Party pursued a vigorous course in direct opposition to the Anschluss policy of Germany and Austrian National Socialism. In this respect the new policy placed the Communist Party on the side of the forces of the Schuschnigg government and, since the illegal Social Democratic Party considered the Anschluss with the *Third Reich* a greater evil than the continuation of the hated authoritarian Schuschnigg regime, also on the side of Revolutionary Socialists. The Social Democrats had shelved the Anschluss policy at their last Party Convention in October 1933, when they annulled the Anschluss clause of the 1926 Linzer Party Conference for union with the *Reich*. But the Austrian Communists actually went farther than merely opposing the Anschluss. They questioned the underlying principle of *"ein*

Volk, ein Reich" and claimed that the Austrians represented a separate nationality. After the *fait accompli* of the Anschluss, the Communist Party unfurled the flag of national independence, placing Austrians on the same level of national opposition to the Nazi regime in the *Reich* as Czechs, Poles and other subjugated peoples of Europe.

During the 1934–38 period, the Austrian Social Democratic Party bitterly opposed National Socialism in Austria and in the *Reich*. It denounced the Anschluss with a tyrannical Germany which would use Austrians as "mere cannon fodder." But it still considered the German Austrians as a mere branch of the German people. The Communists, however, disregarded the *grossdeutsch* orientation of Marx and Engels and that of pre-war German Socialism of Bebel and Liebknecht. They were rather guided by the opposition of the USSR to a Nazi-sponsored union between Germany and Austria. The Anschluss, in the Communist view, would deliver Czechoslovakia and Central Europe to Nazi control, shift the German boundaries closer to the East, and thus threaten the Soviet Union.

In the struggle against the Anschluss, ideology was bound to play an important role. The Communists, adept in ideological propaganda and warfare, were quick to recognize this. Social Democratic leaders, whatever their opposition to a Nazi-led Anschluss, could not, in view of their earlier promotion of the movement for union, deny that they looked upon German Austrians basically as Germans, whatever their separate historic experience, different contemporary outlook, and linguistic peculiarities. The Communists, however, sensed that in countering Hitler's propaganda they would have to make use of the heaviest guns. It seemed best to simply deny that Austrians were Germans. Not only the Socialists but also most Christian Socials under the leadership first of Dollfuss and later of Schuschnigg and the followers of the *Heimwehr* were not prepared to go as far—an unwillingness which no doubt hampered them in their ideological struggle against National Socialism. It made some of the Austrian Rightists disposed to strike a bargain with the Nazis. But the Communists, with shrewd perception of propaganda and of the necessity of waging an effective ideological campaign, disputed the widely accepted thesis that the Austrians were a part of the German nation; they were, they asserted, a separate nation. This gave their struggle the character of a national war of independence and after 1938 gave them a clear goal: The renaissance of Austrian sovereignty and freedom.

The order for a reorientation of the Austrian Communist Party came, according to Ernst Fischer,* leading Austrian Communist after 1934, apparently from Stalin himself in 1938. As Fischer wrote in his book *Das Ende einer Illusion* (1973), referring to the late 1930s: "Dimitrov informed [!] us that Stalin was for an independent Austria, against any form of a Danubian Confederation." He had said, "Why should not the Austrians be a separate nation?"[19] But the theoretical ground for this thesis seems to have been laid much earlier in Austria. According to Fischer, the Austrian Communist Alfred Klahr, having raised the question as to the special national character of the Austrians back in 1933, had answered it positively. Fischer himself first thought that Klahr had gone too far, but ultimately he reached the same conclusion. According to Fischer, Communists in the 1930s did not quickly relinquish the view that the Austrians were part of the German nation. He himself for some time still defended this concept in the Soviet Union against the views of the influential Bulgarian Communist and head of the Comintern George Dimitrov.

While in Russia, Klahr had run afoul of Soviet Communism, though not on account of his conviction that there existed a

---

*Ernst Fischer, originally a Social Democrat and Assistant Editor of the *Arbeiter-Zeitung*, turned after the suppression of the Austrian workers' uprising in February 1934 in bitter disappointment to the Communists: he fled to the USSR and in 1938 became editor of the prestigious *Communist International*. He wrote articles for it under his real name and under the pseudonyms of Peter Wieden or Pierre Vidal. A prominent leader of the Communist Party of Austria, to which he returned in 1945, Ernst Fischer was a maverick and, after his criticism of the Soviet invasion of Czechoslovakia in 1968, was expelled from the Party. He wrote thereafter *Das Ende einer Illusion* (1973), which covers the postwar years in Austria, 1945–55, and his autobiography, translated into English under the title *An Opposing Man* (1974). In a study on "The Development of the Austrian National Character," conceived during his stay in Moscow in the later 1930s but not published until 1945, Fischer had painted the Austrian national character with both its positive and negative traits, and had extolled important Austrian personalities and the struggle for freedom throughout Austria's history. When he read his articles for *Communist International* three decades after they were written, he "blushed for shame." Still, Fischer never disavowed the view that there existed a special Austrian nation, a thesis which he and Austrian comrades had developed in the 1930s.

distinct Austrian nationality. Klahr and other Austrian Communists were rather accused of not being sufficiently critical of Austro-Marxism; of having judged and still judging Otto Bauer's personality in too objective a manner; and on the whole of having been insufficiently "vigilant."[20] There arose in the later thirties the so-called Klahr case in the USSR, a political dispute in the era of the purges, which involved Russian Communists, Austrian and German emigrés, and Dimitrov himself. Klahr escaped the Russian ire, but succumbed to the Hitler terror unleashed against Communists and Jews after his return to Austria.

In his book *Das Ende einer Illusion* (1973) Ernst Fischer no longer thought that the question whether there existed an Austrian nation was still relevant in the viable and neutral postwar Austrian state. But he stressed that, during the years when Hitler ruled, this question was not only theoretically but also practically of "outstanding importance."[21] In all countries which Hitler overran, the national element of the resistance had been much more effective than the mere political, antifascist element.

Perhaps one of the first indications of a radical theoretical about-face of the Austrian Communist Party occurred in an article "National Struggle of Liberation in Austria, a War against Fascism," by F. Wg.—actually the Austrian Comintern representative Peter Wieden (Ernst Fischer)—in the Moscow *Deutsche Zentral-Zeitung* on April 17, 1937. The article puzzled the Austrian envoy to Moscow; in a communication dated April 30, 1937 and addressed to the Austrian Foreign Minister Guido Schmidt, he admitted that it had made him "quite pensive."[22] Wieden suggested to abandon the Social Democratic, and so far also Communist, thesis on Anschluss and German nationalism. Not only Social Democracy but also Communism had gone wrong when it had preached "Anschluss with a Socialist Germany." The thesis so far had always been that Austria and Germany belonged to each other. Now, however, according to Wieden, one must acknowledge that National Socialism had "exploited the fact that Austrians talked German"; actually Germans and Austrians represented different cultures and nations. The conservative Austrian envoy found it ironical and perplexing that Austrian Communists had thus discovered the "österreichischen Menschen" (the Austrian Human Being). But Wieden went beyond such a discovery when he postulated the need for a conscious "Austrian nationalism."

Though Austrian Socialists had not adopted the theory of an "Austrian nation" in 1933, they had, as mentioned, shelved the Anschluss issue for the duration of the Hitler regime. The theoretical question of Austrian national consciousness aside, in many other respects the position of the Austrian Communist Party was quite similar to that of the Social Democrats and the Revolutionary Socialists during the years 1934–38.[23] In a speech at the conference of the Austrian Communist Party in August 1937, Johann Koplenig considered the problem of Austria's independence and her defense against Hitler-fascism "the main political problem" of the country. Just as the Social Democratic Party, the Communist Party asserted that as a result of the July Agreement of 1936 with Germany, Austria had virtually become "a dependency of Mussolini and Hitler." The Austrian dictatorship, as the Ethiopian war and the Spanish Civil War had shown, stood with all its sympathies on the side of the war agitators and of the enemies of the independence of nations.[24]

Austro-Communist Theory on Austrian and German Nationalism

Still, Hitler-fascism, according to Koplenig, threatened Austrian sovereignty and a majority of Austrians opposed the link-up with the *Reich*. The task for the Communist Party lay in giving the will for Austrian independence concrete expression and a democratic and progressive dimension. This meant that Communists must aim their main arrows against National Socialism, "against its agents and close allies in Austria as well as against the authoritarian Austrian dictatorship," since the latter subordinated the interests of Austria and of its people to the interests of German and Italian fascism.

Another speaker at the same Communist Party Conference, Erwin Zucker-Schilling, referring to Austria's "mission" in the "German realm," its "continental mission," and even its "universalist significance," considered it the task of Communism to "block the war-like German imperialism, which under the flag of the swastika . . . wants to conquer the Danubian realm and the Southeast of Europe."[25] Communism, "together with the small states and nations of the Danubian realm [wishes] to defend the sovereignty, independence and peace of the small states and nations of Central Europe," against the expansionist endeavors of German and Italian fascism." Such views hardly differed substantially from the Social Democratic stance and rhetoric. But Communists, as stated, went far beyond the Social Democratic position, denying that Austria was ever part of the German nation and that the "Holy Roman Empire of the Germanic Nation" had anything in common with a nationality in the Marxist meaning and with the concept of nationality in Stalin's definition of the word. As the discussion at the Party Conference revealed, some Communists wondered whether the preoccupation with the theory of nationalism was meaningful, whether there was any pragmatic purpose to preoccupy oneself with "such concepts." But the speaker pointed to the need for juxtaposing to National Socialist ideology a "really firm ideological platform"—which the Schuschnigg regime had failed to do. It had not succeeded in this task, since it had borrowed heavily, perhaps unconsciously, from the ideological armory of Pan-Germanism and Nazism.

A few months earlier, in March 1937, Johann Koplenig at the Conference of Austria's Communist Youth Organization had pointed out that Austrian national consciousness was growing stronger.[26] He charged, however, that it was undermined by the inherent falsifications of the *gesamtdeutsch* (all-German) historic conception which even held many Christian Socials, including Dollfuss and Schuschnigg, many *Heimwehr* leaders, and broad segments of the Catholic intelligentsia captive. The foregoing historic perspective distorted the proper vision of Austrians. They were deluded into thinking that because Germans and Austrians were linked by a common language and close cultural relations, they rather ought to sacrifice themselves to the interests of an imperialist war and to the *Gleichschaltung* plans of Hitler-fascism. Koplenig stressed that the struggle for Austria's sovereignty was not only a struggle for Austrian independence but at the same time a struggle for political and national self-determination. The majority of the Austrian people was "Austrian, not German-national." Whatever the theoretical merit of their new position, the Austrian Communist leaders shrewdly anticipated the powerful impact of nationalism, as distinguished from mere anti-fascism, upon the struggles of European peoples against Nazi Germany—to which especially World War II bears witness.

On the eve of Austria's annexation, Communists, like the Socialists, underlined the importance of Austria's political independence, the need for broadening the narrow base of the Austrian government, and asserted that the defense of Austrian sovereignty was essential not only for the Austrian people but for all peoples of the Danubian realm and for the European balance of power and European peace. But they went farther than the Austrian Social Democrats in asserting the existence of a separate Austrian nationality distinct from the German one. Alfred Klahr, in several theoretical articles in 1937, elaborated upon the thesis developed first in 1933 that the Austrian people were a separate nation.[27] In response to the question whether there existed an Austrian cultural community, separate from Germany, he affirmed it by pointing to a specifically Austrian culture which flowed from the special Austrian historic experience. Traits of the Austrian national character were reflected in the works of numerous Austrian authors and poets; to some of these traits Friedrich Engels had already pointed in a letter to Victor Adler when he spoke of the "gay excitable temperament" of the Austrians; the latter, according to Engels, could be traced back to the "happy Celto-Germanic-Slavic racial mixture in which the German element prevailed." Klahr also quoted Stalin that common language alone did not establish a common nationality; Englishmen and North Americans represented two different nationalities.

In the article "On the National Question in Austria" Klahr raised the question: "Can we, the Communist Party and the revolutionary working class openly acknowledge and foster the development of the Austrian nation?" and replied: "We not only can do this; but we must do it today and actually have done it already."[28] This practical struggle of the Party and Austrian working class in behalf of Austrian independence has already promoted an Austrian national orientation among the people. The victory of fascism in Germany has sharpened the struggle for the national independence in all of Europe, it has also strengthened the will toward independence in Austria, and deepened her national self-consciousness. The annihilation of Austrian independence, be it direct or indirect as in Danzig, would be a blow not only against the Austrian people, but would enhance also the threat to the independence of other nationalities of Central Europe and increase the peril of war.

Some might say, Klahr continued, that Austrian communists fought for the independence of the Austrian state, but not for the national independence of Austria. Yet it was "quite wrong, because quite formalistic," to juxtapose political and national independence, since they are "most closely" intertwined with each other. A different historic course in Austria had shaped a different outlook, temperament, and national character. Therefore, the struggle for the preservation of Austria's sovereignty meant struggle for the preservation of the national character of the Austrian people. The conquest of Austria through Hitler would not only deliver the Austrian population to the most brutal political system known in history, but would also signify its national oppression through German fascism. "There may be national oppression also there where the national oppressor speaks the same language."

Austrian communism continued its struggle against the concept of *Grossdeutschland*, as used by the Nazis, even after the annexation. It was a lie that Austrians had wanted Anschluss with the *Third Reich* and a lie that they had acquiesced to the annexation. Klahr aimed some of his main criticisms against the concept of *grossdeutsch* Romanticism. Immediately after the annexation of Austria, German fascism had begun to assail Czechoslovakia and incite the German minorities against the states in which they lived. It attempted to harness *grossdeutsch* traditions of the past for its imperialistic war policy. However unfair his criticism of the Austrian Social Democracy, he perceived the weaknesses of the *gesamtdeutsch* ideology which indeed had long permeated not only socialist but also Christian social thought. Schuschnigg clearly wanted Austria's independence. But because of his fateful *gesamtdeutsch* conception of Austria as the "second German state," he had furnished the Austrian people the noose around the neck with which German fascism strangled the country and himself. Klahr blamed as equally fateful the result of the *grossdeutsch* orientation of the leadership of the Austrian Social Democracy. It allegedly had not recognized the changed importance of the *grossdeutsch* idea in the era of imperialism. Klahr faulted the Social Democrats for not having assumed the vigorous leadership of the movement for independence soon after 1933. Though the author claimed that the Communist Party already in 1925 had drawn the line against the bourgeois-national *grossdeutsch* Anschluss solution of Social Democracy, he conceded "that only in the last years, also belatedly, it had begun to lead a struggle against the *grossdeutsch* orientation."[29]

Bauer's line of thought, according to Klahr, survived in the circle of the Revolutionary Socialists, which made polemics with them unavoidable. According to the author, the only beneficiary of the Austrian Socialist thesis that the Anschluss was irreversible was National Socialism. Bauer and the Revolutionary Socialists had acquiesced to the *fait accompli* of the Anschluss; their thesis in every respect strengthened reaction and threatened European peace. There existed in reality no "*Gesamtdeutschtum*," but only different German-speaking peoples. Fascist imperialism claimed that, because of the alleged "sameness of blood," there was only one German people, while in actuality there were numerous peoples such as the Austrians, the German Swiss, the Alsatians, the Sudeten Germans, etc. Konrad Henlein, the "Führer" of the Sudeten Germans, should be grateful to Otto Bauer! "The strongest weapon of national fascism is its national demagoguerie. The German proletariat cannot achieve its liberation nor, in the event of the outbreak of war, fight today for peace unless it systematically frees itself from the national-fascist myth and the illusion that Germany had a right to attach to herself all the remaining German-speaking border regions. Otto Bauer's solution, even though it is presented as a slogan of the future, "opens all dams and permits the chauvinist Nazi poison being poured into the workers' consciousness."[30]

In a continuation of his polemics "against Pan-Germanism in the Labor Movement," Klahr took the writer Fritz Valentin to task who, like most Austrian Socialists, writing in *Der Sozialistische Kampf* in Paris, accepted the reality and finality of the Anschluss.[31] Klahr criticized what in his opinion amounted to a recognition of the annexation of Austria and to a rejection of the national struggle for self-determination of the Austrian people. Especially Valentin's observation that through the victory of fascism the unification of Europe had to some extent already started was singled out for criticism. Klahr compared this faulty reasoning with that of geopolitics which tried "scientifically" to explain why the rapacious endeavors of German finance capital were not rapacious at all. He castigated the use of such fascist concepts as "*grossräumig*," "*kleinräumig*," and "*gesamtdeutsch*," and ridiculed those who looked upon the victory of fascism in Europe as a step toward a socialist Europe.

Clearly, the *volte-face* of Austrian Communists in the seemingly esoteric theoretical discussion of the existence of a separate Austrian nationality was startling: an abrupt change had taken place from first endorsing the Anschluss to ultimately opposing the union concept, not only for the duration of Hitler's *Third Reich* but beyond it. This view reflected of course the change in the Soviet outlook on the European scene.

On the Eve of Austria's Annexation

What was the attitude of the Soviets to Austria and the Anschluss on the eve of Hitler's coup against Vienna? In Berchtesgaden German diplomacy had encountered first the stubborn resistance of Schuschnigg, but, according to *Izvestiia*,[32] it had quickly produced strong means to break it. Perhaps the German military maneuvers along the frontier might not have had the desired effect, if Berlin's diplomacy had not secured in advance the "benevolent neutrality" of London and the capitulation of Rome. Through concessions in Central Europe British diplomacy, *Izvestiia* continued, wished to bring about a shift of forces which would diminish the threat to England in the Mediterranean and the Near East. London still hoped to wean Italy away from Germany, but had apparently overestimated the capacity of rational thinking on the part of Italian fascists and of Mussolini in particular. France's position was contingent on that of Britain. An article in *Pravda* of the same day referred to the reorganization of the Austrian government as a "cold Hitler-Putsch."[33] The editorial held out little hope for Austria, though it asserted that the Austrian people did not want to submit to the slavery of Hitler's dictatorship.

"Post Mortem." New Soviet Appeals

The attitude of both the USSR and the Comintern to the *fait accompli* of the German annexation of Austria on March 13, 1938, was given expression in an article in *Communist International*.[34] Long before March 1938, German fascism had made preparations for the invasion of Austria and the enslavement of the Austrian people. Though the clerical-fascist regime of the "Fatherland front" had deprived the Austrian people of their rights and destroyed the parties of the working class, the trade unions, and peasant organizations, the Austrian proletariat, the huge majority of the Austrian peasants—the overwhelming majority of the Austrian people—unanimously rejected the ideas of having anything in common with the German people. Hitler and his associates "lie shamelessly" when they speak of the "liberation of the Austrians and when they assert that they were only fulfilling the will of the Austrian people. "German troops had come to Austria not as liberators, but as invaders, . . . as imperialist conquerors."

It was the "sacred duty" of the German workers, peasants and intellectuals to rise to the struggle in defense of the complete and free right of the Austrian people to self-determination. This required close collaboration, "a united front," between Social Democrats and Communists in the *Reich* and between them and their refugee leaders abroad. Social Democratic criticism therefore of the Moscow trial of the Bloc of Rightists and Trotskyites in a recent issue of *Der Neue Vorwärts*, after the outrages committed by Hitler against Austria, was sharply castigated because it made collaboration betwen Social Democrats and Communists difficult.

The position of the Austrian Communists in the wake of Austria's annexation was given concise expression in a manifesto of the Central Committee of the Communist Party of Austria, published in the pages of the French Communist daily *L'Humanité*, on March 13, 1938. Hitler had brought Austria under his yoke only through military power.[35] He had imposed a foreign government just 3 days before the scheduled national plebiscite for which his own agents had called for many years. He called it off for fear of the electoral defeat he would have suffered. Berchtesgaden actually had increased the people's resistance "a hundredfold." But it had been muted when Hitler sent his artillery, tanks and airplanes against the united front of the Austrian people. The manifesto called upon Socialists and Catholics, workers and peasants, to unite, and appealed to all Austrians to "resist the foreign intruders and their agents." "All differences of outlook, all party differences recede before the sacred task now confronting the Austrian people." Of course the rhetoric of such Communist appeals as to chase Hitler's soldiers out of Austria, to disregard the Nazi terror, and to make " 'Red-White-Red unto Death' a red slogan" was rather empty. The appeal to the peoples of Europe and of the world—

peoples which had just demonstrated their own weakness and helplessness to assist Austria—was similarly fatuous. They were reminded that it was not only the peace at the Danube that was at stake, but the peace of Europe and that every capitulation was an encouragement of Hitler's aggression.

The appeals of other European Communist Parties had identical or similar thrusts. The Central Committee of the German Communist Party, paralleling the Austrian Manifesto and Soviet policy, warned that Hitler, through his newest "crime," was relentlessly moving toward war. Contrary to his claim of having "liberated" Austria, he had in fact robbed the Austrian people of its right to self-determination. The Manifesto of the Central Committee of the Communist Party of Czechoslovakia warned its own people that with the entry of the troops of the *Third Reich* into Austria, which had "capitulated," the danger of a horrible new war had increased.[36] The appeal of the French Communist Party similarly reflected the traumatic impact of Hitler striking a "thunderbolt" against Austria and Europe. Austria had become Germany's "vassal state." The subjugation of Austria by the Berlin government was "only a stage in the realization of the great plan of conquest." From now onwards Austria formed the bridge between two totalitarian states whose threats against France could not be heard with indifference by any Frenchman worthy of his name. The fate of France was being decided both in Central Europe and in Spain. On this characteristically national note, emphasizing the threat to France in her entirety—a note which harmonized with the increasingly national posture of the French Communist Party on the eve of World War II—the French Communist appeal ended.

Communist International continued to echo the sympathy which Austria's destruction by Nazi despotism had aroused not only in Communist circles but everywhere in Europe. The journal reported of meetings in the United Kingdom in behalf of Austria and its working people, organized by Communists, the Labor Party, the Liberals and by peace movement committees and cooperatives; in London and Manchester mass demonstrations had taken place. The Communist Party of Great Britain had issued a pamphlet by Harry Pollitt entitled *Austria* of which over 100,000 copies had been sold. In France, the International Peace Campaign had adopted a resolution protesting against fascism, and Catholics were "disgusted with the 'capitulation' of the Austrian clergy to Hitler."[37]

At the moment of Austria's annexation by Hitler's Germany the USSR was in no position to stem the tide of Nazi expansionism in Central Europe. Like France and Great Britain, the Soviet Union was geographically too distant from the theatre of main events to throw her weight into the scales. Like the Western Powers, she also was neither militarily nor psychologically prepared to render effective assistance. In spite of the increased threat to Czechoslovakia, the USSR apparently did not hold that Austria's annexation would adversely affect her own vital national interests. But Moscow made clear its opposition to it. And after the German annexation of Austria the USSR and the Austrian Communist Party, not to mention Communist parties throughout the rest of Europe, devised promptly the programme of the restoration of Austria's independence.

Such a program of course had little practical and immediate significance. But it must be admitted that similar words were then not heard from the Austrian parties, the Christian Socials or Social Democrats and Revolutionary Socialists; they were benumbed and still incapable of reassessing Austria's state of subjugation or charting her future. The struggle for the liberation of just-conquered Austria thus pitted the tiny Communist Party not only against the Nazi conqueror but also against the Austrian Social Democrats and Revolutionary Socialists. In the article "Marxism and Austrian Independence" Peter Wieden (Ernst Fischer) accused Austrian Socialist leaders of having, by endorsing the *fait accompli* of the Anschluss, once again embraced the Nazi concept underlying the union, that of Greater Germany.[38] Fischer, while denouncing what he called the Nazis' falsification of history, the doctrine of the inevitability and progressiveness of Austria's inclusion into the *Reich,* the creation of a fully united Germany, accused Karl Renner and Otto Bauer, of having come forward as the chief witnesses for a Nazi-dominated Greater Germany. Quoting Bauer's article in Der *Sozialistische Kampf,* Paris, he interpreted his position in favor of a *gesamtdeutsch* Revolution as a repudiation of the struggle for the restoration of Austria's independence. He ridiculed Bauer's recommendation to adopt a "revolutionary" attitude toward the *fait accompli* of Austria's occupation and both his and Renner's stance of "approving" the "Anschluss," though the "union" was effected by force.

According to Ernst Fischer, the struggle of the Austrian people was aimed not only against social oppression but also against national oppression and foreign rule. The military conquest of Austria by German imperialism had aroused deepest hatred of the brown-shirted conquerors. Bitterness against the German officials and jailers had reached into the ranks of Austrian National Socialists themselves. Alongside Communists, Socialists and Catholics, there were now even Austrian Nazis in prison camps and concentration camps. The *de facto* master of Austria was Bürckel, the German governor, not the Austrian Seyss-Inquart. Clearly, Austrian Communist policy was trying to establish an underground Popular Front extending as far to the Right as some disillusioned Austrian Nazis and to prepare the struggle for the restoration of Austria's independence. While the author pointed to what he considered a theoretical weakness of Austrian Socialism, the apparent willingness to accept the "judgment of history," the reality of the Anschluss, he resorted to distortions of his opponents' actual position; he claimed that a direct road led from Bauer's allegedly Romantic theory of nationality to the race theory of the Nazis. After 1848, the author claimed Marx and Engels had not renounced the idea of Greater Germany, because the Russian Tsar, the Austrian Emperor and Napoleon III represented darkest reaction. Today, however, Hitler-Germany was "the most reactionary, the most barbarous state in Europe." The demand for "union of all Germans in the *Third Reich*" signified subjugation of the Austrians, the Czechs, the Hungarians, the Swiss, the Dutch, and others under German fascism. In the struggle against Hitler, against the "Anschluss," a *new Austrian national consciousness** had arisen among the masses of Austrian people." Consequently, it was "one of the important tasks of all anti-fascists to place the struggle against foreign rule, for the independence of Austria everywhere in the foreground." Austrian Communism, in line with the new policy of the USSR, refused to recognize the country's 1938 annexation and the birth of a Greater Germany.

---

*Italics are Fischer's.

During the war and toward its end this position served Communism well. Even prewar German conquests such as the 1938 annexation of Austria were simply annulled by the West—in accordance with Soviet policy since the late 1930s and that of the Austrian Communist Party. In 1943 the Western Powers and the USSR joined in the Moscow declaration on Austrian independence, and thereafter the major Austrian political parties also adopted this very stance.

The abrupt change of the Austrian Communist Party on the Anschluss issue about 1937 turned out to be a trail-blazer in Austrian politics, though it was clearly opportunistically rooted. But after Austria's liberation it failed to pay off politically for the Austrian Communist Party.

Chapter 11

American Ambassadors in Central Europe 1933–1938 and United States Policy

Hitler Assumes Power

In the 1930s, as distinguished from the post-World War II era, the fate of Central Europe was largely decided by "outside" forces, by Germany and proportionately less so by Fascist Italy and the Western Powers, but little by the Soviet Union or the United States. The United States, pursuing an isolationist policy, was militarily and psychologically unprepared and geographically even more remote from *Mitteleuropa* than the U.S.S.R.

Hitler's assumption of power in January, 1933, with its inherent threat to Europe's political and territorial *status quo*, and the preceding Japanese aggression in the Far East in 1931–1932 signified the beginning of a new era for the United States, one marked by war, by violation of international law on a major scale, and by global imbalance of power: it was bound to have a long-range impact upon the United States and its foreign policy. In its initial stage already, Austria became the target of Nazi Germany's imperialism.

Since the mid-thirties waves of aggression further extinguished the independence of Ethiopia, caused the outbreak of the Civil War in Spain and Rome's and Berlin's intervention, and led to the occupation of the Rhineland and, in the Far East, to the invasion of China proper. The American people felt repelled by the aggression of fascism in Europe and Africa and of Japanese autocratic militarism in the Pacific. Though Americans in thought were no longer neutral about European and world affairs, they were not prepared to engage in collective action for the sake of peace. The majority of Americans rather wished to stay out of any war abroad, whatever the issue and however just the cause.[1] As far as Hitler-Germany in particular was concerned, Americans condemned it on many grounds; they criticized the repression of democracy and of civil rights, the establishment of tyrannical government, the arrogant claims made in behalf of German nationality and race and the deprecation of all others, the attack on religion, churches, and Jews, and they abhorred the increasingly evident expansionism which threatened peace and stability and undermined the legal and moral order of European and world civilization. Still influenced by the isolationist mood of the twenties, the anti-war propaganda of the thirties, and opposition to a dangerous armament race, Americans embraced the belief that war never settled anything. Such ideas by weakening the will to timely resistance were likely to play into Hitler's hands.

The widespead revulsion of war's horrors which continued to grip the United States worked in a curious manner also to help the aggressors in Europe rather than its victims; the latter, mostly peoples adjacent to Germany, were pictured in Nazi propaganda as domineering and selfish nations, holding on to their illgotten gains of the Peace Treaties of 1919, rather than peoples oppressed for centuries by master nations such as the Germans. The drumfire of German revisionist propaganda made the more distant English and American nations believe that the *Third Reich* merely wished to remedy grievances and made them ignore her evident desire to go beyond these to the restoration of German domination over non-German peoples. Under these circumstances the policy of appeasement of the 1930s, of piecemeal surrender and retreat before the aggressors appeared to some, especially in Anglo-Saxon countries, neither foolish and ignoble but pragmatic and a just and moral imperative to avoid the scourge of war.[2]

It was the good fortune of the *Third Reich* that it made its historic entry at a moment the American people was preoccupied with a domestic crisis of major proportions and was psychologically unprepared to engage in close international cooperation, not to mention alliance, for the sake of preserving peace and stability in Europe and the world.

On page one of *Mein Kampf* Adolf Hitler had proclaimed the doctrine that Germans and Austrians, being of the same nationality, should form a single state.[3] The well-known slogan "Ein Volk, ein Reich, ein Führer" left no doubt about this fundamental goal of the National Socialist German Workers Party (NSDAP). Thus it was hardly surprising that National Socialist policy toward Austria showed from the very beginning the earmarks of unrelenting aggressiveness toward the neighboring German state. Buoyed by the sudden victory in January 1933 in the *Reich*, the NSDAP had an exaggerated opinion as to its chances for early success against Austria.

B. G. Stockton, writing from the American Embassy in Vienna, in May 1933, held that the provocations unleashed by the German Nazis against Austria, while technically not acts of war, would, if directed against almost any other sovereign state, soon burst into open warfare. But Austria, he held, could without outside help offer no effective resistance to German aggression.[4] Stockton voiced the fear—which during the next five years was often rekindled—that, unless France, Great Britain, and Italy took a "decided stand," "it would soon be too late." He did not even think of including the United States among these powers.

American Ambassadors in Central Europe

Similarly gloomy were the early reports from Berlin which reached Washington. After assuming the Presidency, FDR picked the historian and Democratic activist Wilhelm E. Dodd* as new Ambassador to the Third Reich.[5] Once in Berlin, Dodd established contact with high-placed German officials, including Foreign Minister von Neurath, a conservative who loyally served the *Third Reich*. In regard to Austria, Neurath strongly defended the theory that Germans and Austrians belong into one state. Commenting on this view that Austrians were part of the German people and that "national movements" could not be restricted by political

---

*William Dodd was a leading academician with strong liberal and democratic credentials and one who was in sympathy with FDR's liberal domestic and foreign policies. A distinguished Professor of History at the University of Chicago, later President of the American Historical Association, he was also the author of significant histories and biographies, among them of a biography of Woodrow Wilson. While serving as Ambassador in Germany for four and a half years, this Jeffersonian democrat gained the undeserved reputation of being a poor diplomat; as if the representative of any power on earth, and an isolationist one at that, could single-handedly have arrested the course of events! At the time of his appointment he was 63 years old and not in the best of health. But FDR was persuaded that Dodd's knowledge of German history and culture and proficiency in the German language, dating back to his days at the University of Leipzig, would make a favorable impression upon the Germans.

boundaries nor be suppressed by policy measures, Dodd conveyed to Washington his conviction that such opinions were "rather sweeping in their implications" and warned that, "in view of the broad distribution of German stock in Europe, they opened up almost unlimited prospects."[6]

Before Dodd left for Germany, FDR invited him to the White House. He urged him to work toward three goals, "the continued repayment of all private American loans, the moderation of Jewish persecutions by use of official and personal influence," and the conclusion of trade arrangements on certain items "which would increase German exports and aid them in their debt payments."[7] It was clear that at that moment FDR did not think yet in terms of European or global geopolitics, but rather of limited national eocnomic objectives and traditional concerns of religous tolerance and human freedom.

Dodd's first report to Washington, written with the help of George A. Gordon, Counselor of the Embassy, and of George S. Messersmith,* then Consul General, reflected the jointly held view that Hitler might be slowing down and halting the Revolution. Dodd also appeared to believe that a mutually acceptable compromise on German debts would be worked out and that "strenuous Jewish persecutions" were on the decline. But he was far from certain.[8] Hitler, Göring, and Goebbels seemed to him "adolescents in the great game in international leadership and even national guidance." As he wrote on August 12, 1933, "with a free hand they would soon . . . be at war with France, Austrian annexation being the pretext." George Messersmith similarly considered the top Nazi leaders, including Hitler, "uninformed and little concerned about foreign attitudes."[9] With greater German

---

*G. Messersmith was born in Pennsylvania in 1883. After having spent several years as teacher and administrator in the Delaware school system, he entered the Foreign Service in 1914. Serving first as Consul in Canada, in the Netherlands and the West Indies—where he discovered a secret German code—he was Consul General in Antwerp between 1919 and 1928. Following a short stint again in Latin America, in Buenos Aires, he was in 1930 assigned to Berlin, where he functioned as Consul General. In May 1934 he was appointed Minister to Austria, a post which he held until October, 1937. (See Ruth Alford, biographical sketch in *Calendar of G. S. Messersmith Papers in the University of Delaware Library*, vol. 1.)

experience than the newcomer Dodd, Messersmith was more critical of Berlin and suggested that Hitler had retained von Neurath as Foreign Minister only as a "mere decorative and protective front, because of the confidence that the diplomats here and chanceries abroad" had in him. He was also doubtful that public opinion abroad would eventually bring about a more moderate regime in Germany, views held by some officers in the Department of State.

These same people also criticized Dodd for his unwillingness to mix socially with his counterparts in Berlin. Dodd, however, found the company of prominent Nazis repulsive. It was actually unrealistic and naive to believe that by playing up to Nazi bigwigs it would be possible to moderate Nazi policy and methods. National Socialist Germany was bent on rampage and intimidation for the purpose of expansionism and domination rather than on ingratiating herself with foreign diplomats and public opinion abroad. Dodd's growing disillusionment with Nazi Germany was interrupted only briefly at the conclusion of the German-Polish ten-year non-aggression pact in 1934 which engendered new hopes. But a few weeks later he was convinced that Hitler remained "wholly belligerent."[10] In the back of Hitler's mind was still "the old German idea of dominating Europe through warfare." Messersmith agreed with Dodd that Hitler might want peace for the moment, "but only to have a chance to get ready to use force, if in the end it is found essential."[11]

In a meeting with the English Ambassador Sir Eric Phipps, Dodd took the initiative in suggesting that in return for a British-American pact, England consider linking up with the United States and the Soviet Union to prevent further Japanese encroachments in the Far East. Though FDR personally did not rebuke Dodd for this unauthorized radical proposal of a global policy against imperialist aggression in Asia and/or Europe, he consented to an elaborate nine-point reply dispatched to him by Under-Secretary Phillips in which the latter made clear that the President and he were "somewhat concerned" over Dodd's references to the Far East, since the United States wished to avoid any step which would appear to be aimed at Japan's "isolation." As far as Europe was concerned, the United States would not offer to participate or play the role of an honest broker, "as this would inevitably draw us into the general European picture."[12] Remaining aloof was the guiding motive of American policy.

United States policy, as the exchange of views makes clear, was not to be disturbed by any, even a mere intellectual, challenge to the basic concepts of the new administration, non-entanglement, aloofness, and passivity in foreign affairs both in Europe and Asia. Dodd understood that he had questioned the fundamental doctrine underlying the foreign policy of the new Administration, but, persuaded by his sobering German experience, he had felt constrained to do so. In his reply to Washington, Dodd gave little ground, asserting that he had merely put forward "a personal and informal suggestion." Isolationism, he warned, was a short-sighted policy or "false interest" which more likely than not would ultimately lead to war.[13]

Among numerous points of contention between Berlin and Washington was the vitriolic Nazi propaganda in the United States. In the views of the State Department, Berlin aimed at establishing in the United States "a form of government inimical to our constitution and civil liberties."[14] Secretary of State Cordell Hull urged Dodd to take up this matter informally and unofficially with the German authorities. When Dodd did so, he found the chancellor "uninformed and unreasonable." When the Germans furthermore objected to the American counterpropaganda, pointing to a mock trial of Hitler in the United States, Dodd held his ground, lecturing his German counterparts about freedom of speech and assembly in America. In general, it was Dodd's impression that Hitler "talked as if he would never yield an inch."[15]

According to Ernst Hanfstaengl, the Nazi Party's foreign press officer, Hitler's mind about American and the Americans was already made up. Behind the American Ambassador's back, the Führer ridiculed "den guten Dodd," who, he found, could hardly speak German and made no sense at all. The United States, in any case, was a subject about which Hitler, he was convinced, could not learn anything. The United States was only "a mongrel society." She was "hopelessly weak and could not interfere [!] in any way with the realization of . . . his plans." All he seemed to know about America was related to the depression, "to the gangsters in Chicago, and the scandals surrounding Jimmy Walker . . . of New York." He was convinced that "any country which could not even master its own internal police problems cannot hope to play a role in foreign affairs."[16]

At times Dodd hoped to nudge FDR toward a more activist role in European and world affairs. Before returning to Berlin in May 1934, Dodd in a memorandum prepared for FDR warned that "there has not been so terrible a social and economic situation for Western Civilization since the collapse of the Roman Empire." But he still thought it possible that England and the United States could save the situation. What was required for the United States was to join with Britain and Holland to guarantee the *status quo* in the Far East and to join the League of Nations. It was, however, revealing that he did not send a copy of this memorandum to the State Department in view of the rather strained relations existing between them;[17] he was convinced that the latter was dead-set against an internationalist approach to Germany and European and world affairs. In matters of international politics FDR and Dodd were more flexible and activist than Cordell Hull, though the President moved at a snail's pace.

For close to a year Dodd entertained the hope that the policies of Nazi Germany would show some moderation, in response to selected economic, political, and diplomatic pressures from abroad. While English and French diplomats and politicians continued to nourish such views, Dodd especially after 1934 abandoned these hopes as illusory. As he told the President after reading a Goebbels speech in which the latter proclaimed the Jews "the syphilis" of all European peoples, he was convinced that he had been "humbugged."[18]

The other top American observer on the spot was George Messersmith who commenced his service in Vienna in 1934 which was to last until October 1937. Messersmith was a man of strong democratic and anti-Nazi convictions. Though after Hitler's seizure of power, he had made a point of remaining on speaking terms with Nazi officials, it was reported that Hitler "frothed at the mouth" when Messersmith's name was mentioned.[19] A keen student of German and Austrian affairs, he predicted with great accuracy the likely disastrous turn of events in Europe, unless the Nazis were overthrown in time. When he once discussed his opinion that it was better "to fight a small war now than a catastrophic one later,"[20] some quickly accused him of being a warmonger. But both FDR and Secretary Hull held a high opinion of his abilities and of his personality. There seems little doubt that his assessments of European politics in the 1930s, in particular of the Austrian and German situation, helped to shape the evaluation of these events which came to be accepted by the President and the Department of State. But his and Ambassador Dodd's recommendations for closer cooperation, if not for forging an outright alliance, with West European states fell on deaf ears.

American Envoys Assess Austria's Situation

The February 1934 uprising of the Austrian para-military *Schutzbund* organization was the Socialist workers response to the moves of Chancellor Dollfuss to abolish Austrian multiparty politics and parliamentarianism and underlined the precariousness and vulnerability both of the new authoritarian system and of the very existence of Austria herself. According to Dodd, the Nazis in Austria and the *Reich* were gleeful over this struggle and overjoyed that matters were seen "to be going the Nazi way." International intervention in Austria in behalf of the Social Democrats and political democracy would, according to Dodd, make matters only worse.[21]

On June 2, 1934, Dodd warned Secretary of State Cordell Hull about the recent Nazi resumption of their anti-Austrian campaign. Following the sanguinary reprisals of the Hitler regime against the S.A. leadership and various other individuals and groups in the *Reich* on June 30, 1934, terror acts in Austria greatly increased.[22] On July 25 the Austrian Nazis staged an abortive *Putsch* which resulted in the assassination of Chancellor Dollfuss, but, with Mussolini rushing to Austria's defense and Hitler's subsequent disavowal of Germany's complicity and refusal to offer military help to Austrian National Socialism, in the latter's defeat. George S. Messersmith's reports to the State Department during this troubled period shed light on the agitated situation in the German capital. On June 29, he reported, Goebbels had told Cerruti, the Italian Ambassador, that there would be a Nazi government in Vienna within a month.[23] Similarly, the reports of the American Consul at Munich, written on the eve of July 25, leave no doubt that Hitler had advance knowledge of the schemes of the Austrian Legion and other semimilitary units, all pointing to impending action.[24] The Austrian Legion in Bavaria was to cross the frontier on a signal from the Vienna radio station.

Messersmith's reports continued to stress the central importance of Austria and the Anschluss question. Messersmith heard Keppler, one of Hitler's "really most intimate and trusted" advisers, say "that even he could not talk with Hitler on the question of Austria and that of the Jews, that these two were the questions on which he had convictions and his reaction is always the same. . . . On these two questions there can be no compromise with him." In London, both the 30th of June, the day of the alleged Röhm *Putsch* and the killing of the top S.A. leadership in the *Reich*, and the 25th of July, the day of the futile coup in Austria, had "destroyed the last illusion" which had still lingered on. Thus, in conclusion, Messersmith warned of what was a continuing crisis: Hitler and his associates were determined "to make Austria fall into the lap of Germany." "They will work in a more subtle way, but in just as dangerous a manner."[25] The American emissary entertained no false expectations about the Führer and about the ambitions of the rest of the *Third Reich* leadership, and criticized especially those in the West who tended to dismiss or minimize the threat which National Socialism constituted. "It is strange," he wrote, "that in spite of his [Hitler's] own declarations, in spite of his actions, there are those who persist in giving Hitler credit for better intentions and for greater honesty of purpose and for milder views than he really holds. This I consider one of the most dangerous factors of the European situation."[26]

Messersmith was convinced that Hitler had not the slightest intention of striving for conciliation with Austria, but wished to carry out an "insidious program" which aimed to bring Austria into the *Reich*. He wants "to throw dust into the eyes of Europe and of the Austrian people, but anyone who knows must realize that these are only means to an end, that the ultimate purposes have in no way been changed."[27]

The British Minister in Vienna, with long previous experience in the Foreign Service, held, according to Messersmith, that the preservation of Austria was a necessity for peace in Europe. While he did not look with approval on a government, which suppressed elections and shunned a representative parliament, he did believe "that the present government is probably the only one and the best one that Austria can have for the time being, and therefore it was deserving of support."[28] Messersmith held a similar opinion, being anxious to shore up the Austrian political structure, even in its unrepresentative form, rather than have it reformed and perhaps in the process irreparably weakened vis-à-vis the internal and external Nazi threat.

The assessment of the Central European situation in the reports of Messersmith from Vienna and of Dodd from Berlin complemented each other. Immediately after the July 1934 *Putsch*, the Austrian government, Dodd reported, was more convinced than ever that the NSDAP had not abandoned its aims directed against the independence and integrity of the country.[29] Dodd and his staff had reached the conclusion that Hitler himself was determined to pursue a "moderate" course versus Austria, since he felt that "in time Austria is bound to fall in Germany's lap, so-to-say, and that aggressive action would only produce dangerous results both for German-Austrian relations and for Europe in general, as well as probably retard the achievement of the end in view."[30] Instead, Hitler after the abortive *Putsch* switched from a revolutionary to a "gradualist" approach in the Austrian question, comparable to the switch after the failure of the Munich *Bürgerbräuhausputsch* of 1923 to a legalist approach toward seizure of power in Germany. But the Austrian government felt not reassured, but was rather of the opinion that its sovereignty and independence "are threatened as long as the present German regime remains in power. It was convinced that nothing could change the aim of the present National Socialist government in the *Reich* to incorporate Austria into Germany." Therefore, while the Austrian government was grateful for, and deeply appreciative of, the tripartite declaration by Paris, London, and Rome of February 17, 1934, "it cannot be tranquil." "The powerlessness of Austria against invasion is, however, so obvious as not to require any comment."[31]

Messersmith had a clear conception of the correlation of forces in Europe which could stop Nazi Germany. As he wrote: "As I have indicated in my dispatch of No. 152, I am definitely of the opinion that the firm attitude of England, France, and Italy is essential, if an eventual war is to be avoided." But it is characteristic that he made no suggestion regarding American policy at any time during his long stay in Vienna. Nor did it occur to anyone else in the State Department then or later that a more active

American role was called for. If Italy and France would compose their differences in a reasonable manner, Messersmith continued, then England could join with them in a continental policy "which they can force on Europe. If the three major powers establish unity, then Poland, Yugoslavia, and Hungary will stop wavering and align themselves with these powers." "This will mean the definite curbing of Germany as the principal disturber of European peace" and the possible disintegration of the Nazi regime which is making the German people "the most militaristic and dangerous that Europe has yet known."[32] But Messersmith foresaw the "greatest calamity" if the major West European Powers were unable to settle their differences, and he concluded with this blunt warning: "The major fact still remains that 6 ½ million of Austrians themselves are powerless before Germany with its 65 million, until Germany renounces her aspirations against Austrian sovereignty and independence. This is the kernel of the Austrian problem which is now definitely recognized as the principal factor in the maintenance of a durable peace in Europe, as the absorption of Austria would be inevitably followed by further German expansion to the Southeast."[33]

Both Dodd and Messersmith knew that their position on Germany and especially on National Socialism was held by some people in the State Department to be too critical and one-sided. If his views on Germany, Dodd countered, were being interpreted as "unfriendly," he was plainly "misunderstood."[34] He assured his critics at home that he was never forgetful of the circumstance that the very great majority of the Germans were "a worthwhile and decent people." He also believed that there could be no peace in Europe unless Germany was "happy, contented and strong." "On the other hand," he emphasized, "my views on National Socialism and what it means for Germany, Europe, and the world are based not on prejudice, but on an objective consideration of the facts which we have to face." After the Saar plebiscite he informed the State Department that he entertained no illusions that Germany was now prepared to give up its aspirations in Europe, to shift its interests to regaining its former colonies and pursue other territorial ambitions of Hitler and the NSDAP. Their eyes were set foremost on Memel, Alsace-Lorraine, the Ukraine, "to settle the surplus German population and to get fertile lands which Germany 'must have'. Austria is a definite objective, with absorption or hegemony over the whole of South-eastern Europe definite policy. As long as Hitler and National Socialism remain in power in Germany, Europe will have to deal with these aspirations, pacts or no pacts."[35] "The only thing that can hold Germany in line, is a concert of the powers so close and definite that Germany's policy will be reoriented." Nazi Germany, Messersmith warned, did not keep her promises, even the Soviet government had a better record of keeping its. Therefore, it would be the extreme of folly to put any hope in German promises at this time. With respect to Austria and in other respects, Nazi Germany "may not contemplate direct action, but she intends to work through raising disturbances through so-called German minorities, keeping Europe in a turmoil." When Hitler proclaims his will for peace he may want peace "but only so that Germany can work her will."[36] On February 8, 1935, the American Legation in Vienna referred to alleged "orders" to the NSDAP, received after the Saar plebiscite and pointing to the need of opening up a "fighting territory" "not only in the West, but also in the East and Southeast," especially against the Memel Territory which belonged to Lithuania and "then against German Austria."[37]

Dodd's and Messersmith's Doubts and Fears

Since the German government proclaimed frequently its alleged will toward peace, the American Embassy in Berlin dispatched on September 24, 1934, an eight-page account of "Germany's will for peace." which contrasted Germany's pacific professions with the *Reich's* contrary deeds; it concluded that the evidence of Germany's will for war was overwhelming and deeply disturbing. In early October, in a pessimistic letter to Moore of the Department of State, Dodd expressed his conviction that Hitler was there to stay and that he did not see how resistance to him could even begin. "The German people are thoroughly indoctrinated with the war idea and drilled to the limit. They intend to destroy France, break English power, and annex territory where it seems to be needed, Austria, Hungary, part of Poland, and all of Holland. Pan-Germanism of 1910–1912 is fully alive. If it succeeds therein, Europe will give our people something to think about. They refuse to think now: Borah and Johnson examples. The only nation that can stop this course is the U.S.A., but the

U.S.A. will not do it." And he added with a critical side-remark, referring to the Nye investigation in Congress about munitions manufacturers, in a vein quite different from an earlier observation: "Note the Nye investigation," which, he held, had been turned about "and was now used as an additional argument for American isolation from European and world affairs."[38] Dodd painfully observed that America's isolationist course deprived her of even the smallest influence in foreign affairs. While Hitler had personally notified the French, English, Italian, and Polish ambassadors of his rearmament plans, he had "simply ignored the American diplomat here." Anticipating the President's query "What can one do?", Dodd merely listed what he considered America's wrong political and international moves ever since the end of World War I.[39]

In March, Hitler launched one of his boldest and, in view of the lack of German rearmament, most reckless moves, the occupation of the Rhineland. But France, hesitant to retaliate without support from Great Britain, floundered. The impact of the occupation of the Rhineland was felt not only in Western Europe, but also had obvious consequences in Central Europe. In a report from the American Legation in Berlin to Washington it was pointed out that the Austrian government clearly recognized that the German occupation of the Rhineland had a far-reaching significance for Central and Southeastern Europe.[40] A realistic assessment of the German move into the Rhineland was also furnished by Messersmith in a memorandum dated March 25. The militarization of the Rhineland, he asserted, was "definitely on the agenda and its place in the program is clear." "Austria and Czechoslovakia, the countries most threatened by Germany, were likely the first to suffer as a result of the fortification of the Rhineland."[41]

Dodd anticipated the moment when Germany will have grown to about eighty million people, namely "when Austria (including part of Czechoslovakia) is annexed"; then all of Europe would soon find itself under German control. "If Wilson's bones do not turn in the Cathedral grave," Dodd bitterly complained to FDR, "then bones never turn in graves. Possibly you can do something, but from reports of Congressional attitudes, I have grave doubts." Messersmith, who from Vienna came for a brief visit to Berlin on April 6, 1936, supported Dodd's pessimistic view wholeheartedly. He considered Hitler's latest peace oratory in the wake of the Rhineland occupation a "fraud" and the address itself "full of veiled threats in every direction."[42]

About a year later, shocked about the attitude of the new British Ambassador Sir Nevile Henderson, Dodd reported that he was "representing his country as willing for Hitler to annex Austria and other countries in that zone"; the Belgian Minister too seemed to favor "German expansion in the East." Dodd clearly foresaw that such policies would neither save Belgium nor halt the British road to "decline." The Franco-English equivocation of the last years was, in his opinion, not giving way to resolve, but, on the contrary, was replaced by Western acquiescence, if not outright surrender. Both the French and English Ambassadors, André François-Poncet and Nevile Henderson, were not examples of strength, but symptoms of the decline of the power and spirit of the Western countries.[43]

In October 1937, George S. Messersmith was recalled from his post as Minister for Vienna to assume the key post of Assistant Secretary of the State Department; it was widely held that his knowledge of European affairs and of Central Europe in particular would be more valuable in the capital. On October 11, 1937, Messersmith gave his political judgment about the European situation in a long memorandum to Secretary Hull. Despite the preoccupation of the world and of American public opinion with Japan in the Far East and with Italy in the Mediterranean area, Germany, in his judgment, still held the center of the stage and was the crux of the problem in international affairs. Messersmith warned of the dangers of appeasement policies which the Western democracies pursued. As he wrote: "There is no logical escape from the fact that the lawless nations continue to gain their ends through force or through the threat of force." He especially cautioned that if "too dangerous compromises continue to be made," as they have been made in recent years, "the peace of the world will be definitely endangered and catastrophic war will be the sole outcome."[44]

Throughout 1937 and in early 1938 both FDR and Hull were greatly perturbed by the increasing plight of the democratic powers and the spectacular gains made by the dictatorships. In the judgment of one close to the Secretary of State, Hull was "swinging to the left" from his customary middle-of-the-road position: he was favoring a more activist role for the United States in attempting to stem the menacing tide of the Axis powers. Hull began to think that the best hope of restraining the would-be oppressor nations and bringing the "three jingoist countries Germany, Italy, and Japan to their senses" lay in the adoption of a common attitude by the U.S., Great Britain, and France, "preferably joined by Russia."[45] The analysis and recommendation were sound, but the implementation, also as far as the U.S. was concerned, was faulty, if not completely missing.

Last-Minute Warnings

Washington then was almost continuously warned that the *Third Reich* was preparing a major strike in Central Europe in the spring of 1938. Such reports or rumors reached the Department of State and the President from several European capitals. On December 19, 1937, William J. Carr of the United States Legation in Prague reported to Secretary Hull about an interview with Frederick T. Birchall, European Manager of the *New York Times*, concerning affairs in Austria. On occasion of a visit of the Duke of Windsor to Berlin Göring, according to Birchall, had implied that he expected Germany to be in control of Austria by March of 1938.[46]

On January 15, the American chargé ad interim, Wiley, expressed his concern to Washington that the recent Budapest Conference of the Roman Pact states, Italy, Hungary, and Austria, had made no reference to the independence of either Austria or Hungary, despite some pressure exerted by Gabriel Puaux, French Ambassador to Vienna, on Rome. Count Ciano had demurred to Schuschnigg on the ground that a reference to "independence" was "tactically inadvisable"—a position which was quite ominous.[47] On January 18, 1938, the United States chargé d'affaires in Germany, Gilbert, reported to the American Secretary of State of rumors in the German capital that "some development" in the Austrian question was imminent, though the Embassy was unable to substantiate these rumors.[48] Also, von Neurath, according to a French colleague of Wiley, had alarmed both the French Ambassador in Berlin, François-Poncet, and the politician Flandin, by stating in substance that Germany would not be able much longer to continue looking at Austria with folded arms.[49] Göring had recently sounded the same note in an even more ominous manner. He had told François-Poncet that it would not be long before Austria would be chastised for her sins.

After Berchtesgaden, on February 15, Wiley telegraphed Secretary Hull, from the Vienna Embassy, warning him that Austria's situation was, in his view, "most unfortunate and dangerous." The day before he had asserted to Austria's Foreign Minister Guido Schmidt that the U.S. Government maintained a sincere interest in the welfare of Austria and "hoped earnestly that the Austrian government would firmly resist threats against the independence of Austria." It was clearly a pious hope which Wiley thus voiced, no real assurances of U. S. help were given or intended. Yet it was over this remark that Secretary of State Hull expressed concern; by wire he thus admonished Wiley: "In the future, you should very carefully avoid making any statements which can possibly be construed as implying that your government is involving itself in any case in European questions of a purely political character or is taking any part, even indirectly, in the determination of such questions." America's policy of aloofness and isolationism could hardly have been articulated more clearly. What was at stake was, of course, the question of Austria's independence which Secretary Hull euphemistically preferred to circumscribe as a question having "purely political character." There was no implication that the United States would be interested and prepared to assert herself in questions pertaining to Europe in general or to Central Europe that had non-political significance. Nor could either the State Department or the President claim that they were not fully informed by their Ambassadors throughout Europe, Wiley, Bullitt and others of the threatening character of Germany's most recent and impending diplomatic or military moves and of the likely responses, or lack of it, by France, Great Britain, and Italy. Wiley, pointing to several unfavorable turns in major European countries, especially Eden's having quit the British cabinet,[51] did not share "the prevailing wave of optimism" in Austrian official circles. Germany will want to consolidate her position not only in Austria but also in regard to the Sudeten Germans. "When all this happens—and what is going to stop it?—one would have to be extremely sanguine to hope that the German appetite will be satisfied. My feeling is, and I know Germany very well, that she is embarking on an expansionist

Weg zur Weltmacht policy." After the annexation of Austria, the *Reich* would extend "from the Baltic to within 60 miles of the Adriatic." "Can anyone believe that Germany will not eventually seek an outlet to the coast."[52]

Thus, there cannot be the slightest doubt that FDR, his top advisers, and the State Department were kept abreast of the gathering of clouds over Austria and the growing Nazi threats in Central Europe prior to and immediately after the Berchtesgaden Conference. American representatives in Austria and Germany, first Messersmith and Dodd, in 1937-38 Wiley, did their job competently, reported the impending blow with accuracy and perspicacity and did not attempt to soften it or minimize its farreaching significance for Europe as a whole and for the United States across the Atlantic.* They and other American envoys in Europe anticipated events and on the whole assessed correctly their likely geopolitical, economic, and military significance. U.S. intelligence, notwithstanding exceptions, was not failing; Hitler had announced his blows long in advance, and European observers could hardly claim that they had been truly surprised.

On February 18, 1938, George Messersmith, now Assistant Secretary of State, gave his evaluation of the Berchtesgaden Conference to the Secretary and Under-Secretary of State. The general situation in the wake of the Conference was "further deteriorating." Many people had long entertained illusions regarding Hitler's trustworthiness. "Any idea that a certain group in England has been fostering concerning making lasting and binding agreements with Germany was utterly futile and fatal." The terms imposed upon Austria the other day "will mean her rapid absorption into Germany," unless there was some great change in the major European picture. In the conversations which

---

*More questionable are some reports by Hugh Wilson, formerly Minister to Switzerland, later of the Department of State, and then successor to Dodd in Berlin. His direct message from the German capital to FDR, dated March 3, 1938, about a meeting with Hitler and other high-placed German officials was marked by an abundance of inane generalities and flatteries for the Führer at a moment of widely recognized threats to Austria's existence and to the peace of Europe itself; it contained no warning whatsoever! His letter to FDR, March 12, after the event, is hardly more perceptive (FDR Library, Hyde Park, PSF Diplomatic, Box 45).

Ambassador Bullitt had with General Göring, the latter did not conceal that the Nazi objectives involved the disappearance of Austria's independence. In his own conversations which he, Messersmith, "had in the last 3 or 4 years with high-ranking members of the Party in Germany, they left no doubt that this is their objective, although in the press and in official statements they may cover this over." Messersmith feared that Schuschnigg might meet the same fate as Dollfuss. "In my opinion, whatever we may see emerge from the present situation, we can take it that the independence of Austria is gone in fact, although its outward form may be retained for the present." He still felt that if London and Paris had spoken in a determined manner the present catastrophe would have been avoided, "for Hitler is not yet ready to go to war."[53]

It was more than revealing that Messersmith did not even raise the question of U.S. past and present policy. Every American observer or policy-maker took it for granted that England, France, and Italy for that matter, should be reprimanded, but that American policy was either faultless or that for geographic reasons it was most unreasonable to assume that its foreign policy toward Germany and Austria could be anything else but marked by complete aloofness. Most European commentators, politicians, and journalists did not mention the isolationism of the U.S. as an additional cause of the latest disturbing developments in Central Europe. Though it was quite obvious that this was the case, Europe in its entirety was so inured to this circumstance that it seemed quite superfluous to draw attention to it.

Reactions of FDR and of the Washington Establishment

The thought of the members of the U.S. cabinet about Austrian developments becomes rather evident in *The Secret Diary of Harold Ickes.* Ickes reported of a cabinet meeting on February 19, 1938, just a day before the President was planning to go to Hyde Park. While Sumner Welles immediately after the Berchtesgaden meeting, in reply to an inquiry by FDR, observed that the European situation was getting "worse and worse," the President seemed surprised. He revealed that he had thought it was "settling down" on the basis of the *fait accompli,* referring to Hitler's having assumed control of the army and having delivered an ultimatum to Chancellor Schuschnigg which, "on the surface at any rate, makes it appear that Austria has been brought into the sphere of German influence."Sumner Welles, however, correctly judged that the situation was "disturbing, nonetheless, and not yet clarified."[54]

The opinion of the cabinet, according to Ickes, was that at Berchtesgaden Nazi Germany had forced the hand of little Austria and had virtually made it "a German dependence." He was also convinced that Germany in due course "would move aginst Czechoslovakia and Rumania and some other countries." One cabinet member even thought that Hitler in his speech, scheduled for the next day, February 20, might announce the German annexation of Austria. Though this did not prove to be the case, the apparent gloomy assessment of Austria's future by the U.S. cabinet was not far off the mark. As Ickes summed up the consensus of the cabinet meeting, Austria at Berchtesgaden was in no position to resist Hitler's steamroller and was forced to comply. Apparently Mussolini, in spite of his previous assistance to Austria, had now come to "a secret understanding with Hitler. There is a feeling that, while Hitler is in the ascendant, Mussolini is on the decline."[55] FDR and his cabinet seemed fully aware of the immediacy of the Nazi threat to Austria and even to Czechoslovakia and realistic in their appreciation of Austria's helplessness; the possibility of an effective American intervention of any sort seemed so remote that it was not seriously contemplated and not even discussed.

On March 8 Harold Ickes reported some observations of FDR at a party at the White House. Hitler's demand for the right to protect German minorities wherever they might be was correctly interpreted by FDR as "Germany reserving the right to interfere in any country, not only Austria, Hungary, Czechoslovakia, the Polish Corridor etc.," wherever there was a "considerable German population." The President voiced the opinion that if Hitler adhered to this view, Eden would be more than justified in his position and Great Britain would find itself in a difficult situation.[56] The President thus seemed to take a stand against Chamberlain's policy of appeasement and to have no illusion about the scope and the significance of Hitler's demands. But it is of interest to note that while he empathized with Britain's "difficult situation," it did not quite occur to him that the United States, admitting all differences of geographic distance, found herself in a comparable situation. When after Berchtesgaden the Austrian crisis mounted, the former American Ambassador Dodd, now sidelined, warned an audience in Rochester, N.Y., on February 21, that the "German appetite for expansion of territory and power will not be satisfied with the Nazification of Austria. This will be succeeded by more bold steps . . . Poland is scared and Czechoslovakia, the only democracy remaining in Central Europe, threatened. The program of the dictators will be carried on without arms, and the democracies will probably make concessions rather than fight." Democracy's only hope in Europe, Dodd concluded, "depends on the ability of the Great Powers to cooperate, a fact they have thus far been unable to accomplish."[58]

In these critical days Austria's diplomacy looked with anxiety, though not with great hope, to London, Paris, and Rome. If there was any hope left in Vienna and the major European capitals for the preservation of the country's independence, it was that the Stresa Front could be restored through a last-minute Anglo-Italian settlement. Even the more skeptical Dr. Hornbostel, Director of the Austrian Foreign Office, had at this late hour still unwarranted hopes in regard to the progress of Anglo-Italian negotiations.[58] No Austrian political leader, however, set any hopes upon the United States. It is of interest to note that in the aftermath of Austria's demise no critical words were uttered in Washington's official circles, as distinguished from the American press, about England and France. Washington understood only too well the desire of London and Paris not to become embroiled with the *Reich* over Austria. Geographically more remote from Central Europe than the West European states, the United States after all pursued the same policy, a policy of aloofness, of "splendid isolation."

American Second Thoughts After the Annexation

The Austrian crisis reached its climax on March 11, when the Nazi government delivered its ultimatum to Chancellor Schuschnigg and the latter was compelled to resign. There could be not doubt anywhere that Austria's fate was sealed and that the annexation of the country was a mere matter of days, if not hours. The following reports of Americans on the spot, in Vienna and Berlin, in Paris, London, Rome, and other European capitals, reflected the grim reality of the political situation, the irrevocability of Austria's demise.

On March 12, Wilson reported from Berlin of his meeting with the French Ambassador François-Poncet: "His thesis was simple. The states of the world have made irretrievable mistakes in giving in step by step to Germany. They had merely whetted Germany's appetite, and who could tell who will be the next victim. The only thing that might still save the world would be all states getting together to serve formal notice on Germany that it had to behave or face consequences."[59] "All states getting together"— this recommendation addressed to the American diplomat clearly included the United States. Not only West European policy but also that of the United States, whatever it had been, had proved bankrupt.

On the very same day the American Ambassador sent this report—one day after Schuschnigg's resignation—the German Ambassador, upon his own request, called on Secretary of State Cordell Hull. Without being instructed by his own government, as he disclosed, he wished to explain the action taken by the Reich's leadership. Hull was probably stunned partly by the Ambassador's following emotional outburst, partly perhaps by the realization of the United States' inactivity at a moment of crisis. He merely inquired as to the prospects of peace hereafter, trying to elicit an answer as to the character of the German-Italian relationship. As if Hitler's move into Austria had not shed full light on that! This relationship had no doubt been a key element in first delaying, then in bringing about, the Third Reich's thrust into Austria and was bound to be deeply affected by the fait accompli of the Anschluss. However, in view of what just had taken place in Central Europe, a grievous violation of international law and interstate conduct, the American Secretary's response was inadequate and conspicuously weakly.[60]

On March 13 Hitler reached Vienna. The American chargé in Austria had no longer any doubt that Austria's freedom and independence were part of an irretrievable past. As he telegraphed: "Situation completely liquidated. Austria under German military occupation under guise of a 'friendly visit.' Detachments of SS and SA have been armed. Only question in doubt is whether

Austria is to maintain fiction of independence or whether outright union is intended."[61] That very day this question was decided by Hitler in favor of the latter alternative.

The following day, March 14, the German Ambassador Dieckhoff in Washington, D. C., called again upon the State Department, this time no doubt on instruction from Berlin: he met both with Cordell Hull and Sumner Welles and informed them of the promulgation of the union between Austria and the *Reich*, but he appeared exasperated when Welles met him with an icy silence. In better times Dieckhoff had been anxious to maintain "extremely friendly" personal relations with the leading men of the State Department. But apparently annoyed about his cold reception by Hull the other day and the persistent coolness, he now embarked upon a "tirade" which lasted about 10 minutes. He claimed that no matter what Germany did the rest of the world was always ready to inveigh against her. Welles interjected when the Ambassador claimed that the Austrian people unanimously desired to become an integral part of the German *Reich*. The use of physical force, he asserted, necessarily obscured any determination by the Austrians of what they themselves desired.[62]

On March 17, 1938, only days after the shock waves of the annexation of Austria had reached the American continent, Secretary Hull delivered a major foreign policy address before the National Press Club in Washington, D. C. The speech had been carefully scrutinized in the State Department and been heartily approved by FDR. It was widely disseminated, in five European languages. The speech clearly reflected American official mood in the aftermath of Austria's annexation. Hull, referring to an earlier address which he had delivered on July 16, 1937, on principles of international conduct, the "Eight Pillars of Peace," reaffirmed this program and denounced international lawlessness. The address coming so close after the invasion of Austria spoke for itself. Hull announced that the U.S. would refuse to withdraw from the Far East or to retreat from the protection of American interests wherever they might exist. Though the speech represented a toughening of the American position, it did not go so far as to declare the territories of Germany's neighbors, threatened though they were by Nazi imperialism, spheres of American interest: While Hull denied that the United States had any desire or interest to "police the world," he held out the possibility of the United States pursuing parallel action with other governments having similar interests and also offered the hand of cooperation to other states in the attempt to preserve peace. The most effective contribution, the Secretary proclaimed, the Administration might be able to make to the cause of peace was to have the United States respected throughout the world "for integrity, justice, good will, strength and unswerving loyalty to principles." As Hull pointed out, his speech was not likely to please either a determined isolationist or an "internationalist determined to commit us to alliances."[63] Though the American public would not have condoned the latter policy, it was perhaps the only one which in time might have deterred a resolute aggressor such as Hitler.

The official reaction of Washington to the most violent and far-reaching act in foreign policy committed so far by the Nazi regime, the invasion and annexation of Austria, consisted only in cold-shouldering the German Ambassador. Neither Washington nor Berlin or any other capital could have any doubt that the German *fait accompli* in Central Europe had produced a mere ripple in the United States. Yet in the midst of political triumph of the *Reich*, the criticism of American public opinion was a source of irritation to the German Ambassador Dieckhoff personally and to the leadership of the *Reich* in its entirety, portending sharp future disagreement and mounting opposition.

One officer in the State Department with first-hand knowledge of conditions in Central Europe, both in Austria and in Germany, Assistant Secretary of State G. S. Messersmith, expressed his dismay at the extinction of Austria's independence, but not without voicing some hope for the rebirth of the country in a more distant future, a hope then not widely shared either among Austrians or foreign observers: "First of all, let me say that words would be inadequate to tell you how much my heart goes out to our Austrian friends. The barbaric hordes have swept over Austria again and, while the situation must be recognized as a temporary [!] one, I for one am not yet sure that German domination of Austria is a permanent matter." He personally had no illusions that the Nazi steamroller would not move on. Whether Washington was going to recognize the forcible absorption of Austria or not—so far it had not recognized the puppet state of Manchukuo or Italian sovereignty over Ethiopia—had not yet been decided.[64] Actually, Washington did not extend a de jure recognition to Germany's annexation of Austria; still, it had little choice but to acknowledge the transformation of the Austrian Embassy into a Legation now headed by a Consul General.[65]

Belatedly, in the aftermath of Austria's annexation, Secretary Hull inquired about the attitude of the Italian government with regard to German troops in former Austria and with regard to the possible desire of Germany to acquire access to the Adriatic. The American Ambassador in Rome, Phillips, informed Hull that Mussolini had been "forced to accept the inevitable" and that there had been no criticism that German soldiers were "found across the border." Though Phillips dismissed the likelihood that Germany would make Trieste part of the German *Reich*—"a bitter pill for Mussolini"—he was far from being really reassuring. "It looks to me as if 'by hook or by crook' Germany will secure access to the Mediterranean through Trieste." He had found "Ciano very chary in expressing any views whatsoever with regard to the new situation in which Italy finds herself as a result of the exit of Austria."[66] It was rather puzzling that Hull waited for the annexation of Austria before raising the question of possible further German ambitions aiming at the Adriatic and that he seemed concerned about the presence of German troops in former Austrian territory. Such questions came months, if not years, too late!

This holds also true for another suggestion of Phillips to Hull. A week prior to this letter, Phillips had written in the same vein and had mentioned the virtually unanimous opposition of Italians of all classes to the annexation and what it portended for the future; this despite Hitler's public assurances to Mussolini that the Brenner frontier would be eternally respected. Phillips had suggested that the United States show a desire to develop commercial relations with Italy! He seemed uncertain even about the purpose of his own mission to Italy and virtually apologized to Hull for making these most innocent suggestions, adding: "I assume it is my job here to do everything in my power to improve our relations with Italy."[67] Only under the pressure of geopolitical changes generated by the annexation of Austria, did the American Ambassador propose to "win over," or at least to neutralize, Fascist Italy in the continuing struggle to check Nazi aggressiveness.

On March 23rd, ten days after the annexation of Austria had been proclaimed, Hugh Wilson, writing from Berlin, offered the following analysis of the significance of the recent happenings in Austria, as seen from the German capital. The Austrian victory, he wrote, had been the greatest success achieved during the five years since National Socialists had taken over the German government. "The inaction of other countries at the time of Austria's annexation has led to a feeling of revulsion and contempt for these countries, including even Italy. . . , and the growth of a belief that Germany was invincible."[68]

Wilson apparently confined his observations to European countries, but the passivity of states beyond the Atlantic, especially the U.S., did hardly have to be pointed out to the Department of State. The role American policy had played did by no means enhance U.S. prestige and weight in contemporary world affiars. It was likely to strengthen Hitler's conviction that other German thrusts, such as those planned against Czechoslovakia and Poland, would hardly produce a basically different U.S. reaction. Still, American denunciation of Hitler's annexation of Austria and its aftermath, the persecution of the Jews and of prominent Austrian patriots, the rising threat to Czechoslovakia and U.S. perception of change of Europe's balance of power, while far from deterring the *Third Reich* from its next targets in Europe, must have produced some uneasiness in Nazi ruling circles. A few weeks after the absorption of Austria, Ambassador Wilson reported of a conversation with Göring in which the latter expressed the belief that "America must be counted among the enemies of Germany."[69]

Other Neighbors of Austria and Germany: East Central European States, Switzerland, and Belgium

Czechoslovakia

On the ruins of the Habsburg Empire arose both the First Czechoslovak Republic and the First Austrian Republic. In the late 1930s both were to succumb to the imperialistic drive of the *Third Reich*. From the earliest beginnings after the war and the Paris Peace Conference it was evident that Austria and Czechoslovakia owed their very existence to the break-up of the Habsburg Monarchy and the military catastrophe which had befallen both the Austro-Hungarian Empire and Germany. The new states were to retain their independence as long as Germany's military weakness persisted, i.e., during the entire Weimar period and the first years of the *Third Reich*, until the latter had sufficiently rearmed and began to steer the German nation toward new advantures not only in Central Europe but on the entire continent. Czechoslovakia and Austria never became allies, first because Hitler intimidated both of them, considering any pooling of their defensive resources a "provocation" and "encirclement" of Germany. Secondly, Austria under Schuschnigg, while fighting for independence, nevertheless maintained a strong emphasis on the German character of the Austrian state.

From the beginning Czechoslovakia clearly perceived the danger of the Anschluss movement in neighboring Austria and Germany. She promptly alerted her friends and allies in France, Great Britain, the Little Entente, and in the League of Nations itself, to the growing Anschluss threat.

In the mid-nineteen thirties, Beneš's diplomacy was a carefully balanced performance. While he claimed not to aim at the total exclusion of Berlin from any participation in Austria and Central European affairs in general, he definitely opposed the creation of an Austro-Hungarian bloc. He also feared that between Italy and Germany Austria would be sacrificed. He clearly opposed the extension of either German or Italian influence but was also fearful of the possible collusion of the two powers in Central Europe. He wished that Austria remain Austrian and not become German or Hungarian or Italian. According to an interview Beneš had given to the *Morning Post*, the announced plan of an Italo-Austrian-Hungarian alliance was not likely to have success, since what was required was the collaboration of all states in Central Europe.[1] The smaller states would find a new system of collaboration which in turn both Germany and Italy could tolerate. But Prague apparently, rather than Berlin or Rome, should take the initiative in devising such collaboration.

A few weeks only after the February 1934 civil war in Austria had ended with the Pyrrhic victory of Dollfuss and the authoritarian-fascist ideology, Beneš delivered a major policy statement about Central Europe and the Austrian question. The Austrian Ambassador in Prague Dr. Marek sent to Dollfuss Beneš's exposé with the comment that it was "friendly toward us" and assured Austria of "his true sympathies."[2] In this address Beneš rejected all plans centering on a Danubian Federation despite its many apparent advantages. The only possible solution, he held, was the independence and integrity of Austria, guaranteed by all of Europe. Germany must be assured that Austria be not incorporated into a political and economic system which was directed against Germany. He denied the anti-German proclivity of such a guarantee, but on the other hand asserted that the Central European states were politically "sufficiently mature as not to need the protection of a Great Power," apparently either Germany, Italy, or possibly even France. While he rejected a Danubian Federation as a political structure, he was not opposed to an economic one, which would leave ultimate sovereignty with each member.

Germany clearly opposed any rapprochement between Czecho-slovakia and the Little Entente on one side and Austria on the other as a move likely to procrastinate the Anschluss and even to block it. Thus the *Reich* looked upon the planned visit to Prague of Kurt von Schuschnigg, Austria's Chancellor after the assassination of Dollfuss, as an unfriendly act; Schuschnigg was indirectly told that German authorities would prefer "that this visit not take place." Austrians in turn castigated this step as an "unheard and inexcusable interference."[3] The American Ambassador to Austria, George Messersmith, reported a conversation of the Foreign Minister Egon Berger-Waldenegg with Beneš, in which the Austrian impressed upon his Czechoslovak colleague that, unless Czechoslovakia and the rest of Europe stood by Austria, both countries would be lost. Messersmith concluded that the fears of the Austrian government over the intentions of the present German government had in no sense waned and that any favorable opportunity might be seized to bring about a *fait accompli*.[4]

Though both the Vienna and the Prague government realized that they had common interests vis-à-vis Berlin and that cooperation along economic and other lines against the common threat was an imperative, the problem of German nationalism and of the Sudeten Germans in particular had often a divisive impact. In view of the spectacular growth of Austrian National Socialism and the growing importance of the *Nationalbetonten,* among whom Germans originating in Bohemia and Moravia were most influential, Schuschnigg had to pay close attention to the Sudeten German problem. The Sudeten German question was "not a matter of indifference to us, since it is after all a question of Germans. Many Sudeten Germans have been resident in Vienna for decades. In many cases they occupy high positions and are respected and esteemed."[5]

It was not only the Sudeten German issue which made it difficult for Austria, led by a government which was strongly oriented toward "Grossdeutschtum" and stressed its German character, to cooperate closely with Czechoslovakia. After the Austro-German July 1936 Agreement Schuschnigg assured Gabriel Puaux, France's Ambassador in Vienna, that he understood the need for friendly relations of Austria's with Czechoslovakia and that he personally trusted Dr. Milan Hodža, the Czechoslovak Premier. But the "russophile policy of Prague makes impossible an entente between the two countries." He claimed that Czechoslovakia was "an immense depot of arms of the Soviet air force from which will develop the inevitable Russo-German conflict."[6] Puaux, generally a strong supporter of the Schuschnigg course, countered that the famous camps of the Soviet air force existed only in the romantic imagination of the Hungarians or in the tendentious information of Hitler's propaganda, but Schuschnigg was not persuaded. The *grossdeutsch* ideological blinders worn by the Austrian Chancellor made him suspicious concerning the Czechoslovak neighbor and were in turn to strengthen the anti-Austrian sentiments in the countries of the Little Entente. Ideological blinders of a different kind, the exaggeration of the threat of a Habsburg Restoration, limited the view also of prominent Czechoslovak statesmen.

While Nazi Germany in Beneš's thought was the irreconcilable enemy of Czechoslovakia, Italy, it was hoped, might become a partner in the defense of Austrian independence. But Prague's ambivalent attitude toward Rome, and vice versa, was clearly evident during the entire 1930s. Czechoslovakia wanted Italian assistance in the defense of Austria, but not Italian domination in any part of Central Europe. Prague hoped that Italy would become a stabilizing, not a disruptive force in Central Europe; it wanted its cooperation with the states of the Little Entente in general and her preservation of the *status quo* in particular, not Rome's support for Hungarian revisionism. It desired Rome as a counterbalance against Berlin, but opposed that the two Great Powers, Germany and Italy, divide Central Europe into spheres of influence. Endorsing collective security for all of Europe, in accordance with the general policy and thought of France and the League of Nations, Czechoslovakia wanted complementary collective security arrangements for Central Europe.

Prague was of course increasingly disturbed by the diplomatic detours of Belgrade. The coherence of the states of the Little Entente, tied together by their opposition to Magyar revisionism, was increasingly weakened by the flirtation of Yugoslavia with Germany and Italy, and the loosening of her links to France. The government of Czechoslovakia, according to the Austrian Ambassador in Prague, would not suppress its concerns in view of the continuing incongruency between the foreign policy tactics of Czechoslovakia and Yugoslavia. As early as summer of 1936 Beneš discerned, as he revealed in his *Memoirs*, symptoms of the disintegration of the Little Entente. Yugoslavia and Germany were taking a position toward a Franco-Italian rapprochement which was at sharp variance from that of Czechoslovakia. Germany was accused of making behind the scenes strenuous efforts to postpone an Italo-French agreement and sought to create the impression that the Central European pact would be dominated by the Little Entente. France and Czechoslovakia, however, assured Yugoslavia

that they had her vital interests at heart and were not opposed
to an understanding between the Little Entente, Paris, and Berlin;
"the combination, however, of Berlin, Warsaw, Budapest, Vienna,
Rome" represented a "dangerous game" for European peace and
stability.

The Era 1936-1938. Beneš Glances Back

Looking later back, Beneš emphasized that in the years 1936-
1938 Czechoslovakia's policy correctly diagnosed the ills of Europe
and did everything to retrieve her own situation, that of her
friends, and of all of Europe "in face of fascist gangsterism and
pan-German Nazism and of war itself." By the summer of 1937
only France, Czechoslovakia, and the Soviet Union remained,
according to Beneš, in favor of determined and consistent resistance
to the onslaught of the fascist powers and France was already
wavering, as a result of subversive activities of her own reactionary
elements. Everyone in Europe was "spinelessly, if resignedly,
running from the fight for the defense of democracy and was
'safe-guarding' himself alone by means of blind negotiations with
perfidious Hitlerite Germany and dictatorial Italy."[7]

In his *Memoirs* Beneš was quite critical of the policy of appeasement and its outspoken proponents or actual practitioners
such as Pierre-Etienne Flandin, Pierre Laval, Neville Chamberlain,
but also of Edouard Daladier, Léon Blum, and especially of the
lack of military preparedness of the Western Powers even as late
as January 1938. He was equally caustic about the political leaders
of the Little Entente—the disintegration of which he began to
discern already in the summer of 1936—especially the Yugoslav
Regent Prince Paul and the country's Prime Minister Stojadinovič.[7b]

The fear of the return of the Habsburgs prevailed among many
neighbors of Austria between 1933 and 1934 and increased when
Schuschnigg, by conviction and at heart a monarchist, became
Chancellor in July 1934. While the fear was real in Prague and
Belgrade, it was increasingly a matter of pretense by the *Third
Reich*. By attributing to Austria plans for Restoration, Nazi diplomacy cast upon little Austria the odium of being a disturber
of the *status quo* and of peace. Restoration, it was widely held,
would somehow strengthen Austria's will to resist German pres-

sure. Hitler and his entourage entertained no such beliefs. But they found it tactically profitable to appear taking the issues seriously, since it aroused anti-Austrian feelings also in Prague and Belgrade and prevented the latter from aiding an Austria beleaguered by the *Third Reich*. Propagandistically, Germany had a natural interest in inflating alleged monarchist *Putsch* plans in Austria to deflect attention from its own aggressive schemes aimed against Austria and to hatch military plans under the smoke-screen of frustrating an Austrian legitimist coup.

Yugoslavia

Czechoslovakia was on the whole opposed to the Anschluss which appeared to her a "catastrophe." While at critical moments she was either blinded—exaggerating the danger of a Habsburg Restoration in Austria to its independence—or resigned to "accommodate" herself to the inevitable course of history, the foreign policy and attitude of Yugoslavia, her partner in the Little Entente, toward Austria and the Anschluss in the 1930s ceased to be that of an active opponent of the union.

From the start Belgrade's attitude was marked by contrary tendencies. On one hand, Yugoslavia feared Germany's proximity in the event of Austria's demise, especially in view of her own German minority which was located in the northwestern part of the country; she equally feared the German resumption of the *Drang nach dem Osten* and toward the Adriatic. On the other hand, some Germans had held out the tempting hope to Belgrade that in the event of Austria's annexation by the *Third Reich*, Yugoslavia's territorial claims against portions of Styria and Carinthia would be given due consideration in Berlin; a few gullible Yugoslav politicians embraced these illusions.

Besides, Yugoslavia had serious territorial differences with Italy which dated back to the peace treaties and the early postwar period, and was fearful of Mussolini's expansionist ambitions; Belgrade also entertained the illusion that it would be able to play Berlin against Rome, and vice versa. Yet, in spite of her flirtations with Germany, Yugoslavia remained France's ally and was also linked with Rumania and Czechoslovakia in the Little Entente. Like its other members, Belgrade was opposed to Budapest's revisionism and, like many in Prague, had a paranoic fear of the restoration of the Habsburg Empire. Many Yugoslavs were more hostile to the idea of a return of the Habsburgs than to Austria's Anschluss with Hitler Germany. These fears of a Habsburg restoration, belief in a rapprochement with Nazi Germany, and the subsequent weakening of Yugoslavia's ties with France and the Little Entente, became more pronounced between 1933 and 1938.

After 1933, members of Yugoslavia's governments saw in Austria's Anschluss with the *Reich* no longer a special peril to Belgrade[8]—frequently in contradistinction to the political opposition as well as to public opinion. Yugoslav governments claimed to be more fearful of a strategic encirclement of their country by Italy, Austria, and Hungary, and set their hopes upon the circumstance that the Anschluss would diminish Italy's threat and eliminate the danger of a Habsburg restoration. They even assumed that a German neighbor would not provoke domestic unrest in Yugoslavia and that the *Reich* would make no territorial claims on ethnic grounds. They seemed confident that Yugoslavia would reap far-reaching economic advantages due to increased trade with Germany, completely ignoring the Nazis' unbounded demands for *Lebensraum* in the East and the aggressive character of National Socialist and Hitler's doctrines.

On August 25, 1933, Foreign Minister Jevtić proclaimed that the Yugoslav government would welcome the Anschluss of Austria in any form, since the current situation in Austria constituted a source of unrest.[9] In mid-February 1934 the Yugoslav Foreign Minister revealed to the French Ambassador Naggiar in Belgrade that the attachment of Austria to Germany was sooner or later "inevitable."[10]

During the spring of 1937, however, Belgrade became hesitant on pursuing its pro-German and pro-Anschluss course. Following an agreement with Ciano on March 25, 1937, and a visit of Beneš, Stojadinović began suddenly to stress the value of Austrian independence. As late as December 1937 he revealed to Mussolini that he was "not sympathetic" toward the Anschluss of Austria; he was, however, still unwilling to offer military assistance in behalf of Austrian independence. Differently from previous occasions, he now feared German proximity to the Adriatic and acknowledged also the economic importance of an independent

Austria for Yugoslavia.[11] But there were limits to Stojadinović's pro-Austrian course both in regard to length of time and substance. According to Poland's Foreign Minister Colonel Beck's *Final Report*, Prime Minister Stojadinović informed him "that Yugoslavia would not take up arms to defend Austria should an attempt at Anschluss be made." He admitted that people tried "to frighten" Belgrade with the Germans: "It was certainly also a considerable problem, but the threat on that side was not so direct" as from the Italian side, "the most suspect neighbor" of Yugoslavia. While Stojadinović disliked Beneš's Czechoslovak policy, the Little Entente was, he pointed out, "not only a traditional but also in some circumstances very handy agreement for Yugoslavia."[11b] While not breaking with the Little Entente, held together by common interests against Hungary, Yugoslavia, as far as Austria was concerned, went her own way.

When German military units marched into Austria, Stojadinović ordered Yugoslav border troops to establish contact with representatives of the German army and German administration and to cooperate with them, "in accord with the friendship between Germany and Yugoslavia."[12] At the same time the Yugoslav Ambassador in Berlin, Aleksander Cincar-Markovic, was instructed to notify the German government of this order. The Belgrade government also informed the foreign press of Yugoslavia's strict neutrality concerning the Austrian question and justified it with previously often stated arguments: the solution of the Austrian question concerned the German nation, and the existence of Yugoslavia herself rested also on the nationality principle. The question of equilibrium in international policy was a concern only of the Great Powers.[13]

The split on the Anschluss issue between the Yugoslav government and Yugoslav public opinion found expression within the framework of the authoritarian Yugoslav state and continued to reveal itself even after the annexation of Austria. Ivo Andrič, assistant to Stojadinović and later a famous literary personality, two days prior to Austria's annexation referred to it as "an act of German aggression against Austria."[14] But Stojadinović stuck to his guns; after the annexation he could hardly pursue a different course. In a secret session of the Parliamentary Club in Belgrade he claimed it was "better to have the Germans at our border than the Habsburgs," an apology, but hardly revealing keen political judgement. In this address he also shifted responsibility for the events in Austria upon the shoulders of Schuschnigg, who allegedly had broken his word given at Berchtesgaden.[15] Finally, he blamed the Western Powers for their passivity in regard to Austria. He admitted the danger of Germany building a "bridge to the Adriatic" via Austria and anticipated a joint move of London, Paris, and Rome only in that eventuality. He conceded that he could "not sleep quietly, if I had Germans and Italians as enemies." But Hitler had assured him that the boundaries of Yugoslavia were "sacrosanct" and that Germany was disinterested in the German minorities of Yugoslavia and Rumania. However, when he seriously added, "and you know what a German word and the faithfulness of the *Nibelungen* means," he encountered only laughter.[16]

Rather excessive was also Stojadinović's claim that the Anschluss was "good" for the domestic situation of Yugoslavia, since it was an anti-Communist move, brought home to the Croats the need for internal political consolidation, and warned the Slovenes to refrain from further demonstrations: Yugoslavs could not invade Austrian Carinthia nor demand a plebiscite for 90,000 Austrian Slovenes of whom 40,000 were already alienated from their people. But the parliamentary opposition of the Serb Radicals, of Yugoslav Democrats, and of the Croatian Peasant Party, the most important political groups, differed sharply with him. They criticized Stojadinović and Yugoslav policy for breaking up the alliance with the states of the Little Entente and with those bound by the Balkan Pact, and castigated him for the abandonment of the alliance with France and the virtual adherence to the Berlin-Rome axis. Avoiding the forum of the *Narodna Skupština*, he rather chose that of the Senate. There Senator Dr. Andjelinović warned that the formation of a German state with 75 million inhabitants along Yugoslavia's borders would entail incalculable political, military, and economic consequences; the push of a totalitarian Germany to the *Karawanken* and the Drave could virtually isolate Yugoslavia from Western Europe. What was imperative was the collaboration of the entire Yugoslav people, which presupposed a more democratic orientation of the government in domestic and foreign policy.[17]

Faced with the question of whether Stojadinović during his visit to Berlin was informed by Hitler about the impending

Anschluss, the Prime Minister was evasive. To the question relating to the recognition of Yugoslavia's borders, raised by German national demonstrations in Graz when demonstrators called for a German Marburg (the Yugoslav Maribor), the Premier assured the lawmakers that Hitler had told him of his interest in a strong Yugoslavia and of the absolute inviolability of the Yugoslav-German border. To another question relating to the always acute minority problem of Yugoslavia which affected the common boundary, Stojadinovič referred simply, and not very convincingly, to the continuing friendly relationship between Yugoslavia and Germany as the best guarantee for Yugoslavia's integrity. He further minimized Belgrade's responsibility for the defense of Czechoslovakia, a fellow member of the Little Entente. Officially, the Premier, in a talk with the German Ambassador in Belgrade, von Heeren, expressed his felicitations on occasion of Austria's annexation.[18] There closely followed instructions to the Yugoslav officials as well as to Belgrade dailies to prevent possible demonstrations and protests "in connection with Carinthia and Germany" and to suppress any news about the oppression of Slovenes in Carinthia.[19] The suppression of news relating to Austria and Germany and of Yugoslav concerns appeared the more imperative, since the parliamentary and political opposition unleashed major demonstrations against the Belgrade government. Slovene students in Ljubljana (Laibach) and Maribor (Marburg) were especially active. On March 10, Dr. Maček, Chief of the Croatian Peasant Party, had warned at the implementation of an old-Pan German goal—the German "bridge to the Adriatic." While he feared the "pan-German push" to the sea, at the same time he attempted via Budapest to attach Croatia to the Axis.

Rumania and Poland

Yugoslavia's and Czechoslovakia's partner in the Little Entente, Rumania, was geographically more remote from Austria than her allies, but she was also deeply worried. In the days after the Berchtesgaden Conference between Hitler and Schuschnigg in February 1938, F. P. Hibbard, U. S. chargé d'affaires in Bukharest, in an analysis of the attitude of the Rumanian press wrote thus to Washington: "The general tone is one of alarm, the various commentators speaking repeatedly of an 'invisible Anschluss,' the immediate threat to Czechoslovakia and the potential menace to all the rest of the Danubian basin. There is a general tendency to intimate that the great democratic powers England and France are on trial. . . . Some ask themselves why Italy is so blind or so apathetic to recent events."[20]

Grigoire Gafencu, formerly Under Secretary of State for Foreign Affairs, in an article in *Timpul* called for the formation of a "single bloc by the states of the Little Entente and Rumania's ally, Poland, to meet the danger. . . ." Of all Rumanian papers, only *Universul*, which was independent, nationalistic, and anti-Semitic, believed to detect a "detente" after Berchtesgaden. However, even an article in this paper carried "a reminder of the desirability of the perpetuation of Austrian independence." Clearly, an independent Austria kept Germany at greater distance from Rumania!

Among the pro-French oriented nations and states the *Third Reich* tried to detach from France and to win over to its side were also the Poles. Poland was one of France's most important allies, but ready to "accommodate" herself to Austria's disappearance. Late in 1933 Berlin and Warsaw established contact with each other which in January 1934 was to climax in a ten-year non-aggression pact. Though Poland retained military and other ties with France, there could be little doubt that Hitler had scored heavily and that the system of collective defense laboriously built up by France in the postwar period had received a blow from which it was never fully to recover. Poland, concerned about territorial integrity and survival, made the fateful assumption that Hitler's word could be trusted. Its government was all too willing to watch silently the propaganda campaign of the *Third Reich* against Austria, hoping that annexation would still Germany's appetite and make her forget the tense and disputed German-Polish border, rather than whet her appetite for an eastward expansion. To Poland, Germany's drive toward the Anschluss seemed like a welcome diversion of Germany from Upper Silesia, the Corridor, and Danzig. Besides, the German drive toward the Southeast of Europe promised Germany's preoccupation with the Adriatic rather than with the Baltic.

To the Polish Government whose geopolitical short-sightedness was only surpassed by its ideological preference for authoritarian types of government, the Anschluss did not seem an issue of major national significance. When Laroche, French Ambassador to Warsaw, in February 1934 met with Minister Beck concerning the impending Austrian complaint against Germany at Geneva, the latter answered a direct question posed by his interlocutor in a way quite similar to earlier official utterances: Poland had "no direct interest" in this question.[21] Laroche, according to his own account, disputed this view by pointing out that the disappearance of Austria would have serious risks of an economic nature for Poland —which Beck admitted. The Austrian question, Laroche further insisted, was an affair holding general interest, since the Anschluss, due to the growing power of Germany, was bound to have serious consequences for Poland. Again, Beck did not deny this. The Polish government, in his view, had merely seized an opportunity for normalizing relations with Germany. Accordingly, Lipski in Berlin, on the very eve of signing in January 1934 the German-Polish ten-year non-aggression pact, had received instructions from Warsaw to avoid any conversations with Western diplomats on Austria. Warsaw had made up its mind on Austria and the Anschluss. It did not want to arouse false hopes in the West that its attitude on this issue could be changed in favor of Austrian independence and the West.

The Polish government's myopia concerning the significance of the Anschluss, which was bound to strengthen Hitler's Germany, was quite apparent. The Russian Ambassador to Warsaw, Antonov-Owssejenko reported to have heard from Colonel Beck, that Hitler had told the Polish Ambassador in Berlin, Lipski, "I am not a Prussian."[22] These words were designed to convey the impression that the Führer would interest himself to a lesser extent than the Prussians in problems of the East. Beck and the government of the Colonels banked heavily on such fatuous promises!

Hitler was bent on deceiving the Poles and making them believe that he was more interested in the Anschluss—a "specifically German problem"—than in broaching the question of the eastern frontiers of the *Reich*. He also went so far as to blame Bismarck's policy against Poland.[23] Laroche cautioned Colonel Beck that Poland's indifference against the Anschluss was not only a "major error" of Warsaw, but would also have grave consequences for the policy of France the effects of which to save Austria were well known to him.

On January 14, 1938, Colonel Beck journeyed to Berlin where he met the Führer. "Never before," he reported in the *Final Account*, "was the Chancellor so categoric in his assurances as to the inviolability of the indirect and direct interests of Poland."[24] Planning the move against Austria, though the timetable may still have been flexible, Hitler wanted no trouble from Poland, but calm on the eastern front! Though Hitler tried to speak in "carefully chosen terms" about Austria and the Sudeten Germans, Beck had the "definite feeling that the problem of Austria and the Sudetenland were reaching a climax and dominating Hitler's thoughts."[25]

The plebiscite ordered by Schuschnigg on March 9, 1938, in Austria made, according to Beck—he was then on a visit to Italy—an unfavorable impression not only upon himself, but also upon Italian official circles. In a reply to Ciano's question as to the plebiscite's significance, Beck answered "that it was probably the end." Though Colonel Beck was scheduled to spend ten more days resting in Sorrento, he decided on an early return to Poland, and via Austria. He was evidently fearful not only of a precipitate German move against Austria but also of possibly getting into a "dangerous conflict." He thought that "complete passivity in view of the German expansion would in any case be dangerous." "If we had to maintain our position in Eastern Europe, we should think of finding an assurance for Polish interests, should anyone think of violating them." Who at that moment was likely to "violate" Poland's interests but Germany? Even glancing back, Colonel Beck did not call Germany by name. As he revealed, he was primarily thinking of Danzig, Polish-Lithuanian relations, Teschen, Silesia, and of the possibility, in the event of a collapse of Czechoslovakia, of a common frontier between Poland and Hungary. But he definitely excluded Austria, "a problem which was remote to us and concerned us comparatively little."[26] On his way home, passing through Vienna, he was already received there by the *Statthalter* of Austria, the crypto-Nazi Seyss-Inquart. At the moment of Austria's demise, Colonel Beck may still have felt safe as far as Poland was concerned. But a year and a half later the clouds of war engulfed his country and destroyed Poland's sovereignty and independence. The interests of Austria and Poland had not been so far apart as he had thought.

Hungary

Of all the East European neighbors of Austria and Germany, none was as German-oriented as Hungary, though she too was torn by ambivalent sentiments. All this was rooted in history, especially in her long struggle with Vienna, the establishment of dualism in the old Habsburg Monarchy in 1867 and the spectacular rise of the Magyars, and Hungary's pro-German inclinations in the pre-1914 era. After 1918 revisionism was a major tie between radical German and Magyar nationalism. While German and especially Nazi revisionism pitted German nationalism against the national movement of the Poles, the Czechoslovaks, the Yugoslavs, even the Rumanians and Italians, this did not seem to be quite the case as far as the Hungarians were concerned. But Hitler was ready to abandon the German minorities in Italy and to keep suppressed the demands of the Swabian Germans in Hungary. For the sake of German revisionism, to enhance the chances of altering the map of Europe in favor of the *Reich*, Hitler needed at least temporary friends and allies.

Hungarian revisionism, having long set its hopes upon Italy, began to shift its expectations toward the *Third Reich*. If Hungary was ever to achieve her far-flung goals, only Germany could make that kind of territorial revolution in Central Europe and the Balkans which offered her tangible benefits. On the other hand, German revisionism would lead to the Anschluss, the annexation of Austria, and establish a lengthy German-Hungarian border constituting a continuous threat to Magyar independence. The Anschluss, however brought about, signified for Hungary the possibility of great gains as well as of terrific losses which could reduce the former to insignificance. Since 1921, wrote Count Stephen Bethlen, noted Hungarian statesman, in 1938, after the annexation of Austria, "there has not occurred an international event to equal the international significance of Austria's union with Germany as regards our national future."[27]

Prior to the annexation of Austria in 1938, there was in the interwar period always the chance that Hungary, nominally a monarchy, would become one in fact, with a Habsburg ruler enthroned in Budapest and perhaps attempting to restore the old Habsburg Empire in Central Europe. Or Austria, according to Bethlen, might join the Little Entente, especially if Social Democrats once again got the upper hand: this would compel Hungary, "though contre coeur," to surrender to the idea of a Danubian Confederation. And he raised the grim alternative question: "Was the uncertainty of yesterday better for us than the certainty of today? Was it the lesser evil of the two?" But, as if he wanted to avoid answering the question, he concluded that Austria's union with Germany had "both advantages and drawbacks for us." From a theoretical point of view, there could be no doubt that "a weak neighbor was always more acceptable to a weak country than a powerful one." Considering Hungary's geographic position and the fact that the principal market for Hungary's exports will in future be Germany and "that moreover the majority of our exports to other countries will have to be effected via that country, we shall be more dependent on the goodwill of Germany than ever before." Due to the annexation of Austria, Germany will also have gained "proximity" to other agrarian states of the Danubian basin and will in relation to these states be able to act "as a monopolizing factor." All this, of course, "is disadvantageous from our point of view."

In a conversation in 1935 with Starhemberg, leader of Austria's fascist *Heimwehr*, Hungary's dictator Nicholas Horthy disclosed that due to the injustice of the Peace Treaty of Trianon an improvement of Hungary's relations with Czechoslovakia, Rumania, and Yugoslavia was "almost impossible."[28] He regretted that Hungary's "need to incline toward Germany as the main champion for the revision of the peace treaties was much greater than was beneficial to Magyar interests." Horthy saw here clearly that revisionism with the help of Germany would lead to the reconquest of separated Hungarian territories but that this could only be purchased by complete vassalage toward Germany.

In the evening of the same day Starhemberg also conversed with the Hungarian Premier Julius Gömbös who drew his attention to the machinations of the Austrian Nazis. When Starhemberg voiced puzzlement at this frankness of a Hungarian politician who was on excellent terms with Berlin and Hitler, Gömbös replied: "I have to be on good terms with these people in Berlin, but I am afraid of them. As long as Austria survives, the peril has not yet moved into close proximity. But—never mind if I am frank—I am not so sure that you will survive. . . ." Starhemberg then suggested, as he had previously done vis-à-vis Mussolini—

that it was imperative to juxtapose a Danubian patriotism to that of Pan-Germanism. But Gömbös recalled that the revisionist outlook was the "beginning and the end of the policy of every national [Hungarian] government;" it alone united the Hungarian nation. "The Hungarian nation is too much geared toward this only goal of its politics." Hungary had to entertain good relations with the *Third Reich*, "even if we can hope most sincerely that you Austrians survive and protect us from having a common border with the Prussians."

In 1938 Bethlen claimed, not always convincingly, that the new situation, Austria's annexation, had brought "great political advantages" to Hungary, advantages which will afford her "a great opportunity to rise from the humiliation of Trianon, and once again to become an important, even "its most important [!] factor" in the Danubian region. There followed bitter denunciations of the role of the Little Entente and of Czechoslovakia especially, which has "masqueraded" as a Great Power. Bethlen recalled Bismarck's friendship for Hungary and reminded the Germans in turn that Hungary had rendered the German nation an "immense service by not abandoning her just claims after Trianon."[29] Bethlen concluded by stressing the community of German-Hungarian interests confirmed in World War· I, but warned against any attempt to introduce into Hungary the methods and forms of a state system that appeared to suit the German nation, "but could bring about a fatal reaction" in Hungary. Though playing up to Rome and now also to Berlin, Bethlen had not yet abandoned Hungary's loose ties with the West. He claimed it to be "indubitable" that, in the views of Italy and Germany, Hungary, a friendly state, should occupy a position of "proper significance" in the Danubian basin. But he also appealed to the Western Powers: England and France must see "how really important it is in the interest of European balance to maintain the independence of the Hungarian nation in the Danube basin unimpaired, and to ensure its vitality." It was curious that a Magyar statesman after the annexation of Austria rediscovered the argument used by France and her friends and allies throughout Europe against the Anschluss ever since 1918.

Many in Hungary feared, Bethlen admitted, "that the German voracity will not stop at the gates of Sopron (Ödenburg) and that Hungary will be the next victim." But he dismissed "phantoms of this kind," only designed to "frighten" the Hungarian nation. It would make no sense for Germany to add Hungary "to the already fairly large number of enemies." All of Hungary's resources were in any case at Germany's disposal. Neither was it in Germany's own interest to cut Hungary off from the West, "for the German Empire's shortest route to the Balkans and the East passes through our country." It was also "absurd" that Germany might consider "our country as a settlement area when the Alföld (Great Plain) or the Trans-Danubian districts show already signs of comparative overpopulation." There have been "sporadic German settlements in this country for 200 years," which might give some German fanatics the idea of extending the German frontier to the East." Bethlen, however, was "firmly convinced that no such thoughts are harbored by a single serious-thinking German or by government circles." All of East Central Europe—even Hungary which had more reason to nourish territorial hopes in the wake of the Anschluss—visibly trembled when the German troops marched into Austria.

Switzerland

Of Germany's and Austria's neighbors, Poland, Czechoslovakia, and Yugoslavia were the beneficiaries of the Paris Peace settlement. All of them were therefore early allies of France. Hungary, on the contrary, had suffered grievous territorial losses. While Hungary's hopes rested on the great revisionist powers, Italy and later Germany, Switzerland, Austria's and Germany's neighbor, continued her neutrality policy of the pre-World War I era. However, her ethnic composition as well as her democratic heritage made her vulnerable to the Nazi thrust into Austria and to the Pan-German claims of the expansionist *Third Reich.*

The dissolution of the Austrian Empire and the defeat of Imperial Germany left Switzerland a neighbor of a powerful victorious France. But Switzerland had no ground to fear France, while every reason to fear German expansionism in Nazi garb.[30] There was no pan-Gaullist movement, no French equivalent to Pan-Germanism, either in France or in neighboring French-speaking cantons such as existed in Switzerland. The Swiss feared lest the Anschluss would become only a temptation for the Pan-Germans to declare all people who spoke German as *"Reich*

Germans." Switzerland opposed the Anschluss out of concern for her own independence!

After the Berchtesgaden Conference in February 1938 the *Journal de Génève* in an editorial "Austria and Swiss Sentiments" held that it required greater courage on the part of Schuschnigg to accept the invitation than to refuse it.[31] One may perhaps say, wrote the daily, that the Austrian national sentiment was not very developed, that part of the population showed a sympathy for Hitlerism, that this country, an artificial creation of the Versailles Treaty, did not know how to offer moral resistance like a solidly established state resting on a long tradition (obviously a state such as Switzerland). All this may possibly be true, but the editorialist still expressed his "profound sorrow" over recent developments, which had chilled one's sense of liberty and justice. Dollfuss's death had been a loss for Europe and for Switzerland in particular, "since we have a major interest to see on our eastern frontier an independent nation, necessary for an international equilibrium." It "is not indifferent to us [Swiss] to have one day a single neighbor along the Rhine instead of two." It was most regrettable if one party could use military force to impose its views and the other can oppose it only with a sense of righteousness. This situation has "troubled the heart and spirit of every Swiss citizen for whom national independence is one of the most precious of all goods." The daily recalled the example of the Swiss legendary hero Wilhelm Tell; the use of violence which forces a people to bend to it was intolerable. On March 13, 1938, the *Journal de Génève* in the editorial "The German Army in Austria" wrote thus: The indignation in Europe is general against Hitler's "coup de force." He had won the game in Austria, but he has "gravely compromised the future of the *Reich*." In another article it insisted that the *Reich*'s act of violence had made a "profound impression in Switzerland," though it had not surprised government circles or the parliamentary Foreign Affairs Council. Fortunately, in German Switzerland no political group existed that was comparable to that of the Austro-Nazis. Swiss citizens had the "good sense" to remain immune against doctrines that were "contrary to our national traditions," "but the fate of Austria does not permit us to be indifferent." Abuse of force was always "a detestable thing." "It places in danger all small states which cannot oppose force except by appeals to law and order."

"Our sympathies go out to the Austrian people which is forced to accept a regime which its great majority opposes."[32]

On March 13 the *Neue Zürcher Zeitung* castigated Germany which in her treatment of Austria had defied all rules of international law. "The threat, which was already uttered at Berchtesgaden, was turned into open violence." Two days later the *Neue Zürcher Zeitung*, recalling Austria's key position in Europe, asserted that the actual addition to German power was "incomparably greater than anything she might have achieved through the revision even of all territorial losses imposed upon the defeated *Reich* in 1918."[33] The concepts of law and justice had reached low bottom on the international scene; a view which, according to the daily, was widely shared in Switzerland and most of Europe.

While during the last days of the crisis, in February and March 1938, Swiss public opinion had condemned Germany's reckless methods against Austria as "brutal imperialist aggression," official reaction reflected not only caution but even timidity. On March 21, both houses of the Swiss Parliament called the completed Anschluss of the Austrian neighbor the "realization of the popular will" and reaffirmed Switzerland's traditional neutrality.[34] This declaration may have been an understandable act of pragmatic politics, but it went too far; it had all the characteristics of gratuitous and unheroic appeasement.

Chapter 13

Surrender at Berchtesgaden and its Aftermath

Toward the Conference

Glaise-Horstenau as well as Seyss-Inquart had frequently made suggestions to Chancellor Schuschnigg to meet Hitler personally, claiming that a direct conversation with the Führer would most likely lead to a lowering of the tension between their states. But Schuschnigg long opposed this idea. Early in January 1938 Papen again began to sound out the possibility of a meeting between the two political leaders. In late January, believing he had no longer any alternative, Schuschnigg finally agreed to it.[1] He held that a rejection of Hitler's invitation would merely furnish the Führer with a weapon, enabling him to paint the picture of an unyielding Austrian Chancellor. Yet before consenting to a meeting, Guido Schmidt, Austria's Foreign Minister, demanded from Papen several "guarantees": a prior advance determination of the themes of conversation in Berchtesgaden and the pledge that the July 1936 Agreement with its acknowledgement of Austrian sovereignty and German non-intervention would be preserved without change. Only after Papen in the name of Hitler had given the foregoing assurances, did Schuschnigg accept the invitation. Still, the Austrian Chancellor was extremely naive about the negotiations leading to the meeting. It was his impression that Papen knew little, if anything, about the impending Conference and that Seyss-Inquart knew nothing.[2] Both suppositions proved to be wrong, though none of the personalities involved had an advance knowledge of all the events which were to unfold.

At the postwar trial of Austria's Foreign Minister Guido Schmidt, the accused observed that "the situation in early 1938 had become, judged from a domestic point of view, indefensible."[3] Something had to happen. "All agreements with the Austrian Nazis, without approval from beyond the border, were irrelevant." Both Schuschnigg and his Foreign Minister wished therefore to make a last attempt to clarify the inner-political situation through an accord with Hitler, though this was "perhaps irreconcilable with our conception of sovereignty." Still, Schmidt held that an exchange of views with the German government offered the possibility of improving the situation. On the other hand, he doubted that Schuschnigg was the most skillful adversary for Hitler; he may have foreseen the outcome of a confrontation between Schuschnigg with his cultivated manners and Hitler with his ill-concealed brutality. Schuschnigg himself had come to consider his journey to Berchtesgaden the last means of salvaging Austria's independence. He still would probably have refrained from it had he known in advance that Hitler would ignore the conditions agreed upon for the talks. Schuschnigg later disclosed that he had carefully weighed all arguments pro and con; he had voiced his innermopst doubts and hesitations to a few confidants. But in the end he concluded that a decline of Hitler's invitation might lead to more unfortunate consequences than an inconclusive meeting. Also, though Hitler's aggressive manners in international diplomacy were known, they had not yet fully evolved. Finally, Papen almost implored the Austrian Chancellor to accept Hitler's invitation, since it offered a unique and last opportunity for reaching an understanding. In return for relatively minor concessions Schuschnigg might gain a major triumph.

The Austrian case was carefully prepared at the *Ballhausplatz* and a dossier was assembled consisting of complaints about German press attacks, the glorification of Austrian state criminals— a German student club in Munich had been named after Planetta, the murderer of Dollfuss—and active support of hostile and illegal anti-Austrian agitations. Again, it was naively assumed that, if Schuschnigg would produce the "evidence" of Germany's indisputable violations of the terms of the July 1936 Agreement, Hitler would be embarrassed and beat retreat. When the so-called "Punktationen," agreed upon in discussions between Guido Zernatto and Seyss-Inquart, representing the limits of Austrian concessions to be made in Berchtesgaden, were leaked to the German Nazis, Hitler obtained a considerable diplomatic advantage. Schuschnigg was completely unaware of these happenings, though, considering all circumstances, they had to be expected. Guido Schmidt was informed of the "Punktationen" just before the departure for Berchtesgaden and was greatly perturbed by the magnitude of the concessions which had been made to Seyss-Inquart.[4]

On February 1, 1938, Seyss-Inquart had reported to Wilhelm Keppler, Commissioner of the Führer, that Schuschnigg had declared himself ready to comply with the following demands of Seyss-Inquart: release of all persons still in jail in consequence of the abortive July 1934 Putsch; elimination of economic discrimination against all persons who had been convicted because of Nazi activities; and development of closer relations with the *Reich* through greater participation in Austrian affairs of persons from the ranks of the National Opposition. Seyss-Inquart had gained the definite impression that Schuschnigg was prepared to yield to a greater extent than ever before.

On February 4, Papen took Captain Leopold, the illegal Austrian Nazi leader, to task because of his instructions to resort to acts of terrorism in the Austrian provinces.[5] Apparently, Leopold desired to force the *Reich* authorities into an early intervention in Austria and especially into cancelling the impending Schuschnigg-Hitler meeting about which he must have learned. In view of the continuing internal disputes among Austrian Nazis and their challenge to German foreign policy in particular, the threat to his carefully nurtured project, the meeting in Berchtesgaden, Papen recommended that Captain Leopold be summoned to the *Reich* as soon as possible.

On the eve of Schuschnigg's journey to Berchtesgaden, on February 7, 1938, Wilhelm Keppler, since June 1937 special German Emissary to Austria, dispatched a very optimistic report on the state of Austrian affairs to the new German Foreign Minister Joachim von Ribbentrop.[6] He freely admitted that the Austrian Nazis had already obtained a firm foothold in the Austrian Cabinet, though officially Seyss-Inquart and Glaise-Horstenau were not considered Party members, merely "nationalbetont." According to Keppler, the prospects of the success of an evolutionary solution to the Austrian question had recently considerably improved. During the last two weeks especially, Schuschnigg had been much more willing to comply with the provisions of the July Agreement concerning the inclusion of the National Opposition to share joint responsibility for Austria. Raising the question of why Schuschnigg was now more willing than before to carry out the July Agreement, Keppler held that the changes of the Austrian Chancellor to escape the diplomatic pressures from the *Reich* were "dwindling": the visits of the Hungarian and Yugoslav Prime Ministers in particular had shown him that there was really no longer any room for such a policy. The detailed plans for a forcible solution of the Austrian question which were found in the raid on the Teinfaltstrasse had apparently not failed to make an impression either: "Persons in the Austrian government itself who are in sympathy with us [!]" had told Keppler repeatedly that Schuschnigg was in no position "to let go the few National Socialists who are openly in the Government." The foothold already obtained in the Austrian administration should be further strengthened. Keppler recommended that the Party "by a moderately adroit policy" obtain further concessions, and he held this prospect likely, "particularly so, since a very large part of the population was firmly behind us."

Once more Keppler focused upon the core of the problem which Papen had often illuminated before. "The political efforts of the last few years, especially those of the last six months, had been greatly handicapped by disagreement and opposition on the part of the Austrian leadership." He, Keppler, had taken utmost pains and shown very great patience in trying to bring *Landesleiter* Leopold into line, but his efforts had been of no avail. Like Field Marshal Göring—he might have also added, like Papen, but apparently considered him a lightweight in Party circles—he too was of the opinion that the removal of Leopold was an "urgent necessity." Göring, judging by his reaction to Keppler's report the previous day, had approved the efforts and the progress made so far by Seyss-Inquart. If, in view of the international situation, Keppler concluded, "we continue with the task of solving the Austrian question by way of evolution," the present moment offered good prospects for substantial progress, and he was convinced that "we shall slowly [!] gain political ascendancy over Schuschnigg." Keppler revealed National Socialist objectives to Austria without making any attempt to disguise them. But clearly, well-informed and well-positioned though he was, neither he nor probably anyone else, had an inkling of what the immediate future, the very next days, held in store.

Schuschnigg accepted the invitation to Berchtesgaden in the hope of gaining time. Gaining even a mere six months—which one considered the maximum obtainable in Budapest—[7] might perhaps save Austria from the Nazi catastrophe. Schuschnigg did no longer expect any military support by the Great Powers, but seemed to count at least on a diplomatic démarche by them, especially after the high-level discussions of Anglo-Italian differences. Mussolini himself thought that the negotiations of Ambassador Grandi in London held out the hope of a settlement within a fortnight.[8]

The Meeting In Berchtesgaden

The talks of Berchtesgaden lasted 10 hours. In the first part of the talks, which were between Hitler and Schuschnigg alone, the Führer offered the Austrian Chancellor what he called the "unique opportunity to add his name to those of great Germans," such as Göring, Hess, Frick, and Epp—all of course notorious Nazi leaders. Schuschnigg entertained no doubt that Hitler at best contemplated a "satellite status" for Austria, a hardly camouflaged Anschluss.[9] While underlining his own generosity in opening to him the portals of Valhalla, Hitler at the same time accused the Austrian chancellor of having plotted through his friend, the Jesuit Muckermann, his own assassination—a charge which Schuschnigg indignantly rejected—warned him that he was turning Austria into a second Spain, and recalled threateningly that Vienna was merely a flying hour away from Munich. Schuschnigg was convinced that Hitler was not bluffing, but that a rupture of the negotiations would have unleashed a military response. The plans for "Operation Otto" were indeed long ready. Also, the presence of German military leaders at the Berchtesgaden meeting was, in Schuschnigg's view, no idle threat.

Through Ribbentrop, Hitler let the Austrian Chancellor know that if he refused to accept Seyss-Inquart as Minister of Security, he would give the order for a march into Austria that very hour. Though ultimately obtaining a delay of three days, Schuschnigg was compelled to accept the following points of the protocol: 1) Austria's obligation of prior consultation with Germany in all questions of foreign policy; 2) Recognition of Austrian National Socialism as reconcilable with membership in the Fatherland Front. National Socialist organizations should be permitted to join the Front in a collective fashion. 3) Appointment of Seyss-Inquart as Minister of Interior and as head of the department of

Security; 4) General Amnesty for all persons sentenced by the courts or penalized by the police on account of National Socialist activities; 5) Glaise-Horstenau was to be made Minister of the Army.

Though the Austrian delegation succeeded in improving the Keppler plan in a few points, the improvements were hardly substantial.[10] The version of the communiqué of the meeting which was prepared in Vienna and transmitted to Berchtesgaden by von Papen differed from the original German model and was the one ultimately accepted by both sides; it was published simultaneously in Vienna and Berlin on February 15. It stressed the continuance of the July Agreement of 1936 and claimed that the February 1938 accord was based upon the earlier document; it was designed to supplement, not to supplant it. But Hitler was resolved not to be deterred by mere pledges of non-intervention and of respect for Austria's sovereignty. Twenty-four hours before publication of the communiqué Hitler consented to a suggestion of General Keitel to place Vienna under new and heavy pressure. German authorities were to spread false rumors to the effect that the *Reich* was undertaking military preparations against Austria.[11]

On February 16, Carr, the American Minister to Prague, telegraphed Washington, that the prevailing view in the Hradčany was that Berchtesgaden constituted "the first step toward extinction of Austria's independence" and that Czechoslovakia was "exceedingly apprehensive that it may be the next object of German pressure."[12] A few days later the Polish diplomatic representative in Vienna, who was in close touch with the German Legation, voiced the fear that a new Austrian crisis would arise within one or two months at the latest;[13] he considered the situation hopeless.

American Voices

On February 17, Seyss-Inquart, just appointed to the post of Minister of the Interior in Vienna, was summoned to Berlin and received by Hitler. The American chargé aptly observed: "The circumstance of a newly appointed member of the Austrian cabinet, who is known as pro-German, being thus in effect summoned to Berlin, is construed here as sharply indicative of the nature of the new relationship between Germany and Austria."[14]

On February 17, 1938, Wiley of the American Embassy in Vienna wrote to his fellow American Ambassador William Bullitt in Paris that the Führer had staged a scene in Berchtesgaden which probably had never been equalled. He added: "To me, 1938 smells bad."[15] Turning to a possible United States response, Wiley, U.S. representative in Vienna continued revealingly: "*There is of course nothing that the U.S. can do.** I have murmured a few words of bedside sympathy. That, curiously enough, is all that Schuschnigg got from anyone else, including Great Britain, France, and Italy." Though Schuschnigg will cleverly attempt to out-maneuver Seyss-Inquart, Wiley voiced the fear that Schuschnigg's would be "only a gallant effort slightly to retard developments." The only hope for Austria was to gain time in the expectation that the international situation might change in some way favorable to Austria. But an Anglo-Italian detente, followed by an Anglo-French-Italian agreement to maintain the independence of Austria, seemed very remote. He, Wiley, did not wish to over-dramatize the situation in Vienna, "but it is evidently *the beginning of the end, not only of the independence of Austria, but of existing political values in Europe.*"[16]†

A few days later, on February 21, 1938, Wiley, in a letter to Pierrepont Moffat of the State Department, repeated the view that February 12 had been a "fateful day" for Austria. There is an indirect reply to a warning by Secretary Hull addressed to Moffat a few days earlier—for more or less obvious reasons he avoided answering the Secretary directly—assuring his correspondent that he, Wiley, had not given any pledges of American assistance to the Austrian Foreign Secretary Guido Schmidt; nothing he had uttered to him could have created any false impression in Schmidt's mind![17] Though Schuschnigg with his address of February 24 was to inspire a new enthusiasm in the country, official Austrian optimism was quite limited. At the most it was hoped that Schuschnigg at Berchtesgaden had gained "a respite of six months."

---

*Underlined, A.D.L.
†Underlined, A.D.L.

Austria and Germany In the Wake of Berchtesgaden

Back in Vienna, the formation of a new Austrian cabinet by Schuschnigg had been announced in the evening of February 14. The circular telegram of February 15, sent from Vienna to Austrian diplomatic missions abroad, spoke openly of the pressure exerted upon the Austrian representatives in Berchtesgaden, of the extraordinarily difficult negotiations that had been carried on and of the sharp exchanges which had taken place. It stressed, however, that the recipients of the communication should place main emphasis on the circumstance that the July Agreement of 1936 was in no way either abandoned or weakened and that its reassertion should produce "general calm."[18] In defense of his policy of silence vis-à-vis the Great Powers, Schuschnigg later claimed that the diplomatic representatives of the Great Powers, including of the U.S. government in Vienna, had actually been kept informed about the fateful events. Still, a direct appeal to the governments concerned, while representing unquestionable risks, offered the only chance of alerting public opinion in the West, mobilizing the masses and influencing their governments, as well as galvanizing Austrian domestic resistance to Nazi intimidation from without and within.

According to Berlin, however, Vienna talked already too much. The German government made the Austrian cabinet responsible for alleged "leaks" after Berchtesgaden; these had led to the debate in the French Chamber of Deputies on February 25 and to questions in the British Parliament. Similarly, the Austrian Nationals sharply resented even the most subdued calls for help as an invitation for the intrusion of foreign influence in a strictly German "family" affair, as a provocation.

Schuschnigg later admitted that on February 13, after his return from Berchtesgaden to Vienna, it would have been possible to shock the world by disclosing the whole truth about the Berchtesgaden conference and its aftermath. He questioned, though, whether mere diplomatic démarches which might have resulted from such activity could at this late hour have effectively helped Austria and changed the inevitable course of events; they might well have speeded the coming of the catastrophe. In his opinion, it was imperative to avoid panic at home and retaliation from the *Reich*. He feared lest the certainty of an impending threat undermine Austria's self-confidence and political stability. The country's position was far from being an enviable one, and none of the available alternatives looked overly promising.[19] Intimidated as Schuschnigg himself undoubtedly was, he may have doubted that a terrified state of mind offered to the Austrian people any chance to rally around his government and would have likely generated effective and prompt aid from abroad. Everything considered, the Austrian government erred in not fully and quickly alerting leading politicians and public-opinion-makers abroad. The virtual absence for many days after Berchtesgaden of any direct appeal to the Austrian people and to foreign governments, far from delaying the ultimate breakdown, merely accelerated its coming and made it inevitable.

In a report on the Austrian situation by mid-February, Dr. Vesenmayer of the German Embassy in Vienna recounted the spreading unrest especially among Jews and many Catholics. Legitimists too had abandoned all hope. "The collapse is so complete that if an acceleration of developments fits into the Führer's foreign policy, a number of decisive positions can be captured within the succeeding weeks by means of definite pressure on the part of the *Reich*."[20] The illegal Austrian NSDAP, however, continued to cause great difficulties, though Captain Leopold himself had left for the *Reich* on February 18. They were dissatisfied with merely inflicting what they considered minor wounds on the Schuschnigg regime, instead of aiming at its jugular vein. The radical Nazis, questioning the tactics of Seyss-Inquart and of Hitler himself, tried to provoke Seyss-Inquart, branding him a traitor to the nationalist cause.

On February 16, 1938, a few days only after the confrontation in Berchtesgaden, the German Foreign Minister dispatched the following telegram to the various diplomatic missions and consular offices: The conversation of the Führer and Chancellor with the Austrian Chancellor at the Obersalzberg on February 12 has led to a welcome clarification of the relations between the two German countries. In conversation, German officers abroad should interpret the results of the meeting in Berchtesgaden as a notable progress in the relations between the two German states. "The path to a close and friendly collaboration between the *Reich* and Austria on all decisive questions in the political, cultural, and economic area is now cleared. The Agreement thus represents a valuable contribution to European peace."[21]

This was hardly the true opinion in Berlin, and certainly not the view in the Western countries. Their reaction was well summed up in the reports from the German Embassies in Paris and London. On February 16, the German Embassy in Paris reported thus to the German Foreign Ministry: "France had been following the development of German-Austrian relations with utmost interest. Opposition to a possible Anschluss had not been given up. But even the Leftist press does not give vent to this opposition in concrete terms."[22] In many places they were saying "Finis Austriae." The Agreement was interpreted, the Embassy report continued, as an event of greatest international historical importance, representing the first step in the realization of a Greater German Empire of the Germanic nation. One day later the German chargé d'affaires in London reported to the German Foreign Ministry the tart comment of an English official, Orme Sargent, that although the move had created a feeling of insecurity in London, no appreciable British reaction was to be expected.[23] These assessments turned out to be quite realistic.

In the meantime, Schuschnigg, in accordance with the pledges wrung from him at Berchtesgaden, had thoroughly reorganized the cabinet. The composition of the fifth Schuschnigg cabinet was marked, as mentioned, by the appointment of Dr. Arthur Seyss-Inquart, who, though not without a fight, was also placed in charge of Security.[24] State Secretary Skubl, however, considered a Schuschnigg loyalist, was retained in his post as Director of Security and, at the same time, was made Inspector-General of all law-enforcement agencies, including police. The German Embassy in Vienna looked upon the retention of General Wilhelm Zehner as State Secretary for National Defense and the appointment of Engineer Julius Raab as Minister of Commerce as "blemishes" on the new cabinet. The appointment of Guido Zernatto and of Hans Rott as Ministers without portfolio and of the former Social Democrat Adolf Watzek as State Secretary for the Protection of Labor were also correctly interpreted as representing a "counterbalance" to the appointment of Seyss-Inquart.

The circles of the Fatherland Front feared that their authority would be undermined by the consequences of the Berchtesgaden agreement. The radical Austrian National Socialists on the other hand, while welcoming the concessions, rather minimized them and remained skeptical and impatient regarding further progress and anxious to take advantage of the apparent weakness and confusion of the Austrian government to wrest the remaining power from its trembling hands. The German attaché in Vienna, von Stein, seemed pleased with the appointment of Seyss-Inquart, believed even in the "good will" of Foreign Minister Guido Schmidt, but did not extend the same positive appraisal to Chancellor Schuschnigg himself, castigating "particularly the hitherto completely negative attitude as regards the spirit of the Agreement of July 1936."[25] Schuschnigg and his close associates held out no hopes that the new cabinet would, on its own accord, move "more than will absolutely be necessary" toward a rapprochement with the *Reich*, in spite of the momentum which had been created in the last days.

On February 20, Schuschnigg, having recovered from the traumatic experience of the Berchtesgaden meeting, addressed the Austrian Parliament in a courageous and inspiring speech which reverberated throughout Austria and even instilled some hope abroad. A few days later, on February 26, von Papen, having terminated his Austrian mission and being called back to the *Reich*, in a report entitled "Memorandum of my Farewell Visit to the Federal Chancellor," alluded to Schuschnigg's oration. "I told him" Papen wrote, "that while he had found some very cordial words for Austria's German mission, these had been all but drowned out by his dramatic defense of Austrian independence, which he apparently considered threatened—to say nothing of some unnecessary asides against the *Reich*." "If he assured me that his speech had reestablished his authority in Austria, then I would have to add that the speech had also been the cause of yesterday's Chamber debate in France." Papen thought it very regrettable that the Austrian problem had thus again become the center of discussion in Europe. An Austrian independence, supported by France and Czechoslovak crutches, was unbearable to Germany and would lead to the kind of polemics which might easily endanger the peace concluded only the other day. Papen urged the Chancellor not to delude himself into believing that Austria could ever maintain her position with the aid of non-German European alliances. The Austrian question, Papen proclaimed, would be decided only in accordance with the interests of the German people.[26]

It was a fitting "farewell" for Papen. The address was a characteristic combination of arrogance, offense, and threats against Schuschnigg. Even before Schuschnigg had announced the plebiscite in early March 1938 and Hitler had presented his final ultimatum, the German-Austrian relationship, as exemplified by Papen's reaction in late February, had become intolerable and was near the breaking point. Still, on the very same day (Feb. 26) Hitler in a meeting in Germany with Ribbentrop, Keppler and Austrian Nazi leaders such as Tavs, Schattenfroh, and others, maintained that the Austrian question could never be solved by revolution. The protocol of February 12 signed by Schuschnigg, Hitler explained, was so far-reaching that, if completely carried out, the Austrian problem would be automatically solved. He, Hitler, did not desire a solution by violent means if it could be avoided, "since the danger for us in the foreign policy field declined and our military power grew with each year."[27] As late as February 26, Hitler rejected abrupt "revolutionary" changes in his tactics not out of any revulsion against such methods, but simply because they were no longer necessary. The Austrian plum would soon fall into the lap of the *Third Reich.*

Hitler's tactical decisions had occasioned the removal of Austrian Nazi leaders such as Captain Leopold. But he cautioned them not to interpret his act as a permanent exile for themselves; it was not impossible, he vaguely hinted, that they could later return to Austria. The Führer placed the five leading Austrian Nazis present at the meeting in Keppler's charge, informing them that he had entrusted the Austrian problem to the latter. For years these Austrian Nazi leaders and others had been fanatic and tireless workers for their cause and had brought many personal sacrifices in expectation for later gains. But on the eve of the long awaited triumph there were clear warning signals that not they but German Nazis would reap the choicest fruits of victory.

On February 12, 1938, at Berchtesgaden the Führer had threatened Schuschnigg with Germany's invasion and delivered to him an ultimatum which demanded changes in the Austrian government and particularly the inclusion of Seyss-Inquart, one of the leaders of the *Nationalbetonten* and a hardly disguised Nazi, into the Austrian cabinet. In Paris, Alexis Léger of the French Ministry of Foreign Affairs revealed to ambassador Bullitt in Paris that the acceptance of these demands would spell "the end of Austrian independence."[28]

Anxiety in the French Cabinet

The Austrian climax in early 1938 coincided with the often recurring ministerial crisis in France. On March 13, 1938, Chautemps resigned and was replaced once again by the Blum government with Paul-Boncour as Foreign Minister. The long-drawn-out crisis, which left the French ship of state without a helmsman, has been frequently listed as a major factor in France's diplomatic and military inactivity in Central Europe in February and March 1938. But an analysis of France's foreign policy in the 1930s, especially since the Rhineland occupation, shows rather convincingly that the cause of French passivity lies much deeper, among other matters in the lack of a determined will and policy in Europe.

The depth of pessimism reached by the leading French politicians and members of the cabinet emerged from Bullitt's reports of conversations at a luncheon with Premier Chautemps and Foreign Minister Delbos and a talk with the Minister of War Daladier on February 21, 1938.[29] After Hitler's address to the *Reichstag* on February 20 it had become clear that the Führer intended to incorporate both the Austrians and the Germans of Czechoslovakia in the *Reich*. Still, Chautemps did not yet anticipate that ultimately Hitler would turn the Czechoslovak rump state into a German satellite. About Austria, however, the French Premier had no illusions, her situation appeared to him "hopeless." "He could see no way to prevent Hitler from swallowing Austria in the relatively near future. He confirmed that only three days before he had, through Ambassador Corbin in London, proposed to Eden a joint démarche in Berlin stating "that any future action upsetting the *status quo* in Central Europe would meet with united and firm opposition of Great Britain and France," but he actually entertained no hopes that Europe would join France in such a démarche. "So far as Central Europe was concerned, he was most pessimistic. Every Frenchman with whom he had talked during the past ten days . . . had suggested to him that, if France should permit Austria and Czechoslovakia to fall into German hands and Hungary and Rumania to slip into German control, the power of the *Reich* would be so enormous that France inevitably would be destroyed within a few years." As soon as Austria should be firmly in Hitler's hands, Beneš would feel obliged to enter upon conversations with Hitler. Those talks would probably result in autonomy for the Sudeten Germans of Bohemia. "The definite incorporation in the *Reich* of both the Sudeten Germans and the Austrians would be simply a question of time.[30] Chautemps believed that Chamberlain himself "contemplated with relative equanimity the control by Germany of Austria, Czechoslovakia, Hungary, and Rumania." Chamberlain had telephoned him immediately after Eden's resignation to inform him that there would be no change in British policy. This was polite but not important. The tragedy of France's external position was that the nation which kept its word—the U.S.—could not act in Europe and the nation which could act—Great Britain—could not keep its word." It seemed probable to him that Central and Eastern Europe would gradually fall "into the hands of Germany without war." The "end of the phase of German domination might well come after years through conflict between the German and Russian colossus supported by other states of Europe."

On the same day Bullitt also talked with Delbos, France's Foreign Minister, who was "in acute depression." He would have to give up, he could not think of "any constructive policy"; the entire policy he had attempted to carry out for the past two years had been "destroyed." "The British Government had made it apparent that Britain would do nothing to prevent the absorption of Austria by Germany. France would not alone attempt to protect Austria. It was clear therefore that Austria within a very limited time would fall into the hands of Germany." Chamberlain's note which he had just received asserting that there would be no change in British policy was "of course valueless."[31] "The fact was that Englad had embarked on a policy of turning over central and eastern Europe to Germany in spite of her obligations under the League of Nations." France was "isolated. No other great power would assist her and France alone would not establish collective security." On the same day Daladier too revealed to Bullitt his conviction "that nothing effective could be done to save Austria."

Reaction in the French Parliament

The Berchtesgaden ultimatum, the mounting tension in Austria, and the threats not only to Austria, but also to the Czechoslovak ally had produced a shock effect in France. Its echo was also heard in the halls of the Chamber of Deputies on February 25 and 26, 1938. Virtually all speakers underlined the gravity of the situation. Most emphasized the need for national unity, though voices at the extreme Left and Right blamed France's foreign policy, the first for not having been firm toward the dictators and not having sought strong ties with the Soviet Union, the latter for having allegedly alienated Fascist Italy and for being unwilling to engage in frank talks with Nazi Germany. The deputies dealt with the *fait accompli*, Austria's revamped, Nazi-infiltrated government and the threat to the integrity and independence of the country. Austria had not yet drowned; but most speakers were openly or guardedly pessimistic regarding her chances of staying afloat, though still hoping for a miracle. None of the deputies nor the French government itself pledged military assistance. But Prime Minister Chautemps and Foreign Minister Delbos left no doubt that France would honor her treaty obligations toward Czechoslovakia.[32]

Yet it was undeniable that from the point of view of Czechoslovakia's defense an effective military assistance to Austria would have only increased the chances of Czechoslovakia's survival. But in view of Germany's strong position along the Rhine, a French offensive using the Maginot line as a jumping-off board was out of the question, as the debate disclosed. A thrust into Germany to divert German efforts from Austria was also not feasible in view of the obsession of French military planning with the defense of France proper. As the French deputy Montigny pointed out, there was a striking contradiction between France's foreign policy stressing her obligation to allied Central and Eastern Europe and her self-interest to preserve her military posture on one hand and French military planning on the other; this planning was mired in an outdated conception of defense and took no realistic account of the need for coming aggressively to the aid of France's Central and East European allies.[33]

True, Foreign Minister Delbos asserted that neither on the economic nor the political level was any attempt to "establish hegemony in Central Europe" admissible.[34] He also proclaimed France's willingness to help to create a "better economic reorganization of the Danubian region," but such a pledge came too late. Delbos characterized the immediate Austrian problem as "basically a problem of European security and at the same time one of international honor"—European security and international honor rather than French security and honor—, and recalled that "we cannot by ourselves realize collective security nor set it in motion." Anatole de Monzie was cheered by the circumstance that during the last days the Austrian people had unanimously demonstrated its will toward independence and that "unity" had been established between Austrian socialists, conservatives, and legitimists. But he also qualified France's determination vis-à-vis Austria by saying that France "must defend what it has promised to defend[35]—which did not include that country. Louis Marin warned that Hitler aimed "at an imperialism much beyond the unity of the German race," as he had already developed in *Mein Kampf*, a work cited by many other deputies of different political persuasions. But, according to Marin, the central European peoples would not tolerate that a colonial status be imposed upon them. Germany was tempted to move in all directions, "toward the east, southeast, and southwest," especially toward the open sea. An absorption of Austria by Germany would also be the "most terrible threat" to Italy. Marin claimed to know that it wold be a "grave error" to assume that Great Britain was disinterested in Austria and Czechoslovakia since they were only landlocked countries. The moment when Austria will have disappeared, "Great Britain in the Mediterranean would be threatened," just as Italy would be.[36]

Others, as Louis Deschizeaux criticized the states of central Europe for lack of support to Austria, for their "narrow particularism," Italy for her failure to prevent the German march toward the Adriatic Sea, and England for inadequate aid to the League of Nations. And France's role, he bitterly complained, had been reduced to that of a "brilliant second" to Great Britain.[37] André Albert thought that the Anschluss was already a *fait accompli*, despite the courageous talk of Chancellor Schuschnigg. Turning to the Chamber, he asked, "Will you let the *Reich* Chancellor gain in peace what was lost in war by William II?"[38] France would court danger if she would display disinterest in Central

Europe. The same theme was elaborated by the leading French Communist speaker on foreign policy, Péri, who held that Mussolini had given his consent to Hitler on the *Gleichschaltung* of Austria. France's weak policy vis-à-vis the dictators and the aggression in Spain as well as in the Far East against Japan had created the atmosphere which was responsible for the recent Hitler ultimatum to Austria. France ought to ask herself the question: "On which day will the head of our government be commandeered to appear in Berchtesgaden before Hitler and his generals?"[39]

The French Chamber of Deputies was deeply aroused over Hitler's ultimatum at Berchtesgaden. Though cautious in giving new pledges to Austria, which was immediately menaced, it uttered warnings against further threats of German expansion, minimized the differences between France and Great Britain regarding Central Europe, looked wistfully to the U.S. across the Atlantic, and seemed to understand the need of Frenchmen to draw closer together. Many were also anxious to strengthen ties with Russia, while others hoped to be able to still reach an agreement with Fascist Italy—an apparent illusion at that particular moment. The Parisian government made clear that while it wanted peace it would not accept peace "at any price."[40] Jean Montigny rejected any discussion with the German government, as did a good number of other deputies, as fruitless: "Illusions are no longer possible." He warned against the policy of capitulation, of "temerity."[41]

Montigny did not take quite seriously those interventionists who like Péri allegedly wanted France to intervene simultaneously in Spain, the Far East, and in Central Europe. But there were other interventionists, less ambitious and "more reasonable," who insisted that the government carry out "at least an especially firm, rapid, and energetic action in a painful and sensitive spot, Austria."[42] Ybarnégaray and de Monzie were among them. Montigny, taking issue with the latter group, wondered whether they had economic or military sanctions in mind. The first sanctions, judging by the Ethiopian experience, had proven "ineffective." The military problem, however, was largely a technical problem. After the German rearmament and the occupation of the Rhineland in 1936, France's military situation was quite different from earlier times when the French army could strike into the neighboring highly industrialized Ruhr valley, when Belgium was militarily still tied to France, and before Germany had become industrially more powerful than France and had acquired also a larger army. Finally the French army was organized and trained for a war of defense. Modern military strategy, however, demanded the undertaking of offensive operations.[43] France was also passing through "a crisis of our system of alliances." Italy was no longer in France's camp. Yugoslavia, Poland, and Romania leaned, like Belgium, toward neutrality, and England had made "quite clear to us that she does not want to become engaged in central Europe." Montigny concluded that, in view of these military and diplomatic conditions which every French government must take into account in its deliberations about the Austrian affair, "prudence" was imperative.

While Montigny's analysis was poignant, his own recommendations revealed serious shortcomings. He suggested that France propose a plebiscite in Austria—a few days before Schuschnigg, driven into a corner, was to announce one—one controlled by the United States or neutrals such as Sweden and Norway! He claimed that he did not wish France to "purely and simply accept the successive stages of the Anschluss," since a majority of the Austrians wanted to retain their independence. Certainly France, he concluded, could not act in Austria "in isolation" and had to be aware of her limitations. Paris should talk with Rome and Berlin; "the purpose would not be to capitulate or suffer humiliation."

Only a few deputies referred to the alleged errors of the peace treaties of 1919—especially the dissolution of the Habsburg Empire, by implication also the harsh treatment of Germany, as the deeper causes of the contemporary crisis in central Europe; the great majority apparently did not share these views and saw the cause of the insecurity of Europe in the traditional German striving for hegemony, as did even the champion of the policy of appeasement, Flandin. Pierre-Etienne Flandin voiced bitter complaints of being denounced as a "friend of the German, pro-Hitlerian or pro-fascist"; two years earlier, when he had favored the ratification of a treaty between France and the USSR he had also been "insulted," being called an "agent of the Soviets."[44] France had no right "to accept the risk to play by herself the role of the gendarme in Europe." There was a limit to France's obligations. The French government should carry out a European policy paralleling that of Great Britain under Neville Chamberlain. At the same time he claimed that such a policy was not identical with abandoning Europe, it was no policy of abdication.

None of the other difficulties bound to arise in central Europe, Flandin asserted, will be solved without the help of Italy. He criticized the French government for being unwilling to "subordinate the friendship of Italy to the Spanish affair," and make concessions in the Ethiopian question, creating thus the impression that the Western Powers could at this late hour still gain Mussolini's favor! The old policy of France, he asserted, which rested upon obsolete formulas of the League of Nations, collective security and mutual assistance, was dead. Flandin disclaimed that he did not wish to honor France's treaties. But one should be certain that one was able to keep engagements. "Germany had become powerful." He did not question the value of the historic argument according to which Germany was "a people of conquerors and always aims at hegemony." But France, could, without fear, still arrange for talks with her. If France should be attacked, she would be victorious in the end. She could organize her defenses "behind the Maginot line," until other liberty-loving countries, like those which had helped France in 1914, would join her to assure the victory of her principles. It was quite clear that Flandin was not prepared for France to raise her sword to save Austria and was not ready to do much more to assist Czechoslovakia, France's ally, but counted on England and the support of other powers if Germany should directly challenge France's security.

Flandin was countered by Paul Reynaud, a leader of the traditional Nationalists. Reynaud started his oration with the remark that if Germany, which undoubtedly followed closely the proceedings of the French Chamber of Deputies, hoped that this debate would result in a reversal of France's policy and a French will to "abdicate," she "must have concluded by now that she had been mistaken. None had asked for a revision of the treaties which carried the signature of France. The German thunder had been heard over Austria," and France stood at the crossroads. One alternative stressed maintaining the European equilibrium. The other would lead to the resignation of France, to the abandonment of her allies, and her retrenchment behind the Maginot line. Behind the second alternative lurked the thesis that France was weak, one which Reynaud vigorously disputed. He claimed to know that Poland could not ignore that, if France should be crushed, she herself would wither away and other states of central Europe would in this event also "fall into servitude."[45] Reynaud pointed to France's friends and allies in central and eastern Europe which she could not afford to abandon. Otherwise, "a day will come when the demand of a colossal neighbor will appear to be intolerable to the pride of a noble people; on that day France would be involved in a war "without honor and without friends." Reynaud was prepared to take the assurances of the new British Foreign Minister Lord Halifax in the House of Lords that Eden's resignation did not signify a change in British policy quite literally. France therefore should continue to base her own foreign policy on her defensive treaties and the League of Nations and consider the benefits of her treaty obligation for her own security. These benefits were "greater than the risk they carry for France of being involved in a war." Yet, though he and other deputies referred at times to Austria, at other times to Czechoslovakia, sometimes to both countries, it was not always clear that even Reynaud supported a French military intervention against Germany in behalf of Austria.

Prime Minister Chautemps finally criticized those who held that France's salvation lay in a "complete reversal of her foreign policy." He blamed the League of Nations for its "timidity" and acknowledged the failure of collective security, but upheld the League's principles and called upon France to take pride in her own strength. While Paris should seek an agreement with the totalitarian countries, she would not pursue the policy of abandonment which would "lead to the denial of the traditions of *grandeur*, without guaranteeing security." A policy of renunciation would pose serious dangers for France and would promptly bring about "the inevitable submission of the small nations to great totalitarian powers."[46]

Chautemps associated himself with the declarations of the French Foreign Minister Delbos for whom he had words of praise— "that France could not disinterest herself in the fate of central Europe." Austria, however, was not specially mentioned. Nor should France fail to live up to the alliance which creates the obligation "to protect the independence of Czechoslovakia."[47] His distinction between the two countries was not lost on any Frenchman nor, as a matter of fact, on Nazi Germany. Still, both Premier

Chautemps and Foreign Minister Delbos asserted that Austria's independence was an indispensable element of Europe's balance of power, though neither went beyond it. In regard to Austria at least France and Great Britain were not far apart; but both were far from making tangible and significant pledges of support to Austria.

On the Eve of the Annexation:
Prague, Paris, and London

Thus it was hardly surprising that on the eve of Austria's demise President Beneš of Czechoslovakia, the next obvious target of Nazi expansionism, endeavored to impress upon both Western Powers the geopolitical importance of central Europe in its entirety and of the free Czechoslovak bastion in the heart of Europe in particular. Aware of the difficulty of enlisting Western support for Austria alone, he often coupled Austria with Czechoslovakia and dwelled on Central Europe as such.

The French government was steadily admonished not to ignore France's basic strategic interest in the heart of Europe. According to an utterance of Beneš on March 2, Germany's conquest of Czechoslovakia and Austria would not bring peace to Europe.[48] If Germany should be given control of the whole of Central Europe, he remarked privately, the whole of Europe would be at the mercy of Germany and Russia. This would involve "enormous sacrifices, if not great danger, to Great Britain and France." Beneš warned that Germany and Italy, once in control of central Europe, "would be in a position to wage war." He had strongly urged this point of view in Paris and had explained that, unless the Great Powers such as France and Great Britain clearly perceived this danger and realized that their own salvation lay in the support of the integrity of the Central European states, they themselves would, in due time, be threatened and have to fight for their existence.

During the following days a deep pessimism hovered over the French capital. As Wilson, American chargé in Paris, wrote to Washington on March 1, 1938, Delbos and the French Foreign Office remained "deeply depressed" over the turn of events. The French Government had confidence in Chamberlain's friendship for France, but "also believes that he sees himself in the role of

the British statesman predestined to give peace to the world."
The "constant contact" between the British and French governments, to which Chamberlain recently referred in the House of
Commons, will "probably consist . a few crumbs of routine
information about once every two weeks."[49]

The French government lacked not only genuine confidence in
the English determination to assist it in Central Europe but equally
so in the stability of the new Austrian government, recently
reshuffled in accordance with Hitler's dictate. On March 9, 1938,
the American chargé in Vienna informed the Secretary of State
that the Austrian government had appealed for British and French
financial support. Puaux, France's Ambassador in Vienna, had
frankly told the Austrian Foreign Minister Guido Schmidt that,
before he could recommend favorable action, he would have to
know whether the money would be going to Schuschnigg or to
Seyss-Inquart, a member of the Austrian cabinet, since Hitler had
imposed him on Schuschnigg at Berchtesgaden. "Puaux complains
that he is in an impossible situation. He has urged Schuschnigg
on to resistance, but is able to support him only with sympathy.
So far he has been entirely unsuccessful in endeavoring his
government to adopt a forceful attitude."[50]

Chapter 14

Austria on the Brink: The Passivity of Interested Powers

Rome Surrenders.
Repercussions in East Central Europe

After Berchtesgaden the political leadership in Austria, Schuschnigg included, lived on borrowed time. The Austrian Chancellor told Puaux, France's Ambassador in Vienna, that he mistrusted Italian officials in Rome: "Everything he had confided to Rome had been reported back to Berlin." The British government, according to Schuschnigg, could do a great deal in Berlin, since Hitler eagerly desired an understanding with London; France and Great Britain "must not give Germany the impression that they would be passive in the event that Austria should be attacked."[1] Once again, the Austrian Chancellor had turned for last-minute help to the Western Powers; but it was all in vain.

On the eve of the Berchtesgaden meeting between Schuschnigg and Hitler Ciano believed that "the Führer's intentions towards Austria have not altered for the worse recently,"[2] clearly showing that Rome had no inkling of what was impending. Mussolini, however, was prepared for the "nazification of Austria," and even in its "favor." According to Ciano, Mussolini "had become more radical." Two days later, however, Ciano held that the first reports of the Hitler-Schuschnigg conversation pointed to "a silent nazification of Austria. The Anschluss is inevitable. The only thing to do is to delay it as long as possible." Actually, Rome was in no position even to delay the Anschluss. Ciano seemed confused and vacillating. On February 14 he was all set to form "immediately a secret Italo-German war committee," but on February 17, in a conversation with the Yugoslav representative Cristich about the Austrian situation, the two confided in each other: "Italy and Yugoslavia are in an identical position with regard to Pan-Germanism. They [the Yugoslavs] are worse off than we are—

because they are less strong and because they have not such a solid natural barrier for a frontier." And he concluded: "As the Cockerel had found his way—or almost—into the German pot earlier than necessary, it is indispensable that the bonds between Rome and Belgrade should be further strengthened and we must always bear in mind that Hungary and Poland too are in a similar situation. Cristich agreed. I think we should forthwith study the question of an alliance with Yugoslavia. A horizontal axis will make possible the existence of the vertical axis."

Other Central and East Central European states were no less jittery. In response to Poland's Foreign Minister Colonel Beck's inquiry on Budapest's policy on Austria and Czechoslovakia, Kánya replied that Hungary was prepared to "participate in any action aimed against Czechoslovakia"! Still, "Hungary would prefer to see the continuation of Austrian independence to the proximity of a *Reich* of eighty million inhabitants." Since, however, everything indicated that the Anschluss could not be postponed, it was necessary to contemplate the creation of "a political alignment between Italy, Yugoslavia, Hungary, and Poland"![3] At that moment this very idea also cropped up even in official Italian circles.

On February 17, 1938, after the Berchtesgaden Conference, Kánya requested information from the Palazzo Chigi about most recent developments in Austria and the Italian assessment of the prospects of the Austrian situation.[3b] An official Italian view conveyed by the Hungarian Ambassador in Rome held that the rapprochement between the two German states could not be avoided; but it was the hope of the Italian government that Germany would "not accelerate the natural development."[4] The Vatican, Tardini reported from Rome, considered the Austrian situation as serious; the application of force by Germany faced no real obstacle.[5] According to Ciano in late February, the Anschluss of Austria was inevitable. Italy would, however, like to procrastinate her complete incorporation. In the view of Italy's Foreign Minister, even the fate of Czechoslovakia was sealed![6]

While officially Il Duce pretended not to be aroused about Hitler's moves at Berchtesgaden, in private he was, according to Ciano, in "a mood of irritation." He was angry at the Germans "over the manner in which they have acted in the Austrian business." In the first place "they ought to have given us a warning—but not a word."[7] Apparently Ciano took this to heart, blaming partly and indirectly himself. The following day, February 19, he made the entry that "he invited Schuschnigg to publish details of the part played by Italy in all this Austrian crisis. These rumors about desperate appeals from Vienna remaining unanswered must be contradicted. The truth is that we only learned about the whole thing after the *fait accompli,* when there was no possible alternative and nothing remained for us but to give our approval to what Schuschnigg had done." The truth of the matter was that Schuschnigg had no longer appealed to Italy for assistance since he fully understood that Mussolini would do little if anything. This had been clear to him for a very long time.

The question whether Rome might have provided help at the time of the Berchtesgaden crisis was negatively answered by Ciano in the entry in his diary of February 23: "What in fact could we do? Start a war with Germany? At the first shot we fired every Austrian, without a single exception, would fall in behind the Germans against us."[8] This may not have been quite true, but his following remark in this context has the ring of truth: "A country whose independence is assured by outsiders is virtually finished." The following day (Feb. 24) Ciano reported of the visit of the English journalist Ward Price who disclosed to him Schuschnigg's saying "that Italy's protection of Austria was incapable of practical realization, because, if one Italian soldier set foot on Austrian territory, the result would be a *union sacrée* against us."[9]

Still, until the very last moment of Austria's existence Mussolini's inclinations were far from clear. According to Ciano, Il Duce was "very pleased" with Schuschnigg's militant address in the Austrian Parliament on February 24 which he had heard on the wireless; he was "particularly struck by the enthusiasm of the Assembly, which has given him more confidence in the vitality of Austria. He says that Austrian patriotism was reawakened yesterday after languishing for twenty years, and that the setting of uniforms, flags, and banners hastened to do this. The Duce believes in the necessity of revitalizing political life by means of imagination and display."[10]

But the good news did not last very long. On March 5 Ciano noted in his diary that the news from Austria "gets worse and worse—in Styria the Nazis are in control of everything, the streets and the barracks. In the other provinces they are making rapid progress. People are beginning to talk of Seyss-Inquart as Chancellor, with the specific task of digging the grave of Austrian independence."[11] On March 7 Ciano recorded two interviews of Mussolini with the Austrian Military Attaché Emil Liebitsky. He told him to advise Schuschnigg against a plebiscite.[12] When on the day of crisis, March 11, Schuschnigg asked Rome for advice, Ciano, after consulting Mussolini, wrote into the diary: "We cannot from here assume the responsibility of advising him one way or the other."[13] And Ciano added: "After sanctions, the nonrecognition of the Empire and all the other miseries inflicted on us since 1935, do they expect to rebuild Stresa in an hour, with Hannibal at the gates? Thanks to their policy France and England have lost Austria. For us too it is not an advantage. But in the meantime, we have acquired Abyssinia."[14]

In early March 1938 Poland's Foreign Minister Colonel Beck had visited Rome and had a conversation with Mussolini. After an initial categorical declaration by Mussolini, Il Duce, referring to the Four-Power Pact which had caused "the most serious Italo-Polish conflict,"[15] gave assurances that in the future Rome would not disregard Poland's cause and interests. Then he quickly turned to the matter which he probably found the most alarming, that of the situation in the Danubian basin and above all of Austria. He put to Colonel Beck a "direct question," what he thought of the Austrian problem. Beck admitted that Austria represented "the point in which the interests of our two countries had the most in common." (This must be held against frequent Polish declarations that Poland's major interests were not involved in the Anschluss issue.) But then he held that Austria "had already lost its permanent balance and the future might depend on some trifling accidents. In response to a question by Il Duce, how long the matter could last, Beck answered: " 'Maybe a year, and maybe 48 hours.' The expression of Mussolini's face changed noticeably at that moment. He leaned his head on his hand and after a short silence said with marked concern: 'Then you think it has gone that far?' " But immediately thereafter he added "in a firm tone" that France and England will be mistaken if they thought that he, Mussolini, would "pull chestnuts for them out of the fire."

Once again Mussolini showed resentment at the Western Powers for having been allegedly exploited by them in regard to Austria, and summed up the Austrian problem in a nutshell: "A German neighborhood is certainly inconvenient for anyone, but it is probably unavoidable, and I cannot endanger the vital interests of the Italian nation."[16] The defense of Austrian sovereignty and independence was thus definitely excluded from Italy's "vital interests!" Going beyond it, he also considered "the existence or non-existence" of Czechoslovakia a matter of concern to Italy. Surely, in the last criticial days of Austria's independence, Mussolini, facing judgment day, had radically altered his earlier views as to the geopolitical significance of Austria's independent status for Italy and for European peace in its entirety. Still, his judgment appeared to be beclouded by his avid desire for imperial glory and far-flung nationalist goals.

The following day Colonel Beck, conversing with Ciano, was told by the latter that Italy "had to stick to the policy of the Berlin-Rome axis and could not act against that policy." However, this "did not mean that they did not attach the greatest importance to creating friendly relations between Rome, Belgrade, Budapest, and Warsaw," and Beck added: "It was as if they [the Italians] were looking for reassurance against the hegemony of German influence, . . . It could be understood that Mussolini did not see any possibility of checking German pressure in Austria and Czechoslovakia, but that he seriously apprehended any more extended German action in a southeasterly direction." Italy's fascist leadership tried to block further damage to Italian interests. But all these measures did nothing to help Austria. Austrian independence was in the last throes. Belatedly, Italian fascism conceded that Germany's annexation to Austria would create an entirely novel and dangerous situation for many European states, herself included.

Mussolini was informed of, though not consulted about, Schuschnigg's plan for holding a plebiscite. When Schuschnigg in early March 1938 recalled Colonel Liebitzky, Austrian Military Attaché in Italy, to Vienna, the latter reported to him Il Duce's "satisfaction with the progress of our affairs. He is optimistic . . . Austria should pursue its present policy; things will improve. An impending relaxation of relations between Rome and London would do much to ease the present pressure." But Mussolini referred to the plebiscite as "a mistake"—apparently not a fatal one. Whatever its outcome, it would in his view have unfavorable consequences.

Schuschnigg, however, had reached the conclusion that little choice was left to him. The British Minister in Vienna, Sir Palairet, too voiced the view that the atmosphere of fear, alarm, and uncertainty had to be terminated.[16] Actually, genuine enthusiasm swept throughout Austria when Schuschnigg announced the holding of a plebiscite. But the mood of the Austrian population changed rapidly in the following days when German troops under the sign of the swastika made threatening moves along the border and finally set foot on Austrian soil. The country's annexation became an irreversible reality.

Toward the Berchtesgaden Conference. Reaction in the British Press and Parliament

On occasion of the mid-January 1938 Budapest Conference of the Roman Pact states, Italy, Austria, and Hungary, Italy's policy toward Germany and Austria seemed to hold special attention in Great Britain. On the whole the English press considered the results of the Conference "meager."[17] According to the *Manchester Guardian* the Roman Pact had become only "a pale image" of what it had once been and noticed that the clause emphasizing Austrian independence had been omitted on account of Ciano's "regard for German sensibility." A balanced view of the Budapest Conference was expressed on January 26, 1938, by Sir Robert Vansittart—just "kicked upstairs" to the post of Permanent Advisor to the Secretary of State for Foreign Affairs—to the Austrian Ambassador Franckenstein; Vansittart voiced his gratification that at the gathering of the Roman Pact states Austria, as far as the Anti-Comintern Pact and the question of continued membership in the League of Nations were concerned, "pursued our own policy." But he expressed regret that the conference had not sufficiently stressed the unconditional preservation of Austrian independence by simply renewing the Protocols; Italy had shied away from this course out of fear to "provoke" Germany.

About two weeks later, after a major military shakeup in the *Reich* in early February, foreshadowing an escalation of German aggression, Vansittart disclosed the "deep impression" which these occurrences had made in Great Britain and that "as a result . . . of these personnel changes" Berlin would probably raise its voice demanding colonies. He expected far greater resistance in Britain against restoring German colonies than against any moves of Germany against Austria." The appointment of Ribbentrop as German Foreign Minister caused "great unrest," since one had identified him during his service as Ambassador with aggressive radicalism. Numerous journals held that in view of the push toward a 100% Nazi regime in Austria "any sort of surprise" was possible. People seemed to fear that since his policy to make England join the crusade against Communism and the Soviet Union had misfired, his resentment against Britain would shape his future policy. On February 12, 1938, Schuschnigg made his fateful journey to Berchtesgaden. To the British Foreign Office itself the meeting came rather as a surprise.[18] Eden also observed that the English Government did not know until a few days later how Schuschnigg had been bullied and the extent of the concessions which Hitler had wrested from him.

Immediately after Schuschnigg's return from Berchtesgaden neither the Austrian Embassy in London nor the British press had apparently an inkling of what actually had occurred there.[19] A *Times* editorial ventured to say that Hitler and Schuschnigg had merited the felicitations of their peoples for their deed. The *Manchester Guardian* wrote similarly that the meeting was the "beginning of an attempt to improve Austro-German relations"[20] and the *Daily Express* admired Chancellor Schuschnigg who had allegedly played a masterful card against the Austrian President Miklas to circumvent his objections. It was not before February 15 that the English dailies began to change their tone about the Berchtesgaden Conference. *Times* still wrote only of the difficult days of Schuschnigg in Berchtesgaden and in a half-admiring manner of the "energetic attitude" of the German Chancellor. But *Daily Express* minced no words about Austria having been presented with "a regular ultimatum." It was convinced that Hitler would ultimately triumph, expected Austria to become the Manchukuo of Germany, and favored a policy of British isolation.[21] While English papers had first called the Berchtesgaden Conference a victory for Austria, they quickly designated it her demise. *Times* expressed the vague hope that the "Austrian character" would never find Nazi ways of thought "attractive." As far as the future was concerned, *Times* advised that Britain do "not prevent" the extension of the German sphere of influence into Austria; "By not considering the *status quo* as eternal, one could perhaps eliminate the perils of war." What was obviously still ignored here was that Hitler was not seeking a slight modification, but a complete reversal of the *status quo* in Central Europe, which would have wide-ranging repercussions. Other British dailies judged recent events with greater perspicacity. According to the *Manchester Guardian*, what had happened was the beginning of the end of Austria's independence. The socialist *Daily Herald* talked openly of Austria being a "German dependence." But on February 16, the reaction of the British press to the Berchtesgaden Conference vacillated between wishful thinking and realistic appreciation of Austria's serious situation. Some dailies seemed to focus more on the blow to Italian than to British interests. Others pointed out that British diplomatic action even at this late moment was still possible.[22] But on the same day the American Secretary of State Cordell Hull received a dispatch from the American Embassy in London to the effect that the British press on the whole took it as a foregone conclusion that Austria would fall under the Nazi yoke.[23] It seemed to expect little action, if any at all, on the part of the British Government.

Not only in the press but also in both Houses of Parliament did the Austrian question figure prominently and virtually uninterruptedly in the weeks between Berchtesgaden and the climactic crisis days of March 11-13. On February 16, 1938, the House of Lords heard the unadulterated voice of appeasement. Lord Arnold focussed on Czechoslovakia, realizing that her destiny and that of Austria were closely intertwined. According to Lord Arnold, Great Britain had not a "sufficiently vital interest in Czechoslovakia" to justify her becoming involved in war. "What are called German designs in Eastern Europe should under no circumstances be made a *casus belli*" for Britain. An increase of German population by ten million—as a result of the annexation of the Germans of Austria and of Czechoslovakia—would not be worthwhile to go to war over, even if Britain could prevent it.[24] There was danger in Britain's alliance with France; the best policy for England would be "one of complete freedom from all continental entanglements. Britain should reverse her policy while there was still time.[25]

Lord Arnold was sharply rebuked for making these recommendations which were equivalent to an invitation to Berlin to put forth "altogether extravagant" demands and were likely to lead to "absurd results."[26] Viscount Cecil of Chelwood lamented the "new technique" of indirect aggression which had been developed by Germany. Lord Lothian, a former champion of appeasement who had developed second thoughts about it, expressed astonishment that the new situation in Austria, and in consequence in Czechoslovakia, had not yet been fully debated in the House of Lords. He wanted to know whether the British Government still stood by the joint Stresa Declaration of Great Britain, France, and Italy in 1935 "to the effect that the integrity and independence of Austria was a matter in which we had considerable interest."

On February 18 Mr. Bellenger, a Labor member of Parliament, similarly asked Secretary of State Eden, whether H. M. Government's policy on Austria remained the same as stated by the Foreign Secretary on previous occasions. Whereupon Eden vaguely replied that British policy goals "in Central Europe as elsewhere" were "peace and good understanding."[27] Then Arthur Henderson, former Socialist Foreign Secretary, followed up with the question whether the British Government still stood by the joint declarations of February 1934 relaing to the independence and integrity of Austria. In his reply, Eden, confusing the 1934 declaration with the Stresa Declaration of 1935, drew attention to his often repeated affirmation that Austria's independence was of primary concern to Italy; this must have infuriated Mussolini who for some time had objected to taking sole or primary responsibility for Austria's independence. In any case, Eden's reference that Italy had not consulted the government of the United Kingdom was a weak rejoinder, especially since in the meantime Schuschnigg's ordeal in Berchtesgaden, his brutal maltreatment by Hitler, and the substantial concessions wrung from him had become public knowledge.

After Berchtesgaden the mood underlying the policy of retreat was well expressed in an entry in Sir Alexander Cadogan's diary: "I almost wish Germany would swallow Austria and get it over. . . . What is the good brandishing Austria under Hitler's nose when we can't do anything about it?"[28] This stance was revealing of British frustration and inability to stem the Nazi tide and of the hopelessness of the Austrian situation. If Austria was still important, it was only on account of the likely adverse psychological impact of her extinction upon West European countries, France, Belgium, and the Netherlands, whose will toward active resistance might be unfavorably affected. The same pessimism which rises from the pages of Sir Alexander Cadogan's diary was publicly expressed by Neville Chamberlain after Austria's annexation when he, on March 12, 1938, said in the British cabinet: At any rate, the "Austrian question was now out of the way."[29] The patient indeed had died. But the infectious disease made the survival of the other patient, Czechoslovakia, most unlikely; it actually speeded her demise and accelerated the further spread of the sickness to other parts of Europe. The contagion could perhaps have been stopped if energetic measures would have been taken in time.

Austria, Italy, and Eden's Resignation

On February 21–22, 1938, the Austrian crisis was "completely overshadowed" by Eden's resignation; it not only raised the question of the relationship of Neville Chamberlain with his Foreign Secretary Anthony Eden but also the broader question of the direction of British policy toward Germany, Italy, and the rest of Europe.[30] Both Eden and, after his resignation, Sir John Simon expressed themselves in Parliament with the greatest restraint on Austria-related issues. Of all speakers only Churchill, in the opinion of Franckenstein, made "a positive statement in favor of Austria." "If it were possible for Italy," he said, "to do her duty in supporting Great Britain and France in the defense of the integrity and independence of Austria, I would not hesitate for this price to consent to concessions of Great Britain to Italy." The repeated allusions to Austria in other speeches, however, lacked practical proposals. Whenever Austria was mentioned, the House showed a certain sympathy, but attention concentrated on the negotiations with Italy.

Attlee, Churchill, Lloyd George, and others accused the Prime Minister of having completely retreated before the dictators. The reticence of the British Government regarding Austria and a certain passivity of public opinion on this issue[31] could be partly explained by the inadequate knowledge of the fluctuating Austrian domestic situation. There was perhaps also a reluctance to interfere in Austrian affairs against the will of the country's population. Utterances of the Prime Minster along this line appear to have persuaded the great majority of critics in his own camp and even that of the Opposition to continue their waiting stance.

In contrast with earlier Prime Ministers, Neville Chamberlain took a very close interest in foreign affairs. Eden resented it that the Prime Minster dealt with the Italian Ambassador Count Grandi behind his back. He was equally irritated when Ivy Chamberlain, the widow of Austen, displayed Neville's private letters to her to Ciano in Rome and engaged in significant diplomatic activities, all without his own approval he finally protested about this unorthodox diplomacy. He did not object to the attempt to drive a wedge between Hitler and Mussolini and win the latter over to the Western camp; but he had come to have little, if any, faith in Mussolini, suspecting that he merely wanted to strengthen his bargaining position versus Hitler by appearing to negotiate with Britain and being wooed by Chamberlain. Eden saw no indication of a serious turn in Italian policy; he criticized especially Mussolini's unwillingness to promise to begin the withdrawal of Italian volunteers from Spain, ceasing violent anti-British propaganda, and making any pledges reaffirming his earlier policy of supporting Austria's struggle for the preservation of her independence. Chamberlain, however, pursued the opposite course.[32] When Grandi suggested early in February 1938 to start Anglo-Italian conversations about mutual relations, Chamberlain eagerly responded to these diplomatic overtures; otherwise, in his view, the two dictatorships would only "be driven closer together," and the last shreds of Austrian independence would be lost; the Balkan countries would feel compelled to turn towards their powerful neighbors, and Czechoslovakia would be swallowed up by the *Third Reich*. Then France would either have to submit to German domination or fight, in which case England would almost certainly be drawn in.

The Austrian situation and Italy's policy toward Central Europe were neither the immediate cause, nor a primary issue in the British ministerial crisis, though it occurred against the background of an impending German thrust into Austria. Following his resignation, Eden revealed that his immediate difference with

Chamberlain was the Italian question: it was however, admittedly, not an "isolated problem."[33]

The Italian government well understood Britain's concern for Austria and Central Europe, though it was not prepared to repeat her military threat of the time of the July 1934 Nazi *Putsch*, to stop, if necessary, Germany by armed intervention and to exploit a golden diplomatic opportunity. Ciano, realizing that Europe was "between the fourth and fifth act of the Austrian affair," thought that the remaining time could be used to Italy's benefit.[34]

As far as Chamberlain was concerned, he was ready to enter into negotiations with Mussolini, in contrast to Eden, without definite advance pledges by Mussolini. Eden had scorned a compromise with Italy over Ethiopia in 1936; he still refused a settlement unless Italy made a substantial withdrawal of volunteers from Spain. Chamberlain, greatly exaggerating Il Duce's trustworthiness, believed that the security of Europe depended on an agreement with Italy. It was, however, no longer the Austrian issue which prompted Chamberlain to enter into negotiations with Mussolini.

At a meeting with the English statesmen on February 18, Grandi claimed that if the Anglo-Italian conversations had been started before the Berchtesgaden meeting, Il Duce's attitude "would have been very different."[35] Chamberlain himself appears to have shared this view. How would Mussolini "move troops to the Brenner, as he did before, if he felt that Great Britain was a potential enemy and that the Mediterranean at his back was not secure.?"

By February 18, 1938 Chamberlain most likely seemed to have been mentally prepared to let the *Third Reich* take Austria, provided peaceful means were used and diplomatic proprieties were not unduly ruffled. Eden himself had no longer great illusions regarding the possible defense of Austria. Actually, on Austria Chamberlain and Eden, whatever their other major differences were no longer far apart. Looking back, Eden revealed that he himself would have been ready to journey to Rome—to which, given the circumstances and his mistrust of Mussolini, he strenuously objected—if it would have been possible to save Austria by discussions in the Italian capital. But in Eden's opinion, "Mussolini had no power to hold Addis Ababa and Cadiz as well as Austria." Mussolini, according to Ciano's diary a few weeks earlier, had been "annoyed" with Britain. He said that when the Spanish question was liquidated, "he will invite Göring [alluding to his special interest in Austria and apparently then leading role aiming at her incorporation into the *Reich*] to nazify Austria." Personal frustration and anger aimed against Britain and plain emotionalism entered thus into Mussolini's thinking about Austria, though Italy's major interests in the Brenner pass and in Austrian independence in general should have been apparent. Eden also thought that "Mussolini has, or thinks he has, some kind of *quid pro quo* from Berlin in return for his acquiescence in Austrian events." Vansittart voiced a similarly skeptical view that Mussolini was probably not sincere and may be "playing us along."[36] During the following days in February Eden became increasingly convinced, "especially from our secret sources," that Hitler intended to seize Austria and that Mussolini had yielded. This only strengthened his opposition to open conversations with Il Duce in Rome. "It would be humiliating for us to be talking there when Hitler marched into Vienna and while Mussolini was reinforcing his troops in Spain and asking for recognition of his Abyssinian Empire."

In one of his last functions as Foreign Secretary, Eden, on February 18, 1938, joined Neville Chamberlain in receiving Count Grandi, the Italian Ambassador. Austria, according to different accounts, played a varying role in the following discussions. According to Grandi, it was evident that the fate of Austria was already sealed. When Chamberlain began by referring to Austria, Grandi "regretted what had happened in that country, but denied the existence of any agreement between Germany and Italy in the matter." Grandi admitted, however, that Italy had been expecting matters in Austria to develop this way. He thought Mussolini had done very well to "preserve the integrity" of Austria "during the past three years." Clearly, this sounded like an obituary. Chamberlain posed the direct question to Grandi what remained of Austrian independence. "German action against Austria is evidently intended to change the European balance of power." But Grandi referred to his most recent instructions from Rome not to discuss the problem of Austria. After Eden interjected that Italy had never denounced the Stresa Agreement which provided for consultation between Italy, France, and Britain on the Austrian Problem, Grandi angrily recalled that Eden, the man responsible for economic sanctions against Italy in 1935, was now invoking Stresa!

In his dispatch to Rome Grandi stressed that he did not want to give the impression that Chamberlain had any plans for resisting Germany over Austria. He indeed had none. As Grandi revealed in 1954 to the author Ian Colvin, he personally "preferred" the attitude of Eden on Austria to that of Chamberlain, and for the reason that it was stronger.[37] Actually, there existed no British plan beyond the reaffirmation of the Stresa policy—a reaffirmation which, Grandi made amply clear, Rome was not contemplating. The chasm which had opened up since the Stresa Conference between the Western democracies and Fascist Italy seemed unbridgeable and the subsequent collapse of the Hoare-Laval initiative made it worse.

In Parliament Chamberlain had made the British position on the Anschluss plain. Not denying the "close affinity" between Germany and Austria he had once again warned against a solution of the Austrian problem "by violent methods." He thus concluded his speech in the Commons: "Nothing could have arrested this action by Germany unless we and others with us had been prepared to use force to prevent it."[38]

Eden's resignation shocked many in England, including Churchill who considered him "most resolute and courageous;" as Churchill later disclosed, his "heart sank" and "despair overwhelmed" him when he learned about it. In Parliament, Churchill questioned then the entire philosophy and policy of appeasement and pointed to its underlying illusion; he voiced the conviction that no progress in bringing peace to Europe could be made "if we allow to gain currency abroad that we yield to constant pressure."[39] He questioned the policy "of coming to terms with the totalitarian powers in Europe in the hope that by far-reaching submission not merely in sentiment and pride but in material factors peace may be preserved." Only thereafter did he place the dire Austrian situation after Berchtesgaden into broader perspective, referring to the recent changes in the *Reich* affecting the German army's leadership and to Austria having been laid "in thrall, and we do not know whether Czechoslovakia will not suffer a similar attack."[40] In Churchill's view and that of many Englishmen Austria's fate was already sealed: Czechoslovakia was the next point on the agenda.

The Last Days of Austria: The Plebiscite, Chamberlain, and Nevile Henderson

In early March 1938 most serious warnings reached London and the new British Foreign Secretary Lord Halifax. After receiving on March 4 two telegrams from the British Embassies in Berlin and Paris, the first originating with Sir Nevile Henderson, the second with Sir Eric Phipps, Lord Vansittart warned the government that Hitler, unwilling to "resist his pretension to safeguard the interests of Germans living outside the *Reich*, was prepared to risk a general war" over Austria.[41] The peril was serious enough to make it "necessary to speak plainly in Berlin." At present Hitler was "allowed to rave and threaten without restraint." This criticism of British soft-speaking in Berlin and of Nevile Hendersons' weakly stance was amply warranted. But the main responsibility for British policy lay at 10 Downing Street, with Prime Minister Chamberlain himself, Foreign Secretary Halifax, and with British policy toward Germany, Austria, and the rest of Central Europe in general. Lord Halifax subsequently observed that he received in these days a great deal of "unsolicited advice" from many sides.[42] But Sir Vansittart's warning of March 4 should have been taken more seriously, instead of being simply ignored. Perhaps it was already too late. Over a long period of time, the British government had sent numerous messages to Berlin to make clear that they were likely to object only to the method, the particular link-up of Austria with Germany, not to the substance of German policy aiming at Austria's incorporation. A last-minute warning would have produced no change in Nazi foreign policy and would probably not have arrested the trend of events.

For years the *Third Reich* had asked for a plebiscite in neighboring Austria which, it anticipated, would bare both the pro-Anschluss and pro-Nazi thought of Austrians. But when suddenly confronted by Schuschnigg's announcement of a plebiscite on March 9, 1938, it bitterly opposed it. Pointing to technical and other shortcomings of the impending plebiscite as an alibi, it actually feared that National Socialism would lose the Austrian elections, that the Nazi-inspired Anschluss movement would be discredited, and that the *Third Reich* would suffer a major propagandistic and political setback. Given the British Ambassador Nevile Henderson's questionable utterances and submissive attitude, not to mention Britain's soft stance over a long period of time, this negative reaction of Berlin was hardly surprising. Schuschnigg, Henderson charged in his report to Halifax, "seems to have taken a leaf out of the Nazi book both in the alleged wording of the question and in the manner in which it was to be carried out."[43] Echoing once again German threats, Henderson voiced the fear that Schuschnigg might be "risking Austrian independence in an attempt to save his own position." The British Ambassador Sir Palairet in Vienna, however, took quite a different view of Schuschnigg's decision. While admitting that it was "very dangerous" to play the plebiscite card without Italy's support, in his judgment the independence of Austria was unquestionably at stake; he entertained no doubt about Schuschnigg's motive being "a patriotic" rather than a selfish one, though he questioned his tactics.[44]

The plebiscite was very much on Ribbentrop's mind when he returned to Britain once more before leaving definitely for his new German post as Foreign Minister. In conversation with Halifax he accused the Paris and London governments of interference in Austria and appealed to the British Foreign Secretary to use his influence with Schuschnigg to make him call off the plebiscite. To the contrary, Halifax admonished Ribbentrop that Germany allow the voting to take place without outside interference.[45] When the following day Ribbentrop met with Inskip, Minister for Coordination of Defense, the latter went so far as to reveal to him that, in his view, the British cabinet would not decide in favor of military intervention if the Austrian question was settled by "peaceful agreement."[46] When he quoted Napoleon III to the effect that Germany should not "brusquer l'affair," he merely infuriated the irascible new German Foreign Minister. In his London report Ribbentrop concluded that the British government was not responsible for the hardening of Schuschnigg's position and the Austrian plebiscite.[47] (Berlin, incidentally, without foundation, accused Gabriel Puaux, France's Ambassador in Vienna, of having pushed Schuschnigg into holding a plebiscite.) Ribbentrop disclosed that he personally did not anticipate any anti-German move by France, Italy, or the Allies. But he urged "a very quick settlement of the Austrian questions. If a solution by force be prolonged for any length of time, there would be danger of complications."[48]

Chapter 15

The Death of Austria and Paralysis in the West

The early March days

The atmosphere in Vienna during the first March days of 1938 as well as the sentiments of the angry but also jittery Austrian Chancellor are described in several accounts of Dr. Keppler whom Hitler had given special responsibility for Austrian affairs in mid-1937. In a report dated March 5 Keppler recounted a conversation with Schuschnigg in the latter's private quarters during which Guido Schmidt was present. Schuschnigg was "still quite angry about Obersalzberg; threats had been used. If we wanted to fight, he was prepared to do so too, though he knew it was within the power of Germany to overrun Austria."[1] Schuschnigg also expressed anger at Göring's recent speech in which he had referred to 10 million oppressed Germans, including the Austrians. Schuschnigg declared that he had hardly been able to work with Leopold, the Austrian Nazi leader, but that he esteemed Dr. Jury and believed that he would be able to cooperate with the new people [German Nationals and crypto-Nazis appointed to his Cabinet after Berchtesgaden]." "Dr. Jury was a good National Socialist and in conversations with him he had discovered that many of the views of National Socialism were virtually identical with his own ideas of 1920 to 1925 [!]: He further asked me to study his great efforts on behalf of Germanization especially in the *Burgenland*. He emphasized his absolute loyalty to the German race and to a common policy—in which he would never disappoint us—and declared further that in the long run he considered it right that one [!] German *Reich* be created. As to the date, there is evidently still a difference of opinion. National Socialism was therefore acceptable to him insofar as it did not at the same time mean an anti-Austrian attitude."[2]

Intimidated and isolated, Schuschnigg leaned here over backwards, attempting to impress Hitler's confidant with his German credentials and his *völkisch* professions. The Nazis, however, wanted lasting deeds, not fleeting words. It was the farthest Schuschnigg ever went, virtually accepting *Gleichschaltung,* even incorporation into the *Reich.* "I had the impression," continued Keppler, that Schuschnigg would "by no means submit to force, but that, if treated sensibly, he will come along to a great extent, if this is made possible for him without loss of prestige. We can rely on his loyalty regarding the Berchtesgaden Agreement."

Schuschnigg's wavering attitude before once more screwing up his courage and daring to announce a hazardous plebiscite must be seen against the background of the strengthened position of the Austrian Nazis and his own desperate situation since the Berchtesgaden Conference. In a memorandum on the trip to Vienna between March 3–6, 1938, Major Klausner whom Hitler had recently appointed successor to Leopold as leader of the Austro-Nazis—and who apparently had no foreknowledge of the impending events—pointed to Seyss-Inquart's important position in the government and the Party. "Heil Hitler" greetings and the Hitler salute were permitted almost everywhere in Austria. He also reported that Seyss-Inquart made already use of the SA and the SS even in his official tasks![3]

Schuschnigg's Plebiscite and Hitler's Rage

In early March 1938, Austrian National Socialists worked at feverish heat to bring matters to an internal climax. On March 4 Keppler posed new demands to Foreign Minister Guido Schmidt and the following day to Schuschnigg, though the Austrian Chancellor as recently as February 24 had made clear that Berchtesgaden was his last concession. Keppler had apparently been instructed to make extravagant claims, even exceeding Schuschnigg's pledges rendered at Berchtesgaden, including the formal legalization of the Austrian NSDAP. But his talks with Schuschnigg remained unproductive.

It was actually on March 4, before Schuschnigg's meeting with Keppler, that the Chancellor made the decision to hold a plebiscite in Austria. Several historians of Austria's last days have criticized Schuschnigg for having conceived the idea of a plebiscite and for unleashing the torrent which climaxed in Hitler's ultimatum and in the absorption of the country into the *Reich.* Schuschnigg himself has conceded that he made serious mistakes, which may have speeded the coming of the end: he had erred in not fully anticipating Hitler's reaction to his call for a plebiscite. He had overlooked that from the very beginning Berlin gave the Berchtesgaden Agreement a different meaning than Vienna. Schuschnigg also admitted that a plebiscite held previously, some time between 1934–36, would have been less risky than that scheduled for March 1938 turned out to be; the latter was, as he conceded, actually "an act of despair under most extreme pressure," an "SOS signal,"[4] designed to alert the world.

Though Austria's President Wilhelm Miklas gave his approval to holding the plebiscite, the Austrian cabinet was never consulted about it, all to preserve complete secrecy! As Schuschnigg later admitted, he could not count on the confidentiality of any decision reached in a cabinet which included a Glaise-Horstenau and a Seyss-Inquart! Hitler himself had long favored a plebiscite, but one arranged under circumstances and held under conditions which would have assured a pro-German, if not a pro-Nazi, outcome. According to Schuschnigg, Hitler had talked about a plebiscite even at Berchtesgaden; but it had appeared to Schuschnigg as a mere "farce."[5] As late as March 3, the Führer in a conversation with the English Ambassador Nevile Henderson asserted his interest in a plebiscite which would assure an end to the suppression of German Austrians[6]—meaning of course Austrian Nazis.

The first Austrian suggestions for a plebiscite after Berchtesgaden originated from within the Fatherland Front itself, about February 18, 1938, designed to stem the growing disillusion within patriotic circles.[7] The Front counted then on an absolute majority everywhere in the country, excepting perhaps Graz and parts of Carinthia. On March 6, under utmost secrecy, Guido Zernatto received the order to prepare for a plebiscite for March 13.[8] It was probably through his secretary that this news was leaked to Austro-Nazi circles from which it was promptly transmitted to the *Reich* NSDAP.

Schuschnigg was naive enough to believe that at this late hour he could still induce the Austrian National Socialists to cast their votes on behalf of Austria's independence, all this by using the services of none other than Seyss-Inquart! In an exchange of letters between Seyss-Inquart and Schuschnigg dated March 9 and 10,[9] the Austrian Chancellor insisted that the agreement at Berchtesgaden did not require the legalization of former political parties, but merely demanded the equality of all groupings which acknowledged the program of the Fatherland Front and the Austrian Constitution.

Aroused by the call for a plebiscite by Schuschnigg, Hitler and the leadership of the *Reich* NSDAP claimed that the Austrian Chancellor had deceived and wronged them—notwithstanding Schuschnigg's apparent maltreatment at Berchtesgaden by the Führer. They plainly feared to be defeated at the polls. The plebiscite would reveal to the entire world that the Austrian working class, despite its earlier hostility to the Schuschnigg regime, had rallied to it against the Nazis, and given strong majority support to Austria's independence. Austrian and European public opinion would be morally compelled to support the electoral result as an expression of the true will of the Austrians. Thus, in Berlin's view, the Austrian plebiscite had to be prevented at all costs! A political and diplomatic defeat in Austria would set the clock of Nazi expansion in Europe definitely back. No other country held out such chances of success as Austria at that time. Given the character of National Socialism which fed on continuous success, a defeat in Austria was likely to have also disastrous consequences for the internal cohesion of the *Third Reich*, which had only recently experienced a major military shakeup.

Schuschnigg's Austrian plebiscite constituted a challenge which Hitler could not ignore. On March 10 the Führer ordered the mobilization of the Eighth Army and designated General von Bock as its commander. At the same time Hitler informed General Keitel, Chief of the OKW (*Oberkommando* of the *Wehrmacht*) of his plan to militarily intervene in Austria.

The Incorporation

German Nazis spread rumors to the effect that Czech troops had crossed into Austria, that French Communists recently arrived in the country organized revolts in Austria, that blood was shed by the government, and that Seyss-Inquart had called upon the *Reich* government for help.[10a] But according to Schuschnigg's postwar testimony, Seyss had refused to send such a telegram to Berlin; he had yielded, however, to Göring's impetuous urgings over the telephone. Thereupon Keppler sent the message that Seyss wanted help from the *Reich*.[10b]

Actually, only hours later, Seyss-Inquart changed his mind and called General Muff, German Military Attaché in Vienna, requesting that "the alerted [German] troops remain at the border and do not cross it. If crossing had already occurred at one or the other point, they should be withdrawn."[11] General Muff and State Secretary Keppler who supported Seyss-Inquart's latest request in turn called the *Reich* Chancellery in Berlin. The communication was conveyed to Hitler himself. Ten minutes later the Chancellery received a call from the Führer to the effect that he had decided that the entry of troops could no longer be stopped.[12]

On the 12th of March at 8 A.M. began the intended invasion along the line Scharding and Bregenz. German units entered Bregenz, Salzburg, and Innsbruck, and units of the German air force landed in Vienna. On March 13 the Austrian army was incorporated into the *Reichswehr* and was required to render an oath to Hitler. At his order, the Austrian Legion was to arrive in Vienna not before April 2nd.

These were the circumstances when on March 13 Seyss-Inquart presided over the new cabinet. He informed it that President Miklas had conferred upon him not only the powers of Chancellor but also those of the President. The day before, on March 12, he had been called to appear before the Führer and been assigned the task to decree the union of Austria with Germany. Hitler made it clear, Seyss-Inquart disclosed, that any Austrian resistance would be broken by the German army. The Anschluss decree, drawn up by the German State Secretary Stuckert on March 13, provided for the "reintegration" of Austria with the *Reich*. After having read the decree to the members of the Cabinet, Seyss-Inquart declared it accepted without even asking for a vote. The entire session lasted only five minutes.[13]

Gleichschaltung or Annexation?

During the last weeks and days of Austria's existence, the *Reich*'s Nazi leadership entertained no definite plans for a complete union of Austria with Germany and for the administrative extinction of the former, though Austria's submergence was unquestionably a long-range Nazi goal, one that was never concealed.

On March 11 when Schuschnigg was presented with the ultimatum, Hitler still seemed to have the intention of leaving Austria a certain autonomy, at least for the immediate future, and of linking her to the *Reich* through a personal union under himself.[14]

Few contemporaries had any illusions about Hitler's ultimate goals regarding Austria. But in the postwar era some "*Nationalbetonte*" and Nazi fellow-travellers, wishing to avoid accountability for the 1938 annexation, have claimed that they were "surprised" by Hitler's proclamation on March 13 that the *Reich* was going to absorb Austria forthwith. A few historians have accepted this version and pointed especially to the absence of a definite time-table for the annexation of Austria during the last weeks and days of Austria's independent existence. Though Nazi Germany for years had aimed at the early *Gleichschaltung* or annexation of Austria and had recently increased the pressure upon the Schuschnigg government, Party and *Reich* authorities had, for propagandistic and tactical reasons, officially continued to hold to the "evolutionary" course. But such a course never excluded revolutionary jolts and a climactic revolutionary ending.

Most contemporary observers were convinced that the *Gleichschaltung* of Austria would be a mere step toward her total annexation. Schuschnigg himself had shared this view and rightfully considered the question whether a nazified, *gleichgeschaltet* Austrian state could have emerged in March 1938 rather irrelevant. Indeed, such a limited and moderate concept would never have fitted Nazi totalitarianism for long. Hitler himself claimed that the enthusiastic reception he received in Linz, which allegedly exceeded anything he had expected, finally persuaded him to decide on the immediate annexation of Austria. He did not think it necessary to wait for his own plebiscite which he already planned.

Whether Austria would be *gleichgeschaltet* or fully incorporated into the *Reich*, most Austrians were convinced that the country's independence had reached its end. In the event of Austria's complete absorption, "the total dissolution of the former Austrian state would," according to Schuschnigg, have occurred "in two successive steps."[15] The driving force of Göring, the Führer's apparent last-minute change of mind, and, last but not least, the realization that the Western Powers and Italy would not go beyond mere words of protest, made Hitler decide to go all the way. Yet in his own mind, he had pondered such a move long before arriving in Linz. His remarks on Austria in *Mein Kampf* and elsewhere were always unconditional. A few seemingly contrary statements, pointing to mere *Gleichschaltung* and coexistence of the two German states in Central Europe were made only for the sake of international diplomacy and tactics.

The rapid total integration of Austria with the *Third Reich* seems to have stunned some of the "moderate" Nazi members in the Austrian government. They allegedly were also surprised by the major role played by German rather than Austrian Nazi leaders in the annexation process of 1938. Seyss-Inquart, for obvious reasons, pleaded that the administration of Austria remain in the hands of the Austrian Nazis. But the request was only partially met. A German outsider, Gauleiter Joseph Bürckel of the Palatinate, became the leader of the Austrian NSDAP; Seyss-Inquart was made *Reichsstatthalter*, retaining only a slight grip on the administration.

In the end a plebiscite was held, though under Nazi auspices. The Austrian plebiscite of April 10, 1938, produced the desired result. More than 99% of the electorate approved the *fait accompli*, a slightly higher percentage than that of the German electorate and also slightly higher than the percentage in previous Nazi plebiscites, if one is to put one's trust in Nazi statistics. On the eve of the election Hitler in an address to the German nation credited the achievement of present-day Germany to "his own personal work." Who, he asked, would 100 years hence know the "blockheads" (*Hohlköpfe*) who had tried to ruin Austria? "My name, however, will be inscribed in the history book of this country." The very day Schuschnigg had allegedly broken the Berchtesgaden Agreement on March 9, "the call of Providence had gone out to him."[16]

Hitler's and the German NSDAP's rationale in aiming at the subjection of Austria and the forcible union needs probably no further elaboration. The Führer aimed of course at the domination of all of Central Europe, with its immediate goals being Austria and Czechoslovakia. The annexation of the former would be a stepping stone toward the conquest of Czechoslovakia and open up the Balkans to the imperialist thrust of the *Third Reich* and to expansionism toward Poland and ultimately the Soviet Union. But as late as March 11 Hitler attempted to conceal his imperialist ambitions even in a communication to Mussolini behind the subterfuge of Germany's need for a strong defensive posture. He claimed that the developing close relationship between Austria and Czechoslovakia represented "a most serious threat to the security of the *Reich*. In the course of these [Austro-Czechoslovak] understandings, the Austrian state began gradually to arm along all its frontiers." The purpose of these measures, according to Hitler, was allegedly to effect a Habsburg Restoration at a specified time and "to throw the weight of a mass of at least 20 million men against Germany, if necessary."[17]

Thus the German thrust into Austria was designed to thwart an alleged threat to Germany's security, to prevent the Habsburg restoration with its serious geopolitical and military consequences for the *Reich!* The German invasion of Austria was not only justified on the foregoing grounds—grotesque and staggering to the imagination as they were—but was also the only means of terminating the "persecution" of the Austrians, linked with the Germans of the *Reich* by common blood, origin, and destiny. Hitler had warned Schuschnigg that if the equality of all Germans in Austria—meaning the "equality" of the Austrian NSDAP— were not restored, "we would some day be forced to assume protection over these kinsmen." Though Schuschnigg had signed an agreement and "made me a solemn promise," "he has now dealt a new blow against the spirit of that agreement by re-scheduling a so-called plebiscite."[18a] The Austrian people were now finally rising against the constant oppression and he, Hitler, a son of this soil, could "no longer remain passive" in the face of these developments.

Paralysis in the West, March 11–13, 1938

The official Nazi ultimatum to the Austrian Government demanded, among other things, the resignation of Chancellor Schuschnigg and his replacement by the Minister of the Interior Seyss-Inquart. When brought by airplane to Vienna on March 11, 1938, after 6 P.M., Sir Palairet, British Ambassador, reported its contents to London. Palairet pleaded with the British Government for some message of encouragement that he might give to Schuschnigg, warning that if he yielded "any semblance of independence is gone." But the only thing the London Foreign Office, and at the

urging of Paris only, decided to do was to agree to a joint
démarche to Berlin in Austria's favor at 9 P.M. Halifax sent
Henderson a communication to be delivered to the German
government; the British Government simply acknowledged that
it had been informed of the German "ultimatum."
On the same day, March 11, Nevile Henderson in Berlin made
a vain attempt to have an interview with Hitler; he then sent a
letter to von Neurath—though he was already replaced as Foreign
Secretary—and late at night had a conversation with Göring
which lasted two hours. Göring gave his word that German troops
would be withdrawn from Austria as soon as the situation was
stable. It was allegedly all Schuschnigg's fault, since he had broken
the Berchtesgaden agreement. Once again Henderson, exceeding
his instructions, acted irresponsibly by "reluctantly agreeing" that
the Austrian Chancellor had "acted with precipitate folly."[18b]
Whereupon Halifax took him to task for having put forth "his
own personal opinions."
On March 12 when the major German decision on Austria
had already been made, Henderson, taking apparently Göring's
"word of honor" literally, suggested to Halifax that unless Great
Britain was prepared to use force in behalf of Austria she should
at least insist that the assurances given by Göring be carried out
as soon as feasible.[19] Short of the forcible restitution of Austrian
independence, "the best thing to work for is independence on
lines of pre-war Bavaria." There had never existed a genuine
"independence on lines of pre-war Bavaria," as Henderson should
have known.
When on March 11, 1938, Schuschnigg had telephoned London
for help and asked what Britain would do if he were asked to
resign, Foreign Minister Halifax made it appear as if Austria's
destiny had never been a British interest and concern. He glumly
replied that he could advise no action which might expose Austria
to dangers "against which the British Government could not
guarantee protection."[20] The following day, March 12, the Cabinet
met in emergency session; Chamberlain expressed his conviction
that the Anschluss had been inevitable unless the Powers had
threatened war beforehand. Whatever Austria's importance in the
framework of European and British Security, that had always
been impossible.[21] He ended with a curious matter-of-fact conclusion, expressing a sort of relief that the Austrian question had

ceased to exist. The remark reveals that Chamberlain had counted for a considerable length of time with the possibility of the Anschluss, and undoubtedly the thought had been painful. But this did not warrant a feeling of relief. It must have been evident that the demise of Austria would make the Sudeten German and Czechoslovak problem only more acute. Was Chamberlain already prepared to surrender not only Austria but also the Sudeten Germans? After all, he had always given more attention and weight to the manner of the German takeover than to its inevitable geopolitical consequences. He also made light of past British attempts to preserve Austria for her own sake and for the sake of Europe's equilibrium.

The Germans marched into Austria on March 13, Göring, who had played a key role in the conquest of Austria, had pledged, as mentioned, that the troops would be withdrawn once conditions stabilized. As usual, he obfuscated the real situation, since it was Austrian Nazis and German troops who constituted the desta-bilizing elements. As far as the Western Powers were concerned, they were involved in a sham rearguard struggle. When after the takeover in Austria Parisian officials approached the English Ambassador Sir Eric Phipps concerning the advisability of bringing the Austrian question before the League of Nations, the latter produced the telegram he had received from Halifax, dated March 12, pointing out that the British Government saw "no practical advantage" in such a move; it would only expose the League to "open humiliation."[22] Delbos, though himself at the point of leaving his post as French Foreign Minister, actually agreed with this official British view.

French "Exasperation"

France's role in the critical March days was the very opposite of a determined stance. According to Hornbostel, Léger advised the Austrian government through its Minister in Paris "to play for as much time as possible. Action might be concerted with England and Italy." Allegedly, he added: "If not, 'France would march alone.'"[23] France had no such intention as Léger must have known; he probably wanted only to boost Austria's rapidly vanishing self-confidence. The same day, 7:30 p.m., Wiley reported about the German ultimatum to Vienna: "French and British

Ministers had heard nothing further from their governments and expect nothing." Also on the same day the American Chargé Wilson wrote from Paris that the Quai d'Orsay had inquired whether the British and Italian governments would join with the French government in a démarche at Berlin and had received a negative reply in both cases.[24] Even a joint démarche would have been of doubtful value at that moment. The German ultimatum to Austria and the virtual lack of Western response revealed for all to see the weakness of the West's position and the futility of any further action.

On March 12, 1938, American Ambassador Wilson reported from Berlin that he had called on François-Poncet and had found him "in a state of extreme nerves and exasperation." "His thesis is simple: the states of the world have made irretrievable mistakes in giving in step by step to Germany. They have merely whetted Germany's appetite and who could tell who will be the next victim." Mussolini was now condemned to subservience to Germany; his intelligence, in François-Poncet's view, had been "overrated."[25]

A most revealing post-mortem analysis of French policy, as seen from Paris by leading politicians came from the American chargé Wilson (not identical with Wilson, U. S. Ambassador in Berlin) to the Secretary of State. Léger had pointed out to him that the French government had no legal or moral obligation to go to the assistance of Austria. The French government recently, on four separate occasions, had proposed to the British government to make strong joint presentations in Berlin, the first time just before Eden's resignation and last on March 11. But that very day the British government, after most careful examination of the matter, called in the Austrian Minister—this after the news of the second ultimatum to Schuschnigg became known—and "told him frankly and loyally" that London was in no position to come to Austria's assistance. The British cabinet also informed the French government that their Ambassador in Berlin would make a démarche, which, in Léger's view, was merely formal and for the record.

The paralysis of the West is well reflected in the English and French contemporary press. On March 12, 1938, the German chargé d'affaires in Great Britain, Erst Woermann, reported that the British press, while repeating the officially inspired version that action against Austria seriously interfered with proper Anglo-German relations, entirely refrained from threats of any sort.[26] While German methods were condemned in the press, the general impression given was one of resignation at the death of the Schuschnigg regime and of Austria's independence. The French press, according to Welczek, German Ambassador in France, described the outcome in Austria as a severe blow to the Western Powers. Its indignation was coupled with perplexity and uncertainty. The French dailies, almost without regard for Party differences, pointed to the following circumstances as having contributed to the last blow: the troubled political situation in France and general weakness of French policy, England's aloof attitude toward developments in Central Europe, and Italy's refusal to take joint action with the Western Powers against German expansion in Austria.[27]

German policy toward Italy in the aftermath of the annexation of Austria is revealed in a report from Berlin by the American chargé Wilson.[28] The German-controlled press had not published the letter Hitler dispatched to Mussolini on the eve of the entry of German troops into Austria. Neither had it made public Mussolini's telegram in reply to the Führer's letter which revealed German anxiety as to the attitude Italy would adopt. Hitler's communication tacitly admitted that the proposed action against Austria went further than the understanding between the two leaders presumably reached at their September 1937 meeting, but also pledged respect for the Brenner Pass as the final frontier between the two countries.

The Führer and Il Duce

In the following days new information about the relationship between the Führer and Il Duce reached European capitals and Washington, D.C. The American Ambassador Wilson in Berlin quoted high-placed Italian sources to the effect that Berlin had given Rome no prior information respecting Schuschnigg's journey to Berchtesgaden; nor had Schuschnigg asked for any advice from Italy. After Berchtesgaden the Austrian Chancellor received from Rome only a counsel of prudence. According to the same source, Italy had once mobilized on the Brenner; "to mobilize a second time under these circumstances meant war."[29] Thus, Italy clearly had left Hitler a free hand. As the Amsterdam *Telegraf* wrote on March 12, Italy during the last days had evinced "a marked degree of inactivity."[30]

Actually, Rome's first response to the dramatic moves of Chancellor Schuschnigg relating to the Austrian plebiscite to counter Hitler's overwhelming pressure had not been unfavorable. According to the American Ambassador Phillips in Rome, it was not until the evening of March 9,[31] that the Italian government learned about the impending plebiscite in Austria. The first reaction in the foreign press, diplomatic circles, and in the Italian Foreign Office regarded Schuschnigg's move "as a clever, although a daring one." Count Ciano even informed the Austrian Foreign Minister that the Italian government was pleased with Schuschnigg's decision. Members of the American Embassy, in conversation with Italians of various rank, gained the impression that Schuschnigg's decision in favor of a plebiscite "would probably be fraught with success." When indications, however, multiplied that Hitler was taking a strong line, Rome's attitude toward Schuschnigg's actions began to change.[32] Late March 11, Italian press correspondents were informed that they should treat the crisis from a point of view more or less favorable to Germany. While in early March the Italian press had still shed on Austrian affairs "the cold light of impartiality," on March 12 officials of the press bureau were taking pains to point out that the crisis had no effect upon the Rome-Berlin axis and that, in any case, a Nazi Austria could not adversely affect the Italo-German relationship.[33]

The crescendo of the Italian press chorus was reached on March 13 when a personal letter from Hitler to Mussolini, dated March 11, expressing gratitude to Il Duce and giving assurance regarding the Brenner frontier, was published in all newspapers in Rome. Equal prominence was given to resolutions on the Austrian situation by the Fascist Grand Council, which had met on the night of March 12 and were already discussed. Hitler's letter to Il Duce was personally delivered to Mussolini by the Prince of Hessen. To the knowledge of the American Embassy, this letter was the first direct intimation received by Il Duce of the impending German march into Austria,[34] and its conciliatory phrasing may well have had considerable influence upon Mussolini. From then on, the Italian press tried to make the best of Hitler's military coup. On the evening of March 12 the U. S. Embassy learned through the Austrian Legation that the Austrian Minister in Rome, Baron Berger-Waldenegg, had been unable to see either Mussolini or Count Ciano. Finally, he had been received late that afternoon by a subaltern official at the Foreign Office. That subordinate official, according to the Austrian Legation, had stated that, while in principle Italy had not changed her position with respect to Austrian independence, the "dynamic pressure" of events had made a revision of Italy's position necessary.

The American Ambassador also informed Washington that the British representative, Lord Perth, in accordance with instructions from London, had tried to call Mussolini but was put off by Ciano with the startling remark that such a telephone conversation "might be misunderstood." Ciano informed then Lord Perth that under the circumstances the Italian government could do nothing. On March 14, the Italian press gave great publicity to the enthusiastic reception accorded to the entry of German troops into Austria. The only newspaper dissension voiced was that of the Vatican organ *Osservatore Romano*, which expressed grave fears for the religious issues raised by Germany's absorption of Austria. But as far as the rest of the Italian press was concerned, it unleashed a major propaganda offensive to convince doubters that events in Austria could not shake the Rome-Berlin axis. On March 14, 1938, V. Gayda, writing in *Giornale d'Italia*, distorting the historic record, claimed that "Italy had always refused to join in the encirclement and humiliation of Germany" and that she had not intervened in July 1934 but had merely shown her resolve "to defend Italian territory against any potential repercussions."[35]

Mussolini's Non-Intervention

Mussolini's first reaction to Hitler's surprise coup against Austria was one of complete bewilderment. Before the first German soldier crossed the Austrian frontier on March 12, Hitler had dispatched Prince Philip von Hessen to notify Mussolini of his move and to seek his consent. Actually Il Duce had earlier sent a message to Berlin disclaiming responsibility for the plebiscite. But the Führer, never certain about Italy's reaction until the very last moment, waited for Mussolini's reply. At 10:35 P.M. of March 11 Prince Philip, after his visit to the Palazzo Venezia, telephoned Hitler that the Duce had accepted the whole thing in a very friendly fashion and sent his regards. But he also revealed that Mussolini had been stunned by the move against Austria, though he already knew about it: "At first he said that such a thing was impossible; he pretended to believe that it was only a bluff and that Germany would not go into Austria." Only after the Prince had "told him that it was, unfortunately [!], arranged and could not be changed, he said that Austria was immaterial to him." Clearly, Mussolini, despite all mental preparation to expect the worst for a long time, was shocked, but he quickly accepted the inevitable, claiming that Italy and he personally were not affected one way or the other by the most recent developments. Hitler's response in turn was to express thanks to Mussolini: "You may tell him that I do thank him ever so much, never, never shall I forget that," "never, never, never, whatever happens."[36]

The following day Ciano too, in an interview with the British Ambassador, the Earl of Perth, made the best of an intractable situation. Schuschnigg had disregarded Mussolini's warnings about the plebiscite. One could "not force a people to be independent if they do not wish to be so." When the Earl pointed to "strong" English resentment over "the violent interference of Herr Hitler in Austria's internal affairs," Ciano "carefully avoided any criticisms whatever of Hitler"; it might be that there were only 30% supporters of his in Austria, as the British Ambassador asserted, "but the 30% were enthusiastic, well organized and young," while the other 70% were divided among themselves. He concluded by referring to the allegedly bloodless character of the present revolution—which in this respect was comparable to the Fascist march on Rome.[37] This of course raised it above any further criticism, though the March on Rome obviously did not constitute an invasion of a foreign country!

Schuschnigg himself, long after the event, rejected the thesis that Mussolini had agreed to the Anschluss beforehand: the actual Anschluss in early March 1938 surprised him. As the Chancellor much later told an interviewer, the Duce had all along advised him "not to lose his nerve, but to hold on to Vienna at least, even though some of the provinces had to go, until Italy and England had signed their agreement [one was finally concluded, but not before April 1938!] and then Hitler would not dare attack."

On March 11, 1938, the day on which the Germans sent two ultimata to Schuschnigg and a new Austrian government under

Seyss-Inquart was formed, the Hungarian Minister in Rome reported that Anfuso of the Palazzo Chigi had let him known that the Italian government had decided not to interfere in the impending crisis in Austria, since Schuschnigg in turn had not followed the advice of the Italian government to eschew the plebiscite.[38] This was at best to serve as an excuse, but did not come close to Italy's real motivation.

The communiqué issued by the Fascist Grand Council on the evening of March 12[39] was basically also an apology of the Italian government, "determined not to interfere in any form in Austrian internal policy and obstruct a movement of national character the logical epilogue of which could be readily foreseen." The Italian government declared that the recent public manifestations of the pro-German sentiments and the will of the Austrian people were most impressive. If the Fascist government had accepted the last French proposal for a concerted Allied action, this would have merely aggravated the international situation. The Fascist Grand Council therefore approved the policy and line of conduct adopted by the government toward Austria, since they were inspired by a realistic evaluation of the situation as it related to Italy's national interests.[40] As if to alert both Italians and the Berlin government that Italy, while acquiescing in the annexation of Austria, was not in a hopeless situation vis-à-vis the new German neighbor, the communiqué reported the Foreign Minister's speech disclosing "the satisfactory progress" in conversations with the British Ambassador in Rome!

Among criticism expressed in the Fascist Grand Council itself, but in view of the domestic censorship never reaching Italy's public, was the voice of Cesare Balbo, popular hero, who voiced "fears" for Trieste and criticized German procedures. "Naturally," wrote Ciano, "he does this behind the scene and in whispers!"[41] Mussolini, however, exculpating Hitler and the *Third Reich* countered that if Italy had "eight million [sic] Italians on our frontiers, we should do just the same."

The following day Mussolini in an important address in the Chamber of Deputies,[42] revealed that as far back as April 1937 he had counseled the Austrian government to come to terms with Germany. He had impressed upon Schuschnigg that the independence of Austria was a matter which concerned primarily Austria. In any case, the Rome-Berlin axis was the fundamental base of Italian policy. To those who had asked why the Italian government had not intervened to save Austria, Mussolini replied that Italy had never assumed any written or verbal pledge to protect Austrian independence and that the Austrians themselves would have been the first to resist any such intervention; recent events had shown that the majority of Austrians were in favor of the Anschluss. He added that it was better to accept rather than oppose an inevitable historic development.

With reference to any possible menace posed by the presence of Germany on Italy's frontier, Mussolini stated that Hitler's assurance on this point had been categorical and that, moreover, Italy's frontiers were sacred and would be defended. He said that in German eyes the Austrian crisis had been a crucial test of the Rome-Berlin axis. The relations between Italy and Germany were founded on similar ideologies and manner of life. He concluded that the two fascist states could now march together side by side to bring about peaceful collaboration among all peoples. The American Ambassador Phillips, forwarding Mussolini's address to Washington, D.C., commented that this speech was intended in the first instance to reassure public opinion in Italy and to answer local criticisms which bared the fear of many Italians that their country played now only a secondary role in the Rome-Berlin partnership.[43] Il Duce had also attempted to reaffirm the solidarity of the Rome-Berlin axis and to demonstrate that, although Italy may have had little to say in shaping the recent events, her acceptance of an inevitable development had not weakened her position, and that her fundamental policy continued to be based upon the association with Germany. His reference to the inviolability of Italian frontiers constituted an answer to those critics in Italy and abroad who inferred that one of the next German moves would be "the infiltration of the German-speaking population of South Tyrol."

The very day Mussolini addressed the Chamber (March 13), Ciano gave the Yugoslav politician Cristich who inquired about official Italy's views on Austria, the following blunt reply: "When I signed the Pact with Yugoslavia on March 25 of last year, I was already thinking of all that has actually happened in the last few days. And I discussed the possibility at length with Stoyadinovič. I am now thinking of the second pact which we shall have to forge with Yugoslavia which will unite the destinies of the two countries in the common defense of our respective worlds—but without altering [!] our friendship with Germany. So long as there are eighty million Germans in the heart of Europe, for Rome and for Belgrade German friendship is a fatality, oppressive perhaps, but very real."[44]

Chapter 16

Second Thoughts. International Reactions
to the "Anschluss."

In England

Austria's independence had been extinguished. If there had
been a time and need for reexamining the policy of appeasement,
it certainly was at the moment of Austria's demise. But in his
speech in the British Parliament on March 14, Neville Chamberlain
continued to cling to the appeasement policy, though the balance
of power in Europe had been radically altered. Chamberlain,
while facing a frustrated, confused and divided country, proclaimed
that "gibes and taunts would leave him absolutely unmoved."[1]
He asserted that England had no commitments to take any action.
She was only obligated to consult with Italy and France, an
obligation which had been met. Only outright force could have
stopped German action. Chamberlain was supported by Lord
Redesdale, an old political friend and an appeaser who claimed
that the change in Austria was the result of "the sincere desire
of a large majority" of the Austrian population: "The gratitude
of Europe and the gratitude of the whole world are due at this
time . . . to Herr Hitler for averting a catastrophe" of staggering
magnitude.[2] A few other British politicians, like the old appeaser
Lord Londonderry, felt "relieved from the terrible tension which
was in existence in Austria during all these years."[3]

Resolute opponents of the government and of its policy of
appeasement, however, still shocked by the brutal extinction of
Austria's independence but also aware of the irreversibility of
recent events and of acute danger facing Europe, raised their
voices of criticism and warning. Viscount Cecil of Chelwood
accused Lord Redesdale of disseminating Hitlerite propaganda.
Lieutenant-Commander Fletcher of the Labor Party pointed out
that Hitler had struck over the weekend when members of the
Foreign Office were on vacation. Instead of telling the Minister

at Vienna to make protests, "we ought to lay a wreath on the grave of Austrian independence, for it is a funeral and nothing else."[4] Miss Wilkinson, also of the Labor Party, recalled the change of the political atmosphere in the United Kingdom since Chamberlain had taken office: Under Chamberlain's leadership England would no longer stand in the way of German expansion in the East. "The many dinners given in Ribbentrop's honor where little remarks were dropped; sending an Ambassador Extraordinary in the person of Halifax, while the Foreign Minister Eden clearly did not share the Prime Minister's line of policy—all this showed that British policy was divided."[5] Mr. Gallagher, the one Communist member in Parliament, pointed out that three weeks ago Hitler had demanded a change in the British Cabinet and now Eden had been removed as Foreign Secretary. This removal occurred "at the demand of Germany and Italy." Traitors in Austria had opened the gates to Hitler, and there were traitors in England who would be prepared to do the same in the British isles.

On March 14, Churchill finally gave expression to the anxieties of many in Great Britain and even of some official circles when he warned that the gravity of the event of March 12 could not be exaggerated. Europe was confronted with a programme of a nicely calculated aggression. There seemed "only one choice open, not only to us but to other countries, while time remains to ward off the danger and, if it cannot be warded off, to cope with it," firm alliances with all threatened European nations. "Two years hence, the German army will certainly be much larger than the French army, by which time all the small nations will have fled from Geneva to pay homage to the everwaxing power of the Nazi system, and to make the best terms that they can for themselves."[6] The mastery over Vienna gave Nazi Germany military and economic control of the whole of the communications of Southeastern Europe. With the annexation of Austria a wedge had been driven into the heart of the Little Entente, and Czechoslovakia at this moment was isolated, both in the economic and in the military sense. In conclusion, Churchill recommended that the events of March 11 be not accepted by the British Government as the final solution of the Central European problem.[7]

Woermann, German diplomat in London, summing up English reaction to the German *fait accompli* in Austria found it on the whole quite weak.[8] Even Clement Attlee's demand that the League of Nations be promptly summoned to prevent any further breach of international law seemed to him rather lame.

On March 18, Halifax submitted a lengthy Foreign Office paper to the Foreign Policy Committee which constituted the latest English political thinking after Austria's annexation. The Memorandum assumed that Germany would "by fair means or foul" continue to work for the eventual incorporation within the *Reich* of the German minority in Czechoslovakia. The Memorandum pointed out that Czechoslovakia's integrity was severely affected by the Anschluss and that the country was now open to attack "along the unfortified Austrian border." Germany can easily establish "an economic stranglehold" over Czechoslovakia, controlling, as she did, Czechoslovakia's only effective communications with the sea. Halifax then stressed that mere repetitive statements of British interest in Central Europe or to the effect that Britain could not be indifferent to German action in the area would no longer have "any deterrent effect."[9] He did not have to add that British policy in regard to Austria had amply proven that.

On March 18, in the aftermath of Austria's annexation, the Soviet government suggested a conference on the new European and international situation. France and England responded to it in a less than positive manner. The French government was torn by domestic differences; in Spain Franco's armies continued to make progress. The sentiments and thoughts of Chamberlain were clearly expressed in a letter to his sisters on March 20 in which he referred to the discussion of Churchill's plan of a "grand alliance." This idea which he had discussed with Foreign Secretary Halifax and the Chiefs of Staff was "very attractive," but he found it not practicable. Czechoslovakia, as a glance at the map showed, could be easily overrun by the Germans. Therefore he had abandoned any idea of giving guarantees to Czechoslovakia or to France in connection with her obligations to that country."[10]

Looking back, Churchill rightfully criticized Chamberlain's decision as being based on wrong arguments. The certainty that crossing of the Bohemian frontier line would have produced a European war, "might at that date well have deterred or delayed Hitler's next assault."[11] Chamberlain's rejection of a link-up with Russia and other nations prepared to resist Nazi Germany ignored, in Churchill's view, the brutal alternative of "being mopped up one by one by the aggressor." To Churchill and like-minded opponents of Chamberlain's policy, appeasement among other things meant abandonment of the League of Nations and its charter, and of right and wrong. It signified wooing of Italy and a loosening of ties with the obligations toward France. In this policy there was no ray of hope.

This view was in accordance with an almost simultaneous address (March 17) by Paul Reynaud in the Chamber of Deputies: "The shadow of the German eagle" had fallen upon central Europe: in Austria, patriots who had lost "the reason for living, committed suicide." What was at stake, he concluded, was that the European equilibrium and also the security of France were "threatened by German hegemony."[12-13] But apparently France was neither materially, militarily, nor psychologically ready to meet these threats effectively and prevent the annexation of Austria. The troubled domestic situation and internal political and ideological differences aside, her increasing dependence on Great Britain in foreign policy and military planning had made vigorous independent action quite unlikely.

Italy and Her Neighbors

On March 13 when Hitler reached Vienna, the Fascist government, in accordance with Ciano's instructions, adopted the policy of complete non-intervention. But as Formentini, Italy's representative in Budapest, let the Hungarian Foreign Minister Kánya know, Italy was ready to strengthen her political and economic relations with Hungary![14] The following day, however, the Hungarian government, having in the meantime become Germany's immediate neighbor and apparently little impressed by Italy's belated offer, jumped on Hitler's bandwagon; Kánya instructed the Ambassador in Berlin to express his felicitations in the name of the Hungarian nation,[15] the genuine concern of public opinion and of the Hungarian government notwithstanding!

The ruling circles of Yugoslavia who for several years had adopted an increasingly pro-German stand, also experienced second thoughts at the moment of Austria's supreme crisis. The Hungarian Ambassador in Belgrade reported an utterance of Stojadinovič to the effect that in the event German troops would march into the Italian territory of German South Tyrol, the

Yugoslav army would enter the struggle on the side of Italy.[16] Though the threat may have lacked credibility, the mere circumstance that it was made revealed a great deal about the sentiments of Belgrade!

Italy herself was shaken by the swiftness of the resolution of the Austrian question and the seemingly irretrievable character of Austria's disappearance as a sovereign state. Ciano wished now "the preservation of Italo-Hungarian relations,"[17] established through the Roman Protocols, though one of its members, Austria, and its essential geographic link, had been swallowed by the German colossus! The poverty of Italian fascist and Ciano's thought in particular becomes thus painfully evident. Belatedly, the Italian Foreign Minister, unquestionably in accordance with Mussolini's stance and specific approval, wanted the creation of a "horizontal axis" and advised Hungary to regulate her relationship with Yugoslavia and Rumania "as soon as possible." The Italian general Pariani considered the strengthening of the Italo-Hungarian military collaboration a necessity.[18] Rome's fleeting idea of fortifying the military bond with Budapest came obviously too late, but disclosed the contradictions of its earlier policy toward Austria and of the disarray reigning in the Palazzo Chigi in the critical days of March 1938.

Italy tried to make the best of things and wished to remain on the best possible terms with Germany. On the other hand, the sense of relief conveyed by Hitler in his telegram to Il Duce— "Mussolini, I shall never forget this"—would seem to give the impression that until the very end, the entry of German troops into Austria, Hitler had not been certain of Italy's positive reaction. Many Italians were somewhat nervous about the wisdom of recent steps taken by their government.[19] Similarly, as the Hungarian military attaché in Rome reported in the first days after the Austrian annexation, Italian public opinion had condemned the German methods employed in Austria and Germany's new proximity had caused genuine anxiety.[20]

Il Duce's Apologia

On March 16, after the death-knell for Austria had sounded and Germany was firmly established at the Brenner Pass, Mussolini addressed the Chamber once again.[21] Austria, Mussolini commenced, had ceased to exist, but the Austrian drama had not begun yesterday. Its epilogue had the character "of the irresistible forces of nature." After a brief historical overview, he recalled that in 1918–1919, "the social-democratic period," both Vienna and Weimar had wanted the union. He referred to the 1934 intervention of Rome only as "an act of elementary precaution" rather than what it was, a warning addressed to Hitler. "No Austrian asked us to do so. No Austrian ever thanked us for having done so." He only briefly referred to the period 1934–1936, "the policy of the Roman Protocols," spoke with bitterness of the sanctions of the League of Nations, an openly admitted "effort to strangle the Italian people." Finally, in 1936, after the creation of the axis, he, Mussolini, had advised the Austrian government to seek a rapprochement with Germany. The German-Austrian Accord of July 1936 was brought about with Italy's approval! During the meeting in Venice in April 1937, he had made clear to Schuschnigg that Austria's independence was a question which in the first place concerned the Austrians. The meeting of the two chancellors in Berchtesgaden on February 12, 1938—of which actually Mussolini had not been forewarned by Hitler—represented the "extreme effort to reach a compromise solution which perhaps retarded, though certainly could not prevent [!] the final solution." When on March 7th a confidant of Schuschnigg had asked his opinion about the plebiscite, Mussolini had replied that it was a mistake "in the most emphatic manner: 'This bomb, I said, will go off in your hands'." Hitler's march into Austria had produced a "stream of lamentations, polemics, warnings: an accumulation of futile words which would not arrest history."

To the more or less official circles across the Alps which were asking these days why Italy had not moved to "save" Austria's independence, "we reply that we never had assumed any pledge of this kind." Italy had never made such a promise, had neither given a "direct or indirect, written or verbal" pledge. Actually, the first resistance to any intervention on Italy's part would have come from the Austrians. While Mussolini admitted that Italy had had an "interest in the independence of the Austrian federal state," it was obviously based on the condition that Austrians themselves, "at least a majority," wanted such an independent status. The events of the past four days, however, had shown the "deep-seated longing of people for the Anschluss." Mussolini obviously was anxious to apologize for his inactivity and lack of resolve to stop Hitler, hiding behind an alleged majority will of the Austrians; such respect for the majority will, Italian Fascism ordinarily had never shown either in its domestic or in its foreign policy. But this subterfuge was a cover-up both for the Italian government's change of heart and mind and its rapidly growing weakness in Central Europe.

What had taken place in Central Europe was a "national revolution," one "which Italians are most capable to understand in its historic exigencies and in its methods." He pointed to the history of Italian unification during the *Risorgimento*. What Mussolini deliberately overlooked, if not outright falsified, was the striking difference between the liberal character of the *Risorgimento* and the repressive totalitarian nature of twentieth-century Fascism and Nazism. He had a stake in ignoring this difference, since for opportunistic reasons he always claimed that fascism was the heir and continuator of the *Risorgimento*. In his oration Il Duce also spurned the propaganda of fear disseminated by some individuals who "think they can alarm us with the total figure of the millions of Germans and their presence on our frontiers." Italy calmly admitted that within a few years 50 million Italians would face 80 million Germans. But Germany had ten frontiers and the German-Italian border of two friendly peoples was an "inviolable frontier. The Führer has always been categorical on this point. . . . For us fascists, frontiers, all frontiers, are sacred; one does not discuss them, one defends them." The calculation, Mussolini concluded, of "the democracies, the Lodges [of Freemasons], the Third International," that, because of the Austrian drama, the two totalitarian regimes would clash had proven "mistaken"; such hopes were "childish." The German and Italian nations "whose unification ran parallel as regards time and methods, can march together to give our troubled continent a new equilibrium"; this, Mussolini asserted, will at last make possible the peaceful and constructive collaboration of all peoples.

"A Certain Danger"

An American report from Vienna pointed out that Mussolini's exposé left many questions unanswered.[22] Only two months ago, the writer recalled, the Rome Protocols had been reaffirmed in Budapest. Ciano had then informed the Austrian representatives that Austria could continue to count on Italian support! Now, not only Italy but also allied Hungary was especially affected by Germany's annexation of Austria which with one stroke made both states Germany's neighbors. In the following anxious moments the leading statesmen of both Italy and Hungary thought of strengthening their mutual ties against the *Reich*, though the likelihood of a stronger relationship was a complete illusion; after all, the connecting Austrian link had disappeared. It would have presupposed Yugoslavia joining an Italo-Hungarian bloc and replacing Austria as an intermediate link!

Indeed, this thought also occurred to Budapest, though it did not go as far as to include Yugoslavia. But thirteen days later Hungary's Foreign Minister Kánya was ready to embrace the idea as he publicly revealed. On March 20th he dispatched a circular telegram to all Hungarian Legations informing them of Hungary's hopes to strengthen the friendship with Italy and Poland; Hungary wished to save her own independence![23]

On March 23, Kánya reported to the Foreign Policy Committee of the Hungarian Parliament about the recent Austrian developments. After offering a survey of the history of the Anschluss movement since the end of World War I, he pointed out that Italy, on account of her other interests had left Austria to her own devices and to the Western Powers;[24] the latter, however, had witnessed the annihilation of Austria without offering any resistance. The Hungarian government had held that the fate of Austria would deeply affect the Great Powers, but they had remained inactive. The close proximity of Germany to Hungary signified a "certain danger," but, in view of the German-Magyar community of interest in foreign affairs, the Budapest government was confident of the possibility of a friendly cooperation. The Hungarian government wanted to strengthen relations with Italy and Poland. It even wished, Kánya disclosed, to regulate her relations with the Little Entente! It was ominous that while he was silent about Czechoslovakia herself, he freely conceded Hungary's fear of the German colossus. In his report from Moscow, the Hungarian Ambassador revealed Litvinov's view, more or less similar to Kánya's opinion, that the German occupation of Austria had destroyed the balance of forces in Central Europe. Litvinov had voiced the opinion that Hungary's increasing endeavor to seek rapprochement with Italy was a sign of the anxiety which she felt vis-à-vis Germany.[25] According to Litvinov, his own proposition of March 17 had the purpose to block Germany's further expansion through cooperation of the Great Powers. Italy's, Hungary's, and Czechoslovakia's restlessness found their repercussions also in Geneva., High officials of the League of Nations blamed the Western Powers and their lack of resistance to Germany's aggression. Secretary Avenol especially condemned the foreign policy of Italy[26] which, fearful of Great Britain's moves in the Mediterranean, had relinquished her position in Central Europe.

South Tyrol and the Axis

Despite all efforts Mussolini was unable to make Italians endorse the official Fascist point of view concerning Austria's annexation and the consequences of Germany's newly-won proximity to their country. The fear even of the Fascists was enhanced by subsequent developments in South Tyrol. A few weeks only after Germany's absorption of Austria, on April 3, Ciano discussed with Il Duce relations with Germany. "In South Tyrol propaganda of a kind we cannot tolerate is continuing. The 212,000 Germans there are getting too uppish and there is even talk of a frontier at Ala or Salerno"—all south of the Brenner Pass! "I advised the Duce to talk to the Führer about it. The anti-German current in Italy, fomented by the Catholics, the Masons, and the Jews, is strong and becoming steadily stronger. If the Germans behave impudently in South Tyrol, the Axis may at any moment be blown sky-high. We must give them a hint about the desirability of their absorbing their nationals. Geographically, South Tyrol is Italian territory and, as we can't change the position of the mountains and the course of the rivers, the men will have to move."[27] In a conversation with the new German Ambassador Mackensen Ciano brought up the restrictive measures taken by the *Reich* in Austria, particularly the abolition of the special tariff for Trieste. All this is likely to "exacerbate people—the Germans must not forget that the Anschluss was a shock to many Italians."[28]

On April 23 in a session of the Council of Ministers Mussolini showed Ciano a very recent Leipzig publication in which the question of South Tyrol was agitated again and "offensive language" used about the Italian mountain population. "He was indignant. 'These Germans,' he said, 'will compel me to swallow the bitterest pill of my life. I mean the French pill'."[29] The threat remained an empty one, but it was revealing neverthel ss.

On April 24 Ciano had another long talk with the Duce about the South Tyrol question. Later on Mussolini telephoned him. He had, he told him, clarified his ideas on South Tyrol. "If the Germans behave well and are obedient Italian subjects, I shall be able to encourage their culture and their language. If, on the other hand, they hope to move the frontier post one single yard, they must learn that it can't be done without the most bitter war in which I shall combine the whole world into a coalition against Germanism [!]. And we shall crush Germany for at least two centuries."[30] It was Italians who overthrew Mussolini and, changing sides in World War II, linked forces with the Allies, who later implemented Il Duce's threatening words.

Surely, the opposition of the Western Powers, though humiliated by Hitler's bloodless conquest of Austria, Mussolini's little camouflaged anger and the Soviet Union's denunciation of Hitlerite aggression and subsequent appeal to create a unified front of European nations against further Nazi aggression, bode ill for the continuation of Nazi imperialism's ruthless "pacific" expansion. Resistance of the peoples of Europe to Hitlerite aggrandizement began to appear on the horizon.

The Soviet Union and East Central Europe

From the safe distance of Moscow, Soviet Communism denounced the enslavement of the Austrian nation by German fascism. While the major thrust of its propaganda aimed straight at the *Third Reich*, it did not fail to castigate the Schuschnigg regime for its brutal suppression of the workers' revolution in February 1934 and the establishment of a clerical *Ständestaat*, of an indigenous fascist regime. It also criticized Britain's and France's policy of appeasement of Hitler and Mussolini's surrender of Austria and his alliance with the Führer. In Litvinov's view, Hungary's desire to seek rapprochement with Italy was the result of the German occupation of Austria, which had destroyed the balance of forces in Central Europe. The Soviet Union was convinced that Hitler had carried off a major victory in gaining hegemony in Central Europe and that Czechoslovakia, linked both with France and the USSR, was in extreme danger.

After the proclamation of the Anschluss public opinion in most European countries, not only that of the Western Powers and of the Soviet Union (Fascist Italy preferred to conceal its real views), but also the general mood in East Central Europe, was highly critical of Nazi Germany's flagrant aggression against Austria and her forcible annexation. At the same time all these nations were overawed and intimidated by the German juggernaut. The "Anschluss" clearly imperiled Czechoslovakia and aroused fears in Hungary, Yugoslavia, Poland, Switzerland, Belgium and elsewhere. The annexation of Austria undermined the stability of numerous multinational European states and strengthened the separatist tendencies especially among the Magyar and Carpatho-Ruthenian minorities of Czechoslovakia. The Hungarian government may have welcomed these developments, but, fearful on the other hand, it asked for assurances from the new aggressive neighbor; it urged the German Ambassador in Budapest, Erdmannsdorff, to obtain a declaration from the *Wilhelmstrasse* acknowledging its recognition of the former Austro-Hungarian frontier—close to which a substantial German minority lived—and permit the Budapest government to publicize it.[32] Germany complied with the first of these requests.

According to Hungary's Foreign Minister Kánya, Hungary would have preferred to see the continuation of Austrian independence to the proximity of the *Reich* of 80 million inhabitants," but everything indicated that the Anschluss could not be postponed. Therefore it would be necessary to contemplate "a political alignment between Italy, Yugoslavia, Hungary, and Poland![33-34] And Beneš would even be prepared to make territorial sacrifices to Hungary—a concession never seriously contemplated before![35-36]

After Austria's annexation the concern of her neighbors grew by leaps and bounds. The Yugoslav government fortified the Austro-Yugoslav frontier, and the border districts of Czechoslovakia, especially near Bratislava, were strengthened.[37] Though Italy had decided on a policy of non-intervention as far as Austria and Germany were concerned, Formentini, Italy's Ambassador in Budapest, let the Hungarian government know that Italy was ready to strengthen her political and economic relations with

Hungary.[38] But the following day Hungary jumped on Hitler's bandwagon.

Polish reaction was not identical with that of the Polish government. Many Poles responded to the news of the forcible annexation of Austria "with antipathy." Even the Polish government which considered the partitioning of Czechoslovakia as impending, concluded that the "strengthening of Hungarian-Polish collaboration" was "necessary,"[39] but not to prevent Nazi Germany from altering the *status quo*, but for shortsighted selfish nationalist reasons: to gain a better deal in the spoliation and partitioning of Czechoslovakia!

Not only were East Central European countries such as Czechoslovakia, Hungary, and Yugoslavia terrified by the tempo of the latest developments affecting Austria, but also the German people itself worried expecting that the annexation of Austria would lead to further German expansion toward Eastern and Central Europe. According to the Hungarian Consul in Munich, the inhabitants of the city first feared that the annexation of Austria would lead to war;[40] later, however, it was said that after the Austrians would come the Czechs and then it would be the turn of the Hungarians. The long-range target of Germany's expansionist endeavours would be Southeastern Europe!

On March 23, Kánya, as mentioned, reporting to the Foreign Policy Committee of the Hungarian Parliament,[41] freely conceded his country's fears of the German colossus. His address could have been delivered with little change in most legislative assemblies of East Central European states: They all were seized by fear of expansionist Nazi imperialism, of their own shaky sovereignty and independence and their desire to strengthen, if possible, relations with often equally terrified neighbors.

Belgium's Dilemma and Sweden

A sort of replica of Kánya's oration was delivered in the Belgian Parliament. Smaller countries in Western Europe such as Switzerland and Belgium were not only neighbors of the *Reich* but—in contradistinction from East Central Europe—also neighbors of the major West European states such as France, Italy, or close to Great Britain, which acted as a kind of buffer to Germany's threats or blandishments. Belgium's dilemma and apparent anxiety became evident in a major address by its distinguished Foreign Minister Spaack.[42]

After the annexation of Austria, Spaack was compelled to acknowledge that the linking of Austria with Germany was an accomplished fact. Brussels had noticed that neither Italy, France, nor England, "for reasons best known to themselves," had wished to intervene. While Spaack professed to remain a resolute partisan of the independence of nations, he had, he disclosed, no wish to take a stand on the essentials of the Austrian problem many of which were still beyond his ken. For some time past, he had believed that the Anschluss would take place and, had this occurred "normally," it would have caused him no surprise. He could, however, not conceal the Belgian Government's concern, an emotion which, he was convinced, was shared by the nation at large, over the methods employed. The already heavily laden political atmosphere had once again been rudely disturbed. The lesson, he concluded, to be drawn from these events, was not a lesson in foreign policy, but first and foremost a lesson in international politics: "Woe indeed to small countries which chose to remain divided and disunited." In view of the bi-national character of Belgium which comprised Flemings and French-speaking Walloons, the "lesson" had a special and obvious significance.

The American Ambassador in Brussels, Gibson, offered his own assessment of the Belgian reaction: "To a nation which still preserves vivid recollections of German methods of aggression, the need of a realistic foreign policy, such as M. Spaack advocates, is very evident. The geographic proximity of potential danger, combined with what a Hitler week-end surprise may mean, is fully realized throughout the country." Belgium which had suffered from the German occupation in World War I and feared a repetition of German expansionism by the *Third Reich*, was deeply sympathetic toward Austria. Similarly concerned had been the Prime Minister of The Netherlands, Dr. Colijn, when he on March 8 voiced his anxiety that Germany might seize Austria.[44]

The impact upon more distant countries such as Sweden—no neighbor of Austria of course, but geographically close to the *Third Reich*—was equally striking. On March 28, 1938, the American Minister to Sweden, Fred Morris Dearing, reported to Franklin Delano Roosevelt that Sweden's Prime Minister who for years had opposed large expenditures for defense and armament, three days after Austria's formal annexation and undoubtedly under its impact, had on March 16 proclaimed in the *Riksdag* that "in view of the unsettled conditions on the continent it be necessary for the Government to take more ample and immediate measures for defense.[45] He had also asked that the Government be given a practically free hand in employing this money. "In doing so, he had the backing of all the Party leaders and practically the entire *Riksdag*." Small nations quickly closed ranks when faced with the bullying tactics of the leaders of the *Third Reich*.

Several weeks later, the German Foreign Ministry wrote thus to various diplomatic missions abroad: "As a consequence of the reunion of Austria with the *Reich* we have obtained new frontiers with Italy, Yugoslavia, Switzerland, Liechtenstein, and Hungary." These frontiers, the note proclaimed, "are considered by us final and inviolable."[46] The German Minister in Berne also assured the Swiss Government of Germany's respect for the independence and inviolability of Switzerland and for the continued existence of the independent Principality of Liechtenstein, though at the same time making clear that it would consider any strengthening of Switzerland's relationship with Liechtenstein "undesirable"! Switzerland would then abandon "her policy of neutrality in a manner running counter to our interests."[47] In the foregoing note Berlin recalled that it had informed the Yugoslav government that German policy had "no aims beyond Austria and that the Yugoslav border would in any case remain untouched." The German Foreign Ministry also notified the Hungarian government that German assurances vis-à-vis Italy, Yugoslavia, and Switzerland concerning the new frontiers "were, of course, equally valid for the new German-Hungarian frontier."[48] With German approval Kánya, Hungary's Foreign Minister, had pointed out in the Hungarian Parliament that Berlin considered the German-Hungarian frontier "just as inviolable as the German frontiers with Yugoslavia, Italy, and Switzerland."

In reality fear had begun to grip these neighbors, whether old or new. As the German chargé d'affaires in Rome, Plessen, wrote to Berlin on March 25, Mussolini's own reaction was "based only on grounds of political realism," in his heart he is undoubtedly just as unenthusiastic about the developments of the Austrian situation "as the statesmen of other European neighboring states."[49]

Overseas Mexico and Japan

The delegate of Mexico considered the annexation of Austria a heavy blow against the Covenant of the League of Nations and international law, pointing thus to the truly international ramifications of the German aggression in Central Europe.[50]

But in geographically remote expansionist Japan, the reactions to the momentous events in Central Europe and the lessons drawn therefrom were, whatever the motivation, quite different. On March 15 Noebel, chargé d'affaires in Tokyo, reported to Berlin that Austrian developments had found "an enthusiastic response on the part of the Japanese public."[51] The entire Japanese press had "celebrated the Anschluss as a triumph for the determined, courageous policy on the part of the Führer—a policy "which was instructive [!] for Japan's domestic and foreign policy"—"as a tremendous gain in prestige and power for their friend Germany," and "as fresh proof of the gradual retreat of internally rotten 'status quo' powers." The Foreign Ministry, the army, the navy as well as leading personalities in other circles had congratulated the Embassy or the Military and Naval Attachés, and expressed their deep satisfaction over the increase in power of a friendly group of European states as a result of the Anschluss."

Chapter 17

Conclusion

The First Austrian Republic embraced a seriously divided population. Ideology and politics split its inhabitants into three major groupings each of which was hostile toward the other two; the government camp supported by the Christian Socials and the *Heimwehr* (later by the all-encompassing Fatherland Front) the Social Democratic Party, and the former *Grossdeutschen* and Austro-Nazis. The democratic foundation of the Austrian Republic was shattered not only by the massive attack of National Socialism from within the country and from beyond the border by the *Third Reich*, but also had been earlier undermined by the deliberate assault of the Dollfuss regime, pressured by Mussolini and domestically allied with the fascist *Heimwehr*. Austria's political fabric showed thus the strains of battle between the three camps.

To top matters, the three groupings were battling each other over the overriding issue of the very existence of the Austrian Republic. All three groups were first in the Anschluss camp, though many Christian Socials remained opposed to it. But prevailing opinion compelled even the Christian Socials in 1919 to accept a pro-union plank. Only after the victory of National Socialism in Germany did the Socialists and Christian Socials relinquish their pro-Anschluss stance, belatedly endorsing Austrian sovereignty and independence. The absence of a militant Austrian patriotism and of a vibrant Austrian ideology as well as the circumstance that the First Republic confronted in National Socialism a fanatic and intransigent foe, who defiantly exhibited both his ideological armor and superior force, reduced the contest between the two opponents to an unequal fight.

It is quite unlikely that a Habsburg Restoration would have united and strengthened Austria. A return, on the other hand, to Austria's democratic constitution was not likely. Sooner or later German National Socialism would have effectively used its great military strength, aided if necessary by the "Fifth-Column" tactics of the Austro-Nazis, to break the country's resistance. Aside from indisputable political errors and tactical mistakes committed by Dollfuss and Schuschnigg, the juxtaposition of little Austria and the rapidly growing aggressive German *Reich* was likely to end in the destruction of the former.

Though there may be little disagreement between Austrian and German historians about the coercive character of the 1938 "Anschluss," they have necessarily judged the country's annexation from a different historical perspective. For Austrian historians who have focussed on the movement toward union, certain dates stand out as turning points: Hitler's seizure of power in 1933 and its repercussions in Austria; March 13, 1938, when the Führer proclaimed the annexation of Austria; and finally April 1945, when the German occupation disintegrated and the country was liberated. For German historians, on the other hand, focussing on Hitler's foreign policy in its entirety, Austria is an important, though merely one of numerous pre-war targets of the *Third Reich*'s aggressive foreign policy. Giving thus Austria a rather limited attention, they have tried to place Hitler's objectives in Austria and Anschluss policy into the larger framework of Nazi foreign policy in its totality.[1]

There is substantial evidence pointing to Hitler's and the Nazis' plans and phantasies that the *Third Reich*, if victorious on the European continent, would be laying the groundwork for the struggle for world dominion and at some later stage wage a war between continents. This author, interested in the history of the Anschluss movement ending with Germany's apparent crowning success in March 1938, was not concerned either with the period of the actual Nazi occupation of Austria or Hitler's far-flung European visions or global phantasies. But in studying the history of the Anschluss it becomes apparent that such Nazi objectives as the "liberation" of the Sudeten German region and the destruction of the rest of Czechoslovakia and dominance over all of Central Europe loomed never far behind the long planned incorporation of Austria into the *Reich*.

Hitler never confined his aims to Austria alone. Even the Nazi drive to control or annex both Austria *and* Czechoslovakia was always a mere stepping stone toward further German expansion into the Balkan region, the rest of Eastern Europe, and ultimately

the Soviet Union. The Anschluss movement thus had dimensions
which by far exceeded the territories of Austria and the Sudeten
German region of Czechoslovakia. Though the goals of the *Third
Reich* were indisputably hegemonic and imperialist, numerous
contemporaries—Germans and many Austrian Nazis and fellow-
travellers—were incapable of looking upon the Anschluss movement as being anything but a movement in behalf of national
self-determination. As far as some contemporary Germans are
concerned, this view still lingers on. But to many others, foremost
Austrians, Czechoslovaks and French and other perceptive observers, national self-determination was a perilous weapon, likely
to disrupt European peace and stability and ultimately to destroy
self-determination for Austrians, Czechs, and Slovaks, and most
other nations in Central and East Central Europe and throughout
the continent, all in the name of German national rights.

National self-determination was only the smokescreen behind
which National Socialism operated, aiming, after the "liberation"
of the Austrians and Sudeten Germans, to suppress the freedom
and sovereignty of the great majority of the independent European
nations. Czechoslovak leaders, with Edvard Beneš playing a leading
role, were well aware of the German and Nazi threat in particular;
so were numerous other political figures of most other European
nations. But in view of the divergent policies of the Great Powers
in regard to the Anschluss they were unable to stem the tide of
events.

In the wake of World War I it was the judgment of leading
statesmen both of the victorious powers and of the new states
of Central and East Central Europe that the issues of balance of
power and of European security were closely tied up with the
Anschluss prohibition. From the moment of the Allied victory
over Imperial Germany France's policy had been aimed at making
Germany acknowledge the inviolability of the peace treaties and
thus insuring France's own security. In the words of Louis Barthou
in 1919, the French would have to use their preponderance of
power to maintain the new *status quo ad infinitum.*[2] France's policy
on the Anschluss, toward the prohibition of which she had
successfully worked in 1918–1919 and which had been subscribed
to by all major powers in the treaties of Versailles and St. Germain,
was part and parcel of France's German policy and her determination to perpetuate the separation of Austria from Germany.

France would not abandon this course when the military balance was increasingly upset in favor of the *Third Reich*, though Paris, especially since the occupation of the Rhineland in 1936, had lost all powers of persuasion to block the Nazi thrust into Austria.

At the Paris Peace Conference all Great Powers had rejected the union between Austria and Germany. Permitting Austria to join forces with Germany would have given the *Reich* the very numerical equivalent of the population which it lost at Versailles, about 6 1/2 million people. With the same population as in prewar times, Germany would have emerged more homogenous, ethnically speaking, than she had ever been, since the populace lost in 1918 was only partly German in character. By adding Austria, Germany would have made not only substantial demographic gains, but also geographic, strategic, and economic ones. Germany would have emerged from World War I not as a defeated party, but as the real winner. With one stroke, Germany would have become the neighbor of Italy, Yugoslavia, and Hungary, would have lengthened her boundary with Switzerland and, most importantly, would have surrounded Czechoslovakia to an extent which would have made illusory her viability from the very moment of her birth as a state. Austria was also the key to Germany's penetration of the entire Balkan and of the Adriatic in particular. Last but not least, Germany through the Anschluss would also have gained new strength by adding the resources and manpower of Austria to her own. All these gains were made only after Hitler's annexation of the country.

At the Paris Peace Conference in 1919 Great Britain—as well as the USA— had joined France in opposition to the Anschluss. In the 1920s British public opinion began to change, but this did not yet decisively affect policy. In the early 1930s the Austrian question seemed still a relatively minor one to the British Government, despite the important geopolitical role of Austria in Europe's balance of power. Austria was far from having a prominent place on the world-wide, British imperial agenda, though it had played a significant role in Britain's European policy in the past.

In the mid-1930s, however, British ideologues of appeasement challenged their country's pro-French and traditional anti-German political course and the Peace Treaties and placed preservation of peace at virtually any price ahead of the Anschluss prohibition and the balance of power concept. For the sake of conciliation they were ready to shelve the hallowed and time-tested key concept of Europe's equilibrium and relinquish to Germany control over Central Europe—Austria and Czechoslovakia and even portions of Southeast Europe and East Central Europe. The first step to German domination of these areas was the Anschluss of Austria with the *Reich*.

When in the mid-thirties British politicians began to articulate this new policy, most of them understood that at stake was not only the destiny of Austria but also German hegemony over adjacent states in East Central and Southeast Europe. Thus appeasement actually ran counter to age-old concepts of Britain's foreign policy toward Europe. Compared to earlier historical challenges by France in the seventeenth century and again in the era of the French Revolution and Napoleon, and by Imperial Germany in the early twentieth century, the most recent challenge by the *Third Reich* had a totalitarian character and was territorially the most ambitious one; it thus aroused British resistance to the greatest possible extent. The far-flung defense obligations of the British Empire and the lack of adequate military preparations against challenges by the *Third Reich* provided, however, the background for English modifications of the balance of power concept in regard to the European continent. Under the pressure of Germany's threat of war, Great Britain, even under Neville Chamberlain's leadership, was, after the fall of Prague in March 1939, to revert to reasserting a more traditional balance of power, in regard at least to East Central and Southeastern Europe. By that time, before the outbreak of World War II, the *Third Reich* had already made substantial territorial changes in the heart of the continent.

A more consistent and far-sighted British policy would have steadfastly rejected appeasement in favor of the policy of preserving the political equilibrium in Central Europe; it would have given no *carte blanche* to the German conquest of Austria. It would have understood that, whatever had earlier been said in favor of union, any concession regarding Austria under conditions existing in the late 1930s was bound to be merely the first step down the slippery road to more appeasement, surrender, and war.

Almost during the entire interwar era Italian fascism, virtually unchallenged at home, presented the stern face of authoritarian control and extreme nationalism to her neighbors across the Alps and the Adriatic. Though in the 1920s no common ideology linked Rome with either Vienna or Berlin, the widespread revisionist propaganda in the *Reich* established some common ground between the long-range foreign policy goals of Fascist Italy and Weimar Germany. But in one important sector of the foreign policy field, the Anschluss question, Italy, differently from Germany was long in favor of preserving the *status quo*, of continuing the prohibition of the union. On this vital issue Italy's national self-interest seemed to dictate maintaining weak Austria as a neighbor, "protecting" her own South Tyrolese German minority, and blocking Germany's road to the Italian peninsula and the Balkans. The preservation of Austrian independence and sovereignty also appeared as an issue which would bridge differences between Italy and the Western Powers, France and Great Britain, which existed ever since the Paris Peace Treaty.

On the other hand, Italian revisionism and imperialism of the 1930s, aiming at building a large Empire in Africa and at exporting fascism into Central Europe and the Mediterranean area, faced widespread reprobation. Italian Fascism was looked upon as a pariah in the League of Nations and the world at large. In despairing isolation, Italy searched for a helpful hand—which Germany willingly offered. The high price, however, that Italy had to pay for this economic, political, and propagandistic assistance, was to relinquish Central Europe and Austria in particular to the *Third Reich*. Mussolini's ambition and desire for power, prestige, and adventure proved stronger than the earlier restraining influences which had been brought to bear against the threat of a powerful and menacing German neighbor to the north. Thus not only the democratic Western Powers but Fascist Italy too appeased the *Third Reich*. The history of the Anschluss movement in the 1930s is the history of the appeasement of Hitler-Germany by a powerless Austrian government as well as by the Great Powers.

Footnotes

Chapter 1

1. O. Bauer, *Die österreichische Revolution* (1923), p. 145.
2. *Public Records,* London (thereafter *P.R.*), F.O.628, v.16, Rumbold to F.O., March 21, 1919, and *Politisches Archiv, Auswartiges Amt,* Bonn (thereafter *A.A.*) Nachlass Brockdorff-Rantzau's, Cunninghame, H 234604-605.
• 3. A.D. Low, *The Anschluss Movement, 1918–1919,and the Paris Peace Conference* (1974), vol. 103, *Memoirs,* Amer. Philos. Soc., Philad., p. 258.
4. *Le Temps,* Oct. 19, 1918, and *France, Débats Parlementaires. Annales de la Chambre des Députés,* Dec. 29, 1918, p. 3334.
5. *Affaires Étrangères, French Foreign Ministry,* Quai d'Orsay (thereafer *A.E.*) A Paix, A 1056, Allizé to Pichon, Apr. 1, 1919, pp. 12–13.
6. *Le Temps,* Feb. 11, 1919.
7. *Corriere della Sera* (Milan), Oct. 18 and 20, 1918, and *Secolo,* Oct. 29, both quoted in *A.E.,* Europe 1918–1929, Doss. Gén. I, Consul, Milan, to Pichon, Oct. 29, 1918, pp. 88–89.
8. Low, *op. cit.,* p.314.
9. *National Archives,* Washington, D.C., *American Commission to Negotiate Peace,* v. 303,185.1136/1,Nr.10, Wm Bullitt to Lansing, Feb. 2, 1919, and *Foreign Relations of the United States. Paris Peace Conference* (in the following *F.R.U.S.P.P.C.*), II, 87–88.
10. *F.R.U.S.P.P.C,* XII, 570–73, Halstead to Lansing, Sept. 19, 1919, and Low, *op. cit.,* 331.

Chapter 2

1. A.D. Low, *the Anschluss Movement, 1918–1919, and the Paris Peace Conference.* vol. 103, *Memoirs,* 1974, pp. 83–98.
2. *Arbeiter-Zeitung,* Dec. 12, 1919.
3. Neue Freie Press, morning ed., Dec. 18, 1919.
4. *Bulletin periodique de la presse autrichienne,* No. 114 (March 5–31, 1921, p. 2.
5. *Times,* London, May 20, 1921; also May 14.

6. *Neue Freie Presse,* even. ed., July 9, 1921.

7. *Neues Wiener Tagblatt,* Feb. 9, 1920, and *Neue Freie Presse,* even. ed., Feb. 16, 1920.

8. *Neue Freie Presse,* Jan. 26, 1920.

9. Low, *op. cit.,* p. 160 and pp. 175–76.

10. *All-Deutsches Tagblatt,* Feb. 8, 1920.

11. League of Nations, *Restoration of Austria,* p. 7 and pp. 18–23.

12. *Bundesgesetzblatt f.d. Rep. Österreich,* 1925, Stück 60, Nr. 264, quoted by Margaret Ball, *Post-War German-Austrian Relations. The Anschluss Movement 1918–36,* 1937, p. 157., and also some of the following references.

13. *Neue Freie Presse,* Apr. 18, 1925.

14. *Ibid.,* Aug. 31, 1925.

15. *Bulletin periodique de la presse autrich.,* Nr. 164, July 8–Sept. 1, 1925, pp. 4f.

16. Suval, St. *The Anschluss Question in the Weimar Era* (1974), pp. 38–43.

17. *New York Times,* Apr. 17, 1925.

18. *Neue Freie Presse,* Aug. 28, 1925.

19. *Ibid.,* morning ed. Feb. 5, 1926.

20. W.T. Layton and Chs. Rist, *The Economic Situation of Austria,* Geneva, 1925.

21a. Kleinwaechter, F.F. *Selbstbestimmungsrecht für Österreich* (Stuttgart, 1929), pp. 30f., and Rotschild, K.H. *Austria's Economic Development between the Two Wars* (London, 1947).

21b. For a useful account of the debate on Austria's economic viability in the 1920s, which applies also for the following decade, see Suval, St., *The Anschluss Question in the Weimar Era* (Baltimore, London, 1974), chaps. vii and ix, and also for some of the following references.

22. Tremel, "Die wirtschaftliche Situation der ersten Republik Österreichs," quoted by Suval, *op. cit.,* p. 178.

23. See also Kleinwaechter, *Der deutsch-österreichische Mensch* (Vienna, 1926).

24. Hertz, F., *Zahlungsbilanz und Lebensfähigkeit Österreichs* (Munich, 1925); pp. 3–6 and p. 62; Neumann, Österreichs wirtschaftliche Gegenwart und Zukunft, (Vienna, 1927), pp. 5f., 30, and 83, and Stolper, G., in *Der österreichische Volkswirt,* 16, 1925.

25. F. Kleinwaechter, *Selbstbestimmungsrecht* . . . , pp. 51–52.

26. Johannes Barodin and Kurt Schechner, *Für und wider die Donauföderation,* Vienna, 1928, pp. 23f.; Stolper, *Deutschösterreich als Sozial- und Wirtschaftsproblem,* pp. 130–31 and 145–153; also Karl Janovsky, *Zollunion Prag-Wien oder Anschluss Wien-Berlin* (Reichenberg, 1927, and

Schilder, S., *Der Streit um die Lebensfähigkeit Österreich's* (Stuttgart, F. Enke, 1926), 90. Heft, pp. 59–82.

27. Suval, *op cit.*, pp. 187–88.

28. Wm. Heile, in *Berliner Tageblatt*, Aug. 15, 1925.

29. *Neue Freie Presse*, June 3, 1927, quoted by Suval, *op. cit.*, p. 124; also *Neue Freie Press*, July 7, 1926.

30.-31. Leo Rosenberg, *Lehrbuch des Deutschen Zivilprozessrechts*, Berlin, 1927, quoted by Ball, *op. cit.*, p. 77.

32. Herbert Kniesche, *Die grossdeutsche Wirtschaftseinheit*, Leipzig, 1929, p. 192.

33. M. Ball, *op. cit.*, p. 79.

34. *N.Y. Times*, Oct. 3, 1928.

35. *Wiener Neueste Nachrichten*, July 22, 1928.

36. *Le Temps*, July 24, 1928.

37. *N.Y. Times*, Nov. 2, 1927.

38. *Neue Freie Presse*, July 22, 1928 and Jan. 1, 1929.

39. *Neues Wiener Journal*, Dec. 21, 1928.

40. Low, *op. cit.*, pp. 176 and 417.

41. *Neue Freie Presse*, Sept. 29, 1927.

42. H. Dachs, *Österreichische Geschichtswissenschaft und Anschluss 1918–1930*. Vienna, 1974, p. 7, and 73.

43. *Ibid.*,

44. *Ibid.*, p. 83.

45. O. Redlich, *Geschichte Österreichs*, Gotha, 1921, vol. 6, p. V.

46. Dachs, *op. cit.*, p. 91.

47. *Verhandlungen des Reichstags*, Feb. 9, 1926.

48. G. Stresemann, *Vermächtnis*, III, 360.

49. *N.Y. Times*, Aug. 2, 1927.

50. Telegram from Lugano, Dec. 15, 1928, in *Le Temps*, Dec. 16.

51. Bülow to Neurath, *Documents on German Foreign Policy (DGFP)*, Nr. 385, pp. 708f.

52. *N.Y. Times*, March 4, 1931.

53. *Neues Wiener Tagblatt*, March 22, 1931.

54. *Vorarlberger Tagblatt*, March 23, 1931, quoted by Ball, *op. cit.*, pp. 110–11.

55. League of Nations, *Official Journal*, 12th yr., Nr. 7, 1069–73.

56. *Le Temps*, March 22, 1931.

57. *France, Débats Parlementaires. Annales du Sénat*, 2e seance du 18 mars, 1931.

58. *Le Temps*, Apr. 8 and 12, 1931.

59. *Ibid.*, June 5, 1931.

60. *Times*, March 27, 1931.

61. *Verhandlungen d. Reichstags*, March 31, 1931.

62. *Neue Freie Presse,* morng ed., March 29, 1931.

63. *Wiener Neueste Nachrichten,* March 31, 1931.

64. *Le Temps,* Apr. 29, 1931.

65. *Bulletin périodique* . . . , No. 206, March 9–May 7, 1931.

66. *Rote Fahne,* March 24, 1931; *N.Y. Times,* March 29.

67. League of Nations. *Commission of Enquiry for Union. Minutes of the Fourth Session of the Commission,* 1931, pp. 8–11.

68. *Arbeiter-Zeitung,* Sept. 4, 1931, and *Neues Wiener Journal,* Sept. 1, 1931.

69. Quoted in *Journal des Nations,* Sept. 6, 1931.

Chapter 3

1. A.D. Low, *The Anschluss Movement, 1918–1919* . . . (1974), pp. 207f.

2. *Ibid.,* pp. 192–93.

3. *Archiv f. Geschichte d. Sozialismus,* XV, 214, about Engels; *Arbeiter-Zeitung* (Nov. 22, 1918), about Liebknecht and Bebel.

4. O. Bauer, "Die alte und die neue Linke," *Der Kampf,* (1920), p. 249f.

5. From the vantage point of the Second Austrian Republic, Otto Leichter, *Otto Bauer. Tragödie oder Triumph* (Vienna, 1970), p. 140, disciple, friend, and admirer of Bauer, had conceded the latter's "error." In the critical 1930s Bauer persisted in displaying a confidence regarding the revolutionary zeal and striking power of the German working class which was no longer warranted.

6. O. Bauer, *Die österreichische Revolution* (Vienna, 1923), p. 232.

7. Bauer, "Wandlungen und Probleme der Anschlussbewegung," *Der Kampf,* 1927, pp. 297ff.

8. Leichter, *op. cit.,* p. 139.

9. Otto Bauer, *Werkausgabe* (Vienna, 1975), III, 1039.

10. Bauer, *Bolschewismus oder Sozialdemokratie,* 1921 (also *Werkausgabe,* II, 223–358).

11. Das Linzer Programm, 1926, *Werkausgabe,* III, 1017–1039, especially 1022–24.

12. See Nr. 7.

13. Leichter, *op. cit.,* p. 138.

14. Bauer, see 7., p. 302.

15. K. Renner, "Zollunion und Anschluss," *Der Kampf* (1931), p. 198f.

16. *Ibid.,* pp. 199–200.

17. A.L. Brancato, *German Social Democrats and the Question of the Austrian German Anschluss 1918–1945* (dissert. Bryn Mawr, 1975). A pioneering work which points to several primary sources used in the following.

18. *Volksstimme* (Frankfurt a.M.), May 22, 1922. Commissar Hugo Haase has been repeatedly criticized for his lukeward attitude in 1918–19 on the union issue.

19. See especially *Freiheit;* about its contributors on Austria and the Anschluss, see R. Hilferding, F. Stössinger, H. Haase, and Ed. Bernstein (Brancato, *op. cit.,* pp. 31–32).

20. *Volksstimme,* May 22, 1922, and F. Ebert, *Schriften* (Dresden, 1926), II, 237.

21. Breitscheid, "Europa und der Anschluss Österreichs an Deutschland," *Sozialistische Monatshefte,* vol. 34, Aug. 16, 1928, pp. 658–62.

22. Paul Levi, "Der deutsch-österreichische Anschluss, *"Sozialistische Politik und Wirtschaft,* vol. 5, July 19, 1927, against O. Bauer's article in *Der Kampf,* summer 1927.

23. Gg. Ledebour, "Österreicher und Bretonen," *Die Weltbühne,* 25, Jan. 1, 1929, pp. 4–6. The Socialist International never took an official stance on the Anschluss issue (Brancato, *op. cit.,* p. 73).

24. *Arbeiter-Zeitung,* Oct. 27, 1930.

25. Brancato, *op. cit.,* pp. 102–03.

26. R. Mischler, *Österreich-Deutschland,* Berlin, vol. 8, April 1931, p. 2, July 1931, p. 1, and Oct. 1931, p. 1.

27. See a letter of P. Löbe of Feb. 18, 1950, about his position in 1931, Brancato, *op. cit.,* p. 107.

28. *Verhandlungen des Reichstags,* vol. 445, pp. 1909ff. and vol. 446, p. 2081.

29. Breitscheid, "Europäisieren! Die deutsche Sozialdemokratie und das Zollabkommen," *Arbeiter-Zeitung,* Apr. 1, 1931.

30. Speeches of H. Ströbel and W. Sollmann, *Sozialdemokratischer Parteitag in Leipzig 1931 (31. Mai–5. Juni) Protokoll* (Berlin, 1931), pp. 94, 110; see also Ströbel, "Der Vorstoss der Mitteleuropäer," *Der Klassenkampf,* vol. 5, Apr. 1, 1931, pp. 223–24.

31./32. O. Bauer, *Arbeiter-Zeitung,* Oct. 27, 1930.

33. Brancato, *op. cit.,* p. 118.

34. *N.P.A.,* K 216, 234–39.

35. *Ibid.*

36. *Ibid.*

37. Paul Szende, "Donaukonföderation," *Der Kampf* (1931), 345–349.

38. *Ibid.,* quotes from the *Prager Presse* and *Česke Slovo.*

39. K. Schuschnigg, *Im Kampf gegen Hitler* . . . (1969), p. 166.

40. O. Bauer, *Werkausgabe,* I. Annex: Das Linzer Programm, and III, 1039.

41. Schuschnigg, *op. cit.,* pp. 173–74.

42. *Arbeiter-Zeitung.,* Jan. 19, 1934.

43. *Ibid.*, Jan. 29, 1934; also Bauer, *Der Aufstand der österreichischen Arbeiter* (1934), *Werkausgabe*, III, 957–97.

44. *N.P.A.*, Kat. 852, 585v; *Arbeiter-Zeitung* (Brno) Aug. 18, 1935.

45. *Arbeiter-Zeitung*, Apr. 7, 1935.

46. *Ibid.*, Apr. 21, 1935.

47. *Ibid.*, Jan. 17, 1935, O. Bauer, "Eine heilige Allianz für Mitteleuropa."

48. *Ibid.*, "Friedensschluss Hitler-Schuschnigg," July 19, 1936, pp. 364f.

49. *Ibid.*, 1936, p. 551.

50. *Ibid.*, Feb. 26, 1937, p. 72.

51. *Ibid.*, Sept. 29, 1937, p. 104.

52. Schuschnigg, *op. cit.*, p. 175.

53. Quoted by Buttinger, *In the Twilight of Socialism* (1953), p. 471.

54. *Der sozialistische Kampf (La lutte socialiste)* Paris, June 2, 1937, Bauer, "Nach der Annexion."

55. O. Leichter, *op. cit.*, p. 146.

56. Quoted *ibid.*, p. 147.

57. *Ibid.*

58. *Der sozialist. Kampf,* O. Bauer (Heinrich Weber), "Österreichs Ende," April 1938.

59. See articles of Bauer listed in Nr. 54. and 58.

60. See chap. 10 on the Soviet Union, of this study.

61. Bauer, "Die Selbstbestimmung der Sudetendeutschen," *Der Sozialist. Kampf,* July 1938.

62. *Ibid.*

63. Bauer, "Der deutsche Faschismus und die Internationale," *Der Kampf,* 1933, vol. 26.

Chapter 4

1. Schumpeter's suspicion against the Social Democrats and Dr. Bauer in particular was unfounded: see A.D. Low, "The First Austrian Republic and Soviet Hungary," *Journal of Central European Affairs,* July 1960, pp. 178, and *The Anschluss Movement . . .* (1974), p. 208.

2. *Public Records* (in the following *P.R.*), London, F.O. 606, vol. 27, Intelligence Report B/493, A.C. Coolidge, March 31.

3. *Reichspost,* Dec. 15, 1918.

4. *Times,* March 14, 1919.

5. A. Wandruszka, "Österreichs Politische Struktur," in *Geschichte der Republik Österreich,* ed. H. Benedikt, (Vienna, 1954), p. 331.

6. Seipel, I. *Nation und Staat,* 1916, p. 10.

7. *Ibid.*, p. 14.

8. Schuschnigg, K. von, *Im Kampf gegen Hitler* (Vienna, 1969), p. 61.

9. Verosta, Stephan, "Ignaz Seipel's Weg . . . (1917–1919)" *Die österreichische Verfassung von 1918 bis 1938*, Wissenschaftl. Kommission, Bd. 9 (Munich, 1980), p. 31.

10. Seipel, *op. cit.*, p. 14.

11. *Reichspost*, Nov. 18, 1918.

12. Quoted by B. Ward, "Seipel and the Anschluss," *Dublin Review*, 1938, p. 48.

13. *Österr. Staatsarchiv (in* the following *O.S.)*, Seipel, Dec. 17, 1918, Nachlass Bauer, K 261, B 443, March 25, 1919.

14. *P.R. F.O.* 606, vol. 27, Intelligence Report.

15. H. Lammasch, *Seine Aufzeichnungen* . . . , 927, especially the contributions by G. Herron, Sperl, F.W. Foerster, and F. Schumacher.

16. *Ibid.*, Herron, pp. 186–96.

17. *Ibid.*, Schumacher, p. 200.

18. *N.P.A.*, K 281, "Lammasch" Bauer to de Vaux, March 7, pp. 451–52.

19. *Ibid.*, de Vaux to Bauer, March 18, p. 454.

20. Heilfron, E. ed., *Die deutsche Nationalversammlung im Jahre 1919* . . . I, 3–7, I. Sitzg., Feb. 6, 1919.

21. Hugelmann, K., "Die polit. Parteien u.d. Anschlussfrage," in F. Kleinwaechter and H. Paller, eds. *Die Anschlussfrage* . . . (1930), pp. 322–37.

22. *Ibid.*, p. 333; for the following see pp. 332–34.

23. In its official program adopted in 1920 the DNVP under Count Westarp's influence made, however, no mention of the Anschluss, Hertzmann L. *DNVP, Right-Wing Opposition in the Weimar Republic* (Un. of Nebraska Pr., Lincoln, 1963), p. 85.

24. Feder, G. *Das Programm der NSDAP and seine weltanschaulichen Grundgedanken* (Munich, 1933), p. 42.

25. *Reichspost*, July 11, 1920.

26. Ward, B. *op. cit.*, pp. 31–50.

27. *Ibid.* See also Seipel, *op. cit.*, p. 132.

28. see 26.

29. J. Gessl, ed., *Seipel's Reden* (Vienna, 1926), pp. 19f.

30. Schuschnig, *op. cit.*, p. 53; see also *Stenograph. Protokoll d. Dritten Sitzung. Konstituierende Nationalversammlung*, Oct. 22 1922.

31. A. Wandruszka, *op. cit.*, p. 331; also *Das christlichsoziale Programm. Mit Erläuterungen* von R. Schmitz (Vienna, 1932).

32. See Hugelmann, *op. cit.*, p. 331.

33. Seipel, "Das wahre Antlitz Österreichs," Feb. 11, 1926.

34. Ward, *op. cit.*, p. 45.

35. *Ibid.*, pp. 45–46; Seipel to Bishop Frind, Aug. 16, 1928.

36. *Ibid.*, Report of Tagung d. kathol. Hoschschülerschaft in Österr. at Heiligenkreuz, 1930.

37. Ward, *op. cit.*, p. 45 and 49.

38. Quoted by Sweet, P. "Seipel's Views on the Anschluss in 1928 . . ." *Journal of Modern History,* March–Dec. 1947, pp. 320–23.

39. Seipel, *Nation und Staat,* p. 11; also Wandruszka, *op. cit.,* p. 411.

40. Srbik, H. von, *Deutsche Einheit,* in A. Low, *The Anschluss Movement 1918–38.* . . . *An Annotated Bibliography* (1984), p. 15.

41. Wandruszka, *op. cit.,* pp. 369–421.

42. *Ibid.,* p. 414.

43. *Records Office,* London, F.O. 120, vol. 1135, file No. 292; see also Rosar, W., *Deutsche Gemeinschaft, Seyss Inquart und der Anschluss,* 1971, which is a hardly disguised apologia.

44. Eppel, P. *Zwischen Kreuz und Hakenkreuz,* 1980, pp. 120–22.

45. Hudal, A. *Grundlagen des Nationalsozialismus. Eine ideengeschichtliche Untersuchung,* 1937, p. 239.

46. Reimann, V. *Kardinal Innitzer zwischen Hitler und Rom,* 1967, p. 59; also pp. 114.

47. *Ibid.* Pp. 53–60.

48. Weber, E. ed., *Dollfuss an Österreich. Eines Mannes Wort und Ziel,* 1935, p. 70; also pp. 72 and 77.

49. Wandrsuzka, *op. cit.,* p. 343.

50. *Débats Parlementaries. Annales . . Chambre des Députés,* vol. 136, 640.

51. Jagschitz, G. *Der Putsch der Nationalsozialisten 1934 in Österreich,* 1976.

52. Wandruszka, *op. cit.,* pp. 362–63.

53. Starhemberg, *Memoiren,* pp. 1, 160f.; also p. 157.

54. Institut für Zeitgeschichte, Univ. Vienna, Wenninger, Jan. 17, 1938. See also his letter of Feb. 26, 1938, and Starhemberg's reply.

55. Jedlicka, L., E.R. Starhemberg . . . 1938, *Fallstudien zur öst. Zeitgeschichte 1900–75,* (1975), p. 558, March 27, 1938; see also 54.

56. see 54. Starhemberg's reply.

57. Starhemberg, *Memoirs,* pp. 158f.

58. Starhemberg to Hitler, quoted in B. Berger, *E.R. Von Starhemberg.* Dissert. Vienna, 1967, pp. 185–87.

59. "Sollen wir den Anschluss fordern?" Volksverein, Jan. 1919. Nationaldemokratische Flugschriften, Nr. 3.

60. *N.P.A.,* Österr. 74, vol. 2, Under Secretary of State to Wedel, Jan. 27, 1919. Tel. 39; also Österr. 95, v. 27, "Richtlinien," Feb. 12, 1919, and also "Skizze."

61. *N.P.A.,* Öst. 74, v. 2, Under Secret. of State to Wedel, Jan. 27, 1919, Tel. 39.

62. *Ibid.;* also Low, *Anschluss* . . . (1974), p. 160.

63. Heuss, Th. *Erinnerungen 1905–33,* 1963, pp. 244–45; see also the account of Gustav Stolper's widow, Toni (Kassowitz) Stolper, *Ein Leben in Brennpunkten unserer Zeit,* 1960, pp. 127–29.

64. Fellner F. and H. Maschl, *St. Germain im Sommer 1919,* 1977.

65. Ackerl, Isabella, *Grossdeutsche Volkspartei 1920–1934,* Dissert. Un. of Vienna 1967, "Richtlinien," Vienna, 1919, p. 24, Zeitungsausschnitt-sarchiv. See also Jung, Karl: *Geschichte der Grossdeutschen Volkspartei 1920–34.* Man. Vienna, 1934, AVA, Zeitungsausschnittsarchiv d. grossdeutschen Volkspartei.

66. *Ibid.,* p. 11, "Richtlinien," Vienna, 1920, Archiv.

67. Ackerl, *op. cit.,* p. 314.

68. "Der Verein der Deutschnationalen," Mss, Vienna, 1923, AVA, Zeitungsausschnittsarvhic, Anhang, Nr. 5, Wolf, *Deutschösterreichische Tageszeitung (Dötz),* Oct. 25, 1923.

69. Ackerl, *op. cit.,* p. 264.

70. *Ibid.,* p. 293; see also *Wiener Neueste Nachrichten,* June 23, 1933.

71. Ackerl, *op. cit.,* p. 295, Köpke, letter, March 28, 1933.

72. *Ibid.,* p. 295.

73. *Ibid.,* pp. 310–11.

74. Feldmann, Angela, *Landbund für Österreich, Ideologie-Organisation-Politik,* Un. of Vienna, Dissert. 1966, p. 6; see also "Programm and Leitsätze des Reich-Landbundes, Nov. 10, 1921, in *Nachlass Schumy,* Instit. f. Zeitgeschichte, Univers. Vienna.

75. Feldmann, *op. cit.,* p. 129.

76. *Ibid.,* p. 186.

77. Pauley, B.F., *Hitler and the Forgotten Nazis. A History of Austrian National Socialism,* Un. of No. Carol. Press, 1981, p. 26.

78. *Ibid.,* pp. 30–31.

79. *Ibid.,* p. 57.

80. A.D. Low, "The *Völkischer Beobachter* 1933," *Social Science,* vol. 55, autumn 1980, pp. 196–97.

81. *Völkischer Beobachter* (Munich ed.) Feb 3 (report from Linz, Feb. 2, 1933).

82. *Ibid.,* March 10, 1933.

83. *Ibid.,* Apr. 26.

84.a. *Ibid.,* May 14.

84b. Contemporaries, Nazis and non-Nazis, as well as some Austrian Historians have made a distinction between "moderate" and "radical" Nazis. Others, emphasizing the radical character of National Socialism in general, have raised questions as to the significance of this distinction. Many Austrians had a stake in claiming that the distinction was real, especially former *Grossdeutsche (or betont Nationale)* who later followed the Nazi lead, as well as leading circles of the Austrian government who for years pursued the policy of building bridges toward the Nationals, under the illusion of strengthening thus Austria's defenses against the *Third Reich* (About Nazi radicalism see B.E. Pauley, *Hitler and the Forgotten Nazis* (1981), espec. pp. 91–97).

85. Starhemberg, R.E. *Memoiren* (Vienna, Munich, 1971), p. 209.

86. Pauley, *op. cit.*, pp. 148–51.

87. Starhemberg, *op. cit.*, pp. 209–14.

88. *DGFP, C*, II, Rieth to Berlin, March 29, 1934, Nr. 369, p. 692; Starhemberg, *op. cit.*, pp. 212–13.

89. *DGFP, C*, II, Nr. 389, Apr. 9, 1934, pp. 728f. and *ibid*, Hüffer, Memorandum, Apr. 19, 1934, Nr. 409, pp. 757–58.

90. *DGFPC, C* II, Nr. 389, pp. 728f.

91. *Ibid.*, Bülow, Further Political Handling of the Austrian Question, pp. 728–29.

92. *Ibid.*, Bülow's Memorandum, Apr. 10, 1934, Nr. 393, pp. 735–36.

93. *Ibid.* Department II, Apr. 19, 1934, Nr. 409, Hüffer.

94. *Ibid.*, Muff, May 24, 1934, Nr. 459, pp. 835–37.

95. *Ibid.*, III, C, Frick to For. Ministry, June 14, 1934, Nr. 3, p. 5.

96. *Ibid.*, C, II, Memorandum, Deptmt II, May 29, 1934, Renthe-Fink, Nr. 469, p. 852.

97. *Ibid.*

98. *Braunbuch*, quoted by Schuschnigg, *Im Kampfe* . . . , pp. 161–62.

99. *Ibid.*, C, III, encl. 2 in Nr. 167, "Guiding Principles of German Policy vis-à-vis Austria," approved by Hitler.

100. *Ibid.*, Nr. 151, Hitler, Aug. 8, 1934.

101. *Ibid.*, Nr. 173, Hess, Aug. 21, 1934.

102. *Ibid.*, Nr. 123, Hitler to Papen, July 26, 1934.

103. Rainer's account, Aug. 22, 1939, in *Conspiracy and Aggression*, vol. I, 460–64.

Chapter 5

1. Eichstädt, U., *Von Dollfuss zu Hitler*, pp. 25f.

2. *DGFP*, (1957), C, I, Gömbös to Hitler, Feb. 6, 1933, Nr. 15, pp. 34–35, and Nr. 12, Feb. 6, p. 76.

3. About Hassell's ideas, see Ross, D. *Hitler und Dollfuss. Die deutsche Österreichpolitik, 1933–34* (Hamburg, 1966), pp. 15–16.

4. *DGFP, C*, I, Rieth, Vienna, to Bülow, Feb. 18, 1933, Nr. 25, p. 52.

5. Ross, *op. cit.*, p. 334.

6. *DGFP, C*,I, Köpke to Rieth, Nr. 107, March 22, 1933, p. 193.

7. *Ibid.*, Neurath, Memorandum, Nr. 219, pp. 397–98; also *ibid.*, Memo., Nr. 112, March 23, p. 207.

8. *Ibid.*, see also *DGFP*, Nr. 173, p. 324, and *ibid.*, Hassell, unsigned memorandum, Sept. 24, 1933, Nr. 448, p. 839.

9. *Ibid.*, C, I, Köpke to Rieth, Nr. 107, March 22, 1933, p. 13.

10. *Ibid.*, Hassell to Berlin, Nr. 173, Apr. 20, 1933, pp. 318f.

11. *Ibid.*, p. 320.

12. *Ibid.*, p. 321.

13. *Ibid.*, Memorandum Köpke, March 23, 1933, Nr. 112, pp. 206–07.

14. *Ibid.*, Neurath Memorandum, Apr. 27, 1933, Nr. 191, p. 351.

15. *Ibid.*, Neurath Memorandum, May 10, 1933, Nr. 219, pp. 397–98.

16. *Ibid.*, Köpke Memorandum, May 19, 1933, Nr. 249, pp. 460–61.

17. *Ibid.*, Memorandum, Department II (Heeren), May 20, 1933, Nr. 256, pp. 474–75.

18. *Ibid.*, Hassell to For. Min. Apr. 20, 1933, Nr. 173, pp. 318–20.

19. *Ibid.*,, Nr. 187, Apr. 25, 1933, p. 346.

20. Pauley, *The Forgotten Nazis.* . . . pp. 82–83.

21. *DGFP*, Extracts from Minutes of the Conference of Ministers, May 26, 1933, Nr. 262, pp. 487–90.

22. *Ibid.*, p. 490.

23. *Ibid.*, pp. 489–90.

24. *Ibid.*; also Ross, *op. cit.*, p. 53.

25. Ross, *op. cit.*

26. *DGFP*, Nr. 313, June 15, 1933, Neurath, London, pp. 567–68.

27. *Ibid.*, C, I, Nr. 448, Sept. 24, 1933, unsigned memorandum (Hassell), p. 839.

28. See Ross, *op. cit.*, pp. 55 and 271.

29. *Ibid.*, p. 56.

30. *DGFP*, C. I. Rieth to Bülow, Nr. 346, July 1, 1933, pp. 619f.

31. *Ibid.*, Neurath to Bavaria, Nr. 375, July 22, 1933, and ftnte 2.

32. *Ibid.*, Nr. 376, July 27, 1933, pp. 689–90, ftn. 7.

33. *Ibid.*, Bülow to Neurath, Aug. 1, 1933, Nr. 385, pp. 708–12.

34. *Ibid.*, Neurath to Bülow, Nr. 390, Aug. 4, 1933, pp. 718–19.

35. *Ibid.* Bülow, Memorandum, Nr. 391, Aug. 5, 1933, pp. 719–20.

36. *Ibid.*, Neurath to Bülow, Nr. 390, pp. 218–19 (Aug. 4) and Neurath to Hitler, Nr. 398, Aug. 9, 1933, p. 732.

37. *Ibid.*, Bülow's Memorandum, Aug. 5, 1933, p. 719.

38. *Ibid.*, see 36., p. 718.

39. *Ibid.*

40. *Ibid.*; for Mussolini's complaints about Habicht, see No. 441, Aug. 12, 1933, p. 738 and *Ibid.*, ftn. 2 and 6.

41. *Ibid.*, Nrs. 392 and 393, both Aug. 7, 1933, pp. 720–24.

42. *Ibid.*, Neurath's Memorandum, Nr. 402, pp. 740–41.

43. *Ibid.*, Rieth to Bülow, Nr. 407, Aug. 17, 1933, pp. 763–66.

44. *Ibid.*, Bülow, July 27, 1933.

45. *Ibid.*, see 43. p. 765.

46. *Ibid.* Bülow to Neurath, Aug. 25, 1933, pp. 770–72.

47. *Ibid.*, July 1, 1933, Mussolini to Dollfuss, *Geheimer Briefwechsel* . . . (Vienna, 1949), pp. 16f.

48. *Ibid.*, Dollfuss's reply to Mussolini.

49. Quoted by Ross, *op. cit.* p. 84 and 279; see also *DGFP*, C, I, Nr. 485, pp. 893f.

50. Ross, *op. cit.*, p. 87.

51. *DGFP*, C, I, Smend, Chargé in Rome to Berlin, Sept. 21, 1933, pp. 830 and 828–31.

52. Pauley, *op. cit.*, p. 123.

53. Ross, *op. cit.*, p. 115; also *DGFP*, C, II, Nr. 49, p. 87.

54. Ross, *op. cit.*, p. 114 and 286–87.

55. *DGFP*, C, I, Nr. 465; also Ross, *op. cit.*, p. 97.

56. Suvich in Berlin, Dec. 12 and 13, 1933; *DGFP*, C, II, Nr. 126, Memorandum by For. Min. Dec. 13, 1933, pp. 224–25.

57. *Ibid.*, C, II, Nr. 144, Habicht to Hassell, Dec. 22, 1933, p. 269 and Nr. 153, Hassell to Habicht, Dec. 28, pp. 285–87.

58. *Ibid.*, Rieth to Bülow, Dec. 21, 1933, Nr. 143, p. 267; also *Beiträge zur Vorgeschichte und Geschichte des Julirevolte* (Vienna, 1934), p. 49.

59. *DGFP*, C, II, Nr. 143, p. 265.

60. *DGFP*, Nr. 409, Apr. 19, 1934, p. 757.

61. *Ibid.*; Schuschnigg, *Im Kampf* . . . p. 233.

62. *Ibid.*, Nr. 166, Jan. 8, 1934, pp. 309–11.

63. *Ibid.*, also Nr. 167, p. 311.

64. *Ibid.*, C, I, Neurath to Bülow, Nr. 390, Aug. 4, 1933, p. 718.

65. *Ibid.*, C, II, Nr. 225, Jan. 26, 1934, pp. 431f.

66. *Österreichischer Pressedienst*, Munich, Habicht, Jan. 27, 1934.

67. *Völkischer Beobachter*, Jan. 31, 1934, Hitler before the Reichstag.

68. *DGFP*, C, II, Nr. 229, W. Muff, Jan. 31, 1934, p. 437.

69. *Ibid.*, C, II, Rieth, Memorandum, Feb. 10, 1934, Nr. 247, pp. 464–67.

70. Ross, *op. cit.*, pp. 174–75.

71. *DGFP*, C, II, Memorandum Gilbert In der Maur, Feb. 16, 1934, Nr. 263, p. 498.

72. *Ibid.*, pp. 499–501.

73. *DGFP*, C, II, Hassell, Feb. 15, 1934, Nr. 255, pp. 484–85.

74. *Ibid.*, Neurath Memorandum, Feb. 16, 1934, Nr. 258, p. 491.

75. About the aftermath of the Three Powers Declaration of Febr. 17, 1934, *ibid.*, Nr. 282, Neurath Memorandum, Feb. 27, 1934, pp. 533–34.

76. Th. Habicht's radio address from Munich, Feb. 19, 1934; on Habicht's Munich propaganda, see also Pauley, *op. cit.*, pp. 115–17.

77. *DGFP,* Nr. 278, Feb. 26, 1934, pp. 529–30.

78. *Ibid.,* Neurath Memorandum, Feb. 27, 1934, pp. 533–34.

79. *Ibid.*

80. *Ibid.,* Neurath to Hassell, Nr. 320, March 13, 1934, pp. 588–99.

81. *Ibid.,* Hassell to Neurath, Nr. 332, March 17, 1934, pp. 619–27.

82. *Ibid.,* III, Austrian Legation and Muff to Berlin, Nr. 125, July 26, 1934, p. 255.

83. *Ibid.,* Nr. 151, Aug. 8, 1934, p. 299.

84. *Ibid.,* Nr. 152, Aug. 8, 1934, pp. 300–305.

85. *Ibid.,* Nr. 208, p. 411.

86. *Ibid.,* C, II, Papen, Guiding Principles . . . , Nr. 167, encl. 2, pp. 342–43.

87. *Ibid.,* II, Papen to Bülow, Aug. 19, 1934, Nr. 167, pp. 338–39.

88. *Ibid.,* p. 339.

89. *Ibid.,* III, Nr. 173, Aug. 21, 1934, pp. 352–53.

90. *Ibid.,* Nr. 183, Muff to For. Min., enclosure, Aug. 30, 1934, pp. 372–76.

91. *Ibid.,* Nr. 231, Papen to Hitler, Oct. 4, 1934, p. 460.

92. *Ibid.;* see also *ibid.* C, III, Nr. 55, pp. 118–22, Minutes Conference of Ministers held on July 3, 1934.

93. see 91.

94. Schuschnigg, *Ein Requiem in Rot-Weiss-Rot* (Zürich, 1946), pp. 233f.

95. Schuschnigg, *Dreimal-Österreich,* (Vienna, 1938), p. 277.

96. Three Power Declaration, Sept. 27, 1934, in *Weltgeschichte der Gegenwart in Dokumenten* (eds. M. Freund and W. Frauendienst, 5 vols., Essen, 1940) I, T. I, p. 269.

97. About the Stresa Conference, April 1935, *DDF,* 1ère sér., X, pp. xxvii–xxix and Nrs. 101, 153, and 196.

98. Papen, Oct. 26, 1934; see also Eichstädt, *op. cit.,* p. 86.

99. *Ibid.,* p. 87 (Papen, Aug. 8, 1935) and *Schmidt Prozess,* p. 393.

100. Quoted by Eichstädt, *op. cit.,* p. 87.

101. *GDFP,* C, IV, Nr. 544, Papen, Feb. 6, 1936, pp. 1101–02.

102. *Schmidt Prozess,* p. 403 (also Papen, Apr. 21, 1936).

103. *Ibid.,* pp. 168 and 416.

104. Glaise Horstenau in *Schmidt Prozess, Internat. Gerichtshof,* vol. XVI, 132.

105. *Ibid.,* p. 582.

106. Schuschnigg, *Im Kampf . . . ,* p. 221.

107. *Ibid.*

108. *Ibid.*

109. Quoted *ibid.,* p. 222.

Chapter 6

1. *GDFP,* C, III, Nr. 123, July 26, 1934, pp. 252–53.
2. *Ibid.,* Nr. 146, Aug. 3, 1934, Memorandum by State Secretary Bülow, p. 291.
3. *Ibid.,* Bülow's Memorandum, Nr. 146, pp. 260–61.
4. Papen, *Memoirs,* p. 351; on Austria in general and Papen's own role, see *ibid.,* Part Four, pp. 337–439.
5. *Ibid.,* p. 378.
6. *Conspiracy and Aggression,* I (1946), pp. 459–460.
7. About Papen's relation with Hitler and Habicht, see Papen's *Memoirs,* pp. 340–48; Hitler pledged to Papen that he would not "interfere" in Austrian affairs, p. 361.
8. *Conspiracy* . . . , I, 463.
9. *GDFP,* I, D, Jan. 30, 1937, pp. 386–87. About Berger-Waldenegg's reports from Rome about his talks with Mussolini & Ciano, see *N.P.A.* Jan. 23, 1937, p. 323v–326 and 487v, 499–500 respectively.
10. About differences between Berlin and Vienna regarding the Saar, see *DGFP,* C, III, Nr. 235, Oct. 8, 1934, p. 465; see also *DDF,* IX, Puaux, Jan. 25, 1935 Nr. 89, pp. 118–20.
11. *DGFP,* C, IV, July 27, 1935, Nr. 232, pp. 496–502, espec. 502.
12. *Conspiracy.* . . . , I, 458–59.
13. *Ibid.,* pp. 460–61.
14. *Ibid.,* p. 464.
15. *Ibid.,* Seyss-Inquart to Göring, July 14, 1939, pp. 465–66.
16. Starhemberg, *Memoirs,* pp. 280–81, 218; see also Papen, *op. cit.,* pp. 355–57, 381–82, 394–95, and Starhemberg, *Memoirs,* p. 397.
17. Starhemberg, *Memoirs,* pp. 210–13.
18. *Ibid.,* p. 214.
19. *Ibid.,* pp. 222 and 242.
20. *Ibid.,* p. 222.
21. *Der Hochverratsprozess gegen Dr. Guido Schmidt vor dem Wiener Volksgericht.* . . . (Vienna, 1947), p. 407.
22. Starhemberg, *op. cit.,* pp. 242–44.
23. *Ibid.,* p. 245.
24. *Ibid.,* p. 246; also p. 263.
25. Papen, *op. cit.,* p. 365.
26. Starhemberg, *op. cit.,* pp. 275–77.
27. *Op. cit.,* p. 280.
28. *Op. cit.,* p. 281.
29. *Ibid.,* pp. 253–54.
30. *Arbeiter-Zeitung,* April 14, 1936, quoted in *N.P.A.,* K 852, 650 v.
31. Starhemberg, *op. cit.* p. 258.

32. Schuschnigg, *Im Kampf* . . . , p. 176.

33. *Ibid.*, Promemoria, p. 177.

34. *Ibid.*, p. 183.

35. Kerekes, L., *Allianz Hitler-Gömbös-Mussolini. Dokumente zur ungarischen Aussenpolitik,* (Budapest, 1966), pp. 124f.; also Starhemberg, *op. cit.,* p. 178.

36. Schuschnigg, *op. cit.,* p. 185.

37. *Ibid.;* also *Hochverratsprozess* . . . , p. 8.

38. *Ibid.,* witness Schuschnigg.

39. *Ibid.*

40. *İbid.,* p. 432.

41. Starhemberg, *op. cit.,* pp. 266–67.

42. *Ibid.* p. 267 and 191–92; also *N.P.A.,* Fasz. 466, 2158f.

43. Schuschnigg, *op. cit.,* p. 193.

44. For the text of the July Agreement, see Schuschnigg, *op. cit.,* pp. 187–91 or *DGFP,* D, I, Nr, 152, pp. 278–82.

45. Schuschnigg, *op. cit.,* p. 187.

46. *DGFP,* Doc. Nr. 233, Papen's Bericht an Hitler, July 1, 1937.

47. *Ibid.,* Hassell to Berlin, Nr. 155, July 11, 1936, p. 283.

48. Papen, *op. cit.,* pp. 370–71.

49. *Hochverratsprozess* . . . , M. Hoffinger, p. 137.

50. Schuschnigg, *op. cit.,* p. 195; *ADA,* Ser. D, I, Doc, 152.

51. *Ibid.,* Doc. 166; also Schuschnigg, *op. cit.,* pp. 195–96.

52. Schuschnigg, *op. cit.,* pp. 197–98.

53. Pauley, *Hitler and the Forgotten Nazis* . . . , p. 179.

54. *Ibid.,* pp. 186–87.

55. *Conspiracy and Aggression* . . . , I, 472–73, Papen to Hitler, Sept. 1, 1936.

56. *Ibid.,* Captain Leopold's memo considered by the Austrian Cabinet, Jan. 1937.

57. *GDFP,* D, I, Papen to Hitler, Nr. 214, pp. 401–03.

58. *Conspiracy* . . . , I, 474; Papen to German For. Min., Jan. 27, 1938.

59. *Conspiracy* . . . , I, 476.

60. *Ibid.,* pp. 477–78.

61. Schuschnigg, *Im Kampf* . . . , especially pp. 225–27.

62. *Ibid.,* pp. 199, 207–08, 212, and 230–32.

63. *DDF,* III, Nr. 375, p. 675.

64. *P.R.* (London) 863.00/58, p. 4, Secret. Gen. Adam, to Alt-Österreich Association.

65. *Ibid.,* Schuschnigg 86300/;58, pp. 10–11.

66. *Reichspost,* Feb. 6, 1935.

67. *DGFP 1918–1945*, Set. D, I,, Nr. 181, Memorandum on the reception of Dr. Guido Schmidt by the Führer, Nov. 19, 1936, pp. 338–42; see also Nrs. 325, 328–29, 337.

68. *Ibid.*, p. 341.

69. *Ibid.*, No. 182, pp. 342–48.

70. *Ibid.*, Papen to Hitler, Nov. 24, 1936, No. 185, pp. 348–49.

71. *Ibid.*, German For. Min. memorandum, Nov. 28, 1936, No. 188, pp. 352–54.

72. *Ibid.*, No. 191, pp. 360–62.

73. *Ibid.*, Stein, No. 190, p. 356.

74. See 69.

75. *Ibid.*, See 73. Pp. 356–57.

76. *Ibid.*, No. 191, pp. 360–62, Dec. 2, 1936.

77. *Ibid.*, p. 361.

78. *Ibid.*, No. 196, pp. 366–74.

79. *Ibid.*, p. 373.

80. *Ibid.*, p. 374.

81. *GDFP,* D, I, No. 199, Memorandum of Hassell, pp. 376f.

82. *Ibid.*

83. *Ibid.*

84. *Ibid.*, p. 384.

85. *GDFP,* Hassell's Memorandum, No. 207, pp. 384–85; also Hassell to Goring, No. 208 (enclosures), Jan. 30, pp. 386–87.

86. *Ibid.*, see also Hassell to Berlin, *GDFP,* No. 155, pp. 283–84.

87. *Ibid.*, Papen to Hitler, Feb. 13, 1937, pp. 389f.

88. *Ibid.*, Memorandum of For. Min. No. 212, pp. 396–98 and No. 213, pp. 399–401.

89. *Ibid.*, p. 400.

90. *Ibid.*, Memorandum by For. Min. No. 213, p. 400.

91. *Ibid.*, Papen to Hitler, March 3, 1937, No. 214, pp. 401–03.

92.-93. *Ibid.*, Papen to German For. Min., March 13, 1937, p. 407, and *Ibid.*, Papen to Hitler, No. 220, Apr. 17, 1937, pp. 413–15.

94. *Ibid.*, Austrian For. Min. to Legation, London, No. 220, Apr. 14, 1937, pp. 416–17.

95. *Ibid.*, enclosure 2, Apr. 15, 1937, p. 417.

96. *Ibid.*, No. 222, May 8, 1937, p. 419.

97. *Ibid.*, Papen to Hitler, May 26, 1937, No. 225, pp. 422–24.

98. *Ibid.*, p. 423.

99. *Ibid.*, Papen to Hitler, May 26, 1937, No. 227, pp. 425f.

100. *Ibid.*, p. 426.

101.-102. *Hochverratsprozess* . . . , Schuschnigg as witness, p. 501.

103. *GDFP,* Papen to Berlin, May 26, 1937, Nr. 226, p. 424.

104. *Ibid.*, Nr. 232, p. 433.

105. *Ibid.*
106. *Ibid.*, Stein's report, Oct. 7, 1937, Nr. 259, p. 468.
107. *Ibid.*, Stein to Berlin, Oct. 22, Nr. 264, pp. 474–75.
108. *Ibid.*, Stein to Berlin, Oct. 23, Nr. 266, pp. 476–77.
109. *Ibid.*, Stein to Berlin, Dec. 21, 1937, Re: further development of Austria's political situation, Nr. 273, pp. 483–84f.
110. Rosar, W. *Deutsche Gemeinschaft. Seyss-Inquart und der Anschluss* (1971) pp. 189–90; also Papen, *Memoirs*, pp. 404 and 410, and Schuschnigg, *Im Kampf . .* , p. 219.
111. Schuschnigg, *op. cit.*, pp. 205, 209.
112. *Hochverratsprozess*, G. Schmidt, pp. 501–02.
113. Papen, *Memoirs*, p. 423, insisted in February 1938 that Hitler forbid Leopold to reside in Austria; also pp. 384, 394–96 and 404. About Seyss-Inquart's virtual surrender to Nazism, see Gedye, *Fallen Bastions* in Rosar, *op. cit.*, pp. 235–36 and Seyss's fascination with Hitler's personality, pp. 309–10.
114. Schuschnigg, *op. cit.*, p 218.
115. Rosar, *op. cit.*, p. 121; also 142. Though this biography is a vain attempt at a whitewash, it contains useful information. And Schuschnigg, *op. cit.*, pp. 227, 232.
116. Rosar, *op. cit.*, pp. 117f.
117. *Ibid.*, pp. 139–40.
118. *Ibid.*, pp. 163–64; for the following see especially pp. 166, 196.

Part II, Chapter 7

1. Bérenger, H. Dec. 20, 1932, and Paul-Boncour, Nov. 14, 1933, see *Le Temps*, Dec. 21, 1932, and Nov. 15, 1933, respectively.
2. Wolfers, A. *Britain and France between two Wars* (N.Y., 1966), especially chaps. 13, 14, and 17.
3. *Ibid.*, pp. 95f. and pp. 229f.
4. Poincaré, R., "Histoire politique: chronique de quinzaine," II, 1373, in *Revue des deux mondes*, Dec. 1, 1920.
5. Wolfers, *op. cit.*, pp. 100–09.
6. *Parl. Debates, House of Commons*, Baldwin, July 30, 1934, vol. 292, col. 2339.
7. *Chambre, Débats*, Gaston River, p. 632, Feb. 25, 1938.
8. Wolfers, *op. cit.*, see 2.
9. *Chambre, Débats*, Ybarnégaray, Feb. 25, 1938.
10.-11. DDF, *1932–1939*, III, No. 19, March 20, 1933, p. 41 and No. 20, Annex; memorandum March 20, 1933, pp. 42–43.
12. *Ibid.*, François-Poncet to Paris, No. 23, March 21, 1933, pp. 46–48.

13. *Ibid.*, No. 107, Visits de M. Pflügl.

14. François-Poncet, A., *Memoirs of a French Ambassador in Berlin 1931–38* (N.Y., 1949), p. 94.

15. *Ibid.*, pp. 92–93.

16. *Ibid.*, p. 94.

17. *Ibid.*, p. 119.

18. *Ibid.*, p. 143.

19. *DDF,* vol. 5, No. 272, Paul-Boncour to Corbin, London, Jan. 20, 1934, p. 528.

20. *Ibid.*, No. 275, Jan. 26, 1934, pp. 532–33.

21. *Ibid.*

22. *Ibid.*, Nr. 332, Puaux to Paris.

23. *Ibid.*, Notes du Départment, Audience du Chancellor Dollfuss, Nr. 396, June 16, 1933, pp. 718–20.

24. *Ibid.*, p. 720.

25. *Ibid.*, Nr. 383, Charles-Roux to Paris, June 10, 1933, pp. 697–98.

26. *Ibid.* lère sér., IV, Nr. 129, Annex, Aug. 22, 1933, p. 225.

27. *Ibid.*

28. *Ibid.*, Puaux to Paul-Boncour, Nr. 134, Aug. 23, 1933, p. 231.

29. *Ibid.*, See also *DDF*, VII, Puaux to For. Min., Paris, Aug. 8, 1934, pp. 145–46.

30. *DDF,* III, Nr. 375, Puaux to Paul-Boncour, June 8, 1933, p. 675.

31. *DDF,* IV, Nr. 180, Sept. 5, 1933, Chambrun, Rome, to Paul-Boncour, pp. 307–08.

32. *DDF,* lère sér., V, 13, Puaux to Paul-Boncour, Nr. 246, Jan. 20, 1934, pp. 490–92.

33. Ibid., Puaux, Jan. 22, 1934, Nr. 255, p. 502.

34. *Ibid.*, Puaux to Daladier, For. Min., Nr. 314, Feb. 3, 1934, pp. 602–03.

35. *Ibid.*

36. *Ibid.*, Puaux to Daladier, Feb. 5, 1934, Nr. 332, pp. 629–34, espec. 630.

37. *Ibid.*, prem. sér., V, Nr. 341, Chambrun to Daladier, Feb. 7, 1934, p. 651.

38. *Ibid.*, Corbin to Barthou, Feb. 7–10, 1934, Nr. 352, pp. 662–63.

39. *Ibid.*, Barthou to Puaux, Feb. 12, 1934, Nr. 361, p. 673.

40. *Ibid.*, VI, Puaux to Barthou, March 15, 1934, Nr. 9, pp. 19–23, and Nr. 47, March 29, 1934, Puaux to Barthou, p. 122.

41. *Ibid.*, IV, Noël, Prague, to Paris, Nr. 223, Sept. 16, 1933, p. 379.

42. *DDF,* III, Paul-Boncour to Laroche, Warsaw, Nr. 425, June 25, 1933, p. 774.

43. *Ibid.*, Puaux to Paul-Boncour, Nr. 183, Apr. 25, 1933, pp. 317–18.

44. *Ibid.*, lre sér., III, Nr. 425, p. 774.

45. *Ibid.*, Puaux, Nr. 270, Oct. 3, 1933, pp. 478–79.

46. *DDF*, III, Noel to Paul-Boncour, Nr. 406, June 19, 1933, pp. 739–40.

47. *Ibid.*, V, François-Poncet to Barthou, Nr. 481, March 9, 1934, p. 911.

48. *Ibid.*, V, Laroche to Paul-Boncour, Nr. 49, Nov. 23, 1933, pp. 95.

49. *Ibid.*

50. *Ibid.*, Laroche to Paul-Boncour, Nr. 56, Nov. 26, 1933, pp. 111–12; also Nr. 65, Dec. 1, 1933, p. 134.

51. *Ibid.*, Laroche to Paul-Boncour, Nr. 62, Nov. 29, 1933, p. 128.

52. *Ibid.*, Laroche to Paul-Boncour, Nr. 65, Dec. 1, 1933, p. 134.

53. *Ibid.*, III, Nr. 83, Puaux, Dec. 5, 1933, p. 164.

54. *Ibid.*

55. *Ibid.*

56. *N.P.A.*, Bericht d. österr. Gesandtschaft, Berne, Nov. 2, p. 192.

57. About the trilateral negotiations between Italy, Austria, and Hungary, see Gehl, *op. cit.*, pp. 51–52.

58. See Mussolini's identical threat two months later, in November 1933, *DDF*, IV, Nr. 286, p. 404.

59. Giovanucci, F.G., *Il problema austriaco e l'Italia*, Rome, 1934.

60. Ross, D. *Hitler und Dollfuss . . .*, pp. 147–48.

61. *N.A.*, Bericht der Division Brescia, T-821/368/390/351; also Stuhlpfarrer, in *Österreich 1927 bis 1938*, p. 147.

62. N.A., Amer. Embassy, Vienna, to State D., T-821, reports Febr. 1934 about Italian press.

63. *Ibid.*

64. *Ibid.*

65. Jedlicka, L. "Die Ära Schuschnigg, "in Wissenschftl. Kommission, *Österreich 1927–38* (Munich, 1973), p. 196.

66. Jedlicka, "Die Aussenpolitik der Ersten Republik," in Zollner, ed. *Diplomatie und Aussenpolitik . . .* (Vienna, 1977), pp. 164–65.

67. *Ibid.* and Jedlicka "Mussolini und Österreich 1936" in *Österreich in Geschichte und Literatur*, 1968, p. 533, and "Die Ära Schuschnigg" (see 65.), p. 199.

68. See 62.

69. See 65; also *BDFP*, 2nd ser., VI, Simon to Clerk, Aug. 3, 1934, Nr. 560.

70. *Ibid.* also July 31, 1934.

71. *Survey of International Affairs, 1934*, p. 485.

72. *GDFP*, C, II, Hassell, Rome, Apr. 3, 1934, Nr. 377, p. 706.

73a. *Parliament. Debates. H. of Commons*, Jan. 7, 1935.

73b. *G.D.*, Ser. C, III, Nr. 555, p. 1059.

74. Watt, "Anglo-German Naval Agreement of 1935," *Journal of Modern History*, vol. 28 (1956), pp. 157–58.

75. *F.R.U.S.*, *1935*, I, 284, Litvinov to Bullitt, Telegr. May 29, 1935.

76. *Documents in International Affairs*, 1935, I, 178.

77. *G.D.*, 8033/E 577840, Neurath's Memo.

78. Viscount Templewood (Sir Samuel Hoare), *Nine Troubled Years* (London, 1954), pp. 164–65.

79. Quoted by Heriot, *Jadis*, II, 577–78, Laval to Hoare.

80. *Survey of Internat. Affairs, 1934*, p. 444; see also *DBFP (Documents on British Foreign Policy)*, 2nd ser., VI, Selby to Sir Simon, Feb. 13, 1933, pp. 411f.

81. *DBFP*, V, Sargent's note, June 25, 1933, enclosure in Nr. 233.

82. *Ibid.*, ser. 2, Simon to Phipps, June 17, 1933, Nr. 214.

83. *Ibid.*, Sargent's note, June 29, 1933, Nr. 233; also minute, Graham to Simon, July 11, Nr. 246.

84. *Ibid.*, Vansittart's memo. Nr. 254.

85. *Documents on German Foreign Policy (in* the following *DGFP)*, C, I, Bülow's Memo, July 31, 1933, Nr. 383, p. 698.

86. *DGFP*, C, II, Nr. 188, enclosure, Memo. for For. Min. Neurath, Jan. 17, 1934, p. 361; also pp. 362–63.

87. Quoted by Gehl, *op. cit.*, p. 80; see also *DBFP*, 2nd ser., VI, Jan. 20, 1934, pp. 298f.

88. *DBFP*, Sir Simon to Drummond, Feb. 13, 1934, Nr. 270.

89. *Parl. Debates, H. of Commons*, vol. 286, Feb. 21, 1934, col. 318.

90. *DGFP*, C, V, Nr. 320, Hassell's report, Nov. 10, 1933.

91. *The Times*, London, Feb. 14, 1934, p. 7.

92. *Parl. Debates. H. of Commons*, vol. 286, Feb. 21, 1934, vol. 315–20.

93. *DGFP*, C, III, Nr. 5, Neurath's Memo., June 15, 1934; see also Nr. 7, pp. 10 and 14.

94. *Survey of International Affairs, 1934*, p. 185.

95. *Parl. Debates . . . Commons*, vol. 311, col. 117, March 11, 1935.

96. Wathen, Sister, M.A., *The Policy of England and France . . .* (1954), p. 69. Also Wilson to C. Hull, Geneva, Sept. 4, 1935, 765.84/1036, Ms. Deptmt of State.

97. Quoted by Wathen, *op. cit.*, p. 171.

Chapter 8

1. *G.D.*, C, IV, Hassell, Rome, Jan. 7, 1936, pp. 974–75f.

2. *G.D.*, 6114/454477, Hassell's Memo., Jan. 20, 1936; about Hassell and Italian diplomacy, see E. v. Rintelen, *Mussolini als Bundesgenosse* (1951), pp. 10–11, 29. About the vacillations of Mussolini and of Ciano,

see F. Anfuso, *Rome-Berlin im Diplomatischen Spiegel*, espec. pp. 43 and 59–61. The author considered Ciano the "most friendly toward Germany among us [at Palazzo Chigi]."

3. Kerekes, L. *A Berlin-Róma Tengely* . . . (Budapest, 1962), Nr. 8, Jan. 18, 1936.

4. *Ibid.*, Hungarian Ambassador, Vienna, Nr. 13, Jan. 22, 1936.

5. *Ibid.*, Hungarian Ambassador, Berlin, Nr. 45, Feb. 21, 1936.

6. *Hochverratsprozess*, Schuschnigg as witness, p. 432; see also p. 168.

7. GDFP, C, V, Nr. 304, May 4, 1936, p. 499.

8. *Ibid.*; also Jedlicka, "Ein österr. Militardiplomat . . . Liebitzky," in *Vom alten zum neuen Österreich* (St. Pölten, 1975).

9. see 8. Jedlicka.

10. Zernatto, Guido, *Die Wahrheit über Österreich* (N.Y., 1938), p. 156.

11. Starhemberg, *Memoiren*, p. 222.

12. Papen's report, Feb. 12, 1936; *Hochverratssprozess* . . . , pp. 401–03; G.D. 6114/E54690, Köpke to Hassell, April 6, 1936.

13. Starhemberg, *Between Hitler and Mussolini* (London, 1942), pp. 226f; G.D. 6114/E454690, Renthe-Fink's Memo., May 6, 1936.

14. *Survey of International Affairs, 1936*, p. 430.

15. G.D., 1744/402749-750, Mussolini to Hassell, Circular of German Foreign Ministry, May 26, 1936.

16. G.D., 1744/402744-748, Papen to Hitler, May 29, 1936.

17. Anfuso F., *Die beiden Gefreiten*, 1952, p. 21.

18. *Hochverratsprozess* . . . , p. 432, Also G.D., 1744/402761, Hassell's report, June 6, 1936.

19. *Ciano's Papers*, Mussolini to Frank, Ciano's Minute, Sept. 23, 1936, p. 45; *Hochverratsprozess*, Schuschnigg's testimony, p. 432.

20. Gilbert, "Ciano and his Ambassadors," in Craig and Gilbert, *The Diplomats*, p. 514.

21. G.D., Ser. D, I, Nr. 152, *pp. 277–82*.

22. G.D., 1486/368470, June 4, 1936.

23. *Ciano's Papers*, June 29, 1936, p. 8.

24. Cited by Gulick, Chs., *Austria from Habsburg to Hitler*, II, 1723.

25. Fuchs, M. *Showdown in Vienna* (N.Y., 1939), pp. 277–82; Agreement July 1936 in G.D., Ser. D, I, Nr. 152.

26. *Gazetta del Popolo*, re 1936 Agreement, G.D., D, I, 762.63/325, p. 8.

27. *Ibid., Tribunal*, p. 9.

28. Gayda V. in *Neues Wiener Tagblatt*, Aug. 25, 1936.

29. *Izvestiia*, Nov. 15, 1936.

30. Kerekes, A. Berlin-Róma Tengely . . . Oct. 11, 1936, Nr. 158.

31. *Ibid.*, No. 161, Oct. 24, 1936.

32. *Ibid.*, Nr. 45, Feb. 21, 1936; About the Hitler-Mussolini relationship and National Socialist and Italian Fascist policies toward Austria respectively, see Wiskemann, Elizabeth, *The Rome-Berlin Axis* (1949), p. 48. Hitler is for her the hunter equipped with an almost demonic consequence and persistence and Mussolini his, though not innocent, but still unsuspecting victim (pp. xviii-xix). While preserving his sentimental enthusiasm for the genius of Mussolini, the Führer pursued the expulsion of Italy from the Danubian basin into the Mediterranean. About Mussolini's ideology and foreign policy, see also Petersen, Jens, *Die Entstehung der Achse Berlin-Rome 1933–36* (1973), pp. 188f., 206, 272–82.

33. Kerekes, *op. cit.*, Nr. 156, Sept. 26, 1936.

34. *Ibid.*, Nr. 170, Oct. 30, 1936.

35. *Ibid.*, No. 172, Oct. 31, 1936.

36. *Ibid.*, No. 203, Feb. 22, 1937.

37. *Ibid.*, No. 210, Feb. 27, 1937.

38. *Ibid.*, 218, March 15, 1937.

39. *Ibid.*, No. 342, Jan. 19, 1938, also No. 357, Feb. 15, 1938.

40. *Ibid.*, No. 382, Feb. 26, 1938.

41. *Ibid.*, No. 258, May 5, 1937.

42. *Ibid.*, No. 260, May 28, 1937.

43. *Ibid.*, No. 245, Apr. 30, 1937.

44. *Ibid.*, No. 242, Apr. 28, 1937.

45. *Ibid.*, No. 250, May 10, 1937.

46. *Ibid.*, No. 220, March 15, 1937.

47. *Ibid.*, No. 223, March 20, 1937 (*Izvestiia*).

48. *Ibid.*, No. 227, Apr. 2, 1937.

Chapter 9

1. *Public Records (P.R.)* London, South. Deptmt, *F.O.*, St. Clair O'Malley, Dec. 1, 1935 Memo on Collective Security, W 5075/79/98.

2. *Ibid.*; see also Colvin, J. *Vansittart* (1965), p. 54 and p. 84.

3. *P.R.*, W. Strang, C 585/4/18, FO. Min. Strang, Jan. 31, 1936.

4. *F.O.* 795/125/67, Min. Sargent, Feb. 11, 1936.

5. *F.O.*, C 585/4/18, Min. Carr, Jan. 30, 1936.

6. *F.O.* 795/125/67, Min. Sargent, Feb. 11, 1936.

7. Britain strongly supported Austro-Czech negotiations (Eden to Selby, Jan. 29, 1936)R 127/27/3.

8. *Ibid.*

9. *F.O.*, N 5005/20/38, Min. Lebouchere, Oct. 14, 1936.

10. *F.O.*, C 583/4/18, Mem. Vansittart, Feb. 3, 1936.

11. *F.O.*, Memo O'Malley, Feb. 24, 1936. See also CAB G(36)6; R 3919/1167/67.

12. *F.O.*, C 1906/4/17, Min. Sargent and Eden, March 18, 1936.

13. *F.O.*, C1716/4/18, Cranborne Memo., March 10, 1936.

14. *F.O.*, W 16767/79/78, Cranborne Memo.

15. *London Observer*, Apr. 4, 1936, pp. 2–3.

16. Austen Chamberlain, while in Vienna, observed that British opinion, while placid toward the occupation of the Rhineland, was incensed against Italy.

17. *F.O.*, C 2827/4/18, Sargent, Apr. 10, 1936.

18. *F.O.*, R 2799/73/3 Memo. O'Malley, May 7, 1936.

19. *F.O.*, Sargent, 2799/73/3, May 12, 1936. Wigram, May 12, 1936.

20. *Ibid.*

21. *Ibid.;* see also 2730/1884/3. Eden, May 8, 1936.

22. *F.O.*, C 330/4/18, Cabinet Conclusions 3(36), Apr. 29, 1936.

23. Middlemas K., *The Strategy of Appeasement*, 1972, p. 73, quoted by R. Wagnleitner, "Die britische Österreichpolitik, 1936," p. 68 in Jedlicka & Neck eds., *Das Juliabkommen von 1936.*, 1977, pp. 53ff.

24. *F.O.*, W 4508/79/98, Memo Cadigan, May 1936.

25. *F.O.*, R 3731/1167, War Office Paper, June 20, 1936.

26. *Ibid.*, War Office to Sargent, July 10, 1936.

27. *F.O.*, R 3919/1167/67, Wigram, June 24, 1936.

28. *F.O.*, R 3752/294/67, Eden, June 26, 1936.

29. *F.O.*, C 2737/4/18, Sargent, Apr. 18, 1936.

30. *F.O.*, R 4956/73/3, O'Malley, The Austro-German Agreement, July 14, 1936.

31. *F.O.*, R 4171/73/3, Vansittart, July 13, 1936; R 4956/73/3 O'Malley; The Austro-German Agreement, July 14, 1936.

32. *F.O.*, O'Malley (ibid).

33. *F.O.*, R 4204/73/3, Selby, July 13, 1936.

34. *Parl. Debates. H. of Lords*, vol. 315, Cranborne, July 31, 1936.

35. *F.O.*, R 7096/73/6, O'Malley, Nov. 26, 1936.

36. *F.O.*, 800/292, Wigram, "The European Situation," Oct. 1936, and R4255/126/67. Sargent and question by deputy Vyvyan Adams.

37. *F.O.*, W 9513/79/98. Min. Sir Th. Inskip, mem. Aug. 24, 1936, F.P. (36), 13.

38. *F.O.*, 800/1936/394, Ge/36, 4, Vansittart to Swinton, Sept. 22, 1936.

39. *Parl. Debates, H. of Commons*, vol. 318, Eden, Dec. 2, 1936, cols. 1229f. and R7312/1167/67, FO Memo: Prospects of Italo-German Cooperation in Central and Southeastern Europe, W.R.C. Green, Dec. 3, 1936.

40. *F.O.*, 800/394.Ge/36/6, Chatfield to Vansittart, Dec. 29, 1936.

41. *F.O.*, see Nr. 39 (Dec. 3), Eden, Dec. 16, 1936.

42. *F.O.*, W 18355/18335/50. Memo Vansittart, The World Situation and British Rearmament, Dec. 16, 1936.

43. *F.O.*, 800/268/5. Memo on British Foreign Policy towards Germany, May 10, 1937. Its author, according to Middleman, *Strategy of Appeasement*, was N. Henderson, p. 73f.

44. *Ibid.*, Memo.

45. Despite Mussolini's assurances ever since January 1936, Hitler was more concerned about Fascist Italy's reaction to the Anschluss than that of the Western statesmen, English and French. See chap. 9 of G. Weinberg's *The Foreign Policy of Hitler's Germany. Starting World War II, 1937–1939* (1980). This chapter is one of the most analytical treatments of Hitler's Austrian policy, though focussing on Nazi foreign policy in general. About J. Petersen, *Die Entstehung der Achse . . .* (1973), see Nr. 32, ch. 8. Eichstädt, *Von Dollfuss zu Hitler* (1955), is dated and *grossdeutsch*-oriented. Many other German discussions on the Anschluss are limited to a few pages.

46. Gilbert M. and R. Gott, *The Appeasers*, 1963, p. 32; see also for the following.

47. Owen, Frank, *Lloyd George*, Sept. 27, 1937, p. 737.

48. Angell, Norman, *The Defense of the Empire*, pp. 183–84, quoted by Gilbert and Gott, *op. cit.*, p. 34.

49. Quoted by Gilbert and Gott, *op. cit.*, p. 38. Lothian Papers, Scottish Record Office, Edinburgh, Note of an interview with Hitler, Dec. 14, 1934, Appendix III, pp. 330–37.

50. Quoted *ibid.*, Nr. 39, Interview, Appendix 3(b), pp. 337–45.

51. *Ibid.*, p. 46.

52. Jones, Thomas, *Diary with Letters*, May 23, 1936, p. 208.

53. Gilbert and Gott, *op. cit.*, p. 48.

54. *Dictionary of National Biography, 1941–50*, Orme Sargent "Nevile Henderson," (Oxford Univ. Press, 1959). pp. 376–78.

55. *Ambass. Dodd's Diary 1933–1938*, eds. Dodd, Jr., W.E. and M. Dodd (N.Y. 1941), pp. 421–22.-Sir Walford Selby, *Diplomatic Twilight 1930–1940* former Ambassador to Vienna, was sharply critical of Henderson, speaking of his "betrayal of Austria" and his "disastrous views about Germany." So was even Foreign Minister Viscount Edward Halifax, especially of his March activities. Selby's successor in Vienna, Sir Palairet (*DBFP*, Third Ser. I, 1938, Nr. 14) records Henderson's sharply critical judgment of Schuschnigg's plebiscite move as a "definite defiance" of Hitler and as "precipitous and unwise." On Henderson's "illusions" about Hitler's foreign policy, see also *DDF*, VIII, Nr. 88, March 16, 1938, pp. 59–60).

56. McLeod, I. *Life of N.G. Chamberlain* (London, 1961), p. 206. W. Churchill spoke of Chamberlain's "limited outlook" (*The Gathering Storm*, p. 255) and the historian A.L. Rowse, *All Souls and Appeasement* (London, 1961), p. 63, did not forgive the Premier that he "knew no history."

57. Churchill, *op. cit.*, p. 243.

58. McLeod, I. *op. cit.*, p. 207.

59. Quoted in full by Feiling, *Chamberlain*, p. 208, Nov. 26, 1937.

60. Mowat, C.L. *Britain between Two Wars 1918–1940*, 1955, p. 591.

61. *N.P.A.*, K 66, p. 333v.

62. *DGFP*, D, I, Nr. 31, Memo. Conversation with Hitler, Nov. 19, 1937, pp. 55–67, espec. p. 62.

63. *F.R.U.S.*, 1937, I, General, Bullitt to Hull, Dec. 4, 1937. 740.00/ 239 (Washington, 1954), pp. 186f.

64. *DGFP*, D, I, Lord Londonderry to Major Gall, Dec. 6, 1937, pp. 183–84.

65. Feiling, *op. cit.*, p. 333.

66. Colvin, I. *Vansittart* . . . , p. 168.; see also A. Orde, "Grossbritannien und die Selbständigkeit Österreichs 1918–1938," *Vierteljahshefte für Zeitgeschichte*, 28. Jhrgg, 1980, 2. Heft, April, pp. 224–47. When Austrian independence was lost, British public opinion, in Orde's view, was "paradoxically" more than ever convinced that Austrian independence was the right and necessary solution (247).

67. *F.R.U.S.*, 1937, I, General, p. 122.

68. *Ibid.*, Bullitt to Washington, Feb. 20, 1937, p. 52.

69. *Ibid.*, Apr. 22, 1937, pp. 77f.

70. *Ibid.*, Apr. 30, 1937, pp. 84f.

71. *Ibid.*, May 6, 1937, p. 89.

72. *Ibid.*, p. 90.

73. *Ibid.*, p. 91.

74. *Ibid.*, pp. 91f.

75. *Ibid.*, Bullitt to Secret. of State, Dec. 1, 1937, p. 182.

76. *Ibid.*, Biddle, Warsaw, to Hull, Dec. 8, 1937, p. 190.

77. *Ibid.*, Bullitt to Secret. of State, Dec. 4, 1937, p. 188.

78. *Ibid.*

79. *F.R.U.S.*, 1938, I, Bullitt, Jan. 4, 1938, p. 1.

80. *Ibid.*, Jan. 4, 1938, pp. 2f.

81. *N.P.A.*, K 66, pp. 28v and r.

82. *G.D.*, D, I, Nr. 24, Ribbentrop to For. Min. Nov. 15, 1937.

83. Chamberlain's letter to his sister, March 30, 1937 in Feiling, *op. cit.*

84. *N.P.A.*, K 66, p. 300v, Garvin in *The Observer*; series of articles beginning Nov. 22, 1937.

85. *N.P.A.*, K 66, pp. 301–02, Nov. 22, 1937.

86. *Ibid.*, pp. 302v and r.

87. *Ibid.*, pp. 303.

88. *Ibid.*, pp. 336v and r, Nov. 25, 1937.

Chapter 10

1. A.D. Low, *The Anschluss Movement.* . . . (1974), pp. 366f.
2. *Izvestiia*, Feb. 29, 1932; see also *N.P.A.*, K 55, pp. 201f.
3. *Izvestiia*, March 27, 1932.
4. *N.P.A.*, K 55, pp. 222f., envoy's report, March 29, 1932.
5. *Ibid.*, p. 530.
6. *Ibid.*, K 56, pp. 34–35.
7. *Ibid.*, p. 55.
8. *N.P.A.*, K 56, envoy's report, June 27, 1935, pp. 256–58.
9. *N.P.A.*, K 56, pp. 256–62, and 265, June 27, 1935.
10. *Ibid.*, p. 327, "Stimmen der Sowjetpresse" (June 1935).
11. *Ibid.*, pp. 365–67; see also *Izvestiia*, Jan. 27, 1936.
12. *Pravda*, Jan. 15, 1936; also *N.P.A.*, K 56, pp. 360–63.
13. *N.P.A.*, p. 416, Apr. 21, 1936.
14. *Pravda*, July 14, 1936; *N.P.A.*, K 56, pp. 486f.
15. *N.P.A.*, p. 487.
16. *Ibid.*, pp. 583f; *Izvestiia*, Nov. 16, 1936.
17. *N.P.A.*, K 56, pp. 693–96, International Overview, March 20, 1937; *Izvestiia*, March 20, 1937.
18. *N.P.A.*, K 56, p. 803, Sept. 1, 1937.
19. Fischer, E. *Das Ende einer Illusion*, pp. 61–62.
20. Fischer, E. *An Opposing Man*, p. 291.
21. See 19., p. 59.
22. *N.P.A.*, K 56, pp. 718–21, Apr. 30, 1937.
23. See chap. III of this study.
24. *Die Kommunisten im Kampf* . . . (Vienna, 1955), pp. 14–16.
25. *Ibid.*, pp. 17–20.
26. *Ibid.*, pp. 22–23.
27. *Ibid.*, p. 27. See also Alfred Klahr, "Zur nationalen Frage in Österreich," *Weg und Ziel*, March 1937 and April 1937 (reprinted in *Die Kommunisten im Kampf.* . . . , pp. 26–39.
28. *Ibid.*, pp. 28–29; also Klahr "Die nationale Frage . . ." in *Communist International*, Oct. 1937.
29. Klahr, "Zur Diskussion uber die Annexion," *Weg und Ziel*, Aug. 1938, in *Die Kommunisten* . . . , pp. 93–98.
30. *Ibid.*
31. F. Valentin, "Gibt es eine österreichische Nation?" *Der sozialistische Kampf*, Paris, Nrs. 9 and 10; Valentin, "Der faschistische Frieden und die europäische Revolution, *ibid.*, 1938, Nr. 11; and Klahr's rejoinder in *Weg und Ziel*, Jan. 1939 (reprinted in *Die Kommunisten* . . . , p. 109).
32. *Izvestiia*, Feb. 17, 1938; A.J., "A First Step on the Road to the Anschluss," in *N.P.A.*, K 56, pp. 914–18.

33. *Pravda*, Feb. 17, 1938; A.J. "A First Step . . . ," pp. 919–22.

34. F. Denegel, "The Seizure of Austria and the Masses of the People in Germany," *Communist International*, Apr. 1938, pp. 343–47.

35. *L'Humanité*, March 13, 1938; *Communist International*, Apr. 1938, p. 405.

36. *Ibid.*, p. 406.

37. *Ibid.*, April 1938, p. 405.

38. *Ibid.*, June 1938, p. 542, see also another article by Fischer, pp. 847–59.

Chapter 11

1. Pratt, J.W., *Cordell Hull, 1933–1944*, N.Y. 1964, pp. 572–78.

2. Langer, W.L. and S.E. Gleason, *The Challenge to Isolation, 1937–1944*. (N.Y., 1952), pp. 12–15 and 18–39.

3. A. Hitler, *Mein Kampf* (1943, 1971), p. 5.

4. *N.A.* G.B. Stockton, Vienna, May 13, 1933, 762.63/101, p. 13.

5. Dallek, R. *Democrat and Diplomat. The Life of William E. Dodd* (N.Y., 1968), pp. 190–96.

6. *N.A.*, Dodd to State D., 762.63/115, pp. 2–3.

7. Dodd, Jr. W.R. and Martha Dodd, eds. *Ambassador Dodd's Diary 1933–1938*, with Introduction by Chs. A. Beard, pp. 4–6.

8. Dallek, *op. cit.*, pp. 199–200.

9. *N.A.*, 762.63/95, Dodd, Aug. 12, 1933.

10. *N.A.*, 862.00/3097, 1/2, State D. Mss., Dept. 29, 1933, also *Ambass. Dodd's Diary*, p. 90.

11. *Peace and War. U.S. Foreign Policy, 1931–41* (Wash., 1943), pp. 194–99.

12. Quoted from Phillips MS Diary, Harvard Un. Libr., by Dallek, *op. cit.*, p. 217.

13. *Ibid.*, p. 218.

14. *N.A.*, FDR Libr., Hyde Park, N.Y., P.S.F., Dodd to FDR, Dec. 28, 1933; see *German Documents Series*, C, II, 556–57, letters of von Neurath and Dieckhoff, March 5, 1934.

15. *Ambass. Dodd's Diary*, pp. 88–90.

16. Weinberg, G. "Hitler's Image of the U.S.," *Amer. Histor. Review*, LXIX, July 1964, pp. 1010–11.

17. Dallek, *op. cit.*, p. 229.

18. *Ibid.*, p. 233; see also *N.A.*, Hyde Park, P.P.F. 1043, Dodd to FDR, Aug. 15, 1934.

19. Alford R., *Calendar of G.S. Messersmith's Papers*, Un. of Delaware Libr. vol. I, Introduction.

20. *Ibid.*

21. *N.A.*, Dodd to Hull, June 2, 1934, 762.63/168, pp. 2–5.
22. *Ibid.*, Dodd to State D. June 2, 1934, 762.63/202, and June 29, 762.63/220, pp. 2–3.
23. *N.A.*, Dodd to State D., July 30, 863.00/100.
24. *Ibid.*, Chs. M. Hathaway, Aug. 1, 1934, 863.00/1013; also report of July 25, 1934; see also Dodd to State D., 762.63/370.
25. *Ibid.*, Messersmith to State D., 863.00/1078, pp. 2–4.
26. *Ibid.*, Messersmith to Phillips, Aug. 17, 1934, pp. 1–2.
27. *Ibid.*, p. 4.
28. *Ibid.*, Messersmith to Phillips, Sept. 19, 1934, 863.00/1103, pp. 2–3.
29. *Ibid.*, Dodd to State D., 762.63/244, pp. 7–8.
30. *Ibid.*, Dodd to State D., 762.63/370, pp. 2–3; also Messersmith to Phillips. Aug. 17, 1934, 863.00/1080, p. 4.
31. *Ibid.*, Messersmith to Hull, Dec. 20, 1934, 863.00/1126, pp. 6–7.
32. *Ibid.*, Messersmith to State D., 863.00/1131, p. 5.
33. *Ibid.*, Messersmith to State D., 863.00/1149, p. 16.
34. *Ibid.*, Messersmith to State D., 863.00.1167.
35. *Ibid.*, Messersmith to State D., Jan. 21, 1935, 863.00/1165; see also Messersmith, 863.00/1168, pp. 6–7.
36. *Ibid.*, Messersmith to State D., 863.00/1168, p. 7.
37. *Ibid.*, Messersmith to State, Feb. 8, 1935, 863.00/1126.
38. *Ibid.*, Hyde Park, P.S.F., Dodd to State D., Sept. 24, 1934.
39. *Ibid.*, FDR Libr., Hyde Park, FDR to Dodd, Apr. 16, 1935, PSF Diplom. box 45. and May 9, 1935.
40. *Ibid.*, box 6841, 863.01/261; also box 44, Hull to FDR, March 9, 1936 and March 25, 1936, 863.00/1263 and 863.00/1264.
41. *N.A.*, Messersmith, 863.01/279, pp. 2–4; see also Messersmith, 863.01/265, p. 4.
42. *Ibid.*, Messersmith, Apr. 8, 1936, 863.01/279 and 863.01/280.
43. *Ambass. Dodd's Diary*, pp. 413, 420–22.
44. Pratt, *op. cit.*, p. 273.
45. *Ibid.*
46. *N.A.*, Carr, Prague, to State D., Dec. 29, 1937, 863.00/1367; see also 762.63/411.
47. *Ibid.*, Wiley to State D., Jan. 15, 1938, Hyde Park, Wiley Papers, box 2 Diplom. Files; Austria 7, 1937–38, p. 4.
48. *F.R.U.S.*, 1938, vol. I, General, Gilbert, Berlin, to Hull, Jan. 18, 863.01/566; see also 863.01/569.
49. *N.A.*, Wiley, Jan. 27, 863.00/1368, and Wiley Papers, box 2, Austria 7, 1937–38, p. 4.
50. *Ibid.*, Wiley to Hull, Feb. 14, 762.63/427, pp. 391–92.

51. *Ibid.*, Wiley Papers, Hyde Park, to Moffat, Feb. 21, box 2, pp. 1–5.

52. *Ibid.*, Wiley to Bullitt, Feb. 17.

53. *Ibid.*, P.S.F., Feb. 18, 762.63/478; Secretary Hull himself did not deny that dispatches had long forecast the "annexation of Austria" and "also forecast that the European powers, though protesting, would do nothing to prevent it" (*The Memoirs of C. Hull*, 1948, I, 575).

54. *The Secret Diary of Harold Ickes*, Feb. 19, p. 321.

55. *Ibid.*

56. *Ibid.*, Feb. 19, p. 321; March 8, p. 333.

57. *N.Y. Times*, Feb. 22, 1938, 15:8; see also Feb. 23, 19:4.

58. *F.R.*, 1938, vol. I, General, Wiley to Secret. of State, Feb. 23, 1938, 762.63/464, p. 406.

59. *N.A.*, Hyde Park, PSF Diplom., Box 45, Wilson to State D., March 12.

60. *F.R.*, vol. I, General, Memorandum of Conversation by Secret. of State, March 12, 862.00/1494.

61. *F.R.*, Wiley, March 13, 863.00/1427, p. 433.

62. *Ibid.*, Memorandum of Conversation by Under-Secretary of State, Sumner Welles, March 14, pp. 442–45, 863.00/1436½.

63. *Memoirs of C. Hull*, 1948, p. 577; see FDR's praise of Hull's address, p. 57.

64. *F.R.*, 1938, Messersmith to Riley, March 16, 124.63/97a,-pp. 451–53.

65. *Memoirs of C. Hull*, p. 575.

66. *N.A.*, Phillips, Rome, to Hull, 863.00/1735, Apr. 8, 1938.

67. *Ibid.*, 863.00/1793, Apr. 1, 1938.

68. *Ibid.*, Wilson to Secret. of State, March 23, 863.00/1628, pp. 462–64.

69. *Ibid.*, Hyde Park, PSF, Secretary's File, Memorandum, box 45, Conversation with Göring, Apr. 29, 1938.

Chapter 12

1. For a fuller treatment of Czechoslovakia's policy toward Austria and the Anschluss, see Low, "Edvard Beneš, the Anschluss Movement 1918–38 and the Policy of Czechoslovakia," *East Central Europe* 10, pts 1 and 2 (1983), pp. 46–92, and for literature and sources, p. 53; also *N.P.A.* (Vienna), K 63, p. 358, *Morning Post*, Great Britain, March 1, 1934.

2. *N.P.A.*, K 63, Prague Embassy to Dollfuss, March 22, 1934, "Das jungste Exposé Dr. Beneš's über die Lösung d.österr. Frage," pp. 452v–457v.

3. *D.D.F.*, II, Nr. 72, Jan. 16, 1936.

4. *N.A.*, Washington, D.C., box 6840, 863.00/1239, p. 7.

5. *Ibid.*, box 6840, 863.00/1168, p. 5, and 863.00/1169, March 7, 1935, "Die Tschechoslowakei und die Anschlussfrage."

6. *D.D.F.*, 2e sér. III, Puaux, Vienna, to Delbos, Nov. 16, 1936, No. 492, pp. 774–75; see also G. Puaux, *Mort et transfiguration de l'Autriche 1933–1955*, Paris, Plon, 1966.

7. Beneš, *Memoirs*, p. 27.

7b. *Ibid.*, pp. 30–32.

8. About Yugoslavia's opposition to both Anschluss and Habsburg Restoration, but greater fear of the latter, see G. Reichert, *Das Scheitern der kleinen Entente* (1971), pp. 80–83; also *DDF*, Nr. 142, Aug. 25, 1933, pp. 244–45, and the Austrian Ambassador's report from Belgrade that Stojadinovič preferred the Anschluss, in Jedlicka, L. "Vorgeschichte des 13. März," *Zeitbilder*, p. 382.

9. Quoted by Reichert, *op. cit.*, p. 82; also *DDF*, Aug. 25, 1933, Nr. 142, pp. 244–45.

10. *DDF*, le sér., V, Nr. 481, March 9, 1934, p. 911.

11. Ciano, *Diary*, late Dec. 1937.

11b. Beck, *Final Report*, p. 117.

12. But the Yugoslav army was concerned about Germany's new proximity, Kerekes, *op. cit.*, Nr. 424, March 16, 1938.

13. *Ibid.*, Nr. 425, March 16; also *DGFP*, D, I, Nr. 363, Jansa, Chargé in Belgrade to Berlin, pp. 583–4, and Nr. 351.

14. *Ibid.*

15. *Ibid.*

16. *Ibid.*; Eichstädt, *Von Dollfuss zu Hitler* (1955), pp. 255f.

17. Dr. Andjelinovic's speech in Senate, Belgrade, March 17.

18. Kerekes, *op. cit.*, Nr. 419.

19. *N.A.*, 762.63/502, box 4348, Yr. G. 59, State Decimal File 1930–39 - About Belgrade's anxieties regarding Germany's irredentist endeavours in Yugoslavia, see Ciano's *Diplomatic Papers* (London, 1948), Apr. 15, 1938, pp. 200–01.

20. *F.R.U.S.*, Hibbard, Bukharest to State D. Feb. 1938.

21. *DDF*, V, Feb. 1, 1934, Nr. 308., pp. 593–95.

22. *Ibid.*, Nov. 29, 1933, Nr. 62, pp. 127–28.

23. *Ibid.*, p. 128.

24. Beck, J., *Final Account*, Jan. 14, 1933, p. 140.

25. *Ibid.*, p. 141.

26. *Ibid.*, pp. 144–45.

27. Bethlen, Stephen, "Hungary's Position after the Austrian Anschluss," *Hungarian Quarterly*, vol. 4, 1938, pp. 201–210.

28. Starhemberg, *Memoiren*, pp. 175–81.

29. see 27.

30. Zimmermann, Horst, *Schweiz und Österreich während der Zwischen-kriegszeit*, p. 424; see thereafter p. 60, 192. See also Hans Oehler, "Switzerland and the Anschluss Question," in Kleinwaechter and Paller, *Die Anschlussfrage in ihrer kulturellen. . . . Bedeutung*, 1930.

31. *Journal de Génève*, Feb. 20, 1938, p. 1.

32. *Ibid.*, March 13, 1938, p. 1.

33. *Neue Zürcher Zeitung*, March 13 and 15, 1938.

34. Kerekes, *op. cit.*, Nr. 444, March 22, 1938.

Chapter 13

1. Schuschnigg, *Im Kampf gegen Hitler* (Vienna, 1969), p. 219.

2. *Ibid.*, p. 231; see also about Seyss-Inquart, pp. 226–28.

3. *Hochverratsprozess. . . .*, see concluding speech by Guido Schmidt.

4. Schuschnigg, *op. cit.*, pp. 228–31 and pp. 406f.

5. *DGFP*, Nr. 284, Papen to Hitler, Feb. 4, 1938, p. 499.

6. *Ibid.*, Keppler to Ribbentrop, Feb. 7, 1938, Nr. 285, pp. 500–02; about Keppler see also Schuschnigg, *op. cit.*, p. 226.

7. Kerekes, *op. cit.*, Nr. 373, Feb. 21, 1938.

8. *N.A.*, Wiley Papers, Hyde Park, box 2.

9. Schuschnigg, *op. cit.*, p. 237.

10. *Ibid.*, pp. 226–28 and 238–240.

11. *Ibid.*, p. 243.

12. *F.R.U.S.*, vol. I, General, Carr, Amer. Min., Prague, to State D., Feb. 16, 1938, 762.63/436, p. 396.

13. See 8., Febr. 20, 1938.

14. *F.R.U.S.*, I, General, Wiley, Feb. 21, 1938, 762.00/165, p. 405.

15. *N.A.*, Hyde Park, Wiley Papers, Wiley, Vienna, to Bullitt, Feb. 17, 1938, box 2, pp. 1–2.

16. *Ibid.*

17. *Ibid.*, Wiley to Moffat, Feb. 21, box 2, pp. 1–2.

18. Circular telegram, Vienna, Feb. 15, 1938, to missions abroad, see 8.

19. Schuschnigg, *op. cit.*, pp. 262–64.

20. *DGFP* (or *G.D.*), German Embassy, Vienna, Feb. 18, Nr. 313, pp. 534–37.

21. *Ibid.*, German For. Min. telegram, Feb. 16, Nr. 302, pp. 522–23.

22. *Ibid.*, German Embassy, Paris, to German For. Min., Feb. 16, pp. 526–28.

23. *Ibid.*, Woerman, London, to Berlin, Feb. 17, pp. 525–26.

24. Schuschnigg, *op. cit.*, p. 238.

25. *DSIP*, Stein to Berlin, Feb. 17, Nr. 306, pp. 526–28.

26. *Ibid.*, Papen, Memorandum of Farewell Visit, Nr. 327, Feb. 26, pp. 547–48.

27. *Ibid.*, D, I, Nr. 328, Memo., pp. 548–49.

28. *F.R.U.S.*, Bullitt to Hull, Feb. 15, 1938, p. 394.

29. *Ibid.*, I, General, Bullitt to Secret. of St., Feb. 21, 1938, pp. 24–26.

30. *Ibid.*, p. 27.

31. *Ibid.*, pp. 28–29.

32. *Chambre des Députés*, Débats (microfilm), Feb. 25, 1938, card 22, p. 653.

33. *Ibid.*, Montigny, Feb. 25, p. 634.

34. *Ibid.*, Delbos, Feb. 25, p. 730.

35. *Ibid.*, Anatole de Monzie, p. 610.

36. *Ibid.*, Louis Marin, pp. 612f.

37. *Ibid.*, L. Deschizeaux, p. 615.

38. *Ibid.*, A. Albert, p. 618.

39. *Ibid.*, Péri, pp. 605–07.

40. A. Low, "The Anschluss Movement, 1933–38, and the Policy of France," *Jahrbuch für Deutsche Geschichte*, 1982, pp. 318f.

41. *Chambre, Débats* (see 32.) Montigny, pp. 634f.

42. *Ibid.*

43. *Ibid.*

44. *Ibid.*, Flandin, pp. 638–43.

45. *Ibid.*, Reynaud, p. 647.

46. *Ibid.*, Chautemps, p. 653.

47. *Ibid.*

48. *F.R.U.S.*, I, General, Carr, Prague, to Secret. of St., Nr. 93, p. 410.

49. *Ibid.*, Wilson, Paris, to State D., March 1, p. 29.

50. *Ibid.*, Wiley to State D., March 9, 1938, p. 415.

Chapter 14

1. *F.R.U.S.*, *1938*, I, Wiley to State D., Feb. 19, 1938.

2. Ciano, *Diary*, Feb. 11, p. 73.

3a. *Ibid.*, Nr. 389, March 2, 1938; Ciano, *Diary*, Feb. 11, pp. 73–75, and Feb. 17, p. 76.

3b. Kerekes, *op. cit.*, Nr. 362, Feb. 17, 1938.

4. *Ibid.*, Nr. 371, Feb. 20, 1938.

5. *Ibid.*, Nr. 381, Feb. 25.

6. *Ibid.*, Nr. 382, Feb. 26.

7. Ciano, *Diary*, Feb. 18, p. 77.

8. Ciano, *Diary*, Feb. 23, 1938.

9. *Ibid.*, Feb. 23 and 24.

10. *Ibid.*, Feb. 25.
11. *Ibid.*, March 5.
12. *Ibid.*, March 7.
13. *Ibid.*, March 11.
14. *Ibid.*
15. Beck, *Final Report*, p. 141.
16. *Ibid.* On the other hand, F. Anfuso, *Die beiden Gefreiten*, p. 59, asserts that Il Duce "until the very eve of the Anschluss," had not yet decided to abandon Austria.
17. *N.P.A.*, K 66, pp. 368v and 369r, English press about Budapest Conference, Austrian Embassy, London, Jan. 15, 1938.
18. *Ibid.*, pp. 394 v and r, conversation with Sargent; Kunz, A., Feb. 15, p. 120.
19. *Ibid.*
20. *Ibid.*, pp. 396v and r, Franckenstein, Feb. 17, pp. 396v–399.
21. *Ibid.*, p. 397v.
22. *Ibid.*, pp. 398 v and r.
23. *N.A.*, 762.63/433, Amer. Embassy, London, to Hull, Feb. 16, 1938.
24. *Parl. Debates, H. of Lords*, cols. 684–91, Feb. 16, 1938.
25. *Ibid.*, cols. 691–700.
26. *Ibid.*, col. 710; for the following cols. 714, 711, 766.
27. *Ibid.*, vol. 331, Eden, Feb. 18, (Commons), cols. 2211–12.
28. *The Diaries of Sir Alexander Cadogan, 1938–1945* (1971), p. 47; also pp. 82, 147.
29. *Ibid.*, pp. 83, 152.
30. *N.P.A.*, K 66, pp. 400r–402v, Feb. 23, 1938, Reaktion auf die österr. Vorgänge in England, Franckenstein's report.
31. *Ibid.*, p. 402r; also 400 v and r.
32. Chamberlain N., *In Search for Peace*, 1939, pp. 49–79; see also his *Diary*, Feb. 19–27, 1938, in McLeod, *Chamberlain*, pp. 211–17.
33. *The Memoirs of Anthony Eden. Earl of Avon. Facing the Dictators* (Boston, 1962), p. 682.
34. *Ciano's Papers*, p. 161, Ciano to Grandi, Feb. 16, 1938.
35. Quote by Chamberlain in McLeod, *op. cit.*, p. 223.
36. Colvin, *Vansittart in Office*, p. 188.
37. *Ibid.*
38. Chamberlain, *In Search*, , , pp. 75–76.
39. *Parl. Debates. H. of Commons*, Feb. 21, 1938, cols. 265–66; see also Churchill, *The Gathering Storm* (1948).
40. Churchill in *Parl. Debates* (see 39).
41. Colvin, *op. cit.*, pp. 194–95.
42. Lord Halifax, *Fullness of Days*, p. 2.
43. *DBFP*, Third Ser., I, March 10, 1938, p. 3.

44. *Ibid.*, March 13, p. 38.
45. *DGFP*, D, I, pp. 250–69, record of conversation between Secret. of St. in London and Ribbentrop, March 10, 1938.
46. *Ibid.*, pp. 272–73, March 11, Ribbentrop's memo.
47. *Ibid.*, March 10, p. 263.
48. *Ibid.*

Chapter 15

1. *DGFP*, D, I, Nr. 334, March 5, 1938, p. 557. - Next to *völkisch* and strategic considerations, economic motivation played of course a key role in pushing the Anschluss issue in 1937 and 1938 into the foreground. It was hardly an accident that both Göring and Keppler, greatly involved in the implementation of the last phase of the "Anschluss," had important economic functions in the *Third Reich*. Göring was entrusted by the Führer with the execution of the Four-Year Plan and Dr. Keppler had begun his career in the NSDAP as an economic adviser to Hitler. Both men had carefully assessed Austria's economic resources in various fields. Though official Nazi propaganda touted the advantages which the "Anschluss" would bring to Austria, leading *Third Reich* officials were well aware of the tangible benefits which Germany would draw from the inclusion of Austria into the *Third Reich*. Of recent historians Schausberger, N, *Der Griff nach Österreich* (1978), has focused on economics as the major motivation of the Anschluss, though he somewhat qualified it by speaking of "strategic-economic" considerations. In Hitler's thought, however, as expressed also in *Mein Kampf*, economics was clearly subordinated to völkisch-racial priorities.
2. *Ibid.*, p. 558.
3. *Ibid.*, Memo, March 3–6, 1938, Nr. 335, pp. 559–61.
4. Schuschnigg, *Im Kampf gegen Hitler* . . . (1969), p. 300.
5. *Ibid.*, p. 299.
6. *DGFP*, D, I, Ribbentrop to Henderson, March 4, 1938, Nr. 138 (also 139), pp. 240–50.
7. Schuschnigg, *op. cit.*, p. 301 and pp. 295–97.
8. *Ibid.*, p. 302.
9. *Ibid.*, pp. 304–06.
10a. *DGFP*, D, I, Seyss to Hitler, March 11, 1938, Nr. 358, p. 580; see also *DBFP*, Henderson to Halifax, March 11, p. 42.
10b. *Nazi Conspiracy* . . . p. 715, and p. 641.
11. *Ibid.*, Altenburg, Nr. 364, pp. 584–85.
12. *Ibid.*
13. Schuschnigg, *op. cit.*, p. 311.
14. *Ibid.*

15. *Ibid.*, p. 312.
16. Hitler speech of Apr. 9, 1938, quoted *ibid.*, p. 313.
17. *DGFP*, D, I, Hitler to Mussolini, Nr. 352, March 11, 1938, p. 574.
18a. *Ibid.*, p. 575.
18b. *Ibid.*
19. *DBFP*, Henderson to Halifax, March 12, Nr. 49, p. 25.
20. *Ibid.*, Nr. 25, March 11, 1938, Halifax to Palairet, p. 13.
21. *P.R.*, CAB 23/93, Session March 12, 1938.
22. *DBFP*, Third Ser., I, p. 32, Halifax to Phipps, tel, March 12, p. 32.
23. *Ibid.*, March 11, pp. 421f.
24. *Ibid.*, Wilson, Paris, to State D., March 14, pp. 35–37.
25. *Ibid.*, Tel. 863.00/1440, Wilson (Berlin) to Washington, March 12, p. 428.
26. *Ibid.*, D, I, Nr. 359, March 12, 1938, pp. 580–8.
27. *Ibid.*, Nr. 360, March 12, pp. 581–82.
28. *N.A.*, 863.00/1521, March 18, 1938.
29. *Ibid.*, 863.00/1556, Wilson, Berlin, March 18.
30. *Ibid.*, Telegraph (Amsterdam), 863.00/1556, pp. 4–5, March 12.
31. *N.A.*, Phillips, Rome, to State Deptmt, 86300/1509; actually, Mussolini may have known about it two days earlier, on March 7 (see his speech to the Chamber on March 16).
32. *DGFP*, D, I, Nr. 373, March 13, p. 591.
33. Italian Press Bureau, March 12, 1938.
34. *DGFP*, D, I, Nr. 352, March 11, pp. 573–76; also *ibid.*, Nr. 385, March 14, p. 600, and Nrs. 396 and 397.
35. Gayda, V, in *Giornale d'Italia*, March 14, 1938.
36. *Internat. Gerichtshof* (Amtl. Text, Nurnberg, 1946f.), IX, 336.
37. *N.A.*, Rome Embassy to State D., March 12, 1938, about conversation of Ciano with Lord Perth, p. 5.
38. Kerekes, *op. cit.*, Nr. 406, March 11.
39. *N.A.* 863.00/1601, enclos. Nr. 2 to dispatch Nr. 828, March 18, 1938.
40. *Ibid.*, enclosure Nr. 3.
41. Ciano, *Diary*, March 12, p. 87.
42. *Camera dei Deputati*, March 13, 1938.
43. *N.A.*, Phillips to State Deptmt, 863.00/1509. About the policy of appeasement and some of its main actors in Britain, such as Chamberlain, Halifax, N. Henderson, and Eden on the other side, see Middlemas, K. *The Strategy of Appeasement* (1972). Though he tries to defend Chamberlain's policy, he is not uncritical of it; he considers N. Henderson "an extremist," uninformed of the impending blow against Austria. (p. 74) About slight differences between Eden and Halifax in regard to Austria,

pp. 135–36. He points correctly to the ever widening gap between the public debate on foreign policy as conducted in the Commons and the Press and the Government's private plans (210). R. Wagnleitner, "Die britische Österreichpolitik 1936 . . . . . ." in *Das Juliabkommen von 1936*, eds. Jedlicka and Neck, 1977, pp. 53–83, apparently unaware that an anonymous Memorandum in the files of the Foreign Office in 1937, was the work of N. Henderson, goes too far in identifying his views with that of the Foreign and War Office (p. 80), but is correct in pointing out that British policy toward Austria found its basic formulation in 1936. The English historian Anne Orde, "Grossbritannien und die Selbständigkeit Österreichs 1918–1938," *Vierteljahrshefte für Zeitgeschichte* 28. Jhrgg, 1980, 2. Heft, April, pp. 224–247, points to the ambivalence of British thought on the Anschluss. Following rising fear of German expansionism after 1933, there occurred after the break with Italy and Germany's military growth an alienation of England from Central Europe. But the majority in the British isles became never confused by Nazi propaganda (247).

In regard to France's policy of appeasement, a fuller treatment is the study by Sr. M.A. Wathen, *The Policy of England and France toward the Anschluss of 1938* (1954); it is dated, however. While she does not focus on the anti-democratic policies of Dollfuss and of the *Heimwehr* (p. 37), her judgment on French and British policy is fair and realistic.

44. Ciano, *Diary*, March 13, 1938, p. 88.

Chapter 16

1. Feiling, *Chamberlain*, p. 321.
2. *Parl. Debates. H. of Lords*, vol. 108, March 29, cols. 451–52.
3. *Ibid.*, March 16, col. 140.
4. *Parl. Debates. H. of Commons*, March 14, 1938, vol. 333, cols. 145–46.
5. *Ibid.*, March 14, cols. 88–92.
6. *Ibid.*, Churchill, March 14, pp. 272–74.
7. *Ibid.*, cols. 95–99.
8. *DGFP*, D, I, p. 601, Woerman to the German For. Office, March 14, 1938.
9. *Ibid.*, Paper of For. Off. to For. Policy Committee, March 18, 1938.
10. Feiling, *Chamberlain*, pp. 347–48.
11. Churchill, *The Gathering Storm*, p. 275.
12.13. *Chambre des Députés* (microfilm), Reynaud, March 17, 1938, pp. 647f.
14. Kerekes, *op. cit.*, Nr. 416, March 13, 1938.
15. Ibid., Nr. 419, March 14, 1938.

16. *N.A.*, 863.00/1509, see also Nr. 412, March 12, and Nr. 446, March 28, 1938.

17. *Ibid.*, Nr. 422, March 15.

18. *Ibid.*, Nr. 433, March 18, 1938; also E.v. Rintelen, *Mussolini als Bundesgenosse*, p. 30.

19. *DDF*, 2e sér., VIII, Nr. 486, Blondel, chargé in Rome, to Paul-Boncour, March 17, 1938, pp. 902–04.

20. Kerekes, *op. cit.*, Nr. 433, March 18, 1938.

21. See speech in *F.R.U.S.* (Nr. 170), enclosure Nr. 3 to dispatch Nr. 538, March 18, Rome Embassy; see also comment of Phillips, March 16, 1938, *F.R.U.S.*, (Nr. 160), pp. 450–51; Plessen, Rome, to German For. Min., March 25, 1938, *DGFP*, D, I, 612–13.

22. *N.A.*, Vienna Embassy to State Deptmt, box 6842, 863.00/1603, pp. 2–8, n.d.

23. Kerekes, *op. cit.*, Nr. 440, March 20, 1938, Kanya, circular telegram.

24. *Ibid.*, Nr. 448, March 23.

25. *Ibid.*, Nr. 450, March 26.

26. *Ibid.*, Nr. 451, March 26. Hungarian representative at the League in Geneva to Budapest.

27. Ciano, *Diary*, Apr. 3, p. 96; also Apr. 20, p. 104 and Apr. 21, p. 105.

28. *Ibid.*, p. 105.

29. Weinberg, G. *Foreign Policy of Hitler's Germany . . . 1937–39*, pp. 286–87; see also pp. 304–05 and 308; F. Huter, ed. *Südtirol. Eine Frage des europ. Gewissens*, (Munich, 1963), pp. 321–28 and M. Toscano, *Questione dell Alto Adige*.

30. Ciano, *Diary*, Apr. 2, 1938, pp. 105–06.

31. *Ibid.*, Apr. 24, 1938, p. 106.

32. Kerekes, *op. cit.*, Nr. 438, March 19, 1938.

33.-34. *Ibid.*, Nr. 389, March 2.

35.-36. *Ibid.*, Nr. 399, March 7.

37. *Ibid.*, Nr. 412, 413, March 12.

38. *Ibid.*, Nr. 416, March 13; for the following Nrs. 418, 419, 420 and 421, March 14–15.

39. *Ibid.*, Nr. 429, March 17.

40. *Ibid.*, Nrs. 431 and 432, March 18.

41. *Ibid.*, Nr. 448, March 23.

42. *N.A.* Spaack 863.00/1600, pp. 4–5.

43. *Ibid.*, Hugh Gibson, to State D., 863.00/1600, n.d.

44. *F.D. Roosevelt and Foreign Affairs*, Secd. ser., IX, 193, Nr. 937.

45. *Ibid.*, Nr. 934, Dearing, Stockholm, to FDR, March 28.

46. *GDFP*, D, I, Nr. 402, pp. 621–22.

47. *Ibid.*, Köcher to Berlin, March 14, Nr. 382, pp. 598–99.

48. *Ibid.,* See 46.
49. *Ibid.,* Plessen, Rome, to Berlin, March 25, 1938, Nr. 399, pp. 612–13.
50. *Ibid.,* p. 164.
51. *Ibid.,* Noebel, Tokyo, to Berlin, March 15, 1938, Nr. 387, p. 602.

Chapter 17 (Conclusion)

1. For recent evaluations of Hitler's continental and global foreign policy from the perspective of German history and the necessarily minor role of Austria in this framework, see especially Hildebrand, Klaus, *Deutsche Aussenpolitik 1933–45* (Stuttgart, 1980).

———. *Vom Reich zum Weltreich* (Munich, 1969).

———. *The Foreign Policy of the Third Reich* (Transl. A. Forhergill, Berkeley, 1970), especially pp. 60–65.

———. *Das Dritte Reich* (2. Aufl., Munich, 1980) pp. 22, 30f., 168f.

Hillgruber, Andreas *Deutsche Rolle in der Vorgeschichte der beiden Weltkriege,* (Göttingen, 1967)

———. *Endlich genug über Nationalsozialismus und zweiten Weltkrieg?* (Düsseldorf, 1982).

For a more comprehensive treatment of Austria, see chapter 9 of Weinberg, Gerhard *The Foreign Policy of Hitler's Germany. Starting World War II, 1937–1939,* (Chicago, 1980)

2. *Chambre des Députés, Débats, 1919,* Barthou, Sept. 2, p. 4102.

Selected Bibliography

(For a more detailed bibliography see this author's annotated bibliography *"The Anschluss Movement 1918–1938 . . ."* (Garland Press, N.Y. 1984), in the following section A.)

Bibliographical References

Bibliographies, Enclyclopedias, and Historiographies

Der Anschluss [Vienna], I-VII (1927-August 1933).

Austrian Historical Bibliography, H. Baehm and Fritz Fellner, eds. (Santa Barbara: ABC Clio Press, 1965–   ).

Austrian History Yearbook. Various volumes.

Bibliographie zum deutsch-österreichischen Anschlussgedanken (second edition, Stuttgart: Weltkriegsbücherei, 1929).

F. Bridge, *The Habsburg Monarchy 1904–1918. Books and pamphlets published in the United Kingdom between 1918–1967* (London: University of London Press, 1967).

Dictionnaire biographique du mouvement ouvrier international, vol. I: Autriche, J. Bourdet, G. Haupt, F. Kreissler, and H. Steiner, eds. (Paris: Editions ouvrières, 1971).

Kenneth J. Dillon, *Scholar's Guide to Washington, D.C. for Central and East European Studies* (Washington, D.C.: Woodrow Wilson International Center for Scholars, Smithsonian Institute Press, 1980).

David H. Kraus and Anita Navon, eds., *The American Bibliography of Slavic and East European Studies of 1974* (Columbus, Ohio: The American Association for the Advancement of Slavic Studies, 1976).

Alfred D. Low, "The Anschluss Movement, 1918–1938. Recent Historical Writing: German Natinalism and Austrian Patriotism," *Canadian Review of Studies in Nationalism,* III (Spring, 1976), 212–25.

Alfred D. Low. "The Anschluss Movement." *Canadian Review of Studies in Nationalism Annotated Bibliography of Works on Nationalism; A Regional Selection,* IX (1982), 129–202.

———. "Selected Annotated Bibliography on the Anschluss Since 1970," *ibid.*, VIII (1981), 1–16.

———. *The Anschluss Movement 1918–1938: Background and Aftermath. An Annotated Bibliography in German and Austrian Nationalism.* New York: Garland Press, 1984.

Peter Malina and Gustav Spann, eds., *Bibliographie zur österreichischen Zeitgeschichte 1918–1978. Eine Auswahl* (Vienna: Verlag für Geschichte und Politik, 1978).

Österreichisches Dokumentationsarchiv, *Mitteilungen* (February 1977–).

Österreichisches Dokumentationsarchiv der Widerstandsbewegung (Vienna: Österreichisches Dokumentationsarchiv, 1963).

Wilmer H. Paine, Jr., "Austria Since 1918: A Bibliography:" (mimeographed; provided by author).

Herbert P. Rothfeder, comp., "Checklist of Selected German Pamphlets and Booklets of the Weimar and Nazi Period in the University of Michigan Library." Prepared under the direction of Gerhard L. Weinberg (Ann Arbor: University of Michigan Library, 1961).

Hans Schroth, *Bibliographie zur Geschichte der österreichischen Arbeiterbewegung. Archiv. Mitteilungsblatt des Vereins für Geschichte der Arbeiterbewegung.* (Vienna: Archiv. 1965–67).

Louis Leo Snyder, *Encyclopedia of the Third Reich* (New York: McGraw-Hill, 1976).

Wiener Library, *Books on Persecution, Terror and Resistance in Nazi-Germany* (London: Wiener Library, 1953).

Published Documents

Beiträge zur Vorgeschichte und Geschichte der Julirevolte (Contributions to the Pre-History and History of the July Revolt) (Vienna: Selbstverlag, Bundeskommissariat für Heimatdienst, 1934).

Les délibérations du Conseil des Quatre (24 mars–28 juin 1919). Notes de l'officier interprète Paul Mantoux (Paris: Editions du centre national de la récherche scientifique, 1955), 2 volumes.

Die deutsche Nationalversammlung im Jahre 1919 (The German National Assembly in 1919), Professor Heilfron, ed. (Berlin: Norddeutsche Verlagsanstalt, 1919), 8 volumes.

I documenti diplomatici italiani 1921–1935, Commissione per la publicazione dei documenti diplomatici, ed. (Rome: Libreria dello stato, 1952).

Documents diplomatiques français 1932–1939, Commission de publication des documents relatifs aux origines de la guerre, 1939–1946, ed. (Paris: Imprimeries Nationales, 1963), Series I, 8 volumes; Series II, 15 volumes.

Documents of British Foreign Policy, 1919–1939. E. L. Woodward and Rohan Butler, eds. (London: H. M. Stationery Office, 1946–1957), Series I,

22 volumes; Series Ia, 7 volumes; Series II, 19 volumes; Series III, 8 volumes.

Documents on German Foreign Policy, 1918–1945, from the Archives of the German Foreign Ministry, R. J. Sonntag, ed. (Washington, D.C.: U.S. Government Printing Office, 1949–1954), Series C, 2 volumes; Series D, 11 volumes.

Documents on International Affairs, 1928–1963, John W. Wheeler-Bennett and Stephen A. Heald, eds. (London: Oxford University Press, Royal Institute of International Affairs, 1929–   ), volumes 1931–38 used.

The Financial Reconstruction of Austria. General Survey and Principal Documents, Survey by Sir Arthur Salter (Geneva: n.p., November 1926).

Foreign Relations of the United States. Diplomatic Papers, 1861–   (Washington, D.C.: U.S. Government Printing Office, 1931–1938), volumes 1931–38.

The Trial of German Major War Criminals: Proceedings of the International Military Tribunal Sitting at Nuremberg, Germany, 20th November, 1945 to 1st October, 1946. Taken from the Official Transcript (London: H. M. Stationery Office, 1945–50), 42 volumes.

Great Britain. Parliament. House of Commons. The Parliamentary Debates (Hansard). Official Report, Feb. 1909–Nov. 1943 (London: H. M. Stationery Office, 1909–   ), 14 volumes.

Der Hochverratsprozess gegen Dr. Guido Schmidt vor dem Wiener Volksgerichtshof. Die gerichtlichen Protokolle mit den Zeugenaussagen, unveröffentlichten Dokumenten, sämtlichen Geheimbriefen und Geheimakten (The High Treason Trial against Dr. Guido Schmidt before the Vienna People's Court) (Vienna: Österreichische Staatsdruckerei, 1947).

International Military Tribunal. The Trial of German Major War Criminals by the International Military Tribunal Sitting at Nuremberg, Germany (Commencing 20th November, 1945) (London: H. M. Attorney General, by H. M. Stationery Office, 1946).

Journal officiel de la République Française. Débats parlementaires, Assemblée nationale (Paris: Assemblée nationale, n.d.).

Lajos Kerekes, *Allianz Hitler-Horthy-Mussolini. Dokumente zur ungarischen Aussenpolitik 1933–1944* (Alliance Hitler-Horthy-Mussolini. Documents on Hungarian Foreign policy 1933–1944) (Budapest: Akadémiai Kiadó, 1966).

League of Nations. Treaty Series, The Restoration of Austria. Protocol No. III (Declaration), signed at Geneva, October 4, 1922 (Geneva: Imprimeries Réunies, 1922), volume 12.

Nazi Conspiracy and Aggression. Office of United States Chief of Counsel for Prosecution of Axis Criminality (Washington, D.C.: J. S. Government Printing Office, 1946–1948), 10 volumes.

The Speeches of Adolf Hitler, 1922–1939, Norman H. Baynes, ed. (London: Oxford University Press, 1942), 2 volumes.

The Treaty of St. Germain. A Documentary History of Its Territorial and Political Clauses, Nina Almond, ed. (Stanford: Stanford University Press, 1935).

United States Department of State, *Records of the Department of State Relating to Internal Affairs of Austria-Hungary and Austria, 1910–1929* (Washington, D.C.: National Archives, National Archives and Records Services, General Services Administration, 1967–   ), 69 microfilm reels.

Memoirs and Diaries

(Most works which belong both to the category Memoirs and Secondary Works are listed under the latter category).

D'Abernon, Lord, *An Ambassador of Peace.* London: 1929.

Earl of Avon, *The Eden Memoirs: Facing the Dictators.* London: 1962.

Anfuso, Filippo, *Die beiden Gefreiten.* Munich: 1952.

————. *Rome-Berlin im diplomatischen Spiegel.* Transl. from Italian by E. Heymann, Munich Pohl & Co., 1951.

Beck, Jozef, *Final Report,* New York: R. Speller & Sons, Publishers, 1957.

Beneš, Edvard, *The Memoirs of Dr. E. Beneš. From Munich to New War and New Victory.* New York, Arno Press, 1972.

Braunthal, Julius, *Auf der Suche nach dem Millenium.* Transl. from English by F. Schulz, Munich: Nest Verlag, 1948, 2 vols.

Broucek, Peter, *Die Erinnerungen Edmund Glaises von Horstenau, Bd.1:K. und K. Generalstabsoffizier und Historiker.* Vienna: H. Böhlaus Nachf., 1980.

Ciano, Count Galeazzo, *Ciano's Diary, 1937–38.* London, 1952.

————. *Ciano's Diplomatic Papers,* Ed. M. Muggeridge. London: Odhams Press, 1948.

Deutsch, Julius, *Ein weiter Weg. Lebenserinnerungen.* Vienna: Amalthea, 1960.

Dodd, William, *Ambassador Dodd's Diary 1933–38.* New York: Harcourt, Brace & Co., 1941.

Hoover, Herbert, *The Great Depression.* London, 1953.

Langoth, Franz, *Kampf um Österreich.* Wels, 1951.

Lansing, Robert, *The Peace Negotiations.* London, 1921.

Magistrati, Massimo, *Il prologo del dramma, Berlino 1934–37,* Milano, U.N. & O. Mursia, 1971.

Manstein, Erich von, *Aus einem Soldatenleben 1887–1939.* Bonn: Athenaum, 1958.

Schmidt, Paul, *Als Statist auf der diplomatischen Bühne.* Bonn, 1949.
Stern-Rubarth, Edgar, *Drei Männer suchen Europa.* Munich, 1947.
Stresemann, Gustav, *Vermächtnis,* Berlin, 1932.
Tardieu, André, *La Paix,* Paris, 1921.
Templewood, Viscount, *Nine Troubled Years.*
Vansittart, Sir Robert, *The Mist Procession.* London, 1958.
Weizsäcker, Ernst von, *Memoirs.* London, 1951.

Secondary Literature

Allmayer-Beck, J. Chr. and Adam Wandruszka, Eds., *Spectrum Austriae.* Vienna: F. Molden, 1980.
Andics, H., *Der Staat den keiner wollte. Österreich 1918–1938,* Vienna: Herder, 1962.
Andreas, Willy, *Österreich und der Anschluss.* Berlin, Deutsche Verlagsanstalt, 1927.
Anschluss an Frankreich, Die politische und wirtschaftliche Auswirkung der Protokolle von Lausanne. Vienna: Wr. Neueste Nachrichten, 1932.
Ardelt, R.G., *Zwischen Demokratie und Faschismus, Das deutsche nationale Gedankengut in Österreich 1919–1930.* Vienna and Salzburg: Univ. of Salzburg, 1972.
Auerbach, B., *Le rattachement de l'Autriche à l'Allemagne.* Paris: Beyer-Levrault, 1927.
Avramov, K.P., *Eto ne povtoritsje, Iz istorii zachvata Avstrii gitlerovskoi Germanye b 1938 gody* (This must not repeat itself. From the History of Austria's Seizure by Hitler Germany in 1938). Moscow: Publication Society of Social and Economic Literature, 1961.
Barker, Elizabeth, *Austria 1918–1972.* London: MacMillan, 1973.
Barodin, Johannes and Kurt Schechner, *Für und wider die Donauföderation.* Vienna, 1928.
Bärnthaler, Irmgard, *Vaterländiche Front. Geschichte und Organisation.* Vienna: Europa Verlag, 1971.
Basch, Antonin, *The Danube Basin and the German Economic Sphere.* N.Y.: Columbia Univ., 1944 (1943).
Bauer, Otto, *Acht Monate auswärtiger Politik.* Vienna: Brand & Co., 1919.
―――. *Die österreichische Revolution.* Vienna: Wiener Volksbuchchhandlung, 1933 (also in English, London: L. Parsons, 1925).
―――. *Werkausgabe.* Vienna, 1975.
Beneš, Edvard, *The Austro-German Customs Union Project.* Prague: Orbis, 1931.
―――. *Munich,* Transl. from Czech by S. Pacejka. Prague: Svoboda, 1968 (Paris, Stock, 1969).

_____. *Das Problem Mitteleuropas und die Lösung der österreichischen Frage*. Prague: Orbis, 1934.

Bérenger, J., *La république autrichienne de 1919 à nos jours*, Preface by J. Dorz. Paris: Didier, 1971.

Bewley, Chs., *Hermann Göring and the Third Reich*. Toronto: The Devin-Adair Co., 1962.

Bibl. V., *Geschichte Österreichs im zwanzigesten Jahrhundert*. Vienna: Tag-blatt-bibl., n.d.

Birk, Bernhard, Dr. *Ignaz Seipel, Ein österreichisches und europäisches Schicksal*. Regensburg: G. J. Mainz, 1932.

Botz, Gerhard, *Wien vom Anschluss zum Krieg, Die national-sozialistische Machtübernahme und politisch-soziale Umgestaltung am Beispiel der Stadt Wien 1938–39*. Munich: Jugend und Volk, 1978.

Broucek, Peter. "Edmund Glaise-Horstenau und das Juliabkoomen von 1936" in *Das Juliabkommen von 1936*. Munich, R. Oldenbourg, 1977, pp. 119–135.

Busshoff, Heinrich, *Das Dollfussregime in Österreich in geistesgeschichticher Prespektive unter besonderer Berücksichtigung der 'Schöneren Zukunft' und der 'Reichspost.'* Beiträge zur polit. Wissenschaft, Bd. 6, Berlin: Duncker & Humblot, 1968.

Campbell, F. Gregory, *Confrontation in Central Europe, Weimar Germany and Czechoslovakia*. Chicago and London: Univ. of Chicago Press, 1975.

Carsten, Francis L., *Fascist Movements in Austria from Schönerer to Hitler*. London: Sage Public. 1977.

Churchill, Winston S., *The Gathering Storm*. Boston: Cooper Publishing Co., Houghton-Mifflin, 1948.

Clough, Nathaniel P., *Die deutsch-österreichische Anschlussfrage in der öffentlichen Meinung Amerikas*. Heidelberg: H. Meister, 1933.

Colvin, J. Ian, *Vansittart in Office. An Historical Survey of the Origins of the Second World War*. Based on the Papers of Sir Robert Vansittart. London: V. Gollancz, 1965.

Craig, Gordon A., *Germany 1866–1945*. New York, Oxford Univ. Press, 1978.

Curtius, Julius, *Sechs Jahre Minister der deutschen Republik*. Heidelberg: C. Winter, 1948.

Dachs, H., *Österreichische Geschichtswissenschaft und Anschluss 1918–1938*. Salzburg. Histor. Institut d. Univers. Salzburg, 1974.

Das Jahr 1934:12. Februar. Veröffentlichungen. Bd. 2, Kommission, Munich: R. Oldenbourg, 1975.

Das Jahr 1934:25.Juli. Protokoll des Symposiums in Wien am 8.Okt.1974. Veröffentlichungen, Bd. 3: Wissnsch Kommission, Eds. E. Holtmann, L. Jedlicka and R. Neck. Munich. R. Oldenbourg, 1975.

Dallek, Robert, *Democrat and Diplomat. Life of William Dodd*. N.Y. London, Oxford Univ. Pr., 1968.

Deutsch, Julius, *Civil War in Austria*. Chicago: The Socialist Party National Headquarters, 1934.

Der deutsche Einmarsch in Österreich. Berlin, n.p., 1938.

Dollfuss in Österreich. Eines Mannes Wort und Ziel. Ed. E. Weber, Vienna: Reinhold, 1935.

Droz, Jacques, *L'Europe Centrale. Evolution historique de l'idee de Mitteleurope'*. Paris: Payot, 1960.

Eichstaedt, Ulrich, *Von Dollfuss zu Hitler. Geschichte des Anschlusses Österreich's 1933–1938*. Mainz: Wiesbaden (Veröffentlichungen des Instituts für europäische Geschichte, 1955.

Eisenmann, Louis, Emile Bourgeois et al., *Les problèmes de l'Europe Centrale*. Conférences. Paris: Librairie Felix Alcan, 1923.

Engel-Janosi, Friedrich, *Vom Chaos zur Katastrophe. Vatikan Gespräche 1918 bis 1938*. Vienna and Munich: Herold, 1971.

Erdmann, Karl Dietrich, *Die Zeit der Weltkriege. Handbuch der deutschen Geschichte*. Stuttgart: Union Verlag. 1960 (1959), vol. 4.

Eyck, Erich, *A History of the Weimar Republic*. Transl. by H. P. Hanson and R. G. Waite. Cambridge: Harvard Univ. Press, 1963, vol. 2.

Fellner, Fritz and Heidrun Maschl, eds., *St. Germain im Sommer 1919*. Salzburg W. Neugebauer, 1977.

Fischer, Ernst, *An Opposing Man*. New York: Liveright, 1974 (Translation of *Das Ende einer Illusion 1945–55*). Vienna: F. Molden, 1973.

Foerster, Friedrich W., *Europe and the German Question*. New York: Sheed and Ward, 1940.

Franckenstein, Sir George, *Diplomat of Destiny*. New York: Alliance Book Corp. 1940.

François-Poncet, André, *The Fateful Years. Memoirs of a French Ambassador in Berlin 1933–1938*. (Transl. from the French by J. LeClerq) New York: Harcourt Brace and Co., 1949.

Friedrich Fritz, *Der deutsche Einmarsch in Österreich*, 1938, Militärhistor. Schriftenreihe, Heft 8. Vienna: Österr. Bundesverlag, 1968.

Frisch, Hans von, *Die Gewaltherrschaft in Österreich 1933 bis 1938. Eine staatsrechtliche Untersuchung*. Leipzig and Vienna: J. Günther, 1938.

Fuchs, Martin, *A Pact with Hitler. The Death of Austria*. (Transl. from German by Chs. H. Lumley, London: Victor Gollancz, Ltd., 1939.

Funder, Friedrich, *Als Österreich den Sturm bestand. Aus der Ersten in die zweite Republik*, 3rd ed., Vienna and Munich: Herold, 1957

———. *From Empire to Republic. An Austrian Editor Reviews Momentous Years*. Transl. by B. Waldstein. New York: A. Unger, 1963.

Funke, Manfred, ed., *Hitler, Deutschland and die Mächte*, Düsseldorf, Droste, 1976. M. Funke, *ibid*. "Die deutsch-italienischen Besielungen-

Antibolschewismus und aussenpolitische Interessenkonkurrenz . . ." pp. 823–846.

Gedye, G.E.R., *Betrayal in Central Europe. Austria and Czechoslovakia. The Fallen Bastions*. New York and London: Harpers Bros. Publishers, 1939.

Gehl, Jürgen, *Germany and the Anschluss 1931–1938*. Foreword by Alan Bullock, London, New York, Toronto: Oxford Univ. Press, 1963.

Goldinger, Walter, "Das Projekt einer deutsch-österreichischen Zollunion von 1931," in *Österreich und Europa*, Festgabe für Hugo Hantsch zum 70. Geburtstag, Vienna, Graz, and Cologne, Styria, 1965.

Goldner, Franz, *Dollfuss im Spiegel der U.S. Akten*, St. Pölten: Niederösterreichisches Pressehaus, 1979.

Görlich, Ernst Joseph, *Die österreichische Nation und der Widerstand*. Vienna, Europa-Verlag, 1967.

Gregory, John Duncan, *Dollfuss and His Times*, London, Hutchinson Co. Ltd., 1935.

Gruber, Karl. *Ein politisches Leben. Österreichs Weg zwischen den Diktaturen*, Vienna, F. Molden, 1976.

Haas, Hans, "Österreichisch-italienische Beziehungen von Villa Giusti bis St. Germain," in *Innsbruck-Venedig*, eds. A Wandruszka and L. Jedlicka, Vienna: Verlag d. österr. Akademie d. Wissenschaften, 1975.

―――. "Österreich und das Ende der kollektiven Sicherheit. Zur Rolle der französischen und sowjetischen Politik der Friedenssicherung in Bezug auf Österreich," *Auflösung des Habsburgerreiches*, eds., R. G. Paschka and Karlheinz Mack. Vienna: Verlag F. Geschichte u. Politik, 1970.

Habsburg, Otto von, *Briefe aus der Verbannung*. Ed. Karl Freiherr von Werkmann, Leipzig: R. A. Hoger, 1935.

Hacker, W. ed. *Warnung an Österreich. Neonazismus*. Vienna: Europa-Verlag, 1966.

Hannak, Jacques, *Karl Renner und seine Zeit*. Vienna, Europa-Verlag, 1963.

Hartmann, Ludo Moritz, *Grossdeutsch oder Kleindeutsch? Ein Appell*. Gotha: F. A. Perthes, 1921.

Heer, Friedrich, *Der Kampf um die österreichische Identität*, Vienna, Cologne, H. Böhlau, 1981.

Heinisch, Theodor, *Österreichs Arbeiter für die Unabhängigkeit 1934–45*. Vienna: Europa-Verlag, 1968.

Henderson, Nevile, *Failure of a Mission. Berlin 1937–39*. New York: G. P. Putnam's Sons, 1940.

Hertz, Friedrich, *Zahlungsbilanz und Lebensfähigkeit Österreichs*. Munich, 1925.

Heuss, Theodor, *Friedrich Naumann, Der Mann, das Werk, die Zeit*, Stuttgart and Tübingen, Rainer Wunderlich Verlag Hermann Leins, 1949 (1937).

Hildebrand, Klaus, *The Foreign Policy of the Third Reich* (Transl. by A. Fothergill), Stuttgart, W. Kohlhammer, 1977.

Hildebrand, Klaus, *The Foreign Policy of the Third Reich*, transl. by A. Fothergill, Los Angeles & Berkeley: Un. of Calif. Press. 1970.

―――. *Das Dritte Reich, 2. Aufl.* Munich, Vienna: Oldenbourg, 1980.

Hillgruber, Andreas, *Deutsche Rolle in der Vorgeschichte der beiden Weltkriege.* Göttingen; Vandenhoeck & Ruprecht, 1967.

―――. *Deutsche Grossmacht-und Weltpolitik*, Düsseldorf: Droste, 1977.

―――. *Endlich genug über Nationalsozialismus und zweiten Weltkrieg?* Düsseldorf: Droste, 1982.

Hindels, Josef, *Österreichs Gewerkschaften im Widerstand 1934-45.* Vienna: Europa-Verlag, 1976.

Hiscocks, Richard, *The Rebirth of Austria.* London and New York: Oxford Univ. Press, 1953.

Hitler, Adolf, *Mein Kampf* (Transl. by R. Manheim) Boston: Houghton Mifflin, 1971 (1943).

Hofer, Josef Theodor, *Weggefährten vom österreichischen Freiheitskampf, 1933-45.* Vienna, F. Scheibl Verlag, 1946.

Hohenecker, Leopold and Gustav Otruba, *Von St. Germain zum Staatsvertrag 1918-1945.* Vienna, Bergland, 1967.

Holborn, Hajo, *A History of Modern Germany, 1840-1945*, New York: A. Knopf, 1968.

Hoor Ernst, *Österreich 1918-1938*, Vienna, Österr. Bundesverlag, 1966.

Horak, Kurt and Franz Klar, *Hitler ist nicht tot*, Vienna, Verlag Jungbrunnen, 1968.

Hudal, Bishop Alois, *Grundlagen des Nationalsozialismus. Eine ideengeschichtliche Untersuchung*, Vienna, G. Gunther, 1937.

Hugelmann, K. G., "Die politischen Parteien und die Anschlussfrage" in *Die Anschlussfrage in ihrer kulturellen, wirtschaftlichen und politischen Bedeutung*, eds. F.F.G. Kleinwaechter und H. v. Paller, Vienna and Leipzig; W. Braumüller, 1930.

Hummelberger, Walter, "Österreich und die kleine Entente, "*Das Juliabkommen von 1936*, Wissenschaftl. Kommission, Munich: R. Oldenbourg, 1977.

Ingrimm, Robert, *Der Griff nach Österreich.* Zürich: Europa-Verlag, 1938.

Jacobsen, Hans-Adolf, *Nationalsozialistische Aussenpolitik 1933-38*, Frankfurt, a.M.: A. Metzner, 1963.

Jagschitz, Gerhard, *Der Putsch der Nationalsozialisten 1934 in Österreich.* Graz: Styria, 1976.

―――. "Zwischen Befriedung und Konfrontation. Zur Lage der NSDAP in "Österreich 1934-36" in *Das Juliabkommen von 1936*, Munich: R. Oldenbourg, 1977, pp. 156-187.

Janovsky, Karl, *Zollunion Prag-Wien oder Anschluss Wien-Berlin*, Reichenberg, 1927.

Jambor, W. ed., *Der Anteil der Bundesländer an der Nationswerdung Österreichs.* Vienna and Munich: Kurt Wedl, 1971.

Jedlicka, Ludwig, *"Die 'A'ra Schuschnigg," Österreich 1927 bis 38,* Vienna: Verlag für Geschichte und Politik, 1973.

_____. "Die Auflösung der Wehrverbände und Italien im Jahre 1936" in *Das Juliabkommen von 1936.* Protokoll des Symposiums in Wien am 10.u.11.Juni 1976. Munich: R. Oldenbourg, 1977, pp. 104–118.

_____. "Aufteilungs-und Einmarschpläne um Österreich 1918–34," *Festschrift für Franz Loidl.* Vienna: Hollinck, 1975, I, 141–66.

_____. "Die Aussenpolitik der Ersten Republik," in *Diplomatie und Aussenpolitik Österreichs. Elf Beiträge zu ihrer Geschichte.* Ed. Erich Zöllner. Vienna: Österr. Bundesverlag, 1977.

_____. *Ein Heer im Schatten der Parteien. Die militärpolitische Lage Österreichs 1918–38.* Vienna: H. Böhlau's Nachf., 1935.

_____. "Ernst Rüdiger Starhemberg und die politische Entwicklung in Österreich im Frühjahr 1938," in *Fallstudien zur österreichischen Zeitgeschichte. 1900–75,* St. Pölten: Niederösterr. Pressehaus, 1975.

_____. "Gauleiter Josef Leopold," *Geschichte und Gesellschaft. Festschrift für Karl Stadler zum 60. Geburtstage,* eds. G. Botz, H. Hautmann, and H. Konrad. Vienna: Europa-Verlag, 1974, pp. 143–62.

_____. "Das Jahr 1934," *Österreich 1918–38,* Vienna: Institut für Österreichkunde, 1970.

_____. "Österreich und Italien, 1922–38," *Innsbruck-Venedig,* eds. A. Wandruszka and L. Jedlicka, Vienna" Verlag d. österr. Akademie d. Wissenschaften, 1975.

_____. *Vom alten zum neuen Österreich. Fallstudien . . . ,* St. Pölten: Niederösterr. Pressehaus, 1975.

_____, ed. *Bericht der historischen Kommission des Reichsführers, SS. Die Erhebung österreichischer Nationalsozialisten im Juli 1934.* Prague: Europa-Verlag, 1965.

Jens, Jessen, *Österreich und die grossdeutsche Volkswirtschaft.* Schriften des national-sozialistischen Reichswehrverbandes in Österreich, Heft 3, Vienna: Selbstverlag, 1938.

Kafka, Gustav, "Das Ende Österreichs," *Österreich 1918–1938,* Ed. Institut f. Österreichkunde, Vienna, Institut f. Österreichkunde, 1970.

Kaindl, Raimund Friedrich, *Österreich, Preussen, Deutschland. Deutsche Geschicthe in grossdeutscher Beleuchtung.* Vienna and Leipzig: W. Braumüller, 1926.

Kann, Robert A., "Österreich, das Erbe und die Erben," *Österreich 1918–1938,* Wissenschaftl. Kommission, Symposium Oct. 1972, Vienna, Verlag f. Geschichte und Politik, 1973, pp. 20–25.

_____ and Friedrich D. Prinz, eds. *Deutschland und Österreich,* Munich, Jugend und Volk, 1980.

Katzenstein, Peter J., *Disjoined Partners Austria and Germany since 1815.* Berkeley: Univ. of California Press, 1976.

Kaufmann, Fritz, *Sozialdemokratie in Österreich,* Vienna, Amalthea, 1978.

Kerekes, Lajos, *Anschluss 1938,* Budapest: Akadémiai Kiadó, 1963.

_____. *A Berlin-Róma tengely Kialakulasa és Ausztria annexioja 1936–38.* Budapest: Akademiai Kiadó, 1962.

Kleinwaechter, F.F.G., *Der deutsch-österreichische Mensch und der Anschluss.* Vienna: Vienna: A. Luser, 1926.

_____. *Selbstbestimmüngsrecht für Österreich.* Stuttgart: 1929.

Klemperer, Klemens von, *Ignaz Seipel, Christian Statesman in a Time of Crisis.* Princeton Univ. Press, 1972.

Koerner, R. Richard, *So haben sie es damals gemacht. Die Propagandavorbereitungen zum österreichischen Anschluss durch das Hitler Regime 1933–38.* Vienna: Ges zur Förderung wissenschaftlicher Forschung, 1958.

Die Kommunisten im Kampf um die Unabhängigkeit Österreichs. Vienna: Stern Verlag, 1955.

Konrad, Helmut, *Widerstand an der Donau und Moldau. KPO and KSC zur Zeit des Hitler-Stalin Paktes.* Vienna: L. Botlzmann Institut für Geschichte der Arbeiterbewegung, 1978.

_____. *Social Democracy and Anschluss. Historische Wurzeln. Anschluss 1918 und 1938,* in *Nachwirkungen,* ed. K. R. Stadler, Vienna, L. Boltzmann Institut für Geschichte der Arbeiterbewegung, 1978.

Koplenig, Johann, ed. *Österreichs Kampf um seine Unabhängigkeit,* Paris, Editions Promethée, 1939.

Kordt, Erich, *Wahn und Wirklichkeit,* Ed. K. H. Abshagen, Stuttgart: Union Deutsche Verlagsanstalt, 1948.

Kreisky, Bruno, *Die Zeit in der wir leben. Betrachtungen zur internationalen Politik.* Ed. M. Lucbert, Vienna, F. Molden, 1978.

Kreissler, Félix, *La prise de consciene de la nation autrichienne. 1934–1945–1978.* Paris, Presses universitaires de France, 1980, 2 vols.

_____. *Von der Revolution zur Annexion. Österreich 1918 bis 1938.* Vienna: Europa-Verlag, 1970.

Laun, Rudolf, *Deutschösterreich im Friedensvertrag von Versailles. Kommentar zum Friedensvertrage.* Ed. W. Schücking, Berlin: F. Wahler, 1921.

Layton, W. T. and Ch. Rist, *The economic situation of Austria.* Report presented to the Council of the League of Nations, n.p.n.d.

Leichter, Otto, *Otto Bauer,* Vienna: Europa-Verlag, 1970.

Lennhoff, E., *The Last Five Hours of Austria.* With an introduction by P. Frischauer, London: Rich and Cowen LTD., 1938.

Leser, Norbert, "Die nationale Selbstfindung der Österreicher" in *Der Anteil der Bundesländer an der Nationswerdung Österreichs.* Ed. W. Jambor. Vienna and Munich: Kurt Wedl, 1971, pp. 344–64.

Lhotsky, Alfons, *Aufsätze und Vorträge*, eds. Hans Wagner and Heinrich Koller, Munich: R. Oldenbourg, 1974.

Lloyd George David, *The Truth about the Peace Treaties*, London: V. Gollancz, 1938, vol. 2.

Löbe, Paul, *Der Weg war lang. Lebenserinnerungen von Paul Löbe*. Berlin-Grunewald: Arami Verlag, 1965.

_____ and Hermann Neubacher, *Die Österreichisch-Deutsche Anschlussbewegung*, Leipzig, Unikum, 1926.

Lorenz, Reinhold, "Österreich in Mitteleuropa 1867–1918," *Österreichs Erbe und Sendung im deutschen Raum*, eds. Josef Nadler and Heinrich v. Srbik. Salzburg and Leipzig, A. Pustet, 1936.

_____. *Der Staat wider Willen. Österreich 1918–38*. Berlin: Junker & Dunnhaupt, 1940.

Lott, Walter and Werner Reese, eds. *Gesamtdeutsches Denken in Österreich und die Reichsgründung*. Munich, J. F. Lehmann, 1938.

Low, Alfred D. *The Anschluss Movement 1918–1919, and the Paris Peace Conference*, vol. 103, *Memoirs*, Philadelphia, American Philosophical Society, 1974.

_____. *Die Anschlussbewegung in Österreich und Deutschland, 1918–1919 und die Pariser Friedenskonferenz* (abbreviated German version of the foregoing work). Vienna: W. Braumüller, 1975.

_____. "Austria between Two Soviet Republics. In the Mirror of the Soviet Press," postdoctoral thesis, Columbia Univ., 1957 (typewritten).

Ludwig, Eduard, *Österreichs Sendung im Donauraum. Die letzten Dezennien österreichischer Innen-und Aussenpolitik*. Vienna: Verlag d. österr. Staatsdruckerei, 1954.

Luža, Radomir, *Austro-German Relations in the Anschluss Era*. Princeton, Princeton Univ. Press, 1975.

Maass, Walter B., *Country without a Name. Austria under the Nazi rule 1938–45*. New York: Frederick Ungar Publ. Co., 1979 (German original appeared in 1975).

MacDonald (Proudfoot) Mary. *The Republic of Austria, 1918–34. A Study in Failure of Domestic Government*. Reprint ed., London and New York: Oxford Univ. Press, 1946.

Malfer, Stefan, *Wien und Rom nach dem Ersten Weltkrieg. Österreichisch-ialienishche Beziehungen 1919–1923*. Kommission für neuere Geschichte Österreichs, Bd. 6, Vienna: H. Böhlaus Nachf., 1978.

Mamatey, Victor S., *The United States and East Central Europe 1914–1918. A Study in Wilsonian Diplomacy and Propaganda*. Princeton, Princeton Univ. Press, 1957.

Massiczek, A., *Die österreichische Nation zwischen zwei Nationalismen*. Vienna: Europa Verlag, 1967.

Meissner, Otto, *Staatssekretär unter Ebert-Hindenburg-Hitler*, Hamburg: Hoffmann & Campe, 1950.

Metnitz, G. A. von, *Die deutsche Nationalbewegung 1871–1933*. Berlin: Juncker & Dunnhaupt, 1939.

Meyer, Henry Cord, *Mitteleuropa in German Thought and Action, 1815–1945*. The Hague: Martinus Nijhoff, 1955.

Micaud, Chs. A., "The Anschluss," in *The French Right and Nazi Germany, 1933–38. A Study of Public Opinion*, New York: Octagon Books, 1964 (1943), pp. 133–159.

Mitteräcker, Hermann, *Kampf und Opfer für Österreich. Ein Beitrag zur Geschichte des österreichischen Widerstandes 1938–1945*, Vienna: Stern Verlag, 1963.

Mosca, Rodolfo, "Die österreichische und die italienische Aussenpolitik vom Vertrag von St. Germain bis zur faschistischen Machtergreifung," *Innsburck-Venedig*, Vienna: Verlag d. Österr. Akademie d. Wissenschaften, 1975, pp. 183–196.

Munch, W., *Der Anschluss Österreichs und das Echo im Reich (1918–22)*, Bad Kreuznach: 1968, and Braunschweig: G. Westermann, 1949.

Neck, Rudolf and Adam Wandruszka, eds., *Anschluss 1938*, Wissenschaftliche Kommission, Veröffentlichungen, Bd. 7, Munich: R. Oldenbourg, 1981.

Neubacher, Hermann, "Die Organisationen für den deutsch-österreichischen Zusammenschluss," in *Die Anschlussfrage in ihrer kulturellen, writschaftlichen, und politischen Bedeutung*, eds. F.F.G. Kleinwaechter and H. von Paller, Vienna and Leipzig: W. Braumuller, 1930, pp. 136–56.

Nolfo, Enno di "Die österreichisch-italienischen Beziehungen von der faschistischen Machtergreifung bis zum Anschluss (1922–38)," *Innsbruck-Venedig*, Eds. Adam Wandruszka & L. Jedlicka, Vienna, Verlag der österreichischen Akademie der Wissenschaften, 1975, pp. 221–72.

Die österreichische Verfassung von 1918 bis 1938. Protokoll des Symposiums in Wien am 19. Oktober 1977. Wissenschaftl. Kommission, Bd. 6, Munich, no publ., 1980.

Offner, Arnold A., *American Appeasement, U.S. Foreign Policy and Germany 1933–38*. Cambridge: Harvard, 1969.

Oudard, Georges, *Croix gammée sur l'Europe centrale. Mars-Septembre 1938*. Paris: Les editions de France, 1938.

Papen, Franz von, *Memoirs*, Transl. by Brian Connell. London: A. Deutsch, 1952.

——— . *Der Wahrheit eine Gasse* (original of the foregoing work). Munich: P. List, 1952.

Papesch, Joseph Friedrich, *Fesseln um Österreich*. Hamburg: Hanseat. Verlagsanstalt, 1933.

Pauley, Bruce F., *Hitler and the Forgotten Nazis*, Chapel Hill: Univ. of No. Car. Press, 1981.

Payer, Friedrich, *Deutschösterreich und wir, Der Aufbau,* 2. Heft, ed. Conrad Hausmann Stuttgart: Deutsche Verlagsanstalt, 1919.

Pembaur, Walther, *Im letzten Kampf um Österreich,* Vienna: J. Günther, 1939.

Petersen, Jens, *Hitler-Mussolini, Entstehung der Achse Berlin-Rome, 1933–1936,* Tübingen: Max Niemeyer, 1973.

Pezet, Ernst, *Fin de l'Autriche, fin d'une Europe.* Preface by Edouard Herriot. Paris: Self-edition.

Pollitt, Harry, *Austria.* London: Communist Party of Great Britain, 1938.

Poltavskii, M.N., *Avstriiski narod i anschljuss 1938g* (The Austrian Nation and the Anschluss 1938), Moscow.: n.p., 1971.

———. *Diplomatiia imperializma i malie stranii evropi (1938–45)* (The Diplomacy of Imperialism and the Small Countries of Europe 1938–45), Moscow: n.p., 1973.

Preradovich, Nikolaus von, *Der nationale Gedanke in Österreich 1866–1938,* Rankegesellschaft, Heft 8, Göttingen: Musterschmidt Verlag, 1968.

———. *Die Wilhelmstrasse und der Anschluss Österreichs 1918–33,* Berne and Frankfurt a.M. Herbert Lang, 1971.

Puaux, Gabriel, *Mort et transfiguration de l'Autriche 1935–1955.* Paris: Plon, 1966.

Raschhofer, Hermann, *Gross-oder Kleinösterreich. Funktion der kleinösterreichischen Ideologie.,* Mitteleurop. Schriftenreihe, Bd. 2, Berlin: Volk und Reich, 1933.

Rauschning, Hermann, *Hitler Speaks. A Series of Political Conversations with Adolf Hitler.* London: Thornton Butterworth, Ltd., 1939.

Reichold, Ludwig, *Scheidewege einer Republik. Österreich 1918–68.* Vienna: Europa Verl., 1968.

———. *Geschichte der ÖVP.* Graz: Styria, 1975.

Reimann, Viktor, *Bruno Kreisky. Das Portrait eines Staatsmannes,* Vienna: F. Molden, 1972.

———. *Innitzer, Kardinal zwischen Hitler und Rom,* Vienna and Munich, F. Molden, 1967.

———. *Zu gross für Österreich. Seipel und Bauer im Kampf um die Erste Republik,* Vienna, Frankfurt a.M., 1968.

Rennhofer, Friedrich, *Ignaz Seipel, Mensch und Staatsmann,* Vienna, Cologne, Graz: H. Böhlaus Nachf., 1978.

Richter, Karl F., "Die Beziehungen zwischen der Tschechoslowakei und der Republik Österreich in der Zeischenkriegszeit," in *Gleichgewicht-Revision-Restauration. Die Aussenpolitik der Ersten Tschechoslowakischen Republik im System der Pariser Vorortverträge,* ed. Karl Bosl, Munich: R. Oldenbourg, 1976.

Rintelen, Anton, *Erinnerungen an Österreichs Weg. Versailles-Berchtesgaden-Grossdeutschland.* Munich: F. Bruckmann, 1941.

Rintelen, Enno von, *Mussolini als Bundesgenosse. Erinnerungen eines Militärattachés in Rom, 1936-43.* Tübingen and Stuttgart: Rainer-Wunderlich Verlag Hermann-Leins, 1951.

Rohrwig, Otto Reich von, *Der Freiheitskampf der Ostmarkdeutschen. Von St. Germain bis Adolf Hitler.* Graz, Vienna, Leipzig. Leopold Stocker, 1942.

Rosar, Wolfgang, *Deutsche Gemeinschaft. Seyss-Inquart und der Anschluss,* Vienna: Europa-Verlag, 1971.

Ross, Dieter, *Hitler und Dollfuss. Die deutsch-österreichische Politik 1933-34,* Hamburg, Leibniz Verlag, 1966.

Rothschild, K. W., *Austria's Economic Development between the Two Wars.* London: F. Muller, 1947.

Sailer, Karl Hans, Ed. *Geheimer Briefwechsel Mussolini-Dollfuss.* Vienna: Verlag der Wiener Volksbuchhandlung, 1949.

Sakmyster, Thomas L., *Hungary, the Great Powers and the Danubian Crisis 1936-39.* Athens: Univ. of Georgia Press, 1980.

Schärf, Adolf, *Österreichs Erneuerung 1945-55.* Vienna: Wiener Volksbuchhandlung, 1955.

Schausberger, Norbert, *Der Griff nach Österreich. Der Anschluss.* Vienna: Jugend und Volk, 1978.

――――. "Ökonomisch-politische Interdependenzen im Sommer 19¬6," in *Das Juliabkommen von 1936,* Munich: R. Oldenbourg, 1977, pp. 280-298.

――――. "Österreich und die nationalsozialistische Anschlusspolitik" in Funke M., ed. *Hitler, Deutschland und die Mächte,* Düsseldorf: Droste, 1976.

Scheu, Friedrich, *Der Weg ins Ungewisse. Österreichische Schicksalskurve 1929-38,* Vienna: F. Molden, 1972.

Schilling-Schletter, Alexander, *Dr. Walter Riehl und die Geschichte des Nationalsozialismus,* Leipzig: Forum, 1933.

Schmitz, Oskar A. H., *Der österreichische Mensch.* Vienna and Leipzig, Wiener Literar. Anstalt, 1924.

Schneefuss, Walter, *Österreichs Zerfall und Werden eines Staates.* Leipzig: W. Goldmann, 1937.

Schoppe, Hanns, *Presse im Kampf. Geschichte der Presse während der Kampfjahre der NSDAP (1933-38) in Österreich,* Brno, Vienna, and Leipzig: R. M. Rohrer, n.d.

Schuschnigg, Kurt von, *Austrian Requiem* (Transl. by F. von Hildebrand) New York: G. P. Putnam's Sons, 1946.

――――. *Im Kampf gegen Hitler. Die Überwindung der Anschlussidee,* Vienna: F. Molden, 1969.

Selby, Sir Walford, *Diplomatic Twilight, 1939-1940,* London: J. Murray, 1953.

Shepherd, Gordon, *The Austrian Odyssey*, London: McMillan & Co., Ltd. and New York: St. Martin's Press, 1957.

Siebert, Ferdinand, *Italiens Weg in den zwerten Weltkrieg*, Frkft a.M.-Bonn: Athenäum, 1962.

Springenschmied, Karl, *Der Donauraum. Österreich im Kraftfelde der Grossmächte; geopolitische Bilderreihe.* Leipzig: E. Wunderlich, 1935.

Srbik, Heinrich Ritter von, *Österreich in der deutschen Geschichte*, Munich: F. Bruckmann, 1938 (1936).

Stadler, Karl R., *Österreich 1938–45, im Spiegel der NS-Akten*, Vienna and Munich: Herold, 1966.

Starhemberg, E. R. von, *Memoirs* (Transl. from the German original *Zwischen Hitler und Mussolini*), London, Harper & Bros., 1942.

Staudinger, Anton, "Zur Österreich-Ideologie des Ständestaates," *Das Juliabkommen von 1936*, Munich: R. Oldenbourg, 1977, pp. 198–240.

Steinbauer, Gustav, *Ich war Verteidiger in Nürnberg. Ein Dokumentenbeitrag um Österreich.* Klagenfurt: E. Kaiser, 1950.

Steiner, Herbert, "Otto Bauer und die Anschlussfrage 1918–1919" in *Die Auflösung des Habsburgerreiches. Zusammenbruch und Neuorientierung im Donauraum*, eds. R. G. Plaschka and Karlheinz Mack, Munich: R. Oldenbourg, 1970, pp. 468–82.

Stern-Rubarth, Edgar, *Graf Brockdorff-Rantzau. Wanderer zwischen zwei Welten.* Berlin; R. Hobling, 1929.

Stolper, Gustav, *Deutschösterreich als Sozial-und Wirtschaftsproblem.* Munich, Drei Masken, 1921.

——. ed., *Deutschösterreich. Neue Beiträge über seine wirtschaftlichen Verhältnisse*, Schriften des Vereins für Sozialpolitik, Bd. 162, Munich and Leipzig: Duncker & Humblot, 1921.

Strauss, Emil, *Tschechoslowakische Aussenpolitik, eine geschichtliche Einführung.* Prague: Orbis, 1936.

Strong, David, *Austria (Oct. 1918–March 1919).* New York: Columbia Univ. Press, 1939.

Stuhlpfarrer, Karl, "Österreichs aussenpolitische Lage 1934," in *Österreich 1927–38.* Munich, R. Oldenbourg, 1973.

——. "Zum Problem der deutschen Penetration Österreichs," *Das Juliabkommen von 1936*, eds. L. Jedlicka and R. Neck, Munich: R. Oldenbourg, 1977, pp. 315–27.

Suval, Stanley, *The Anschluss Question in the Weimar Era. A Study of German Nationalism in Germany and Austria 1918–32*, Baltimore: Johns Hopkins Univ. Press, 1974.

Szecsi, Maria and Karl Stadler, *Die NS Justiz in Österreich und ihre Opfer.* Vienna: Herold, 1962.

Tansill, Charles Callan, *Back Door to War. Roosevelt's Foreign Policy, 1933–41.* Chicago, Henry Regnery Co., 1952.

Taylor, A.J.P., *The Origins of the Second World War*. Greenwich: Fawcett Publ., 1961.

Tersannes, J., *Le problème autrichien et la menace du rattachement à l'Allemagne*. Paris: Editions Bossard, 1921.

Till, Rudolf, *Pax Austriaca. Sinn und Geschichte des österreichischen Staatsgedankens*. Vienna: Bobenberg, 1948.

Tončic-Sorinj, Lujo, "Austria-Crossroad between East and West," in *20 Jahre Republik Österreich*. Vienna: Austrian Ministry for Foreign affairs, Deptmt. of Documentation and Information, 1967.

Verosta, Stephan, "Josef Schumpeter gegen das Zollbündnis der Donaumonarchie mit Deutschland und gegen die Anschlusspolitik Otto Bauers (1916–19), in *Festschrift für Christian Broda*, Preface by B. Kreisky, Vienna, Europa-Verlag, 1976.

Vincentis-Perticone, Maria de, *Il problema dell-Austria. Alla vigilia della Seconda Guerra Mondiale*. Milan, n.p., 1967.

Wache, Karl, ed., *Deutscher Geist in Österreich*. Munich: Dornbirn, 1933.

Wagner, Dieter and Gerhard Tomkowitz, *Ein Volk, ein Reich, ein Führer. Der Anschluss Österreichs*. Munich: Piper, 1968.

Wagnleitner, Reinhold, "Die britische Österreichpolitik oder 'The Doctrine of Putting off the Evil Day,'" in *Das Juliabkommen von 1936*, eds. L. Jedlicka and R. Neck, Munich: R. Oldenbourg, 1977, pp. 53–83.

Warum fordern wir den Anschluss? Vienna: Hölder-Pichler-Tempsky, 1926.

Wathen, Sister Mary Antonia, *The Policy of England and France toward the Anschluss of 1938*. Washington, D.C. Catholic Univ. of America Press, 1954.

Weinberg, Gerhard, *The Foreign Policy of Hitler's Germany: Diplomatic Revolution in Europe 1933–36*. Chicago: Univ. of Chicago Press, 1970.

———. *The Foreign Policy of Hitler-Germany 1937–39*, Un. Chicago, 1980.

Weinberger, Lois, *Tatsachen, Begegnungen und Gespräche. Ein Buch um Österreich*. Vienna, Österreichischer Verlag, 1948.

Weinzierl, Erika, "Aus den Notizen von Richard Schmitz zur österreichischen Innenpolitik im Frühjahr 1933," in *Geschichte und Gesellschaft*. Festschrift für Karl Stadler zum sechzigsten Geburtstag. Vienna: Europa-Verlag, 1974, pp. 113–42.

———. *Der Österreicher und sein Staat*. Vienna: Herder, 1965.

Wengst, Udo, Graff, *Brockdorff-Rantzau und die aussenpolitischen Anfänge der Weimarer Republik*. Frankfurt a.M.: Peter Lang, 1973.

Winter, Ernst Karl, *Bahnbrecher des Dialogs*. Selected and introduced by Alfred Missong, Vienna: Europa-Verlag, 1969.

———. *Monarchie und Arbeiterschaft*. Beihefte zu den "Wiener Politischen Blätter," No. 1, Vienna: Wiener Politische Blätter, 1936.

Wiskemann, Elizabeth, *The Rome-Berlin Axis*, London: Oxford Univ. Press, 1966 (1949).

Wisshaupt, Walter, *Wir kommen wieder.* Vienna: Wiener Volksbuchhandlung, 1967.

Wright, Herbert Francis, *Attitude of the U.S. toward Austria,* 78th Congress, 2nd sess. House doc. no. 477. Washington, D.C.: Catholic University, U.S. Government Printing, 1944.

Zernatto, Guido, *Die Wahrheit über Österreich.* London and New York: Longmanns, Green & Co., 1939 (1938).

Zimmermann, Horst, *Die Schweiz und Österreichs Anschluss and die Weimarer Republik. Die schweizerisch-österreichischen Beziehungen von 1922–31.* Berne: Lang, 1967.

———, *Schweiz und Österreich während der Zwischenkriegszeit. Eine Studie und Dokumentation internationaler Beziehungen im Schatten der Grossmächte.* Wiesbaden, Franz Steiner Verlag, 1973.

Zimmermann, Ludwig, *Deutsche Aussenpolitik in der 'A'ra der Weimarer Republik.* Berlin: Musterschmidt, 1958.

Articles

Bauer, Otto, "Address at the Party Conference, Oct. 14–16, 1933," in *Archiv. Mitteilungsblatt des Vereins für Geschichte der Arbeiterbewegung,* 3 (1963), pp. 45–67.

Broucek, Peter, "Edmund Glaise von Horstenau als Offizier, Historiker, und Journalist," *Geschichte und Literatur* 22 (1973), pp. 143–54.

Cullin, Michel, "Ernst Karl Winter et Alfred Klahr," *Austriaca. Cahiers Universitaires d'Information sur l'Autriche* 4 (July 1978), pp. 171–84.

Gasiorowski, Zygmunt J., "Czechoslovakia and the Austrian Question 1918–1928," *Südostforschungen,* 16 (1957), pp. 87–101.

Gould, S. W., "Austrian Attitudes toward the Anschluss October 1918–September 1919," *Journal of Modern History,* 22 (September 1950), pp. 220–231.

Gruber, Karl, "Austria Infelix," *Foreign Affairs,* 25 (Jan. 1947), pp. 229–239.

Hauser, Oswald, "Der Plan einer deutsch-österreichischen Zollunion von 1931 und die Europäische Federation," *Historische Zeitschrift,* 179 (Feb. 1955), pp. 45–92.

Haushofer, Albrecht, "Ein Volk, ein Staat," *Zeitschrift für Geopolitik,* 2. Aug. 1931, 1–6, pp. 26–95.

Jedlicka, L., "The Austrian Heimwehr," *Journal of Contemporary History,* 1 (1966), pp. 127–44.

Kann, Robert A., "Karl Renner (Dec. 14, 1870–Dec. 31, 1950)," *Journal of Modern History,* 23 (Sept. 1951), pp. 243–49.

Kerekes, Lajos, "Österreich zwischen Anschlusspolitik und Donaukonföderation, 1918–1919," *Vierteljahrshefte für Zeitgeschichte*, 22 (Jan. 1974), pp. 18–45.

Klein, Anton, "War die Erste Republik tatsächlich der Staat wider Willen?" *Österreich in Geschichte und Literatur*, II (Nov. 1967), pp. 457–470.

Kvacek, Robert, "Der Kampf um Österreich in den Jahren 1933–38 und die tschoslowakische Aussenpolitik" (in Czech) *Sbornik historicky*, 12 (1964), pp. 261–87.

Low, Alfred D., "The Anschluss Movement, 1933–38, and the Policy of France," *Jahrbuch des Instituts für deutsche Geschichte*, Univ. of Tel-Aviv, 1982, pp. 295–323.

————. "Austria between East and West: Budapest and Berlin, 1918–1919," *Austrian History Yearbook*, 4–5 (1968–69), pp. 44–62.

————. "The First Austrian Republic and Soviet Hungary" *Journal of Central European Affairs*, 20 (July 1960), pp. 174–203.

————. "Otto Bauer, Austro-Marxism, and the Anschluss Movement 1918–1938," *Canadian Review of Studies in Nationalism*, 6 (Spring 1979), pp. 33–57.

————. "The Soviet Union, the Austrian Communist Party, and the Anschluss Question 1918–1938," *Slavic Review*, 39 (March 1980), pp. 1–26.

————. Edward Beneš, the Anschluss and the Policy of Czechoslovakia, *East Central Europe*, 10, 1983, pp. 46–91.

Miller, Susanne, "Das Ringen um die 'einzige grossdeutsche Republik' Die Sozialdemokratie in Österreich und im Deutschen Reich und die Anschlussfrage 1918–19," *Archiv für Sozialgeschichte*, 11 (1971), pp. 1–67.

Mraz, Gottfried, "Die Bedeutung des 'Anschlusses' für die Beurteilung des Nationalsozialismus durch die römische Jesuitenzeitschrift 'Civiltà Cattolica,'" *Mitteilungen des österreichischen Staatsarchivs*, 31 (1973), pp. 503–17.

Orde, Anne, "Grossbritannien und die Selbständigkeit Österreichs 1918–38," *Vierteljahrshefte für Zeitgeschichte*, 28 (Apr. 1980), pp. 224–48.

————. "The origins of the German-Austrian Customs Union Affair of 1931," *Central European History*, 13 (March 1980), pp. 34–59.

Ritter, Harry R., "Hermann Neubacher and the Anschluss Movement 1918–40," *Central European History*, 8 (1975), pp. 348–69.

Ross, R. J., "Heinrich Ritter von Srbik and 'gesamtdeutsch' History," *Review of Politics*, 31 (Jan. 1969), pp. 88–107.

Schausberger, Norbert, "Der wirtschaftliche Anschluss Österreichs 1938," *Österreich in Geschichte und Literatur* (May 1971), pp. 249–73.

Sweet, Paul, "Seipel's Views on the Anschluss in 1928: An unpublished Exchange of Letters." *The Journal of Modern History*, 19 (Dec. 1947), pp. 320–24.

Ward, Barbara, "Ignaz Seipel and the Anschluss," *Dublin Review*, 203 (July–Sept. 1938), pp. 38–50.

Weinberg, Gerhard L., "Secret Hitler-Beneš Negotiations in 1936–37," *Journal of Central European Affairs*, 19 (Jan. 1960), pp. 366–74.

Dissertations and Theses

Ackerl, Isabella, "Die grossdeutsche Volkspartei, 1920–1934. Versuch einer Parteigeschichte," Doct. Dissert. Univ. Vienna, 1967.

Baumgärtner, E. G., "Die österreichische Presse und ihre Stellungnahme zur Anschlussfrage 1918–38," Doct. Dissert., U. Vienna, 1951.

Benedikt, Ursula, "Vinzenz Schumy, 1878–1962. Eine politische Biographie." Doct. Diss., Univ. Vienna, 1966.

Berger, Barbara, "Ernst Rüdiger von Starhmberg. Versuch einer Biographie," Doct. Dissert., Univ. Vienna, 1967.

Brandstätter, Rudolf, "Dr. Walter Riehl und die Geschichte der nationalsozialistischen Bewegung in Österreich," Doct. Dissert., Univ. Vienna, 1969.

Braun, Fritz, "Der politische Lebensweg des Bürgermeisters Richard Schmitz," Doct. Dissert., Univ. Vienna, 1968.

Eppel, Peter, "Die Haltung der Zeitschrift 'Schönere Zukunft'zum Nationalsozialismus in Deutschland, 1934–38," Doct. Dissert., Univ. Vienna, 1978.

Fabri, F., "Zur Psychologie des österreichischen Nationalgedankens. Unter besonderer Berücksichtigung des legitimistischen konservativen Denkens (1918–38)," Doct. Dissert., Univ. Mainz, 1955.

Feldmann, Angela, "Landbund für Österreich. Ideologie-Organisation-Politik," Doct. Dissert., Univ. Vienna, 1966.

Harasek, Anneliese, "Bundesprasident Wilhelm Miklas," Doct. Dissert., Univ. Vienna, 1967.

Hübener, Karl-Ludolf, "Illegale österreichische Presse von 1933 bis 1938," Doct. Dissert., Univ. Vienna, 1969.

Jagschitz, Gerhard, "Die Jugend des Bundeskanzlers Dr. Engelbert Dollfuss," Doct. Dissert, Univ. Vienna, 1967.

Lang, Hilde Verena, "Bundespräsident Miklas und das autoritäre Regime 1933–38," Doct. Diss. Univ. Vienna, 1972.

List, Evelyne, "Die Propaganda des Austro-Marxismus am Beispiel der sozialdemokratischen Anschlussbewegung 1919–33," Doct. Dissert., Univ. Vienna, 1976.

Mairer, Werner, "Ignaz Seipel und Benito Mussolini. Der Denker und der Realist," Doct. Dissert., Univ. Graz, 1973.

Mauser, Rosa, "Die Genesis des politisch-sozialen Ideengutes des Bundeskanzlers Dr. Engelbert Dollfuss," Doct. Dissert., Univ. Vienna, 1960.

Mayrhofer, Friedrich, "Dr. Franz Dinghofer (1873–1956)," Doct. Dissert., Univ. Vienna, 1968.

Myers, Duane Paul, "Germany and the Question of the Anschluss, 1918–22," Yale Univ. 1968.

Neubauer, Maria, "Österreich und seine Geschichte im Werke und in der Politik Winston Churchills," Doct. Dissert., Univ. Vienna, 1970.

Röglsperger, Helga, "Die Politik Frankreichs gegenüber Österreich von 1918 bis 1922," Doct. Dissert., Univ. Vienna, 1973.

Schirra, Rainer, "Die öffentliche Meinung und das Juliabkommen von 1936," Doct. Dissert., Univ. Vienna, 1961.

Schlag, Gerald, "Edmund von Glaise-Horstenau," Seminar Study, Institut für Zeitgeschichte, Univ. Vienna, 1963.

Vogelmann, Karl, "Die Propaganda der österreichischen Emigranten in der Sowjetunion für einen selbständigen österreichiichen Nationalstaat (1938–45)," Doct. Diss. Univ. Vienna, 1973.

Wagner, F., "Der österreichische Legitimismus 1918–38. Seine Politik und Publizistik," Doct. Dissert., Univ. Vienna, 1957.

Index